VOLTAIRE

Books by Jean Orieux, Translated into English

VOLTAIRE
TALLEYRAND

VOLTAIRE

BY JEAN ORIEUX

Translated from the Original French
by Barbara Bray and Helen R. Lane

DOUBLEDAY & COMPANY, INC.
GARDEN CITY, NEW YORK
1979

ISBN: 0-385-08567-2
Library of Congress Catalog Card Number 74-25095
Translation Copyright © 1979 by Doubleday & Company, Inc.
All Rights Reserved
Printed in the United States of America
First Edition

To M.B.
in token of affectionate admiration

ACKNOWLEDGMENTS

Voltaire's name is known the world over, and everyone has formed an opinion of him. But pro or con, the way we form our opinion of him is always the same. When he first arouses our interest, our picture of him seems quite clear. But as we dig deeper into his life, the profusion of facts, his constantly shifting public poses, and the contradictions of his personality make our heads swim. His every gesture has been amply documented, yet Voltaire himself vanishes in the light. He scintillates, but all we can grasp are mere reflections of his true self. To capture him takes time, effort, and allies.

I was fortunate enough to find such allies, and I thank them for all their help. I shall not forget the willingness with which Monsieur Desgraves, the head of the Bordeaux Municipal Library, and his assistant, Mademoiselle Boutteaux, put at my disposal both their collections of books and their learning. Monsieur Bessen, the municipal librarian of Libourne, likewise lent me most generous aid in my researches. I thank Monsieur René d'Ukermann for spending so much of his valuable time searching out books and sending them on to me in Marrakech; I am grateful to him most of all for conversations about the Age of Voltaire, in which he is so thoroughly at home. I am particularly indebted to Madame Bethouart, whose unfailing acuity of judgment has been of inestimable aid in the writing of this book, which she has kindly allowed me to dedicate to her.

Madame Chibois and Madame Pefferkorn have been vigilant readers and have acted as the most sensitive of sounding boards. Madame la Comtesse de Breteuil first introduced me to Madame du Châtelet, née Breteuil, who is now a close acquaintance of mine. My work has often been made easier thanks to Monsieur Bruno Radius, the French consul general at Marrakech, and to Monsieur Tanguy, the cultural attaché at Las Palmas. Finally, I must thank Morocco and the Moroccans, whose flawless hospitality enabled me to work in the most relaxed atmosphere and to live with Voltaire among a friendly people—the climate and the courtesy of our hosts suited both of us perfectly.

Among my guides in print I feel special gratitude and admiration for Monsieur Pierre Gaxotte, all of whose writings on the eighteenth century, Frederick II, and Prussia suffused "my" Voltaire, the moment I had exhumed him from the archives where he lay buried, with such a breath of truth that he came to life as though he were again breathing the air of his own time. I also owe a great deal to Monsieur Jean Guéhenno for some masterly pages of his in the April 1937 issue of *La Nouvelle Revue Française:* they threw a new light on my subject which I have done my best to keep brightly glowing.

Among other works mentioned in the bibliography, that of Monsieur Gustave Desnoiresterres was especially important: it is full of valuable though sometimes deeply buried treasures. I have set many of the facts I learned from his book in a different and more modern light than that shed by the kerosene lamps of the era of Napoleon III.

I felt I could best express my gratitude to Mr. Theodore Besterman, and even more my admiration for this charming gentleman and scholar, by writing a book that is a frank acknowledgment of the debt I owe him. I suspect that Mr. Besterman, who lives in Voltaire's house at Les Délices, has also acquired the wit and style of its original owner.

My most powerful ally has been the indomitable spirit incarnate in Voltaire himself. Since I lack his genius, it must surely have been that spirit that gave me the courage to follow him step by step through every one of his eighty-four years, without once experiencing the slightest trace of boredom or fatigue. Such is the miracle of "St. Voltaire."

For it is indeed a matter of miracle, or perhaps of magic. To tell the story of Voltaire's life is to attempt the impossible. So perhaps I owe the reader some sort of explanation as to how I have approached the task.

PREFACE

Voltaire's life is a ballet, the liveliest sort of ballet imaginable. It is danced more often by a will-o'-the-wisp than by a man: he is an utterly elusive star. How can one capture the reflections of a dancing mirror, of a diamond catching the light of sparkling chandeliers? D'Alembert, defining Voltaire, admitted that he was indefinable. He called him "Monsieur Multiforme"—Mr. Proteus. How was I to create a unique and inimitable character out of this dazzling, bewildering multiplicity?

It seemed to me that I must actually play a bit part myself in the fascinating *opera buffa* that occupied the European stage for nearly a century—that I must pretend to be Voltaire himself. Hence this book was written as Voltaire lived—to the rhythm of an allegro by Mozart. Nothing reveals Voltaire's fundamental nature more truly than his lightning changes of pace. Tone, subject, the roles he assumes all shift incredibly rapidly. There are those who have called these sudden metamorphoses diabolical. He has often been consigned to hell, including a hell on earth in his own lifetime, though he himself wrote: "The earthly paradise is wherever I am."

It was in fact his life itself that captivated me. The reader will not find here a literary study of Voltaire's works: that was not the object, though it goes without saying that mention and discussion of his most characteristic writings figure in these pages in so far as these works influenced or were influenced by the events of his life.

Nothing could be more astonishing than the path of Voltaire's destiny as a writer. Though extremely flighty in many ways, he pursued his chosen career with unflagging tenacity from first to last. At the age of fifteen he already knew exactly what he wanted to be—both very rich and a very great poet—and he won on both counts. His social success had to go hand in hand with his literary success. As he sat in class as a schoolboy, he realized that talent without money is an affliction and money without talent a meaningless achievement. And he was certain that he would be able to escape both these misfortunes.

There are those who maintain he was not "serious." This is true. He did everything he could to avoid seeming to be; but he is infinitely important nonetheless. We tend to forget how many people, in their innermost attitude toward life, have been marked by *Candide*. Voltaire was the almost perfect incarnation of a certain turn of mind which existed in France before him but found its decisive form thanks only to his pen. When he recast the humanism of Molière and La Fontaine, Marot and Montaigne in the dazzling form of his *Micromégas* or his *Letters*, the French became more French than they had been before. Even those of his countrymen who reject his "revelation" still think, speak, and write in a way that reflects his style. Mallarmé said: "The world was destined to end in a book." It might also be said that the French language, beginning with the *fabliaux* and *farces* of the Middle Ages, was destined to end in a marvelous story called *Candide*.

Though he made his own genius and that of his countrymen famous all over Europe, Voltaire had almost no interest in engaging in nationalist propaganda. There is no trace in him of patriotic pride. He is far above such chauvinism. He gallicized the best contemporary Europeans, not in order to annex them to France but to make them cultivated "gentlemen." That is one of his greatest claims to fame. For him and those who understood him, Europe was something very real: the Europe of the Age of Enlightenment, the most civilized and humane of fatherlands, with no frontiers save those of the mind. This far-flung society composed of the elite of all nations was for him the triumph of civilization. It was in large part his own handiwork.

I have endeavored to bring out other of Voltaire's claims to fame which have been somewhat forgotten or obscured because of the apparent frivolity of his personality. Voltaire was a fighter, one who did battle every day of his life for happiness. Not a vague mythical happiness, but an earthly one within everyone's reach. Man must be rescued from the clutches of tyranny and want. Man can be happy only when he assumes all his human responsibilities—when he lives in freedom and reasonable material comfort. Fanaticism, ignorance, and poverty engender blind stupidity, slavery, and war. Happiness is the fruit of intelligence and courage, the fruit of civilization; it is the free man's nobility and grandeur. As for the life beyond this earth, there is nothing to be hoped for there. Every man forges his own destiny here below. One has only to watch Voltaire in action to see a man who constructs his life as an actor builds his part, who plays his role like an actor of genius.

Voltaire's greatness appears again in his feeling for human solidarity. He was an unbeliever who believed in man—without being blinded by illusions. For him, man is the masterpiece of the universe. Every infringement of liberty or justice is intolerable. When Jean Calas is drawn and quartered at Toulouse, Voltaire feels that he himself is being tortured, and cries of pain and anger are immediately forthcoming from

Geneva. Not only is Calas a victim of terrible injustice, but all mankind along with him: Voltaire, you, me. It was you and I and every man that Voltaire defended.

Such a person deserves to have a few years devoted to him. In fact, I can claim no credit: it was out of sheer pleasure that I chose to live in the company of this most intelligent and well-bred of men, the most attentive friend and host, sometimes the most outrageous and surprising of men, but unfailingly the most human. I spent six years of my life in perhaps the best company there has ever been—that is not a labor but a privilege. Everything about Voltaire is fascinating, his bad side as well as his good. He has countless faults and even a number of vices—dancing, pirouetting, dazzling vices. In telling the story of his life I have respectfully left them the not inconsiderable place they deserve. As Voltaire's friend Lord Bolingbroke said of Marlborough: "He was such a great man that I have forgotten his faults." We can forget Voltaire's; but in order to forget them we must first know what they are. I have done my best to portray them as faithfully as his virtues, leaving it to the reader to forget or to gloat over them, as he pleases.

To leave nothing out of a study of so tumultuous, rich, and iridescent a life one would have to live almost as many years as Voltaire himself. There is still much that might have been added. But as Voltaire himself put it: "The secret of being boring is to tell everything," and it seemed to me that nothing could be more Voltairian than to spare the reader such ennui.

JEAN ORIEUX

ILLUSTRATIONS

1. Voltaire, at age twenty-four, after Nicholas de Largillière.
2. Madame du Châtelet. Engraving by Delpeche.
3. Madame de Pompadour, by François Boucher.
4. Engraving depicting the triumphal procession in which Voltaire's remains were transported to the Panthéon, July 11, 1791.
5. Sketches of Voltaire by Jean Huber.
6. Voltaire's bedroom in his Paris residence, corner of Rue de Beaune and Quai Voltaire.
7. The house at Rue de Beaune and Quai Voltaire, where Voltaire died.
8. Frederick the Great with his dinner guests at the Château de Sans Souci, by A. V. Menzel. Foremost among Frederick's guests is Voltaire (left, in profile).
9. Engraving of Voltaire being crowned with a laurel wreath by Le Kain, as Madame Denis looks on.
10. View of the north side of Voltaire's Château de Ferney, by Signy.
11. Meeting of philosophers. Engraving attributed to Jean Huber.
12. Paris, with view from downstream of the Pont Royal, 1740, by C. L. Grevenbroek.
13. View of Paris from the Belleville heights, circa 1740, by C. L. Grevenbroek.
14. The crowning of Voltaire, drawing by Moreau Le Jeune on the subject of Voltaire's "apotheosis."
15. Voltaire, at age forty, by Quentin de la Tour.
16. Voltaire, at age forty-two, by Quentin de la Tour.
17. Voltaire, 1775, at age eighty-one, in an engraving after V. D. Denon.
18. Voltaire in his last years, a bust by Houdon.
19. Counselor of the Parlement, after an engraving by Sebastien Leclerc (1637–1714).
20. Illustration for La Fontaine's *Contes*. Engraving by J. Dambrun, after Fragonard.
21. Rue Quincampoix. Engraving showing crowds besieging Law's bank.

PART ONE

The eartly paradise is wherever I am. (*The Man of the World*)

In the great game of human life one begins by being a dupe and ends up being a rascal. (*Contant d'Orval*, Volume I)

To dissemble: a virtue of kings and chambermaids. (*Remarks*)

It is a superstition of the human species to have imagined that virginity could be a virtue. (*Remarks*)

Nothing would be more intolerable than to eat and drink if God had not made this activity so pleasing and so necessary. (*Dialogues and Conversations*, 25)

The Enfant Terrible

"I was born with two feet in the grave," Voltaire once said. And indeed when François-Marie was born in Paris on November 22, 1694, he was so puny the nurse thought he couldn't last an hour; so Voltaire was given provisional baptism and properly christened later. This enabled him to fib about the date of his birth, and he used to say he was born a year earlier at Châtenay—for some reason he liked to make himself out to be older than he was. But a letter written by a Poitou cousin present at his birth records the actual date.[1]

Voltaire was not the only one to create confusion on the subject of his birth and family background. His enemies spread the tale that he first saw the light on a farm (they were referring to his father's comfortable country house at Châtenay); others said his father was janitor to a notary and ran errands for the clerks and clients. These falsehoods infuriated Voltaire, even though he did not shrink from employing the same methods himself on occasion.

In fact, what his enemies had to say was as nothing compared to the rumors he himself circulated. Voltaire hinted quite openly that his mother had had lovers and that he was the son of one of them. (Anything rather than be an Arouet!) At one point he claimed it was the Abbé de Châteauneuf, the freethinker, who was his father. On another occasion he inclined rather toward Monsieur de Rochebrune, a good gentleman from Auvergne who wrote songs and was a frequent visitor in the Arouets' salon. Voltaire said Monsieur de Rochebrune had a great affection for him, but there was nothing astonishing about that. Young François-Marie might not have been very robust, but he was so intelligent, so quick, so much at ease with grownups that one did not need to be his father to take an interest in him. It is even probable that a legal and legitimate father might have viewed his offspring's boldness with a less indulgent eye than his guests.

Be that as it may, here is young François-Marie equipped with three fathers—an abbé, a witty nobleman, and a royal notary. Why this trio? For the pleasure of inventing witticisms; to make himself interesting; to provoke, to shock, to be in the limelight. To his friend the Duc de Richelieu he addressed a poetical confidence calculated to amuse a person who was even more of a freethinker than himself:

> Le bâtard de Rochebrune
> Ne fatigue et n'importune
> Le successeur d'Armand et des esprits bien faits.

I fear Rochebrune's bastard/Is a source of vexation/To Armand's heir and other highly respectable persons.

He wrote these lines in 1744, when he was nearly fifty. In fact, he would have preferred to be the abbé's bastard: it would be so much more titillating for an unbeliever to be the son of a man of the cloth!

There is no evidence, however, to justify Voltaire's dubious fantasies. Madame Arouet used to visit Ninon de Lenclos, but that does not mean that she had frequented a house of ill repute. In her day Ninon had had so many lovers it would be tedious to try to count them; but at the time when Madame Arouet paid her visits the famous courtesan was in her eighties. In her late years she had only friends from the cream of society —and, no doubt, one or two lovers. But even during the Fronde, when her salon was one of the liveliest in Paris, it was never thought of as disreputable.

The Arouets

Qui sert bien son pays n'a pas besoin d'aïeux (He who serves his country well needs no ancestors). This line from Voltaire's *Mérope* indicates how he felt about families; families in general and his own in particular. He despised them. He wanted to be the first of his lineage and name. Why François-Marie Arouet chose to call himself Voltaire we cannot be sure. The Comte de Dompierre d'Hornoy told me of a family tradition according to which the name Voltaire derives from a nickname given to François-Marie as a child: "Petit Volontaire" (Headstrong), shortened first to "Vlontaire" and then to "Voltaire." There are those who stretch a point and maintain that the name is a rough anagram of "Arouet l.J." (Arouet *le Jeune*, i.e., Junior). Others say it refers to some family estate. But there is no trace of a place of that name, though heaven knows the lawyers of the *ancien régime* kept minute records of the ownership of every patch of land. Perhaps he called himself Voltaire because he did not want to be called Arouet like his father or his older brother Armand or all the other Arouets. He would have liked to burst on the world like Minerva, a child of genius sprung full-blown from the mind of the Supreme Being. But he was born in the bed of a notary and, willy-nilly, he was an Arouet.

He haughtily disowned his forefathers, but this was only conceit. To turn your nose up at your family lineage you need to have had ancestors worthy of your lofty scorn, and Voltaire's were not sufficiently illustrious to merit such calculated disdain. They were respectable enough, however, and in truth deserved something better than contempt from their descendant.

We should know nothing at all about the Arouets if we had only Voltaire to rely on. He never spoke of his family except in the most offhand manner. Yet he owed a great deal to them. In this family, typical of a certain breed of Frenchmen, we find evidence of many of Voltaire's own characteristics, indeed some of his finest. The rise of the Arouets in the course of two centuries is an object lesson in hard work, intelligence, and perseverance. There are clear records of their uninterrupted climb up the social ladder. There were no setbacks and no mistakes: with every generation the Arouets moved up another rung.

The family came originally from a little Vendéean village called Saint-Loup, in the green, wooded, and somewhat remote region of Gâtine in the northern part of the old province of Poitou. It was a typical peasant area, shut in on itself and clannish. The first Arouet we have any record of was a tanner at the end of the fifteenth century. Tanners were numerous in those parts, where cattle raising flourished and water was pleasant. In 1495 this first Arouet rented a plot of land adjoining the river to wash and dry hides. Thanks to the local production of hides, wool, and woven cloth, the sixteenth century was a fairly prosperous period for the village. The Arouets soon moved on from tanning to producing wool and weaving cloth. By 1523 one Hélènus Arouet had become the owner of land in Saint-Loup. He became a person of standing in the region, sometimes referred to by the titles of his various properties: Lord of the Fairies' Mount, Lord of the Swan's Ford, names mindful of a medieval fairy tale.

Gâtine was by no means a prestigious region. The old aristocracy did not live there, and the manor houses were not châteaux but forts with nothing luxurious about them. The local elite consisted mainly of officers of the crown, most of them petty magistrates recruited from among the sons of newly rich tanners and merchants. They automatically acquired nobility on being appointed to these posts that invested them with a fraction of the King's authority. This was the supreme ambition of the head of every enterprising family, and from the sixteenth century onward the Arouets sought such connections. Though they themselves did not yet possess titles, they associated with this new gentry. Some members of the family even held modest positions of prestige, such as steward of the manor.

The first Arouet to take a really decisive step to better his fortunes elsewhere was named François, the son of another Hélènus Arouet who had married into the noble family of Marceton, and the grandson of Pierre Arouet, whose wife belonged to the noble family of Parent. In 1625 François sold everything he had in Saint-Loup, left his tannery behind, and set himself up in business in Paris as a dry-goods merchant. This step was daring but calculated, for it was not by chance that he set up as a wool and silk merchant. Under Louis XIII it was the great luxury trade and the most lucrative. It was also the commerce that brought the merchant class into direct contact with the nobility.[2]

François opened his new shop at the Sign of the Peacock, in the Rue Saint-Denis. In 1626 he married Marie de Mallepart, who came from a family of rich merchant drapers. Her father owned or had owned a bank in Frankfurt and had been ennobled for services rendered. It is notable that from the beginning no Arouet ever married without calculating the consequences of what might be a step downward socially.

François and Marie Arouet had seven children. Of the marriage of one of their daughters, Marie, and Mathieu Marchant were born the only cousins Voltaire ever recognized, perhaps because they were contractors with important positions at court and in the army, and it was they who were responsible for the family's definitive entry into the nobility, since one of their daughters married the Marquis de Bièvres.

The seventh child of François Arouet and Marie de Mallepart was François, Voltaire's father, born in 1650. In 1675 he purchased the office of *conseiller de roi*[3] at Le Châtelet, where the principal royal law courts in Paris were located. After nearly two centuries, the Arouet family had finally achieved its goal: acquiring an office that brought nobility with it. The purchase of this office and setting up legal chambers cost a fortune: the equivalent of between two and two and a half million francs.[4]

On June 7, 1683, François married a young lady whose family name was Daumart. Her father was something a bit grander than a cloth merchant: a gentleman of the robe, a clerk to the Parlement,[5] which was an honorable, indeed a royal office, but one that did not confer nobility.

Nevertheless through his marriage to this clerk's daughter François Arouet entered the set of families connected with the Parlement. His wife's brothers, like himself, were eventually granted titles of nobility.[6]

François Arouet registered his coat of arms with the college of heralds, and his escutcheon was to be Voltaire's. The Arouets had been keeping it in readiness for two hundred years. They were what are known as canting or allusive arms, a sort of heraldic pun, for they showed three scarlet tongues of flame; in the ancient language of Poitou, *arrouer* meant "to burn." Voltaire could hardly have chosen this coat of arms with three blazing *flammes gules* more aptly if he had done so himself.

And yet he jeered at what he owed his forebears. In 1741 he wrote to the Abbé Moussinot, his business agent in Paris: "I sent you a power of attorney with my signature. But I omitted to include the name of Arouet, which I confess I often do quite deliberately. I am sending you other documents on which the name appears, in spite of my scant respect for it."

One day a certain Monsieur de la Fonds, a provincial amateur historian who lived near Loudun, hoping to impress Voltaire, wrote him a most polite letter announcing that he had just discovered that a poet called Arouet had lived in Loudun around the year 1429. But Monsieur de Voltaire coolly replied that he cared neither for fifteenth-century poets in general nor for Arouets in particular. As it happened, this local scholar was mistaken, for the name of the poet was really Adouet. But there was no mistake about Voltaire's contempt for the family name.

What did François-Marie Arouet really have against his family line: centuries of toil, of impeccable respectability, of upright behavior and dignity? There is no sign that they possessed a humorous side. They were undoubtedly austere folk whose chief virtue was moral strength. In the course of two long centuries they had not left behind a single trace of wit, not one picturesque anecdote, one stroke of imagination; not so much as a letter or a page of personal recollections. They admittedly filled many notebooks—but all of them were business ledgers. For two hundred years every column of figures had been added up correctly, every transaction carefully noted down. All their possessions were protected by the royal seal—as were their children, their marriages, their houses. Yet even their health was never the subject of any particular comment. Doctors killed them as they killed most of their patients in those days; but these physicians sent the members of the family to their graves either in early infancy or in old age—that is to say, before they could go into business or after they had made their tidy fortunes. The Arouets and their like were the backbone of pre-revolutionary France: neither war nor pestilence nor financial catastrophe could shake them. They were the rock on which the nation was built. No doubt this was what so exasperated Voltaire.

And yet he himself possessed something of their imperturbable rock-like quality. Not for nothing is one descended from seven generations known to be dedicated workers, honest to a fault, and possessed of a respect for money amounting almost to a passion. But in him Arouet blood had been mixed with Parisian: the Mallepart and Daumart strains warmed and lightened that of the old Vendéeans, lending it an alien fire. This bright glow was fed, however, by the deeper embers of his heredity, and though these flames might mask the Arouet foundations they never quite consumed them. Every so often in the course of his long life, behind the Voltaire we know—worldly, Parisian, freethinking, sacrilegious—we catch a glimpse of an old-style Arouet from Saint-Loup letting drop a typical notary's expression: And in the privacy of his study Monsieur de Voltaire keeps his accounts for all the world like the dutiful son he was determined not to be. Hence there are certain chinks in his philosophical individualism, through which more than once there appears the implacable face of a traditional Arouet, his quill adding up long columns of figures and working out complicated accumulations of interest.

In one way Voltaire was right: he had made himself, invented himself, as few other men have done. The world of the bourgeoisie irritated him no end; his natural habitat was the aristocracy. He forgot one thing however: if the aristocracy opened its doors to him he owed that fact to his father. True, he made a place for himself in this milieu through his own talent; but it was by virtue of the respectable name of Arouet and the esteem in which men of noble families such as Richelieu, Saint-Simon, and Sully held his father that he first gained entry into these elite circles.

By 1692 Voltaire's father was no longer a notary. He had sold this office and now appears in the college of heraldry as "conseiller du roi, collector of spice taxes in the Royal Exchequer"—a by no means unprofitable occupation. What sort of person François Arouet was is a matter of conjecture rather than knowledge. Almost incredible as it may seem, no letter exists from Voltaire to him. He was an austere man of unyielding rectitude, and so he wished his offspring to be. Neither of his sons gave him much satisfaction, though he probably preferred Armand, the elder.[7] François-Marie frightened him, inspired him with a sort of contempt, and never brought him anything but humiliation and bitterness. Armand presented a striking contrast to his brother François-Marie. "Two mad sons," their father would say. "One crazy with religion and the other with irreligion." Armand had been tonsured, a first step toward taking holy orders, and had considered joining the Oratorians. He was a strange man, full of curious ideas, never at peace; his religion was an anxious and tormented one. He was an extremist, a fanatic, who belonged to the group of the controversial Jansenist sect known as convulsionaries: he was one of those who must have miracles. Every so often he would roll on the floor in order to call down grace. But coming from the family he did, he never allowed his religious concerns to interfere with his temporal interests. He lived with his father and managed to get his hands on the major part of the fortune the latter left. He hated François-Marie. One of his bitterest disappointments was to die without issue, knowing that part of his own estate would go to his impious brother.

There was also a sister, Marguerite, the conseiller's fifth child. Voltaire loved her: she was the only person in his entire family for whom he seems to have felt any affection. On January 28, 1709, she married Master Mignot, conseiller du roi and a supervisor in the Royal Exchequer.[8]

Such was the sort of nest into which our hero was born. But, alas, the essential element is missing. Voltaire was to all intents and purposes a motherless child, for Madame Arouet died when he was seven. He never speaks of her. Practically nothing is known about her except a remark she made about the celebrated literary figure Nicolas Boileau, who was one of the Arouets' neighbors.[9]

There are those who have tried to represent the Arouets as society people. Others have gone so far as to imagine that they were worldly and frivolous. Voltaire himself contributed something toward this belief, but in fact it is untrue. If Ninon de Lenclos and certain nobles entrusted their legal interests to Monsieur François Arouet it was simply because he possessed the traditional virtues of his profession: solidity, integrity, rectitude. His clients became his friends—there is no better testimony in his favor. One of the visitors to the Arouet home was a canon of the Sainte-Chapelle, the Abbé Gedoyn. François Arouet had also known the great Corneille. Voltaire writes: "He used to tell me Corneille was the most wearisome creature and most boring conversationalist he had ever met." Corneille himself modestly admitted that he had nothing to say for himself in company. The Abbé de Châteauneuf, François-Marie's godfather, was a member of this circle. He made a splendid addition. It was he who taught the boy his first verses, and arbitrated, or even provoked, the frequent bitter arguments the youngster had with his older brother Armand. The spectacle of an abbé[10] fostering animosity between two brothers, setting two clever but irritable children to quarreling, is a curious one. Such was the company the respectable Arouet family received. No doubt they entertained fellow lawyers and their own most distinguished clients with considerable ceremony and lavishness, and probably Madame Arouet would respectfully return these visits, but nothing could be less like a fashionable salon than the Arouets' richly furnished but boringly stuffy drawing room.

After his mother's death in 1701, François-Marie went on living at home for another three years. When he was ten he was sent to be taught by the Jesuits at Louis-le-Grand. There were three arrangements available to boarders at the school. The ordinary one cost four hundred livres and the pupils slept in a dormitory and ate in the refectory. The sons of great nobles each had a private room and a tutor and valet to themselves. But for François-Marie his father chose the mean between those two extremes, an arrangement whereby the pupils lived five to a room under the supervision of a prefect. The prefect allotted to young François happened to be the famous Abbé d'Olivet, who was later Voltaire's colleague in the Académie Française.[11] Miraculous to relate, each retained a great regard for the other and pleasant memories of their early acquaintance. They might easily have drowned the pupil-teacher relationship in gall and venom. That they did not is to the credit of both. "You sat at my feet then," the abbé said later in the Academy; "now I sit at yours."

Voltaire's schooldays were not always easy for him, but he did not complain. The winter of 1709 was unusually severe. The cold was so intense that master and pupils had to huddle together round the stove. François, a frail child who felt the cold intensely, was continually chilly and peaked. All his life it was the same: even on a cool summer evening he would crouch over a fire. The best pupil in the class, instead of being in the front row facing the teacher, sat nearest the stove. An apocryphal story has François-Marie, who was not the best pupil in the class and hence did not occupy the coveted position nearest the stove, give another boy a shove one day so as to try to get a bit nearer the fire. "Move over," he said, "or I'll send you to Hades." "Why not hell?" said the other. "It's even hotter there." "You can't be any surer of one than you can of the other," François replied.

In the mouth of a fourteen-year-old at a Jesuit college the remark is bold but not improbable. One might quote a few other of his supposed comments without actually vouching for their authenticity.

One day another boy asked François to give back the mug he had hidden somewhere to tease him.

"Give it back or you won't go to heaven."

"Heaven?" François replied. "What's the boy thinking about? Heaven's the great dormitory that everyone goes to in the end."

On another occasion Father Lejay, with whom he did not get on at all, is supposed to have laid hold of François and cried out prophetically: "Wretched boy! You will grow up to be the standard-bearer of deism in France!"

But this prediction, reported in 1786 by Théophile Duvernet, one of Voltaire's earliest biographers, is too good to be true. Nothing could be easier than to "foresee" Voltaire's deism eighty years after the event, eight years after his death. The written report of Father Pallou, the boy's confessor, is far more to the point: "This boy is consumed with the desire for fame." Here we are dealing with facts.

François-Marie was a friend too of the young Duc de Fronsac, Armand de Richelieu,[12] son of the Duc de Richelieu, who was a client and friend of Monsieur Arouet. He was also on intimate terms with other boys: Fyot de la Marche, who became the presiding magistrate of the Parlement of Dijon and who wrote Voltaire letters full of gaiety and a kind of admiring respect; and a certain Le Coq who never made his way in the world but who turned up every so often to receive help that Voltaire never confessed to giving.

Between Voltaire and his teachers there was a sort of natural understanding. He and they loved the same authors for the same reasons. If he had been educated at a Jansenist or even a Calvinist school he would still have become famous. But to grow up to be Voltaire, the young Arouet had to be incubated by the Jesuits. From the Jesuits the young boy learned that supreme combination of intelligence and art known as taste. At school he learned the language in which he was later to write *Mérope* and *Candide;* and there he also acquired a certain cast of mind, a subtlety of thought, the art of significant understatement. Such things can be acquired only by intimate contact with masterpieces, after long exposure to thoughts that have been expressed in classical forms, established beyond debate. In the case of Voltaire, the fathers were preaching to one already converted: their literary principles must have seemed to him like nature itself—or rather, like his own nature. His entire work breathes air of classic purity that permeated the lessons at Louis-le-Grand.

At school his lessons were no burden to him: he enjoyed them and was eager to please, which he did by playing up to his teachers and by producing good results. He was fond of the masters and they of him. All his life he retained that gratitude and affection: "For seven years I received my education at the hands of men who devote themselves tirelessly and without reward to the task of forming the minds and manners of the young. Since when has it been the fashion to be ungrateful to one's masters? Nothing will ever make me forget Father Porée; and he is as dear to all those who studied under him as he is to me. No man ever made virtue and learning appear more attractive." (That was the secret, the golden rule for Voltaire. He learned it at his desk at school, and was to go on proclaiming it all his life.) "The hours when he taught us were hours of delight. I would have liked to see him installed in Paris as in the Athens of antiquity, so that all might come and hear such lessons at any age. I myself would often have gone to hear them. I had the good fortune to be formed by more than one Jesuit of the stamp of Father Porée, and I know he has successors worthy of him." Voltaire wrote this in 1746.

Though he paid homage to their teaching, Voltaire did not always deal with other aspects of the Society of Jesus so gently. Nevertheless they never had a more affectionate pupil. He sent them his books and anxiously awaited their verdict. To Father Tournemine, one of his former teachers at Louis-le-Grand, he wrote: "Most dear and reverend Father, is it really true that you like my *Mérope?* Did you find in it some of the generous sentiments you taught me as a boy?" Once, as he was not in Paris, he pleaded his cause with Father Brumoy through a friend, Thiériot, "In the name of heaven hasten as soon as you can to Father Brumoy, one of the priests who were my teachers and must never be my foes. Speak to him affectionately but persuasively. Father Brumoy has read *Mérope* and liked it. Father Tournemine is enthusiastic. Please God I have deserved their praises! Assure them of my unshakable attachment; it is but what I owe them. They brought me up, and whoever is ungrateful to those who formed his mind is a monster."

He paid tribute not to his own father but to his real spiritual fathers, the Jesuits who shaped his mind. The obligation that Voltaire felt toward them is a typical Arouet trait. One of his most deep-rooted characteristics was always to be aware of what he owed others. He also was aware of what others owed him, and if they failed to give him his due it was they who were the "monsters."

And how could his teachers, for their part, have forgotten him? At twelve, in the breaks between lessons, he did not often play; instead he talked with them. What interested him most was contemporary history, or, as we would say today, politics. Father Porée once said: "He loved to weigh in his small scales the great issues of Europe."

What really singled him out at school was his skill at writing verses. The Abbé de Châteauneuf had introduced him first to La Fontaine, then —when François-Marie was nine—to a ribald poem by Jean-Baptiste Rousseau. When François-Marie was only twelve he spoke of a tragedy he had already composed, called *Amulius et Numitor*, which has unfortunately disappeared. Some occasional youthful verses have survived however. One day in class he was playing with his snuffbox, tossing it up and down (snuff had been prescribed as a remedy against colds). The teacher confiscated the box and demanded a forfeit for its return—a petition in verse. The twelve-year-old Arouet lost no time in composing a plea in rhyme, aping with considerable skill the conceits of a courtier.[13]

One more poem traveled beyond the walls of Louis-le-Grand, inspired by motives of charity. While still a schoolboy Voltaire had begun to use his pen in defense of the unfortunate—in this case a war veteran who had served under the Dauphin and sought a New Year's gift from him. The poem was read at court, and the veteran was duly given some golden louis. Voltaire's reward was to go and be dandled by Ninon de Lenclos. The aged enchantress, ever on the lookout for youthful talent, wanted to meet and congratulate the young poet, son of her notary and godson of her friend the Abbé de Châteauneuf. It was the abbé who took François-Marie to see her. Voltaire wrote of the occasion long after: "The Abbé de Châteauneuf took me to her house in my extreme youth. I was then about thirteen years old, and had written some verses worthless in themselves but deemed creditable enough for one of my years." Voltaire tells us that the abbé was "the master of the house," which clearly means that Ninon was the abbé's mistress. Incredible as it may seem, she was then over eighty.[14]

In order that the mind and manners of the young poet should be fully formed, he no doubt had to be told that there was yet another master in Ninon's house. This was the Abbé Gedoyn of the Sainte-Chapelle, whom Voltaire already knew. Ninon's boudoir was a side chapel swarming with clerics, and if anyone wanted to see the canon they went to her house. No one had any objections: it was an age that created scandals only about money.

Nevertheless, François did find the loves inspired by Ninon somewhat strange. He did not see her through the eyes of ardent middle age, and his view of her is no doubt nearer the truth: "She was a wrinkled, decrepit old creature with nothing left on her bones but yellow and still darkening skin. By the time she was eighty all the most repulsive marks of age reigned in her face, as did all its infirmities in her heart." He speaks of her without emotion, as a "curiosity," a monument of a bygone age, a relic of the age of gallantry. She did not move him: his senses were not affected. But the literary monuments of the previous century had not withered, and it was they that touched and stirred him, and always would. Iphigenia would be fresh and young and moving forever, and it was as such a figure that she struck a chord in young Arouet.

As a consequence of her meeting with young Arouet, Mademoiselle de Lenclos left him two thousand livres with which to buy books. It was a handsome gift and a generous and charming gesture, one that prolonged the memory of a woman who had shone through one century in the mind of the young man whose genius was to illuminate the next.

François-Marie also gained a certain celebrity for an *Ode to Sainte Geneviève* written in these early years. The piece has something of the eclogue about it and its religiosity is in the vein of courtly compliment. He begs the patron saint of Paris, if his ardor should win her favor, to allow him to lay his works at her feet. In later life, Voltaire was none too proud of this ode, not because it was doggerel but because it was devout. His deadly enemy Elie Fréron was to excavate it one day and parade it everywhere, for everyone to laugh at Voltaire's piety. Today's reader merely smiles at the quaint versification.

While François was still at Louis-le-Grand he had the honor of being complimented by the most celebrated poet of the day, Jean-Baptiste Rousseau. This was Voltaire's first encounter with the literary tribe, and a prophetic one. It was prize day at the end of the school year of 1710 and the reigning poet asked to meet young Arouet, whose budding talents he had already heard about. This is how Rousseau later described what he saw in a portrait written thirty years after the meeting: "A young schoolboy who looked sixteen or seventeen, of unprepossessing countenance [*mauvaise physionomie*], but with an alert and lively expression, who came and embraced me with all the grace in the world."

One must make the necessary allowance for ill will. The piece was written after the two had become enemies. That "unprepossessing countenance" is pure malice. At seventeen François, though he was not handsome, had an expressive face and a winning smile. Rousseau could hardly do less than admit the sparkle in François's eyes: it dazzled everyone. Nor could he very well deny his "grace": François was a natural courtier, and though some have criticized and some have praised his efforts to please, no one ever denied his charm.

Voltaire never forgave Rousseau for those words *mauvaise physionomie*. It was easy enough to take his revenge later: Rousseau was as carroty-headed as his name suggests, pale, freckled, with eyes of different colors and a crooked mouth. "I know well why my face does not please him," Voltaire said. "It's because my hair is brown and my mouth not twisted."

When Rousseau went on in later years to attack Voltaire's *Henriade* as well, the latter's revenge became even more cruel. The public then learned that Rousseau's father was a cobbler who had worked for the Arouets, and that Rousseau himself had neither manner nor manners, only morals that left much to be desired. Voltaire wrote: "He [i.e., Rousseau] ought to have added that he paid me this visit because his father had been my father's shoemaker for twenty years, and that my father had taken the trouble to get him employment with an attorney, where he would have done well to remain. But he was discharged for having disavowed his birth. He might also have added that my father and other relations and likewise all my teachers then forbade me to go and see him. And such was his reputation that whenever a boy at school transgressed in a certain way they used to say to him, 'You'll grow up to be just like Rousseau.'"

True or false, there it is. That was what one got for saying that François-Marie Arouet had an unprepossessing countenance on speech-day at Louis-le-Grand in 1710.

The Education of a Freethinker: The Temple

The circle that surrounded François outside school was nothing if not stimulating. It was distinguished by wit, manners, culture—and amorality. François saw and understood everything, and in spite of the discipline that reigned, it was impossible for a boy not to be influenced by the conversations he listened to with such rapture. The rakes of the Temple,[15] as the group was called, were excellent talkers. Just as their birth made them the aristocrats of society, so their airy attitude toward laws, beliefs, and morals made them the aristocrats of intellect and freedom. François was dazzled, captivated. Here he felt at home, among his equals—perhaps having already half persuaded himself that in reality he was the offspring of a freethinking aristocrat. Thus when addressing the Prince de Conti at a dinner where all vied with each other in wit and daring, it seemed quite natural for him to offer this astonishing pleasantry: "Those gathered here are princes or poets all!" Before a prince of the blood this was boldness indeed. But it got by: Conti was young and a wit himself.

The words help illuminate their author. A prince who was a poet, a poet who was a prince—for him they were the same thing. The prince-poet had nothing in common with ordinary people. François-Marie Arouet knew he was going to live on the heights and not in a notary's chambers—not even a royal notary's. Nor did he aspire to a magistrate's mortarboard: what he must have was a crown. He was going to be a king —with or without the permission of other kings.

It was his mentor Châteauneuf who first took François-Marie to the Temple. In 1706, when he was twelve, François began to spend his days off from school there. His education presents a strange alternation: on weekdays, the offices, sermons, and brilliant lessons of the holy fathers, and on Sundays inspiration in the Temple of Impiety. When he was a little older he became a regular guest at the famous suppers that left the devout horror-stricken. From this distinguished company he borrowed the tone, the purity and elegance of their language, and their sovereign contempt and sarcasm for "everything that is most sacred."

It is difficult to understand why later freethinkers allowed the great tower of the Temple to be destroyed: it had been the cathedral of irreligion under the *ancien régime*. Its rites were never more dazzlingly celebrated than at the beginning of the eighteenth century. At that time the Grand Prior of the Knights of St. John of Jerusalem, to which the Temple then belonged, was Lieutenant General Philippe de Bourbon-Vendôme, brave, brilliant, but ravaged by dissolute living. The grandson of Henri IV and his mistress Gabrielle d'Estrées, he was the high priest of "libertinage." Voltaire did not meet him until 1715 because until then Bourbon-Vendôme had been in exile: the court of the aged King and Madame de Maintenon regarded him as a limb of Satan. Appearances certainly seem to support their point of view. In his absence the altar of free thought was tended by distinguished substitutes: the poets La Fare and Chaulieu, and two great friends and fellow pupils of François-Marie's, the Duc de Sully and the Duc de Fronsac.

There were also minor characters such as the Abbé Servien, who had set all Paris laughing by going on the stage of the Opéra and singing a ditty in praise of the King, only with the words cleverly reversed. The applause brought down the house. The abbé lacked neither wit, culture, nor the social graces, and he probably owed his election to the Académie Française to his songs and the excellence of his conversation. On the day of his reception there was such a crowd that he had difficulty fighting his way to the door. "I see," he observed, "that it is more difficult to get into this place than to be admitted to it." All doors were open to him, but the only places he chose to frequent were those where he might indulge his audacity freely. He was a familiar figure at the Opéra and in the arcades of the Palais Royal; it was his habit to carry a muff and deliver his witticisms with his nose buried in its fur. He made a specialty of expressing the most horrifying ideas in the most ornate style and in a gentle, caressing voice. A strange intimacy existed between him and his Sully nephews.

A short while before the King's death the abbé was arrested, and he and his muff carried off to Vincennes. There was great lamentation. François-Marie Arouet, who was always fond of his masters whether they were on the side of good or evil, lost no time in consoling Servien by sending him a quaint Anacreonetic ode, full of high-flown references to the Graces, weeping and beating their breasts at the sight of the abbé's misfortunes.

It was among these people that young Arouet was to put the finishing touches to his education. They demonstrate the tone of Paris as it was then, at the end of Louis XIV's long reign and the beginning of the Regency.

First Flirtations with the World of High Society

By the time he was sixteen years old, François-Marie knew he wanted to be a man of letters. To the entire Arouet clan François-Marie's ambition was not only ridiculous, it was disgraceful. " 'Tis the condition of a man who means to be of no use to society, to sponge on his relatives, and to starve to death," Monsieur Arouet declared. Though young François-Marie scorned this opinion, he did begin to study law. But from the beginning he was horrified by the coarse language and manners of both teachers and students. He found their personal standards of cleanliness most questionable as well. The law school itself was little better than a barn. He would never resign himself to being trapped in such surroundings: he needed to be understood by dukes and princes, and could blossom only in the lap of luxury. It was not without apprehension that Monsieur Arouet would see his son hobnobbing on equal terms with young noblemen of whom he, the elderly notary, stood in awe. Yet he was powerless against the future. His son would be the peer not only of dukes but of kings, and his sovereignty would overshadow theirs.

Meanwhile a titled lady engaged François-Marie to revise the verses she composed. This was the beginning of a sort of pedagogic vocation—correcting the poetical exercises of the great. It was so much more amusing to versify with a duchess than to gossip with smelly lawyers! In payment the duchess sent him a hundred livres, and this rather handsome sum went to his head. He bought an old carriage, hired horses and lackeys, and spent an entire day driving around Paris, playing at being a lord. Unfortunately, the whole rig overturned while rounding a corner. That evening, not knowing what to do with it all, he sent the coach to his father's stables and dismissed the lackeys. During the night Monsieur Arouet's horses, made nervous by their strange stable companions, started to whinny and lash out at their stalls, wrecking the stables and waking the whole neighborhood. When Monsieur Arouet heard what had happened he was as upset as his horses, and turned his son out of the house. Next day he got the local wheelwright to sell the carriage and the old nags.

Whether or not this little anecdote is entirely true, Voltaire's enemies would later vow that it was. In any case it was hardly a serious matter: François-Marie, at sixteen, was merely engaging in a symbolic little ges- of independence. His other independent habits of coming home at all hours of the night and dropping in for meals when it pleased him pro- duced encounters with his father that undoubtedly were irritating to both.

One night François found the doors of his father's house closed against him and went and asked the concierge at the Palais to take him in. The concierge, not knowing where to put him, pointed out a sedan chair that had been left in the courtyard, where he could snooze till daylight. Two young magistrates arriving early were amused at the spectacle, and gently carried the chair and its contents and deposited them outside a café by the river, where the early customers had a good laugh at the expense of the victim, still sound asleep in the chair in broad daylight.

His father was so worried about his son that he was ready to buy him a post in the Parlement. He would have been glad to purchase peace at any price, even that of the mortarboard and ermine-lined gown of a prési- dent,[16] in the hope that such honors and duties would curb his offspring's frivolity. François-Marie rejected the cap and gown in no uncertain terms. "Go tell my father I will have none of an honor that may be bought. I shall win for myself one that costs nothing."

Insolence apart, this expresses a very modern sentiment, the pride of the self-made man. It smacks of rebellion, and even has a prophetic re- semblance to Mirabeau's famous "Go tell the King we are here by the will of the people. . . ."

Voltaire was later to say: "I threw myself into the arts, which are still somewhat degrading in that they cannot make a man privy counselor to the King." This was true. To be a writer did entail a certain degradation in those days: for in society as it was then a man could not be someone unless he was something. But a man of letters was nothing. He did not even own the products of his pen. François-Marie Arouet was to change all that. Voltaire was the first man of letters of middle-class origins to possess power and dignity and social esteem, and to defend ceaselessly the rights of all writers.

It was not to dissociate himself from the class to which he belonged that François-Marie repudiated the Arouets, but to raise to a higher class the things he stood for: freedom of thought and freedom to write. It was not simply the emancipation of a young dandy so that he could lead the life of a debonair social butterfly in peace; it was the breaking of an old yoke, the rise of a new element in society. But this would become appar- ent only later. During Voltaire's youth we see little but worldly frivolity and triviality; elegant witticisms that evaporate as swiftly as a duchess' perfume; compliments; smiles. He dressed to perfection, walked well, talked like a prince, and moved in society with innate grace and ease. In this era of pomp and circumstance, a salon was a sort of theater, and a stage was the place where François-Marie felt most at home. He was witty, clever, polished—an ideal toy for a duchess, but a toy of the highest quality. That was how he began, and he knew what he was about. At seventeen he was convinced that his genius made him the equal of a prince. All his life he endeavored to persuade Europe of the same thing; and he succeeded.

He was already getting his hand in: he was working at writing. Scatterbrained though he might seem, he produced long exercises in style and composition. He read, talked, listened. For him, to talk was to learn and to collect his own thoughts—there was no such thing as talking for the sake of talking. Even his trivialities were well-turned phrases.

Chaulieu and La Fare encouraged him to write verses. In 1712, when he was eighteen, he entered a poetry competition sponsored by the Académie Française. Louis XIV had suddenly remembered a vow made by his father Louis XIII, dedicating France to the Blessed Virgin, and had had an altar built in Notre Dame to commemorate it. Now the Académie asked poets to submit an ode to the Virgin. Voltaire produced one, as he had done earlier in honor of Saint Geneviève, and Jean-Baptiste Rousseau complimented him, not on its piety but on its wit.

He rather expected his entry would win the prize. Jean-Baptiste Rousseau, however, had warned him against the vanity of literary awards: "We do not see men like Corneille, Racine, or Despréaux writing for prizes. They feared it might harm their reputation, knowing well that 'twas on the most mediocre compositions that academic laurels were most likely to be bestowed."

Not very complimentary to the jury, but prudent advice. It was the Abbé Dujarry who won the prize. Young Arouet was dreadfully hurt. He thirsted for poor old Abbé Dujarry's blood. It was not the abbé's fault; he had written his ode in good faith; but Arouet was out for vengeance: "He is one of those professional poets one meets everywhere and could wish to meet nowhere—a parasite who pays for a good dinner with bad verse." He was sharpening his pamphleteer's claws on the unfortunate abbé's back: "Of course 'tis merely to honor his advanced age."

This is how Voltaire was to be. Any contretemps or obstacle and he flew into a biting, scratching rage.

The young author's principal goal, however, was that of every writer in those days: fame. To become famous one had to produce some great work, and in this era the greatest and most sublime genre was thought to be tragedy. He had already chosen his subject: Oedipus. When reminded that Corneille had already treated this subject, he replied that he would outdo Corneille. (Not a very dangerous boast: Corneille's *Oedipe* is a play most people prefer to forget.) Though there was no early prospect of performance, Voltaire's tragedy was soon finished and he kept reworking it. But it was not yet really mature, and neither was he.

François-Marie Falls in Love

Monsieur Arouet had lost all patience with the life his son was leading and had sent him to Caen. But the results had been disappointing: François-Marie behaved in Caen as he had in Paris. He dazzled a local Catholic noblewoman, Madame d'Osseville, and they were seen everywhere together, from the fine houses in Caen to the country mansions just outside the city. The lady could not take her eyes off him, fairly swooning at the sound of his voice. But she nearly choked with rage when she learned that he had recited libertine verses in someone else's salon. She would endure neither atheism nor infidelity, and closed her doors to him. All this caused a certain local scandal: but for all Voltaire's life, wherever he went, scandal followed in his wake. He soon found compensation for his prudish lady's rebuff in the shape of Father de Couvrigny, a Jesuit, a circumspect freethinker, and a man of culture, who proclaimed everywhere that young Arouet was a genius. Father de Couvrigny was a valuable companion; with him François read books he had never come across before, and had long discussions from which he emerged if not better behaved at least more skillful and knowledgeable. In 1713 he returned to Paris.

His father immediately approached an old friend, the Marquis de Châteauneuf—the abbé's brother, then ambassador to Holland—entrusting the incorrigible François-Marie to his care. Let them make of him what they would—attaché, secretary, counselor or page—but let them tame him, or at least relieve a father of a son's disturbing presence.

His visit to The Hague provided François with countless surprises and diversions, of which the sweetest were badinage and love. Needless to say, the French Embassy and its staff and documents saw little of him. He headed straight for a circle of French refugees—Protestants for the most part, but also political refugees. It was a large group and heterogeneous; while many of its members were respectable, many others were not. It was the latter that François-Marie took for his confidants. His incursions into this dubious world, drawn by curiosity, gave rise to an adventure, accompanied by a scandal, and, if the truth be told, a certain amount of publicity to which he was not entirely insensitive.

At The Hague, François-Marie made the acquaintance of a Huguenot lady, a certain Dame Dunoyer, who had fled France to escape religious persecution and come to Holland in search of freedom of conscience—among other liberties. That she had already found freedom of morals her behavior amply demonstrates. Her business dealings were enhanced by the presence of two charming daughters whom she had taken away from their father, a French captain still in France. He had managed to reconcile his faith and his patriotism, but lost his wife and daughters in the process. Dame Dunoyer did not hesitate to tell her intimates that it was her husband's authoritarianism rather than His Majesty's dragoons that had caused her to flee the country. She was given to these bursts of sincerity. She freely admitted that she was ugly, for example, but also readily confessed that it had never diminished the number of her lovers. She was as lacking in scruples as she was in beauty. Claiming she "knew what men were like," she relied on their vices rather than their virtues to manipulate them. Her methods earned her quite a good living. Before coming to The Hague, Dame Dunoyer had set herself up in business in England, but when the English learned the nature of her activities she was obliged to seek a new clientele elsewhere.

Her talents were certainly varied. To amorous intrigue and sophisticated mendacity she added calumny. For she was also a writer: her voice was one in the dreadful chorus of insults that rose up abroad against France. She wrote scurrilous pamphlets on the court, the Church, the judiciary. François-Marie was amused rather than shocked and said that there wasn't a word of truth in all her gossip. But in fact there were occasional truths among this trash.

François-Marie listened to Dame Dunoyer but had his eye on Olympe, her younger daughter. She was known as Pimpette, a much more suitable appellation for a young creature not exceptionally pretty, but lively, impulsive, charming, flighty, and no fool. For the first time François found himself head over heels in love. For him it was a new experience, but Pimpette, with the benefit of her mother's training, already knew all the ins and outs of the love game. In spite of her own reputation, Dame Dunoyer intended to make good matches for her daughters. "One should get married at least once," she used to say. "In the first place for pleasure and in the second for advantage." She succeeded in marrying the older girl off to one Monsieur Contantin, an elderly but well-to-do officer. Moreover, she nearly succeeded in marrying off Pimpette to the famous Jean Cavalier, leader of the Camisards, a group of openly rebellious Cévennes Calvinists. The Huguenots revered this champion of the Protestant cause and when he came to Holland he was feted by all the refugees. Dame Dunoyer took him aside and offered him her all, but he would take only Pimpette. He promised to marry the girl, then suddenly fled to England. No one ever discovered whether he ran away from the mother, the daughter, or both.

Some thirty years later Voltaire's enemies would sneer that, although he had been the Camisard's rival, Voltaire could get only what the Camisard had tossed aside. They would also maintain that this was not surprising since young François-Marie looked rather like a forlorn waif at the time. Yet a police inspector wrote, "Arouet is tall and thin and looks like a satyr." He was not tall; and if it was his mocking smile that made him look like a satyr, satyrs can nevertheless be fascinating. Pimpette was as taken with François-Marie as he with her. Neither Dame Dunoyer nor anyone else at The Hague was under any illusion about the relations between the two young people, for they took no trouble to hide their affair. The mother was the last person to stand on ceremony about such open secrets and was the first to turn them to her advantage. If François-Marie had been a man of substance she would have forced him into marriage. She scolded her daughter for starting on the cake without thinking about the bread and butter, and she was determined to protect her daughter from the consequences of her folly.

Gathering together whatever dignity remained from better days, she presented herself at the French Embassy in the role of outraged mother: a Frenchman attached to the embassy had compromised the innocent Pimpette, sullying both the girl's reputation and that of her mother, a woman of unquestionable virtue and, what was more, a Huguenot who would tolerate no such outrage to morality. Reparation must be made. The ambassador had only just taken up the post (there had not yet even been time for him to present his credentials) and he most certainly did not want any scandal from this "outraged" mother capable of wielding a venomous pen. At this point Captain Dunoyer intervened, in an attempt to recover not his wife but Pimpette. In exchange for the return of his daughter he offered to convert to Catholicism and to oblige Pimpette to do the same. The aged Louis XIV, reconverted to the strict practice of his faith and to prudery under the influence of Madame de Maintenon, would be certain to approve. And so he did, instructing his ambassador at The Hague to second the father and do everything possible to facilitate Pimpette's return to the bosom of France and the Church. But the scandal being stirred up by the mother threatened to spoil everything. It was necessary to prevent Dame Dunoyer from knowing of her husband's negotiations. She did not want to give up her position either as a heretic or as an exile. Not only were they her most profitable sources of income, but they also freed her from marital tyranny. If her husband, France, and the Church took Pimpette away from her, what would she live on in her old age?

The day after Madame Dunoyer had presented herself to the ambassador, Monsieur de Châteauneuf summoned François and told him he was sending him back to his family at once. François begged, argued, implored, undoubtedly with great guile, wit, and charm, but the ambassador remained unmoved. All François could obtain was a twenty-four-hour delay—to be spent, alone, in his room. He toyed with the idea of eloping with Pimpette, rushing to Nîmes, and throwing himself at the captain's feet to beg for his daughter's hand—but it took a fortnight to get to Nîmes by coach. Finally he thought of the time-honored solution: penning a letter to the young lady. She must follow him without hesitation or complaint. "If you hesitate a moment you will have merited all your misfortunes. Let your virtue here show itself entire: watch me depart now as resolutely as you will later follow," he writes her. He also tells her that he is locked in his room, with a guard outside his door, and instructs her to send him three letters: one for the captain, one for her uncle, and one for her sister, to enlist their immediate support.

But just as he was about to send the letter he discovered that all his messages were being intercepted—getting no farther than the embassy. He too knew a trick or two, however. He promptly disguised his valet, a rascal from Normandy, as a peddler of snuffboxes, and sent him to offer his wares to Dame Dunoyer. The ruse succeeded, and the valet gained access to Pimpette. The poor girl was half dead with grief, but the valet told her François meant to see her and carry her off to hide in the outskirts of The Hague. She must steal out of the house at midnight. Pimpette was quite ready to do so, but her mother was on to all the stratagems of thwarted lovers and made Pimpette sleep with her in her own bed.

The situation was resolved by a melodramatic scheme invented by François. He sent Pimpette a suit of his clothes and a cloak, together with a letter of instructions: "Be on your guard still with your respected mother, be on your guard with yourself—but count on me as on yourself to do everything possible to deliver you from the abyss in which you lie." (There is a certain piquancy in his description of Dame Dunoyer's bed as an abyss.) And what might seem possible only on the stage actually happened. Pimpette, dressed in François's clothes, crept into the house to which the ambassador had confined him, and exchanged letters with him. After seeing Pimpette in disguise he wrote: "I know not whether to address you as Mademoiselle or Monsieur. Though you are adorable in your lace cap, you make no less charming a gentleman. Even the porter here, who is not in love with you, thought you a most handsome youth."

Obliged finally to leave Holland, François gave Pimpette the address of his father's house in Paris. But she was madly in love and wanted to throw herself at the ambassador's feet and ask for pardon for François and protection for herself against her cruel mother. François forbade her to do any such thing however: he knew the consequences would be catastrophic for both of them. The ambassador meant to nip their affair in the bud, and anything that interfered with his purpose was doomed to failure. "My dear Pimpette, but follow my advice this once and you shall take your revenge all the rest of my life, for I shall vow to obey you forever," François writes her to dissuade her.

All this was too much for poor Pimpette, and she fell ill. Her mother no longer had to keep her in bed—fever took care of that. Of the two it was Pimpette who had been genuinely in love. Her letters may have been naïve, but her words scorch the paper. François was admittedly smitten by her charms, but his letters to her are always those of a rhetorician. Though the inspiration came from his heart, his mind always remained in control. He addresses her in the formal *vous* form: "Adieu, dear heart, 'tis perhaps the last time I shall write from The Hague. I vow to be constant forever. None but you can make me happy—I taste happiness already when I recall your tenderness toward me. Adieu, adorable Olympe, adieu, my dear one. If kisses might be set down on paper, I would send you an infinity of them through the post."

Pimpette, in torment, feverish with wild schemes for rejoining her lover, wrote to him, using the familiar *tu* form: "I shall say nothing of my health. 'Tis what concerns me least. I think too much of you to have time to think of myself. I assure you, my dear heart, that had I any doubts concerning my love I would rejoice in my present pain. Yes, my dear child, life would be but a burden to me without the sweet hope of being loved by what I love most in the world."

She was ready to risk any stratagem again in order to see him; but she foresaw that he would not allow her to. This time it was she who was all ingenuity and daring, he the voice of prudence. "Refuse me not this favor, my dear Arouet. I ask it in the name of all that is most tender—I mean in the name of the love I bear you. Adieu, my darling child, I adore you and swear that my love will last as long as my life."

There is no mistaking these accents: they are not those of fashion but of a woman passionately in love. The maternal protectiveness of her "my dear child," "my darling child," attest to a more genuine fervor than her dear Arouet had felt.

And so he departed for France. He wrote to her "from the bowels of a yacht" that he had an aching heart and was seasick. He promised to win over her father, "unless he has already been told what has happened." He went on: "Feel toward me as you now do as long as I shall deserve such feelings, and you will love me all your life." It was the same language he was to use with the duchesses he would shortly be seeing again. Fine phrases and prudence—that was what Arouet's first grand passion really amounted to. On arriving in Paris he threw himself into the arms of Father Tournemine, one of his old teachers from Louis-le-Grand. Strange as that may seem, there was method in it. He had just written him three letters confiding his misfortunes and his hopes. They were most edifying missives: Was not Olympe a soul to be saved? Had not Providence chosen François's love as the instrument to bring a heretic back into the Church? Whoever did not further this love would therefore be opposing the workings of divine grace, which was unthinkable. François's rhetoric worked, and Father Tournemine was won over.

François wrote Pimpette to tell her what he was up to. He begged her to write to her father and insist that she wanted to return to the bosom of the Church; and also to write to a relative of hers who was Bishop of Evreaux and beg for his help. ("And whatever you do, don't forget to address him as 'Monseigneur,'" he warns her.) So here was Arouet, a votary of the Temple, moving heaven and earth, presumably, to bring Pimpette, the poor lost sheep, back into the fold. But it was the fold of

François-Marie Arouet rather than that of the Church he really was attempting to bring her back to.

One might wonder whether this was cynicism or merely a scatter-brained adventure. Like all the contradictions with which Voltaire's long life is strewn, we are sometimes told they are inexplicable. What lies behind them in this case is his impatience to gain possession, a restless instinct to get what he wanted no matter what the means, provided they were quick—regardless of the consequences for religion, Pimpette, Father Tournemine's good faith, and even for his own peace of mind and reputation.

But at this juncture Monsieur de Châteauneuf wrote to François-Marie's father, telling him the whole story. The notary was so enraged that friends thought it best to hide François-Marie from his wrath—they were afraid for his life. As it was, the elder Arouet applied for a *lettre de cachet:*[17] He wanted his son put in prison or sent to the West Indies. Meanwhile François-Marie continued to beg Pimpette to come to Paris. He had found somewhere for her to go: a convent for young women converts. Once she was there he would rescue her at the first opportunity, and all would be as she desired: "But should you be so inhuman as to insist on remaining in Holland, I give you my certain promise that I shall kill myself at the first news I have of it." All this was very romantic but also very calculated. If the affair verges on tragedy it does so only lightly, for François-Marie was simultaneously acting out a comedy for his father. Young Arouet was made for society, and to get on in the world as it was then it was necessary to play-act. For the moment the theater he acted in was not the great one; but he was getting in training. People were talking about the son of the worthy conseiller du roi and not always charitably. But the important thing was that they should talk and that he become known.

The idea of the elegant young favorite of duchesses in the wilds of the New World was ludicrous. So for Monsieur Arouet's benefit François played the part of the prodigal son returning repentant, and begged to be allowed to throw himself at his father's feet before disappearing forever into the jungles of the Indies. The interview took place according to the traditional scenario, a tableau anticipating the melodramatic family dramas depicted by Greuze: the father pardoned the son on condition that instead of going and burning to a cinder in the tropics he would go and molder in the chambers of a Paris notary.

François-Marie capitulated so as to be able to stay in Paris, to correspond with Pimpette, to write poetry, to continue to see his friends. But the punishment that went with all this turned out to be a terrible one: Pimpette was costing him dearly. There he was—a clerk in some dusty hole reeking of moldy documents, where the language was as turbid as the thick ink, and where he would have to draw up ridiculous rigmaroles

in appalling style for clients whose sordid squabbles he wouldn't or-
dinarily have touched with a pair of tongs.

He had accepted the terms but was more determined now than ever to
become something quite different from what his father meant to make of
him. He hated old Monsieur Arouet, but he obeyed him, and duly served
in purgatory in the office of Master Alain, royal notary.

Meanwhile, at The Hague, Pimpette's passion was burning fiercely—
too fiercely to last. She was not of a very literary turn of mind, and
Arouet's letters by no means gave her as much pleasure as the actual presence of her "darling child." And while he pressed on with his plans for
the conversion of the daughter, the mother had other ideas. A handsome
and discreet young Frenchman, Guyot de Merville, had caught her eye
and she had opened the doors of her house to him. Pimpette saw him and
opened the doors of her heart. François-Marie continued to write most
tender letters—which the daughter merely glanced at but the mother
kept. The references to herself were not always flattering, but little did
Madame care: she eventually published them as a collection entitled
Lettres historiques et galantes (*Letters Historical and Gallant*), flaunting
the name of François-Marie Arouet. The collection did not pass unnoticed, and this was just what Dame Dunoyer wanted. She had succeeded
in compromising young Arouet and confirming the deplorable reputation
he already had among the bourgeois and the devout. The person who was
most annoyed by the volume, however, was Arouet's successor in Pimpette's favors. For years De Merville's hatred pursued François-Marie,
but he took no notice. Then one day, after he had become Voltaire, rich
and influential, De Merville came and asked a favor, and Voltaire was as
deaf to his supplications as young Arouet had been to his insults.

When François-Marie learned that he had been supplanted in Pimpette's affections he was heartbroken. But his grief was as short-lived as it
was intense. He soon realized that Pimpette had done him a service by
forgetting him, and was duly grateful. It may not have been romantic,
but it was eminently sensible and typically Arouet. He bore her no
grudge. On the contrary, a few years later, in 1721, he tried to help her in
her business affairs. He always spoke of her with affection, and when she
became Comtesse de Winterfeldt he paid tribute to her virtues. She eventually led a dull and respectable life very different from her beginnings.
Contrary to her madcap mother's maxim, she married neither for pleasure
nor for interest, but for common sense and virtue.

And so ended the sad but edifying tale of Pimpette and François-
Marie. The poet had fallen in love—in his own unusual way. His first
affair of the heart is revealing in that it so little resembles passion. And
yet Voltaire was a passionate man. But the grand passions that consumed
him all his life were fame and liberty in all their guises. These were the
only idols to which he paid tribute. It was to them he dedicated his fervor, zeal, and tenacity, and his immense capacity for work. His extraor-

dinary sensibility might make him commit acts of folly as well as splendor, but it is in that service and not in worldly, high-flown compliments to Pimpette that we discover the accents of genuine passion. He would never fight for his mistresses. But for his own glory and for liberty he would do battle with the whole world.

II

Men are like animals; the big ones eat the little ones, while the little ones sting them. (*Remarks*)

A fair number of people who have not been able to keep a servant girl and a valet in hand have tried to rule the universe with their pen. (*Dialogues and Conversations*, Dialogue 24)

The eagerness to show off one's wit is the surest way of not having any. (*Contant d'Orval*, Volume II)

Kings have the same relations with their ministers as cuckolds with their wives: they never know what is going on. (*Remarks*)

If members of the magistrature sometimes sell their votes in court, they resemble therein certain beauties who sell their favors but do not talk about it. (*Dialogues and Conversations*, 22/14)

It is a proven fact that there is more good than evil in the world, since in point of fact few men wish for death. (*Contant d'Orval*, Volume I)

The Law, Poetry, and Another Scandal

A man of intelligence never really wastes his time no matter what he is doing or reading or observing. François-Marie nearly died of boredom in the chambers of Maître Alain, notary, but he was making discoveries. The more or less devious methods he learned in dealing with other people's affairs he was later to make use of in his own. He was a master in this as in everything—an Arouet, perhaps the most wily of them all.

What is more, at Maître Alain's he found a new friend, a man named Thiériot, a notary's clerk like himself. Though the two of them were still in their teens, François, with his usual horror of familiarity, always addressed his new friend as "Monsieur" and, as with Pimpette, never used the *tu* form with him. Yet he and Thiériot remained friends all their lives —though it was a friendship that Thiériot often put to the test.

The real bond between them was their love of poetry. The aptitude they shared for versifying made them both equally unfit for legal hairsplitting and resentful of their forced labor as law clerks. Not, of course, that their talents were comparable, since Thiériot had none. But he liked poetry—especially François's poetry. And both knew that another world beside the world of the notary existed.

Though François's first literary endeavor, the ode submitted to the French Academy, had not earned him a prize, his attack on his rival who had won had attracted a certain amount of attention. In 1714 the twenty-year-old Arouet published a satiric poem, *Le Bourbier* (*The Mire*), into which he pitched *all* the people he hated. Already his fake archaic style was brilliant, full of energy and cruel wit. It was a success, or rather a scandal—Voltaire's first literary scandal. There would be hosts of others, but already the mechanism was set in motion that was to function tirelessly until the poet's dying breath.

His *Le Bourbier* earned him a little glint of fame of a rather dubious kind. Still, it was the beginning of the celebrity he sought. When the intoxication of it had passed, he reflected on it all. "I vowed never again to fall into that detestable way of writing."

But it was too late for such resolutions. He was to fall into that way of writing all his life, deriving from it the most remarkable effects and the most disagreeable consequences. But even though these consequences were sometimes shocking enough to make him ill with rage and terror, they also brought him his most delicious transports—the transports of pride.

Another poem with an ominously scurrilous title, *L'Anti-Giton* (*The Anti-Pansy*), also published in 1714, was scarcely calculated to appease his father's wrath at his capacity for creating scandal. Despite this titillating title, the poem itself was not scurrilous: it was simply a light-hearted satire on a nobleman noted for his sexual inversion. There was never anything obscene, filthy, or even coarsely vulgar in Voltaire's writing, speech, or behavior. The poem was dedicated to Mademoiselle Duclos, because he and she had laughed together about certain homosexuals of the theater and the town. Voltaire defends convention without being intolerant toward the unconventional. There is nothing in this trifle to shock taste, though more than a touch to shock morals. Voltaire wrote coolly: "I had rather see the morals of the public depraved than its taste."

This time his father wanted to settle things once and for all, and he would have been quite ready to have François-Marie imprisoned had not an old friend intervened. This was Monsieur de Caumartin, who offered to take charge of the young man. Arouet, who would willingly have handed his son over to the Devil himself, was only too glad to pass him on to this eminently respectable gentleman who bore him off to his Château de Saint-Ange, near Fontainebleau. François was quite prepared to accept a château, and also the society of an octogenarian who in the seventeenth century had been a *conseiller d'état*[1] and an *intendant des finances*[2] in the provinces.

Caumartin was cultured, virtuous, and exceedingly rich. Saint-Simon, who knew him well, says he knew history, genealogy, politics, and the day-to-day events of the old court of Louis XIV. His memory was so good that he could quote whole pages from books he had read thirty years before, and the conversations of Mazarin, Colbert, Louvois, and the King, princes and favorites of the *Grand Siècle*. "He was extremely well informed in matters of high society," Saint-Simon wrote, "and, as well as being a man of much wit, he was also most obliging and gentlemanly." During this retreat, which gave public opinion and Monsieur Arouet a chance to digest the *Anti-Giton*, Monsieur de Caumartin told François-Marie the story of his life—that is, the history of Versailles from its beginnings early in the reign of Louis XIV down to the last years of the seventeenth century. He told it with such skill that François was spellbound. His host brought the *Grand Siècle* to life again, conjuring up both the setting and the *monstres sacrés* who played in that great spectacle, dazzling Europe with its tragedies, ballets, and melodramas. Monsieur de Caumartin took François behind the scenes and showed him the machinery; he introduced him to princes and the generals and to the great King now dying at Versailles. He showed him the ministers and the geniuses of the age, its puppets and dancers, and the surrounding swarm of hornets, wasps, and butterflies. How brilliant it all was! And it was during his few weeks of exile at Saint-Ange that the twenty-year-old François first started to take notes on a future work that years later would dazzle the world, his *Le siècle de Louis XIV* (*The Age of Louis XIV*), incubating this eulogy to the *Grand Siècle* in a mind as minutely organized as his father's files.

Once he had gathered all its fruits, he did not linger at Saint-Ange. He already had a passion for the theater and actors. Was he not one of them? He had already composed his *Oedipe*, and was eager to further his career as a writer for the stage. But it is one thing to write a tragedy and another to get it accepted, understood, and applauded. François now began a concerted campaign to achieve this second goal. It is easy to imagine him fluttering in and out of the boxes of the Comédie Française, flattering and amusing those present, saying sharp things about those absent and those who were his rivals. Always lively, courtly, flaunting his cuffs and three-cornered hat and the short sword under the skirt of his coat, he was everywhere, taking note of everything, talking to everyone, talking of his play. He was all enthusiasm: nothing so sublime, he said, had been written for the theater since Racine. Racine was a god; but he was now in heaven. On earth there was François-Marie Arouet, the reincarnation of

the god of tragedy. If anyone doubted it they had only to stage his
Oedipe.

Meanwhile, through singing the praises of Mademoiselle Duclos,[3] the
actress to whom the *Anti-Giton* had been dedicated, François had fallen
in love with her. He declared himself, was listened to, the blossom was
about to bloom. But the Comte d'Uzès swept by and plucked the flower,
leaving François breathless at the ways of the great. When he had got
over his annoyance he wrote: "Every morning la Duclos takes a few
pinches of senna and cloves, and every evening a few of Comte d'Uzès."
That was the only revenge he took.

His campaign on behalf of his *Oedipe* was faring no better. The Académie Française had been deaf to his ode and now repeated their mistake
with his tragedy.

With the death of Louis XIV in 1715, the current of libertinage,
hitherto subterranean, or almost, suddenly burst out into the light.
Atheism was everywhere, morals were suddenly relaxed. That is to say,
what people used to do clandestinely they now did openly, without hypocrisy. They were only following the lead of their betters.

Philippe d'Orléans, the Regent, was a friend of the Grand Prior of the
Temple, Philippe de Bourbon-Vendôme. Shortly after the King's death
the Regent recalled Bourbon-Vendôme from exile and restored the Temple to him and him to society.

The Temple suppers at Vincennes resumed with new vigor. Arouet
had his own regular place. François professed the epicureanism of the
group, but the delicate health he had suffered from since childhood forbade him to be more than a Platonic disciple. He talked, but he never
acted out his words. He wished people would eat and drink less. He was
amazed that people needed wine to intoxicate themselves: were not words
enough? This attitude resulted not only from his health but also from his
taste. He was ready to be ribald but not obscene, blasphemous but not
coarse. He toyed with dissoluteness, but always with gloves on. Arouet
and the freethinkers of the Temple agreed in substance but differed in
style. He was more modern. While they were aristocratic *libertins* in the
seventeenth-century manner, he was what our century would call an
intellectual and what his own century would come to call a *philosophe*.
Those who frequented the Temple cared little what other people thought
or believed. So long as they were left to enjoy themselves in peace they
asked nothing of anyone; when the devout delivered themselves of sermons against them, all they felt was a pitying amusement devoid of aggressiveness. They did not attack the Church. They simply did not
bother about it, except for the fact that they were men of the cloth and
held their prebends and titles of abbé, prior, canon, or bishop from the
Church.

But Arouet was already a propagandist: he wanted to demonstrate his
irreligion in public, to bear witness to it and glory in it, to be a mission-

ary of impiety. His was not the serene irreligion of his noble friends: he wanted to make converts, to promote irreligion all about him.

At the Temple suppers, the conversation centered on poetry and the theater. He got his friends at the Temple to read his *Oedipe*, and it was discussed and criticized. They may not have had irreproachable morals but they had excellent taste. "The other evening did my tragedy much good," he wrote to the Abbé de Chaulieu. "I think if I supped four or five times with you I might write something really worth while. Socrates gave his lessons in bed. You give yours at table and they are doubtless the merrier for it." He knew how to flatter, and how to express elegantly what he set most store by. One of the precepts that was to rule his life was that one must combine instruction with delight. Dreary learning is dead learning. For Arouet, intelligence was synonymous with enjoyment.

Another place he frequented was the Château de Sceaux, on the outskirts of Paris. There too his manners and conversation made him a success. The Duchesse du Maine, who kept an almost royal court there, asked him to read *Oedipe*. He read it well—he always read his plays as an actor would have done—and with the utmost conviction of the author's genius. He earned both praise and criticism, and was equally skillful in expressing his thanks for the one and learning from the other. He heeded the advice of princes so gracefully, they were inclined to praise him all the more. All this was not just the idle pastime of a frivolous society. Their frivolity was the adjunct of a solid and self-assured taste, thoroughgoing, intimate knowledge of the rules of art and language. Though the tone was bantering, it was in all seriousness that Arouet reworked his tragedy, cutting a scene here, a phrase or a line there, and speeding up the action. He worked everywhere and all the time—especially when he seemed to be merely enjoying himself. Château life was toil for him—gilded, sparkling toil.

The Comedy Ends Badly

Tragedy was only one side, the official side, of his budding talent. He also had a bent for caustic comedy. Under the Regency, authors with a gift for clever satire found an outlet in the fashion for lampoons and mocking verses, all more or less anonymous, scurrilous, and libelous, attacking the Regent and his family. The only attention the Regent paid them was to read the witty ones. François-Marie could not resist the temptation to join in, but these printed pasquinades became so numerous that the chief of police intervened.

He was accused of having written certain verses with his usual light touch, informing Paris of the incestuous relationship between the Regent and his daughter, the Duchesse de Berry. Rather a dangerous subject for teasing doggerel. Arouet swore he was not the author. But his friend Pierre Cideville said he had seen these verses while Arouet was writing them. It was characteristic of Voltaire that he could not prevent himself from reading around, in strictest confidence, what he had written in secret about the most intimate facts of some of his contemporaries' lives. Of course such secrets ended up as the talk of the town. The argument Arouet used to defend himself now was the one he used all his life: the verses could not be his because they were too bad; he could be accused of anything except being a bad writer.

In this case, he succeeded in casting doubt on the attribution, so instead of being sent to prison he was sent to virtual exile in Tulle. Arouet heard the news with horror. Were there any duchesses in Tulle, that provincial hole? His father took pity on him and intervened with the Regent to have François-Marie banished instead to Sully-sur-Loire, explaining that there were relatives there who could keep an eye on his wayward son.

But his relatives scarcely laid eyes on François, for he immediately installed himself in the château of his friend, the young Duc de Sully. Formerly the Chevalier de Sully, Maximilien-Henri had recently been elevated in rank following the death of his elder brother. François had often spent evenings with Maximilien-Henri in the Temple: he was one of the nephews of the vivacious libertine Abbé Servien. They spoke excellent French at Sully. François's room was in a tower where the poet Claude Chapelle had been imprisoned for two years a century before and where for two years he had been continually drunk. François proceeded to get drunk not on wine but on delightful company. The young duc was unmarried and the life he and his friends led was an unending *fête galante* in the park and on the banks of the Loire. Any excesses were harmonious ones, for which poetry, ballet, and the theater offered elegant pretexts. It was all perfectly ideal for François-Marie Arouet. There was even a theater—but all the world was a stage, even the woods. It was always to be like that: wherever Arouet appeared, trestles and boards rose out of the ground and everyone was brought on stage. Intrigues sprang up at the play itself, to be continued and resolved in boudoirs or beneath the trees.

At Sully Voltaire fell in love with Suzanne de Livry—a butterfly love, like all his others. Her uncle was lawyer, procurator, and steward to the duchy of Sully: the Livry family held these posts by heredity. Suzanne too belonged to the duchy, in a different sense: she enhanced the delightful atmosphere of the castle with her youth and beauty. That was how Arouet made her acquaintance. He at once converted her to the arts of the theater and of libertinage. They acted with famous actors and great lords, but love of the theater obliterated all differences: noble amateurs did not despise celebrated professionals, and the latter forgave the aristocrats their lack of skill. Suzanne possessed the sacred fire, and Arouet gave her lessons. They lived in the tenderest fairyland, though it was far from an entirely make-believe one. They loved each other, made no secret of it, and set out together for Paris. Arouet was to direct her in her theatrical career: she wanted to be an actress or die in the attempt. They amused themselves driving round Paris in hackney carriages and were seen smiling tenderly at each other in suburban pleasure gardens.

Arouet was so debonair, confident, and unsuspecting that he often took his friend Génonville along, a pleasant, handsome, witty young man with perfect manners. Génonville was the same age as Arouet, and what was bound to happen duly happened: the fire kindled before his very eyes by the two lovers started a flame in him. He did not hide it from Suzanne, who took the view that as the two young men were such good friends, and both equally charming and in love, it would be unfair not to treat them alike. One day on entering Suzanne's room François found Génonville in her bed. He stamped and raged, and talked of ingratitude and treachery. He even brandished his sword. At this the guilty pair wept. But the sight of their tears moved him too, and soon all three were in one another's arms mingling tears and tender phrases of repentance and forgiveness.

Later on François thought it over. He wondered whether his love for Suzanne could have lasted longer than his friendship for Génonville and concluded, for various reasons, that it could not. First of all, Suzanne had no real talent for acting: fire perhaps, but a lot of smoke as well, and Arouet was not one to be attached for long to the vapors of illusion. Her charm did not rest on talent or intelligence or application either. Another thing was that she was in the habit of casually saying that "Monsieur Arouet was a somewhat chilly lover [*Monsieur Arouet était un amant à la neige*]," which leads one to presume that in Génonville she found warmer qualities.

François gave up Suzanne. She continued her charming career, and Génonville was faithful to her for a little while. Arouet had forgotten everything except Génonville's friendship, and readily forgave him. Meanwhile the Temple was disintegrating.

François wrote to the Regent to clear himself and obtain pardon. He had said so often how much he was enjoying his exile that he was afraid he might be taken at his word and never get back to Paris. The thought terrified him. He could not stay at Sully. For one thing, he had enemies in Paris, and needed to be on the spot to protect himself. Moreover, he knew himself very well: "I am not made to dwell long in one place," he wrote while still a very young man. He was indeed to travel many roads in his long life, harried and pursued by the authorities or simply a prey to his own restlessness. He was so changeable, he would sit on ten different chairs in one evening, and by the end of his life he had lived in a hundred different houses. At the age of twenty he already knew that his true homeland was exile, or rather, perpetual motion.

The Regent forgave him, and Arouet was summoned to thank him for being recalled to Paris. And although just a few weeks later he had already composed a new poem as scurrilous as the last, the Regent merely smiled. The police noted it in his dossier and remembered.

When he returned from Sully he left his father's house and installed himself in a furnished apartment. After a lively and exhausting period reacquainting himself with the delights of the town, he went back for a rest to Caumartin's château at Saint-Ange. There he spent the Lenten season of 1717, and he tells us that his diet was definitely "not confined to smoked herring and salsify." Also at Saint-Ange was one of the marquis's sons, the Abbé de Caumartin. The Caumartins, father and son, both adored gossip and were good at enlivening it with mischievous comment. The abbé, witty and cultivated, was already, at the age of only twenty-six, a member of the Académie Française. He knew all there was to be known about the court and the town. So it was a well-assorted trio, with each member capable of delighting the other two.

But Arouet had one fault of which he never rid himself. He would often get carried away by his own wit, and what he said on such occasions might be very discomfiting to others, and ultimately to himself. Following his exile at Sully, he hated the Regent so much that he could not resist making libelous gibes about him in conversation even when members of the Regent's entourage were present.

In the spring of 1717 the police seized a violent lampoon in verse against the Regent and the administration. It was called *J'ai vu* . . . (*I've seen* . . .). The poem offered a list of all the scandals and abuses, real and imaginary, that the author had witnessed, and ended:

> J'ai vu cex maux et je n'ai pas vingt ans.

> (I've seen all these evils and I'm not yet twenty.)

The author was an obscure fellow named Lebrun who had written an inane opera entitled *Hippocrate amoureux* (*Hippocrates in Love*). But it was generally believed that François-Marie was the author. A sort of unconscious conspiracy was his undoing: his friends, who considered it a good poem, believed they were enhancing his reputation by claiming they had seen him write it. Meanwhile his enemies denounced him for other reasons, and the real author, frightened by the poem's dangerous success, did his best to convince people it had been written by Arouet rather than himself.

This time the Regent was shocked. Meeting Arouet in the Palais Royal, he called him over and said, with a menacing allusion to the title of the poem:

"Monsieur Arouet, I wager I could show you something you've never seen."

"What is that, monseigneur?"

"The Bastille."

"Ah, monseigneur, let us say I know all I care to about it."

But this report did not stop the Regent from keeping his promise. On the morning of May 16, 1717, a police inspector brought Voltaire the following peremptory invitation: "It is the desire of His Royal Highness that Monsieur Arouet be arrested and taken to the Bastille." It was signed "Philippe." After his first outcry François went along quietly.

Since the time he was first suspected of having written *J'ai vu*, the Regent, uncertain that he was the author, had waited two years before having him arrested. But meanwhile there had appeared a new and even more pernicious poem called *Puero regnante* (*A Child on the Throne*). This was a venomous attack against the Regent, and its central theme was that when the king is a mere youth his kingdom is prey to pillage and debauchery. A police report accused Arouet of publicly boasting that he "had written insulting verses against Monseigneur the Regent and Mademoiselle his daughter, the Duchesse de Berry; including, among others, a poem entitled *Puero regnante*." He was also accused of saying that "as he could not avenge himself on the Regent in a certain manner, he would not spare him in his satires." When "someone" then asked him what the Regent had done to him, he sprang up angrily and replied: "What, do you not know what that b———— did to me? He exiled me because I proclaimed publicly that his Messalina was a whore."

Isabeau and Bazin were the police officers who had arrested him. The "someone" who had asked him why he hated the Regent was an informer whom François had made his confidant: a bold captain by the name of Beauregard. The impulsive François would unburden himself to anyone provided he had good manners and could carry on an interesting conversation. Beauregard had met Arouet in a café, where he had no doubt been spying on him. François invited him home. Why not? He was an officer, a brave soldier, and could spin fascinating tales of his experiences on the battlefield. When François modestly hung back, Beauregard cleverly pumped him for information. "People say you wrote such and such a ballad." "What!" François replied. "Do you think I'm capable of such feeble stuff?" "But they say that *J'ai vu* is such a fine poem that it would make Jean-Baptiste Rousseau's name." "Ah, now that one I did write. I wrote it at Monsieur de Caumartin's place in the country. I can even show you the manuscript!"

It was this that sent him to the Bastille—boasting of having written verses that were not his simply because a spy admired them.

Another day Beauregard encountered his friend Monsieur d'Argental at Arouet's apartment. The spy, without a word, pulled a copy of *Puero regnante* out of his pocket. The heedless Arouet immediately burst out: "That one wasn't written at Monsieur de Caumartin's—I wrote it long before I left Paris. . . ."

He gave himself away before he was even accused. "What," said Beauregard, "you claim this poem is yours? But I was recently told on good authority that it was written by a Jesuit schoolmaster."

Arouet was annoyed at this and answered that the Jesuits were like the jay in the fable that dressed itself in peacock's feathers, and that he had written the *Puero* and could produce the manuscript. He then went on at great length, describing the debaucheries of the Regent's daughter, who he said was about to bear a child sired by her father; he even named the house in Auteuil where preparations were being made for her secret confinement for the birth. After that, reported the virtuous spy, Arouet added a hundred things "impossible to be set down."

As for the traitress-mistress mentioned in François's poem, he doubtless meant Suzanne de Livry, whom he had brought back to Paris with him and seen stolen from under his nose by his friend Génonville.

François Hoaxes the Inspector

That Whitsun morning, May 16, 1717, he was driven to the Bastille in the eighteenth-century equivalent of the Black Maria, accompanied by Inspector Isabeau. François was mad with silent rage. But unwittingly he already possessed his revenge. Isabeau, to judge by his unemotional and doggedly detailed reports, seems to have been a thoroughly humorless man. A touch of humor and he might have avoided the trap. But he did not know Arouet: he took him for a common lampooner and was not on his guard.

His orders were to seize not only the poet but all the papers in his apartment. Finding very few, he concluded that Arouet must have hidden or destroyed them.

"Where are your papers?" he asked.

"They're all on my desk," snapped François.

"I don't believe it. There must be others. Where have you hidden them? Tell me where they are and save me the trouble of breaking the locks."

Then a wicked idea popped into François's head.

"Down the water closet," he said.

Monsieur Isabeau was in a quandary. He reported to his senior officer and asked what he should do. The commissioner of police replied curtly: "Go look for them in the place where they are."

Monsieur Isabeau did as he was told, but it was no easy matter. In the eighteenth century everything was ordered not by decrees and orders and committees but by customs and usages that had the force of law. Thus in Paris each street or group of houses had an official (usually a woman, for it was a privilege reserved for the female sex) in charge of its cesspool. No one could alter, mend, or empty the cesspool without this official's knowledge and instructions. So Monsieur Isabeau was obliged to apply for the collaboration of *Madame l'Intendante Merdière* (Madame Sewer Mistress)—as the common people called her. After a first investigation turned up nothing, Isabeau reported to his chief: "The sewer mistress found no paper, since the cesspool is full to overflowing with water." He went on to explain that Madame l'Intendante had let a candle down into the conduit on a string; then, peering down through the seat of the water closet, she reported that the pipe showed no traces of any papers; Isabeau himself would guarantee this. His report is a minor masterpiece of professional conscientiousness. With a perseverance worthy of a better object he continued:

> The letters, if there, would have floated on the water that covers the solid matter. Nonetheless, monsieur, if you think it suitable that a search should be made below, I believe it could be done without entirely emptying the latrines.
>
> Inspector Isabeau. May 21, 1717

"Make a thorough search," his merciless superior replied.

Inspector Isabeau and Madame Sewer Mistress did so, though apparently they set about it so clumsily that they damaged the cesspool, which was in the cellars. The woman who owned the house then entered the picture, complaining, pleading, invoking the law. Not only was she being asphyxiated by the stench, but the King's officers had caused the loss of heaven only knew how many bottles of beer and wine which she had just had laid in at great expense. She brought a lawsuit against the Crown and won it. The King was obliged to reimburse her for the damage caused by an unlucky blow from a pickax in Monsieur Arouet's latrines, which contained nothing but what the police could do without.

Isabeau then realized that Arouet had played a trick on him, and informed his chief. He declared that the perfidious poet had given him false information, "incited thereto by his natural propensity to cause unnecessary trouble." This is the only acrimony the worthy Isabeau permitted himself.

Arouet, on arrival at the Bastille, was stripped of all he had on him, and he was greatly inconvenienced by being so bereft—especially as far as dress and toilet were concerned. He immediately sent for "two calico kerchiefs, one for the head and one for the neck; a small cap, two cravats, a nightcap and some essence of clove." Also other oils and unguents, not forgetting some for the mind: among the other odds and ends he requested we find volumes by Homer and Virgil—his "household gods," as he called them.

As always, Arouet's supreme resource was work. For him it was the "panacea." Illness, disappointment, malice, exile—he overcame them all with pen, paper, and books, and with the mental liberty he enjoyed even in prison. The miracle was that as soon as he sat down in front of a piece of paper he forgot his despair. He became himself again in the act of creation. No one could have suspected this energy in a man who seemed so delicate, restless, and frivolous, apparently frittering away his powers. But he was the opposite of what he seemed: tough, tenacious, single-minded, even obstinate, possessed of enormous will power and earnestness when he was working. Here is the old Arouet background that he denied, or rather disguised. No one yet suspected the strength of this frail and ambitious young man. He concealed it beneath a worldly blitheness that deceived everyone—even, in his youth, himself. But alone in his cell in the Bastille, face to face with his despair, he discovered the best hope that life can offer, the hope inherent in a new piece of work.

In the margins and between the lines of the few books he was allowed he wrote the beginning of his epic poem, *La Ligue* (*The League*), which all Europe would come to know under its published title, the *Henriade*. Sleeping he composed it, and waking he wrote it down, or so Président Hénault claims Voltaire told him.

In 1718, for Suzanne de Livry, he had had Largillière paint his portrait, the handsomest one we have of him. His face was so mobile, it was extremely difficult to catch a true likeness. He is wearing a blue velvet coat and a somewhat complacent smile. Two fingers of his left hand are tucked into his waistcoat. His cheeks are already slightly hollow, and later on they were to become quite furrowed.

This is how he saw himself at that time: "I am supple as an eel and lively as a lizard and industrious as a squirrel." He observes his own physical traits with surprising accuracy. No one has ever seen himself, or others, with more lucidity. With these piercing eyes he saw himself as an eel, with all the agility needed for slipping between the constable's fingers and for eluding theories, systems, ready-made ideas, and tyrannies—even if this agility sometimes carried with it a certain slipperiness. The main thing was never to be held back by anything except pleasure. He knew himself to be agile, fugitive, and mercurial, like the chilly, furtive, nimble lizard. A sudden noise and he disappeared into a hole in the rock: Saint-Ange, Sceaux, Sully, The Hague, and many others. He saw himself, finally, as a charming little aristocrat in the fur pelt of a squirrel, delicate, clean, and energetic. He nibbled at libraries and was always adding to his store. He might seem to be showing off his skill in flying from oak to elm, but in reality he was gathering precious fruit. He would leap from branch to branch, from salons in town to country houses, from the Duchesse du Maine to the Prieur du Vendôme, from notary's chambers to embassy, then on to a rotten branch that ditched him into a cell in the Bastille. Everywhere he would find what he needed: ideas, friendships, books, characters, and money. He would eventually accumulate a vast fortune. Life was long. Fame was not to be acquired with gold, like public office; both fame and fortune had to be worked for. So for the rest of his life the squirrel would indefatigably store up protectors among the great, libraries in country houses, bills of exchange in every capital, and an unparalleled network of international friendships.

But much of all this still lay ahead. In Paris in 1718 he was not forgotten, but if people remembered him it was only to speak ill of his name.

But was this not the best possible proof of his growing fame? People vied with each other in predicting that he would never again see the light of day, that the Regent hated him so much, he had been thrown into a dungeon where he would shortly molder away. Those most kindly disposed toward him predicted that he would be transferred to some distant fortress; for life, naturally. In short, everyone wrote him off, with more or less ferocity and hypocrisy: he was already a thorn in everyone's flesh. Nevertheless, on April 11, 1718, like a lizard suddenly darting out of a crack in a wall, Arouet emerged into the sun's first rays. His imprisonment had lasted eleven months.

The conventions had to be respected. Those who had enjoyed the King's hospitality in the Bastille did not return immediately to public life. By way of transition, His Majesty's former pensioners were required to observe a brief period of exile. Arouet waited out his quarantine at Châtenay, in his father's comfortable country house. It was not the Antipodes. It was almost Paris. Yet he complained bitterly.

He wrote to the Regent and to the chief minister to plead his innocence. He wrote to the lieutenant of police that he had never spoken ill of the Regent and the court. The lieutenant, who had all the reports in front of him, must have had a good laugh. "If Monseigneur the Regent had been but a private person, I should have wished to have him for my best friend!" Arouet wrote. But no one wanted him to play the eel; all they asked was that he should be quiet. Impossible! He begged them to put an end to his exile at Châtenay: "You may easily imagine the torments of a man who can see Paris from his country house but is not free to go there." All he asks is three days in Paris—just enough time for the squirrel to flaunt his tail.

He was not so unfortunate as he pretended. The Baron de Breteuil kindly interceded for him and got him permission to visit Paris for a week instead of three days. The Breteuil family in general were to be his guardian angels. They were intelligent and generous, and belonged to the enlightened elite that was at once the honor and ornament of society. Some years later the baron was (unwittingly) to bestow on Voltaire the prodigious gift of his daughter Gabrielle-Emilie, Marquise du Châtelet, who would give Voltaire eighteen years of happiness. Meanwhile her father gave François Arouet a week's leave.

He rushed to Paris. But a week was not enough! Again thanks to Monsieur de Breteuil, he was granted an entire month: July 1718. Next he got his stay extended to the month of August, and then, in September, was given leave to remain in Paris indefinitely, though the permission could still be withdrawn at any time. His liberty was finally restored in full on April 1, 1719, a year after he was let out of prison. The transition had been artfully managed. François-Marie Arouet could not complain of government neglect. They were keeping an extremely vigilant eye on him.

His visits to Paris were not given over to dissipation. If he amused himself it was always in the service of his ambition. He was a past master at praising people, but above all at praising himself. Like everyone with literary pretensions, he could be insufferable. But he could also be irresistible. That was how he contrived to get *Oedipe* staged.

The public of the salons, in whose hands success rested, were in favor of his tragedy; but the Comédie Française was against him. They wanted radical and far-reaching changes in the text, not for artistic reasons, but out of consideration for the audience. They thought they knew what the public wanted better than the public itself. The terrible story of Sophocles' Oedipus struck them as far too distasteful. It needed to be given a fashionable turn, a Regency style, with ribbons, powdered hair, beauty spots, scarves, and cambrioles. Jocasta as a lady out of Watteau! The actors wanted scenes of gallantry inserted before, during, and after the dreadful act of incest—the actresses liked to play at being coy, and the men at being dandies. They wanted to cut a scene that Arouet had taken almost directly from Sophocles: they found it dull.

François, being young and wanting to have his play performed at any price, watered it down as best he could to satisfy the foolish creatures he had to deal with. Finally, with great reluctance, the Comédie Française agreed to perform *Oedipe*. The first performance took place on November 18, 1718, while its author was still on probation.

Naturally, the scene that went over best with the audience was the one Arouet had borrowed from Sophocles and which the players themselves had thought unactable. The play was a success but, incredibly enough, a *succès de scandale*. Arouet seemed fated to create scandal. In certain passages the audience saw allusions to the late king, whose death had been the subject of public rejoicing. Three years later Louis XIV was still hated for the puritanical despotism of his last years.

Certain passages made the audience sit bolt upright, and once they had seen an allusion in one scene, they looked for allusions in others, and of course found them even where they did not exist. It is not certain that the lines were really aimed at the dead King; but there were others that glanced off royalty in general.

The audience already had a presentiment, a vague sense that people would not believe forever in the greatness of kings and the divine right of their sons. Arouet's lines gave form and substance to what before had been only dimly apprehended. Henceforth the presentiment became a feeling, then an idea, then a theory, and finally, in 1789, a fact.

Arouet's anti-clerical trumpet call burst upon the stage of the Comédie Française, echoed throughout Paris, and brewed up storms that would never die down again. This was an unheard-of result for a tragedy that was to all appearances so regular, classical, and Racinian. The lines exploded beneath altars like a charge of dynamite. Father Nonnotte, a Jesuit and one of Arouet's enemies, saw "a diabolical enthusiasm" in the play, and said that its author used high-flown language to accuse the Lord's anointed servants of the "blackest horrors." The war of militant anti-clericalism had begun.

Arouet delivered his thunderbolts gaily. On opening night he could not resist going onstage during the performance, to exult and play the fool. He started playing the clown, carrying the train of the High Priest, and everyone laughed. Hardly suitable during a tragedy: he could not have done better if he had deliberately set out to wreck the show. This was the conclusion of the Maréchale de Villars, who was in the audience. She was amused to learn that the joker was the author himself, and asked to be introduced to him. They took to each other at once and resolved never to part. This was going fast; but they didn't go far.

During the performance Arouet's father roamed about restlessly, and from the back of a box was heard to mutter, "Oh, the rascal! The rascal!" It was Jean-Jacques Rousseau, or perhaps his disciple Bernardin de Saint-Pierre, who told this story. We do not know whom they had it from, but even if it is not true it might well have been: Monsieur Arouet was torn between admiration and fear—and also vexation at seeing his son lost forever to the practice of the law.

The Prince de Conti complimented Arouet in verse, saying that he made people believe Racine had risen from the dead. No flattery could be more welcome to the young playwright than to be compared to his idol. With an astounding familiarity, as if to a friend, he replied: "Monseigneur, if you were a great poet I would see to it that you had an annuity from the King."

The jest was well received, but the game was a dangerous one, at which even the most skillful player was bound to burn his fingers. François-Marie would burn his. How could he do otherwise? To be prudent was to limit one's freedom: wit could flourish only in liberty, and often only in outrageous impertinence.

The play ran for forty-five performances, which for those days represented an enormous success. Pamphlets appeared for and against it, and the salons buzzed with praise and imprecations. François-Marie could not have been more pleased. The play met with equal success when it was printed the following year. Jean-Baptiste Rousseau, the poet, who was living in Vienna at the time, wrote Arouet to thank him for the book: "I have long since looked upon you as a man destined one day to be the glory of his age, and I have the satisfaction of seeing that everyone who does me the honor of listening to me has arrived at the same conclusion."

Jean-Baptiste Rousseau had not yet become a rival and an enemy. He was being sincere; he wrote the same thing to several people. In Vienna the Empress and the court had read *Oedipe* and were delighted with it. "I hope we shall meet in Brussels," Rousseau went on, "and that we shall have leisure to talk of various matters too long to be set down here."

They did meet in Brussels—with unexpected results.

High Society and Low Company

The turbulent Paris of the Regency harbored a cosmopolitan society that was both colorful and somewhat disturbing: in this it already resembled modern Paris, European Paris. François-Marie became friendly with a Baron Goertz, who claimed to be the envoy of Charles XII of Sweden. Ambassador Goertz was always brimming over with astounding projects to reshape the map of Europe, to dethrone a monarch, ruin a port, or take a province away from one king and give it to another. His chosen confidant for these murky maneuverings became young Arouet, a debonair genius who was fascinated by these machinations of history, and thus entered into the life of one of its most extraordinary kings. François-Marie was so frequently at the baron's house, it was rumored that Charles XII wanted to carry him off to Sweden.

Jean-Baptiste Rousseau was jealous, and rightly pointed out that the King of Sweden could not understand a word of French and knew nothing of poetry. "A poet would not cut a very fine figure at such a court," he wrote. As Arouet was determined to cut a fine figure wherever he might be, he was not likely to be lured away to Sweden. But while he was playing the role of confidant and possible future favorite of a half-mythical king, he was already gathering anecdotes for the story of a real and living hero, and shaping the idea for the masterpiece that would appear more than ten years later as the Histoire de Charles XII (History of Charles XII).

Voltaire had no objection to alighting on rotten branches, and Baron Goertz was by no means a sound one. But his second perch, Baron Hogguers, an Austrian or a Swiss (no one is quite sure which), was positively worm-eaten. Giddy, full of fantastic ideas and political information, overflowing with secrets of state and of royal bedchambers, of public funds and privy purses, he was, like Goertz, half diplomat and half adventurer. He was affluent in the manner of his kind—that is to say, he spent extravagantly while on the brink of ruin. He had much knowledge and no discernment; many ideas, but most of them quite mad. This shady baron lived on a sumptuous estate at Châtillon, where he dispensed lavish hospitality. There were always innumerable guests at his gatherings, for the host had neither the time nor the taste to discriminate, and parasites flocked there.

It was circles such as this that had inspired Arouet to write his poem Le Bourbier four years before, but though the title is enough to indicate what he thought of such people, he did not cease to fish in these waters. He was fascinated by the confidences of adventurers covered with diamonds and lace, and flattered by their trust. Always afraid the title of poet might seem a slight one, he was delighted to be taken seriously by men who were unscrupulous but nonetheless astute. He needed to be noticed, to be constantly in the limelight. He was not taken in by those whose regard he sought, for he had too much intelligence and too little naïveté to cherish any illusions about them. But when his affluent host drew him aside and whispered, "Between you and me, His Royal and Imperial Majesty is only a hairsbreadth from bankruptcy . . ." Arouet was intoxicated with vanity. He saw himself as secret minister in the great affairs of Europe. Nor was this an empty dream. But the glaring contradiction between Arouet lucid and Arouet blinded by vanity and ambition was to both give him an enormous boost up the social ladder and bring him many difficulties.

Police reports on young Arouet's movements show us that the forces of law and order did not look on these associations with a very friendly eye. The Regent was aware of François-Marie Arouet's friendship with characters whom the government tolerated only with reluctance and whom it would be glad of an excuse to expel. François was only playing, of course; but it was a dangerous game.

He even found a way of turning his wretched sojourn in the Bastille to good account. Though a born courtier, he was too wayward and too fond of freedom to be an entirely successful one. But when he bothered to take the trouble he was irresistible. He sent a poem to the Regent entitled *La Bastille*. It contained no trace of bitterness or resentment: everything was powdered and curled, done up in ribbons. The Regent was not disinclined to see Arouet, and Arouet did not need to be asked twice. To the Regent's thanks for the poem he replied: "Monseigneur, I should be most pleased if His Majesty would continue to provide my board, but I implore Your Highness never again to provide my lodging."

The grace and vivacity of the jest once again caused its impertinently familiar tone to be overlooked. The allusion to board was not an idle one: it referred to a pension the Regent had awarded him for *Oedipe*. This pension was perhaps intended not so much as a reward for his merits as a poet as a golden inducement to seek the protection and rewards of the court by writing works that pleased the Regent. Arouet must certainly have seen the implication, but he continued to prick the Regent with his biting wit, refusing to become a tame pet.

The Regent gave him yet another sign of his good will. He presented him with a huge gold medal to mark the success of *Oedipe*, offering him also a chain on which to hang it round his neck. The goldsmith went to Arouet's to ask him what kind of chain he would like. "A well-chain," he answered with his usual cheeky disdain for the Regent's favors.

François-Marie wanted a great name to whom to dedicate his *Oedipe*. He set inquiries afoot among kings and princes to see who might deign to accept the honor. The Regent did not answer: the play dealt with a story of incest that was an uncomfortable reminder of what Arouet had alleged about him in his poems. Arouet then applied, without success, to the dowager Duchesse d'Orléans. Then he offered the King of England and next the Duc de Lorraine "the first fruits of his talent," adding: "'Tis to the gods one owes them, and you are my god." Still without success. Perhaps those to whom he applied knew how little he really cared for gods, or for kings.

The dedication was signed Arouet de Voltaire. This was the first time the name "Voltaire" had appeared in print, though a letter signed Arouet de Voltaire is dated 1718. Why should he have chosen 1719 for this? He wrote to Mademoiselle Dunoyer, an actress: "Do not be surprised, my dear, at this change of name. I have been so unfortunate with the other, I mean to see if this one will bring me luck."

Perhaps he really thought that, having offended so many people with verses signed by or attributed to Arouet, he would free himself of the old suspicions by using a new name. But to do that he would have needed to change his genius as well.

"Arouet" was abolished, removed from the playbill, to exist henceforth only in the scribbles in the parish register of the Curé of Saint-André-des-Arcs. François-Marie had chosen a new name and character and role for himself, and his life would be the play. The stage was already set: Europe in the eighteenth century, the Europe of courts and courtiers. The remainder of the cast would be the flower of civilization in the Age of Enlightenment. And so, in 1719, in the dedication of *Oedipe*, Voltaire was born.

In Paris there are a great number of little circles presided over by a woman who in the decline of her beauty makes the dawn of her mind a brilliant spectacle. (Letter, 1723)

It is easier to come up with insults than with good reasons. (*Dialogues and Conversations*, 1724)

The best government is that in which there are the fewest useless men. (*Dialogues and Conversations*, 4)

I like to see free men make the laws under which they live themselves, as they have made their dwellings. (*Dialogues and Conversations*, 4–6)

A victorious general has committed no errors whatsoever in the eyes of the public, just as a general who has been beaten is always wrong, no matter how sage his conduct has been. (*Contant d'Orval*, Volume I)

Announcing truths, proving something useful to men is a sure recipe for being persecuted. (*Contant d'Orval*, Volume I)

The spirit that reigns in the theater is the faithful image of the spirit of a nation. (*Contant d'Orval*, Volume 1)

One Has to Live. . . .

During 1720, 1721, and 1722 we see a new appetite developed in Voltaire: the appetite for money. He was now at home in a number of quite different circles but all of them were rich. With a talent and an innate need to manage things, he began to take an interest in business. He acted as intermediary between financiers and aristocrats, between traders and officials. Some of the money that came and went stuck to his fingers as profit. After Voltaire was restored to favor with his pension and medal, not to mention the chain, the Regent himself became involved in these dealings. Voltaire wrote cryptically to his friend the wife of Président de Bernières: "The gentlemen of the Excise might well hold off for a few days. The person you know [probably Richelieu] has the repeated assurance of Monsieur le Régent as regards the more important matter. . . ."

Yet Voltaire was never one of the Regent's close friends. At that time such a relationship would have been possible, but apparently Voltaire made no attempt to cultivate the Regent. He met him one evening at the opera and they talked of Rabelais. The Regent admired Rabelais and was full of praise for *Gargantua*, but Voltaire, when he was young, found Rabelais coarse and barbarous, and the Regent's enthusiasm irritated him. Later he revised his opinion and made a sort of "digest" of Rabelais for his own use: only a hundred or so pages were allowed to survive, but they were the best.

Voltaire was still living in the Rue Calandre, where he had been arrested. His father had suspended his allowance. He had Ninon's bequest of two thousand livres, but it is not likely that much of it was spent on books. He dined out, he hired cabs, he dressed with elegance. He spent a good deal: his noble friends cost him a pretty penny, for he was not their parasite and in order to keep company with them, even in their country houses, it was necessary to live expensively. The Regency was an age of extravagance, at least in the circles in which Voltaire moved, but even in his youth the heir of the Arouets knew how to handle money.

The financial ethics of the Regency were deplorable from the State's point of view, and idyllic from that of all the speculators, tax farmers, traders, and extortionists large and small. Excesses were so flagrant that the Regent set up a Chambre de Justice in the monastery of the Grands Augustins. This court inquired into and punished the officers of the crown who flaunted the scandalous fortunes they had acquired through corruption: 4,400 families were denounced, and ruined by confiscation. but of the 160 million livres thus confiscated, the royal treasury recovered only 70 million. High finance and trade were both disorganized, with no advantage either to the State or to the people. Business was paralyzed. What happened was that between the Chambre de Justice and the money it confiscated there rose up a race of new "officials." They "sorted out" the money involved to such good purpose that the greater part of it stuck to their hands.

As well as state scandals there were private ones. There are dozens to choose from, but one that was well known to Voltaire himself indicates the tone of the society in which it happened. The Marquis de La Fare, who was both hard up and extravagant, married a Mademoiselle Paparel. Her father was a contractor: that is to say, he was entrusted with the supply and maintenance of an army. He was treasurer of the Royal Constabulary. For his financial crimes, he had to appear before the Chambre de Justice, but before being sentenced, as he expected, he transferred all of his possessions to his son-in-law, who treated them as a thief would treat stolen goods (which they were), and kept them. He rounded it all off by letting his father-in-law die of want. This hardly mattered, as the Chambre had condemned him to death anyway. But seeing him die of hunger thanks to his son-in-law, they decided it was unnecessary to apply the sentence. The story has a moral ending. La Fare, the son-in-law, not only died penniless but, after having run through Monsieur Paparel's four million livres, left half a million livres of debts in addition.

Voltaire was thinking of such strange financial dealings of the Regency when he wrote *Zadig*, in which he said that, as far as finance is concerned, justice is caprice. "In Persia 'tis said sixty-three noblemen were impaled"; and quite rightly too. But: "In other countries," *Zadig* goes on, "they would have set up a Court of Justice which would have cost three times the amount of the money stolen and put nothing at all into the royal coffers."

We seem to be reading not about the eighteenth century but our own. In this, as in many other qualities and observations, Voltaire is close to us. Voltaire saw that it was more dangerous to have "wrong opinions" than to misappropriate public funds, and that swindlers were less likely to see the inside of the Bastille than those who spoke their minds too boldly. So he joined the middlemen, and the crumbs of their trade served him as pocket money. In his eyes it was imprisonment, not theft, that was the crime against humanity. The thief deprives his victim merely of his money, which is a comparatively minor evil. But to throw a man in prison is the worst wrong you can do him. A man in a cage is man fallen from his proper state, and imprisonment is an infamous thing, even if the prisoner himself is infamous. Paparel in prison is a wreck, an outcast of humanity. Paparel free is a magnificent financier. The moral is, leave the swindlers free to disport themselves. Of course, Voltaire was only concerned with thieves on the grand scale, the artists in bankruptcy, the Houdinis of peculation. Leave them alone and you will have flowing finances, lively trade, patrons, salons, and a flourishing opra. What more can be required of a society? How nimbly the eel glided among the heaps of gold.

Voltaire expressed his views in an *Ode à la Chambre de Justice*. Really, he protested, if people were no longer allowed to steal from the King, what was France coming to? What used to be the land of freedom (for crooks and swindlers) had been turned into a huge prison. Voltaire was not too proud, later on, of this masterpiece of cynicism, which he wrote at the request of his friends, the brothers Pâris, a pair of dazzlingly successful financiers. They were as rich as Croesus: a tax of a million and a half livres was nothing to them. It was they who introduced him to speculation, and he took to it like a duck to water.

Arouet and the Duchess

The Maréchal-Duc de Villars lived in the Château de Vaux, some twenty-five miles from Paris. Ever since the splendors of Fouquet, who had built it in 1656–59 and was two years later accused of fraud and confined to prison for the rest of his life, Vaux-le-Vicomte had been one of the most splendid gathering spots of elegant society. Monsieur de Villars's dazzling uniform was not the main attraction: at every reception people thronged to behold the charm of his lovely and witty duchess. Though past her first youth, she still seemed to retain its freshness. The maréchal was so delighted by all his grand visitors that he referred to the château in his letters as "Villars" instead of Vaux.

Ever since the triumph of *Oedipe*, Voltaire and the duchess had been inseparable. Villars, a very important personage, who had conquered Prince Eugene of Austria at the Battle of Denain, gave them his martial benediction and congratulated Arouet on his tragedy: "The nation is under a great obligation to you." To the elderly conqueror of the European Coalition the young poet graciously replied: "It would be under a greater one, monseigneur, were my writings the equal of your deeds."

At these words the maréchal felt all his laurels grow green again. He loved literature; not that he understood much about it, but men of letters were useful trumpeters of glory, so to be in good company he got himself elected a member of Académie Française.[1]

Voltaire hurried to Vaux at the slightest bidding, enchanted by the maréchale. She was a very great lady. Président Hénault said she was "tall and admirably formed, with a gracious manner and the unmistakable air that can be acquired only at court"—and the président was a connoisseur of wit, good living, good manners, and pretty women, all of which were to be seen at their best at the maréchal's château. This was exactly the sort of society, and the duchess was exactly the sort of woman, to whom Voltaire thought himself indispensable, because they were so to him. But in spite of all his experience in worldly circles, Voltaire was made a fool of. Of course this was done with style too; the duchesse was as accomplished a coquette as a Marivaux heroine. And her relations with the young poet were colored by a kindly affection for him. But Voltaire tried to persuade himself that she had a deeper feeling for him which modesty alone prevented her from declaring. He thought he knew all there was to be known about the tricks of love and the stratagems of salons, but he let himself be carried away by her smiles and languishing glances and delicate attentions, which were only meant to flatter his well-known vanity. Yet what the maréchale refused Voltaire she accorded almost under his nose to an urbane abbé who had had many predecessors and would have many successors. The Abbé Vauréal, "a poor priest but a fine lover," it was said, divided his favors between the Maréchale de Villars and the Comtesse de Guitaut. His skill in choosing, as Tartuffe put it, "the altars where his heart paid sacrifice" made him Bishop of Rennes.

It was not the ardors of Voltaire's heart that the duchess was intent on, but rather those of his mind—his charming manners and delightful conversation, his affectations and tricks, his verses and letters. People kept seeking him out. They made him waste a great deal of time. It pained him to see his own fires being stirred up simply to provide bright sparks for a supper party. When he saw what was happening, he went back to his work and only rarely accepted invitations. He wrote to his friend the Marquise de Mimeure:

"They contrived to ferret me out of my hermitage to beg me to go to Villars, but they will not make me lose my peace there. I now wear a philosopher's cloak that I will not doff for anything in the world."

And he added in a letter a few days later: "You make me sensitive to the fact that friendship is to be valued a thousand times more than love. I find something ridiculous in the idea of myself as a lover, and should find something even more ridiculous in the idea of women loving me. So that is decided. I renounce it for life."

It might be supposed that this premature renunciation of love at the age of twenty-four was caused by pique, and no doubt that did play a part. But there was something else. Voltaire saw himself as he was—and he was not made for passion. He would have other loves, but a burning-hot flame would inevitably change into a warm friendship.

So he drew up his balance sheet for 1719. He had not lost his maréchale, because she had never been his. But he had lost time, and on that score he did not easily forgive himself. As for the maréchale, she had lost the most attractive toy a great lady could have presented the guests at her court. Voltaire was really the winner in the long run, for he had found himself again: if the adventure left a tinge of bitterness behind, it was less for a mistress' refusal than for a book unwritten.

Backstage Gossip

Voltaire among adventurers, among financiers, among duchesses: these people seem to have nothing in common; but what they shared was something Voltaire could not resist: luxury. All that civilization offers of beauty, gracious living, refinement of mind, manners, and fashion, all that we call comfort, this was Voltaire's natural habitat. He could breathe only in marble halls, eat only off silver plates or porcelain, be witty only dressed in silk, and be at his most brilliant only for women decked in diamonds. But at the same time he did not disdain the wings of the Comédie Française and the dressing rooms of the actresses. There too he was among legendary princesses, and if the background was only of canvas, still it represented the palaces of kings and Caesars. He breathed the sublime air of Racine's tragedies at the same time that he carried on with the players.)

The success of *Oedipe* had made the author a well-known man and he was now at home at the Comédie Française) In memory of former happiness he wanted to have some good parts assigned to Suzanne de Livry, who was eager for a career in the theater, and he insisted that she be given the role of Jocasta in his *Oedipe!* This weightily tragic role was of course too much for her meager talents, and as Monsieur de Caumartin put it: "The success of the author has not been transmitted to the sharer of his couch." She was hissed, both by the audience and by her fellow actors, in particular by a certain Poisson who imitated her country accent. Voltaire was determined to defend his lady, and he did not mince words. They stung Poisson, who wanted a duel. Voltaire refused. What, he said, conveniently remembering his birth, a man of his condition, son of a royal notary and comptroller of spices at the Chambre des Comptes, cross swords with a ham actor? Ham actor! This insult was the last straw for Poisson, who threatened Voltaire with a beating. Up to this point all the exchanges had been through third parties, each belligerent making complaints and threats among his friends, and gossip doing the rest. But at the word "beating," Voltaire informed the chief of police and demanded protection, and at the same time thought up a little stratagem which, though it may seem surprising to us, was not so unusual in 1719.

Poisson, like Voltaire, was on intimate terms with Baron Hogguers: the actor and the baron in fact shared the same mistress. Voltaire had a message delivered to Poisson saying that the baron wanted to see him urgently. Poisson was afraid of a trap and before setting out had the neighboring doorways and corners searched. And what should his friends find but Voltaire in a dark cloak, accompanied by two bullies with cudgels, waiting to set upon him. Poisson hurried indoors again, finding "the company too numerous," as he put it. He then lodged a complaint. But with the help of dukes and duchesses and the Minister of Police, Monsieur de Machault, Voltaire lodged a countercomplaint, and it was Poisson who was arrested. But as no one wanted him to perish, it was agreed that Voltaire should write at once to the Minister of Police, withdrawing his complaint and asking that Poisson be set free. However, instead of couching the letter in the terms that Monsieur de Machault had himself prescribed, Voltaire wrote one in verse, full of compliments both to the minister, who was thanked for his kind co-operation, and to Poisson, who was declared innocent and forgiven. Poisson was then released. But Monsieur de Machault was irritated, for Voltaire, proud of his epistle, had circulated copies of it all over, and all Paris was laughing at this comedy in which neither the actor nor the poet nor the minister played a very admirable role.

Château Life—Under Duress

A new scandal now broke out—the scandal of the *Philippiques*. This was another attack on the Regent, Philippe d'Orléans, in the form of a ferocious, lively, diabolically spirited pamphlet which made everyone think at once of Voltaire. The Regent had been suspicious of him ever since the *Puero regnante*, and the Regent also mistrusted him for his associations with people who for various reasons were on bad terms with those in power. Voltaire's good friends Richelieu and the Villars were suspected of coveting power, and the Duchesse du Maine, plotting at Sceaux, already saw herself on the throne; moreover, the dubious barons Goertz and Hogguers had chosen him as their confidant.

The real author of the *Philippiques* was a certain La Grange-Chancel. When he saw that people were suspecting Voltaire he thought it an excellent joke and wrote a couplet saying:

> On punit les vers qu'il peut faire
> Plutôt que les vers qu'il a faits.

They punish the lines that he might have written/Rather than verses he has actually written.

But he laughed too soon both at Voltaire and at the police.

Voltaire was innocent; his hatred against the Regent had gradually died away. He proved this later in his defense of the prince, who had many virtues (though even greater faults) that Voltaire eventually found attractive; he then tried to destroy the calumnies he himself had done so much to spread. But now, though Philippe had pretended to forget Voltaire, two years after the ignoble *Puero regnante* episode he still remembered him well. So it was intimated that because spring and fine weather had come—it was May 1719—Voltaire might find the air healthier in a spot as far away as possible from Paris. It was not imprisonment but a form of exile.

Voltaire went from château to château, but it was again at Sully that he settled. At the elegant château of his friend the duc he worked, and wrote another tragedy, *Artémire*, also set in ancient Greece. He, and everyone else, believed in miracles: *Oedipe* was nothing, *Artémire* would be a hundred times better. Adrienne Lecouvreur wanted to play the lead, which was in itself a guarantee of success. The Abbé de Bussy went about telling everyone that *Artémire* would eclipse the glory of all the tragic poets both of antiquity and of the previous century: why, at a private reading of the play the abbé had shed so many tears he had caught a cold!

Successes predicted by cronies have a habit of ending as failures. And this was what happened to *Artémire* on February 15, 1720, shortly after

Voltaire's return to Paris from exile at Sully. Infuriated by the hoots and gibes, he rushed onto the stage and apostrophized the audience. He must have been a skillful actor, for his harangue was a perfect *coup de théâtre*, and completely changed the audience's mood. A miracle occurred: those who had hissed the play applauded its author.

But even this could not resuscitate *Artémire:* it was dead. Voltaire soon accepted the verdict of the public. He did rewrite the play and, yielding to the pressure of the Maréchal de Villars, completely changed it. It was put on again: again the audience rejected it. So that was the end of it.

Realizing that he was no longer in disgrace with the Regent, Voltaire asked his permission to read him *La Ligue* (*The League*), the poem he had begun writing in the Bastille, which was eventually to be entitled *La Henriade.*[2] Voltaire told the Regent that he was singing the praises of the latter's ancestor, Henri IV, to whom the Regent bore a particular resemblance.

Voltaire's friend Thiériot, the former notary's clerk, was to copy out the epic's nine cantos, while its author paid a visit to another friend, the Duc de Richelieu, in the château that his uncle had built.[3] There he wrote to Thiériot, "I am at present in the handsomest château in France—no prince has statues so many or so fine. Everything reflects the grandeur of the cardinal. The town is built like the Place Royale.[4] The château is vast, but what pleases me most is Monsieur le Duc de Richelieu, for whom I have the tenderest affection—but not more than for you." Apparently, in Voltaire's heart the duc and the lawyer's clerk were equals.

From château to château he went, with the manuscript of *La Henriade* as passport: from Richelieu to Sully, from Sully to La Source (the home of Lord Bolingbroke, the English statesman who had been forced by his enemies to flee to France in 1715). With his innate skill at public relations, Voltaire read certain passages in private here and there to a dozen or so people. Thiériot, continuing to receive instructions, copied and distributed suitable extracts in chosen places, and whispered some of its more shockingly outspoken verses to needy hacks who would pass them on. The poem was already famous before it was finished. Extracts circulated everywhere, the author's new name, Voltaire, was on every tongue. He had done all he could to attain this notoriety, but he had succeeded too well and took fright. The news from Paris was rather alarming. He wrote Thiériot to ask how his son (the poem) was getting on in the world, whether it had many enemies, and whether he was still presumed to be its real father.

But his vanity was tickled by these private readings, where he performed like an actor before a perfect audience. On one occasion, however, to his surprise, a certain Monsieur de La Faye criticized him severely for his treatment of Henri IV. The hypersensitive Voltaire gathered all his papers together in a fury and threw them on the fire, crying: "Very well, they are only fit to be burned!" And Président Hénault braved the flames to rescue the manuscript. He was quite proud of this feat (not knowing that Thiériot had spare copies) and congratulated himself for the rest of his life on having saved a masterpiece.

The Law Affair

While Voltaire was traveling from one château to another, he still took an interest in the news of the capital. He knew everything that went on: the pens of many of his friends were as ready as their tongues. In Paris in that summer of 1720 the Law affair was the talk of the town. The ingenious Scot who had been made Comptroller General of Finance had had the idea of substituting for coins paper money backed by the King's guarantee. The Parisians were delighted with the new little notes and amused by the fortunes which in a frenzy of speculation they proceeded to amass from one day, and even from one hour, to the next. The Rue Quincampoix, where Law's Banque Royale stood, became an open-air stock exchange, a Babel. Michelet wrote a vivid description of it:

"The rogues of all the countries and provinces of Europe, not to speak of our own Gascons and Dauphinois and Savoyards, took up their positions early in the day, having hired all the shops to use as offices. All along the gutters of the narrow street a crowd of buyers, sellers, barterers, speculators, gulls, and rascals shoved and jostled each other. There were no noblemen [they acted through intermediaries], but there were many gentlemen, lawyers, monks, and even doctors of the Sorbonne. No modesty veiled their naked fury: insults, tears, blasphemy, and wild laughter rent the air. Then there were the thousand imbroglios. One abbé would give burial certificates in exchange for bank notes. Some women dealt in their own persons, human share certificates paid up in mothers and daughters. When the evening chime closed this street of frenzy, Babel boiled over into the cafés and shops of the neighboring streets, and into the houses of pleasure whose roguish damsels were always ready to relieve the winners of the contents of their wallets."

The tinkle of money, the rumors of fortunes won and lost, reached Voltaire's ears. He wrote to congratulate his friend Génonville on not being seduced by Law's *système*.

Voltaire, like his friend, held aloof from Law's *système*. But if Génonville refrained out of insouciance, Voltaire did so out of prudence. He was not a man to be carried away by crazes, especially popular ones. He loathed promiscuity of ideas, opinions spread by contagion rather than thought, and all collective enthusiasms. When half of France was growing rich on paper and the other half ruining itself by losing its gold, he wrote Génonville that he could hardly bring himself to believe what he heard.

"Have you really all gone mad in Paris? I never hear talk of anything nowadays save millions. They say that everyone who was well off is now reduced to poverty, and all those who once lived in beggary now live in opulence. Is this true, or is it a chimera? Has half the nation discovered the philosopher's stone in paper mills? Is Law a god, a charlatan, or a rascal who poisons himself with the same nostrum that he dispenses to others? Are people satisfied with imaginary riches? 'Tis all a chaos I cannot succeed in making sense of, and which I imagine you understand no better than I. As for me, I follow no other chimeras than those of poetry."

Voltaire had excellent advisers in the Pâris brothers, who were sworn enemies of the "system," speculated on its downfall, and made a fabulous fortune out of the debacle. Their friend Voltaire was carried along in their wake and saw his fortune multiplied tenfold.

When Law's notes finally crashed Voltaire wickedly summed up his system: "It reduces paper to its intrinsic value."

But the cunning ones came out of it well. The Prince de Conti, told in advance of Law's collapse, applied to his bank in time to convert his bank notes to gold. Three carts were needed to carry the coins away: they were said to amount to fourteen million livres. On the following day the Duc de Bourbon did likewise. The common people thought that the princes of the blood were making money hand over fist by speculating in Monsieur Law's paper bank notes. It did not enhance the princes' popularity. This explains the allusion in a witticism of Voltaire's: one day he was at the theater with the Prince de Conti, and the prince gave the signal for the applause to begin. When the audience obeyed, Voltaire remarked, "You did not think you had so much credit, did you, monseigneur?"

In the summer of 1721, Voltaire found himself at Sully. The current diversion was the Abbé de Fontenelle's book, *Entretiens sur la pluralité des mondes* (*Conversations on the Plurality of Worlds*). The object of the book was to popularize Descartes' astronomical theories, and the abbé's ingenious exposition attracted a wide audience. Everyone began studying the stars, for it meant that one could go out at night into the park. But fashion now required that everyone should be "scientific" as well, particularly in astronomy. Ladies and gentlemen fell upon learned treatises as eagerly as they had upon Law's bank notes: all their talk was of gravitation, though understandably enough no one was very clear what it was that gravitated, and around what, or how, or why. Still, it was always pleasant to chat and gaze at the sky and sup in the moonlight. The Château de Sully was like some sumptuous aviary, full of trilling and cooing and the rustle of dazzling wings. Voltaire was under no illusions about the seriousness of all this study, but it was charming all the same.

The Squaring of Family Accounts

On January 1, 1722, Monsieur Arouet died of dropsy. The relations between father and son must have improved, for it is said that at the time of

Monsieur Arouet's death both his sons were living under his roof. Voltaire's bereavement does not seem to have caused him much grief. But his quarrels with his brother over the inheritance were to make up for that.

Armand had the advantage in being the elder; and he had law and the lawyers on his side. The fortune Voltaire had counted on escaped him. This infuriated him, and he wrote to his friend Madame de Bernières: "My fate takes such a diabolical turn at the Chambre des Comptes that I may one day be obliged to work in order to live, I who once lived in order to work." He had started a lawsuit against Armand: "I have many pressing matters to attend to, not the least of which is the suit I have again brought to court to break my father's will." He was to lose his case.

Monsieur Arouet so much disapproved of François-Marie that he had drawn up his will to Armand's advantage. There was nothing in common between Voltaire and his elder brother, a Jansenist[5] like Monsieur Arouet and like most others of his profession. But if lawyers were Jansenists from a sort of austerity and moral integrity, Armand was one out of extremism. And Monsieur Arouet preferred a mad Jansenist to a mad *libertin:* the first was merely disagreeable, the second downright disgraceful.

Armand had taken time off from his devotions to have his father's official post in the Chambre des Comptes transferred to him. He managed it just in time: the transfer was signed only two days before Monsieur Arouet's death. But it was all in order. The post was the most important part of the estate: in 1701 it had brought in 240,000 livres. Voltaire would have liked, not the post of comptroller of spices in the Chambre des Comptes, but some substantial compensation: half of its value, for example. Instead he had been left only 4,000 livres a year: a respectable income, but nothing like the fortune that came to Armand.

His friendly relationship with the Pâris brothers had enabled him to build up a little portfolio: three shares in the Indies Company formed by John Law and five bank notes of 1,000 livres. All this gave him an annual income of about 500 livres, to which was added his pension from the Regent, which the prince was kind enough to raise from 1,500 to 2,000 livres on hearing of Monsieur Arouet's death. He felt sorry for the poor orphan!

So in 1724 the orphan had a yearly income of nearly 6,500 livres. He also had the royalties from his *Oedipe,* but they did not amount to much, and he did not exact them in full. In lordly fashion he left most of the profits from performances to the actors.

Temptation Resisted

Around this time the Maréchale de Villars decided she wanted Voltaire back but too clever herself to risk making overtures that might meet with a rebuff, she had her husband approach him instead. It was a clever move but a somewhat shortsighted one. The maréchal was old and kindly disposed toward Voltaire. He sent him an invitation to Villars, painting in glowing colors the pleasures that awaited him. They were certainly tempting: the theatricals often staged at the château, the charming theater, the actors and actresses, the enthusiastic audience. All that was missing was Voltaire. But the latter begged off, insisting he must obey his doctor's orders. He maintained he was dying: for the first time we hear the plaint that was to echo all through the immensely long life which he claimed was one long agony. Yes, he was in the most precarious state, and if he left his doctor's care for a single day he was as good as dead. Did the maréchal want to kill him?

The doctor in question, Monsieur Vinache, primed by Voltaire, went around Paris telling everyone that the air at Villars would be poison to his patient. Vinache was a sort of charlatan; he had helped the Regent, an ardent devotee of alchemy, search for the philosopher's stone that presumably could turn base metals to gold. Neither Vinache nor the Regent found it, but the charlatan did better than the prince. He invented an elixir which he claimed had cured certain patients suffering from delusions and which he sold to many others, who did not get better but brought him a fortune of 100,000 livres.

Voltaire did not go to Villars, though he sighed mightily as he read the maréchal's tempting letters: they had just performed Corneille's tragedy *Polyeucte*; two of the King's grenadiers had played Pauline and Stratonice. They had had to be decked out in female costumes and made up as women, a task eagerly performed by the Maréchal de Noailles's daughter, until it came to dressing them in their hooped petticoats, whereupon the young lady's modesty received a rude shock.

There was play acting everywhere, even in the servants' quarters. The maréchal wrote Voltaire how a chambermaid had fallen madly in love with a gardener. The girl's mother expressly forbade her to marry the man. She might have given her consent had Madame la Maréchale been good enough to celebrate the wedding at the château and pay all the expenses. But Madame la Maréchale was well known for her thrift and preferred lecturing the mother on her cruelty to her daughter to frittering away a hundred *livres* on a chambermaid's wedding. The maréchal made fun of his wife over this, though he too had a reputation for penny pinching. When he was installed as governor of Provence, custom prescribed that a purse of gold should be offered to the new governor who, also according to custom, would thereupon refuse it. But the Maréchal de Villars refused to refuse it. He was pointedly reminded that the Duc de Vendôme had refused to accept the purse. "Ah, but he was a prince who was inimitable," the maréchal cried and pocketed the purse.

Though he kept his purse strings tight, he had a very loose tongue and told Voltaire everything. The Maréchal de Villars wanted Voltaire to be one of the family. He wrote him all the local gossip, recounting such tales as how a *valet de chambre* had had his head bashed in by the coachman of one of the guests and how the village priest had been reprimanded by the authorities for speaking ill of the Trinity.

It is remarkable to see a highborn marshal of France seeking out a young poet, the son of a notary, in this way. It is partly a sign of the social changes that were in the air, and also proof of how deeply rooted Voltaire now was in the high society that was so attached to him, no doubt partly because he was one of its most dazzling ornaments, and partly because it sensed how essentially he belonged to it. Yet Voltaire refused to yield to this great aristocrat's wooing. He most probably resisted because the maréchal's wife had resisted him—and not resisted others.

Scapin Has Ambitions

Voltaire had other dreams beside wealth, social prestige, and literary glory. His political ambitions led him to court the King's minister, Cardinal Dubois. The cardinal was a despicable character, as Voltaire knew as well as anyone did. This did not stop him, however, from indulging in the most abject flattery. But in so doing he was merely following the lead of Fontenelle and Massillon, the Bishop of Clermond-Ferrand and a famous preacher and orator. The latter had signed a testimonial to the good character of the depraved Dubois when he was a candidate for a cardinal's hat—a rank in the Church that was more or less a necessity for a prime minister in holy orders.

But Voltaire went even further, comparing Dubois to his famous predecessor, Cardinal Richelieu, naturally to the latter's disadvantage:

> Ton génie et le sien disputaient la victoire
> Mais tu parus et sa gloire
> S'éclipsa un moment.

Your genius and his contended for victory/But you appeared and his glory/Was eclipsed for a time.

This already bordered on sycophancy, but even so it was not enough. Voltaire therefore made even more unmistakable overtures. In his characteristic fashion, he organized his campaign like a play, with scenes ranging from the sublime to the ridiculous.

Ferreting about Paris, Voltaire had come across a certain Salomon Levi. The French court had already employed Levi as an agent against Austria. He had also served the Maréchal de Villars in Austria and supplied information to the Maréchal de Villeroi, commander of the French troops in Germany. Athirst with ambition, Voltaire cared little as to whether Levi was a double or even triple agent. Salomon said he was intimate with a private secretary to the Emperor, and Voltaire congratulated himself on having chosen as his entree into the world of secret diplomatic dealings this very fountainhead of information invaluable to the court's Austrian policy.

On May 28, 1722, he wrote to Cardinal Dubois, offering his services as a diplomatic agent—or, as his enemies put it later, a spy.

"I can more easily enter Germany than anyone in the world, on the pretext of visiting Rousseau, to whom I wrote two months ago that I wanted to come and show my poem [*The Henriade*] to Prince Eugene and himself. I even have letters from Prince Eugene in which he does me the honor of saying he would be very glad to see me. If these considerations may induce Your Eminence to make use of me, I beg you to believe that you will not be dissatisfied with me and that I shall be eternally grateful to Your Eminence for having allowed me to serve you."

He asks only to "be made use of," to be given a mission, to be put on the list of secret agents. He does not mention the possibility of a formal post at the embassy, convinced that if only he could be put to the test he would succeed and then be able to exploit that success and enter the heady world of royal diplomacy. Cardinal Dubois set little store by this amateur spy's offers of his services, however, and left him to his amateurism.

An Unfortunate Encounter

Voltaire had been told of the role his "friend" Beauregard had played in his being sent to the Bastille, and it produced in him the sort of furious and persistent hatred which he was to conceive more than once in his lifetime. It must be admitted that Beauregard deserved no better. A captain in the Provence regiment, he made war not on the battlefield but in the cafés of Paris, against poets imprudent enough to make fun of the Regent's mistresses. In 1720, three years after his imprisonment, Voltaire found himself face to face at Versailles with the man who had denounced him. There was a scene. The poet seethed with rage and called Beauregard all the names he had so amply earned. But they were in the King's palace: a scandalized crowd gathered. Beauregard, who kept better control of himself than Voltaire, promised he would soon give him cause to regret his outburst.

Voltaire had been extremely imprudent. His terrible excitability was always playing such tricks on him. Beauregard was the protégé of the Minister of War, Monsieur Le Blanc, to whom he was very valuable. When Voltaire learned of this he was not in the least dismayed: as often, a feverish excitement deprived him of all restraint and self-control.

A great deal could be said on the subject of Voltaire's nerves and his almost morbid sensitivity to certain stimulants. He was allergic to certain people and ideas, certain beliefs and philosophies. A hated name had only to be mentioned in his presence and he was off. There was no longer any question of reasoning and mastering his feelings, only of submitting to his passion and accepting all its consequences, however harmful or absurd. Hence when he was publicly warned to be careful in his dealings with Beauregard because the Minister of War would avenge him, his only answer was: "I knew spies were paid, but I did not know their reward was to eat at the minister's table."

To appreciate the gravity of all this one has to know that the minister, Le Blanc, was on about the same moral level as Beauregard. When Beauregard asked to be allowed to get rid of Voltaire, Monsieur Le Blanc replied: "Very well, but do it in such a way that nobody sees."

Voltaire's life story came close to being a very short one. But fortunately Beauregard was a fool. He ought to have known that if Voltaire was not killed outright his cries would be heard all over Paris. And that was precisely what happened.

Voltaire's carriage was stopped on the Pont de Sèvres; he was pulled out, cudgeled, and knifed in the face by Beauregard.

Voltaire filled all Paris with denunciations and swore revenge.

He pursued his enemy with incredible tenacity, neglecting both work and pleasure, going from one magistrate to another until he persuaded one at Sèvres to issue a warrant for Beauregard's arrest. Beauregard was obliged to take refuge with his regiment: he must have been very frightened to flee to the army!

While absent from the capital, Voltaire wrote Thiériot from Brussels, urging him to stir up the lawyers: "Do what you can to make you-know-who return in handcuffs." On his return to Paris, he wrote, his main concern would be to have the villain arrested and put on trial. "As regards the man in handcuffs, I intend to be in Paris in a fortnight. . . . I shall there be able to have the villain seized and, with the help of my friends, to see to it myself that he is duly punished."

Two years went by and Beauregard was still at large: "Demoulin [Voltaire's lawyer] is working on my behalf to get Beauregard punished. The expense is ruining me," he wrote.

But what did expense matter so long as Beauregard was hanged—which was what Voltaire dreamed of. Fortunately Le Blanc fell from power and was replaced by Voltaire's friend, the Baron de Breteuil.

The lawyers drew up more papers and Beauregard found himself at last where Voltaire wanted him: in a prison cell, handcuffed.

We do not meet Beauregard again. The Abbé Desfontaines, who was to become an implacable enemy of Voltaire's, reported some years later that the poet was awarded three thousand crowns as damages for the blows dealt him on the Pont de Sèvres, and that he rejoiced over them like a miser. But this is calumny. In matters of hatred or friendship, money was nothing to Voltaire. He would ruin himself to do harm, and he would ruin himself to do good.

Journey with a Lady Companion to the Low Countries

At the end of the winter of 1722, Voltaire went on an escapade with a recent friend in whose company he enjoyed many pleasures without having to pay for them by a single moment's boredom. The lady was the Marquise de Rupelmonde. She was the daughter of the Maréchal d'Aligre and had been married to a Flemish nobleman who died in the service of the King of Spain. In gratitude this monarch gave the widow a pension of ten thousand livres, which she had been receiving for so long that she had quite forgotten its source. According to Saint-Simon, she was of a frolicsome disposition, and her nicknames at court were "The Blonde" and "*Vaque-à-tout* [Busybody—perhaps in various senses of the word]." He adds that she was not blond but "carroty as a cow" and "of an unparalleled effrontery," poking her nose everywhere and with a finger in every pie.

Voltaire set forth with her to Flanders. He seems to have been amused at the idea but not altogether at ease. He made it a condition that they would stop in Brussels for him to visit Jean-Baptiste Rousseau and read him *La Ligue*. She agreed. It was she who was in charge: coach, horses, coachmen, and servants were all hers. Voltaire was her guest.

They stopped first at Cambrai, where a peace congress was being held, and they stayed for several weeks. The town was overflowing with ambassadors, ministers, women, spies, actors, generals, field marshals, prelates, and cooks of various nations.

Cardinal Dubois was Archbishop of Cambrai: Fénelon, the former archbishop and the famous author of *Télémaque*, often referred to as the Swan of Cambrai, had been replaced by an owl. So Voltaire reopened the Salomon Levi question and sent a (quite unsolicited) report to the cardinal-minister on the progress of the negotiations at Cambrai. He flattered the cardinal by praising the beauties, riches, and excellent air of the city: "We have just arrived, monseigneur, in your diocese, where I think all the ambassadors and all the cooks in Europe have agreed to meet. It seems all the ministers in Germany are come to Cambrai only to drink to the Emperor's health. As for the worthy ambassadors of Spain, one attends mass twice a day and the other directs the players. The English ministers send a good many messengers to Champagne, and none to England."

And the French ministers? The cardinal was already supposed to know what they were doing. Voltaire's information must have seemed accurate enough to the cardinal, for this self-appointed observer summed up the gathering as follows: "We shall see this congress of Cambrai spend one half of its time establishing its procedure, and the other half doing nothing at all, until some unforeseen events cause it to be dissolved."

While waiting for its dissolution, people enjoyed themselves. Every party included theatricals, and Voltaire sought to play as active a role in them as possible. But the privilege of actually directing the actors belonged to the Spanish ambassador, who had no intention at all of yielding it to the author of *Oedipe*. And so the quarrel began. Prince Windischgrätz, the plenipotentiary, wanted to have Racine's comedy *Les Plaideurs* put on; Madame de Rupelmonde held out for *Oedipe*. Two parties were formed: in speech and writing, verse and prose, everyone vaunted his or her own choice and exhorted the others to give way. Voltaire spared no effort in support of Madame de Rupelmonde's choice —that is to say, his own play—and praised himself shamelessly. Madame de Rupelmonde shrank from no sacrifice, and in the end *Oedipe* was chosen.

But the war soon flared up again on another question. It was Lent; and the canons of Cambrai refused to give the members of the congress a dispensation. A cry of horror went up. People hadn't come to Cambrai to fast! The matter must be discussed. Voltaire joined the discussion and presented several excellent arguments. In observing Lent, would not the Catholics offend the Protestant delegates by an assumption of moral superiority? And might not the negotiations founder if conducted by diplomats suffering from such privations? And lastly, wasn't it better to feast in the middle of Lent rather than fast amidst such absurd conditions?

But the obstinate canons would not listen. The congress must observe Lent.

So appeal had to be made to their superior, the Archbishop Dubois, cardinal-minister at Versailles. The answer was soon forthcoming: he overrode the canons, said they were stupid, and gave the whole congress a dispensation in the name of Christian modesty, which forbids us to call attention to ourselves by ostentatious devotion.

From then on cooks and players could do as they liked.

When Voltaire and his Egeria had exhausted the pleasures of Cambrai they went on to Brussels. The odd couple left a murmur of scandal behind them. They had been misguided enough to take offense at allusions to their relationship, and to defend themselves with such heated resentment that they had become something of a laughingstock. In fact, society at Cambrai cared little about the intimacy between a young freethinking poet and a former belle at the court of Louis XIV, possessed of some remains of beauty if not of virtue, and there was no need for them to pretend to be outraged at the veiled references to their affair.

On the highroads in the enormous coach, Voltaire and his lady, less gallant than in public, bickered over philosophy. Madame de Rupelmonde did not like to waste her time on any but the loftiest subjects. Voltaire explained Lucretius to her, but the explanation soon turned into blasphemy and banter. He wished the ancient's philosophy might teach her to "scorn the horrors of the tomb and the terrors of the afterlife." She adored this kind of lesson, though she had learned its moral long since; but as the teacher was Voltaire she dutifully repeated that what must be done was to overcome "the sacred lies of which the earth is full." It was in this spirit that he dedicated to her his *Epître à Uranie* (*Epistle to Urania*), a witty but thoroughgoing condemnation of Christianity: the fumes of the suppers in the Temple rose to intoxicate him again after ten years: his shafts were sharp and fierce.

In Brussels, Voltaire seems to have called attention to himself by behaving so outrageously in church that the congregation wanted to throw him out. It was Jean-Baptiste Rousseau who told this story many years later, though there is nothing to confirm it. By then the poets hated each other so fiercely that any lie was pressed into service. When told of the allegation Voltaire answered airily: "You say I am supposed to have been irreverent at mass? . . . Perhaps I had one of my fits of absent-mindedness. I am extremely sorry." What he really regretted was not his own irreverence but being attacked by such a wretched detractor: "But, come, is it for Rousseau to reproach me? Do you think it seemly that the author of so many licentious epigrams, of infamous rhymes against his friends and benefactors, of the *Moïsade* . . . should reproach me, sixteen years after the event, of having caused disorder in a church?"

Indeed, Rousseau was in no position to question Voltaire's behavior, having been exiled to Brussels for life (we are told by the latter) for having written an "infamous" publication. But Rousseau put on the best front he could to make people forget his past—while Voltaire did all he could to make people remember it, including any authorities who looked as though they might be in need of reminding. Rousseau spread it abroad that Voltaire was in Brussels as a member of a lady's suite, one of her "retainers." Voltaire fiercely replied that Rousseau was the son of one of old Monsieur Arouet's servants: "It is natural that a servant should use the expressions of a servant: to every man his own language."

These exchanges did not take place until a long time after the visit to Brussels. When Voltaire first arrived there, Rousseau welcomed him with open arms: he was a heaven-sent visitor, he was Paris, poetry, the theater, success, and home. He was also himself, with his shining wit that illuminated everything, a sun among the candles of Brussels. Whatever he may have said afterward, Rousseau was dazzled at the time, especially as Voltaire went out of his way to be charming. Rousseau was his elder, and a great poet in those days, and Voltaire wanted to be loved and admired in return. He at once sent Rousseau *La Henriade*, asking him to read it and give his opinion. Rousseau kept the poem six days and was delighted with it. He wrote: "Monsieur de Voltaire has just spent eleven days here during which we were hardly out of each other's sight. I was charmed to see this young man of such great promise. He was good enough to entrust his poem to me for six days. I can assure you it will do its author very great honor. Our country had need of such a work: its terseness is admirable and the verses of consummate beauty. . . ."

All went well, then, until Voltaire later made fun of Rousseau's poetry, whereupon everything changed. Rousseau would have people believe that Voltaire was able to remain in Brussels only through his patronage, that it was he who had caused all doors to open to Voltaire. But of course neither Madame de Rupelmonde, who was Flemish by marriage, nor Voltaire was in need of such services.

Rousseau foolishly complained of all the trouble he had taken to introduce the disreputable pair into society. He had had to suffer "all the importunity, extravagance, and quarrelsomeness that an out-and-out scatterbrain can inflict on a serious and self-controlled person." He also declared himself profoundly shocked on reading *La Henriade*. His first reactions have just been quoted: but later he said he was revolted by the poem's "satirical and passionate attacks on the Roman Church, the Pope, priests secular and in holy orders, and against both political and ecclesiastical governments." How jealousy changes a man's opinions, and how severe turncoat zealots are!

Rousseau had read the *Epistle to Urania* as well, which sixteen years later he called a work "full of horrors against all that we hold most sacred: against religion, and against the very person of Jesus Christ, to whom a word was applied such that I cannot recall it without a shudder." He claimed he had reproached Voltaire vehemently for having given him such a dreadful work to read. According to Rousseau, the scene took place in a carriage, Voltaire tried to defend himself by using "abominable arguments," and Rousseau threatened to throw him out of the window rather than listen to him. In fact, he had limited himself to stopping up his ears. "Then he was silent, and begged me only not to speak about the poem. I promised, and I have kept my word." He had a strange way of doing so, however.

The quarrel had really arisen not out of Voltaire's lack of respect for Our Lord but out of his impertinence toward the works of Rousseau. The young poet did not even have the courtesy to repay the older one for his praises of the *Henriade*. Rousseau read him his *Jugement de Pluton (Judgment of Pluto)*, a poem against the Parlement of Paris, which had exiled him. It was dull. "This is not our real Rousseau, our great Rousseau," Voltaire said bluntly.

But that was a pinprick. The dagger thrust was still to come. Rousseau was aware of his own decline following his exile, and to recover his reputation had composed a vast vehicle of thousands of alexandrines that was to bear his name forward to future generations. He had boldly entitled it *Ode to Posterity*. On a later visit by Voltaire to Brussels, in 1739, Rousseau showed the work to him.

"I doubt if this ode will ever reach its destination," Voltaire remarked.

The witticism spread like wildfire, and it ruined Rousseau's reputation. That was the unforgivable sin. They parted, enemies for life.

More Complications: Troubles with a Poem and with a Poet

(Voltaire was back in Paris at the end of October 1722. He spent November there and left for the Château d'Ussé, in Anjou, at the end of December. On the way he visited the exiled Lord Bolingbroke at La Source. Voltaire was delighted with the château, his host, the company, and with his own work.

"I encountered in this Englishman all the erudition of his country and all the politeness of ours. I have never heard our language spoken with more energy and correctness. He is a man who has spent all his life in the midst of pleasures and business, and yet has succeeded in learning everything and forgetting nothing."

Lord Bolingbroke had been living in France with the Marquise de Villette since 1717. She was born Mademoiselle de Marcilly and had in her youth been sought in marriage by the Chevalier de Villette. But it was her fiancé's father, the marquis, whom she married, preferring the brave mariner to his son. When he left her a widow in 1707 she was forty-two years old. This was quite an advanced age in those days. When she met Bolingbroke in 1717 she was fifty-two. But he was an eccentric and had no eyes for anyone but her. He loved her and she him. A slight complication was that there was a Lady Bolingbroke in England. The pair behaved as though she didn't exist and lived together as a model couple. Lady Bolingbroke obligingly died in 1719; but it would have been unseemly for the lovers to marry at once. A few years later, while they were traveling, they quietly wed, and no one knew about the marriage until much later. Bolingbroke amused himself by improving his Château de La Source and enjoying its woods and gardens and the spring that gave the place its name.

Bolingbroke was an omnivorous reader, and the success of *Oedipe* brought Voltaire to his attention. He wanted to meet him, and it was D'Argental, Voltaire's schoolmate and lifelong friend, who introduced them. Voltaire brought Henri IV with him to La Source, in the form of his poem *La Ligue*, which delighted everyone. This was the beginning of a friendship founded on mutual admiration, esteem, and affection. Once more Voltaire had discovered true aristocrats: not saints, but representatives of highly cultured society whose alleged sins were more attractive than the most resounding virtues.

(He spent several months during the winter near Chinon in the valley of the Vienne at the magnificent Château d'Ussé. He had everything there: the beauty of the place, the best society, and leisure to work. The Marquis d'Ussé's first wife had been a daughter of the great Vauban—a terrible virago. But she died, and the ways of the second marquise were much more agreeable. There was an Abbé Grécourt at the château who composed songs so ribald he was asked to sing them only while out hunting: such words could only be uttered in the open air. The marquis was a friend of Président Hénault, who said he was the best man in the world. His absent-mindedness was proverbial, and Hénault also attributes to him a characteristic that is very rare: "He imagines he was created only for others." Monsieur Hénault adds that he was an excellent actor in the so-called "bourgeois" tradition, and Voltaire loved him for this small talent as much as for all his virtue.

Life in such châteaux was perfectly balanced; it included at once the pleasures of country life, of society, and of work. When he read his poem aloud Voltaire observed the reactions and revised it accordingly. He wrote letter after letter to Thiériot about the promotion of *La Ligue*. He expected it to bring him fame and fortune, and the more he worked at it the more he loved it. Thiériot was to spread it about that Voltaire had gone to Holland for the sole purpose of arranging for its publication. Above all, Thiériot was not to breathe a word about Voltaire's contre-tempt with Rousseau in Brussels.

Nevertheless Voltaire was anxious. He knew he had sung the praises of Henri IV and of France, but there were shafts and quips among the praise, and he knew Paris and his society and literary friends too well not to fear repercussions if he were to apply for permission to print his epic in the capital. An idea occurred to him. He would print the poem himself at his own expense and publish it by subscription in a limited edition. He distributed a prospectus naming The Hague, where he had already made an agreement with a printer called Le Vier, as the place where the subscription was to be raised. In the provinces arrangements were to be through the chief bookseller, and abroad through the booksellers in the principal towns.

He saw that as many subscription leaflets as possible were sent out, and even intimated that he already had the royal privilege allowing him to print and publish the *Henriade*. He was deceiving himself more than any-one else. He was so sure that the privilege was as good as his that he wrote a dedication to the King. It is an excellent piece of eloquence, one that might have been described as "patriotic" if the word had existed then. Its fervor and sincerity are moving: Voltaire really did intend to produce a poem to the glory of Henri IV and of France—though perhaps of a Voltairian France. The poem's sincerity was even too evident: certain eulogies of Henri IV read like criticisms of Louis XV.[6] But the King never read the dedication. The book was refused by the censors.

This was a catastrophe. What was to be done? There was no question of giving the subscribers their money back. Voltaire decided to have the poem printed secretly at Rouen. He had friends there who could be relied on: Président de Bernières, and, even more, his wife the marquise; his friend Cideville, counselor of the Parlement of Normandy; and Thiériot, who went to stay with the Bernières at La Rivière-Bourdet in order to supervise the printing.

The Marquis and Marquise de Bernières, the président of the Rouen Parlement and his wife, were a charming couple. They had a château near Rouen, called La Rivière-Bourdet, and a fine town house in Paris on the Rue de Beaune. Madame de Bernières was beautiful and intelligent, and a fearless friend. She and Voltaire lived in the closest intimacy, though it cannot be said for certain that they were lovers. Everyone believed they were, except Monsieur de Bernières. It was he who arranged for Voltaire to have an apartment in their town house next door to his wife's. There is nothing, apart from suspicion, to indicate that his wife deceived him. Voltaire stayed at La Rivière-Bourdet long and often; it was from there that he supervised the printing of *La Ligue;* there in 1723 he wrote a new tragedy, *Mariamne,* and treated a chest complaint by drinking ass's milk. He wrote to Madame de Bernières and Thiériot, from Rouen: "I return this evening to La Rivière, to divide my attentions between *Mariamne* and an ass."

He found interesting company in Rouen. There were salons full of wits, plays, excellent music. He acquired friends, and publicity. He aroused curiosity by talking about his poem, and he collected subscriptions: "You will easily understand that a man who is about to publish an epic needs to acquire friends."

In January 1723, Voltaire was still at Ussé. He liked it there and wrote to the Marquise de Bernières: "My love of study and retirement leaves me no desire to return [to Paris]. I have never lived so happily as since I have been far away from all the talk and scheming and slander I once endured."

He was, and remained, torn between his need for work and solitude and his need for Paris. Paris was too much for his nerves but he was a Parisian par excellence. He seemed to enjoy whipping up the slander and scheming, and always returned to Paris after he had renounced it. But although the life there intoxicated him, it soon became painful. He was fascinated yet frightened by it, as children are by fire, and played with it as they do.

He was back in Paris in February 1723 and soon found cause for annoyance. A minor gadfly poet, Alexis Piron, had written a satire on fashionable authors which was performed by strolling players at the fair.

To attack Voltaire he had chosen *Artémire,* the latter's worst play, which had been withdrawn from the repertoire of the Comédie Française. Piron said that the whole tragedy had only two good lines in it: the first two. Which wasn't much, in five acts.

When Voltaire met Piron later, he said acidly, "I am delighted to have contributed something to your masterpiece at the fair."

Piron looked astonished and asked what he had contributed.

"The two good lines of mine that you quote," Voltaire replied.

"Oh, I didn't know," Piron shot back. "No one in Paris recognized them or wanted to claim them. I just put them in without knowing the author. Are they unfortunately yours?"

This sort of thing was torture to Voltaire, however impervious he might claim to be. He was too much alive to the pleasure of making witticisms to be insensible to the pain of being their object.

And Piron, like others, would pay for this one.

A Marquise and an Unpolished Poet; a Lord and an Epic

Since 1715 Voltaire had frequented the salon of the Marquis and Marquise de Mimeure. The marquis was a field marshal and a member of the French Academy, and both he and his wife were charming. Saint-Simon cannot speak too highly of them. Their town house was in the Rue des Saints Pères, and the cream of society visited them there. Voltaire was on familiar though not intimate terms with them. The Mimeures lost a good deal of money through the Law's "system," and Voltaire wrote playfully to the marquise to console them: "Whatever happens, it cannot deprive you of the pleasures of the mind. But if they [the financiers] go on at this rate they will leave you nothing else, and frankly that is not enough to live comfortably and to keep up a country house where I may have the honor of spending some time with you." Which is as much as to say, don't let them ruin you if you want me to come and stay with you.

Madame de Mimeure was always very friendly toward Voltaire, who continued to visit her after her husband's death. The same year yet more sumptuary edicts were issued against the excessive expense women lavished on their dress. Madame de Mimeure, though a widow and advanced in age for those days (she was fifty-three), protested loudly. She wanted to sink into yet deeper ruin but this time by her own efforts, which is of course a different matter. She asked the Regent for a dispensation in consideration of services rendered by the late marquis. She got what she wanted and appeared once more in gold brocade and covered with diamonds, to the great chagrin of those feeble creatures who had still to dress as best they could in linen and drugget. But her triumph did not last long.

It was at Madame de Mimeure's that Voltaire had met Piron. He was witty but crude, a provincial without social graces and deplorably dressed. Even if he had been a vessel of the Holy Ghost, Voltaire would have had to make fun of him. Madame de Mimeure tried to make him dress properly, but he spoiled his clothes by his bohemian ways. He used his pockets to carry bread and cheese and even flagons of wine.

Early one morning Piron called unceremoniously on the marquise to bid her good day. She did not take offense but smiled and told him that Voltaire was there. Voltaire, in fact, had been acting the spoiled child of the house, and his hosts had not appeared to be at all displeased. "Since you are so eager to meet him," the marquise said to Piron, "go in and see him—he's keeping warm in my room." And she continued her toilette.

Piron really was dying to meet the dazzling Voltaire, who had conquered Paris without effort, while he, a writer up from the country, had had to work like a slave for only a semblance of success. He found the poet sitting meditating in front of the fire, hunched up in an armchair with his legs sprawled out as close as possible to the flames. Piron's greeting received only a nod and a blank look in reply. Voltaire had judged the bowing and scraping stranger by his appearance and took no notice of him. Piron gradually edged nearer to the fire. The only sound was the logs crackling. Piron spoke. No answer. The poor Burgundian didn't know what to do next. He felt humiliated. He didn't dare to speak again. They watched each other covertly. Voltaire, resolved not to speak, blew his nose. Piron sneezed. One looked at his watch. The other took a pinch of snuff. It was unbearable. Voltaire then astounded his companion by taking a crust of bread out of his pocket and starting to nibble at it like a squirrel. Piron's spirits rose a bit, and he took his flagon of wine out of *his* pocket and emptied it down his throat. Then Monsieur de Voltaire drew himself up, got to his feet, and said severely:

"Monsieur, I understand a joke as well as anyone, but your jest, if that's what it was, is in extremely bad taste."

Voltaire, his speech now restored, explained: "I am just recovering from an illness which makes me perpetually hungry."

To which Piron replied: "Go on then, monsieur, eat. *I* am just up from Burgundy, which makes me perpetually thirsty."

Voltaire accorded him a faint smile and left the room. Soon afterward Madame de Mimeure hurried in, all upset, and asked Piron what he had done to Voltaire. He had just passed by her, muttering crossly, "Who is that utterly mad toper sitting by your fire?" *Had* he been drinking this morning? she asked angrily. Piron described the scene, and she laughed.

In fact, Voltaire did not look kindly on this intruder in a house where he was the reigning favorite. He despised Piron for his bumpkinish appearance, and he was vexed by his undoubted wit: the most unbearable thing for one wit is to have another hanging about. But he was obliged to put up with Piron, because Madame de Mimeure was fond of him, though not so fond of him as her companion, Mademoiselle de Bar, who constantly played up to him. His good nature pleased the two women, who pretended not to notice Voltaire's sulky looks. He was cross with them and took off for the capital again.

In April 1723 he went to a performance of La Motte's tragedy: "I have been to see *Inès de Castro*, which everyone finds very bad and very touching; they condemn and cry at the same time." In the eighteenth century to weep meant to admire: the more people wept over anything, the finer it was.

Voltaire also spent precious time searching for a sinecure for his friend Thiériot, who was with the Bernières at Rivière-Bourdet helping make arrangements for the publication of the *Henriade*. But Thiériot was difficult to place. Voltaire applied to the bankers Pâris-Duvernet, and when he thought his own tenacity might be becoming irksome to them, he delegated his friends—Génonville, the Maréchal de Villars, Président de Maisons. The brothers Pâris had often demonstrated their good will; but they were not blind. They would willingly have found a good situation for Thiériot among their vast concerns if he hadn't been so unpromising. Thiériot in short was lazy and headstrong: his real vocation was to be a parasite who performed odd jobs. Furthermore, he was not very reliable. But to Voltaire he was sacred: he was his friend. Voltaire knew all his faults, no doubt, but they weren't to be spoken of. The bankers didn't like to refuse; they promised and procrastinated. In the end they did not take Thiériot on. But Thiériot was not nearly so disappointed as Voltaire. All Thiériot wanted was what he already had: to be lodged in a lordly fashion, in this elegant household or that, to do a few errands, to listen and repeat, spread one rumor and silence another, scrounge expenses, and receive generous rewards from his friend Voltaire. Everything went on as before.

In September 1723, Voltaire was at last able to escape from Paris and get away to his *présidente*, his ass, the pure air of Normandy, his friends at Rouen, and his proofs of *La Ligue*. And also to a great sorrow, the death of Génonville, in the great smallpox epidemic of 1723.

Génonville was the young lawyer—cultivated, brilliant, eager, full of promise—with whom young François-Marie Arouet had shared Suzanne de Livry. Once, writing to Madame de Mimeure, Voltaire said: "I sometimes hope that you never meet him, for if you did you could no longer tolerate me."

Ten years after Génonville's death Voltaire's grief was still strong enough to inspire the *Epître aux Mânes de Génonville* (*Epistle to the Spirit of Génonville*):

> Toi dont la perte après dix ans
> M'est encore affreuse et nouvelle.

Thou whose loss, after ten years,/Is still dreadful and new.

(With all his changeable moods, in the midst of the restless and confused life he led, Voltaire's capacity for friendship was the stable element in him. He was strongly attached to his friends and wanted to attach them strongly to him. He used them and let them use him. A moment of forgetfulness or neglect hurt him: he would send off a note at once to make up. A letter was a link: a current could pass by means of a compliment, a witticism, a jest half satirical and half tender. When minds communicated with one another like this, Voltaire felt better. He could see a fellow spirit holding out a mirror in which he could recognize, and admire, himself. He needed highly intelligent friends to co-operate in such a commerce, which was for him perhaps the ideal and perfect form of love.)

He returned to Paris in mourning for Génonville and presented his tragedy *Mariamne* to the actors at the Comédie Française. He wanted *Mariamne* to be played by Adrienne Lecouvreur. She had great talent and had been his mistress in the days of the *Anti-Giton*. Then he went to be admired and made much of by his friend Président de Maisons.

Another Perfect Friend

Président de Maisons belonged to a wealthy family that had enjoyed royal favor for more than a century. His grandfather, chancellor to Anne of Austria, had founded the family fortune. Young Maisons himself was a sort of child prodigy. He performed all his duties with grace: he was as amiable as he was intelligent; and Louis XIV had made him président of the Paris Parlement at the age of twelve, to console him for the death of his father. The Regent continued this favor and allowed him to sit on the bench when he was only eighteen. He gave no one any cause for complaint. But he was interested in science rather than in law. He did research, in the then prevailing manner: that is, fiddled about with this and that and finally discovered something new without always quite knowing what. Monsieur de Maisons was lucky enough to know what it was he discovered. It was a color: Prussian blue. He also created a botanical garden on the outskirts of Paris in which he was the first to grow coffee trees that produced ripe beans. All this was very important to him, but what matters here is that he was Voltaire's friend, and a perfect gentleman.

The président's grandfather had commissioned Mansart to build the fine Château de Maisons, where he entertained everyone in French society particularly distinguished by birth or merit. Voltaire had a room at Maisons, and liked it there. It felt as far away from Paris as Sully, yet he could see the roofs of the capital from the window and could go there and return to Maisons in a day. He had decided to make a long stay at Maisons. But he was forced to stay there whether he wanted to or not— by smallpox, which nearly carried him off as it had Génonville. Barbier, a lawyer who wrote memoirs about this period, says: "Countless people died, and the King made a great saving on annuities."

One evening both Voltaire and Monsieur de Maisons were taken ill. They were both bled, as was the custom. Next morning Monsieur de Maisons was better but Voltaire much worse. In view of his frail constitution the doctor was pessimistic; the servants informed the patient, adding that his coffin was already being prepared. The parish priest of Maisons, one of the few people not afraid of contagion, came to see him, and out of gratitude Voltaire made his confession. He also made his will, regretting that he would be leaving his friends and that he had not been able to put the finishing touches on his *La Ligue* and *Mariamne*. He was frightened by the fact that a famous fortuneteller had predicted that he would die that year. He laughed about it afterward, but at the time, in the grip of fever, he really thought the prophecy would come true, especially as everyone quoted the example of Madame de Nointel, who had been told by the same fortuneteller that if she passed her forty-first year she would live to be a hundred. Soon after her fortieth birthday, in perfect health, she had a sudden headache on leaving a dinner party and died the next morning.

Monsieur and Madame de Maisons nursed Voltaire with the greatest courage and kindness and succeeded in saving his life. As soon as Thiériot heard that Voltaire was ill he came to be with him and, despite the great risk, never left him day or night. Adrienne Lecouvreur also came to see him. He couldn't find praise high enough for Monsieur de Gervasi, the physician who attended him. Voltaire said that if the latter had attended Génonville his friend would still be alive. By November 15, Voltaire was out of danger. On the sixteenth he was sitting up in bed writing verses. By December he was well enough to travel to Paris.

His departure was not without drama. He wrote in a long letter: "I had scarcely got two hundred yards from the house when part of the ceiling of my room there fell in flames. The neighboring rooms, the apartments below, and all their valuable furniture were consumed."

Voltaire was horrified. It looked as if in return for all his host's and hostess' kindness he had set their house on fire! He couldn't understand how it happened, for he had left only a nearly burnt-out log in the fireplace. The explanation was that a beam that passed through the chimney had gradually overheated and burst into flame, no doubt because of the fires kept going night and day in Voltaire's room during his illness.

"I was not the cause of this accident, but I was the unfortunate occasion, and it grieved me as sorely as if I had been really guilty. My fever returned, and I assure you that at that moment I was angry with Monsieur de Gervasi for having saved my life," he wrote in a letter to a friend.

The De Maisons did all they could to console and reassure him. Monsieur de Maisons took such pains that, as Voltaire wrote further on in the same letter, "It was as if *he* had burned down *my* château."

The Inconstancy of the Muses and the Fidelity of Friends and Fevers

Voltaire immediately plunged into the life of the capital again. *La Ligue* was clandestinely brought to Paris and clandestinely distributed. But it was an open secret. The book was to be seen lying about everywhere in salons and antechambers. It could not be bought at a bookseller's but it could be delivered to homes deemed worthy of having a copy. Pseudo secrecy did more for its success than if copies had been given away. People of fashion greeted one another by reciting verses from it, and serious scholars such as the philosopher Pierre Bayle regarded it as a great work. "Senecas and Lucians of today," he wrote, "you must learn to write and to think from this marvelous poem, the glory of our nation, and a reproach to you."

To modern readers the poem seems cold, even pompous, but to those of the eighteenth century it seemed light verse. Voltaire stirred the cumbersome draperies of the *Grand Siècle*, daring to mingle history with smiles and insinuations. Great men were no longer cast in bronze or marble but attired in the Louis XV costumes and institutions; religions no longer appeared in clouds of incense. In short, although the poem contains nothing that seems very subversive to modern eyes, some of its original readers saw heresy in it, some license, some irreligion, some anarchy —and everyone smelled a whiff of brimstone. Jesuits and Jansenists both attacked it, for opposite reasons. Voltaire's old enemy, the Abbé Desfontaines, accused him of being a Jansenist. The court considered that he treated the throne with shocking familiarity. Stupidity, hypocrisy, self-interest, fear, and, as far as other poets were concerned, jealousy as well were behind the hue and cry raised against the poem.

On March 6, 1724, Mademoiselle Lecouvreur played in *Mariamne*. She put all her talent and artistic ardor into it, and all her heart. But the play, in which Mariamne, the heroine, is poisoned by the despot Herod, was a failure. Contrary to the classic rules of stage decorum, which forbade any death scenes to occur directly on stage, Mariamne lifts the poisoned cup to her lips and collapses in full view of the audience. On opening night, as she did so, the audience tittered, and a wag shouted, "The Queen's a toper," whereupon everyone roared with laughter. The play was doomed —as it had been from the very first act, for it was frankly a bad play from beginning to end.

Voltaire fell ill. Not that he was ever in good health; he was continually complaining. He had faith in doctors, particularly the last one he had spoken to, and was always taking medicine and surrounding himself with precautions. He protected his health as vigilantly as his work: the latter with the ramparts of châteaux and the former with ramparts of pills. He kept asking people what they took, obtaining new remedies, and downing them instantly. He once quarreled with Madame de Rupelmonde because, seeing among her various bottles some pills he had never seen before, he stole them and swallowed them. But she needed them and refused to forgive him. Madame de Rupelmonde's were pleasant-tasting, and he thought about them till his dying day: "I wish I could still steal her pills," he would say.

For the moment the malady he was suffering from was the failure of his tragedy: he shivered, had severe stomach cramps, he grew even thinner. But he kept on working, in bed, despite his colics.

When the fine weather came he left with Richelieu for Forges, a watering place some sixty miles from Paris. Président de Bernières had a house there, and at once a splendid circle formed around Voltaire and

Richelieu. It was country life at its freest. Both his pleasant sojourn and the cure delighted Voltaire. On July 20, 1724, he wrote: "The waters do me more good than I expected. I am beginning to breathe and to know what health is. Up till now I was only half alive. God grant that this little ray of hope may not soon be extinguished."

Unfortunately colic was soon to blot out this ray of hope, leaving him again only "half alive." But his "half life" was lived twice as intensely as other people's whole ones, and in the end turned out to be twice as long.

He was soon to be stricken with grief as well as illness. The Duc de Melun, a friend of his and an even more intimate one of the Duc de Richelieu's, was killed while hunting at Chantilly by a cornered stag that pierced him through with its antlers. Richelieu was heartsick, and Voltaire was ill too. It was not only sorrow, with him: he had begun to feel lightheaded and dizzy from the waters at Forges and stopped taking them. He remained in bed in the daytime and rose at night, to gamble. He gambled heavily and lost. He called it "doing his annual wash." However, as this way of losing money was not at all in the Arouet tradition, he stopped as soon as he thought the laundering had gone far enough.

He returned to Paris in July and stayed in the Bernières' town house on the banks of the Seine. But the noise from the quais nearly drove him mad. He stopped his ears with cotton, but that wasn't enough, and he succumbed to what he called a "double tertiary" fever. No doubt it was malignant. He fled.

He went to furnished lodgings, from which the Duc de Sully tried to carry him off to his château. Voltaire preferred La Rivière-Bourdet. But he didn't leave at once, for he wanted to finish L'Indiscret (The Meddler), a farcical curtain raiser which he had begun at Forges.

He found his new quarters so inconvenient, either because of the neighborhood or the bedbugs, that he returned to the Bernières' town house.

Voltaire was vexed to find that many of his books and articles of furniture and clothing had been stolen, for which he blamed the Bernières' concierge, who had turned his quarters at the entrance into a common tavern.

Another annoyance was a skin eruption. "You will find me covered all over with a horrible itch," he wrote to Madame de Bernières. "When you return we will not embrace, but our hearts will speak to one another." Meanwhile he was entirely rewriting Mariamne. "I think it was that wretched Mariamne that half killed me, and that I am struck down with leprosy for having dealt too severely with the Jews." What had spurred him on despite all these vexations was the fact that he had learned that redheaded Jean-Baptiste Rousseau, in the depths of exile, had the audacity to be writing another Mariamne, and that an obscure Abbé Nadal had actually written a tragedy called Mariamne that the Comédie Française had accepted and were going to perform. They did so, and it was a flop. The

Abbé Nadal accused Voltaire of having sent Thiériot with a claque to howl down his play. Voltaire replied to Nadal in Thiériot's name:

"Truly, monsieur, there is no one, great or humble, who does not find you ridiculous and I, who am kindly by nature, am sincerely grieved to see an aged priest so basely abused by the multitude. I still pity you, despite insults and despite your works."

A fortnight after Nadal's failure, the Comédie Française presented Voltaire's *Mariamne* again, entirely done over. He had cut the disastrous denouement with the poison cup, but apart from that it was as tedious and flat as before. But the audience liked it, and he was hailed as a great poet on the strength of his feeblest work to have yet come before the public.

This success was followed by a long-sought-after opportunity to find a sinecure for Thiériot. The King had just appointed the Duc de Richelieu ambassador in Vienna, a highly important post, and Voltaire, who for some time had been soliciting a sinecure for Thiériot, asked Richelieu to take his friend on as a paid member of his staff. Richelieu, who was less choosy than the bankers whom Voltaire had previously approached on Thiériot's behalf, agreed to do so. Voltaire was delighted and communicated the good news. Thiériot turned up his nose and declined. Voltaire, disappointed, thanked Richelieu and conveyed Thiériot's decision. He did nothing to force the latter to accept; but he was vexed.

Voltaire suspected Madame de Bernières of persuading Thiériot to refuse the post as being beneath him. He was staying with her, she made much of him, and he wasn't at all keen on work. Voltaire reproached her for loving her friends selfishly, for her sake rather than their own. She was betraying Thiériot's real interests in keeping him, and Voltaire exhorted her in a letter to make Thiériot think seriously about it, "and reflect that this is the best chance he will have, and that he would little deserve the respect and friendship of decent people if he missed this opportunity to make his fortune just in order merely to lead a useless life."

Voltaire was speaking like his father here, and like a true friend. But Thiériot cared little whether or not he was useless, so long as he was happy. He would rather have decent people's protection than their respect, and as to his fortune, that was already made. Its name was Voltaire.

But to please Madame de Bernières, who had apparently been persuaded by Voltaire's arguments, and to please Voltaire himself, Thiériot decided to give Richelieu a trial, and he wrote saying he would accept the post. So Voltaire reopened the question with Richelieu, which put him in rather a bad light and was time-consuming in the bargain.

But even after all that Thiériot finally decided not to go, and Voltaire merely wrote him: "You have caused me something of an embarrassment by your irresolution. You have made me give two or three different answers to Monsieur de Richelieu, who thought I was trying to make a fool of him. But I forgive you with all my heart."

To all his other vexations was added Madame de Bernières's jealousy over his relations with Madame de Mimeure. She wanted Voltaire to herself. This was a difficult matter for someone with such wide interests as Voltaire. At Madame de Bernieres's he reigned supreme. The only drawback was that she wanted him to be everything there and nothing anywhere else, and Voltaire liked to be the favorite here, there, and everywhere.

When Madame de Mimeure had to have a breast removed—and one can imagine what such an operation must have involved in the eighteenth century—Voltaire went to see her. Madame de Bernières learned of his visit and wrote him a scathing letter. Voltaire answered: "You must be fond indeed of reproaching people to scold me for going to see a poor dying woman who sent her relatives to fetch me. You are a poor Christian if you will not allow people to be reconciled with others on their deathbeds." And in order not to ruffle her feelings too much he added: "This very Christian errand of mine does not engage me to live with Madame de Mimeure again. It was just a small duty I performed in passing."

It was with her, Madame de Bernières, his long-time intimate, that he wanted to end his days. He was only thirty, but already he talked of retirement. His itch persisted, however, as did his colics and his fevers. He felt, and thought of himself as, an old man, or at least so he said. But he brightened up when he acquired a new physician, Bosleduc. Doctors came and went, but his ailments went on, and so did he.

Miracle at Charonne; Near Miracle at Versailles

Like everyone else in Paris, Voltaire rushed off to Charonne to see a woman who had been miraculously healed. At the procession of Corpus Christi in 1742, in the parish of Sainte-Marguerite, a humble woman, one Madame La Fosse, was cured of a bloody flux. Voltaire, like St. Thomas, touched and saw. Everyone talked of the miracle and said that the Protestants would be confounded.

Voltaire was involved in all this, in his own fashion. On June 27, 1725, he wrote to Madame de Bernières: "Everyone in Paris says I have become devout and quarreled with you, because I am not at La Rivière and am often at the miracle woman's in the Faubourg Saint-Antoine. But the truth is I love you with all my heart and, to my shame, God hardly at all." On August 20, again to the présidente, he wrote: "Do not suppose I do nothing in Paris but put on tragedies and comedies. I also serve both God and the Devil tolerably well. I have the reputation of still possessing a little gloss of devotion to which the miracle of the Faubourg Saint-Antoine has lent new luster. The miracle woman came to my room this morning. See what honor I confer on your house. . . . Monsieur le Cardinal de Noailles has written a fine pastoral letter on the occasion of the miracle, and as the crowning touch (either of honor or absurdity), he alludes to me in it. I have been formally invited to the Te Deum which is to be sung in Notre Dame in thanksgiving for the healing of Madame La Fosse."

This allusion to Voltaire in the cardinal's letter and the invitation were a joke perpetrated by one Abbé Couet, whom Voltaire knew and who sent Voltaire the pastoral letter. He must have enjoyed the typically Voltairian pleasure of "compromising" Voltaire by involving him in these pious ceremonies.

Voltaire and those who thought as he did had plenty to get their teeth into, it is true: the Age of Enlightenment had a greater weakness for miracles and charlatanism than the Dark Ages.

To go on with the play acting, Voltaire continued to try to get his *L'Indiscret* staged. The Duc de Richelieu had read it at Forges, where it was written; he liked it, the public liked it, and so did Madame de Prie, the favorite of the Duc de Bourbon, then Prime Minister. She ruled over the duc, who ruled over the King, who rules over everyone else. It was through her that Voltaire was invited to Louis XV's marriage with Maria Leczinska. He intended to pay his respects to the young Queen and to offer her some verses if she proved worthy of them. His doubts as to whether she was deserving of them did not prevent him from writing them before he really knew. But she wept at *Mariamne*, which proved his verses had not been wasted.

He was told that the Queen's father, Stanislas of Poland, would like to read the *Henriade* and meet its author. The Queen received him, but Voltaire talks of all this as though he had accepted her invitation only to please Madame de Prie. "Only a fool would be pleased with all that." Voltaire was not a fool, but nonetheless he could not conceal his satisfaction. The Queen spoke graciously to him and called him "my poor Voltaire" and a few weeks later granted him a pension of fifteen hundred livres, which he had not requested. He now looked on the court with a different though not an egotistical eye: "It is a step toward obtaining what I do ask for. . . . I complain no more about life at court; I begin to have reasonable hopes of being useful there to my friends."

There now followed a few months' respite. The favor of the court gave him a sort of serenity, his health seemed less troublesome because he was happy, and he felt certain he was on the road to success, honors, and high office. He never forgot his great ambition, to be appointed to some lofty official post and to have a title. In France the title made the man. But the King did not say a word. This was disturbing. Voltaire's ally was Madame de Prie, who was powerful, perhaps more powerful than the Queen. She was a sort of queen of the revels, omnipotent but transient. It was necessary for Voltaire to use this ephemeral queen to gain the favor of the permanent one. It would be the second miracle of the year.

He thought he had succeeded. In his exhilaration, he believed that talent and intelligence, skillfully draped in politeness and flattery, conferred privileges on him. The great noblemen who were his friends had spoiled him somewhat. They treated him familiarly, as a friend and equal, though he was always careful to accord them the courtesies their birth demanded. But he enjoyed a special dispensation, and even his friends occasionally murmured at the liberties he took. His shafts did not always wound, but they sometimes scratched.

But in this exciting game there were no dupes. Everyone had his eyes wide open. Everyone, in spite of his silken exterior, was mercilessly lucid, if not hard as steel. The wit that played with all beliefs, even the most sacred, and all subjects, even the most scabrous, was always on the brink of danger, always skirting sacrilege and treason, immorality and anarchy.

Louis XV had as much wit as anyone. He kept watch from a distance over Voltaire's sayings, afraid of the hidden claws and above all of the insouciance that shocked and disconcerted him. He kept apart because he could not have tolerated some of the liberties that Voltaire's noble friends tolerated. In order not to have to punish them, he preferred not to assist at the squirrel's irreverent gymnastics in the sacred oaks of Saint Louis.[7] This is why the King behaved with reserve toward Voltaire. That is why the favor granted him at court was only half a favor.

Charity Ill Bestowed

But the credit Voltaire enjoyed benefited one strange character.

Pierre Guyot Desfontaines was born in Rouen in 1685, of a respectable family of lawyers and magistrates related to the Bernières. A pupil of the Jesuits and a Jesuit himself, he was for some time a teacher in that order. But he was restless by nature, preferred a freer life, and obtained a benefice in Thorigny, in Normandy. He did not remain there long however. There were too many obligations: saying mass, reading his breviary, confessing, baptizing, marrying, and burying people. He preferred a literary career. He could write, and he had both taste and learning. To make himself known he wrote an ode *Sur le mauvais usage qu'on fait de la vie* (*On the Ill Use Men Make of Life*), thereby proving that he was a very bad poet. He renounced poetry but preserved a kind of resentment against poets, especially good ones. His prose was as excellent as that of all educated people at that time. Malice gave him an extra edge.

In 1723 he savagely attacked *Inès de Castro*, the tragedy by the unfortunate La Motte. The police were no less cruel to Desfontaines himself when they arrested him because of his relationships with young chimneysweeps. It was a serious matter: he risked the stake if his judges decided to press the case. Théophile de Viau had been burned in effigy for the same thing. Two years later, in 1726, one Deschauffours actually died on the stake for the crime of sodomy. So the Abbé Desfontaines was far from comfortable in his prison cell.

It was Voltaire who saved him. He was ill, but he rose from his sickbed to throw himself at Cardinal de Fleury's feet and plead for Desfontaines's release. The latter was let out of prison on May 29, 1825. On the thirtieth he wrote to thank Voltaire, and these protestations should be remembered later: "I shall never forget, monsieur, the infinite obligations you have placed me under. The kindness of your heart is even greater than your wit. And you are the truest friend I ever had. The zeal with which you have aided me honors me more than the malice and slander of my enemies have insulted me with and the unworthy treatment they have inflicted on me. I am obliged to retire for a time."

So much for fine words. But the abbé was still not satisfied. He considered his forced exile unjust. Voltaire must obtain permission for him to return immediately. Desfontaines even suggested the phrasing of the letter of recall which the minister would merely have to sign. He devoted six lines of the letter to gratitude and forty to impudence and recrimination.

Voltaire took up the cudgels again. No victim of misfortune appealed to him in vain. As he was in high favor at court at the moment, he was able to obtain Desfontaines's pardon on June 7, 1725, a month after the man had been released from prison. This was a record, but it was not enough: Desfontaines needed a pension, or at least some sort of assistance. Voltaire was then given to understand that it would be better for Desfontaines to keep quiet for a while: "Certain impressions were still too fresh." But Desfontaines was well looked after: he was staying with Madame de Bernières and crowing over his good fortune with Thiérot, with Voltaire's blessing.

The trouble Voltaire took to nourish this viper was soon to have its reward.

The Great Betrayal

The friendship of the great is not without its dangers. Voltaire was so accustomed to it that he forgot the risks involved.

He had calmly persuaded himself that he was a prince because he was a poet, and his friends had allowed him to persist in this illusion. If Richelieu or Sully or Villars or Conti had even gently admonished him, perhaps he might have been more careful. But his insouciance cost him the most cruel humiliation of his life.

One day in December 1725, Voltaire met the Chevalier de Rohan-Chabot in Adrienne Lecouvreur's dressing room at the Comédie Française. Voltaire still had a great admiration for her, and their previous liaison survived in the form of a faithful attachment that was not love but an active and affectionate friendship. The Chevalier de Rohan, jealous no doubt of the familiarity between the actress and the poet, took it into his head to act the *grand seigneur*. Was he not a Rohan? The family device was "*Roi ne suis. Prince ne daigne. Rohan suis.*"[8] Rohan's attitude was so stupid and coarse, so different from that of Conti, for example, that against such a background it stands out like a stain on a silk waistcoat. He put on haughty airs; a Rohan swaggering like Monsieur Jourdain. He pretended not to know Voltaire's name.

"What is it—Arouet? Voltaire? I suppose you do have a name?"

Voltaire was not used to being spoken to like that, and he was not one to be retiring.

"Voltaire," he replied. "I am beginning my name and you are ending yours."

There were other persons present. The chevalier raised his cane against Voltaire, who drew his sword to defend himself. Mademoiselle, who knew how things ought to be done, conveniently fainted between the cane and the sword. The chevalier put his stick back under his arm, Voltaire sheathed his sword, and when Rohan had left Mademoiselle Lecouvreur came to.

But the affair was not over.

Three days later Voltaire was dining at the town house of his friend the Duc de Sully, where he was almost one of the family. During the meal Voltaire was told that a messenger was waiting for him outside. Voltaire, suspecting nothing, went downstairs. In the street stood two closed carriages, and he was asked to mount the steps of one of them to speak to the occupant. As soon as Voltaire approached he was met with a hail of blows. From the second carriage he heard the Chevalier de Rohan's voice calling, "Don't hit his head, something good may come out of it."

In recounting the incident later Rohan said, "I was the one who gave the orders to those who did the job." A crowd of dull-witted spectators looked on and considered it very kind of the gentleman to spare the poet's skull.

Voltaire rushed back to the dining room, furious and disheveled, and told the other guests what had happened. They were stupefied. He called on them to help him—first of all the Duc de Sully, whose guest he was, and on whose doorstep he had been assaulted. He begged Sully to go with him to lodge a complaint: his assailants had tried to murder him. But the duc calmly refused. The faces of all those present were impassive; everyone was silent. Voltaire realized then that no one was going to aid him: Voltaire carried no weight at all when a Rohan was in the other pan of the scales. He was only an entertainer, a good person to ask to dinner, an amusing guest to invite to the country.

He knew this injustice existed but had not realized it existed for him. The insult lay not in the blows but in the silent approbation, complete and universal, of those he had thought his friends.

He had been put in the Bastille but had soon forgotten his grudge against the government. His friend the Duc de Richelieu had been in the

Bastille too: it happened to everyone who flouted the authorities. But blows delivered at the whim of a private person were insulting. The worst of it was that no one considered such things very extraordinary. The Abbé de Caumartin remarked, not meaning any harm: "Where should we be if poets didn't have backs?" Obviously it was for the Caumartins and the Rohans to provide the cudgels, and the poets to provide the backs. The same Prince de Conti who had turned a pretty compliment on Voltaire's *Oedipe* invented an equally pretty phrase on his cudgeling. He said the blows "had been well received but ill given."

Voltaire tried to brazen it out for a few days. He showed himself everywhere, at court, in town. Marais, a sharp-eyed barrister who kept one of the most detailed diaries of the century, intended only for his own eyes, wrote in his journal: "No one pities him, and those he thought were his friends have turned their backs on him." Marais was delighted.

Voltaire besought the Duc d'Orléans: "Monseigneur, I ask you for justice."

The duc, in Voltairian style, replied: "But you've already had it!"

He had begged Madame de Prie to intercede with the Prime Minister, with the King himself. She listened but gave no answer.

No one wanted to get on the wrong side of the Rohans. They were powerful, clannish, and numerous: in the Church, the army, and at court. The chevalier himself was not particularly illustrious. He was reputed to be a coward and a usurer. He was an officer, and became a lieutenant general in 1734; but his greatest claim to fame is his assault on Voltaire.

Voltaire was no warrior either, but his thirst for vengeance took the place of valor. He decided to kill Rohan. He could have had him murdered, but he magnanimously decided to kill him in proper form. Not knowing where to turn, devoured by hatred and shame, Voltaire began to shun society and frequent shady fencing masters and cutthroats who knew how to handle a sword. He was unwashed, unshaven, without wig or proper linen. He was openly sinking into the dregs of society. He did not know that the police were following him and that a spy made a daily report on his comings and goings and the people he saw. He was learning new thrusts and parries from his new friends, the better to kill the man who had insulted him.

The Rohans were afraid of an attack, but Voltaire's friends laughed. They knew he was a coward and didn't expect him to do anything, though they wouldn't really have minded if he did what the police reticently called "something foolish"—that is to say, run Rohan through, or get someone else to do it for him. Voltaire summoned a relative from the provinces to act as a second for the duel to the death he was planning— proof that he no longer had any confidence in his Paris friends. For a man for whom friendship was the strongest, finest, and most constant emotion, it must have been a bitter experience.

Voltaire was preparing his revenge with all the energy and tenacity he put into everything he set his heart on. If he kept low company it was not in despair but in the hope of getting what he wanted. It was not his intention to kill or be killed in defense of his honor, but to kill with the maximum chance of success and the minimum risk.

Voltaire proudly demanded satisfaction through a duel, and the chevalier agreed. But the next thing he did was seek the protection of his family and demand the execution of a warrant of arrest against Voltaire that the police, alarmed by his behavior and the company he was keeping, had had ready for the last fortnight. The authorities hesitated a little, but finally the Duc de Bourbon gave in. And so Voltaire was first beaten, then betrayed, and then, on the night of April 17, 1726, imprisoned in the Bastille for the second time—much to the relief of his brother Armand, who bore him no good will and wished above all to avoid scandal, and to the relief of Madame Mignot, his favorite sister. She knew that "the greatest poet of our age," as public opinion described him, would be shattered like glass if he collided with the Rohans.

One voice alone was raised, with dignity and force—that of the Duc de Villars, who had fought against the enemy on the battlefield, not against poets among the ladies. He admitted that all parties were to blame: "Voltaire for giving offense to the chevalier, the latter for the capital crime of having a citizen beaten, and the government for leaving this notorious misdeed unpunished and putting the beaten in the Bastille to reassure the beater."

The maréchal was thinking of the law, a consideration that seems to have escaped his contemporaries. This conspiracy of silence was what shocked Voltaire most in the whole affair. The civic spirit which he and Villars and probably a few others felt was not yet ripe among Frenchmen in 1725.

The court gradually realized how disgraceful Voltaire's imprisonment was. His imprisonment did not enhance the Rohans' reputation: they were made to understand that though they had got what they wanted they had set people against them. But people's resentment was silent, and passive.

One sign of the Prime Minister's uneasy conscience is a letter to the governor of the Bastille: "Monsieur de Voltaire's genius is such as requires to be treated with care. His Royal Highness has charged me to write that it is the King's wish that you procure him all such amenities and liberties of the Bastille as are not incompatible with the security of his detention."

Hence Voltaire was installed in an apartment containing furniture belonging to the King, and visitors began to arrive. The friends who had made themselves so scarce as to be invisible now came in swarms. Visits to Voltaire in prison became the fashion. It is difficult to say whether society had been more odious in its cowardice than it was now in its effusive demonstrations of support for him. Voltaire's arrest seemed superfluous to them: the beating he had suffered would have been quite enough, and to shut Voltaire up deprived the public of the pleasure of a fresh scandal. It was in fact an error on the part of the government: Voltaire, made ridiculous by his cudgeling, was rehabilitated by the glory of state imprisonment. So many people came to see him that visitors had to be limited.

The same day that visits to Voltaire were restricted, the order was signed for his release. The authorities were not eager to retain so awkward a captive. He was let out of the Bastille on May 1, 1726, and given permission to leave France at once for London.

He did not forget to say farewell to his illustrious fellow prisoner, Madame de Tencin, who had been sent to the Bastille because one of her lovers had committed suicide. She was accused of having urged him to it. In fact she seems not to have been responsible at all. She was the sister of Madame d'Argental, to whom Voltaire wrote: "We were like Pyramus and Thisbe. Only a wall separated us, but we did not kiss through the chink."

Madame de Bernières, Madame du Deffand, whom Voltaire had met in 1720, and Thiériot came to Calais to bid him good-by. He had asked Madame de Bernières to lend him her post chaise for the journey to Calais; the police officer who was to accompany him there would bring it back again to Paris.

Before proceeding to London, Voltaire sneaked back from England for a short secret visit to Paris in search of Rohan. He did not find him, and, as he wrote to Thiériot, the fear of being discovered made him leave Paris more quickly than he had come. He went on: "It seems very likely that I shall never see you again. . . . There are only two things left for me to do with my life: one is to risk it honorably when I can, and the other is to end it in the obscurity of some retreat consonant with my way of thinking, my misfortunes, and the knowledge I have of men." If the first alternative was perhaps rather literary, the second was more serious. He wanted to forget his country and his countrymen, Paris society, dukes and duchesses, ministers and their favorites, and the horrible falseness of friends in aristocratic circles. Soon England would smile on him and help him to forget.

It is far easier to lead men by way of the ideas they have than by trying to give them new ones. (Preface to *Mariamne*, 1730)

Newton said that an Englishman had converted his first wife but could not contrive to convert the second because his arguments had more validity in days of yore. (*Remarks*)

[On historians who forget the common people and are interested only in crowned heads]:
Historians resemble in this respect those tyrants of whom they speak: they sacrifice mankind for a single man. (Anecdote recounted by Chabanon)

A historian is a chatterbox who pesters the dead. (*Remarks*)

History is a witness and not a flatterer; the only way to oblige men to say good things about us is to do good things. (*History of Charles XII*, chapter on Schulembourg)

In writing history nothing is to be disregarded; and it is necessary to consult, if one can, kings and valets. (*Historical Miscellanea*)

There is nothing truly beautiful unless all nations recognize it as such. (*Literary Miscellanea*)

My love for my country has never closed my eyes to the merit of foreigners; on the contrary, the better citizen I am, the more I seek to enrich my country with treasures that were not born within its bosom. (*Contant d'Orval*, Volume II)

Spending must be the thermometer of fortune; and luxury in general is the unmistakable mark of a powerful empire. (*Contant d'Orval*, Volume I)

It is necessary to belong to a party, otherwise all parties unite against you. (*Literary Miscellanea in Honor of Monsieur Lefebvre*, 1732)

I shall always be persuaded that a clock proves the existence of a clockmaker and that the universe proves the existence of a God. (*Contant d'Orval*, Volume I)

London 1726: the New Arcadia

Everything was perfect once Voltaire reached London. He had made up his mind that it would be. His Anglomania, kindled by his friendship with Lord Bolingbroke, now found its real justification. He praised England to the skies; though as soon as he could he left, never to return. But even so he never ceased singing that country's praises, either because he half believed what he said or perhaps to annoy Versailles and Paris. In this he succeeded very well; and they did not forget.

England was never painted in such bright and smiling colors: "The sky was as cloudless as on the finest days in the south of France, the air cooled by a mild west wind that both enhanced the peace of nature and disposed the mind for pleasure: so much are we machines, and so much do our souls depend on the action of the body. I stopped near Greenwich on the banks of the Thames, a river that never overflows its banks. . . . O gentle river that puts all the rivers of France to shame . . ."

The cudgeling, the Bastille, the cowardice of his friends had made France uninhabitable for him, a country where everything was dreadful, cruel, and perfidious, even the rivers. And now here was the Thames swarming with rich merchant ships, and among them a gilded barge in which the King and Queen took the air, surrounded by other barges rowed by men in silk and gold. One glance told him that the rowers were "free citizens": the joy of liberty and plenty leaped to the eye.

It was eminently natural for Voltaire to want to begin afresh, to turn over a new leaf when the old ones were so full of disagreeable things, and to see nothing but virtue in novelty simply because it made him forget.

When he arrived in London he went to stay with Lord Bolingbroke, who had been repossessed of his fortune and was held in the highest esteem by men of fashion and letters. It may have been at his home that Voltaire met Swift, Pope, and Gay. But Bolingbroke was not quite as cordial as Voltaire had hoped. Voltaire's intention had been to dedicate *La Ligue* to him, but Bolingbroke courteously declined the honor. Voltaire's urbanities and courtly flattery irritated him slightly, and without openly refusing he quoted Cicero: "I fear praise because I fear ridicule." And in a letter to Madame de Ferriole, a friend they had in common, Bolingbroke wrote: "I shall let him have the satisfaction all his life of thinking he fools me with a bit of verbiage."

In this first year of exile he had two misfortunes: he lost his sister, Madame Mignot, and he lost his money. The death of his favorite sister, perhaps the only Arouet he loved, affected him a good deal. He was interested in her family and often asked Thiériot to see her and send him news of her health and her affairs. He wrote to Madame de Bernières: "It was my sister who should have lived and I who should have died. Fate made a mistake. . . . I really thought it would be she who would wear mourning for me."

His grief was so sincere that it brought him closer to his brother for a time. He wrote to a family friend, Mademoiselle de Bessières, begging her to persuade his brother to send news of his health, but the zealous Jansenist did not reply. Voltaire was so mistrustful of his brother that, when in 1728 he was contemplating a short clandestine visit to France to make arrangements for the printing of a new edition of *La Ligue,* he wrote to Thiériot (in English): "I would not be so much as suspected of having set my foot in the country, nor of having thought of it. My brother especially is the least proper person to be trusted with such a secret, not only on account of his indiscreet temper but also of the ill usage I have received from him since I am in England. I have tryed all sorts of means to soften if I could the pedantick rudeness and the selfish insolence with which he has crushed me these two years. I own to you in the bitterness of my heart, that his unsufferable conduct toward me has been one of my greatest grievances."

Voltaire was hurt by his brother's hatred. And the horror his own irreligion inspired in Armand doubtless had something to do with the ever increasing contempt Voltaire came to feel for the devout. It was inadmissible for him that Armand should earn credit from heaven for hating his own brother, and acquire indulgences by making a votive offering for the redemption of Voltaire's "diabolical" soul in the chapel of Saint-André-des-Arcs. (This ex-voto could still be seen on the wall there as late as 1786.)

As for his money, he lost that on account of a Portuguese Jew called Medina who managed to go bankrupt just before Voltaire arrived with his bills of exchange "for the sum of about eight or nine thousand French livres, reckoning all." King George sent him a hundred guineas as consolation, but he was in considerable difficulties: he could no longer draw his pensions from the French court, he had lost his income from the post he had bought in the city of Paris, and his brother's horrible lawsuits prevented the settling of his father's estate, which would have been enough in itself to assure him a decent living.

But the friends he made in England consoled him. The Bolingbrokes offered him their money and their house, "but I refused all, because they are lords and I have accepted all from Mr. Faulknear [sic], because he is a single gentleman." Everard Falkener had a country house outside London which was simple by comparison with Richelieu's château, but comfortable, and pleased Voltaire by a moderate luxury, less pompous but milder and more peaceful, not to say more bourgeois, than the princely luxury in which French nobles lived. Falkener was a merchant who was later knighted and became first an ambassador and later a minister. Voltaire was full of admiration for a country where such a thing could happen to a merchant, conveniently forgetting that neither Colbert nor Le Blanc was a nobleman, to name only two in his own country.

Voltaire was very touched by Falkener's "true and generous affection," but he admired both him and England through chattering teeth, for he was ill and in difficulties. He nursed both his ailments and his sorrows with his usual remedies, work and curiosity. His boundless activity had always saved him from boredom and despair. He found intellectual nourishment everywhere. Everyone who was anyone in London came to the refuge Falkener had offered him. But he missed meeting Newton, who was dying. His splendid funeral astonished Voltaire. What a wonderful people the English were to accord their greatest scientist the honors that France gave only to kings!

Voltaire took a malicious pleasure in showing that a man of letters was much more respected in England than in France. In England, to describe oneself as a writer was a recommendation; in France it engendered mistrust. Voltaire gave examples. In France the poet Addison would have been made a member of some academy and given a pension—that is, if a fashionable lady took the trouble to obtain it for him—and would soon have been in trouble if anybody saw an allusion in one of his plays to the concierge of one of the powers that be. In England, however, Addison was a minister. In France, if he had protectors, Newton might perhaps have been given a pension of twelve hundred francs, whereas in England he had been Master of the Mint. Another English poet was a minister plenipotentiary, and Dr. Swift was Dean of Saint Patrick's and held in higher esteem than a cardinal. . . .

Though he had missed meeting Newton himself, Voltaire did meet Newton's friend Samuel Clarke, a metaphysician who impressed him enormously by the depth and boldness of his speculations on the mysteries of the universe: "Clarke leapt into the abyss, and I boldly followed!" Voltaire was seized with a kind of intoxication on letting his thoughts play on subjects that were forbidden by religion in France. After one of these thrilling conversations he exclaimed enthusiastically to another Englishman who was present: "Mr. Clarke is a greater metaphysician than Mr. Newton!" The other replied coldly: "It may be so. But it is as if you said that one played football better than the other."

Voltaire never forgot these words. They put metaphysics in its place, simply, politely, but ruthlessly.

He paid a visit to Congreve, who feigned surprise that a foreigner should trouble to visit an ordinary English gentleman. "If you were only a gentleman," Voltaire said, "I should not have had the honor of being here today."

In order to indulge in his best-loved pastime, conversation, Voltaire had to learn to speak English perfectly. He set about this task eagerly and indefatigably, and succeeded marvelously, if we are to believe his English judges rather than his enemies in Paris.

With one or two exceptions the English appreciated his virtues without being blind to his faults—they found them interestingly piquant too. After Voltaire had delivered himself of a brilliant diatribe against *Paradise Lost* and its "disgusting and abominable story" of original sin and death, the poet Edward Young declared:

> You are so witty, profligate, and thin
> At once we think you Milton, Death, and Sin.

Voltaire soon spoke and wrote the language so fluently that he composed his letters to Thiériot in English. When he returned to France he had to make quite an effort, he said, to go back to French: "I had almost grown used to thinking in English, and I felt that the terms of my own language no longer presented themselves to my fancy with the same abundance as before. It was like a stream whose source has been deflected; time and trouble were required for me to make it flow once more in its own bed."

The best evidence of how at home Voltaire became in English is given by the most impartial of judges, the ordinary people. Sympathy with the French does not seem to have been the dominant feeling in the streets of London. One day Voltaire was set upon by a crowd who had recognized him as a Frenchman by his dress. They chased him and were about to pelt him with mud. He had the presence of mind to clamber up onto a milestone and make a speech: "Good Englishmen, am I not already unfortunate enough not to have been born among you?" he began. He went on to praise their country and criticize his own. He expressed himself so well that he was applauded by those who had wanted to do bodily harm to him.

Apart from this chance encounter with a crowd, Voltaire saw only the cream of society, in London as in Paris. Among them were Lord Hervey and his wife, who had a Parisian air about them. Hervey was a poet in the style of Chaulieu, and Voltaire bombarded them with verses in English. He spent three months with another aristocrat, Lord Peterborough. Lord Bath, who became a minister, welcomed Voltaire, as did his enemy Walpole, one of the most remarkable statesmen in England and in Europe. Voltaire was very glad to visit the Duchess of Marlborough. She was writing her memoirs in a slipshod way, more anxious to rend her enemies than to tell the truth. When Voltaire asked if he might read the manuscript she asked him to wait a little: "I am at present rewriting the character of Queen Anne. I have come to love her again under the present government."

There was another surprising encounter in London, this time with Mademoiselle de Livry.

Suzanne had been tolerated at the Comédie Française only because of Voltaire: her performances were regularly hissed. The company had finally asked her to withdraw. Voltaire considered this disgracefully severe: if every other state institution sacked its employees for inefficiency, he said, very few people would have jobs. Mademoiselle de Livry, without a protector, was in a desperate situation. She maintained her virtue was above profit; be that as it may, her talent was beneath reproach. She decided to go and act in London, but the English saw through her immediately and she was out of work again. A French innkeeper took her in and she moped in her room with the door carefully bolted. Her youth and beauty called forth the admiration of her host, who sang her praises to his French customers. The Marquis de Gouvernet, who belonged to the La Tour du Pin family and was passing through, was curious to see the lady.

She refused to let him in, despite repeated supplications, and finally they were obliged to force the door. She had not opened her veins or drunk poison; she was not even thin. Her dress was simple and elegant, and she spoke beautifully. It was simply out of false pride that she had refused to see him. The marquis fell head over heels in love with her and wanted to marry her. She declined, because she was too poor. She was a better actress in her garret than on the stage. But the marquis thought of a discreet and elegant solution. He gave her three lottery tickets and had a false list of winning numbers printed, among which was one of Mademoiselle de Livry's. After some becoming hesitations, she agreed to become his bride. It was like an episode from Marivaux's *Vie de Marianne*, or the plots of Voltaire's *Contest;* it is like Voltaire himself, at once the mirror and reflection of his age.

But Voltaire did not foresee the denouement. When, still loyal and affectionate, he returned to Paris and presented himself at the door of the now Madame la Marquise de Gouvernet, once the mistress of François-Marie Arouet and Génonville, once the poor little actress promoted by Voltaire, her porter refused him admittance at her instructions.

He avenged himself in verse. But the *Epître des tus et des vous* (*The Epistle of Thees and Yous*) was not vindictive. He reminded her of the past, which was doubtless what irked her most. But the bad old days were past, and Suzanne had a uniformed porter.

Voltaire's curiosity about the exotic novelties to be found in England did not prevent him from working. He was writing his *Histoire de Charles XII*. He had already published the first version of *La Henriade* in Paris under the title of *La Ligue*. In London he reworked and modified it and gave it its definitive title. Among the modifications was one dictated by resentment: his friend the Duc de Sully's betrayal had made the name Sully so odious to him that he removed it from *La Henriade*. Everything that related to his former friend's ancestor, the great Sully, friend and minister of Henri IV, was suppressed. Originally the poem had included praise of the minister, which he certainly deserved but which had been made even warmer by Voltaire's friendship for his descendant. Now Voltaire refused to write the name. It is rather a tricky thing to write the history of Henri IV without mentioning Sully! In this Voltaire was like the Duchess of Marlborough: resentment counted for more than the truth. But at least there was no pretense: the truth was in the sincerity of the falsification. Nor did the poem attempt to be real history. It was an epic, and epics always partake of fable, especially when, like the *Henriade*, they tend toward satire.

How did Sully take the insult (for insult it was)? Paris expected the poem to contain bitter allusions, with praise of the great Sully serving as pretext for nasty blows at the "little" one. But there was nothing but silence. This made the affront even more resounding. Voltaire would have spared himself many humiliations had he kept to this method of revenge.

As he corrected the proofs he went on, with his usual skill, placing copies by subscription. The English responded beautifully: the King and the court and his friends all subscribed. Swift raised subscriptions in Ireland. The splendid new edition of his epic, magnificently printed, with engravings, was dedicated to the Queen of England: she had not refused. It would have been better for him if she had. All's fair in love and war: he had been forced to leave France, the English had received him kindly, and now he was showing his gratitude. Nevertheless at the French court, in spite of the contemptuous indifference affected there, this gesture, itself a product of disgust, was considered disgusting. People felt a mistrust or even hatred which expressed itself in slander. Voltaire's goings-on were criticized even by people who were not necessarily supporters of the Chevalier de Rohan.

Certain rumors circulated by the Abbé Desfontaines about Voltaire in London were the inventions of pure malice; but they have been accepted and are still sometimes used against Voltaire. Desfontaines said that Voltaire came to be so disliked by the English that he had to flee from London. Also, that Voltaire, dining with Pope, had said things so insulting to the Catholic religion that Pope's mother, who was a Catholic, left the table, and Pope, who revered her, had Voltaire ejected. All this is ridiculous. Voltaire did not insult people at their own tables, especially old ladies of ninety whose sons were writers he loved and admired. And if he had done so, Pope would never have forgiven him, whereas their friendship never flagged. They were both cantankerous, and if they had quarreled people would have been sure to hear about it.

Desfontaines also alleged that Voltaire had been beaten by a London bookseller. This too is absurd, but it is true that Voltaire fiercely defended his author's royalties against a bookseller as avid as himself. He knew how to take care of himself. "I am not such a fool," he said, "as to abandon all my property to a printer." He was the author, after all, and it was he who had organized the sale, distribution, and dazzling commercial success of the book. It was only just that Voltaire should reduce the bookseller's claims; and for once there was no scandal.

The success of the *Henriade* in England was not repeated in France. There, instead of the three hundred and forty-four copies sold in London, Thiériot had obtained only eighty subscriptions. The figure does not reflect much credit on French readers, nor does the sequel reflect much credit on Thiériot.

On Pentecost Sunday 1728 some demon possessed Thiériot to go to mass, though this was not at all his habit. While he was at his rare devotions, thieves broke into his rooms and carried off his precious stock of the *Henriade*. They all disappeared, silently and without a trace, stolen secretly and sold in the same way.

It was whispered everywhere that Thiériot himself had performed the new miracle of the Pentecost. Without knowing the details, Voltaire, in London, realized what had happened. Thiériot had robbed him.

Voltaire said nothing about it. That sort of thing affected him less than an insult or an adverse criticism. His first care was to see that every subscriber received a copy—at Voltaire's own expense. As for Thiériot, Voltaire punished him with nothing more severe than a few allusions: he did not like anyone to think he had been taken in: "This adventure, my friend, may discourage you from going to mass, but it will not stop me from loving you always and thanking you for your trouble."

He forgave the man he looked on as the loyal friend of his youth. But it was Voltaire who was loyal. Such constancy and patience are remarkable in one who was so nervous and irritable. "He was young," he said later, when someone was trying to make him angry with Thiériot. Both Voltaire and Thiériot were thirty-three at the time.

Voltaire's exile in London lasted three years, and it seemed very long. He did not suffer from anything in particular, but he was homesick, which is everything. The child of Paris needed the air of Paris—full of the miasmas of envy, denunciation, and slander, full of the poisons and elixirs of intellect and art.

Back in Paris: Voltaire with a Finger in Every Pie

On March 15, 1729, the troublesome poet returned to France. But not to Paris: to quarantine in Saint-Germain-en-Laye, a town on the Seine on the outskirts of Paris. He lodged with a wigmaker called Châtillon in the Rue des Recollets. It was a hovel. Voltaire painted no idyllic picture here, wrote no couplets about the Seine or gilded barges or boatmen in silk and velvet. France was sullen and cruel to him; but he loved her in spite of himself.

The first piece of news was chilling: the cardinal-minister, Monseigneur Fleury, informed him courteously that the King had decided to discontinue his pensions. He was not surprised, but it was a blow. He hoped the Queen would go on paying the pension she had given him. She owed it to him to do so, "since Monsieur her husband has taken away his against all right."

He was again as he had been before his exile, writing letters in every direction, pleading, flattering, being gallant, sending Thiériot all over on confidential errands, ready in short for any boldness or imprudence. For any generosity also: Thiériot was to have five hundred livres out of his pension from the Queen as soon as the matter was settled. Moreover the *Histoire de Charles XII*, which Voltaire had brought back with him from London, was to be printed and Thiériot was to receive six hundred livres of the proceeds. Voltaire would brook no refusal: "It is to be so or we are no longer friends." No danger of a quarrel in such circumstances: Thiériot agreed.

Voltaire went to Paris secretly to see to certain matters, but it was risky. With Richelieu acting as intermediary, the poet appealed to Maurepas, director of the King's household. At the end of April 1729 he was given permission to reside in Paris.

Instead of returning to his apartment as the Bernières' he stayed in a modest house in the Rue Traversière-Saint-Honoré. He had a mania for moving: he had had ten different lodgings in London, and it is impossible to count all the places he lived in Paris. This time he changed domiciles because his relations with the Bernières, though still amiable enough, had grown cool, and he did nothing to restore them to their former warmth. Madame de Bernières, like Madame de Mimeure before her, had become merely another shooting star in the Voltairian firmament.

Voltaire's first concern in Paris was to get his finances on a sounder footing. He had made progress with his English friends in the art of making money increase and multiply. But haste and imprudence were to undo his enterprise and make Paris again a risky place to be.

He still had a certain amount of capital. The Arouet estate had been settled and he had his share. The performance of his tragedies had left him a little nest egg, and the *Henriade* a large one. Although Thiériot had made inroads, he still had a considerable sum left.

Voltaire knew both how to enjoy Paris and how to extract profit from it. In conversations he sowed but he also reaped. At a dinner party given by a certain Madame Dufay, one of the guests explained how Lepelletier, the new comptroller of finances, had reorganized the lottery in which prizes were allotted to numbers borne by certain state bonds. Voltaire observed that if anyone bought all the tickets he would be bound to win a million livres. He and some others arranged to do so, and brought it off.

The comptroller of finances was furious at having the inadequacy of his system exposed in this way, and refused to pay. But the Conseil obliged him to, and Voltaire received five hundred thousand livres as his share. But he also now had a mortal enemy in Lepelletier, and he was advised to travel.

He did not flee without letting fly a sarcastic poem at the comptroller of finances, which he neglected to sign. The Parthian shot was justfied in his eyes because the comptroller shouldn't have lost his temper at being outwitted.

Voltaire went to take the waters at Plombières with Richelieu, who borrowed some money from him, after signing a note drawn up in the strictest legal form, providing for stiff interest and collateral. On the journey Voltaire learned that the Duc de Lorraine had issued bonds which were to become so profitable that no one outside Lorraine was allowed to buy them. The profit was so tempting that Voltaire made a detour through Nancy. He was very tired, he had a fever and scarcely ate; he slept little and had colic. But he talked and calculated endlessly. He spent two days in Nancy in bed, thus losing the two days he had intended to gain by traveling by chaisepost. He was half dead. But on the third day he was up again, seeing and pleading with the necessary people. It was no use: he was not from Lorraine and couldn't have any shares. But he did get fifty, owing to the fortunate resemblance of his own name to that of one Haroué, a gentleman of Lorraine belonging to the house of Beauvau. "I have tripled my gold, and hope soon to enjoy my doubloons in the company of people like you," he wrote gaily to Président Hénault.

When he got back to Paris he tried to get his tragedy *Brutus* performed. The subject was not Caesar's friend but the much earlier Lucius Junius Brutus, consul in the fifth century B.C., who is betrayed by his son Titus, forgives him his treachery, but condemns him to death. The play was in fact a dramatization of the conflict between the Senate of Rome and the threat of tyranny of the would-be invader, Tarquin, and an assertion of the superiority of democratic government never before put before a French audience in the theater. But the actors of the Comédie Française found it dull and tried to dissuade him. Voltaire resigned himself, but alleged that Crébillon, a rival dramatist, and the Chevalier de Rohan had plotted to get the actors to turn down the play. Voltaire rewrote *Brutus*, taking criticism into account, and it was finally staged at the Comédie Française in 1730. But it was only moderately successful at first, though it steadily increased in popularity over the years.

The *Histoire de Charles XII* had been printed, but it had been seized. Voltaire set great store by it and decided to go on and sell it clandestinely as he had *La Ligue*. Like the latter, a new edition was to be printed in Rouen. His friend Cideville was put in charge of the operation. It is rather odd to see a counselor of the Parlement of Normandy, soon aided by Monsieur de Pontcarré, its chief président, involved in an affair which they would have had to condemn had it been officially brought before them by the public prosecutor.

Thanks to his friends, Voltaire was assured that authority would look the other way, and he came to Rouen to supervise the printing. To mislead the police, and also for fun, he pretended to be a traveling Englishman. He hid away in a vile inn where "Arachne drapes the walls,/The sheets are short, the beds are hard." He worked tremendously hard among the cobwebs, correcting *Charles XII*, going over the *Henriade* for the new edition, and writing two new tragedies at the same time, though again suffering from fever.

But even in hiding he was not at peace or able to devote himself quietly to his work. He was harassed as always; afraid, and with reason. A poem of his was circulating about the death of Adrienne Lecouvreur, overflowing with indignation at the way the great actress had been treated. She had died in Voltaire's arms in March 1730, three days after playing in his *Oedipe*, but because she was an actress and thus automatically excommunicated, she had been buried like a dog in waste ground on the banks of the Seine. Was it not revolting to dump on the garbage heap the body of a woman whom all Paris had applauded, praised, and entertained?—for Mademoiselle Lecouvreur, the foremost tragedienne of her day, had been received in society. Voltaire rebuked the French for their injustice and barbarity, and to shame them he sang the praises of England, where everything was mildness, justice, tolerance, and so on.

His anger is understandable. Adrienne had meant a great deal to him, and even more to his friend D'Argental, who had loved her passionately. Voltaire made his friend's grief and the insult to Adrienne his own. But the poem's passionate tone and flaming eloquence are explained even more by a feeling which Voltaire had always had and which came to haunt him increasingly until the end of his life: the fear that after his death he too might be thrown on the rubbish heap. The sincerity of his condemnation is all the more terrible because he saw himself in the poor mortal remains of the great actress. Voltaire was convinced that he would die before he was forty—his health hardly allowed him to hope for more —and Voltaire the freethinker wanted to rest in consecrated ground and to receive the blessings of the Church. Death seemed to him to be alleviated by the sacraments. He did not believe that a priest's prayers could guarantee him eternal life. There was nothing mystical about his attachment to these forms: death was death in any case. But Voltaire remained the child of the holy fathers who had been his teachers, and in the arms of Mother Church death, horrible death, though it might not become more divine, did become more human. What angered him most about Adrienne's shameful burial was its inhumanity.

The poem circulated—though Voltaire disclaimed responsibility for it. But he had entrusted it to Thiériot, who naturally spread it abroad. All Paris repeated its verses. The anger of the clergy rumbled ominously;

there was talk of Voltaire being arrested again. His printer, Claude-François Jore, who was later to publish the *Lettres philosophiques* (*Philosophical Letters*),[1] hid him at Canteleu, a few miles from Rouen. Jore does not give a very friendly account of his guest. According to him, Milord Voltaire was a skinflint who didn't pay for the eggs and vegetables supplied to him, and who reduced by half the wages of the manservant Jore had found for him, even though Jore was paying him out of his own pocket. In return Voltaire offered Jore an old clock, but in fact he never got either money or clock. Voltaire moved again and went to stay with a friend of Jore's. There he was well looked after and made much of, but when he departed he left the chambermaid a mere eighty sous. She had hysterics: she claimed she'd been waiting on him for seven months.

How true was all this? At the time that Jore circulated these stories about Voltaire, he was involved in a lawsuit against him and was doubtless doing his best to blacken Voltaire's name. It is true that his overshrewd author presented him with very strict accounts. In business Voltaire was very strict, even harsh. But it wasn't true that Voltaire had stayed at Jore's friend's for seven months. And admittedly Voltaire tended to be stingy when he suspected that people were trying to cheat him. But it seems very unlikely, from considerations of mere decency, that Voltaire would have allowed someone else to pay his valet, and the story about the old clock is difficult to credit. Jore and his associates thought they were dealing with a milord easily gulled. In fact they were faced with a worthy son of old Monsieur Arouet, and they were not the only ones to be mortified in their dealings with a poet who knew how to count.

By 1731, Voltaire was back in Paris. He read his new tragedy, *La Mort de César*, on the death of Julius Caesar, to Monsieur de Maisons and ten Jesuit fathers. They liked it. He was still uneasy as he feared the dandies of Versailles more than these austere priests. Between the thorns of *César* on the one hand and those of *Charles XII* on the other, he couldn't sleep.

He worked out two possible ways of enabling *Charles XII* to conquer Paris: either to have the entire edition brought by road from Rouen to Versailles, store it at the Duc de Richelieu's, and have it distributed in Paris by men wearing the duc's livery; or, if transporting the books by road was too costly, have them shipped by barge to the Duc de Guise's mansion at Saint-Cloud. Guise had offered to see to the matter "by himself." The fewer accomplices there were the better the chances of success. So *Charles XII* traveled to Paris by water and entered the city in the form of twenty-five hundred clandestine volumes. The police knew nothing about it.

That autumn Voltaire had a terrible blow: his friend Monsieur de Maisons died on September 13, 1731, of smallpox. It was a repetition of the death of Génonville: the two resembled each other in wit, generosity of heart, manners, and the extent of their wealth; they both had every possible gift. Voltaire was deeply fond of such fortunate beings and considered them the masterpieces of our unhappy breed, the few elect who redeem the wretched herd. Where lesser men envied, he loved fate's darlings. It was a characteristic way of rendering thanks to divine injustice. Voltaire had no vast esteem for humanity in general, but he loved and felt himself a part of it. He rebelled because some insensate power had deprived him and deprived mankind of one who did honor to all: "The death of Monsieur de Maisons has left me in a state of despair not far from total dejection."

"He died in my arms, not through the ignorance but through the negligence of the doctors." Crushed by this bereavement, Voltaire went sobbing from door to door, embracing those who understood and seeking consolation from them. He told everyone of his grief and his resentment. He was exhausted, and thinner, weaker, more feverish than ever.

And of course he had nowhere of his own to live. He slept with some friends, dined with others, supped elsewhere: not that he had no refuge, but because he had too many. In fact, this nomad loved to sit by a fireside meditating, this restless spirit was perseverance itself, this social butterfly an indefatigable worker. For nothing can be reduced to a simple formula with Voltaire, who seems so transparent. Sometimes the mystification is deliberate on his part, and it is then that it is most transparent. Voltaire mystified in broad daylight, as he breathed, as he spoke, as he charmed. But his apparent clarity of character concealed deeper mysteries, for he was the most breath-taking of all conjurers in an age which boasted many.

In 1731, however, he found a temporary resting place that suited him perfectly: the town house of the Comtesse de Fontaine-Martel.

Voltaire's new Egeria, who lived in the Palais Royal, gave him an apartment in the ground floor of her mansion overlooking the garden. She was over sixty, which in those days made her a perfect ancient. She was also afflicted with eczema.

Her age and her malady were providential: they made the virtue of both hostess and guest above suspicion. At first it seems surprising that Voltaire should ever have gone there. The lady was repulsive, miserly, and bad-tempered. But Voltaire had compensations: in her home he was undisputed king of a distinguished salon. A prince of the blood sometimes risked coming to partake of the drugs the comtesse's cook served by way of supper. Also, his hostess was a freethinker or, to put it more plainly, a thoroughgoing atheist and a rabid *philosophe*. As far as dramatic entertainment went, she spurned mass, thought opera sublime, tragedy sublimer still, and Voltaire most sublime of all. She had his tragedies performed in her house. What more could he have wished for?

Voltaire set to work and put on a tragedy called *Eriphyle*. Its admirable versification won it some applause, but the success was so faint, it seemed more like a failure. Voltaire withdrew the play and began it again. He wrote three acts, read it aloud, took note of the unfavorable judgments of his critics, and corrected it again. Voltaire's professional conscientiousness and the attention he paid to a serious public are admirable in one who was sometimes so impatient and so vain. When he saw that no good would come out of *Eriphyle* he put it away and started on another. *Zaïre*.

Zaïre was written in twenty-five days. The Palais Royal lent itself admirably to such feats. Voltaire had been criticized for not putting enough love into his plays. Was there very much in his life? He decided to put in more love in the form of a passionate attachment of the Sultan of Jerusalem to his Christian captive, Zaïre, and the audience was in ecstasies. People wept at the first performance. They sweated too, for it was August 13, 1732, and Voltaire's tragedy, set in a Mideast seraglio, was given in the torrid heat of the airless auditorium of the Comédie Française with a thousand candles burning.

Success did not preclude criticisms or stop Voltaire from noting them and setting about making corrections. But the actors had had enough of these endless alterations, and one of the most popular of them let Voltaire understand that he intended to ignore any further changes. He was an objectionable character who affected the same lofty airs in real life as he used on the stage. Voltaire, instead of losing his temper, skillfully set about bringing him around. At a dinner party given by the actor a splendid pie, sent by an unknown donor, was brought in. When opened it was seen to contain a number of partridges, each holding a piece of paper in its beak. On them were written the corrected lines of *Zaïre*. The actor was won over and agreed to learn them.

Zaïre was the greatest theatrical success of its time, and Voltaire, now the recognized master of the French stage, was henceforth considered the equal of Corneille and Racine. He was thirty-eight, and became the hero of his age with tragedies which ours finds unreadable and almost unactable. But he remains one of France's most famous writers because, as well as these "sublime" tragedies, he penned airily witty works, so light that they fly through time unscathed.

A good many barbs mingled with the paeans to his success. Jean-Baptiste Rousseau, still in exile and more embittered than ever, launched a vitriolic attack, and Voltaire knew that the enemy lurking in the shadow of Saint Gudule was implacable. The envy manifested in Paris was as bitter as that in Brussels. Voltaire recounted how certain literary colleagues had advised him not long before to give up writing. Asked what his reply had been, he said: "I put on *Zaïre*."

Madame de Martel gave a private performance of the tragedy with Voltaire in the role of old Lusignan, Zaïre's father, a part he loved all his life. He declaimed, he emphasized, he exaggerated, he threw himself into it with such abandon that his acting was terrible. His rasping voice pierced walls and people's eardrums. In the play Lusignan is an old man just released from twenty years in a dungeon. Voltaire gave him the chance to make his voice heard at last, and in spite of the cries of protest from the audience, he would not desist; he was possessed. For him the theater was a kind of supernatural transport.

At the same time as he corrected Zaïre he polished his book on England, the Lettres philosophiques. He worked with the perseverance of an ox and the nervousness of a hare. He felt his book, full of praise for English institutions and scarcely veiled condemnation of French ones, was bound to cause more dangerous scandal. But nothing could prevent him from saying what ought not to be said, and it was for that reason that his name would one day be famous the world over as the sworn enemy of all received ideas, all prejudices, all authorities of whatever kind. Hoping to procure the support of the government, he deliberately deceived Cardinal Fleury, to whom he read some passages from it, choosing harmless ones which the chief minister indeed found very amusing and innocent. The cardinal would have been furious with the complete text—as indeed he was when he eventually saw it.

Voltaire was so thin at that time that a stranger who caught a glimpse of him gave him only one month to live. He led too restless a life for one in his precarious health. He need not have used stage make-up to play the sepulchral Lusignan: he looked as if he already had one foot in the grave.

But as it turned out it was he who buried the Comtesse de Fontaine-Martel. He attended her in her last moments and made her die according to the rules, whether she liked it or not, forcing her to have the last sacraments administered to her because he was afraid he would be held responsible if she died without having received them. So she agreed to see a priest to spare her friend from scandal. Voltaire described what happened in a letter: "I fetched a priest half Jansenist and half politician, who went through the motions of confessing her and then gave her the rest of the rigmarole. When this play actor from Saint Eustache asked her aloud whether she believed that her God and Creator were in the eucharist she answered 'Oh yes!' in such a tone that in less lugubrious circumstances I would have burst out laughing." These ceremonies over, the lady retained her wit right up to the end. Realizing that her last moments had come, she asked what the time was. When told it was two o'clock, she answered, "God be praised, no matter what the hour I always have an engagement."

At the comtesse's he had written a poem called Le Temple du goût (The Temple of Taste) in which he expressed his views on the art of writing and on the books and authors of his time. Some were praised and some were ridiculed, and there was another scandal. The scandal really resided in the malice of readers already ill disposed toward him and the envy of other writers: if Voltaire had published *Tom Thumb* his enemies would undoubtedly have conspired to have it confiscated. His *Temple du goût* hurt no one save a number of bad writers and Jean-Baptiste Rousseau, who had more or less brought Voltaire's scathing counterattack upon himself. But Voltaire made enemies even among those he had praised. Among others a certain Monsieur de Caylus gave Voltaire to understand he would do better to omit the complimentary passages relating to him in the next edition. Needless to say, these complaints were accompanied by threats.

But Voltaire had one great sastisfaction: the King and Queen had *Zaïre* put on at the royal palace at Fontainebleau. So Voltaire made his re-entry at court, sponsored by the Duc de Richelieu. He met Piron there. Neither of them was any too pleased: each considered the other out of his element. Piron shows us Voltaire at court, not without malice, but with perspicacity too. There seemed to be ten of him. He was everywhere at once; bowing, talking, not listening to a word, seeing everybody, waving to someone in the distance, dropping phrases right and left. "He rolls about like a pea among crowds of scalawag scatter-asses," Piron reports in his characteristic style.

"Ah, good day, my dear Piron," Voltaire said one day when they met. "What are you doing here at court?" (Piron might have asked the same question.) "I have been here three weeks." (It was really three hours.) "They performed my *Mariamne* the other day, and they are going to do *Zaïre*. When is *Gustave* to be performed?" (*Gustave* was Piron's still-born tragedy.) "How are you? . . . Ah, Monsieur le Duc, a word, I've been looking for you everywhere. . . ." he said then, turning away and leaving Piron standing there. Next day, meeting Voltaire again, Piron said without preamble, "Very well, thank you. At your service." Voltaire asked him what on earth he meant, and Piron reminded him that on the previous day he'd been asked how he was and had not been able to answer sooner.

Voltaire continued work on his *Lettres philosophiques* with the greatest care and a geuine attempt to respect the truth. Though he wished to accord them a particularly honored place, he was afraid of being inaccurate in dealing with Newton and his system. For him, Newton was the future. In Voltaire's eyes he had already dethroned Descartes; he was a universal genius at whose feet all science and every country should sit. Voltaire's was a prophetic idea absolutely contrary to the official scientific views in Paris. Orthodox scholars had taken fifty years to learn Descartes, and it would take them another fifty to unlearn him. Though Voltaire was the first Frenchman to urge his fellow countrymen to renounce Cartesian physics, he was the second to become acquainted with Newton's laws. The first was Pierre Maupertuis, a French mathematician and astronomer, and it was to him that Voltaire sent his manuscript to be checked and corrected. It was the beginning of a long relationship that, predictably enough, was to end stormily.

A new scandal was launched in 1732 concerning the *Epître à Uranie*, which Voltaire had written for the Marquise de Rupelmonde in 1722, and over which he had had the scene in the carriage with Jean-Baptiste Rousseau. Now the poem was circulating in print. Voltaire claimed that the text had been stolen and printed without his knowledge in order to get him into trouble. Was this true, or had he given the poem to the printer himself? Everyone concerned told lies. But certain people took the occasion to attack Voltaire fiercely, and they were in a good position to make their ferocity effective. When the Chancellor d'Aguesseau asked his secretary's opinion about what should be done with Voltaire, the secretary replied: "My lord, Voltaire ought to be shut up in a place where he can never lay his hands on pen, ink, or paper. He is a man whose wit could ruin a kingdom."

An astonishing compliment, but a dangerous one. The Archbishop of Paris asked the chancellor to take severe measures against Voltaire. The latter was summoned by Monsieur Hérault, superintendent of police, who questioned him closely as to the authorship of the epistle.

"I didn't write it," Voltaire said. "It's by the Abbé de Chaulieu."

The Abbé de Chaulieu had been dead for fifteen years, but Voltaire's wit worked again, the authorities pretended to believe him, and he got off.

But a critic wrote: "There's a nasty little author for you, who ought to be sent packing across the sea again!"

And another *lettre de cachet* was deposited on the chief minister's table, the presage of another stay in the Bastille. But Voltaire's friends prevented the *lettre de cachet* from leaving the minister's portfolio. At the same time, however, he was refused all permission to print. Only unlicensed printers, peddlers, and shady booksellers profited by this pointless persecution: anyone who could afford to pay could buy a clandestine book as easily as one that was authorized.

As for systems, one must always reserve the right to laugh next day at one's ideas of the evening before. (*Dialogues and Conversations*, 24/17)

Happy is he who lives only for his friends; and unhappy he who lives only for the public! (Letter, July 6, 1733)

As was said by a man who spent his entire life feeling, reasoning, and joking, if everything is not fine, everything is passable. (*Dialogues and Conversations*, 24/3)

I am more and more convinced that the greatest men are as likely to be wrong as are lesser spirits. I think that the power of the mind is like that of the body: the most robust lose it on occasion and the weaker give a hand to the stronger when the latter are ill. (Letter, July 8, 1733)

No one is more convinced than I that all men are equal, but with this maxim one runs the risk of dying of hunger if one does not work. (Letter, October 27, 1733)

The miseries of life, philosophically speaking, no more prove the fall of man than the miseries of a coach horse prove that horses were all big and fat once and were never whipped, and that since one of them took it into its head to eat oats, all its descendants were condemned to pull coaches. (Letter to Monsieur de la Condamine, 1734)

You know that I consider great men as first and foremost and heroes as the last of men. I call those men great who have excelled in what is useful or agreeable. Pillagers of provinces are merely heroes. (Letter, July 15, 1735)

If someone attacks me as an author, I hold my tongue. But if someone tries to make me out to be a dishonest person, my horror makes me shed tears. (Letter to Monsieur Berger, September 1735)

One of the reasons that ought to make us respect women who take advantage of their wit is that they do so only out of predilection. (*Alzire*. Epistle to Madame du Châtelet)

It was ridiculous once upon a time to be learned, because the sciences themselves were ridiculous. A man who knew everything that was taught in school knew only inconsequential things; but today even a woman is permitted an education because the reading of good books and mathematical truths have nothing about them that is not respectable. (*Remarks*)

I am afraid that marriage is one of the seven deadly sins rather than one of the seven sacraments. (*Remarks*)

God gave us the gift of life; it is up to us to give ourselves the gift of living well. (*Remarks*)

The Appearance of the Goddess

In May 1733, Voltaire went to live opposite the door of the church of Saint Gervais, which he called "the only friend *Le Temple du goût* won me": he had praised the door in his poem, and the door had not been offended!

He had not chosen a very cheerful place. He was in an alley called the Rue du Long Pont, "in the worst quarter of Paris, in the oldest house, more deafened by the sound of the church bells than a sexton. But I shall make so much noise with my lyre that the bells will not trouble me." Fools made fun of him, believing that he really had gone to live there so as to admire the door of Saint Gervais. But Voltaire had a much more positive reason. He wanted to keep his eyes on Monsieur Demoulin, who lived on the same street. The latter was a grain and straw merchant who had had the idea of making paper out of straw. It was an excellent idea, but Demoulin had no money. Voltaire supplied the capital and, using Demoulin's name as a front, thus became a manufacturer of wrapping paper. This new interest did not stop him from being ill, or from writing, or from giving suppers at home. In spite of his complaints his lodgings, as usual, were not uncomfortable: his visitors found him very agreeably installed.

One evening after passing along the narrow street with some difficulty, a fine carriage deposited three chance visitors at his door, come to lure the poet out of his retreat. He asked them to stay to supper, but since it was their first visit they politely refused. He made them promise to return.

His visitors were the Duchesse de Saint-Pierre, her lover, the Comte de Forcalquier, son of the Maréchal de Brancas, and the Marquise du Châtelet, who had no lover for the moment. She hadn't wanted to come alone so the others had brought her. Soon she would dare to come alone. It had been the duchesse's idea to drop in on Voltaire and bring along her good friend Madame du Châtelet and Forcalquier. They formed the most delightful quartet in the world, and went and dined that same day on fricassee of chicken at an inn at Charonne. Voltaire and the marquise never forgot that dinner, at which there was sealed an understanding, a love, a friendship which lasted seventeen years and ended only with her death. The evening was one of those successes that a fortunate chance sometimes, for some reason, introduces into life. Forcalquier was handsome, worthy, and full of life; his company must have been far from dull. A friend of his, Mademoiselle de Flammarens, once remarked: "He lit up the room when he entered it." And the Duchesse de Saint-Pierre was exquisite, radiant with happiness at having such a lover, and anxious for everyone else to be radiant too.

Voltaire and Madame du Châtelet adored one another from that evening on, and the world was not slow to hear the news. One of the most learned and elegant women of her time had just embarked upon the most famous liaison in the literary history of the eighteenth century. Even if Voltaire had not become the century's greatest author the couple would deserve the admiration of posterity, for they managed to create an unbelievable harmony between a bluestocking and a turbulent poet. Their relationship was a miracle—one that malice respected and the Marquis du Châtelet gave his blessing to.

Voltaire had known Emilie du Châtelet a long while. She was still a child when her father, the Baron de Breteuil, had helped Voltaire get out of the Bastille. Voltaire had always been on the best of terms with the family to which he was now to become more intimately linked. The two lovers did nothing to conceal their liaison: the liberty enjoyed in that century by certain privileged beings is astonishing. Many married couples at that time led a less harmonious life together than Voltaire and Madame du Châtelet. In fact, the relationship between Voltaire and Emilie was the real marriage, not that between Emilie and the Marquis du Châtelet.

Gabrielle-Emilie Le Tonnelier de Breteuil was born on December 17, 1706. So she was twenty-seven when she made her appearance in Voltaire's "humble lair" near Saint Gervais. She had been married for seven years to the Marquis du Châtelet, but it had not taken her all that time to discover that her husband was a decent sort but not much more. The Châtelets were not too well off whereas the Breteuils were rich, and the couple's finances depended much more on the wife's family than on the husband's. Unfortunately Emilie had kept her Breteuil tastes, together with others no less expensive, such as a mania for gambling and a frenzied love of jewels. She was the first to laugh at these faults and the last to correct them. One suspects, however, that it was not for these reasons that Voltaire was dazzled by her, and was for the first and last time in his life wildly and deeply in love. He was never to know the frenzies or intoxications of passion, but it is plain that through his attachment for Madame du Châtelet he did experience its occasional outburst of violence and an exquisite tenderness.

Did she fascinate him by her beauty? This does not seem very likely, in spite of the habitual compliments paid her. But she was not so unattractive as she appears in the malicious description of her by Madame du Deffand that is repeated from generation to generation every time the names of Voltaire and Madame du Châtelet are linked. Madame du Deffand's portrait is famous simply because it is so spiteful. Despite the false over-all impression that it creates, certain of its details are nonetheless true. Here are its main outlines:

"Imagine a tall gaunt woman with no hips, narrow-chested, with fat arms, fat legs, enormous feet, a tiny little head, a sharp face, a pointed nose, two little sea-green eyes, a dark complexion, red and flushed, a shapeless mouth, and sparse and very badly decayed teeth. Such was the lovely Emilie. . . ."

Why should she have been known as "the lovely Emilie" if she had really been as unattractive as Madame du Deffand makes her out to be? Out of irony perhaps? More likely, certain people truly found her a handsome woman. Madame du Deffand's ill will is obvious, but she adds some interesting touches. She spares nothing, neither the curls nor the gewgaws nor the jewels, nor the glass ornaments Emilie decked herself out in: "As she tries to be beautiful in spite of nature and magnificent in spite of her means, she is often obliged to do without stockings, chemises, handkerchiefs, and other such trifles."

Madame du Deffand, who always has a wicked tongue but usually is more subtle, has this time let her hatred run away with her. It is impossible to believe that the very relative lack of wealth of the Châtelets, which after all allowed Emilie to possess diamonds, would not permit a change of stockings or chemises. But there is some truth in the description of her predilection for trinkets and jewelry. When on her most extravagant days Emilie appeared in public dripping with diamonds (some of them perhaps paste), covered with powder and rouge, and festooned in rainbow-colored ribbons from head to foot, people said, not without malice, that she looked rather like a mule in fancy harness carrying relics in a religious procession.

Madame du Châtelet had questionable taste in matters of dress and Voltaire did not endure it without complaint. The strange thing is that Emilie agreed that she lacked taste but simply could not do without her gaudy baubles. The portraits we have of her do not show her as ugly at all. Others claimed that her sea-green eyes were very beautiful and that her gaze was kind, extremely intelligent, glowing. It was the most noticeable thing about her: she too lit up a drawing room as she entered it. With such eyes she did not really need all those diamonds. It was this brilliance that Madame du Deffand could not forgive and that fascinated Voltaire.

Certainly she was no pretty little doll, no Dresden porcelain figurine. But she had her own sort of beauty. And after all, who knows whether her big arms and legs and feet did not hold a certain attraction for Voltaire, the squirrel? Although certain people, especially Madame du Deffand, took pleasure in criticizing Emilie as ugly, Voltaire adored his Emilie as she was, and above all for the superiority of heart and mind that made her worthy of him. He loved her, too, because she was his daily distraction. She amused him with her whims, and he forgave her obstinacies, her noisy fits of temper, and, from time to time, her infidelities. In a word, she was enchantingly intolerable. And she brought her lover the joys of friendship and the pleasures of love, as well as all its cares and quarrels and tender reconciliations. She brought him everything—except boredom.

The Marriage of Don Juan, Followed by a Farce and Two Tragedies, All Failures

The transports of love did not interfere in the slightest with Voltaire's other activities. The paper factory was closely supervised. He also began writing the libretto for a stately biblical opera, entitled *Samson*, for which the illustrious Rameau was to write the music. Voltaire also busied himself with another plot: the marriage of the Duc de Richelieu, the Don Juan of the age, to the second daughter of another friend, the Duc de Guise. Guise had undertaken to distribute the entire edition of *Charles XII*, shipped by barge from Rouen to Saint-Cloud, and it was in remembrance of such services that Voltaire had fixed up the duc's second and not very marriageable daughter with the most brilliant nobleman at court.

Both the Duc and the Duchesse de Guise were freethinkers, and they were rather astonished to be presented with a prospective son-in-law even more daring than they were. But that was no impediment; the real obstacle was one of birth. The Guises were princes of Lorraine, and theirs was almost a royal house, whereas Richelieu was only the grandnephew of the cardinal, the grandson of the latter's sister, Madame Vignerot. The Guise relations turned up their noses at the idea of accepting a mere Vignerot into their princely family. But Voltaire arranged everything. The Guises were not very well off, and Richelieu was immensely rich. Voltaire intimated that Richelieu would take his bride without a dowry, and the thing was done. All the Guise uncles, nephews, and cousins were obliged to swallow Richelieu, whom they called "the Vendéean goatboy." At the sumptuous wedding feast Richelieu nearly died of boredom: he was interested neither in his wife nor in the guests. He had invited half of France: the other half, the Guises, stayed away.

Voltaire would have worked at anything. He would willingly have written ballets, and performed them too if his legs hadn't been so thin. He would have manipulated puppets. He said that all the talents God has given man should be exploited, that nothing that is in us should be neglected, and that the refusal to make use of any faculty is an act of foolishness and a moral failing. The Church uttered cries of alarm at the consequences of such principles. Voltaire went on to say it was a great pity that Newton, the sublimest of men, had not written an opera. If in addition to his other achievements he had been able to compose a love scene for an opera and choreograph a ballet he would have been not merely a genius but a god. With such a zest for living, Voltaire could never be bored. He felt full of inexhaustible resources, belonging not merely to him but to mankind as a whole. Man was the most wonderful being in creation: he contained everything, and his infinitely varied talents burgeoned and renewed themselves in a continual creation of his own. No external authority could prevent the appearance of the perpetual miracle of intelligence. This was one of the basic credos of Voltaire's religion. "We are not born merely to read Plato and Leibnitz, to measure curves and put facts together in our heads; we are also born with a heart that needs to be filled. . . . We must introduce all imaginable fancies into our minds and open the doors of our hearts to every science and every feeling. Provided they do not enter in confusion, there is room for all." And Madame du Châtelet, converted to this doctrine of the universality of man, wrote: "It is a strange restriction of the mind to love one art or science to the exclusion of all others. . . . One may have preferences, but why exclusions? Nature has given us so few portals through which pleasure or instruction may enter our souls; why should we open only one?"

So they were both open to the four winds of the spirit. It is to be noted that they place pleasure and instruction on an equal footing. Down what dangerous paths did their motto, "Nothing excluded," lead them? Voltaire's own idea of dissipation is reassuring: "Work is the honor and the lot of mortals, and I perceive each day that it is the very life of man. It concentrates the powers of the soul and makes men happy."

Madame du Châtelet, who sang well, played Rameau's music on the harpsichord. She didn't like the composer himself. He was—as well as being a very great musician—churlish and a pedant. When Voltaire was alone with him he addressed him as "Orpheus," and the other accepted it as no more than his due. But it was a different story when Voltaire wrote to his old schoolmate and intimate friend Pierre Cideville: "Rameau . . . is a musical pedant, finical and boring." In public he went about saying that Rameau was writing the finest opera in the world. "Mine," he would add modestly.

While in the midst of preparing his opera, a tragedy, a real-life one, occurred: the near death of his friend Richelieu. Voltaire knew full well the disadvantages of the sort of marriage he had done so much to bring about. He had given the young bride a warning in verse:

> Ne vous aimez pas trop, c'est moi qui vous en prie,
> C'est le plus sûr moyen de vous aimer toujours.
> Il vaut mieux être amis tout le temps de sa vie
> Que d'être amants pour quelques jours.

Do not love one another too much, I pray,/For that is the surest way to love one another forever./It is better to be friends for the whole of your lives/Than to be lovers for a few days.

But the Duchesse de Richelieu was given no chance to be either friend or lover. And Richelieu was the lover of every woman except his wife. Directly after the wedding he left her and went back to the army. There he encountered the Prince de Lixin and the Prince de Pons, now his cousins by marriage, who treated him with obvious disdain. Richelieu was not a patient man, and on June 2, 1734, he fought a duel with Lixin, killing him and receiving such serious wounds himself that for a few days his life was despaired of. Voltaire nearly died of grief himself.

Another Flight

Voltaire was staying with the Guises at Monjeu when the *Lettres aux anglais* appeared in Paris and brought him troubles of his own. His "guardian angel" D'Argental warned him in time of an order for his arrest, and he fled.

Such was the first effect of the *Lettres aux anglais* or *Lettres philosophiques*, which had been printed by Jore in Rouen. After receiving Maupertuis's explanations about Newton, Voltaire had finished his book, quite converted to Newtonism. "Your first letter baptized me in the Newtonian religion," he wrote to Maupertuis in 1732, "your second confirmed me in it. I thank you for your sacraments. . . ."

But now he had a surprise. He did not know the book was already on sale, and without permission. Thereby hangs an obscure tale of printer and author of a kind all too frequent in the eighteenth century. Authors were very poorly protected by the law; it was a sort of catch-as-catch-can between them and the booksellers. Voltaire had sent Thiériot to London to supervise the printing of an English edition of the *Lettres* and had promised the English publisher that the French edition would not come out until after the English one had appeared. But instead of expediting the English edition Thiériot simply amused himself. Voltaire tried to urge him on by offering him a share in the rights. "Nothing is so pleasant as to be able to make at the same time one's own reputation and one's friends' fortune," he wrote.

1. Voltaire, at age twenty-four, after Nicolas de Largillière. (Musée Carnavalet. Photo Lauros-Giraudon)

2. Madame du Châtelet. Engraving by Delpeche. (Bibliothèque Nationale. Photo Roger-Viollet)

3. Madame de Pompadour, by François Boucher. (The Wallace Collection, London. Photo Crown)

4. Engraving depicting the triumphal procession in which Voltaire's remains were transported to the Panthéon, July 11, 1791. (Photo Roger-Viollet)

5. Sketches of Voltaire by Jean Huber. (Photo Roger-Viollet)

At this Thiériot began nagging the English publisher, who wa⸍ ready to bring out the book. But Jore, who was still waiting for th⸍ Voltaire had promised him, did all he could to outstrip his rival in spi⸍ of vigorous protests on the part of Voltaire, whose only authority to publish was a few smiles from the cardinal-minister, obtained with an incomplete text. There was a long-drawn-out quarrel, Voltaire ordering Jore not to publish, Jore demanding compensation if he so agreed. But in fact Voltaire was being led up the garden path, and while he was occupied with other things, Jore issued the book in Paris of his own accord.

In England the famous *Lettres* in praise of the country, its institutions, and its manners aroused a certain mild interest. The book was considered not bad for a Frenchman but not good enough for England. And there the matter rested.

In France there was a tidal wave of indignation and a sort of holy horror tinged with a vague uneasiness more significant than all the strident protests. England came off far the better in Voltaire's comparison between the two countries. But over and above that, there was something wounding about the tone in which the book was written, whether the opinions it offered were just, as they sometimes were, or unjust. It was this tone that angered many French readers (though not all; some agreed with Voltaire's ideas). The sharp epigrammatic edge of the writing made it seem like an act of revenge. Voltaire was to a certain extent revenging himself on the entire nation for the cudgeling he had received at the hands of a highborn bully and the cowardice of several of his aristocratic "friends." The book also troubled people's consciences. It cast poisoned darts at religion and French institutions. To old Cardinal Fleury, it seemed to make fun of hallowed institutions, feudal privilege, and royal absolutism. Instead of being heavily castigated by a long-winded and virtuous reformer fulminating against injustice, France's political apparatus was compared, in the simplest, most straightforward manner, to the wise customs of England. Voltaire made use of an irony by which the odiousness of French customs often seemed to be surpassed only by their ridiculousness, and their cruelty only by their absurdity. It was not the actual criticisms that were new. For a long time people had been murmuring or preaching against the same abuses. Incendiary sermons of almost incredible verbal violence had been forthcoming from certain pulpits, but they were just part of the game, producing more smoke than fire. These ponderous attacks were really intended to stimulate and strengthen Church and throne, whereas Voltaire's lightning darts were meant to kill the institutions they were aimed at. That was what was new about the *Lettres*, as those in power fully realized.

The chief minister and the Parlement acted with unusual swiftness. The book was condemned to be publicly burned as scandalous and contrary to religion, morality, and the respect due the authorities.

How many "crimes" were seen in the book when it appeared! It was a crime in the 1730s to prefer Newton to Descartes, to advocate vaccination against smallpox, to praise Shakespeare in the land of Boileau. And the book committed other "crimes" as well, in the eyes of many of Voltaire's countrymen and contemporaries.

As for Shakespeare, Voltaire only half liked him. It was admirable that he should even have tried to like him, and that he should have half succeeded without understanding him. But France could not forgive Voltaire for not having condemned Shakespeare out of hand. To us, Voltaire's criticism of Shakespeare seems timid or, rather, beside the point. He was too classical to appreciate such a "barbarian." But he did have some inkling of Shakespeare's wild beauties, his strength and grace. Voltaire would have *liked* to like him, but he was afraid to. He could neither bring Hamlet into the Temple of Taste nor go out of it to meet him. Trying to serve Shakespeare, he translated him, and the old saying that to translate is to betray was never more apt. Shakespeare is adapted to the taste of Regency salons, with Othello turned into a dandy in wig, satin, and lace. Yet, by betraying him, Voltaire made Shakespeare known and accessible in the homeland of Racine and La Fontaine. Shakespeare began to exist in France because of Voltaire. No one would have read the *Lettres anglaises* if he had not been the Voltaire who had made a name for himself with his *Brutus*, his *Oedipe*, his *Zaïre*, and all the other plays whose most obvious merit today is that their dullness killed off a genre that had long been dying. Though unreadable today, Voltaire's tedious odes and tragedies had been valuable exercises and had prepared the way for Voltaire the thinker.

Madame du Châtelet and Voltaire's great friend Richelieu had been lovers, though probably for only a few short days, for Richelieu was by nature a bird of passage. They had quarreled and made up, and were now friends again. When prison loomed for Voltaire following Jore's unauthorized publication of the *Lettres*, she confided in her old flame out of fervent affection for the new. "I have not the courage to think of my friend, with his wretched health, in a prison where he will certainly die of grief if not of illness," she wrote Richelieu.

Voltaire's continued illnesses made prison a dangerous prospect. He was often doubled over with colic, and lived on bread and milk. He could no longer bear being shut up: four walls and a locked cell would be his coffin. D'Argental got word to him that the best thing would be to let himself be arrested, and afterward his friends would extricate him. Voltaire did not agree, and fled from Monjeu to Lorraine, which was still independent. "I have taken a mortal aversion to prison; I am ill, stifling air would have killed me, and they would have put me in a dungeon."

This is quite probable: the minister was furious and was being besought on all sides to put a stop to Voltaire's mischief once and for all.

As soon as he arrived in Lorraine, Voltaire hurried to the bedside of Richelieu, who was in camp recovering from his wounds. The officers feted Voltaire: *lettres de cachet* meant little in army circles. Voltaire was staggered by the sumptuous way these noblemen lived while on campaign: Richelieu was accompanied by seventy-two mules bearing his luggage, thirty horses, and a multitude of valets. Voltaire was so intrigued by his new surroundings that he went ferreting around everywhere and was taken for a spy and roughed up a bit by sentries who had not read the *Lettres anglaises*. But the battlefield itself held no attractions for him, and he withdrew to more peaceful regions when the army prepared to make an attack.

The court was very angry at Voltaire's impertinence and at the honor the army had paid this fugitive from justice. Emilie exhorted him to go abroad, to Brussels or London: the danger must have been great to reduce Emilie to such an extremity. She could not live without him, but he must go into exile because his very life was at stake. Voltaire's reply is touching. He names no names because his letters were intercepted: this makes his discretion all the more moving: "As long as I am loved so warmly in France by a few, I cannot seek any other refuge: one's homeland is where friendship is."

But Voltaire did find a refuge, one that represented both safety and love and was the next best thing to a homeland. He found it at Cirey, in Lorraine. The château of Cirey belonged to the Marquis du Châtelet, who made everything perfect by giving the lovers his blessing.

Alarums and Excursions Before the Retreat

But Voltaire and Madame du Châtelet could not be there together yet. Emilie had to bestir herself in Paris, not to obtain Voltaire's pardon (it was too soon for that), but to try to halt the proceedings against him. She was as active as she could be, which is saying a good deal, for like Voltaire she possessed irrepressible energy, and unlike him she enjoyed an iron constitution. She attended to a thousand different things at once, from the most frivolous to the most serious. But she was serious and diligent about everything she undertook. At the moment, in addition to Voltaire's business, there was also mathematics. She threw herself into improving her knowledge; her teacher was the famous Maupertuis. One doesn't know whether to admire or to suspect their assiduity and ardor. Emilie was the more fanatical of the two: she could not spend a single day without geometry, or rather without her geometer. If he put off the lesson she would rush to his apartment or search him out in the Café Cradot and drag him off. She paid visit after visit to her dear friends the Duchesse de Richelieu and the Duchesse de Saint-Pierre. She called on ministers; wrote; dressed, changed, changed again; got herself up like an opera star; devoted entire afternoons to looking after the Duchesse de Richelieu, who was ill; solved six difficult geometry problems; and spent hours daubing her face with powder and rouge.

Voltaire, alone at Cirey, was just as frenziedly active. He had an army of workmen: a regiment of painters, another of carpenters, and another of masons. The château was rather dilapidated, and at his own expense Voltaire set about making it not only habitable but also comfortable and elegant. Or at least a part of it: Emilie's and his apartments and the public rooms made up a luxurious ensemble. The rest remained as run down as before. . . . Later on, guests would complain about their quarters. They froze or were nearly overcome by the smoke from the fireplaces in their rooms: all the drafts between the Rhine and Champagne whistled through the chinks.

Despite all the excitement of the alterations, and the delicious thought of having found at last the haven he had always sought and never been able—or perhaps never really wanted—to find, Voltaire felt that it was absolutely necessary for him to be in Paris. He talked about going there in secret: "One could bury oneself snugly in a suburb, one could sup with you," he wrote to Emilie. "One would be hidden away like a treasure, and decamp at the least alarm. One has business affairs, after all, and must set them in order and not run the risk of seeing one's little fortune suddenly melt away."

Voltaire's "little fortune" was worth a few risks.

But he did not make the secret journey. In October 1734, Emilie came to Cirey, but apparently Voltaire was not there. Shortly afterward he wrote her a letter from the Low Countries. It seems likely that the lovers had quarreled and that Emilie's enthusiasm for geometry and the geometer had had something to do with it.

On his return from the Low Countries there was a resounding reconciliation. He was so happy to forgive her that everything seemed wonderful, even the harebrained changes she had made in the plans for altering the house. He could hardly recognize them. But the goddess was there, and nothing else mattered.

She wasn't there for long, however. When the first effusions had cooled down, Voltaire sent her off to Paris to deliver to the Comédie Française the tragedy that he had just completed. It was called *Alzire:* D'Argental was to read it and make whatever corrections he thought fit.

Meanwhile Voltaire had had enough of directing operations on the house and brought in a foreman to supervise the workers. Soon after, in the midst of all the plastering and hammering, he finished the eighth canto of *La Pucelle (The Maid).* How had he managed to get it done; or, for that matter, to write *Alzire?* In that restless year of 1734 he had composed a tragedy and eight cantos of an epic, and rebuilt a château . . . among countless other things.

He got enormous enjoyment out of writing *La Pucelle.* The idea of this mock-heroic epic on the life of Joan of Arc had first come to him during a dinner party at Richelieu's. They were making fun of Jean Chapelain's ridiculous *Pucelle,* an unintentionally grotesque poem on the

Maid of Orléans. Richelieu told Voltaire he ought to treat the same subject and burlesque it deliberately. Voltaire declined, but the idea took root. And now the first eight cantos had been written.

He had a marvelous time writing them: irreligion and disrespect flowed gleefully from his pen. What did it matter how unbridled he was, since the poem was to remain secret? Or, rather, only Richelieu would read it. Or perhaps a few other friends as well—or at least have it read to them. Where was the danger, since the poem would never be printed? No one would even be allowed to see the manuscript, which would be kept safely under lock and key. So Voltaire could throw caution to the winds and be fiercer and wittier than ever. There was a certain perversity in this elaborate concern for secrecy that went hand in hand with an obvious desire to let others in on the secret. And all this when there was still a warrant out for his arrest, and he was officially threatened with banishment for life! He was incorrigible.

Fortunately he had friends. D'Argental, above all, went to endless trouble to get the warrant for Voltaire's arrest suspended. When Hérault, the superintendent of police, wrote to tell Voltaire that this had been done, he used terms that were not only courteous but kindly. He advised him to silence his enemies "by acting like a sensible man who has already reached middle age." It was good advice, but Voltaire would never be sensible, and the maturity of "middle age" had nothing to do with the case. Voltaire was forty in 1734, and would go on astonishing sensible people with his follies until nearly the end of the century. Voltaire must have laughed as he read Hérault's letter with *La Pucelle* on his desk before him.

Three weeks later, on March 30, 1735, Voltaire returned for the fourth time to Paris. The first thing he did was write a note to Hérault, telling him that he would have liked to visit him in person to express his gratitude, but that his poor health prevented him from doing so. All his thoughts were devoted to Monsieur Hérault, he assured him. If a tear came into the kindly police superintendent's eye it did not remain there long. He must surely have soon learned that Voltaire was to be found everywhere in Paris except at home.

Voltaire wanted to know and see everything. What had happened in Paris since the year before? There had been a revolution; or, rather, a change of fashion. In the salons people no longer talked of poetry; versifying was considered frivolous now. All the talk at present was of physics and geometry. Voltaire was staggered: poetry was not a fashion. He was piqued as well: everyone in Paris who counted thought Maupertuis a genius. With his circles and triangles and his rigmaroles, Maupertuis had dazzled duchesses and had even won Emilie's heart for a time. The Duchesse de Richelieu made such good progress that she was able to refute a Jesuit who attacked her views on Newton's theory of attraction. Such were Maupertuis's pupils. Not that Voltaire had anything against mathematics; on the contrary. It was the best way to understand Newton. He did not reproach Emilie for the immense progress she had made in the natural sciences: he himself was an avowed disciple of Newton and Maupertuis. But that was no reason for banishing the muses and discouraging their admirers, and no excuse for leading his charming Emilie astray.

As for *La Pucelle*, its existence was an open secret. People talked of it in Paris as the most sacrilegious poem ever written. It was marvelous publicity, but Voltaire's friends began to tremble for him again and adjured him to hide the poem. A month later he was back in Lorraine, and went to call on the Duc de Lorraine at Lunéville. He did not see him, but he did spend entire days in the physics laboratory there and emerged converted to the new fashion.

He then returned to Cirey. Emilie was there with her elder son and a tutor, with her neighbors Mesdames de Champbonin and de La Neuville to round out her little circle. Voltaire brought a certain Linant with him, a dull, addlepated parasite who in Paris had gone to bed at seven in the evening and risen at noon. At Cirey, Linant decided to renounce holy orders. Voltaire let him do as he liked. Linant grew exacting and insolent, criticized his board and lodging, and complained of having sacrificed his "position" to be with Voltaire. Voltaire lectured him, pointing out that his complaints only harmed himself and made people think badly of him. But Voltaire continued to put up with him nonetheless. Once he had pledged his friendship to anyone he never tossed them out, as all Voltaire's hangers-on knew full well. What patience he showed to the chubby Linant with his red, freckled moonface. He had no talent: his eyes were so weak he could barely read, he stammered, he knew little Latin and scarcely more French. Yet Voltaire offered him as tutor to the young Du Châtelet. The marquis wanted a priest. Voltaire did not. Voltaire won. "No priests in houses of women such as Emilie!" he said.

Linant's other faults were crowned by his bold presumption. He wanted a mistress in the château, and one day put his sweaty, pudgy paw down the front of Madame de La Neuville's dress. She took a very dim view of this clumsy advance, and nothing less than a set of verses by Voltaire would assuage her wrath.

Nonetheless Voltaire did not dismiss the boorish culprit.

The Villainous Desfontaines

It was during Voltaire's first sojourn at Cirey that the Abbé Desfontaines found his first opportunity to harm his benefactor.

Voltaire had given an unpublished tragedy to the pupils of the Collège d'Harcourt, who wanted to perform one of his plays. The tragedy was printed, full of mistakes and printer's errors, without Voltaire's knowledge. Voltaire wrote and asked Desfontaines to make it known that he had had nothing to do with the publication of this garbled text. Desfontaines not only failed to do so; he also wrote a savage criticism of the play, affecting to believe the published text to be authentic. To crown everything, he published Voltaire's letter. The worst thing about the whole affair was not simply Desfontaines's duplicity: Voltaire was proscribed in France at this time and was thought to be in Brussels. By publishing the letter Desfontaines let everyone, including the police, know that Voltaire was at Cirey.

It was a villainous trick and aroused in Voltaire an implacable resentment. He wrote and told all his friends how much he hated Desfontaines, and at their insistence the abbé tried to make amends by publishing a piece in praise of the play. The play did not in fact deserve all this fuss. But, in exile, Voltaire's anger mounted. He did not feel himself sufficiently revenged: he had not yet replied to the attack. As chance would have it, Desfontaines's apologies did not reach Cirey until just after Voltaire's famous riposte had been sent off. It was an article that appeared in *Le Mercure*. When Desfontaines saw it he thought it was Voltaire's treacherous method of replying to his own laudatory article. It was now his turn to be furious: he snatched up his pen and set about tearing the poet of Cirey to pieces. He accused him of writing tragedies contrary to the rules of drama and of morality. This from a man who had barely escaped burning for immorality! (And had been saved by Voltaire!) Desfontaines entitled this firebrand *Libelle du divorce* (*Lampoon Concerning Divorce*).

It was now open war between the perfidious abbé and Voltaire, who was exasperated to the point of fury on learning that even while Desfontaines was still in prison he had started writing a lampoon against his benefactor. Later, Desfontaines was to produce a pirated edition of *La Ligue*, making use of a stolen copy. It was probably stolen by Thiériot, whose relations with Desfontaines were most dubious. But Thiériot was not averse to a little treachery. It is clear that Thiériot and Desfontaines were lamentable characters; but it was far worse that Voltaire should sink to wallowing with them in slander and denunciation and Grub Street blackmail. In wrestling with such creatures he could only besmirch himself. Admittedly Desfontaines's ingratitude and Thiériot's betrayal were enough to infuriate a man who was irascible and sensitive to the point of hysteria. But Voltaire is not entirely excusable. He had rubbed it in a little too much that Desfontaines owed everything to him, including perhaps his life, and that in return he expected unreserved and even shameless praise. Such quid pro quos were not unusual then. But Desfontaines, who was just as canny a bargainer as Voltaire, resented the latter's claiming his due with arrogant barbs. There is no denying the fact that his mad vanity as an author often made Voltaire reckless at his own expense, and unbearable to other authors. The most intelligent man in the world could sometimes behave like a conceited whippersnapper. As soon as praise grew faint his brow would furrow and his eyes grow stormy. If someone expressed reservations about his talents he would cry out against injustice and stupidity. If there were actually open criticism he would fly into a rage and dance about the room, poking the fire savagely, hitting the furniture, brandishing the offending paper in the air. Afterward the torrent of gall would ebb away in a hundred libelous letters. He told everyone how much better it would have been if Desfontaines had been burned for his predilection for chimney sweeps. If the lamentable critic had been burned once and for all there would have been no further need to burn his lamentable articles.

All this had little to do with literature. Was it not time entirely wasted in a life usually so devoted to work? Not quite. Hatred made Voltaire live with a special intensity; any emotional paroxysm intoxicated him; that is the secret of his love for tragedy and for Racine. People thought he was half killing himself with hatred and wrath, but in fact he had a strange constitution: while he breathed fire and slaughter against Desfontaines he ceased being troubled with colics and fevers. His enemies tortured him but did not lay him low. On the contrary, they stimulated him. Sickly and ailing, he might have coddled himself into lethargy had it not been for the red-hot pokers aimed at him by people such as Desfontaines.

Be that as it may, his insults only redounded to his own disadvantage. The superintendent of police, at the insistence of the abbé and his friends, told Voltaire he must make public amends. Voltaire, much against his will, wrote a few sugary lines and Desfontaines pretended to be satisfied with this bone thrown his way, for it was in his interest not to break completely with Voltaire. He still had need of him and of the articles he might write for his paper, *Le Mercure*. The shameless abbé lost no time in asking Voltaire's permission to publish a poem the latter had written about his hosts at Cirey. Voltaire refused out of respect for the Châtelets, who wanted to keep the poem in the family. Desfontaines printed it nonetheless. Where did he get the manuscript? It was the same old story over again. Voltaire writes something in secret, and everyone hands the manuscript around. Did someone steal it? Did he give it to Thiériot in order for him to pass it on? One can't help but feel a nagging suspicion now and then. . . .

The Marquis du Châtelet was furious that all the tongues in Paris had been given this opportunity to wag at the delights of the *ménage à trois* at Cirey and lodged a complaint against Desfontaines with the Keeper of the Seals. At that very moment sentence was passed against the abbé in another connection. Voltaire's reaction at this point defies understanding: he takes pity on Desfontaines and gets Châtelet to withdraw his charge. "What has become of the abbé?" Voltaire writes. "Where have they put this dog that would bite his masters? I would still give him bread, mad as he is." This is not weakness but humanity; Christian charity, even. But naturally Desfontaines was not in the least grateful.

Stolen Properties

Yet another literary skirmish began with a case of plagiarism of a kind very common in the eighteenth century. Voltaire had just written his tragedy *Alzire* and sent it in secret to Thiériot in Paris. Jean-Jacques Le Franc, the Marquis de Pompignan, somehow got access to the work and Le Franc quickly wrote an imitation which he entitled *Zoraïde*, and gave it to the actors of the Comédie Française. Voltaire learned that Monsieur Le Franc's *Zoraïde* was going to be put on before the *Alzire* of Voltaire. He cried out that this was unfair; he would die of shame if *Zoraïde* was performed first, because then it would look as if he were plagiarizing Le Franc, whereas in fact the opposite was true.

Le Franc strutted like a turkey cock in front of the actors of the Comédie Française; they laughed. He was haughty with them; they began to murmur. He ruffled his feathers, pecked, and he and his *Zoraïde* were left out in the cold. *Alzire* was restored to its proper place and was a critical and financial success. It ran for twenty consecutive performances and brought in a tidy sum which Voltaire magnanimously turned over to the actors.

Alzire is almost completely forgotten today, except perhaps by the unappeased ghost of Racine's son Louis, also a writer of tragedies, who went about complaining that Voltaire had stolen a line from him and put it in the play. One day when Voltaire was reading *Alzire* aloud in a salon and Louis Racine kept moaning, "That's my line! That's my line!" the Abbé de Voisenon went over to Voltaire and said, "Give him back his line and let him clear out of here." Which line it was has never been discovered.

The Printer from Rouen

Jore was a difficult fellow and Voltaire made a blunder. He was not usually so naïve but, wanting to settle matters with Jore and thinking to appease him, he wrote to him setting down all the details of the extremely complicated transactions they had both been involved in with regard to the *Lettres anglaises*. He hoped this proof of his own good faith would persuade the other to come to a friendly agreement. But Jore, once in possession of Voltaire's frank accounting, brought a court action against him. Voltaire lost, and was threatened with having his assets seized if he did not pay the sum Jore claimed was due him. Voltaire went to Paris, where he realized that opinion was against him. In spite of the intervention on his behalf by Monsieur Hérault, the superintendent of police, his enemies published a lampoon on his avarice, his shady maneuvers, and his simperings. The picture it gave of him was a hideous caricature; unfortunately the pen that drew it was a skillful one. But despite fact that many details were correct, the portrait that emerged was false. The authenticity of the places and dates mentioned and the anecdotes recounted was irrefutable. Desfontaines did not sign his name to this small masterpiece of perfidy, but it was his handiwork. The abbé had supplied the malice, Jore the materials—and the money. Another shady development complicated the matter still further: someone had stolen from Voltaire (yet again!) a revised copy of the *Lettres anglaises* in which the corrections, far from lessening the virulence of the text, increased it. As soon as this manuscript came into Jore's hands he printed it, distributed it widely and sent a copy to the King's chief minister, Monsieur de Maurepas, who loathed Voltaire. Maurepas and the police had had quite enough of him: his troublemaking left them little time for anything else.

Voltaire realized that the affair had to be brought to an end, and offered Jore the money. Jore, feeling himself in a strong position, brought another court suit against him. Once more Voltaire had to run about enlisting the aid of influential friends. Monsieur Hérault came to his rescue once again, Jore's claim was dismissed, and he got nothing. But Voltaire was fined five hundred livres to be turned over to a fund for the poor. He had in effect been found guilty. He accepted this judgment but he was bitterly angry; he did not cry out against it, but he moaned. He is seen here in one of his least attractive roles, pleading poverty, saying he was being brought to ruin and that the poor would now be better off than he was. Everyone in Paris smiled sarcastically at this unconvincing comedy. Jore amused himself by proving that Voltaire had an income of thirty thousand livres. Voltaire made the best of it and resigned himself to the inevitable. He even thanked the minister, who had done nothing to help him, and his conscience was moved so far as to express a little, a very little regret at owing the dismissal of Jore's suit against him to "the intervention of the powers that be" rather than to justice. In that case why had he never stopped imploring that intervention, or intriguing to sway the course of justice in his favor? And his remorse did not prevent him from later soliciting other privileges, just as everyone else did. There are certain occasions when one wishes Voltaire had remained silent. But they are rare: usually he speaks so eloquently.

The Abbé d'Olivet, François's former tutor at Louis-le-Grand, says that Voltaire was eager at this time to become a member of the Académie but that the affair with Jore had done him the greatest possible harm. The ministry was against him; the Duc de Richelieu and the Duc de Villars for him. The shrewd abbé thought it would do Voltaire's reputation good if he were to disappear from the scene for a time: his friends would unobtrusively open the doors of the Académie but later, much later. Voltaire knew very well that this was a foolish hope, so he forestalled disappointment. He wrote vaguely, not mentioning names: "Someone spoke to me today about a place in the Académie, but in the circumstances in which I find myself neither my health, nor my liberty, which I prize above all else, permits me to think of it."

In fact he thought about nothing else. It was the Académie that did not think of it, except perhaps to refuse him membership. He thought of it again at distant Cirey, but wisely said no more about it.

Skirmishes

The unvarying pleasures of Cirey might have made him lethargic if the quarrel with Jean-Baptiste Rousseau had not flared up again. An Amsterdam printer published *L'Epître à Uranie* without Voltaire's knowledge. The Marquis du Châtelet had been against printing it, and he had been right. But the rapacity of Dutch printers in the eighteenth century knew no scruples. Rousseau, still exiled in Brussels, fought back by circulating fierce lampoon against Voltaire, to which Voltaire replied in kind. He recalled Rousseau's father, cobbler to Monsieur Arouet; his own valet, who had been Rousseau's cousin and who apologized every day for his relative's dreadful poetry; the beating Rousseau had received at the hands of Monsieur de La Faye (how could Voltaire bring himself to speak of cudgelings?)—in short, everything that could be guaranteed to wound the unfortunate Rousseau.

To relax his nerves Voltaire wrote a comedy called *L'Enfant prodigue* (*The Prodigal Son*). As he was doubtful about its merits he spread the rumor that it was by Gresset, the author of a popular parrot-poem. Gresset was very annoyed, although the play enjoyed a certain success and even met with Desfontaines's approval. But Voltaire's resentment was not assuaged. Several months later he took his revenge with an *Ode à l'ingratitude* which alluded to Desfontaines by name, as the "priest come from Sodom to Bicêtre." From then on Desfontaines attacked him without respite, though he would probably have desisted if Voltaire had not baited him: he had been silent for six months previous to the appearance of the *Ode*. Voltaire was soon to pay dearly for the provocation.

VI

A parish catechist tells his pupils that there is a God, but Newton proves it to wise men. (*Philosophical Dictionary:* "Atheists")

I love fine arts to such a degree that I would find even the success of my rivals interesting. (Letter to Thiériot, January 26, 1736)

I have an instinct that makes me love what is true but it is only an instinct. You find that I explain myself quite clearly; I am like little streams—they are transparent because they are not very deep. I have endeavored to present ideas in the way in which they have entered my head. I take a great many pains to spare our Frenchmen difficulties, for, generally speaking, they would like to learn without studying. (Letter to Pitot, June 1737)

Nothing is truer, sire, than the fact that in this world we are under the direction of a power as invisible as it is strong, more or less like chickens that have been cooped up for a certain time in order to put them on the spit later, and who will never understand by what caprice the cook has thus caged them; I wager that if chickens reason and construct a system with regard to their cage, not one of them will guess that they have been put there in order to be eaten. (Letter to Frederick the Great, 1738)

Resting is permitted, so long as it is on one's laurels. (Letter to the Abbé Yart, 1738)

It is no small task to give pleasure. (Letter, January 8, 1740)

Remember, the secret of the arts
Is to correct Nature. (Letter to Formont, 1738)

The Charms of Exile

Meanwhile the work of improving Cirey had been going on for two years. Voltaire and Emilie threw themselves into everything: alterations and decorating, study and poetry, lawsuits and business. Their days were full to overflowing.

Their object was to make the house where they were happy into a sort of temple dedicated to love, friendship, and assiduous intellectual labors.

As both had taste and ample money, plus a penchant for pomp which expressed itself in Emilie's case in the form of furbelows and in Voltaire's as a passion for theatricals, they turned provincial Cirey into a very imposing residence, no mean feat in 1734. To do so they had to cope with tragedies, algebra, and digging all at the same time. The gardens were completely redone, to provide "views" and tiers of balustraded terraces. Inside the house, porcelain tubs were installed, for Emilie bathed often. "It cooled her ardors," according to Longchamp, Emilie's butler. Emilie's fondness for frequent ablutions earned her a reputation for eccentricity. She had other "peculiarities" as well: she studied English, physics, and geometry. She also entertained many visitors, for ladies and gentlemen of quality were always eager to make a detour to call on the hermits of Cirey. Their studious retreat caused almost as much talk as the scandals stirred up by Desfontaines and Jore. Moreover, it was a scandal to live in solitude in the country, rejecting Paris and the court. Every visitor to Cirey was besieged with questions afterward. Even unasked, they couldn't help talking about it. How could anyone resist trying to find some intriguing explanation of this incomprehensible flight into the wilderness? How could Emilie de Breteuil and François-Marie Arouet, both frequenters of the most elegant salons in Paris, live outside the shadow of Notre Dame? The air of the moors and forests, the dreadful air of solitude, must surely be fatal to worldly people of scintillating wit, who like diamonds and pearls only came to life in the light of chandeliers. What astonished the Parisians was that, when they asked whether Emilie and Voltaire were not becoming dull and listless, the answer was that they were in splendid form and as brilliant as ever.

In 1736 the Chevalier de Villefort was one of the visitors to Cirey, and he reported on the two enchanted enchanters. The place he describes seems strange, indeed even mysterious: a house in the wilds where two eccentric hermits enjoy all the refinements of civilization and culture.

The chevalier arrived as night was falling. He went through first one courtyard, then another, then another. He rang the bell. There was a long wait. The entire household seemed to be asleep. At last a chambermaid appeared in the dusk, carrying a lantern. Villefort followed his guide through an antechamber, then through long corridors and a succession of dark, empty rooms. They halted, and he mustered up his courage and asked to see the marquise. The maid left him there while she went to announce him to the Enchantress. He waited till the maid returned, then on they went again, practically groping their way in the dim light from the lantern. Then suddenly a door was flung open, and lo and behold! there before him was a splendid salon. The chevalier was rooted to the spot with wonder: "The ruling divinity of the place was so decked out with so many diamonds that she would have looked like a Venus at the opera if, despite the indolence of her attitude and her richly bejeweled attire, she had not been leaning over papers covered with Xs and Ys, at a table strewn with instruments and books on mathematics." The fairy queen of algebra in the costume of an opera Cleopatra!

The stranger was accorded a distant, aristocratic, somewhat absent-minded bow, and his hostess, reluctantly disentangling herself from her Xs and Ys, offered to have him taken to Monsieur de Voltaire's apartments. It was assumed that the visitor would have come all this way only in order to see the poet. The Enchanter's apartments were connected to those of the Enchantress by a hidden staircase, probably the one built inside a chimney by Madame du Châtelet during Voltaire's flight to the Netherlands. The chevalier climbed up and up. There was a door at the top. He knocked. No answer. What could be going on inside—the search for the philosopher's stone? At last the door was opened, and the visitor was informed that he had arrived at an inopportune moment: it was not yet the hour for conversation. Time passed and a schoolbell rang, fortunately announcing that the dinner hour had come.

The dining room was just as odd as the other rooms. There were no servants. At each end of the room there were two dumbwaiters, one to deliver the dishes and the other to remove them. At each course everyone went and fetched his own plate, already filled. The food was exquisitely prepared, the repast lengthy. Then the bell rang to signal another change of activity.

It was now time for reading moral and philosophical works, perhaps to aid digestion with a gentle somnolence. An hour went by, then the bell rang once more. Bedtime. Everyone dutifully obeyed.

On the stroke of four next morning the visitor found himself being literally shaken out of his slumbers. Had he not heard the bell? Did he not wish to attend the poetry session just about to begin in the gallery downstairs? Surely he did not mean to miss these important matins! Just like those soft Parisians to shirk predawn versification exercises on a November morning in an icy château in a region noted for its exceptional cold. Voltaire and Emilie never missed this office, at which they were at once priests, acolytes, and congregation.

When friends in Paris told Emilie of the chevalier's account, she said it was just "a fairy story made up out of the whole cloth. What you tell me has neither head nor tail, rhyme nor reason."

It is true that Villefort had embroidered his tale and made her out to be the fairy queen of an enchanted château. But his description of the time-table there was not at all fanciful. The day's activities were ruled by the bell, so that it was almost impossible to waste a quarter of an hour. Voltaire had a kind of instinctive horror of idleness and inertia. His passionate love of life made him cherish each hour of the day and fill it with its own particular pleasure: reading, reflection, and the broadest possible variety of activities.

Voltaire's answer to this gossiping guest was: "I defy Monsieur le Chevalier de Villefort to have expressed or even to have understood how happy we are at Cirey." That was the important thing, and that was what the people in Paris did not understand: happiness was friendship, love, luxury, and order—the almost monastic or military order that Voltaire constantly sought after, amid all the apparent disorders of his life.

Fresh Alarums and Other Excursions

More disorders soon came his way. Among Voltaire's friends at the Temple had been a certain Abbé de Bussy who later became Bishop of Luçon. The bishop had just died, and among his papers was found a poem by Voltaire called *Le Mondain* (*The Man about Town*). It had in fact been printed and circulated in Paris in 1736 without the author's knowledge. And now there were new proceedings against Voltaire because of the poem's impieties. One of the crimes alleged against him, Voltaire reported, was that he had described Adam as having long fingernails and bad manners. "What century are we living in?" he cried.

He would be obliged to set out on his travels again. His retreat was no longer a safe one. There was another danger, and one that threatened Emilie even more than himself. Although it was two years after the beginning of the liaison between the poet and the marquise, some cousins of the marquis suddenly decided that it was unseemly for their cousin's wife to live under the same roof as Voltaire while, two hundred leagues away, her husband fought the King's enemies. They prepared to bring charges against the marquis in a court of law. Seeing that the marquis would have no choice but to act, Voltaire packed his bags in haste.

Where was he to go? He was tempted to take refuge with Frederick, Crown Prince of Prussia, with whom he was conducting an epistolary flirtation. Frederick had made the first advances, and Voltaire had replied with alacrity. He was delighted to be addressed as an incomparable genius and installed on the throne of intelligence and talent by a royal highness who would doubtless one day become a king. This prince would surely be the most noble monarch of the age, the flattered poet decided. And he was eager to see him with his own eyes.

He was reckoning without Emilie. She smelled a rat and suspected that she would lose him. Afraid for herself, she persuaded Voltaire that danger threatened him. She feared he might become too enamored of the prince, who was not only intelligent but also heir to a crown to which Voltaire already kowtowed; she pointed out the threat represented by the old King Frederick William. He treated his son disgracefully. He had put him in prison and had had his best friend decapitated under his very eyes. It was not difficult to show Voltaire that the old man would look askance at a French philosopher-poet no doubt all prepared to fill his heir with pernicious opinions on paternal authority. At that rate Voltaire might easily find himself sent off into some Pomeranian dungeon, or even, without further ado, into the beyond. Emilie had no difficulty in getting this argument across, and to console Voltaire she promised that when the prince became king they would go and see him together. Until then, it wasn't safe. She was deceiving herself if she thought Voltaire would ever ask her along. But for the moment at least Voltaire declined Frederick's invitation.

Having been convinced that Prussia was unhealthy, he returned to the Netherlands. He avoided Brussels, which was contaminated by Jean-Baptiste Rousseau. But he received word that Rousseau had been given permission to return to France. At the very moment when he was being pursued, his mortal enemy had been pardoned. This was too much. It was all very well for him to be pursued—it had come to be a habit with the authorities. But at least let them persecute Rousseau too. It must be seen to at once. Voltaire arranged for the chief minister to receive a copy of the poem Rousseau had written against royal magistrates and the King. He also saw to it that it reached the Parlement, which was almost as badly savaged in the poem as if Voltaire had written it himself. The lawyers and présidents were furious and the ban against Rousseau was reinstated. The good news greatly increased the pleasure Voltaire took in his warm reception in the Netherlands.

His tragedies were performed in all the towns he passed through. He also heard that Zaïre was being played with success in London. One piece of news especially delighted him: an author's vanity can feast on what seems tragic to common mortals. An actor named Bond greatly admired the play and acted the part of old Lusignan with such passion that, at the moment when he was supposed to recognize his daughter and be carried away by emotion, he had a heart attack and dropped dead on the stage. Voltaire was enchanted at the idea that his dramatic genius was so great as to destroy its interpreters. But there was more to come. The performance was not interrupted, for another member of the company immediately insisted on taking over the part, only regretting that he was not a great enough actor to interpret this killing role as definitively as Mr. Bond had by dying onstage.

No wonder Voltaire adored the British. He wouldn't have caught any Frenchman wanting to die acting Zaïre!

With such ample tribute paid to his merit, Voltaire enjoyed his visit to Holland in 1736. Although the lawsuit never really amounted to much he was not in any hurry to go back to Cirey. But Emilie wanted him to return. His new work, *Les Eléments de la physique de Newton* (*The Elements of Newtonian Physics*) was about to be published, and she insisted on his supervising the printing. It was essential. The little book was to put within reach of the educated public the theory which orthodox French physicists would have none of and which Voltaire was going to force them to accept. But he was enjoying himself in Holland. Emilie insisted, Voltaire got cross, Emilie wept and threatened. Suddenly she was afraid her Voltaire was being taken away from her. In despair she appealed for help to the D'Argentals: "I implore you on my knees to be harsh with him and inform him that if he is obstinate and does not come back he is lost. This I firmly believe. . . . If you had seen his last letter you would not blame me. It bears his formal signature and he addresses me as Madame. It is so strange and incongruous, I am out of my mind with grief."

Emilie was madly in love. Again, Voltaire's love was less anguished and passionate than that of his partner. But there was no need for her to worry. He was already on the way home, happily putting himself under the sway of his goddess once again. His homecoming was delightful.

He wrote secretly to the Abbé Moussinot, one of his confidants and his unofficial business agent, to ask what subject was proposed by the Académie des Sciences for the prize that year (1738). But no one must know it was Voltaire who was asking: "I am not a scholar," he wrote. But he wanted to become one, or at least proficient enough to appear to be one. When he learned that the subject was "*De la propagation du feu*" (*The Propagation of Fire*) he sent Moussinot, again secretly, to find out as much as possible about it from Fontenelle. Then the abbé was to go to an apothecary's: "Buy a pound of quinine from him and send it to me, and get whatever information you can out of him as to the nature of fire." The abbé performed all these errands without letting on that Voltaire was preparing to compete for the prize.

The Abbé Moussinot was a respectable fellow whose integrity was so well recognized that he was treasurer of his chapter, in addition to serving as Voltaire's. He made investments, bought paintings, and collected interest for Voltaire, willingly discharging even the more delicate task of jogging the memory of debtors who forgot when their interest was due. This was an important function because of the sums involved, and a tricky one as well, since debtors such as Richelieu, Villars, and other noblemen did not think of repayment as the inevitable consequence of borrowing. Moussinot made it inevitable without offending anyone. This made him invaluable to Voltaire, who lent large amounts at considerable interest: Emilie was such a spendthrift.

She was also secretly competing for the prize offered by the Académie des Sciences, and doing research into the nature of fire. They had each applied themselves to the same problem without telling the other, only giving themselves away when the results were announced. This means that they must have left each other to work in complete freedom, in spite of their jealous natures and in spite of living on intimate terms together under the same roof. A splendid example of good breeding!

H. R. H. Prince Frederick of Prussia

The prince's letters had been charming, and a gift to Voltaire completed his conquest. He sent him a walking stick with a gold knob in the form of a bust of Socrates, accompanied by eulogies. Voltaire was overwhelmed; but could anyone have resisted the prince's flattery? "If I ever come to France the first thing I shall ask will be: Where is Monsieur de Voltaire? Neither the King, the court, Versailles, Paris, nor the fair sex nor pleasure will be the reason for my journey. Only you alone." Voltaire thereupon dubbed him "the Solomon of the North." He could do no less. Frederick had not only offered him his house in London as a refuge, he also sent him an ambassador, Baron von Keyserling. Frederick gave Keyserling these instructions as the latter departed for Cirey: "Remember that you are going to the Earthly Paradise, to a place a thousand times more delightful than Calypso's isle: that the presiding goddess yields nothing in beauty to Telemachus' enchantress: that in her you will find all those spiritual attractions so preferable to those of the body: that this marvelous creature devotes all her leisure to the search for truth. . . ." And so on.

The letter was meant to be shown to Emilie, not so much to please her as to betoken Frederick's resentment. Voltaire had not concealed the fact that what had prevented him from joining the Solomon of the North in Prussia was the warmth of the friendship that bound him to Cirey. This was enough to make Frederick detest Emilie. While Frederick praised her extravagantly, he also took care to reveal his eagerness to lure Voltaire away from her: "Pray convey to Madame la Marquise du Châtelet that I could not bear to yield Monsieur de Voltaire to any but her, just as there is no one save her worthy of possessing him."

Frederick tolerated the situation because there was nothing else he could do; but he did not resign himself. He would find other excuses later to summon Voltaire, and Emilie was not at all reassured. A squirrel jumps, an eel slithers, a lizard escapes. That was Voltaire, and she knew it.

Ambassador Keyserling was a small man tormented by gout, but when not incapacitated, he was full of vivacity and zest. He was a great talker and a scholar. Princess Dorothea, Frederick's sister, maintained that he was "a great scatterbrain and chatterbox, who pretended to be a wit and was nothing but an overturned bookcase."

At Cirey, Keyserling was given princely honors, including fireworks and set pieces with the name of Prince Frederick and "To the Hope of Mankind" in colored lights. It was so splendid that Madame de Graffigny, one of the permanent guests at Cirey, reported: "We have seen such things as only fairies and Monsieur de Voltaire could bring about in a place such as this."

Keyserling was enchanted. They let him talk as much as he liked, and he chattered on endlessly. He departed laden with gifts, including Voltaire's manuscripts: the beginning of *Le Siècle de Louis XIV* (*The Age of Louis XIV*), which he had already started but not yet finished; poems; tragedies; essays. But this was not enough—Frederick had insisted on his ambassador's bringing back *La Pucelle*. It was pointed out to him once again that the manuscript was in the possession of the Goddess, who would not part with it for anything. It belonged to her and her alone. In short, here was yet another reason for Frederick to despise Emilie. But he relished the accounts Keyserling gave on his return. He looked in his eyes and held him by both hands—the hands of someone who had seen Voltaire! There and then, so as not to be outdone, "Solomon" christened Voltaire "The Virgil of the Age." And hoping against hope, Frederick began to sing his siren's song again. Emilie was on tenterhooks. Every time a letter arrived from him she spent a sleepless night.

Two Nieces and a Brother

The Arouet family now surfaced again in the persons of Voltaire's two nieces, Marie-Louise and Marie-Elisabeth Mignot, whose father died in 1737. Their mother, Voltaire's sister Marie-Marguerite, had died in 1726.

He decided to take the two orphans under his wing. Family feeling may not have been as withered away in him as he led people to believe. He wanted them to be near him so that he could give them a suitably aristocratic upbringing and eventually arrange good marriages for them. Everything indicates that he loved his sister dearly and transferred this affection to her daughters.

His first idea was to marry one of his nieces to the son of Madame de Champbonin, the faithful country gentlewoman who was a close neighbor at Cirey. But Mademoiselle Mignot of Paris had no wish to come and be a country wife in the backwaters of Lorraine. The Abbé Moussinot made the proposal on Voltaire's behalf. Voltaire asked him to make it quite clear to his niece that he would not be cross with her if she refused; she had only to follow her own inclinations. He wanted Moussinot to make plain to the young ladies the difference between their uncle Armand the fanatic and their uncle Voltaire. It was not a point difficult to demonstrate. Armand was a devoted disciple of the "Convulsionaries." He suffered himself, and he wanted to make others suffer. To a friend of his who was also a Jansenist but did not thirst for martyrdom and tried to calm him down, Armand said: "If you don't want to be hanged yourself, at least don't attempt to dissuade others from seeking that fate." Armand was not unique among his contemporaries, and he and his like must be remembered if Voltaire and his age are to be understood. Along with

Richelieu and Voltaire and a few other brilliant and flamboyant *libertins* in the foreground, there were countless numbers of believers, bigots, and even fanatics; and the provocation offered by *libertinisme* served only to increase their fanaticism. Churches, ministries, and Parlements were full of people who were for the most part believers, and the more insolently their enemies behaved the more determined they were to make their faith respected. These people were powerful: they had the whole arsenal of laws, courts, and police at their disposal. Nowadays these pretended "persecutions" sometimes raise a smile, but when Voltaire, gravely ill, threw himself into a carriage to dash over atrocious roads in the midst of winter, he was flying from no imaginary danger. A dungeon was a dungeon, and if once the minister who had put you there forgot you, it was likely to be your tomb. Voltaire's blood ran cold at the thought.

His brother was one of these frightening people, and Voltaire was duly frightened of him.

Marie-Louise Mignot waited impatiently for a suitable husband to be found for her, and as none turned up she chose one for herself: Monsieur Nicolas-Charles Denis, Esquire, a notary and a supply officer at the War Ministry. He had a respectable competence, a pleasant face, and a good character. He was in love with Marie-Louise and she with him.

Voltaire provided her with a dowry. If she had married young Champbonin she would have had a dowry of eighty thousand livres and twelve thousand livres of silver plate. But as she had chosen Monsieur Denis her uncle gave her only thirty thousand livres: Denis was richer than the Champbonins. The young couple came to Cirey. Madame Denis was astounded at her uncle's attachment to Madame du Châtelet. It made her jealous. What business was it of hers, and what could this little goose on her honeymoon understand of the deep and complex relations between these two brilliant, worldly beings? At any rate she realized that it was all beyond her, and as she was vulgar, this feeling expressed itself in carping and envy. She wrote: "I am in despair, and think him lost to his friends. He is bound in such a way that it seems impossible to me that he could break his chains. They live in a fearful solitude . . . a country where there is nothing to be seen but mountains and uncultivated brush." In point of fact, there were no mountains at Cirey, the guest rooms there were always full, Voltaire and Madame du Châtelet received the eulogies of a crown prince, and hundreds of the most flattering and affectionate letters.

"And such is the life led by the greatest genius of our age," Marie-Louise concluded. Perhaps she would have wished him to lead her sort of life instead. Perhaps she already had ideas for the future. Surely something could be gained from having an uncle so illustrious, and above all so rich.

As for Voltaire's second niece, Marie-Elisabeth, on June 9, 1738, she married Nicolas-Joseph de Dompierre, lord of Fontaine-Hornoy, royal treasurer-in-chief at Amiens. Thiériot was to look after the wedding presents, which included twenty-five thousand livres from the bride's uncle François-Marie.

Voltaire did not attend either marriage. He did not think such formalities worth the sacrifice of a few days at Cirey.

Newton in France

The *Eléments de la physique de Newton* got Voltaire in still more serious difficulties. He could not get permission to have it published in France: French scientists were unanimously against it. He therefore had it printed in Amsterdam. His advocacy of Newton made him guilty of yet another heresy, and as much anathema to the scholars as the Académie des Sciences as he already was to the theologians at the Sorbonne.

The Amsterdam printers, eager to get the book on sale quickly in spite of Voltaire, who wanted if possible to put himself right with the authorities, played a nasty trick on him. Not trusting them, he had given them an incomplete manuscript, intending to give them the last part in his own good time. The printers finished the manuscript themselves and published it in April 1738 without the author's knowledge. Voltaire was furious. Underneath his title, *Eléments de la physique de Newton*, he had written *"mis à la portée de tout le monde* [put within reach of all]," to attract readers of modest means. His detractors put it about that this should be *"mis à la porte de tout le monde* [rejected by everyone]." He was sick with rage.

Despite the printer's errors, the sarcasms of his critics, and the hostility of scholars, the book was of considerable importance. The *Journal de Trévoux*, a Jesuit publication, said that hitherto Newton's work had been buried in the studies of a few rare scholars scattered over Europe, "like a secret to be whispered, and then only to ears especially apt. Then Monsieur de Voltaire appeared, and at once Newton is understood, or on the way to it; all Paris echoes with Newton; all Paris babbles Newton; all Paris studies and learns Newton. . . ."

It is an excellent indication of Voltaire's role as a popularizer and his influence on science, a major current in European thought in the eighteenth century. Voltaire may not have given birth to any political or scientific system, or discovered unknown feelings or strange harmonies, but he gave value, meaning, and efficacy to the discoveries of others. The flash of genius shines for its possessor alone; Voltaire possessed that other light which enables all men to contemplate and comprehend the truths first glimpsed by a privileged few. What is astonishing about Voltaire is that the intelligence which diffused the most original and fruitful scientific thought of modern times was the intelligence of a poet. A public was now given the most masterly physics lesson of the century by a man whose principal claim to fame rested on his mordant wit, his courtly compliments in fashionable salons, and his pseudo-Racinian tragedies.

What diligence and tenacity: to apply himself to the rudiments of mathematics and physics at the age of forty and more; to read and understand the sublime Newton and then to descend to the level of the common reader without sacrificing either the intelligence of the author of the *Principia* or the elegance of the author of *Zaïre*.

Shortly after the book's appearance, the result of the prize competition sponsored by the Académie des Sciences was announced. Neither Voltaire's nor Emilie's essays on the propagation of fire had won, or even received honorable mention. But Monsieur de Réaumur, the renounced physicist, wrote them a nice letter which particularly pleased them. Certain people of fashion made fun of Emilie. Others paid the two of them compliments that were worse than the sarcasms—the doctor of theology at the Sorbonne, for instance, who treated Voltaire, Emilie, and Newton as if they were all one and compared Voltaire to Theseus and Emilie to Ariadne, though ponderously belaboring the metaphor by insisting that, while the clue that led Theseus through the labyrinth had its counterpart in a physical bond, between Voltaire and Emilie there existed "only a spiritual bond free of impurity" as they made their way through the maze of the *Principia!* To think that Newton could give rise to such foolishness! Paris was amused. Voltaire and Emilie were astonished.

Evil Communications

Jore now returned to the attack. He was in desperate straits and ready for anything, even blackmail. Propositions and letters succeeded one another. At last Voltaire received a horrible cringing letter from Jore in which the printer acknowledged all his misdeeds, declared that Voltaire owed him nothing, that he, Jore, had cheated him in the past and was still trying to cheat him. Jore had made this confession in exchange for a sum of money from Voltaire. The exact amount is not known. It must have been considerable if rascality is sold by weight.

The strangest thing of all was that three years later Voltaire was still giving Jore presents!

When Voltaire lodged in the Rue du Long Pont in 1733 it was a Monsieur Demoulin who lent him his name for his dealings in grain, straw, and paper. Voltaire trusted Demoulin, who controlled large sums of money under the distant eye of the poet of Cirey and the easygoing supervision of the worthy Abbé Moussinot. It so happened that twenty-four thousand livres disappeared into Demoulin's pocket. When Voltaire complained, Demoulin, an informer as well as a thief, threatened to reveal his secret partner's speculations in grain. Voltaire might have been expected to breathe fire and slaughter. But not a bit of it: all he was losing was money. Neither his vanity nor his feelings were hurt, nor his literary taste nor his philosophical ideas attacked by Demoulin; he therefore wrote Moussinot to deal with him kindly. "He must certainly blush for shame at the way he has treated me. He takes twenty-four thousand livres from me and then attempts to disgrace me! But if you lose twenty-four thousand livres there is no need to make another enemy as well." So they made their peace with each other. Demoulin promised to give back three thousand livres but never did so, and all Voltaire ever received for the remaining twenty-one thousand was a very humble, repentant, and affectionate letter from Demoulin, explaining his inability to pay the huge sum he still owed, and at the same time assuring him that "never has a lover loved his mistress as much as Demoulin has loved Voltaire."

This might have been overdoing it, but for Voltaire effusions of sentiment could never be too exaggerated and he was completely taken in by this thieving hypocrite. "I forgive you with all my heart, without a trace of bitterness remaining," he wrote back.

Voltaire's detractors say he was stingy. If so, his stinginess was not like anybody else's. He was good at losing money and good at giving it away. His real weak point was vanity. His enemies knew this, and the Abbé Desfontaines made diabolical use of it. Voltaire reacted violently and, it must be admitted, naïvely. Besides being the author of the "*mis la porte de tout le monde*" pun, Desfontaines had violently criticized the *Eléments*, saying it was "rejected by all the physicists in Europe," and telling Voltaire he was past the age for seeking new outlets for his scant talents as a poet. At his time of life—Voltaire was forty-four—he should content himself with writing a few verses every so often. The abbé hinted that Voltaire, past his prime and living in retirement at Cirey, had his glory behind him. His Newton studies were mere schoolboyishness, accompanied by a touch of senility.

All this was conveyed slyly and treacherously, in a roundabout fashion. Voltaire was seized with the sort of rage that makes a murderer of even the gentlest dreamer—and he was far from being that. He had to avenge himself. He rummaged through all Desfontaines's works and in November 1738 wrote a savage pasquinade entitled *Le Préservatif* (*The Preservative*). Once again he recalled all that was known about and against the ignoble priest, an active homosexual. It was an unworthy production and a waste of time. He did not put his own name to it but had it signed by a literary adventurer called the Chevalier de Mouhy, who was in Voltaire's pay and spied for him on all the printers and writers in Paris. When they saw Mouhy's name, everyone naturally realized immediately that it was Voltaire who had penned this genuinely vicious lampoon.

Again, if Voltaire had not stooped to answering him, Desfontaines, who had long been in disgrace, would have lost all his readers and finally fallen silent. People only took an interest in him because after each of Desfontaines's attacks they read what Voltaire said about him and wanted to know what lay behind these violent quarrels. No writer has ever served the cause of his enemies so well as Voltaire.

Madame du Châtelet knew this. She implored, wept, screamed, sulked, hid his papers. But nothing could stop Voltaire from indulging in his dangerous mania. And nothing was more harmful to his reputation and interests.

So it came about that in December 1738 he wrote a comedy called *L'Envieux* (*The Jealous Man*), in whom the principal character, Zoïlin, was plainly Desfontaines. Everyone recognized this immediately; what publicity for an obscure pamphleteer! Zoïlin was weighed down with so many vices that the comedy was absolutely leaden, and the Comédie Française refused to stage it. This only served to increase Voltaire's anger against Desfontaines, the unwitting—and ungrateful—model for Zoïlin.

But Desfontaines nonetheless realized that the affair served his interests admirably and did all he could to keep it going. He wrote one of his most virulent pamphlets against the hermit of Cirey. Its title made no pretense at concealment: it was called *La Voltairomanie* (*Voltairomania*).

The abbé found a new charge in addition to those that were forever being rehearsed: he accused Voltaire of having lived as a parasite in Président de Bernières's household. And at this point Thiériot again entered the picture, for in his pamphlet Desfontaines sang his praises. Thiériot was no parasite; *he* did not sponge on the Bernières' or on anyone else; it was not he who had said that Desfontaines, when he came out of the prison from which Voltaire had freed him, had written a pamphlet against his benefactor. It was Voltaire who had invented all this and pretended that the innocent Thiériot was responsible.

This testimonial in his favor was a strange gift for Thiériot to receive from such a pen. The truth was that Thiériot was in collusion with Desfontaines. He had already betrayed his master and friend by robbing him. Now he sold him by refusing to deny Desfontaines's allegations.

The day this pamphlet arrived at Cirey, Voltaire suddenly fell ill. Emilie did not show it to him, fearing that it would kill him. It made her ill herself. She wrote to D'Argental, the ultimate resource: what should be done? Reply or not reply?

It was Emilie who wrote Thiériot, castigating him for the shameful role he had played in the affair and pleading with him to disavow Desfontaines and declare publicly that he had seen him writing the pamphlet. Thiériot had in fact seen him and done nothing to prevent him from writing or publishing the allegations against Voltaire.

Why? Thiériot's usual motive was money: you paid him, and he did what you asked. But Desfontaines was penniless. In this instance Thiériot had acted out of pure baseness. He was one of those weak, faithless characters who accept kindness as their due and afterward derive a sort of satisfaction from avenging themselves on their benefactors. They feel humiliated by their kindness yet at the same time despise them and secretly bite the hand that has fed them. When Thiériot stole the edition of *La Henriade* and was not arrested for it, he saw in this an expression not of the magnanimity of his master but of his weakness and stupidity. Voltaire could have had him hanged; and Thiériot would have thought the better of him if he had.

Everyone at Cirey was in a turmoil but all parties tried to hide their consternation. Finally there had to be an explanation: Emilie had concealed the fact that she had read the horrid pamphlet, and Voltaire, who had read it on the very first day, had done likewise. Voltaire had actually been the first to receive it, and that was what had made him so ill that Emilie had felt it necessary to keep it from him. Each thought the other knew nothing, and tried to spare him or her pain. What power the Desfontaines' of this world have!

Thiériot did not reply to Madame du Châtelet's entreaties. Weeks later he wrote back a vague and frightened letter to Voltaire saying he remembered nothing. Voltaire penned him a moving, affectionate reply, begging him to state clearly and publicly that he had seen Desfontaines write his lampoon against the man who had saved him from the most ignominious death.

There was no answer. And it was at this point that Monsieur du Châtelet took up his pen—Emilie's husband springing to the defense of Voltaire, his wife's lover! He did not beg Thiériot but rather ordered him to write what he had been asked. Monsieur du Châtelet added a draft of the sort of letter required, together with some vague threats of the kind to which people such as Thiériot are not insensible.

The marquis's attitude was admirable. He could easily have washed his hands of this messy literary squabble and left Voltaire to his own devices and gone back to his regiment. But he resolutely adopted the role of friend and host. It was all the more to his credit because in spite of the *lassier allet* of current manners the position Voltaire occupied at Cirey was rather ambiguous, when all was said and done.

Madame de Bernières also rose magnificently to the occasion. She wrote an indignant letter disproving the abbé's charges and proving that Voltaire had rented his apartment and paid not only for his own board but for Thiériot's as well. She recalled the sums the latter had received from his master. She also mentioned that Thiériot had received all the profit from the *Lettres philosophiques,* and two hundred guineas from the English edition.

"Good old Bernières!" Emilie exclaimed when she read her letter. Voltaire's friend, the présidente, was also to be pitied. He had not seen her since departing for London. The Bernières were not getting on very well at that time, and friends avoided their house. The président died, Madame de Berniéres sold La Rivière-Bourdet and remarried, following her own inclinations rather than the advice of her friends. The husband was a certain Monsieur Prudhomme, a bourgeois as his name indicated, neither a man of the world nor a wit. She gained a husband but she lost her friends.

Emilie kept repeating, "Good old Bernières, I love her with all my heart." Voltaire shed tears of affection and nostalgia over the memory of the old days, the beautiful friendship, the beautiful friend. But in spite of all these effusions Madame Prudhomme was not invited to Cirey.

Meanwhile Thiériot remained silent. He could not have been very easy in his mind: at this very moment he was betraying Voltaire in yet another way. On Voltaire's recommendation he was Prince Frederick's correspondent in Paris, and for a consideration he acted as his informer. He sent the prince secret intelligence and all the scurrilous pamphlets circulating in the capital, including a copy, doubtless the first one off the press, of the *Voltairomanie*. Voltaire knew nothing about it, but Frederick, who loved gossip, was only too pleased that Thiériot sent him a goodly share of it.

Emilie could not contain herself. She wrote to Frederick and told him what sort of a person Thiériot was. He must have laughed at her indignation and her naïveté. He knew very well what sort of a person Thiériot was. He only used him because of his baseness. What amused Frederick was the cruel spectacle of the most intelligent of men caught in the toils of his own vanity and stooping to the level of people like Desfontaines and Thiériot. Frederick despised humanity and loved to seek out the weaknesses of even its most eminent representatives. Emilie's ardor and integrity, and the candor of her love, only added extra spice to his enjoyment. He wrote back to her saying that Thiériot's services were rendered most punctiliously, that his desire to be useful was much appreciated, and that the man was considered worthy of esteem. Which was as good as saying that Frederick had no intention of giving up Thiériot because of the latter's quarrel with Voltaire. If Voltaire did not immediately see what sort of person Frederick was, it was because he did not want to see. But Voltaire adored royal highnesses, especially when they weren't French.

As for Thiériot, he entertained his café companions by reading them Emilie's supplications. He met with such success that he even talked of publishing Voltaire's and Emilie's tearful letters. And Voltaire—unpardonably—forgave him. But Emilie was less charitable and informed Thiériot in no uncertain terms that she was prepared to muster all the Châtelets and all the Breteuils to use more powerful and more painful weapons than words against him.

Voltaire continued to write him imploring letters. And one day Thiériot began to wear a miniature of Madame du Châtelet. He answered letters in a friendly manner and associated himself with those friends of Voltaire's who were demanding a recantation from Desfontaines. When Frederick ordered Thiériot to make his peace with Emilie he was able to answer that one can only be reconciled to people with whom one has quarreled—and can one have done so with a woman whose portrait hangs round one's neck, surrounded with three hundred crowns' worth of diamonds? Thiériot was clearly a resourceful fellow.

Voltaire was overjoyed, and clasped Thiériot to his bosom. The worthy Madame de Graffigny was amazed: "The friendship Voltaire has for this man is astonishing," she wrote. She and Emilie felt more like having him drawn and quartered.

But Voltaire, aided and abetted by Thiériot, felt like having Desfontaines drawn and quartered. He wrote to D'Argental not to let anyone in Paris sleep until Desfontaines was brought to account: "I shall die or I shall have justice," he proclaimed. Now that he had sunk his teeth in the man, he would never let go. He was all long-suffering for some people and all implacability for others.

He called D'Argental "my guardian angel" but he was afraid he might be Desfontaines's angel too, whereas, to fulfill his role as angel to Voltaire, D'Argental ought to be a devil to his enemy and get him subjected to horrible punishments. But instead Thiériot was to receive new rewards.

A cry of horror went up when Voltaire learned that the Jesuits wanted to reconcile him with Desfontaines. Never! He determined to go to Paris and stir up hatred wherever Desfontaines had friends. Emilie, frightened by his fury, begged him to stay at Cirey. Every day there were scenes: sometimes he would give in, sometimes he would rebel. Should he go or shouldn't he?

Then Desfontaines denied that he was the sole author of the *Voltairomanie* and announced his accomplice: Jean-Baptiste Rousseau, the exile of Brussels. It was not surprising. If Voltaire had only penned a few amicable words in reply a few months earlier when Rousseau made friendly overtures to repair the rift between them by sending him an ode and reams of compliments, he would have had one enemy less. But instead he had answered that "it was not a good enough ode to effect a reconciliation" and that, as he himself was a connoisseur of both odes and integrity, Rousseau must correct both his verses and his behavior if he wished to put an end to their quarrel. To add fuel to the fire he also wrote: "An honest man must always despise a dishonest one to the very end." Rousseau's reply to that was his collaboration with Desfontaines on the writing of the *Voltairomanie*.

It is painful to see the lengths to which these two men's mutual hatred carried them. Rousseau made a secret journey to Paris and Voltaire heard of it. There is a letter in his own handwriting asking a lawyer whether it would be possible to have Rousseau arrested and have the case against him reopened at the Châtelet court. Fortunately for the momory of Voltaire, even more than for that of Rousseau, the letter produced no effect.

His enemies conspired to torture him. There was one page in the *Voltairomanie* entitled "Masterpiece by an Unknown," which gave an insulting burlesque account of the Beauregard incident. The poet is beaten by a handsome and noble officer, and says thank you.

The author of this "Masterpiece" was a writer of cheap squibs called Saint-Hyacinthe, who claimed to be the son of Bossuet, "the eagle of Meaux," no less. He had an evil tongue, and Voltaire said he was born for the rod and the noose.

Amidst all this flood of invective there is one moving note: Voltaire felt that his humanity itself was wounded by the sarcasms and laughter of the common herd. He knew who he was and what he was worth, and there is a noble side to his suffering. The man who was already on the way to becoming the glory of his country and his age felt himself at this time to be "no more than a public buffoon, supposed, whether it redounded to his dishonor or not, to furnish everyone with cheap entertainment and to exhibit his wounds upon the stage." His passion for theatricals was being all too amply satisfied. It all seems very modern. He had chosen to live a public, almost histrionic life, with all the inconveniences as well as all the satisfactions this entails. How he would have enjoyed, how he would have deliberately stirred up, publicity in the modern sense of the word. As it was, he practically fabricated the life of a film star for himself before the cinema was even invented.

He never forgot the wounds dealt him in public. Five years later he was still launching attacks against the author of the "Masterpiece," which brought another cruel riposte from Saint-Hyacinthe. He thanked Voltaire for having enriched the language with a new word: henceforward to beat a poet was to "Voltairize" him.

At last a settlement was proposed: Desfontaines was willing to disown the *Voltairomanie* if Voltaire would disown *Le Préservatif*. Voltaire nearly choked with indignation: a mutal agreement between the two of them would be the death of him. He would never consent. Emilie sided with him.

Finally Monsieur Hérault, who had been patiently coping with Voltaire for twenty years, got a recantation out of Desfontaines by threatening him with prison. What, only prison? Voltaire cried. He would have liked him hanged or strappadoed. The outcome fell short of the total vengeance Voltaire had dreamed of, but everyone wanted to get the matter over and done with. Voltaire did not even have the satisfaction of publishing Desfontaines's recantation, for it was kept locked away in the police files. Monsieur Hérault had doubtless followed the proper course: the less said the better. This lamentable comedy does throw valuable light on its actors, however. When Monsieur d'Argenson questioned Desfontaines as to his motives for writing such libels against his benefactor, the abbé answered cynically: "I have to live."

"I don't see the necessity," Monsieur d'Argenson replied.

This exchange puts the level of the whole affair in the proper perspective and demonstrates what people thought of Voltaire's adversary. Desfontaines did not emerge from his obscurity again. But he had a host of successors.

Life at Cirey

Despite people such as Desfontaines and Thiériot, the round of life at Cirey went on undisturbed: "Do not imagine that the busy and delightful life at Cirey, in the midst of the greatest magnificence and the best entertainment, and, better still, of friendship, can be troubled for an instant by the hoarse croakings of an old scoundrel like Rousseau." In spite of the rages and tears, the colics and the fevers, life at Cirey was far from sad. The most serious work and the most varied pleasures were all pursued simultaneously, as if Voltaire and Emilie were ten different people at once and every day was forty-eight hours long. They loved, hated, worked, played—and above all they laughed. Voltaire loved to laugh and to make other people laugh. He often regretted not having fully exploited his comic vein.

We can share in the life at Cirey almost day by day thanks to Madame de Graffigny's delightfully indiscreet and voluminous correspondence. When they took her in at Cirey, Voltaire said she was "a great example of the misfortunes of this world." For consolation she had friends: Richelieu, Voltaire, and Emilie in particular. But she also had a brutal husband who had never recognized his wife's inexhaustible capacity for love. She had had a terrible life because of him and had nearly died of his physical abuse of her when he was chamberlain to Duc Léopold of Lorraine: in those days a husband had to beat his wife senseless before he was shut away as insane. Such things horrified Voltaire. Poor Madame de Graffigny was the great-niece, on her mother's side, of the famous engraver Callot. (She used to tell how her mother, not knowing what to do with all her uncle's copper plates, had had them made into saucepans.)

Madame de Graffigny was an amiable woman whose misfortunes had not spoiled her good nature. She trusted life and people. She was spontaneous and affectionate, forever laughing at her own sorrows and weeping over other people's. She was almost penniless, and Voltaire and Emilie had taken her on as a permanent guest. She was as improvident as La Fontaine's grasshopper and whenever money from her tiny pension arrived she would squander it at once. But no matter, she enjoyed herself doing so.

Madame de Graffigny arrived at Cirey in December 1738—at two in the morning, waking the whole house. Her coach was covered with mud; it had been almost buried several times on the journey. Voltaire and all the household came to greet her. He was in his dressing gown, nightcap, and furs, with a candlestick in his hand and perishing with cold. He welcomed her with tears in his eyes. Emilie received her kindly, watching with a mixture of astonishment and amusement as Voltaire kept kissing the traveler's hands and Madame de Graffigny kept babbling of the hairbreadth escapes she had had en route.

But if Madame de Graffigny was admittedly a chatterbox, she was also a keen observer and recorder. In a letter to M. Devaux, "Pampan," her most intimate friend and confidante, she writes: "First his antechamber, no larger than your hand, then the bedchamber, which is small, low, and hung with crimson velvet; as is an alcove, where the hangings have gold fringes. These are the winter furnishings. There are not many tapestries but a great deal of paneling, in which there are set charming paintings, mirrors, handsome lacquered corner cupboards . . . and an infinity of things in that style, rich, rare, and above all quarters so clean that you could kiss the parquet floor. Also an open chest of silver plate. All that superfluity, which is so necessary, can dream of."

Here she has slipped in an apposite line from Voltaire's *Le Mondain*— "*le superflu, chose si nécessaire*." It sounds like a mere clever witticism, but it is really a profound reflection, one of Voltaire's key thoughts. Civilization creates luxury, and man naturally adapts himself to it. Superfluity is a necessity for civilized man, which is as much as to say that "nature" for man is a matter of culture and not of virgin forests. All this was a foretaste of Voltaire's future philosophical skirmishes with another, more famous Rousseau, Jean-Jacques, who was sharpening his arrows in the mountains of Savoy as Madame de Graffigny fingered a ring case at Cirey and counted a dozen or so rings set with cut stones and diamonds. Then she walked along the gallery, admiring two statues that stood between the windows: the Farnese Venus and Hercules. Facing the windows were cabinets full of books and physics apparatus, and "a stove that made the air like spring." For Voltaire warmth was not a luxury but life itself, and for Madame de Graffigny it was paradise after her journey through the icy winter cold. The gallery was paneled and painted yellow.

There was also a dark room where the laboratory equipment and machines were kept, and a door that could be left ajar so that one could hear mass without leaving the vernal air of the gallery. This was a pious convenience that Voltaire allowed himself, probably in memory of Montaigne, who could also listen to mass without leaving his library. Pious? Perhaps, but perhaps not only that. One is tempted to think the arrangement was also intended to reassure visitors as to the occupant's religious devotion.

What impressed Madame de Graffigny most of all was Emilie's apartment. "Voltaire's apartment is nothing in comparison. The room is paneled and painted pale yellow with pale blue bands, with an alcove hung with charming printed wallpaper in the same colors. The bed is of blue moiré. Everything is in yellow and blue, right down to the dog's basket," she writes.

"It is carved like a snuffbox!" she goes on. She also reported that there were a Veronese and several Watteaus, a painted ceiling, an amber-topped escritoire sent by Frederick (accompanied by some verses), an armchair upholstered in white taffeta, embroidered muslin curtains, a standing wardrobe with a marble floor and flax-gray paneling. "No, there is nothing prettier in the whole world," she assures Devaux.

But the supreme refinement, unheard of in those days, was the bathroom. It had a marble floor and the walls were covered with porcelain tiles. A little adjoining room had willow-green paneling and contained a sofa and little carved gilt chairs for resting after the exertions of one's bath. There were glass-fronted bookcases; everything was painted, elaborate, shining. There was a miniature chimneypiece: "It is a jewel you could put in your pocket," Madame de Graffigny wrote. "If I had an apartment like that I'd have someone awaken me at night just to look at it."

But poor Madame de Graffigny's room was at the top of the house just under the eaves, and all she could do was try not to notice how miserable it was, and sleep soundly all night. She froze in it; no attempt had been made to renovate what was "the width and height of a covered market. All the four winds play through the chinks round the windows, which I shall stop up if the good Lord spares me my life. The hearth was so huge that it consumed half a cord of wood a day, and still the room was ice-cold. The wall coverings were ugly. There was no view through the ancient mullioned window. The closet and wardrobe were full of cracks. "In short, everything except the lady's and Voltaire's apartments is utterly disgusting. The gardens look pretty from my window. Slip in that way," Madame de Graffigny wrote to Devaux.

Such was the retreat. Now for its inhabitants, the "nymph" and the "god," as she called Madame du Châtelet and Voltaire.

Emilie was stingy about the servants' wages and board. In Paris people laughed at the sparseness and poorness of the table she kept. She bought wine two bottles at a time, a horrible red *vin ordinaire* from Suresnes that she called burgundy, and a white "champagne" sharp enough to waken the dead and kill the living.

There was some excuse for her when she was in Paris: Monsieur de Châtelet was not very well off. But at Cirey it was Voltaire who paid, and he wanted to live lavishly. She bowed to his tastes but clung to her tightfisted habits. They often resulted in sudden departures on the part of the servants, which annoyed Voltaire. As to the timetable at Cirey, as Monsieur de Villefort had seen, it was that of a barracks or a monastery. Madame de Graffigny also complained of its severity. The nymph and the god rose at five, and no one else was supposed to leave his or her room before ten unless invited to do so. The master and mistress worked in their rooms until that hour: the others could either do likewise or keep quiet. At ten everyone met in the pale yellow gallery for coffee. That lasted an hour. Then everyone went back to his or her room or out for a walk, according to weather or mood. At noon there was what Madame de Graffigny called the "cabbies'" dinner. These "cabbies" were Monsieur de Châtelet if he was there, and the plump, affable Madame de Champbonin and her son, the one whom Voltaire's niece had declined to marry. Monsieur de Châtelet dined apart because learned talk put him to sleep, and his wife and Voltaire nearly died of boredom listening to him tell stories of his campaigns. So the separate tables pleased everyone. After the divinities had dined together, the guests were allowed to join them and converse with them. The talk was of what people had been reading and the problems they proposed to solve: geometry served as an aid to digestion. If some lawsuit was at a critical stage they talked of that; if Desfontaines was behaving himself and the equations had come out right, the subjects were literature and poetry. With a witty remark Voltaire would finally rise, bow, and gently shepherd the guests to the door with courtly compliments and manners that enchanted everyone. Then he would return either to his room or to the physics laboratory, where he would work till supper, at nine o'clock.

Madame de Graffigny liked to describe her own life and that of the others at Cirey: her sole occupation while there was writing letters, eight hours a day. Sometimes, at about four o'clock, Voltaire and Emilie would partake of a collation together. According to Madame de Graffigny, it was unwise to venture into the gallery at that hour unless one had been invited. But sometimes one was invited. And then poor Madame de Graffigny would come and sit at the divinities' feet and nibble her bread and butter as if it were manna from heaven. The words the god and the nymph let fall made her forget her own sad life. We can easily believe her: the intimate conversation of Voltaire with Emilie and Madame de Graffigny, who also was a lively conversationalist, must have been delightful. Afterward she would go back up to her room transported with admiration. But there it was cold and dark and lonely again, and she would have a crying fit until the bell rang for supper. Then her idol, the candelabra, the warm air, the silverware, and the fine food would make her forget her troubles again, and she would talk and laugh gaily with Voltaire, who enjoyed and joined in her laughter.

Emilie was a glutton. But food overheated her blood, and she had given up wine. When she had been eating too much she would go on a diet. "Dieting costs me nothing," she said. "I merely stay in my room at mealtimes." And in her room she worked.

When he wasn't too unwell Voltaire did justice to the luxury he insisted on at table. He would be the gayest and most stimulating of all those present. Perhaps his dazzling talk at such times was his real masterpiece. This scintillating flurry of seemingly mere clever small talk really was an expression of the most brilliant thoughts, crystallizing discoveries worked out during hours of study. To the profane these flashes of insight might seem the product of improvisation or inspiration. In reality, however, they were the consummation of long perseverance and profound reflection, despite their being delivered with sovereign ease and nonchalance.

Voltaire was unrivaled in the art of conversation, for as well as wit he had the perfect courtesy which is another luxury, another charm. He knew how to be profound without being solemn and frivolous without being superficial; he could interest, touch, and intrigue people without ever making them sad or forcing them to struggle to understand some obscure expression. He gave everyone the satisfaction of understanding. High society adored him for such exchanges: it saw its own reflection in him. Poor and unsuccessful writers hated him: but this was inevitable. He gave the impression of merely playing with his marvelous talent, though in fact he worked harder than ten long-winded hacks.

Sometimes Voltaire visited his guests in their rooms, but only rarely. To make sure of not lingering he would never sit down, saying "the greatest extravagance is to waste one's time."

Since some exercise was indispensable, the marquise rode and Voltaire hunted deer—from a carriage. He was a very bad shot. He used to send presents of game to his friends, but it was always from the bag of better marksmen in the hunting party.

But the really important occasions were the theatrical performances. At Cirey, theater was not an amusement—it was a religion. Voltaire's passion for the stage was shared by the others. They had only a tiny theater —Madame de Graffigny said it was a theater for puppets—but the stage was spacious enough. There were two rehearsals a week, on Mondays and Tuesdays, and two performances: on Wednesdays and Thursdays. Emilie made young Champbonin design posters imitating the playbills of Paris, which were put up on the gates of the château. The chief pieces in the repertoire were the tragedies of Voltaire. By way of relaxation there were occasional puppet shows, and they also put on a comedy by Reginard.

Sometimes, in the evening, Voltaire would give a magic lantern show. Madame de Graffigny describes one such occasion: "After supper he gave a magic lantern show, with comments that made us nearly die laughing . . . no, there was never anything so droll. But, as he was cleaning the reservoir of the lantern, which was full of spirits of alcohol, he upset it over his hand, which was enveloped in flames. You can't imagine what a fine hand he has but what was not fine was that it was burned. This disturbed the entertainment somewhat, but a moment later he went on again."

They also tackled opera. Emilie had "a divine voice," or so everyone said, including herself. Some evenings she would sing an entire opera, quite a feat after a day of Newton. Her brother, the Abbé de Breteuil, vicar general at Sens, often visited Cirey. He and Voltaire struck such sparks together that the conversation on those evenings became a fireworks display. Maupertuis came by too, and was very charming. They nicknamed him Archimedes: he made them drunk on mathematics night and day for several weeks. Madame de Graffigny kept to her room. She was intimidated by the excited conversation at table and thought they were all mad.

After a year with these divinities, Madame de Graffigny tired of the life at Cirey. The enchanters were not always enchanting. Some times there were dreadful scenes between the god and his nymph, which she was drawn into and which left her shattered. The anger of two such personalities was terrifying. Not for them, for they were always reconciled after having exchanged invectives and sworn to part. Or at least so it seemed from their expressions, for they quarreled in English. They also used English when they exchanged endearments in public. No one else spoke English at Cirey, or practically anywhere else in French circles at that time.

Madame de Graffigny relates a scene less violent than some, but nonetheless revealing. One evening Voltaire came to supper in a suit of plain wool cloth. Madame du Châtelet objected: she wanted him to wear silk. He refused to change because he felt chilly and was afraid of catching cold. She insisted and sent for a valet, who couldn't be found. Voltaire stubbornly refused to go up to his room. The two of them stamped their feet and shouted—in English. Voltaire left the room, and the guests sat down at the table in consternation. Emilie sent for Voltaire. The reply came that "Monsieur had colic and would not be dining."

Guests had been invited that evening for a performance of a play and they were disappointed. Madame de Graffigny went to see what was happening and found Voltaire, not writhing with colic, but laughing and joking with Madame de Champbonin in her room. Madame de Graffigny sat down with them, and all three went on enjoying themselves, forgetting Emilie. Emilie sent for them all, and Voltaire was seized with colic again. He went down, but with bad grace. His face was ashen and there was a bleak look in his eyes. He sat and sulked in a corner of the gallery. When the guests left the room the conversation between him and Emilie began again in English. After a few words his eyes lit up, his smile returned, the two of them stood up, clasped hands, and went back to speaking French. A moment later the performance of the play began.

According to Madame de Graffigny, scenes like this were the only indication that there was anything between Voltaire and the marquise save simple friendship; they behaved, she wrote, "with admirable decorum." But she added that Madame du Châtelet "makes life a bit difficult for him."

Another day he sulked because she would not allow him to drink Rhine wine. So he refused to read *Jeanne*, the scandalous work he was in the midst of writing, later retitled *La Pucelle*. At last they were persuaded to make their peace with each other, and in great secrecy six or eight people listened to the poem that no one was supposed to know any-thing about.

During a visit to Paris, Emilie read some of her own verses one evening at the Duchesse de Luxembourg's. Voltaire remarked rather spitefully that she couldn't have written them because they were good. She spat out an angry reply and they began to shout at each other, in English and French. Suddenly, his hand going to his knife, Voltaire roared: "Don't keep looking at me with those wild, squinty eyes of yours!" It was a ter-rible scene, and the worst of it was that he had used the familiar *tu* to her in public!

Even so, it was not so bad as what happened to the unfortunate Mad-ame de Graffigny. Soon after Christmas 1738, Voltaire rushed into her room in a frenzy, collapsed into a chair, and blurted that he was a dead man if she did not save him. "Write to Pampan," he shouted, "and say he must withdraw the copies he's circulating." She was willing to write to "Pampan"; but what copies was he talking about? Suddenly Voltaire leapt up like a jack-in-the-box and started to dash round the room. "There's no use lying, madame," he cried in a terrible voice. "It was you who sent it."

Now it was Madame de Graffigny's turn to collapse. What *was* he talk-ing about? Finally it emerged that the manuscript of *Jeanne* had been stolen, and copies made and circulated. Voltaire was as good as hanged, and it was all her doing. She cried and wept and called on heaven as her witness that she was entirely innocent. She threw herself at his feet, and he at hers. She swore she had not stolen his *Jeanne*, he implored her to give it back to him. But how could she repair a wrong that she had not committed? But this was nothing—she still had to face Emilie, who rushed in, brandishing a letter and screaming: "Here is proof of your in-famy. . . . You are a monster. I took you in not out of friendship, for I never felt any for you, but because you had nowhere to go. And you have the baseness to betray me, to kill me, to steal a poem out of my desk and have copies made of it. . . ."

One wonders whether Voltaire and his friends play-acted more on the stage or in real life. Voltaire tried to calm Emilie, but she eluded his grasp and raged up and down the room hurling insults at Madame de Graffigny. At last the poor woman asked to see the "proof": it was a let-ter to her from Devaux. The Nymph and the Enchanter were in the habit of intercepting their visitors' letters, both coming and going. They had found an allusion to *La Pucelle* in Pampan's letter and deduced from it a mad machination that did not exist. They loved plots and saw them everywhere. Poor Madame de Graffigny, innocent but prostrate, half out of her mind with shame, pain, and indignation, offered to show Emilie all of Devaux's letters in order to get rid of her. The row did not end till five in the morning.

Madame de Graffigny could not stay at Cirey, but neither could she leave. She had nowhere to go, and she was penniless. At about noon Voltaire came to see her. He felt contrite and tried to comfort her. Madame de Champbonin and the marquis came too. Emilie's only apology was a curt: "I am sorry about what happened last night." But that was not enough to heal the wound. As all this had happened in the midst of the Desfontaines affair, Emilie was afraid that Madame de Graffigny might go to Paris and join the enemy pack, regaling them with juicy items of gossip. So the proud Emilie did what she had never done for anyone else, and took Madame de Graffigny for a drive round the park in her own carriage. If the poor wretch was not overcome with gratitude after that . . . ! She also promised her a copy of one of her own books on metaphysics.

Before creating this grotesque scene, Voltaire might have remembered that he had read several cantos of *La Pucelle* aloud at gatherings in Paris, and in particular in the presence of Monsieur de Maurepas, the chief minister. If copies were circulating he had only himself to blame for having been indiscreet enough to parade his impiety.

Voltaire kept offering Madame de Graffigny his humblest and most heartrending apologies. She could not forget what had happened; but she forgave him. She never forgave the "shrew," as she thereafter referred to Emilie the "nymph" in her letters.

Another blow was to befall her. Voltaire, thinking it would please Madame de Graffigny, invited Monsieur Léopold Desmaret, one of her former lovers in Lunéville, whom she had fondly nicknamed "*Gros Chien* [Big Doggy]," to come to Cirey. But "Gros Chien" immediately informed her he no longer loved her. She left Cirey in March 1739, her spirits crushed.

Expeditions

Voltaire and Emilie were preparing at that moment to depart for Brussels to look after the Châtelets' fortune, which needed careful attention. Voltaire was just the person to attend to it. One of the people who had been taken in at Cirey was a relative of Monsieur du Châtelet's, the Marquis de Trichâteau, who was very rich and had no heirs. Having succeeded in luring him to Cirey, the Châtelets made much of him. When Trichâteau died he left his property to the Châtelets. The inheritance was a considerable one, but the estates were in Flanders. They included a principality near Cleves which made Emilie a princess. But the title meant nothing to her. Voltaire did his best to get Frederick to buy the lands and the title, but the prince turned a deaf ear, though the offer was renewed several times. Frederick had an eye only for good bargains, especially with his friends. Madame du Deffand, as spiteful as ever, was furiously jealous of Emilie's new title. What worried Emilie most was all the bother of the inheritance and the lawsuits that would be necessary to establish her rights. So it was to help the Châtelets that Voltaire left Cirey on May 7, 1739, also leaving behind *La Pucelle* and *Le Siècle de Louis XIV*, just begun. Their intention was to hurry up the legal proceedings in Brussels and make sure their claims got a proper hearing—by greasing the magistrates' palms if need be. Voltaire was half dead when he and Emilie and the marquis set out. Monsieur de Châtelet was so worried that in an attempt to reassure himself he wrote to Monsieur d'Argental: "Our friend's health is so deplorable that my only hope for his recovery rests in the bustle of a journey." An excellent remedy, to send someone at death's door out on bumpy roads in a jolting carriage, at the risk of accidents and at the mercy of innkeepers. And yet it worked: the hardships that would have half killed someone robust improved Voltaire's health and revived his spirits.

When they arrived at Valenciennes the poet and the lady physicist paid visit after visit and eagerly accepted all invitations to dinner, especially the governor's. After a week they left Valenciennes to install themselves in Brussels. In order not to waste any time Emilie had brought with her a teacher of mathematics—Monsieur Samuel Koenig, a disciple of Maupertuis, who had recommended him. She lamented the slowness of her progress and feared that she was a poor pupil and that Koenig took no interest in her. She worked hard. But lawsuits and study did not take up all their time: they also received and were received. It was necessary to show old Rousseau that even in his own territory he was nothing once Voltaire appeared on the scene.

On June 28, 1739, Emilie and Voltaire gave a party in the house they had rented in the Rue de la Grosse Tour. They had the façade cleaned for the occasion, and in the process two men fell from the roof and died in the street at Voltaire's feet. "Imagine what it is like to see two poor workmen fall to their death and be spattered with their blood. I see I am not the sort of person to give parties. This sad spectacle spoiled all the pleasure of the most delightful day in the world," he wrote.

Voltaire observed that Brussels society was more attracted by gambling at cards than by belles-lettres. He deplored this, but consoled himself by remembering that he had been received like an ambassador. Since his vanity was satisfied, all was well. Rousseau had not appeared at any of these gatherings, and his name was never once mentioned. Voltaire regarded this silence as an homage to his own supremacy. The people of Brussels might be illiterate, but they could recognize real talent.

By September they were in Paris, Emilie staying with the Duc de Richelieu, Voltaire in a furnished apartment in the Rue Cloche Perche. He had not been in the capital for three years and threw himself into a frenzied round of visits, dinners, and evenings at the theater. He was lionized everywhere: "I am like that ancient who died beneath the flowers people threw to greet him," he wrote.

He was brimming over with energy. He insisted on the actors learning, rehearsing, and performing his tragedy *Mahomet* in three weeks, although the work had not yet been authorized. The lovers were preparing to leave Paris when Voltaire fell ill: again he was certain that he was dying. Three days later he climbed into the coach, a little thinner, a little less inclined to believe his death was imminent. They went back to Cirey. They arrived in the first days of November 1739, and almost immediately thereafter started packing again. By November 16 they were in Liège; the Brussels lawsuit required their presence.

During the journey Voltaire learned that the chief minister had condemned the beginning chapters of *Le Siècle de Louis XIV*, which had appeared in a collection of other texts by Voltaire. He was angry and bitter, and for good reason. The work did honor both to himself and to France. "You may judge whether it is the work of a good citizen—of a good Frenchman, of a lover of humanity, and of a man of moderation," he protested. Voltaire's description of the spirit in which the book was written is perfectly accurate.

It is painful to see such a fine work condemned merely because some dull courtiers thought its praise of Louis XIV reflected adversely on Louis XV. Voltaire concluded: "The book and I will survive." This too is quite true.

The authorities were making life harder and harder for him. Soon after he learned of the ban on his *Louis XIV* there came another piece of bad news. Monsieur de Maurepas sent him word that he was not to return to Paris: the court considered him to be in exile at Cirey and wished him to remain there.

For the moment, so long as he was where Emilie was, he did not feel exiled. Voltaire liked it in Brussels. The lawsuit he was helping through the courts for the Châtelets was going well. As he lacked the necessary documents for going ahead with *Le Siècle de Louis XIV*, he rewrote *Mahomet* and threw himself with fervor into his correspondence with Frederick of Prussia. Both parties were carried away; they were at the apogee of their mutual admiration. Frederick planned to put out a magnificent edition of *La Henriade*, at his own expense. It was the first time he had ever thought of paying for anything. As it developed, he did no more than think of so doing, and nothing more was heard of the project.

Voltaire, for his part, was carefully supervising the publication of Frederick's *Anti-Machiavel*, a treatise full of lofty moral reflections on the exercise of power. Voltaire had the greatest enthusiasm for it as the work of a philosopher-king and a lover of the human race. The tone of their letters is astonishing. Voltaire wrote that his new tragedy, *Mérope*, was as much Frederick's as his own and offered to dedicate it to him out of gratitude for two or three suggestions the latter had made regarding the text—which Voltaire had not followed.

Frederick wrote even more flatteringly: "Take care of the health of a man who is dear to me, and never forget that since you are my friend you should devote all your care to preserving the most precious blessing heaven has bestowed on me."

And Voltaire capped this exchange of extravagant compliments by writing: "Monseigneur, the thought of you occupies me day and night. I dream of my prince as a man dreams of his mistress."

It was not love; only overexcited vanity.

But already there was a cloud, or, rather, a light mist gathering on the horizon in the form of the prince's jealousy of Emilie's relations to Voltaire. Frederick covered her with flowers, but only in order to smother her. He wrote to her:

"Indeed, neither in Europe nor in the world at large do I find a lady with the strength of mind to have produced works on such deep subjects as you treat of merely in play."

But his true opinion of her was another story: he thought her a goose with only a veneer of learning, and found her books ridiculous. But her worst fault in his eyes was that she had Voltaire tied to her apron strings.

It was still possible for Voltaire to believe Frederick to be what he seemed, and what Voltaire wanted him to be. Had this prince not had an unhappy childhood under a brutal father? Could one imagine a more touching victim of tyranny? Voltaire was convinced that Frederick must hate tyranny and persecution, and that his thoughts on the omnipotence of kings must be "philosophical"—that is to say, the same as his own.

I like people who are capable of deserting the sublime to joke; I wish that Newton had taken up light comedy. (Letter to Monsieur Berger, 1735)

There are certain errors that are only for the common people; there are others that are only for philosophers. (*The Philosophy of Newton:* Discourse on the changes that have taken place on our globe)

It is quite true that men rob and butcher each other, but in so doing they praise equity and gentleness. (*Dialogues and Conversations*, 18/2)

Confound philosophers who do not know how to unbend! I consider austerity to be a disease; I prefer a thousand times being ill and subject to fever, as I am, to thinking sad thoughts. It seems to me that virtue, study, and gaiety are three sisters that must not be separated; these three divinities are your attendants; I take them as mistresses. (Letter to Frederick the Great, 1737)

I envy animals two things: their ignorance of bad things to come and of bad things that are said of them. (Letter to Thiériot, 1739)

What is needed to be happy is the body of an athlete and the soul of a sage. (Letter, October 27, 1740)

Frederick succeeded to the throne of Prussia on May 31, 1740. On June 6 he wrote to Voltaire that he was "disgusted with human greatness." This was no more than Voltaire expected of the philosopher who had now become King. But he was overwhelmed with joy at what followed: "Pray see in me only a zealous citizen, a somewhat skeptical philosopher, but a truly faithful friend. In God's name, write to me only as a man, and join me in despising all titles and outward glory."

It was so flattering that Voltaire believed it. He answered, courtliness doing duty for sincerity: "Your Majesty commands me when I write to him to think not so much of the King as of the man. It is an order after my own heart."

But he had nonetheless addressed Frederick as "Your Majesty."

"I know not how to deal with a king, but I am quite at ease with a man with love of humanity in his head and heart," he went on. "Love of humanity" was already part of the philosophic-sentimental vocabulary. King Frederick's practical demonstration of it remained to be seen, but henceforth Voltaire, conscious of the discrepancy between "Your Majesty" and such noble ideas, addressed him as "Your Humanity."

Emilie had lost several points during this period of Voltaire's heady devotion to Frederick. She could have gained them back very quickly if only Voltaire had come to his senses. He might have done so when Frederick asked him to stop the publication of the *Anti-Machiavel*. The ideas he had had as Crown Prince he considered unsuitable now that he was King. He thought that certain of them might give offense. Voltaire, nothing loath, undertook to recast the book. What Frederick wanted, however, was to stop its publication. But the printer at The Hague, Van Duren, did not want to lose the profit he expected to make from a book written by a king.

Voltaire promised Van Duren huge sums if he would renounce his rights, and Van Duren, in the hope of getting even more, refused. Voltaire hastily wrote him, asking to have the manuscript back, saying the King had asked him to make some corrections, but intending, of course, to get it safely back in his own hands. The printer suspected as much and agreed to the corrections on condition that Voltaire would come and make them at the printing shop. So he went and spent several hours a day there, watched over by Van Duren's son, scratching at the King's manuscript. "I have crossed out so much, and intercalated such dreadful nonsense and rubbish between one line and another, that it no longer resembles a book at all. This is what is called blowing up the ship to avoid being captured by the enemy," he wrote.

But Frederick considered himself not only a man but also a man of letters, and did not approve of this procedure. If he refused to have his book published he objected even more to having it sabotaged, and disavowed this bastard work. Voltaire was astonished but did not like to criticize "His Humanity." In his own opinion he had improved the book, if anything; and he may have been right. Frederick nonetheless preferred the unimproved version that he had written himself.

Voltaire did not spend all his time at the print shop. He went out a good deal; he was on familiar ground. Jean-Baptiste Rousseau and Piron were both at The Hague. He did not meet Rousseau. Rousseau maintained that he would have been willing to drop around to see Voltaire, but as his previous offer of reconciliation had been so harshly rejected he had kept his distance.

Frederick was dying to meet Voltaire and Voltaire was dying to meet "His Humanity." They arranged to meet at Cleves.

The long-anticipated meeting took place on September 11, 1740, at the Château of Moylard, near Cleves. It was a curious encounter: Voltaire must have been blind to think it sublime, when everything went wrong and everything was calculated to displease him. Frederick was accompanied by Maupertuis and by Francesco Algarotti, an Italian count—handsome and witty, charmingly polite, flattering, somewhat sugary, full of savoir-faire and intelligence, and with a lightly worn but extensive culture. There was also Keyserling, and Monsieur Rambouet, a royal magistrate, grotesque, dirty man, with coarse linen and an unkempt wig, who was both sly and powerful. Such for this occasion was the court of His Prussian Majesty.

They were all lodged in dilapidated quarters in the attic. The King was ill with fever. In the bare room, by the light of a candle, a little man in a dressing gown of coarse blue cloth lay shivering on a camp cot: this was Voltaire's first glimpse of his idol. "I bowed to him," he wrote, "and began our acquaintance by feeling his pulse as though I were a chief physician." Then without further ado he sat down on the edge of the bed.

The fever passed and the court sat down at table. "The conversation consisted of a searching discussion on the subject of the immortality of the soul, liberty, and Plato's hermaphrodites." Voltaire reports that as the master, the Enchanter, spoke, the guests were enraptured by his words. The court may have been seedy, but courtliness was as much in order as ever. While the King held forth about the hermaphrodites of Plato, Monsieur Rambouet took to the road bearing an ultimatum from Frederick to the citizens of Liège, proclaiming that, unless they paid the Prussian King a million ducats, two thousand of his troops would surround the city and it would be bombarded by Prussian artillery. Voltaire himself was asked if he would be so good as to draw up a proclamation advising the people of Liège to pay up before it was too late. And he did so. How could you refuse anything to a philosopher-king who was your host at table and addressed you as "Virgil?" Later, much later, Voltaire realized that the philosopher-king's wish to meet the philosopher-poet had served as a cover for his deviously sly political and military maneuvers. The Enchanter's charm had blinded Voltaire to his cunning, and he had been so carried away as to become Frederick's accomplice in a contemptible act of banditry.

But for the moment it was still the honeymoon. Voltaire reported that he had dined—very badly, to be sure—"with one of the most likable men in the world, one who would be the delight of society and sought after everywhere even if he were not a king; a philosopher without austerity; an example of gentleness, affability, and charm."

Frederick came to see him in his room. "I had to make an effort to remember that the person I saw sitting at the foot of my bed was a monarch with an army of a hundred thousand men." (The people of Liège saw, on September 14, to what "philosophical" uses that army was being put when Frederick's troops moved in.)

Frederick was equally charmed by Voltaire, and wrote to a friend that this man he had so long anticipated meeting had "the eloquence of Cicero, the sweetness of Pliny, the wisdom of Agrippa, etc." He adds: "I could only admire and be silent. La du Châtelet is very lucky to have him."

While Voltaire was out "on loan" from Emilie, she hurried to Paris in his defense. She employed all her credit to repair his damaged reputation, which was in dire need of such restoration. The authorities considered that his lampoons, his disgraceful tussles with printers and pamphleteers, his protestations and freethinking poems were too high a price to pay for his tragedies, his letters, and his conversations.

Voltaire returned to The Hague to try to get the *Anti-Machiavel* out of Van Duren's clutches. He stayed in the palace belonging to the King of Prussia; it was half in ruins, but it was a king's palace, and the king who owned it was his friend. He even admired the cobwebs. He would have liked to return to Paris, but Paris was forbidden. So, disregarding poor Emilie's wishes, he decided to join Frederick at Remusberg, in Germany. Frederick, though no doubt delighted, had no illusions. If Voltaire came to him it would be because he could not go where he wanted. "Prussia will only be a poor second choice," he wrote to Algarotti. But Frederick was glad to have him, and in order to leave his "Virgil" quite free he promised to have him conveyed back to Brussels as soon as Madame du Châtelet returned there for the opening of her great lawsuit.

This second encounter arose not only out of their affinities and their eagerness to bask in each other's glory. There were other reasons involved. Frederick was rather pleased with the French court's persecution of Voltaire: the more disagreeable Paris became to him the better Frederick's chances of luring him away to Prussia. And Frederick knew that Versailles looked askance at Voltaire's friendship with the King of Prussia. What Frederick wanted was a complete rupture between Voltaire and the French court.

Voltaire saw things quite differently. He would have liked to have a "situation"—an official title, a post. He had had only a glimpse of court so far, but it had been enough to show him that it might become his Promised Land, his proper setting. But for that he still had to make an entree and play a leading role there.

Paris, qui m'a vu naître,
Me laisse sans éclat
Et ma manie est d'être
Un ministre d'état,
Des finances le maître,
Au moins ambassadeur
Comme feu prieur.

Paris, which saw my birth,/Leaves me unhonored,/While my one idea is
to become/A minister of state,/The master of finances,/Or at least ambassador,/Like the late prior.

He thought his opportunity had now come. As he knew the chief
minister was uneasy about Frederick's designs on Silesia, and that the
Prince de Beauregard, the French ambassador, had been unable to find
out anything about them, Voltaire thought he could please the King—the
French King, for once—by offering to supply the minister with information concerning Prussia's intentions. He wrote to Cardinal de Fleury, informing him that he could quite easily make Frederick II France's ally.

But the cardinal, no novice in these matters, wrote Voltaire an urbane
letter which, without actually declining his offer to bring about such an
alliance, did not actually accept it. In passing, he also gave him some excellent advice on the respect due to Mother Church.

Once Voltaire had arrived in Prussia, the cardinal sent him another,
more veiled letter. It spoke of the admirable principles contained in a
book called *Anti-Machiavel*, in particular the one concerning the keeping
of promises. It would be a good thing if Voltaire were to bring this article, and the book that contained it, to the attention of the King of Prussia, and the cardinal would be glad to hear his reactions. Voltaire understood from this that he was not actually commissioned to act but that his
thoughts on Prussia and on Frederick's plans would be received by the
government with a certain interest.

He answered in his inimitable manner: "I have obeyed the orders that
Your Eminence did not give, and shown your letter to the King of Prussia."

The morality of Voltaire's semi-official spy mission is a matter of opinion. Was it entirely fair to go and worm secrets out of Frederick while
posing as a philosopher? The King was much craftier than Voltaire, and
only an anti-Machiavellian on paper. Still, the least that can be said is that
they were a couple of foxes, and the proceedings were worthy of the
pair.

Voltaire's entry into Germany had in fact been like the first chapter of
a burlesque spy story. On November 11, 1740, just before Hertford, the
coach broke down, and he had to ride into town on an old nag, dressed in
his pumps and silk breeches. When the sentry asked his name he said
"Don Quixote," and it was under that name he entered Hertford.

He and Frederick were reunited at Remusberg. Again Frederick was charmed. To Algarotti, whom he called "The Swan of Padua," he wrote: "Voltaire has arrived all sparkling with new beauties, and much more sociable than at Cleves."

There was poetry, dancing, feasting, scandal about all Europe, cards. Frederick played the flute for his Virgil. Voltaire risked a little money at cards. He didn't dance or eat and drink. But he talked. Frederick's sister, the Margravine of Bayreuth, was there, and she was as fond of Voltaire as her brother was. The philosopher-king seemed carried away with admiration: he spoke and thought of nothing but poetry and music and his hero. Who would ever have thought there was such a place as Silesia, and that at this very moment two hundred thousand troops of his excellent army were preparing under his orders to invade it? And who would have suspected that those airs on the flute and that philosophic billing and cooing covered the clink of coins? Voltaire wanted to be reimbursed for his traveling expenses, and Frederick would not agree. At the very moment when Voltaire was exerting his greatest charm, Frederick wrote to Charles-Etienne Jordan, a writer attached to his court: "Your miser will drink the dregs with his insatiable desire to get rich. He will get thirteen hundred crowns. His lightning visit of six days will cost me a hundred and fifty crowns a day! A rich reward for a madman! Never has a great lord's jester had such handsome wages."

Voltaire returned to Brussels with the money handed over so grudgingly, but he came back no wiser than he had started. If he had read the letter to Jordan he would have known that he was only a jester—of the highest class, certainly, but too expensive. What was most annoying of all was that Frederick knew everything that had been cooked up by Cardinal de Fleury and his emissary.

Voltaire's arrival in Brussels was not exactly a triumph: awaiting him were the lawsuit and Emilie's jealous tears. He felt guilty, so guilty that he wrote to D'Argental to ask him to intercede for him and obtain her forgiveness for his six-day stay with Frederick and the letter ended: "Never has Madame du Châtelet been so far above kings."

It would have been better for her if the comparison had never arisen, for clearly for several days she had been judged "below" the King of Prussia. But she behaved perfectly. As soon as she and Voltaire were together again she stopped complaining and resumed her usual cheerfulness. "He has finally arrived, in tolerable health apart from an eye inflammation. All my troubles are over—he swears to me they are over forever," she wrote D'Argental. But there was also Frederick, and she was under no illusion as to his sentiments about her. "I believe he is against me, but I defy him to hate me more than I have hated him these last two months. A ludicrous rivalry, you will agree," she added.

Jordan reports that Voltaire, hoping to ingratiate himself with Frederick, had spoken so disparagingly of Emilie that the King was shocked.

But at the same time it fed his hopes that Voltaire would return to Prussia. "The poet's brain is as light as his style, and I flatter myself Berlin will prove attractive enough to make him return here soon, the more so as the marquise's purse is not as well lined as mine," he wrote.

Such was the "friendship" between Frederick and Voltaire. Frederick's innuendo was false. No financial interest entered into Voltaire's liaison with Emilie. It was he who spent all his money on Cirey, and he was glad to do so. This love and generosity were beyond Frederick's comprehension. It was unfortunate, however, that Voltaire descended at times to the same vulgar level as his royal philosopher-host.

Small Matters of Literature and Business

Back in Brussels, Voltaire set to work once again, rewriting *Mahomet* —a Voltairian Mohammed who bore little resemblance to the prophet of Islam. He was dying to see the play performed, but he was not in Paris to present it to the actors, conduct rehearsals, and envelop it in the usual cloud of scandal and curiosity.

On the way to Paris he and Emilie stopped in Lille, where Voltaire's niece, Madame Denis, lived. Her husband exercised the lucrative function of military supply officer. As soon as Voltaire made his appearance in Lille all the important people in the town flocked around him. Soon after his arrival he contacted one Monsieur de La Noue, an actor and writer of tragedies in charge of the town theater, whom he had met previously. He had even asked him, on Frederick's behalf, to get together as soon as possible a company of actors for the theater in Berlin. When everything was ready the actors sent word to Frederick, who was busy waging war and for the moment required no other pleasure or glory. He therefore sent the mummers packing, and La Noue, who had staked all his money and all his credit on the venture, was ruined and in despair. But he bore Voltaire no grudge for having misled him with false promises, nor even for having written a play on Mahomet, though he had written one himself. "Our two *Mahomets* embraced at Lille," Voltaire wrote to Cideville. But Voltaire's eclipsed the other: the worthy La Noue put his rival's play on and it was a triumph. Voltaire thought the Lille audience was the most intelligent in the world. Even the priests were enthusiastic. Among them was an Abbé Valori whose brother was French ambassador in Berlin: Voltaire requested him to send the brother a full account of his triumph. Frederick would certainly not be unmoved by it.

At the same moment that Voltaire was sending Frederick news of *Mahomet*'s triumph in Lille, Frederick was sending Voltaire news of his victory at Molditz. The two letters crossed. There then ensued the astonishing spectacle of Voltaire interrupting the performance and coming on stage to ask a French audience to applaud Frederick of Prussia's victory, despite the fact that the victory was an affront to France. Voltaire, drunk with vanity, said: "You'll see, the Molditz drama will make mine a success too." And both dramas did in fact turn out to be successes.

During all these years of study, continually interrupted by his travels and filled with the writing, rewriting, and rehearsing of plays and the preparation of never ending lawsuits, Voltaire still found time to be ill every other day, and above all to augment his fortune. He now lent money to lords. This seemed foolish enough, for they were troublesome debtors, but Voltaire had noticed that though they took a long time about it they always paid up in the end. The speculations he entered into with men of business, on the other hand, did not always turn out so well. In his opinion these people were vulgar and reckless, and bound to end up bankrupt sooner or later. There was one called Charles Michel whose bankruptcy caused Voltaire to lose an enormous sum.

According to his enemies, both past and present, Voltaire was a miser, tightfisted to the point of baseness. If this was really true the Michel affair ought to have enraged and appalled him. But in fact, though resignation was by no means his chief virtue, he took it philosophically. He did not really feel strongly about questions of money. He was fond of money because it was indispensable to his way of being a gentleman. Whether he lost large amounts or spent them or gave them away did not matter—it did not jeopardize his lavish, aristocratic way of life. This is not the attitude of a miser.

Why, then, did he insist on getting back his traveling expenses from Frederick? The explanation is that it was not a matter of a sum to be gained or lost but of something owed him. Frederick had told him to come, and the person who gives the orders ought to pay the bill. Though sometimes stingy with servants, Voltaire usually paid people amply for services rendered. Whenever he ordered anything, the next sentence was always "the money is on deposit with such and such a banker," or "the bearer will hand over such and such a sum." His claim on Frederick was not made out of a morbid appetite for money but out of a kind of moral and intellectual need for clarity and precision. He was the son and grandson of men who had kept their accounts to the penny for centuries. He expected the same scrupulousness from other people, and it is not surprising if their dilatoriness, indifference, or dishonesty sometimes made him impatient or peevish. Frederick's niggardliness is more repulsive than Voltaire's insistence. If the money that Voltaire gave away or spent on others or allowed others to steal from him is set against the sums he claimed back on occasion with a graspingness unworthy of him, the balance shows that he was generous, often munificent.

In the autumn of 1741 he and Emilie were in Paris. They stayed with the Comtesse d'Autrey, who by a strange coincidence lived in the house that had formerly belonged to the Comtesse de Fontaine-Martel. Voltaire, doubtless remembering playing the role of Lusignan in the private performance of his *Zaïre* that had been given there, must have felt quite at home.

Madame du Châtelet's lawsuits wearied her, but thanks to Voltaire's skill they also made her rich, and she wanted to have a fine town house in Paris. She bought the elegant Hôtel de Lambert, built by Le Vau and decorated by Le Sueur and Le Brun. But there was no furniture and it needed repairs; in short it was uninhabitable. Though Voltaire never lived there, he at once took charge of the work. He chose the gallery where the library was to be, and was soon up to his ears in elaborate plans for the mansion. Voltaire the supposed "miser" thus embarked on expenditures of several tens of millions of his own money to improve a house that was not his and that would eventually go to Emilie's children. As at Cirey, he spent a fortune.

Scandals at Court and in the Theater

On December 21, 1741, Emilie returned to Cirey without Voltaire. He was dying to exert his charm at Versailles. But no minister or favorite gave him the long-awaited sign that would gain him entree at the court. He therefore decided that the air there did not agree with his austere ideas and resigned himself to being merely a "citizen philosopher." "I no longer have the health of a courtier," he explained to friends. It was true. He had the soul of one, but not the physical endurance. It was an exhausting life, an impossible one for someone who suffered from colic three days out of seven, and tertian or quartan fevers the rest of the week. A courtier had to stand about for hours, and walk, hunt, dance, eat and drink, play, laugh and cry at the King's bidding. He had to be ready for anything, like a soldier on active service. He couldn't allow himself to feel the cold and muffle himself up in fur caps and thick woolen stockings or put on his dressing gown at five o'clock in the evening as was his habit. A courtier had to be able to waste entire days and nights exchanging small talk, gaming, or doing nothing but stand about waiting. And so Voltaire moved out of the little apartment he had taken in Versailles, just in case. The court would have none of him: he would have none of it. A true philosopher.

Before long he was to give the court reason not only to be standoffish but also to hound him mercilessly. All Paris was passing from hand to hand the copy of a letter Voltaire had just written to the King of Prussia. Contrary to his representations, Frederick had concluded a separate peace with Austria, without even informing France, his ally. Président Hénault imparted the news to Madame du Deffand, who was taking the waters at Forges: "Have you heard about the latest scandal? A letter from Voltaire to the King of Prussia, the maddest thing imaginable. He has written him that he was quite right to make peace, that half Paris thinks so, that he barely beat Cardinal de Fleury to it, and that now all he has to do is amuse himself." What Voltaire had said about opinion in Paris was unfortunately true, but he had libeled Fleury, who was a loyal ally.

The letter had a disastrous effect at Versailles. Madame de Mailly, the current favorite, was furious and demanded that Voltaire be made an example. The latter swore that he had had nothing to do with the letter, that its style was beneath him, and all the usual disclaimers of authorship. But Madame du Châtelet herself recognized the letter. Unable to woo Versailles, he had wooed Berlin. Only as second best, as Frederick would have said, but he had certainly chosen the wrong moment to congratulate the King of Prussia on betraying France.

Hénault recommended "a decampment to Brussels." So much for the decorating of the Hôtel de Lambert, the delights of Cirey, the triumphs at the Comédie Française. *Mahomet* was never to get any farther than Lille.

Voltaire wrote to Madame de Mailly, imploring, cajoling, promising, requesting an audience. Everyone who was anyone in Paris was against him. Madame du Deffand put the problem with her usual malicious lucidity: it was not a matter of finding out whether or not Voltaire had written the letter, since everyone knew that he had. The question was to know how the letter had gotten from Frederick's pocket into the salons, the alcoves, and the streets of Paris. "To discover how it came to be spread abroad, that is where the real mystery seems to me to lie," the marquise said.

The police, thieves, Voltaire's rivals at the Prussian court—all were suspected. Voltaire even suspected the aged Cardinal de Fleury. Everyone was suspected, save the real culprit, Frederick, who was laughing up his sleeve: he had had his agents distribute copies of the letter to all the embassies in Paris—including his own, to divert suspicion. His motive was his desire to bring about a final break between Voltaire and France, and to get him exiled for life. Whereupon Voltaire, having nowhere to go, would fall into the arms, or rather the clutches, of his philosopher-king.

The story had a surprise ending: Louis XV took no interest in the matter. Either through lassitude or indifference, he took no measures against a pen-pusher whom he neither admired, liked, nor respected. Thus, without realizing it, he played a clever trick on Frederick: Voltaire remained in Paris, in peace. No one was more astonished than Voltaire, who never learned of Frederick's treachery.

Mahomet was about to be put on at the Comédie Française. The atmosphere was not exactly propitious. Voltaire had the play presented to the cardinal, but Fleury made no comment and let matters take their course.

The first performance was given on August 19, 1742, before a brilliant audience: princes, great dignitaries and titled aristocrats, ministers, ambassadors, judges. The author's scandalous reputation had filled the theater. *Mahomet* was a huge success that night, but the next day disaster struck: it was realized that *Mahomet* was not the Mohammed of the Koran. What the foolish had taken to be an attack on the alleged prophet of Islam was in fact an attack against Christ. Actually it was not any one religion but religion itself, whatever the nature of its prophet, that Voltaire had chosen as his target. A theologian incited people in the streets to violence against Voltaire, saying that because the names Mahomet and Jesus Christ both had three syllables it proved that the first was used to disguise the second. People untouched by fanaticism, people of taste, didn't need to count the syllables to share this opinion. Lord Chesterfield, who had read *Mahomet* in Brussels, was not deceived for a moment. He wrote that he had found thoughts in it more brilliant than just, had immediately perceived that Voltaire had attacked Christ in the character of Mahomet, and expressed surprise that this was not observed at Lille.

The play's most violent enemies were the Jansenists. There was a great uproar during every performance and the play was banned after the third night. Voltaire was furious: "I shall dedicate *Mahomet* to the Pope, and I expect to be named bishop *in partibus infidelium,* since that is my true diocese," he wrote.

Courting the Court and the Academy

Hardly had the curtain gone down on *Mahomet* than Emilie and Voltaire, on August 22, 1742, were again on the road for Brussels. They stopped at Rheims, to attend theater performances, dinners, and balls. Emilie was in fine form, and this restored Voltaire to the best of spirits. "Never has she danced better, never shone better at supper, never eaten so much or stayed up so late," he wrote.

By September 2 they were in Brussels. Frederick, "in siren's accents," immediately summoned him to Aix-la-Chapelle. Voltaire hastened thither, but it was a brief visit: he set out on a Monday and was back by Saturday. They had only time to libel half of Europe together. Frederick reminded Voltaire of what he was offering him: a house in Berlin, lands in Prussia, a pension, titles. . . . Voltaire politely declined; he was still trying to avoid offending Versailles. He had even asked Cardinal de Fleury's permission to visit Frederick and had tried to get sent officially to Prussia—he wanted to be of service. But the court was not interested, and the cardinal did not even deign to reply.

Emilie was bored in Brussels, but for once Voltaire found this prolonged stay in one place restful. He was always ill, and yet he managed to work fourteen hours a day.

The relation between his maladies and his work is interesting: "Your friend is slightly ill," Emilie wrote to D'Argental, "and you know that when he is ill he can only write poetry." When ailing he composed verses, when well he philosophized; and whatever his state of health, he kept his accounts. But as he was almost always ill, he devoted most of his time to poetry. Emilie cared little for poetry, but she came to like it for love of her poet.

In November 1742 they were back in Paris. Voltaire resumed his wooing of Cardinal de Fleury, and with such success that the minister wrote: "You are pure gold, monsieur. I acquainted the King with your letter, and he was well pleased with it." Voltaire would have made a splendid courtier: a few months earlier Versailles had wanted him hanged! If he had not been so awkward, if he had not had such a penchant for melodrama, he would have had a most brilliant career at court. On the other hand, if he had not had that extraordinary power to flatter and charm, he would have been hanged ten times over. Unfortunately, with one stroke of the pen or lash of the tongue he undid months of subtle flattery.

Voltaire and trouble were almost synonymous terms. He had barely arrived in Paris when a volume of scandalous texts bearing his name appeared. Monsieur Hérault was once again alerted. Voltaire protested that it was slander, that the texts were not his, that someone was trying to destroy him. The printers must be brought to trial and strung up by the neck. The culprit was one Didot, a forebear of the Didots who later became a renowned family of printers. He was arrested, but he had a wife and eight children and pleaded poverty. After swearing never again to sell forbidden books, he was released. Voltaire knew what printers' oaths amounted to and had him watched by the police. Sure enough, once out of prison he started to sell the same forbidden books as before. Voltaire brought a new charge against him, Didot was arrested once more, again he promised to mend his ways, and again he was let go. One might continue the story indefinitely: it constitutes a major part of the history of bookselling in the eighteenth century. The sale of banned books never stopped. The authors went to prison, and so did the booksellers. They were eventually let out, and went on as before. Voltaire, like all the rest, had forbidden books printed and distributed all his life. Apart from a few inconveniences, the system proved to be almost as liberal as the principle of "freedom of the press." And it was much more exciting.

Voltaire had never deprived himself of the pleasure of lampooning either the Academy or the academicians. But it was the same with the Academy as with the court. He did not feel entirely fulfilled as long as he was not a member. And at the age of forty-eight he still did not belong to either. He could hardly blame anyone but himself—or rather, the hatred his pranks engendered—for his talents, his manners, and his way of life would have made him quite naturally a member of both. What he needed were powerful friends to silence the resentment against him.

He counted largely on Cardinal de Fleury—and the King—to bring round the academicians who were against him. But the cardinal let him down. Voltaire wrote to Frederick: "Two days ago the cardinal, who has been quite ill, took it into his head, having nothing better to do, to go say mass at a little altar in a freezing-cold garden." This was at the end of

December 1742; the cardinal was ninety. As the price for not wanting to be, in his words, a "mollycoddle" like the Baron de Breteuil and have mass said indoors, Fleury caught pneumonia following these outdoor devotions and died at the beginning of January 1743.

Voltaire therefore was obliged to wait for another opportunity to have himself put forward for the Academy. Actually, outside Paris no one could understand why he was not already a member. All Europe thought he was one, that he was its finest ornament. To a traveler who informed him that Voltaire was not a member of the Academy, a German prince answered: "Then who is?"

Seeing the place at the French Academy slipping through his fingers, Voltaire decided to canvass for one at the Academy of Sciences. He reminded people of his *Mémoire sur la nature du feu* and his *Mémoire sur les forces vives*. And he found supporters. Fontenelle's chair was then vacant, and who was better fitted to fill it than Voltaire? Fontenelle had been a wonderful popularizer, and Voltaire was an even better one. His enemy, La Beaumelle, found a particularly poisonous way of describing this particular talent: "This occupation suits Monsieur de Voltaire particularly well, since he is the best person in the world at writing what others have thought."

Monsieur de Réaumur and Maupertuis gave him wholehearted support and even made him promise to give up poetry for science. At Cirey, this would have delighted Madame du Châtelet, but Madame de Graffigny and Madame de Champbonin would have wept. Madame de Graffigny wrote: "The lovely lady [Emilie] persecutes him all the time to make him stop writing [poetry], but the fat lady [Madame de Champbonin] and I do all we can to thwart her. It is a dreadful thing to prevent Voltaire from writing poetry." One day, to her delight, Voltaire told Madame de Graffigny, who was making a vain attempt at reading Newton, "Never mind Newton, that's all just dreaming. Long live poetry!"

But neither verses nor physics would open the door of the temple to him: he was refused membership in the Academy of Sciences. Among the academicians there were fanatical Leibnitzians and worthy bigots who swore they would break all their test tubes and retorts if Voltaire was admitted.

So he turned once more to the Académie Française, where he had been told that the King would not oppose his election. He thought a dazzling —and respectable—literary success would silence his enemies. *Mérope*, one of his best tragedies, which he had been working on for several years, brought him that success.

He spread it about that the Comédie Française had refused the piece. This was not true, but the story enabled him to engage in a little play acting. He read *Mérope* to the Abbé de Voisenon, who embraced him with tears in his eyes and said it was a work of genius. Well, Voltaire told him, the actors had just refused it. Voisenon rushed straight to the Comédie

Française and told them they had turned up their noses at the most sublime masterpiece of the French theater. Overcome with confusion, they accepted *Mérope*.

The actors in fact had not refused *Mérope*. They merely wanted to put it on after the play they were currently rehearsing. Unable to bear this postponement, Voltaire made up the story about its being refused, and thanks to his shrewd and disingenuous little scene, *Mérope* was staged first.

It was a triumphant success, perhaps the greatest in the history of the French theater. The thunderous applause both for the play and for the author went on and on. Voltaire tells how, as he was hiding in the box of the young Duchesse de Villars, the audience insisted on his showing himself, and the audience in the pit demanded that the lady kiss him. She did so, we are told, and the audience went wild. Again, Voltaire has embellished the truth. He was in Madame de Boufflers's box, with the Duchesse de Luxembourg, and all he did was kiss the latter's hand.

He had gone to infinite trouble to ensure the play's success. Not only had he rewritten it, taking into account his friends' criticisms, but he himself had directed the rehearsals with a professional minuteness and ardor, acting along with the actors. He was transfigured. There were no more colics or fever, he was everywhere at once, assuming every face and voice. It was he, always at death's door, who breathed life into the rest. One of them, Mademoiselle Dumesnil, exclaimed in exasperation: "But one would need to be *possessed* to do what you want me to do."

"Yes, indeed, mademoiselle," he answered, "one has to be possessed to excel in any art."

At all events Mademoiselle Dumesnil surpassed herself, thanks to the play, to the author's advice, and to her own genuine talents.

One of the most ecstatic admirers of *Mérope* was the Abbé de Bernis, a stout, chubby, debonair man of the cloth, and at that time hard up. He said he was prepared to pardon idolatry if the idol was Voltaire. Coming from another churchman, this impiety would have been no small praise; from the worldly Abbé de Bernis it was merely a compliment.

It was not certain that the Academy would take such a liberal view. The insuperable obstacle was Voltaire's militant and insolent impiety. His avowed enemy at the Academy was Boyer, Bishop of Mirepoix. To disarm the devout, Voltaire wrote a letter to the chief minister. The Academy wanted him to be religious, so religious he would be; in fact he was an exemplary Catholic already. He referred to "those pages of his work sanctified by religion." He described *La Henriade* as "nothing other than a eulogy of virtue submitting to Providence." His enemies reproached him, he said, "with [being the author of] some *Philosophical Letters* or others."

Everyone in Paris read this letter with stupefaction. Some laughed and others were furious, but no one was taken in by it. Monsieur de Voltaire's "devotion" was as celebrated as his talent as a poet. The angriest reaction of all came from Frederick. As he saw it, Voltaire was betraying irreligion.

Voltaire explained later that it was the irascible Bishop of Mirepoix who had forced him into all this: "He ought to have known," he said "that it is a very sad virtue to play the hypocrite." Voltaire did not allow himself to be too depressed by this virtue when its possible reward was a place in the Academy. He had another fiery opponent too, the Archbishop of Sens. "But," Voltaire wrote, "I shall do all that is necessary to disarm and pacify [him]." "All that is necessary" meant that there was no room left for scruples. Voltaire went to see the Bishop of Mirepoix and proposed a bargain: Madame de Châteauroux, the King's current favorite, hated the bishop, but Voltaire offered to get him restored to her graces through his friend Richelieu if the bishop would support his election.

But "the ass of Mirepoix," as Voltaire called him, was obstinate. When Voltaire asked, "Would you then refuse me a place in the Academy?" Boyer answered, "Yes, and I shall crush you."

Thenceforward this ass with a miter and Voltaire were mortal foes. Maurepas, the chief minister, was on the side of the bishop: he was a dangerous enemy and was said to have served as model for Gresset's comedy, Le Méchant (The Backbiter). Voltaire's chances were ruined altogether when someone told the King it would be unseemly to elect Voltaire to the place left vacant by Fleury. Was the greatest infidel of the age to deliver a eulogy to the cardinal? The King therefore opposed Voltaire's election.

On March 22, 1743, the Bishop of Bayeux was chosen to fill the empty chair. The worthy prelate did nothing to increase the Academy's prestige. Voltaire swore that he had renounced the Academy forever. What he really meant was until the next time a seat became empty.

Berlin, or the Second Best

While this setback embittered Voltaire, it delighted his friend Frederick. It served his interests, and he struck while the iron was hot. "Master your feelings," he wrote to Voltaire. "Scorn the nation that knows not how to value the writings of a Belle-Isle and a Voltaire, and come to a country where people love you and are not bigots."

Paris had become hateful to Voltaire. Crébillon the elder, who was the censor for theatrical works, refused to approve Voltaire's latest tragedy, Jules César. Voltaire heard the news as he was coming out of a rehearsal, at midnight. It was the last straw. He at once promised Frederick to leave France and come to the Prussian court.

Emilie was in tears: she was being deserted. Everyone in Paris was laughing at her woe, for they knew all about Voltaire—his loves, successes, squabbles, and reconciliations. But Emilie thought only of Voltaire, the ungrateful Voltaire already on the way to Holland. In an attempt to lure him back to Paris, she did all she could to get *Jules César* put on. She knew Voltaire, and also knew that, though Frederick might seem a stronger attraction to him than she was, the theater was the strongest attraction of all.

Tired and ill, Voltaire fretted at Frederick's palace at The Hague, awaiting his orders to proceed to Berlin. Frederick, "the coquette," was deliberately making him wait. But Voltaire did not waste his time. He never did. With the skillful help of his friends D'Argenson and Richelieu he succeeded in overcoming the French court's disfavor and getting himself entrusted with a secret diplomatic mission on behalf of the Ministry for Foreign Affairs.

Once again he had made his entrance onstage as a secret agent. We know the outline of the play; it is an amusing one. But the best part, the dialogue, is missing. All we have left is the moral, which is deplorable.

Voltaire, ever the actor, pretended to Frederick that he had left France in a rage. He says that Louis XV encouraged him to adopt this ruse. But this does not seem very likely. Nonetheless, he found this play acting amusing: skeptical of everything and everyone, he forgot to mistrust his own vanity.

Voltaire expected to make profits out of both Versailles and Prussia. Frederick had made fabulous promises, which François-Marie Arouet, the notary's son, had meticulously recorded; Versailles had not actually promised anything, but the King was known to discharge his debts faithfully. If Voltaire is to be believed, he was even prepared to pay in advance. As soon as Voltaire was appointed envoy by the ministry, he got his cousin Marchand appointed supplier of fodder to the army. Marchand was only a figurehead; the profit was really to go to Voltaire. Not content with that, he asked for and obtained the right to supply military uniforms to the army. This was big business. It was not Voltaire's first venture of the kind: in 1734 the Pâris-Duvernet brothers had helped him get into the business of supplying provisions for the army, and he had realized six hundred thousand livres profit from it. In 1741 his friend D'Argenson had given him the opportunity to benefit by another profitable supply contract.

While Voltaire was in Berlin his cousin Marchand neglected to deliver the thousand military uniforms that had been ordered. The Minister of War was furious and threatened to withdraw the contract and award it to someone else. It was Emilie who intervened to save the situation: she advanced money and had the uniforms delivered. Another profitable deal. "Fortunate are those who serve you," Voltaire wrote the minister. He might have added, "as are those who serve themselves in the process." But as a stern philosopher he wrote of the war: "How much longer will the people be ruined, and allow themselves to be sent off to be scoffed at, hated, and slaughtered in Germany, just to line the pockets of Marquet and company?"

Marquet was an army contractor; and the words "and company" included Voltaire himself.

To pacify Emilie he took her into his confidence about his secret mission. He explained that he had left her only because he was forced to, that he did not like Frederick and hated Prussia. He had gone merely out of patriotic duty. Emilie had heard this story before and was not convinced: "I believe nothing without proof," she wrote. Voltaire sent her the minister's letters, but she insisted on seeing Voltaire's reports to the minister as well, and the instructions the minister sent to what can only be called his spy. It was not long before obliging diplomats informed Frederick too of the interesting arrangements between his Virgil and the court of France. It is a frightening thought that he might have been more severe.

Voltaire's debut as an agent had begun amid the cobwebs of The Hague. Frederick's steward there, Count Podewik, was involved with the wife of a Dutch minister, who filched her husband's secret reports and passed them to him. He in turn gave them to Voltaire to read, and Voltaire transmitted the gist of them to Monsieur d'Argenson—under the supervision of Emilie. Thus Versailles got its information, and Voltaire took advantage of "the fortunate obscurity that enables me to be received everywhere as more or less an intimate." The mission he had been charged with was to detach Frederick from his English alliance and bring him back to the French. It was a difficult task: the French army, with its lack of organization and undistinguished leaders, was less than impressive to Frederick. Conveniently situated as he was at The Hague, Voltaire endeavored to create a diversion by stirring up trouble between Frederick and Holland. He had learned that Holland was supplying arms in Prussian territory. He informed Frederick of this, pointing out that a justifiable war against the wealthy Dutch republic might bring in substantial war indemnities payable in florins, and that such an operation need only briefly interrupt Frederick's versifying and philosophizing.

Versailles would have liked such a conflict to come about, but Frederick refused to fall into the trap. Voltaire did not give up the idea, however. "I shall attempt to brew up this little cup of poison," he wrote to the minister.

At last Frederick was ready for Voltaire to go to him, not at Aix-la-Chapelle as arranged, but in Berlin, where Voltaire arrived on August 30, 1743. All was embraces and compliments, and Voltaire stayed in the King's palace. This intimacy was useful for his political designs. Frederick, who was somewhat reticent, mostly listened while Voltaire talked, but sometimes he would enter into discussion. This was only by way of amusement, for he did not let Voltaire see what he was really thinking. Voltaire attempted to outguess his royal host. When pressed, Frederick admitted that he didn't trust Versailles: he knew that the French minister was intriguing in Vienna against Prussia. Voltaire pretended to be outraged, and said the Austrians were spreading lies: "Have they not slandered you before? Did they not say last May that you were about to form an alliance with the Queen of Hungary against France?" Frederick was rather taken aback to find Voltaire so well informed. He protested: "I swear to you nothing is further from the truth."

In his report Voltaire notes that the King could not swear to the truth of his statement without lowering his eyes. One of the actors in this comedy still had some way to go. But the other was not a man to be taken in by an equivocal oath. Voltaire embarked on the composition of a poem on the alliance with France. Europe would be at peace, after being sacked; a good brisk war and the Continent would be at Louis's and Frederick's feet. The philosopher and pacificist takes to diplomacy and soon there is a war on. But Voltaire did not finish his poem. Frederick's musicians awaited only His Majesty's flute to soothe the savage breasts of the two poets who had just been carving up Europe.

Frederick played the flute fairly well. He composed too, but not as well. To please Voltaire he put on for his friend an opera whose score he had written himself, with an Italian libretto. How could anyone resist such flattering attention? A king rarely did as much even for a visiting monarch. And being, or believing himself to be, on such intimate terms with Frederick, how could Voltaire refrain from questioning him as to his political projects? The questions were written down one half of the page: opposite it was a blank where the King was to write his answers. This amazing document came into the hands of Beaumarchais, who made a copy of it. One would have to be Voltaire to subject an absolute monarch, in the middle of the eighteenth century, to a tyranny which only the free citizens of twentieth-century democracy will now put up with at the hands of inquisitive bureaucrats. Frederick had already begun to have suspicions about the object of Voltaire's visit. But he answered the questionnaire—à la Voltaire, with jests and snatches of song, ironies which make it only too clear how seriously he took Voltaire's diplomacy.

But Voltaire stubbornly returned to the charge. He wanted a serious message in Frederick's own hand to send to Louis XV. But he insisted too much. At last Frederick replied sharply that there would be no message: "The only message I can give you for France is to tell her to behave herself better."

In spite of this snub, Voltaire wrote to Versailles that his mission was progressing slowly but surely. The father of Candide was sometimes a blind "optimist."

When Frederick was preparing to visit his sister, the Margravine of Bayreuth, whom Voltaire had already met, the Solomon of the North played a little game with him. Voltaire begged Frederick to allow him to come along, and although he did not say no, from the nature of his silence it was clear that it did not mean yes. Voltaire was told that he could rest during the King's absence: His Majesty was concerned about the poet's health. Voltaire protested that his health had never been better and that he would follow his Solomon to the North Pole. But he still was not invited. Nonetheless, he went along in Frederick's entourage and his arrival in Bayreuth was a triumph for him: the margravine adored him, and Ulricka, Frederick's other sister, was even more charmed by him. Voltaire paid extravagant and daringly familiar court to her, but all was saved by the tone and wit and manner in which he did so. Larking about with a royal personage in eighteenth-century Germany was a dangerous game. But he brought it off safely and was in seventh heaven. He had theater, politics, intrigue, gallantry, an entourage of princes, luxury, and an audience always ready with lavish praise. What could be better? He wrote: "Bayreuth is a delightful retreat, where one can enjoy all the pleasures of a court without the inconveniences of grandeur." The remark, of course, was a sly dig at Versailles.

He remained at Bayreuth for a fortnight, an unforeseen extension of his German visit. He had sworn to Emilie that he would not stay more than ten days in Berlin. But the worst of it was that he failed to write her for a fortnight. On the last day he sent her three or four lines to tell her he was staying with the margravine.

Emilie was distraught and wrote letter after letter to the D'Argentals. The truth was that Voltaire had forgotten Emilie, intoxicated as he was with the incense he was burning at the feet of the two princesses. The courts in Germany were really delightful and offered him pleasures that France did not; he was better appreciated there. The German aristocracy, while just as cultivated and hospitable as the French, was much less formal and intellectual, more sensitive and simple. Voltaire liked England, but he had grown bored there; in Germany he was never bored. Emilie knew and dreaded this. She was jealous of Frederick, Ulricka, the margravine, and all of Germany. How could she forgive the court at Bayreuth for having so engrossed him that he did not write for nearly a month, except three or four lines—"the sort of note he might send from his room to mine"?

And what was he doing in Bayreuth? "How should I know? Will he perhaps stay there for the rest of his life? Indeed I should believe so if I did not know he has matters of business that must be attended to in Paris. He is mad about the German courts. But is that any reason to make me die of anxiety?" she wrote D'Argental, begging him to inform Voltaire about "the state he has put me into." As Emilie struggled with her papers and her attorneys in Brussels, weeping, Voltaire sent the following poem to Ulricka, who was later to become Queen of Sweden:

Souvent un peu de vérité
Se mêle au plus grossier mensonge.
Cette nuit dans l'erreur d'un songe
Au rang des rois j'étais monté.
Je vous aimais, princesse, et j'osais vous le dire.
Les dieux à mon réveil ne m'ont pas tout ôté,
Je n'ai perdu que mon empire.

Often a grain of truth/Is mingled with the grossest lie./Last night in the illusion of a dream/I had ascended among the ranks of kings./I loved you, Princess, and dared to tell you so./The gods at my awakening did not take everything away from me,/For I had lost only my kingdom.

His courtly wooing had in fact not been ill received. But the poem was the subject of comment when it was sent to Paris and somehow began making the rounds. It was said that Frederick had taken Voltaire's declaration amiss and compared him to a dog baying at the moon. But these ill-natured remarks were made by Piron, not Frederick. What is certain is that Frederick chaffed Voltaire about his love for his sister—and for the French ambassador's cook, who willingly granted him her favors. Voltaire replied that he had fallen back on the cook because "I did not have an army of three hundred thousand men at my disposal to carry off the princess."

That his boldness was not resented is shown by the fact that he was later sent portraits of Frederick, of the Queen Mother, whom he was authorized to visit without waiting for an invitation, and of Princess Ulricka.

But though the Prussian royal family were easygoing about such things, Frederick became very touchy about politics, and at the end of Voltaire's visit he kept him at a distance. Voltaire noticed this and wrote to the minister about it. He found himself in a very awkward position—the King was suspicious of him, and Monsieur de Valori, the French ambassador, was jealous of him. The latter was vexed that he should have been sent an understudy in the person of Voltaire, and without warning. Moreover, he, like everyone else, knew about the "secret" mission. Voltaire dealt with both flanks. He explained to Frederick that he was simply seeking a rapprochement between him and Louis XV for the good and for the glory of both monarchs; and Frederick accepted the explanation. And he explained to Monsieur de Valori that, as his mission was secret, all the credit, if he succeeded, would accrue to the ambassador, and hence he was really doing him a good turn. Monsieur de Valori also accepted the explanation.

Frederick was as good as Voltaire at brewing up poisons. He had sent Monseigneur de Mirepoix all the letters in which Voltaire had made rude remarks about His Eminence. Frederick and Voltaire were equally perfidious; but Frederick was crueler. He was playing at cat and mouse but, whereas he was in no danger, Voltaire risked receiving a mortal blow from either side. Of course he had put himself in this position of his own free will. But he was a mere poet in an age when talent earned certain privileges but when the life of the individual counted for little in the machinations of kings or ministers, or even against the cudgels of a Chevalier de Rohan for that matter. Voltaire nonetheless found out about Frederick's double dealing. "Voltaire has ferreted out, I know not how, our little treachery against him, and is extremely piqued; he will unpique himself, I hope," Frederick wrote to Monsieur de Rottembourg, his ambassador in Paris.

It was certainly a most peculiar friendship. Voltaire wrote to the minister: "He thinks to win me for himself by destroying me in France, but I swear I would rather live in a town in Switzerland than pay so dearly for the favor of a king capable of mingling treachery with friendship."

Despite so swearing, Voltaire nonetheless continued to enjoy Frederick's poisoned favors. His vanity was too great for him to renounce King Frederick who, if he was not a real friend, was at least a partner of the same mettle as himself. Their malicious games had become indispensable to both of them. On October 12, 1743, they took leave of one another with the usual compliments. But confidence between them was dead: one had scented the spy, the other had scented the traitor. This time there was no haggling over money: all Voltaire's expenses were reimbursed.

He bought a new coach which broke down on the second day of the journey and threw him in the mud, together with his trunks and cloaks and caps. He was bruised, but no bones were broken. The peasants who came to his rescue started filching his belongings, and he took refuge in a nearby village. But no sooner had he begun to calm down than the village caught fire and he was obliged to flee. He betook himself to the château of the Duc de Brunschwig, who welcomed him with open arms. Voltaire spent five days amid the pleasures of this charming court, while Emilie wept day and night in Brussels. Then he proceeded from château to château, on what he called "a celestial journey in which I go from planet to planet until I come at last to the chaos of Paris."

But before Paris there was Brussels. Emilie was overjoyed to see him again and forgave him through her tears. He behaved as though he had merely gone out for the morning and was back for lunch.

The Court Unbends

The two of them left without delay for Paris, where Voltaire was impatient to claim his reward for his services. On their arrival in early January 1744, Voltaire was disappointed to find that the ministry considered his services to have been unimportant. According to Voltaire, he had been the victim of a conspiracy. He reported later that Monsieur Amelot, the minister who had employed him, stammered, and for this reason was dismissed by the King's favorite, Madame de Châteauroux. Voltaire contended that he had been dragged down with Amelot when the latter fell from favor. The episode sounds like something out of *Zadig;* but the truth was quite different. Monsieur Amelot was dismissed not because he stammered but because he was inefficient. moreover, Amelot fell from favor in April 1744, and Voltaire had left Paris at the end of January for Brussels. He had come back to Paris empty-handed, and so he went away again. But his heart was full of bitterness.

This time Emilie kept him at her side. She was certain he would not go back to Berlin—she had made him swear he would not. "If he were to break this vow," she said, "it would be a double sacrilege," for he had so vowed in the presence of Monsieur d'Argental as well. Her confidence is touching. But vows meant nothing to Voltaire when he made up his mind to go or stay, be ill or well, write, speculate, or invent a witticism that was certain to get him in trouble. He was bound by nothing, except in business by contracts and in daily life by work.

Work offered a means of keeping him from straying. So his friends Richelieu and D'Argental, together with other nobles who formed what were called *cabinets*—that is to say, coteries to thwart the ministries by exerting their influence on the King directly—suggested to Voltaire that he write entertainments for the court. These sparkling, frivolous friends relieved the King's boredom; the policies they advocated had only one object: to undermine those of the ministers. The result of these antagonisms was of course the political catastrophe that overtook France under Louis XV.

Richelieu was master of the royal revels, and to please him Voltaire undertook to write *La Princesse de Navarre*, half opera, half ballet. He threw himself into the work with his usual fervor, whatever the undertaking, and this time further stimulated by the hope of gaining a firm foothold at the fascinating but recalcitrant court. He submitted his manuscript to his friends, who criticized it mercilessly. He balked a bit but eventually took their remarks into account, including the illegible observations of Richelieu, to whom he wrote: "It is true that you write like a cat." But he added, "You are a great critic, no one is more witty than you at teatime."

This sort of work was tricky. It must displease no one—a task that was even more difficult than pleasing everyone. He would have preferred to write a tragedy.

He and Emilie retreated to their haven at Cirey, arriving in June 1744. It seemed more beautiful a place than ever. Voltaire felt so happy he dated his letters from "Cirey-en-Félicité." Président Hénault visited them on his way back from Plombières and Voltaire was flattered by his astonishment and delight. "In short, I assure you one thinks it must be a dream," Hénault wrote to D'Argenson. Voltaire read him *La Princesse*, and he liked it all the better because Voltaire had dutifully adopted all his corrections. "He has succeeded in being both touching and comic," Hénault wrote.

During this visit to Cirey, Emilie was undergoing a sort of anti-science cure. Koenig had inoculated her with "Leibnitzism," and now she was ridding herself of its effects. She was taking lessons with one Father Jacquier, a Newtonian. Voltaire was delighted with the progress Newtonism was making in France.

The writing of the court entertainment introduces a new character into the life of Voltaire. Jean-Philippe Rameau was to write the music for *La Princesse de Navarre*. Rameau was afflicted with a disagreeble temperament, soured by his long and difficult struggle to establish himself as a composer, which caused him to become inordinately proud, once he was successful. To him the words of an opera were entirely unimportant. One day he shouted at a singer: "Faster! Faster!" She answered that she couldn't articulate the words any faster, and even if she could they would not be understood. "What does that matter?" he answered. "All that needs to be heard is my music."

His librettists were mere slaves whom he treated with incredible rudeness. Nor did he shrink from tampering with the text supplied by the author of *Zaïre*. Voltaire naturally got wind of his meddling: indeed, Rameau himself made no attempt to conceal it. Voltaire's friends expected the worst. But he only gave the meddlesome composer a pitying smile. Although Rameau was obviously an eccentric, he had great gifts. However Voltaire's forbearance was not due to his respect for Rameau's talents alone. It was absolutely necessary that the entertainment be performed, with or without Rameau's alterations, so there must be no rupture between the two of them. What did the music or the rudeness of its composer matter provided the librettist got the chance to install himself firmly at court? "This trifle is the only resource I have left, if I may say so, since Monsieur Amelot's dismissal."

On September 14, 1744, Emilie and Voltaire returned to Paris. The King had been at death's door at Metz and the entire city was rejoicing at his recovery. Belief in the monarchy was still so strong that Louis the Well-Beloved was welcomed in Paris with transports such as few kings have inspired. He was astonished but, unfortunately for his descendants, he was not moved by them.

Madame du Châtelet wanted to join in the general rejoicing, see the fireworks, and shout "*Vive le roi*" with the artisans and shopkeepers. She and Voltaire were caught in a monstrous traffic jam in the Rue Croix des Petits Champs. Two thousand carriages were milling about, surrounded by a huge, excited crowd. To make matters worse, Emilie's coachman was from Cirey and this was his first visit to Paris. They did not know what to do. If they stayed where they were and spent the night in their carriage they would not get a wink of sleep and would go hungry till the next morning. So Emilie boldly leaped out, decked as she was in all her usual paint and finery and sparkling with diamonds, and dragged her nervous poet through the sea of people. Without receiving so much as a shove or a bruise or an insult, they covered the distance to the Place Vendôme, where Président Hénault had his town house. He was not there, but that was incidental. They went in, sent round to a neighboring eating house for a roast, and had a bottle brought up from the cellar. During their merry repast they drank the président's health and wrote him a letter to tell him how many glasses they had raised to him and to send him their best wishes.

This time the poet did not present himself at court empty-handed. He had written a suitable poem, Les Evénements de l'année 1744 (The Events of the Year 1744), subtly singing the King's praises. The poem was conveyed to the King, and the Cardinal de Tencin was asked to tell Louis that Voltaire had come specially from Cirey to Paris to celebrate His Majesty's return. "In a word, let the King be informed that I put three candles in the window," he instructed the cardinal.

The campaign to gain the King's favor had begun.

In January 1745, Voltaire went to stay in the Hôtel de Villeroy at Versailles for the rehearsals of La Princesse de Navarre. He pretended to see nothing and nobody, and maintained that the place left him completely indifferent: "At Versailles I am like an atheist in a church." But he practiced all the devotions of a perfect courtier. It was tiring to be "the King's jester at the age of fifty," he wrote. He posted ceaselessly back and forth between Versailles and Paris. He continually praised those at Versailles, "the King highly, Madame la Dauphine subtly, the royal family discreetly." And all because he enjoyed this hustle and bustle, any hustle and bustle. On February 8, 1745, he wrote and told D'Argenson what he expected from the court. In the first place, he wanted the office of Gentleman in Ordinary to the King's Chamber. This was merely a small favor, an amenity, and, "small favor being merely a bagatelle, there may be added to it the little post of historiographer. And in place of the pension as pertaining to the historiography I ask only the remuneration of four hundred livres. All this seems to me quite modest, and Monsieur Orry is of the same opinion. He agrees to all these trifling sums."

Voltaire had apparently already consulted Monsieur Orry, the Comptroller General of the Royal Treasury, so that when the King or his chief minister should be informed of his request, Treasury approval would be immediately forthcoming. So the affair was settled. In any case, Voltaire deserved the post of historiographer more than anyone else, and it should have been offered to him without his having to ask for it.

In the midst of the arias and declamations of La Princesse, in the thick of the intrigues and excitements attendant upon the staging of a lavish court spectacle, Voltaire learned of the death of his brother Armand on

February 18, 1745. Voltaire had not been at his brother's deathbed, but he attended his funeral. His unloved brother had played one last trick on him. Instead of choosing his brother François-Marie, his nearest heir, as executor as he ought to have done, Armand had named his nephew-in-law, Monsieur de Fontaine d'Hornoy, Marie-Elisabeth's husband. Voltaire was hurt by this insult. He would have been more capable than anyone else at managing and multiplying the money Armand left, and honesty would have prevented him from harming his nieces' interests. Admittedly, Voltaire lacked neither weaknesses nor deviousness, but his integrity in family matters is unassailable, despite his critics' claims to the contrary.

His brother left him only a life interest in a small part of his fortune. But to thank Monsieur de Fontaine for acting as his executor, Armand left him a diamond worth six thousand livres. That was what you got, Voltaire realized, for poking fun at the Jansenists. They might forgive you "in God's name," but not in their wills.

Armand's funeral did not take up much of Voltaire's time. The theater at Versailles did not yet exist, so for the performance of *La Princesse* a temporary theater was set up in the royal riding school. It was a huge auditorium, but nonetheless it was too small to hold all those who claimed the right to attend. Everyone pushed and shoved; the ushers urged people to move as close to each other as possible. Part of the audience had to be shooed out: the fainting and swooning took up more time than the performance itself. *La Princesse de Navarre* was the principal attraction the program of festivities in celebration of the marriage of the Dauphin and Maria Teresa of Spain, which lasted for a week and were divided between Paris and Versailles. The town rushed to court, the court hurried back to town. Voltaire found such an atmosphere highly stimulating. The exhausted actors did not look as if they could hold out a day longer. The King was due to arrive for the gala performance at six o'clock. He did not get there till seven, and it ended at midnight. Apparently the author was the only person who was enthusiastic about the evening. His play was reasonably successful and no more. There were objections to the mixing of comedy and sentiment, and to some the comedy appeared crude. The bride had a taciturn Spanish temperament, and Voltaire's verbal arabesques did not draw a single smile from her. She was not amused by his "jests," and in her opinion the whole thing lacked "nobility and grandeur." Paris found the entertainment long and tedious on the whole, though it had its witty moments. But as no one detected anything scandalous between the lines, or discovered any treasonable allusion in the play, it was a *"succès de cour."* The audience was politely bored.

For this commonplace, conventional, and sycophantic work so at odds with the remainder of his life's work, Voltaire received the King's compliments and the promise, from His Majesty's own lips, of the post of historiographer and a pension of two thousand livres. These promises were fulfilled a month later. So great a reward for such sorry stuff inspired Voltaire to write:

> Mon *Henri IV* et ma *Zaïre*
> Et mon américaine *Alzire*
> Ne m'ont jamais valu un seul regard du roi.
> J'eus beaucoup d'ennemis avec très peu de gloire.
> Les honneurs et les biens pleuvent enfin sur moi,
> Pour une farce de la foire!

My *Henri IV* and my *Zaïre*/And my American *Alzire*/Never earned me so much as a glance from the King./I had many enemies and little glory./Now at last honors and rewards are showered upon me,/For a fairgrounds farce.

It is impossible to disagree with him.

Anyone who imagined he would chew over old grievances would be misunderstanding him. He rejoiced, rather, in the present favor he was enjoying. The court's praise of his "fairgrounds farce" intoxicated him. He would have sold his soul for the tainted but enchanted pleasures of the court. But he was careful not to admit it. He wrote to the moralist Vauvenargues that he now frequented the court out of neither pleasure nor self-interest but out of gratitude. He thereby meant to suggest that he was fulfilling a disagreeable but very moral obligation. But we know that his duty as he really saw it was not to the King but to his own interests. He was not satisfied with his post of historiographer. Nor had he forgotten that the Académie Française owed him a chair, a chair he had to have. Impiety had heretofore closed the door to him; piety would open it. But who was to give him the necessary testimonial of piety, fidelity, and Christian humility? Why, the Pope, of course!

The Victory of Voltaire (and the King) at Fontenoy

Just as he was about to devote himself to this important project he was obliged to make a little journey which delayed the execution of his schemes. One of Madame du Châtelet's sons was seriously ill with small-pox at Châlons. He hurried to the sickbed to comfort the boy and his mother, abandoning the court, his pleasures, and his ambitious projects. In so doing he lost time that could never be made up and ran the risk of fatal contagion for the sake of Emilie and her son.

When he returned to Versailles no one would receive him. He was in quarantine. No exception to the rule was permitted. Voltaire wanted to see the minister, but there was nothing to be done. "I must simply sacrifice myself to the prejudice that excludes me from Versailles for a period of forty days because I visited someone who is ill at a distance of forty leagues!"

Nevertheless Voltaire was entrusted with the drafting of a letter from the King to the Tsarina, who had offered to act as mediator in the War of the Austrian Succession. The letter contains a sentence that would be surprising if he did not know that it was Voltaire, and not Louis, who wrote it: "Kings may aspire to no other glory in their own kingdoms but that of making their subjects happy." A century before Voltaire this would have been just a pious commonplace with no political meaning. In the age of Louis XV it had a political meaning, but only for the enlightened few.

Voltaire's post of historiographer brought him the honor of celebrating in verse the most famous military victory of the age: Fontenoy. D'Argenson wrote to tell him of the victory, a pleasant surprise after many French defeats. Voltaire was filled with enthusiasm.

So he wrote his dithyramb, full of glory and encomiums, heroes and laurels. D'Argenson, who had actually been in the battle and seen the horrible butchery, reminded his friend of "the dead, the dying, the reeking wounds." This was a new way of talking about war. Voltaire too had a horror of what D'Argenson called "the inhuman rush for the spoils." It was the dawning of a new kind of feeling: "sensibility" and science made a simultaneous entry into the lives of people of breeding. But the hour had not yet come for shedding tears over the ordinary soldier in an official poem such as Voltaire's. His business was to praise the King, the princes, and the court, and he succeeded very well. What earned him the most admiration was the incredible number of proper names he had managed to introduce. Everyone wanted to be mentioned in this great "combat report" written in alexandrines, which they knew would circulate all around Europe and which they expected would become an immortal work. Hence to be mentioned by Voltaire in his poem on Fontenoy meant to enter the halls of fame. The King was not displeased with the poem. Lord Chesterfield said it crammed in the names of more living, dead, and wounded than the official army report. There was not much room left for poetry.

Those who were not mentioned were naturally furious. Voltaire was besought on all sides to add more stanzas: "My head is in a whirl," he wrote. "I know not how to deal with all the ladies who want me to praise their cousins and lovers." As he had written the first version too quickly and new details kept cropping up, not to mention new names, he announced that he would publish further editions, each one more complete and up to date.

People laughed at his announcement and at his snobbishness. He quoted only the most distinguished names in the book of heraldry. Someone wrote a parody which began, "Comrades, ordinary soldiers, I sing only of you," and mentioned only such "titles" as Fanfan la Tulipe.

Someone else wrote *La Requête du curé de Fontenoy* (*The Petition of the Curé of Fontenoy*). Referring to all Voltaire's additions, it said: "One hopes that by the hundredth edition it will begin to take shape. . . . If the poem is not considered good enough to provoke criticism, the author will provide some himself in an attempt to stir up interest and promote the sale of his own work."

For once Voltaire took all these gibes good-naturedly. He had written the poem with the object of pleasing the King and the court, and that object had been attained. What was more, the poem was being read, recited, and sold everywhere. He wrote to D'Argenson: "Do you think it would be ill received, monseigneur, if you were to tell the King that in ten days there have been five editions of his glory? Pray do not forget to execute this little court maneuver."

In fact, the poem itself was a "court maneuver." But in that day and age, not to mention others, everyone was willing to resort to such devices, and no one, including his critics, who also engaged in such maneuvers, performed them with half Voltaire's skill.

VIII

The Pope is an idol whose hands are tied and whose feet are kissed. (*Remarks*)

Courage is not a virtue but a fortunate quality common to rascals and great men. (*Contant d'Orval*, Volume I)

From the time of the ancient Romans, I know of no nation that has enriched itself by victories. (*Contant d'Orval*, Volume I)

Money is made to circulate, to make the arts blossom, to buy the industry of men: he who puts it aside is a bad citizen. It is by not saving it that one makes oneself useful to one's country and to oneself. (*Contant d'Orval*, Volume I)

It is the lot of mankind for truth to be persecuted from the moment that it begins to appear. (*Contant d'Orval*, Volume II)

Is politics nothing other than the art of deliberately lying? (*Contant d'Orval*, Volume II)

He who has nothing new to say must keep silent or at least contrive to have his uselessness forgiven by means of his eloquence. (*Historical Miscellanea*, Fragment on history)

The best politics is to be virtuous. (*Panegyric of Louis XV*)

I have lost a friend of twenty-five years' standing, a great man whose sole defect lay in being a woman. . . . A woman capable of translating Newton and Virgil, who had all the virtues of a gentlewoman, will doubtless merit your regrets at her passing. (Letter to Frederick the Great, on the death of Madame du Châtelet, October 14, 1749)

To the Academy via Rome

Voltaire was determined to get into the Academy, but to do so he had to efface his reputation for impiety. Ever since *Mahomet* had been banned in Paris in 1742, he had been eager to have his piety attested to by the Pope in person, and improbable as it seems, he managed to carry off the feat.

Pope Benedict XIV, a man of letters rather than of religion, was a good Pope for the Age of Reason. Like Virgil, he was known as the "Swan of Mantua." He was too subtle, too much of a Roman, to be easily taken in, even by Voltaire.

Voltaire's request could not be presented directly: so he mounted his attack on Rome on two fronts simultaneously. One would have been enough; two was almost too much, for the second attack nearly spoiled everything.

Voltaire persuaded his friend D'Argenson to get the French ambassador in Rome, the Abbé de Canilhac, to convince the Pope of the piety of the author of La Henriade and Zaïre. Both D'Argenson and the ambassador were highly skeptical, but Voltaire insisted that the Pope was very well disposed toward him, and read and admired his works.

Meanwhile, to make doubly sure, Voltaire had also commissioned a special ambassadress, Mademoiselle du Thil, a friend of Madame du Châtelet's. Mademoiselle du Thil, who somehow managed to combine orthodox Catholicism with admiration for Voltaire's work, had a friend named the Abbé de Tolignon. The abbé, well indoctrinated by the lady and by Voltaire himself, was sent off to Rome bearing various Voltairian relics: a special copy of Mahomet, some verses dedicated to His Holiness, and an inscription to be engraved beneath the portrait of Benedict which Voltaire was hoping to receive. "I am one of his admirers as well as one of his flock," it read.

In return Voltaire begged the Pope to send him some medals. The Abbé de Tolignon obtained two. "Two enormous medals," Voltaire exclaimed, "and a letter from the abbé of His Holiness' Bedchamber!"

When the Abbé de Canilhac then presented himself to the Pope and said his piece, the Pope listened with some surprise: he had heard all this before. However, he did not breathe a word about the gifts he had previously received and the other medals already sent, and simply promised two more, even bigger ones, to the ambassador, "for the feast of Saint Peter," he said. The Pope did not wish to offend anyone, but neither was he deceived.

Benedict XIV had listened benignly to both the emissaries Voltaire had dispatched to the Holy See to plead his cause, and believed what he chose to believe. But Voltaire was afraid that the two abbés might find out they had both been sent on the same mission and be furious. Benedict's discretion saved him. In due course D'Argenson transmitted the Pope's portrait, and Voltaire wrote him: "Monseigneur, I have just received the portrait of the chubbiest Holy Father we have had for a long time. He looked like a devilish good fellow who knows what all this business really amounts to." Voltaire did not forget that the object of the whole exercise was to impress the King, the court, and above all the Academy: "You might now tell His Most Christian Majesty what a Most Christian subject I am," he added.

The Pope had also accepted the dedication of *Mahomet*. In a letter dated August 17, 1745, Voltaire presented himself as an "admirer of virtue" dedicating "to the head of the true religion a work against the founder of a false and barbarous one." He placed the book and its author at the Pope's feet, asking His Holiness to protect them both. If anyone was upset now when *Mahomet* was performed, he must be a heretic.

The Pope found the tragedy admirable, the inscription for the portrait charming, Voltaire's poem on Fontenoy splendid. "You cannot doubt the singular esteem I feel for such celebrated talents as yours," he wrote him.

Voltaire set about making as much capital as possible out of the Pope's favors. "Truly, heaven's blessing cannot be too widely spread abroad, and His Holiness' letter cries out to be published. It is only right, my worthy friend, that respectable people should know I am protected against them by the mantle of God's Vicar," he wrote to D'Argenson.

A Courtier's Work Is Never Done

Voltaire's star at Versailles had risen considerably since writing the poem on Fontenoy, which Louis XV had said was beyond criticism. "I think the King the finest connoisseur in the kingdom," Voltaire wrote. The court was so pleased it wanted more, and Richelieu commissioned a court entertainment in praise of the King and Fontenoy. It was to be called *Le Temple de la gloire* (*The Temple of Glory*) and was to be noble, heroic, and lavish. This suited Voltaire perfectly; the only drawback was that the composer was again to be the insufferable Rameau.

In a letter to Richelieu on this subject, dated August 20, 1745, the name of the Marquise de Pompadour occurs. It was at this time that the favorite took this name and became the King's "official mistress." As she was of bourgeois origin the court had assumed that she would never be granted this lofty status. Her real name was Madame Lenormand d'Etioles, and Voltaire knew her family well. He used to visit her mother, Madame Poisson, who was mistress to the farmer-general Lenormand de Tournehem. The Poisson women had been mistresses for generation after generation. Antoinette, the new Marquise de Pompadour, was said to be the daughter of Monsieur Lenormand, who had married her to his nephew Lenormand d'Etioles, his sublessee. They liked to keep the tax farming and their women in the family. They lived in style, and Mademoiselle Poisson had had the most refined education. Everyone knew of her beauty, her charm, her wit, her talents. She was good at music, she painted, she was quite a skilled jewelry maker. Her extraordinary career was no miracle: it was due to her personality and to the self-confidence that had been instilled into her from the age of nine. Her mother used to say, "My daughter is a royal morsel." Guided by his own star, Voltaire came into Antoinette Lenormand d'Etioles's orbit, and with the aid of Richelieu he helped to forward the designs of Madame Poisson and her daughter, who was grateful to him forever after. (Voltaire is to be found at every crossroad of the eighteenth century, as well as in all its secret corridors!)

In 1745 he paid several visits to Etioles. He drank a bottle of Tokay there which he pronounced superior to one Frederick II had sent him. This was praise indeed, and the Poissons must have appreciated it.

Before the favorite was officially recognized, Voltaire had written some verses about her which doubtless pleased the King. Voltaire knew how to invest his flattery as well as his money.

He had a rival for Madame de Pompadour's affections, of whom, it should be noted, he was not jealous: the frivolous, vain, and eloquent Abbé de Bernis. This pleasant, good-natured young man, pink and chubby, bore no one any malice and amused the divine Antoinette. She had need of amusement, and she attached the abbé to herself and to France. He was good at inventing facile, flowery verses, ephemeral as spring blossoms but fragrant while they lasted. Perhaps it was this gift that earned him his nickname, *"Babet la Bouquetière* [Babet the Flower Seller]." This did not keep him from becoming a member of the Académie, a minister, and a cardinal. Madame de Pompadour even had him given two ministries—rather excessive for someone who seemed overburdened when asked to carry so much as a pair of fans. It was he who was entrusted with the task of answering the passionate letters the King wrote every day to the favorite. Louis XV was delighted with these replies and showed his satisfaction: one day he met Bernis carrying under his arm a roll of tapestry that the marquise had just given him for upholstering the chairs in his apartment. Louis asked to see it, and, as Bernis undid the material, the King drew out a roll of gold louis and gave them to him, saying, "This is for the nails."

Such was the atmosphere in which Voltaire lived at Etioles or Champs, accompanied by Madame du Châtelet, ever faithful both to her studies and to the gaming tables. Meanwhile he worked at *Le Temple de la gloire*. He informed the minister that he was ready to write up the King's most recent campaigns "very historically," with an abundance of documents and details. But Voltaire wanted the King to be informed, to encourage his historiographer, to say to him, too, "This is for the nails." His friend D'Argenson, the minister of war, asked him to draw up a diplomatic protest to Holland, which had broken a treaty with France and was using against her an army of prisoners on parole. Voltaire acquitted himself well: the style of the protest was lofty and firm without being too imperious. D'Argenson was pleased, especially as he had given Voltaire only two days, and the royal historiographer had sat up two nights in order to be ready in time.

Madame du Châtelet was then invited to accompany the court to Fontainebleau in the Queen's train of coaches. Departures on such occasions were extremely complicated. Questions of precedence were ticklish, and ladies often fainted quite away. Emilie, always rather free and easy, got into a coach before the Duchesse de Luynes and two other ladies, sat down inside, and invited the others to join her. They turned on their heels and went off to another coach. When she arrived at Versailles, Emilie sensed a considerable chill. The Duchesse de Luynes had complained to the Queen. The Duc de Richelieu came and formally escorted Emilie to the Duchesse de Luynes, who was supposed to conduct her to the Queen, in whose presence the duchesse would receive the necessary apologies from Madame du Châtelet. Richelieu had made Emilie promise to excuse herself as best she could, for the Queen was offended. Thus reprimanded by her former lover, Emilie did as she was bid, the duchess and the Queen accepted her apologies, and everyone was all smiles again. But for Emilie it must have been an unpleasant moment.

Voltaire, suffering from colic, did not arrive till the following day. His indisposition did not prevent him from paying his respect or from working. To write the history of Fontenoy he needed to show the battle from both points of view; he therefore needed some English witnesses. It happened that his friend Falkener, now Sir Everard, with whom he had stayed in London and to whom he had dedicated Zaïre, had been appointed secretary to the Duke of Cumberland, who had been in command of the English army at Fontenoy. Voltaire wrote off to him at once for information, even offering to post to Flanders to see Falkener if possible. But remembering, perhaps, his disastrous adventures in Prussia, Voltaire prudently abandoned the journey.

Back at Versailles, the King called for the promised festivities, during which Le Temple de la gloire was to have been presented. The festivities took place on November 27, 1745. There was a procession of classical heroes, all famous and all cruel. Finally Trajan appeared, victorious, magnanimous, adorned with all the virtues and showering blessings round him. Trajan was, of course, Louis XV, apotheosized.

The King liked the music offered him but said nothing about the poem, not because he disliked it but because Voltaire had shocked him. It was said that he had approached the King and said in his usual nonchalant manner, "Is Trajan satisfied?" Louis, it was reported, gave him an icy stare, and an equally icy barrier henceforth stood between them.

The episode was much embroidered. The King's cold look was the only readily verifiable detail. But rumor had it that Voltaire had embraced the King with odious familiarity, that the royal guards had flung themselves on him, that he had plucked at the King's sleeve, and that Richelieu in turn had plucked at his. Voltaire was then supposed to have said to Richelieu, "How dare you pluck at my sleeve?" It was all malicious gossip.

Fréron, for instance, got wind of the contretemps over Le Temple de *la gloire* and wrote of his long-time enemy: "It is well known he had never been lucky in the construction of his temples. I know of four of them: the Temples of Taste, Fame, Happiness, and Friendship. . . . If I dared I should suggest that he build a fifth: the Temple of Pride."

In actual fact Voltaire had simply been the victim both of his own boldness of speech and of the King's temperament. The king often withdrew into a haughty silence which was merely a mask for his genuine shyness. Voltaire was not the only victim of this characteristic and it did not impair the favor in which he stood at court. He did not really take *Le Temple de la gloire* seriously; he knew what occasional verse amounted to. What he was waiting for was the first vacant chair at the Academy.

Madame du Châtelet was delighted to see Voltaire growing attached to the court, and even more to see the court growing attached to Voltaire. She thought Berlin had lost its charm. But that charm was still working on others.

Frederick was recruiting. It amounted to a mania with the kings of Prussia: the father had filled his barracks by carrying off the King of France's subjects, and now the son embellished his Academy by wooing the writers and scholars of Paris with flattery and favors. In 1745, Frederick managed to persuade Maupertuis to be president of the Academy in Berlin. Versailles granted him leave of absence, thus serving the ends of Prussian propaganda. When writers and scholars sang the praises of the monarch who made them so welcome, it was easy to conclude that they had come to him because they were more comfortable there than at home.

Voltaire, who had never been so well treated at the French court as he was now, had an excellent opinion of it, lived only for it, and would clearly have liked to go on living for it. He was asked to write a second version of *La Princesse de Navarre*. It was a very tiresome assignment, and also rather humiliating. It made him look like the court jester. But the honeymoon was not yet over, and he agreed to rewrite it.

It was on the occasion of this not very brilliant entertainment that Jean-Jacques Rousseau made his first humble appearance in Voltaire's life and in literature. La Popelinière, the farmer-general, lived in great state and surrounded himself with a large but somewhat mixed court of noblemen, writers, artists, actors, high society, lesser society, and the rest. This court was known as "the menagerie." Richelieu used to come there in search of entertainments for the court. The outstanding figure was Rameau. The La Popelinières had launched him, and his success was the reward of their efforts and of their patience. Toward the end of 1745 he was collaborating with Jean-Jacques Rousseau, whom he treated with the utmost contempt. Rousseau had written an opera, *Les Muses rivales* (*The Rival Muses*), which La Popelinière had had put on. Rameau first praised to the skies each passage that he liked, then said that it was plagiarized. Richelieu was enthusiastic about the opera and wanted to have it performed at Versailles. But Rameau was furious; Madame de La Popelinière supported him, and Richelieu therefore chose something else. To soothe Rousseau's hurt feelings, however, he gave him the job of arranging Voltaire's unfinished poem, *La Fête de Ramire* (*Ramire's Feast*), as a court entertainment. Richelieu asked Rousseau to write to Voltaire to ask permission to make alterations and write in bridging passages. In fear and trembling, Rousseau did so. His letter began: "Monsieur, I have been working these fifteen years to make myself worthy of your glance." (For one who insisted that he scorned flattery he was not doing badly.) Rousseau's letter would doubtless have moved even a heart less susceptible to praise than Voltaire's. Voltaire gave him full permission to do whatever was necessary. Voltaire was charming and affable. Yet Rousseau described the latter's courtesy as "base obsequiousness." He said that Voltaire had been polite to him only because he, Rousseau, was on such excellent terms with the Duc de Richelieu and Voltaire was afraid that, if he offended Rousseau, Rousseau might cause trouble between him and the duc. It is evident that Jean-Jacques didn't know his Paris. How could he possibly have imagined that Voltaire needed the help of an unknown like himself to win over the Duc de Richelieu? Jean-Jacques was already making himself out to be a simple, humble soul, but in reality he was clearly crazy with pride.

La Fête de Ramire was presented in due course on December 22, 1745. Neither Voltaire nor Rameau attended the performance. Rousseau was present, but his name was not mentioned. Rameau had objected to having his illustrious name set side by side with Rousseau's unknown one, and Madame de La Popelinière connived at its omission. Voltaire seems not to have taken any interest in the matter one way or the other.

What he continued to take seriously was his task as royal historiographer. He buried himself in the archives of the War Ministry for days at a time, reconstructing the Battle of Fontenoy. As always, he did a thorough job of things as a matter of principle. But he also wanted people to be grateful, and expected praise for his diligence and pensions for his purse. "I am goodhearted enough," he wrote, "to do for nothing what Boileau failed to do for a handsome salary." He was stretching things. The poet Boileau certainly had not done much as a royal historiographer, but what had Voltaire done apart from the poem on Fontenoy? And he already had his pension. But it was not sufficient; he wanted royal "favors." He wrote to D'Argenson: "Hence tell the King and Madame de Pompadour that you are pleased with the historiographer, and be kind enough to say a word to the King about the work in which his own glory plays so great a role."

Then someone began circulating a rumor that Voltaire had fallen from favor. He was furious. How dare anyone say that the best poet of the age was out of favor at the court of the best of kings? His indignation, though sincere, was so theatrical that it seems affected.

Admission into the Academy and a Sorry Affair

In March 1746, Président Jean Bouhier, a member of the Academy, died. Although the long sought after chair was now open, Voltaire was seized by a fever of conflicting fear and desire. He had had such rebuffs from the Academy before that he was afraid to solicit the coveted chair in person. He wrote to the D'Argentals in the third person: "Voltaire learned yesterday of the death of Président Bouhier, but he forgets all présidents, living or dead, when he sees Monsieur and Madame d'Argental. People have already spoken to V. about who is to succeed Président Bouhier; V. is ill; V. is in no state to exert himself; V. is growing gray-haired and cannot decently go knocking on people's doors even though he counts on the King's support. He thanks his dear angels. He would be very flattered if he were indeed wanted, but will always be afraid to take steps on his own behalf."

So his "angels" were to go about ringing doorbells for him, and he thanked them in advance. For his own part, aloud and on paper, he emphasized what a good Catholic he was and how much he admired the Jesuits. He reminded people that he had received the Pope's blessing: "I feel sure that the declared good will of our common Father assures me that of his most important children."

Louis XV pronounced in his favor, so he was as good as elected. But to be elected was not enough: he wanted to be wanted, sought out, and welcomed as a friend. For Monseigneur de Mirepoix and other members of the Academy it was a different situation. They admitted Voltaire because they could not do otherwise. His enemies were silent, and that was as much as could be asked of them. Montesquieu's harsh comment gives an idea of the atmosphere: "Voltaire is not handsome, he is only pretty. It would be a disgrace to the Academy if Voltaire becomes a member, and one day it will be a disgrace if he is not one." The Academy's choice was between the present shame of accepting Voltaire and the future one of having refused him. They chose the immediate and passing danger.

Voltaire's election brought many of his enemies to life and seemed to multiply their numbers. The worst was one named Roi, who had attacked Voltaire before. Now, in 1746, he republished his *Discours prononcé à la porte de l'Académie* (*Speech Delivered on the Threshold of the Academy*) in 1743, and his *Le Triomphe de la poésie* (*The Triumph of Poetry*) written in 1736, with up-to-date notes on the life of Voltaire.

Roi is forgotten today. In 1746 he was considered an excellent poet and a most disreputable man. He had been in prison, not for the daring of his thought but for faking legal documents: he was a conseiller at Le Châtelet.

On the day of Voltaire's election the Académie and the salons of Paris received Roi's parcel of vilifications. The blow was well prepared: Voltaire's happiness was poisoned before he had had time to taste it. He had come to think that, because he was a courtier and because he had received the blessing of the Pope, he was beyond the reach of calumny. He now had a rude awakening. His enemies such as Desfontaines, Fréron, and La Beaumelle all knew one another and got together against him. Roi was dangerous because he was consumed with desire to get into the Academy himself. Every time a chair fell vacant he suffered the tortures of the damned, and each announcement that someone else had been elected to a place he would never occupy drove him wild with rage. Hence the torrents of vituperation.

Ten years before, Roi had tried to put himself forward as a candidate. Fontenelle had him informed that no one in the Academy would agree to sit beside him; he was already notorious. The poor wretch was often imprisoned and beaten. In 1754 the Comte de Clermont had him so savagely cudgeled by his Negro servant that he was said to have died as a result. In fact he did not die until 1764. Perhaps he suffered for ten years, but he stayed in bed for only ten days.

Roi's hatred of Voltaire had burned even hotter when he proposed an entertainment and the court rejected it in favor of his rival's *La Princesse de Navarre*. He had then written a parody of the *Poème de Fontenoy*. Voltaire had revenged himself by including in the frontispiece of *Le Temple de la gloire* a statue of Envy which was drawn to look like Roi. To make sure there would be no mistaking him, the statue wore the ribbon of the Order of Saint Michael. Voltaire was quite capable of descending to such low tricks—but he paid for them dearly. In this particular affair he perpetrated so many that he ended by losing both face and case, even though his enemies were despicable.

Voltaire ignored all the small fry and concentrated his bitterness and his vengeance on Roi. He personally directed the campaign against the slanderer and his publishers. He scrutinized shopwindows and pointed out to the police the houses and shops of booksellers he suspected of selling Roi's attacks on him. He went to have one of the book-hawkers arrested, but when he led the police to the hovel they found the man was dying. The story got about: the new academician had personally conducted the police to arrest a man on his deathbed. This was only a beginning.

Voltaire had worked hard on the speech he would deliver when he was received into the Academy. Contrary to the usual custom, he made a real speech. Until then new members had merely delivered a short formal encomium to Cardinal Richelieu and an even briefer one to Chancellor

Séguier (the Academy's two foremost founders), and finally some empty politenesses about their predecessors.

Voltaire made his reception speech at the session of Monday, May 29, 1746. He recalled the fact that the Académie was the guardian of the French language and gave a description of the origins of the language and the effect great French authors had had upon its evolution and consolidation. He proclaimed its universality. All this seemed very novel; and it was indeed unprecedented then, though to us it appears quite normal, because Voltaire is closer to us than he was to many of his contemporaries, especially the academicians of 1746. In his speech he referred to foreigners who spoke and wrote French, and naturally included pinches of incense for Frederick, Catherine, and Benedict XIV. He then moved on to the academicians: Montesquieu, Fontenelle, his former tutor the Abbé d'Olivet, and even Crébillon, whom he hated and envied and who even more heartily hated and envied him. All were smothered in praises. He would have liked to flatter Maupertuis too, but the court suppressed this passage: there was no need to congratulate a deserter. This might have been a warning to him about the court's sentiments toward those who took their talents off to Berlin. He also included his friend the Duc de Richelieu, repeating the King's words to Richelieu on the battlefield at Fontenoy: "I shall never forget the service you have rendered me." Finally it was the turn of the King himself: "Would that I could see the statue of this humane monarch in our public squares, sculpted by our modern counterparts of Praxiteles, and surrounded by all the symbols of public felicity. Would that I could see written at the foot of his statue the words that are in our hearts: 'To the Father of his Country.' "

It might be supposed that these laudatory remarks were just part of the game: all one had to do was express them elegantly, exaggerate a little, not examine them too closely, and everyone was happy. But it is worth examining Voltaire's speech more closely. The King is praised not for his victory but for his humanity, and his statue is adorned not with trophies but with "the symbols of public felicity." This was something new. And the title "Father of his Country" was at least fifty years ahead of its time.

At the time, people did not analyze Voltaire's speech so minutely, but they were disconcerted by it, and in Paris, when people did not understand something, they sneered at it. It was observed that Voltaire's speech was made up of ill-assorted bits and pieces: the most brilliant pupil of the most brilliant rhetoricians had done badly in his most important academic test. It became a drawing-room game to read the speech aloud, altering the sequence of the paragraphs: it was supposed not to make any difference in what order they were read.

Meanwhile the police continued to arrest Roi's accomplices, and on their list was a certain Travenol, who played the violin at the Opéra. He hated Voltaire and had been doing his best to circulate Roi's *Discours prononcé à la porte de l'Académie*. When they came to arrest the violinist, Travenol's wife and invalid daughter set up an infernal howl. After six days this breadwinner, who had influential friends, was released. Rumor had it that Voltaire was responsible for persecuting helpless children, and though he was incapable of such cruelties, appearances were against him.

A certain Travenol came and threw himself at Voltaire's feet. But he was the wrong one: Travenol the violinist had fled, and it was his eighty-year-old father who had come in his stead to plead for him. Voltaire could not bear to have an old man at his feet, so he raised him up, they mingled their tears, and Voltaire promised to do all the old man asked. They had a meal together at Voltaire's table, complimented each other, and parted the best of friends. Then Voltaire had second thoughts. Had he perhaps been taken in? Indeed he had. Fresh pamphlets circulated and were traced to Travenol the younger. Voltaire was furious. The old man went to the Abbé d'Olivet, who took pity on him and conveyed a letter to Voltaire in which the father admitted his guilt and begged for forgiveness. But Voltaire, unmoved, brought charges against him, using the letter as evidence of his guilt.

The Travenols' lawyer was one Louis Mannory, who had long borne a grudge against Voltaire for having once put him off with promises when he had tried to borrow money from him. Voltaire said he had given him money, though with no hopes of getting it back; Mannory denied this. Apparently Mannory had not received any money, but Voltaire had sent him to Thiériot's brother, who was a clothier, to be outfitted with a decent suit in which to appear in court. Voltaire was justifiably outraged at the way in which Mannory had repaid his generosity.

The judgment in the Travenol case satisfied no one. Voltaire received only verbal consolation; his calumniators were lectured, but it was he who had to pay the court costs. Yet he had demanded the severest punishment; the strappado was the least of them. He made a public outcry as usual, explaining that public order itself was endangered when he, Voltaire, was slandered. Perhaps his frenzy was half sincere. The first thing Travenol did when he was set free was to write verses to celebrate having got off so lightly. With Mannory aiding and abetting him, he demanded damages for the distress that Voltaire's cruelty had caused his wife and daughter.

Although the judges had deemed Travenol incapable of writing anything, he now published pamphlets containing attacks on Freemasonry, thus demonstrating his supposed respectability.

Voltaire's thirst for revenge was still unsatisfied, and he brought new charges against Travenol. The violinist had excellent advisers, and the judges and public opinion were on his side. The judges had to choose between impiety that was rich, famous, powerful, and intelligent on the one hand and, on the other, the poverty of a modest and pious artist. For of course Travenol was pious, and of course he had never written any poems or possessed or distributed insulting pamphlets. As Travenol could not afford to pay the court costs, the public prosecutor himself advanced him the money for them. Voltaire had lost the case before it even began.

When the tradesmen to whom Travenol owed money tried to seize his effects at the Opéra they were prevented from doing so by officers of the law. Partiality no longer even bothered to hide itself behind a mask. Travenol published a libelous pamphlet against his colleagues at the Opéra. By now it was abundantly clear that he was a scoundrel and that he wrote scurrilous verse; he was accordingly dismissed from the Opéra. But even this could not change the picture the judges and public opinion maintained of him. Voltaire again lost his case, and again he paid the court costs. Travenol was again dismissed with a sermon; Roi and his friends nearly split their sides laughing; Voltaire gnashed his teeth; and all Paris mocked.

The "Rogue" Worth More Than He Seems to Be

The Travenol affair again demonstrates the complexity of Voltaire's character: he was capable, on the one hand, of blind rancor unworthy of him and, on the other, unable to resist the pleas of an old man who turns out to be a sly conniver. Marivaux, who did not like Voltaire but had an excellent insight into the character of others, said of him: "This rogue has a vice other rogues lack: he sometimes has virtues."

Not only sometimes, but often; and often, unfortunately, virtues inextricably commingled with his "roguery." The mixture is a disconcerting one, and some, in order not to be disconcerted, have preferred to see only the roguery. But this is an oversimplification. To redeem Voltaire somewhat, they occasionally add that he had talent. But it is not Voltaire's talent that redeems his faults: it is his virtues.

One sure guide to Voltaire's real character is his gift for friendship. His countenance was too often disfigured by hatred, hatred called forth by attacks on him by jealous enemies which often he himself inspired. But if this dark expression is set aside, his face is radiant not only with marvelous intelligence but also with kindness. His virtues shine forth most brightly in his letters, which survive, and his brilliance in his conversation, which does not, though it perhaps contained the essence of a whole civilization.

A rogue does not write to an unknown young man of letters. Voltaire wrote to Vauvenargues. Voltaire was dazzled by this young officer's letters: he sang his praises everywhere as a writer and as a philosopher. He had recognized at once Vauvenargues's hidden virtue and sensed the moral grandeur in certain of his lofty and melancholy reflections. Vauvenargues was sick, poor, and unknown: Voltaire divined the imperishable quality of his mind.

When ill-health forced him to leave the army Vauvenargues went to live in Paris, where he and Voltaire met quite frequently. Another young man, Jean-François Marmontel, who was a protégé of Voltaire's, used to marvel at these meetings.

"The conversations between Voltaire and Vauvenargues were the richest and most fruitful anyone has ever heard. On Voltaire's side, an inexhaustible abundance of interesting facts and illuminating reflections. On Vauvenargues's, an eloquence full of affability, grace, and wisdom. Never was argument conducted with such mildness, wit, and sincerity. And what charmed me even more was Vauvenargues's respect for the genius of Voltaire on the one hand and, on the other, Voltaire's tender veneration for Vauvenargues's virtue."

This relationship did honor to both men.

Voltaire Changes Secretaries and Coats of Arms

But neither the Travenol case, nor illness, nor business, nor visits to court or to Paris prevented Voltaire from writing another tragedy: *Sémiramis*.

The manuscript accompanied Voltaire and Madame du Châtelet wherever they went. In August 1746 they were staying with the Duchesse du Maine at the Château d'Anet. By September they were at Fontainebleau with the court.

In between there had been a domestic disaster: all Madame du Châtelet's servants had left on the same day, and Voltaire's, out of solidarity, had followed. Madame du Châtelet was exacting and stingy with her domestics. Voltaire was often obliged to oil the wheels by giving them secret tips. Moreover, Emilie was apt to be bad-tempered as well as tight-fisted. She was a philosopher only when in her laboratory and when in her library reading her esoteric books on science: anywhere else she was subject to whims and rages. To add to the general disorder, Voltaire's secretary chose this moment to die. This was the worst loss as far as Voltaire was concerned, but he remembered that Emilie's butler had sometimes helped his late secretary copy his manuscripts. He managed to get hold of the butler before he left, and made him his secretary. He was a man called Longchamp whom Emilie had brought back with her from Brussels after one of her many journeys there in connection with the lawsuit. With a certain amount of difficulty Longchamp had got used to Madame du Châtelet's caprices and odd ways. It was a long time before he would confess that she changed her shift in front of him, "naked as a marble statue." He wasn't made of marble. She had him heat the water for her bath and then got into it as if there were no one there. (Another lady, Madame d'Anville, had her valet actually lower her into her bath, but at least she took the trouble to have herself sewn up in a bag first.) Poor Longchamp could not get over it: "My entire person was no more and no less to her than the kettle I held in my hand."

He escaped these ordeals by taking up service with Monsieur. It was difficult work to begin with, and Longchamp's impressions are very revealing. The first morning, in the absence of all the other servants, he was obliged to be both valet and secretary. When Voltaire woke up he asked for his portfolio. Longchamp started to look for it. It was right under his nose but as the arrangement, or disarrangement, of the room was new to him he was unable to find it. Voltaire got impatient and pointed to a chair, crying, "There, can't you see!"

Then the trembling Longchamp was ordered to dress Voltaire's wig. He brushed and combed it as best he could, but when he handed it to Voltaire he was told it was too heavily powdered, and Voltaire said he would see to it himself. Voltaire demanded a comb, found the one he was handed too small, flung it on the floor, and asked for another. There was no other. Longchamp was told to pick up the other one then, and Voltaire set about vigorously disheveling his wig for himself. This done, he threw it on his head all askew, put on his coat, and went off without a word to breakfast with his Emilie.

One might judge Voltaire severely from this account, but Longchamp himself did not. At first he did not think he would remain long in Voltaire's service, but he soon realized that what he had taken for roughness was really only uncontrollable nervousness which subsided immediately once it exploded: "I saw afterward that, just as his outbursts of temper were fleeting and in a manner of speaking superficial, so his indulgence and kindness were solid and lasting."

Longchamp prudently engaged himself for the Fontainebleau visit only, but he remained in Voltaire's service from 1746 to 1754.

At Fontainebleau Voltaire was obliged to play the courtier, though he pretended to neglect his obligations. "Here I am at Fontainebleau, and every evening I resolve to go to the King's *lever*. But every morning I stay in my dressing gown with *Sémiramis*." But in fact he managed to acquit himself of his social duties as well as to complete his new tragedy. *Sémiramis* was slightly more tedious than the others, but Voltaire's contemporaries were fond of that sort of theater.

On December 22, 1746, he received from the King his appointment as Gentleman in Ordinary of the Bedchamber. It was to Madame de Pompadour that Voltaire owed his new title. It enabled him to claim that in him the Arouets of Saint-Loup had reached the very summit of society. He took this occasion to dust off his coat of arms and modify it a little.

Paris was blasé about such things and Voltaire's new dignity caused no stir there. But, strangely enough, it did cause a stir in Saint-Loup, in Poitou, the cradle of the Arouets, which Voltaire's great-grandfather Hélènus had left in 1620, a hundred and twenty-six years before. The moth-eaten gentry of Saint-Loup were furious that a mere Arouet should be ennobled and received by the King. One of them wrote to a relative, in a letter as full of spelling mistakes as of indignation.

"Esteemed Uncle, I learn that the King, moved thereto by ill-intentioned persons, honors with the title of Gentleman of his Bedchamber an individual called Arouet, of Saint-Loup, the son of a Mademoiselle Daumart, who has made himself a reputation under the name of Voltaire. The King will surely not affront the nobility by dispensing this upstart from furnishing proofs of his, which he will be obliged to seek on his mother's side, because on the father's they were all commoners; to dispense him from supplying proofs would be an insult to gentlemen of title and bearers of arms from father to son since time immemorial. I have decided, my dear uncle, together with other gentlemen in these environs who do not care to cheapen themselves, that we shall be justified in shutting our doors and our titles against this Voltaire. . . . You will tell us your opinion of all this when we dine at Vernay this Sunday." Coming back to earth after this high-flown tirade, this champion of nobility added: "The bay is tired after yesterday's ride; if the gray had been here I would have come to you instead of writing."

Useless Members of Society

The beginning of 1747 was taken up with historical research into the war of 1741. As usual Voltaire had frequent bouts of illness despite the fact that he had discovered some marvelous new pills which he recommended to everyone and swallowed in quantities that would have killed a man in robust health. Nonetheless he did not fail to fulfill his courtier's role. He sent an epistle to the Duchesse du Maine about the victory at Lawfeld on July 2, 1747. Everyone said it was not as good as the poem on Fontenoy, and they were right: besides, the poem was written for a king and the epistle only for a noblewoman. But the duchesse was pleased, at least, and invited Voltaire and Emilie to stay with her at Anet.

Emilie changed rooms three times in three days, the last time complaining of smoke. People laughed at the work that supposedly kept her at her desk all day. It was only during the day that she craved silence: at night she joined the others and was all activity. Voltaire had already begun entertaining the rest of the company and distributed gallant verses here and there. They would have been quite happy to have him if he hadn't had Emilie tied around his neck.

She was a difficult house guest. She had already raided the rest of the rooms for tables: she needed at least seven or eight for her papers, books, mathematical instruments, jewels, trinkets, and make-up. Everything was scattered about.

The couple had been invited in order to be entertaining, and the other guests considered them too unsociable. The days seemed endless, and they appeared only at night. "They will neither play nor take walks," wrote the Baronne de Staal. "They are useless in a milieu where their learned writings serve no purpose."

But at suppertime Voltaire would repay in an hour all the hospitality he had received. Even Emilie acted well, and sang beautifully—as everyone admitted. But criticism was soon forthcoming. "She is the sovereign and he the slave," the baronne concluded.

They did not stay long at Anet. Hastily gathering their papers and baggage together, they hurried off to see Richelieu, who had to go to Genoa and wanted to see Voltaire before he left.

The Danger of Saying "Knave" and Writing "Conquest"

By October 14 the two friends were again with the court at Fontainebleau. It will be recalled that Emilie was stingy over her servants' board; yet she was a reckless gambler. One evening, playing at the Queen's tables, she started to lose badly. The four hundred louis she had on her disappeared in a few moments; and she had not accumulated them without difficulty. Voltaire watched with mounting vexation: he hated wasting time and money in that way. Nevertheless he handed over to Emilie the two hundred louis he had in his pocket. They were swallowed up as quickly as the rest. He ventured a few remarks, but they were curtly rejected. So he resigned himself to dispatching a footman to borrow another two hundred louis at an exorbitant rate from a business acquaintance. But Mademoiselle du Thil, who had been of such help in stage-managing the appearance of his emissaries at the Pope's palace, happened to be present, and she gladly lent a hundred and eighty louis. The divine algebrist flung them all down, but instead of multiplying they all disappeared. Voltaire begged her to withdraw from the game, but she only jumped down his throat again and went on playing, giving her word in place of stakes. Then the real disaster began. She lost eighty-four thousand livres, which with the nine hundred louis she had lost earlier made a hundred and three thousand livres. Madame du Châtelet was not a rich woman. Voltaire had been following what happened with the silent fury and clairvoyance of one who has foreseen all and been powerless to prevent it. He had seen her rush headlong to her ruin. As she made her last unlucky throw of the dice he could not contain himself any longer and said, in English, "Do you not see that you are playing with knaves?" Few people spoke English in France at that time, but there must have been some present who did, for Voltaire saw with alarm that the crowd was beginning to whisper, repeating the insulting word he had just uttered. It was a dangerous word to use at the Queen's tables, around which sat princes of the blood and the most powerful ladies in the kingdom. The best thing to do was to vanish as soon as possible before any reprisals could be taken, for he had as good as committed treason. He was not really in the wrong, but the vices of the court were to be spoken of indirectly or not at all.

Emilie and Voltaire fled in the first post chaise they could find, which fell to pieces at Essonnes. They had no money to pay the wheelwright who mended it, so he would not let them go. Fortunately a passing traveler recognized them and paid the bill.

Voltaire was deeply apprehensive of the vengefulness of titled aristocrats, and with good reason. One Chevalier de Rohan in a lifetime is quite enough. He decided to take refuge with the Duchesse du Maine at Sceaux. But he could not just burst in in broad daylight without permission. So he holed up on a farm and sent a laborer around to the château with a note. The man soon returned bearing a warm invitation.

Voltaire entered Sceaux at midnight. He was led through the darkness to a hidden entrance into the château. A mysterious staircase led up to a tiny, unsuspected apartment at the top of the house, in which Voltaire spent more than two months in absolute secrecy.

At about two every morning he would descend like a ghost to the bedchamber of the witty duchesse. Everyone else was asleep except a footman who had been let in on the secret and set up a table beside the bed. There Voltaire, in his nightcap and dressing gown, supped on exquisite dishes royally served. As he partook he exchanged witty conversation with his hostess, propped up on her lace pillows. They both delighted in these encounters. His solitude during the day made this opportunity to speak all the more precious, and he felt himself loved and understood. The lady who constituted his sole audience was one of the most active and cultivated of women, with an intelligence akin to Voltaire's and infallible taste. So a princess of the intellect chatted by candlelight, in a setting only less sumptuous than Versailles, with the most intelligent man of the most intelligent age in history. As a return for her hospitality and protection, Voltaire read aloud to her each night what he had written during the day. They were the lightest of stories, written with a pen that scarcely touched the paper: *Babouc, Memnon, Scaramouche, Micromégas, Zadig.* Invented to amuse a tiny, almost dwarflike duchess for an hour, they have become immortal.

Longchamp shared Voltaire's captivity and copied out his work. They had a Savoyard lad of twelve to do their errands. One day Voltaire couldn't get his foot into his shoe and sent it to the shoemaker. The shoemaker found a purse full of gold in the toe, and the boy started to cry, thinking his honesty was being tested. He wept and trembled all the way home, afraid of losing the purse in the snow. When he told his story his master laughed, calmed his fears, and gave him a tip. Voltaire had emptied his pockets one day and carelessly thrown their contents into a cupboard. The purse must have fallen into a shoe and lain there forgotten.

By February 1748 the danger was over. Madame du Châtelet had interceded at Versailles and in Paris, the offending word "knave" was forgotten, and Voltaire could show himself in public again. He made his first appearance, characteristically, on the stage of the theater at Sceaux. With the assistance of Emilie, the Vicomte de Chabot, and the Marquis de

Courtanvaux, who was an excellent dancer, he put on two comedies: *La Prude* (*The Prude*) and *Les Originaux* (*The Eccentrics*).

One of the little dancing girls aroused general admiration. Her name was Mademoiselle Guimard, and she was to become the most famous dancer of her time.

The Duchesse du Maine and everyone else who had read the manuscript of *Zadig* admired the work so much that they made Voltaire promise to publish it. He gave the beginning to a printer in Paris, saying he was still writing the end. Then he gave the end to a printer in Rouen, saying he was rewriting the beginning. He then assembled the two parts, had two hundred copies bound, and sent them as a present to the Duchesse du Maine. The two printers were naturally furious. Voltaire had to pay out large sums to both and allow them to print the beginning and the end together in future editions. It might have been simpler to do so from the start.

At court Voltaire's *L'Enfant prodigue* was performed privately for the King and his friends. The Ducs de Chartres, Nivernais, and Gontaut and Madame de Pompadour gave excellent performances. Voltaire was not invited to attend. But Madame de Pompadour told him about it and got the King to promise that in future the authors of plays performed in private were to be invited. Voltaire wrote her a poem, which became the occasion of still another scandal. The Queen's party was horrified by an allusion to Madame de Pompadour's "conquests" in the final line. The uproar caused by this bold mention of the relations between Louis and his mistress might soon have died down if the protests had come only from the Queen and a few former beauties in her entourage. But there were also the King's daughters to be reckoned with. They hated the favorite and Voltaire, and persuaded their father, who adored them, to send the favorite's poet away from court.

Paris, as usual, exaggerated the rumblings at Versailles and said that Voltaire was banished. There is no evidence that he was formally banished, but at any rate he preferred once again to decamp—this time to Cirey. Madame de Pompadour did not try to prevent him. Voltaire's verses tended to be more and more compromising, and this last set had made her lose a trick in the complicated game she was playing at court.

Voltaire wrote to D'Argental and to Président Hénault to explain, and above all to get them to explain to others, that all the rumors about him that were making the rounds were false: "It seems, my angels, that I cannot leave Paris without being exiled!" He was simply traveling for pleasure, he maintained, even though his departure had been somewhat precipitate. There followed an encomium on the royal family to put people off the scent. He did not refer to the poem to Madame de Pompadour and denied having written to Madame la Dauphine. No one but he had even mentioned any letter to her. At fifty-four years of age he was acting precisely as he had when he was twenty: when accused of writing the *Puero regnante* he denied having had anything to do with *J'ai vu*. One thing is certain at all events: Voltaire was running away.

One Heart Is Lost and Another Takes Its Place

In winter the journey to Cirey was a harrowing one. And Emilie, who prided herself on being different from everyone else, would travel only at night. As usual, their coach was overloaded. The cold was terrible, and the holes in the roads were concealed by frozen snow. The two lovers huddled in their furs, squashed up against trunks and buried under boxes at every jolt. The coach had been loaded in haste, and they traveled in as much discomfort as the poorest passenger in a public conveyance. A few leagues from Nangis an axle broke, and the body of the coach was dragged along the ground, in imminent danger of overturning. Fortunately it came to a standstill safely, amid the frantic cries of its occupants. Voltaire yelled the loudest: he was caught between two boxes of books and being crushed to death! Emilie had fallen on top of him, but at least she could breathe. The maid was on top of Madame. They were all dragged out, and once he was set on his legs again Voltaire calmed down and sent to the nearest village for carpenters. Meanwhile he and Emilie spread out the cushions from the coach on the snow by the side of the ditch, and sat and admired the stars.

With the help of ropes and four peasants the coach was set back on its wheels. But the repairs were a makeshift job at best. The workmen, dragged out of their beds into an arctic night, anticipated a handsome reward. Emilie reluctantly paid out twelve livres, and the men went off grumbling. The travelers let them grumble, climbed in, and set off again. The travelers again shouted for help. No sign of the peasants. The travelers called out again, begging and pleading for assistance. Still no sign of the peasants. Then Voltaire got out his purse, there was a gleam of gold in the pale starlight, the peasants returned, and the travelers were able to reach Nangis. There they left the coach and asked for hospitality at a neighboring château. They toasted themselves in front of a roaring fire, ate, drank, and retired to huge feather beds as day was breaking. They stayed there for two days while the coach was being repaired, and finally it limped back to Cirey without further incident.

They stayed four months. As soon as they arrived, the old company—Madame de Champbonin and all the rest—gathered round again. Before the trunks were unpacked a theater was being set up, and soon a rollicking performance of Voltaire's farce, *Le Boursoufle* (*The Man Who Was Puffed Up*) was in full swing.

During that winter, in February 1748, they went off to visit the court of King Stanislas of Lorraine at Lunéville. He was a good King and a good man. His subjects resented him at first but came to love him as much as he loved them, and his reign remains one of the best periods in the history of Lorraine.[1] In point of fact, he reigned without actually ruling: a French administrator Monsieur de la Galaizière appointed by Versailles, saw to the business of government. His court was a delightful place where all were on friendly terms and everyone knew everyone else. Manners were polite and affable, and not nearly so stiff as at Versailles. Like other miniature courts, it imitated the elegance of Versailles but avoided both its formality and its corruption. In this it was much like the German courts that Voltaire was so fond of. King Stanislas was surrounded by a perfect comic-opera cast. First of all a mistress, one of the most beautiful women in Europe, whose gentleness and wit were unspoiled by fame: the Marquise de Boufflers, who belonged to the family of the princes of Beauvau, the highest nobility of Lorraine. In contrast to her was Stanislas' Jesuit confessor, Father Menou—a somewhat sinister figure, whereas the marquise was all light. Voltaire, who later had dealings with him, called him "the boldest and most scheming priest I have ever known." He added that Stanislas' heart was divided between these two and that the Jesuit cost the King more money than the favorite. He had gotten more than a million livres out of the King, built a magnificent house for his order, and set aside twelve thousand livres for his table. Another twelve thousand livres was to be spent as he wished. The favorite, on the other hand, was allowed "only just enough to buy skirts," according to Voltaire.

The confessor was naturally jealous of the favorite and would have liked to evict her from her half of Stanislas' heart. The two were always at sword's points, and after mass the worthy King "had great difficulty reconciling his mistress and his confessor."

The King also had a dwarf, called Bébé, who was so tiny that one day he got lost in a meadow, as an ordinary man might get lost in a forest. On occasion he was served up at table in a pie, to caper about among the plates and glasses. He was allowed to say anything he pleased, and sometimes it pleased him to be spiteful. He was a subject of conversation even at Versailles. Madame de Pompadour was amazed that he had never been able to learn his catechism and that no one had ever succeeded in making him understand that there was a God. Poor Bébé would have needed a good deal of grace to rise to such thoughts.

Such was King Stanislas' court. But Voltaire and Emilie were not making the journey to Lunéville in order to see Bébé. That kind of amusement was not to their tastes at all. What Madame du Châtelet wanted was a pension for her husband.

The marquis belonged to one of the oldest families in Lorraine, but it was not very well off and therefore his country owed him a pension. Emilie knew she would be well received by Stanislas, who had been told about the wonderful style of life at Cirey. Since Cirey was in Lorraine, Stanislas felt they owed him a tribute of wit. Stanislas was not hard to please, but he did not always feel like amusing himself with his dwarf, and the plottings of his confessor and his favorite grew monotonous. With Voltaire there, it would all be different. Voltaire was sure Stanislas was awaiting his arrival eagerly, but his reason for thinking so, though typical of him, was entirely imaginary. He said, with conviction, that Father Menou was planning to get Madame de Boufflers ousted as the King's mistress and replace her with Madame du Châtelet. It seems an unlikely project: Madame du Châtelet was quite unsuitable, for one thing, because of her despotic character, her scientific ambitions, which were not at all to Stanislas' taste, and her age. And above all, the King was extremely fond of Madame de Boufflers. It is very likely that such a project had never entered anyone's head but Voltaire's, and he probably spread such a story about to blacken Father Menou's reputation.

Despite his jealous fears, Voltaire arrived in Lunéville in as good spirits as Emilie, expecting considerable satisfaction for his vanity and perhaps other advantages. It was very pleasant to be made much of by the King, especially as it was Stanislas' daughter, the Queen of France, who had nearly got him thrown out of Versailles. He also greatly enjoyed the company of Madame de Boufflers. He admired and praised her, and willingly yielded to the spell of the marvelous woman—definitely not a bluestocking—who had been nicknamed "*La dame de Volupté* [the lady of Pleasure]." Her conversation and judgment showed impeccable taste and discernment, and she dressed with the elegance of Versailles. In Voltaire's eyes she also possessed the superhuman virtue of being quite naturally devoid of any idea of sin or the slightest trace of religious belief. She created around her an atmosphere of unclouded happiness and freedom from remorse which Voltaire breathed in with joy. She had written an epitaph for herself:

> Ci-gít dans une paix profonde
> Une dame de Volupté
> Qui, pour plus de sécurité,
> Fit son paradis en ce monde.

Here rests in deep peace/A lady of Pleasure/Who, in order to make sure of things,/Placed her heaven in this world rather than the next.

Everyone except the confessor was delighted when Voltaire and Emilie arrived to lend their sparkle to the court at Lunéville. At last there would be fascinating dinners, plays, and new intrigues. Madame de Boufflers and Emilie became bosom friends at once. Voltaire put first things first and saw to the setting up of a theater. They began by putting on the two comedies of his that had been staged at Sceaux. They were equally successful at Lunéville and Stanislas liked them so much, he insisted on two performances. Then they performed *Mérope*, and everyone wept, with even the author joining in.

In the audience there were a number of charming and talented people. One of them was to take a leading role. He was handsome and well built, with a distinguished mixture of affability and reserve; he could write poetry, and above all he was young. He was the Marquis de Saint-Lambert, and a captain in the army. In his poetry the cool element in his character gains the upper hand; it leaves the reader cold as well. Yet dispite the fact that he lacked true poetic talent he made two important appearances in the annals of eighteenth-century French literature. In the first instance he gained a brilliant victory by stealing Emilie away from Voltaire, and in the second he spirited Madame d'Houdetot away from the melancholy Jean-Jacques Rousseau. Such were Saint-Lambert's masterworks in the realm of literature, apart from his poem *Les Saisons* (*The Seasons*), which may be saluted from a respectful distance.

When he first arrived in Lunéville he had addressed himself to Madame de Boufflers. He might well have succeeded, for the marquise was not one to deprive a brilliant cavalier of a victory whose pleasures she was quite willing to share. But it so happened that Saint-Lambert was one of Stanislas' officers, and Stanislas did not want his captain to be his rival. Madame de Boufflers, the most obliging woman in the world, gracefully acknowledged the King's right to object. She would rather refuse a new lover pleasures he did not yet know than deny them to an old and irreproachable lover for whom they had become both a habit and a right. There was also another, more concrete motive. The King already shared the marquise with his chancellor, Monsieur de la Galaizière. This arrangement was a settled matter. One evening the marquise, slightly tipsy and weary of the tender but empty compliments of the King, finally said to her aging lover, "Is that all?" The King replied, "No, madame, that is not all, but my chancellor will tell you the rest." But only the chancellor was allowed this privilege.

And so it came about that Saint-Lambert's eye alighted on Madame du Châtelet, who soon threw herself into his arms. It was almost inevitable. Even at his best Voltaire had never been anything but an "*amant à la neige*," and now age, sickness, and a sort of coolness arising from satiety had virtually extinguished this ardor. It is only too clear that Emilie had been bored in bed with Voltaire for years. But she wasn't made for that sort of existence, and it explains, perhaps, her rages and tears and reckless gambling. No doubt Voltaire still loved her as much as ever—but in a different way. As early as 1742, Frederick had made fun of Voltaire when he imprudently confided that his and Emilie's relationship was no longer anything but affectionate and intellectual. True or not, Emilie was frustrated.

She had endeavored to bring about a better understanding between herself and Voltaire, but the results were disappointing and she had given up. In a poem full of delicacy and melancholy Voltaire admits that at fifty-four there are rites he no longer celebrates. He apologizes to Emilie, and consoles her and himself. There is no sadder or more moving allegory of resignation. After love has broken down:

> Du ciel alors daignant descendre
> L'Amitié vint à mon secours;
> Elle était peut-être plus tendre
> Mais moins vive que les Amours.
>
> ....
>
> Touché de sa beauté nouvelle
> Et de sa lumière éclairé,
> Je la suivis; mais je pleurai
> De ne pouvoir plus suivre qu'elle.

From heaven then deigning to descend/Friendship came to my aid;/She was perpahs more tender/But less lively than Love/. . . . Touched by her new beauty/And illuminated by her light,/I followed her; but wept/That I could now follow only her.

That was why Emilie, too, wept so much, and why she hoped Saint-Lambert would dry her tears. The operetta was to end in tragedy, but as
Voltaire's "indifference" was no secret. Referring to Voltaire's atti-
twists.
Voltaire's "indifference" was no secret. Referrring to Voltaire's attitude toward Madame du Châtelet, the Abbé de Voisenon commented: "He wrote more epigrams against religion than verses to his mistress."

Emilie had confided in her friends the D'Argentals. Her words are moving because she is both sincere and distraught when she confesses that she has "one of those affectionate, unchanging hearts that can neither disguise nor moderate their passions, who know neither flagging nor weariness, whose tenacity survives even the certitude that they were never loved. But I was happy for ten years through the love of the man who had conquered my soul . . . when age, illness, and perhaps satiety too had diminished his desire, it was long before I noticed it: I loved enough for two. . . . It is true that I have now lost that happy state, and not without its costing me many tears." When she arrived in Lunéville she had had enough of tears and had left resignation behind. She wanted a lover. Saint-Lambert crossed her path, and she took off after him.

A note from Madame du Châtelet shows that it was she who had made all the advances and that Saint-Lambert was conceited enough to take advantage of her eagerness. "I can repent of nothing," she wrote him, "because you love me. And it is to myself that I owe it. Had I not spoken to you at Madame de la Galaizière's you would not have loved me. I know not if I should congratulate myself on a love that depends on so little."

Her fears were not unfounded. Saint-Lambert was thirty, she was forty-one, and his love depended principally on what she called her "tenacity." This was hardly the best guarantee of a mutually shared passion. The beginning of the affair was thrilling but not really a source of great happiness. Through fear, she soon became tyrannical. She made him give up taking a journey he had been planning to make. She wanted them both to sacrifice everything to each other, but Saint-Lambert made it clear that he accepted only partial sacrifices and was himself willing to make only superficial ones. Once again she could say, "I loved enough for two." Saint-Lambert was not Voltaire, but she loved him nonetheless.

They wrote to each other even though they met every day. Emilie hid her letters in Madame de Bouffler's harp, from which, when the guests had left, Saint-Lambert would collect them. "I adore you, and it seems to me that when one loves one can do no wrong," she wrote in one missive.

During Carnival, Voltaire and Emilie organized all sorts of parties and entertainments: the court had never enjoyed itself so much. But a certain amount of scandal was caused in the weeks following by the fact that the two visitors did not even pretend to observe Lent. Other people were of the same opinion as Voltaire and Emilie, but at least they made an outward show of respectability. The King liked everyone to make his Easter devotions. He made no comment, but it was said at Versailles that he was annoyed at Voltaire's and Emilie's behavior.

In May, Emilie was obliged to return to Cirey. Voltaire left afterward for Versailles, where he had arrived by May 15. Saint-Lambert was overwhelmed by the missives he received from Emilie: not only were they numerous, but she was really madly in love and they were rambling and obscure. Moreover, she had other troubles in addition to the pangs of love. Instead of giving Emilie's husband the command she had solicited, King Stanislas gave it to another, younger officer. She was so angry she vowed never to set foot in Lunéville again. Stanislas had really not had any other alternative: the marquis's rival had much more claim to the appointment than he had. But in order to avoid hurt feelings the King created a new post and awarded the Marquis du Châtelet a not inconsiderable pension of three thousand crowns. Emilie was overjoyed, not only because of the money but also because she would be able to go back to Lunéville.

At Versailles, Voltaire devoted most of his time to *Sémiramis*. At rehearsals the actors surpassed themselves. "They made me weep, they made me tremble," he reported. The play does not produce the same effect on modern audiences. When he left he entrusted his "daughter" *Sémiramis* to the care of the D'Argentals. "It is a noble thing to protect helpless orphans. If it were not for you *Sémiramis's* father would die of apprehension."

And Voltaire and Emilie returned to Lorraine together. The shadow of Saint-Lambert lay between them, but it was slight, for Voltaire had no suspicion that his Emilie had fallen madly in love with the dashing young cavalier.

Sémiramis *Fails*

In the summer of 1748 Stanislas held court at Commercy, where he had had the palace done up in magnificent style, and it was there that Emilie went, accompanied by Voltaire. Along the way, at Châlons, Emilie decided she would like to take a bowl of soup at the Auberge de la Cloche. She ordered it to be brought out to the coach, and the proprietress of the inn, realizing who her customer was, brought the soup herself in a silver bowl on a porcelain dish. When she told Emilie the bill came to one louis, Emilie screeched in indignation. The mistress of the inn was adamant. Voltaire then intervened, and they all began screaming at each other. A hostile crowd assembled and sided with the grasping proprietress. It looked as if there was going to be trouble. Longchamp solved the problem by throwing a louis on the ground and having the coach drive off, just in time. Emilie had had a narrow escape, but she couldn't bear the thought of having parted with all that money.

The incident suggests that there were limits to the people's patience and that those limits could not be transgressed with impunity.

Voltaire was so ill during this journey that he traveled completely swathed in wraps. When they got to Commercy he wrote D'Argenson that he was at death's door.

But he soon revived enough to act, compose verses, and write one letter after another. He got King Stanislas to invite the D'Argentals to Commercy. Madame du Châtelet wrote: "We live out of time here. True, twenty-four hours are not too much to rehearse two or three operas and as many plays."

The Queen of France invited her father to Trianon, and at the end of August Stanislas left Commercy to go and see his daughter. Voltaire decided to go too, to see *his* "daughter," *Sémiramis*, for the poor girl had enemies; first and foremost, Crébillon. Voltaire knew when he chose the subject that Crébillon had already written a *Sémiramis*, but he wanted to show his superiority over his hated rival. Unfortunately his rival was also the censor and could strangle *Sémiramis* in the cradle. In fact Crébillon cut only a few lines, though Voltaire considered even that unfair. The King offered to pay for the décor of the play because Voltaire had dedicated it to the Dauphine.

It was at the first performance of *Sémiramis* that Voltaire protested publicly against the presence of spectators on the stage. The privilege was not abolished until 1759 however, through the efforts of the Comte de Lauragais. At the premiere of *Sémiramis*, Voltaire was furious: in the scene at Ninus' tomb, a ghost was supposed to appear, but there were so many of the audience sitting on the stage that the actor could not get through. Voltaire called out: "Messieurs! Make way for the ghost, if you please, make way for the ghost!"

Apart from this hitch, the audience was also divided into two factions, one mobilized by Voltaire and the other by Crébillon, Piron, and other enemies of the author. Voltaire was very good at organizing this sort of battle. He had four hundred seats at his disposal and employed a special claque who did not object to using their fists or their walking sticks. One of the terrors of the pit was a man whom Voltaire had hired named La Morlière, whose influence was so great that a play was as good as finished if he condemned it. He was not illiterate: he had taste, and booed out of conviction as well as out of self-interest.

Despite La Morlière's zeal, *Sémiramis* was not a success. "It's Voltaire," someone remarked, "but bad Voltaire." This is a fair enough assessment, but Voltaire could not reconcile himself to it. He wanted to know what the public really thought. So he borrowed the Abbé de Vieilleville's cassock and three-cornered hat, and a huge wig beneath which he nearly disappeared, then went and sat in a corner at the Café Procope, opposite the Comédie Française, hiding behind a newspaper to listen. All the literary people present vied with each other in tearing *Sémiramis* and its author to pieces. Voltaire eavesdropped for an hour, then went home sick with rage and disgust.

But Paris had not finished with him yet. Crébillon had just written a tragedy entitled *Catilina*, and he managed to persuade Madame de Pompadour to allow him to read it to her. Voltaire was terribly jealous, but the worst of all was that the King hid and listened to the reading, declared himself delighted with it, and wanted it to be performed. After that Madame de Pompadour did not dare take up the cudgels for Voltaire's *Sémiramis*, which the King did not like.

The actors at the Comédie Française behaved badly. They took no notice of Voltaire's suggestions and were the first to decry *Sémiramis*. They made it clear they were acting it against their will. This was not to be borne. Until then Voltaire had turned his author's profits over to the entire cast of his plays; in the face of their ingratitude and insolence he now wrote: "I will not sacrifice any of my rights for people who will not thank me for it and in any case do not deserve it."

But still he did not take the profits himself. He had them transferred to the actresses Mademoiselle Clairon, Mademoiselle Dumesnil, and the actor Granval, who thoroughly deserved being so rewarded.

To pour a little balm on these wounds the superintendent of police informed him that the six lines that had been censored could be restored.

Another Encounter with Death

Voltaire was not only overwhelmed with disgust; he was also shivering with fever and doubled up with colic. When he heard that King Stanislas had returned to Lunéville on September 10, 1748, he decided to abandon

Paris, theater, actors, audience and all. He would have been well enough if the play had been a success, but when his vanity was hurt the blood seemed to dry up in his veins. Bundled up from head to foot, deathly pale and in great pain, he set out once more for Lorraine with his faithful Longchamp. At Château-Thierry his fever rose still higher. He was scarcely recognizable: all one could see were burning eyes in a white face, thin, pale lips, and a beak of a nose beneath tightly stretched skin and protruding cheekbones. They pressed on to Châlons, but there Longchamp took fright. Voltaire looked like a corpse. Longchamp sent for the bishop and the administrator of the district, said that his master was dying, and told them he did not wish to be held responsible for his death. But Voltaire refused to go either to the bishop's house or to the administrator's. He went to bed in an inn, sent for a doctor, listened politely to his advice, and declined with equal politeness to follow it. He had eaten nothing since leaving Paris, and he continued to eat virtually nothing. A little tea and bread-soup were enough to keep him going. He did manage to dictate some letters, however, and sign them with a shaky V. He spoke of nothing but the rascally Crébillon, the wretched *Sémiramis*, the rogue of a printer who was publishing *Zadig*, of all his enemies. He used his rapidly failing strength to curse them, to call down horrible tortures on them, and to imagine ways of wreaking his vengeance upon them in the future.

After six days of what he was certain were his death throes he decided it was time to resume his journey. He did not want to die in the dreadful town where the proprietress of an inn had cheated his Emilie out of a louis. If he must die he would die somewhere else. They arrived in Nancy in the evening. Voltaire went to bed, drank a little broth, and watched poor Longchamp, who was also nearly dead—of hunger and fatigue—down a leg of mutton, a dozen thrushes, and as many robins. The dying poet's eyes glistened. Longchamp offered him a taste, and Voltaire put away two robins and a great glassful of wine. He then slept until three the next afternoon. His eyes were bright, his voice rang, and he ordered the horses harnessed to set off for Lunéville.

There he was reunited with Emilie. He wept fond tears and fell into her arms, then joined the others, full of gaiety and wit if not of strength, asking what play was being performed that evening. He set the court acting again and was once again in his proper element: life.

Continuation and End of a Tragicomedy

Emilie was not happy in her passion for Saint-Lambert. Their relations were stormy at best. She was suspicious and exacting, in a word intolerable, and her lover did not tolerate her very well.

Voltaire knew nothing of what everyone else at the court knew. But he too had storms to weather. The news reached him in peaceful Lorraine that a plot was being mounted against him in Paris: the actors at the Comédie Italienne[2] were going to put on a grotesque parody of his *Sémiramis,* a tissue of ribaldry and slander against the author of the boring but noble tragedy. Voltaire's fever returned. He begged Stanislas to ask his daughter to get the burlesque banned. Stanislas did as he was asked, but the Queen had no intention of defending a poet she detested. She had already been convinced that he was a limb of Satan, and now she had just been told that he had recently published the impious *Zadig.* Not that she had read or ever would read it. What she had heard about it was enough. She had been told it was so immoral that Voltaire denied having written it. The Queen told her father that she did not concern herself with literature or authors.

So Voltaire applied elsewhere, knocking on every possible door. His strangest application was to the superintendent of police, the successor of Monsieur Hérault, whose aid he had so often solicited and whom he had caused so much trouble. He explained that it was absolutely necessary to prevent the parody from being performed because he had a niece, Madame Denis, who had been left a widow and was on the point of getting married again to a gentleman of quality. If the parody were performed, Voltaire, Madame Denis's uncle and guardian, would be so dishonored that the marriage could never take place.

Hence it is in connection with the burlesque on *Sémiramis* that Voltaire's niece again enters the picture. That she was now a widow was true. That she was about to remarry was not. But it made a good argument for suppressing the farce.

The new superintendent was well disposed toward Voltaire, Madame de Pompadour also interceded, the King did not care to see his historiographer made fun of, and the skit was not performed at court. But it was not banned in Paris: Maurepas, who hated Voltaire, authorized the Italian players to perform it. By a lucky chance Richelieu and Madame de Pompadour succeeded in getting it forbidden at the last minute, though not before Voltaire had had several weeks of agony over the stupid affair.

But his private life was about to cause him even worse pain. One evening in October 1748, at Commercy, Voltaire found the door of Emilie's apartment open. There was no servant to announce him, and he simply walked in. He went through another door; still nobody. Then he opened the door into Emilie's boudoir and, lo and behold, there were his Emilie and Saint-Lambert in an unmistakably compromising situation. He let out a cry, fell into a rage, stamped his feet, and showered Emilie with insults and threats. This painful and ridiculous scene became even more humiliating when Saint-Lambert, calm and collected, stepped between the other two and offered Voltaire satisfaction in a duel. It was scarcely an act of great courage: Voltaire at fifty-four was already an old man, ailing, and completely unskilled at handling a sword, while Saint-Lambert was a soldier of thirty-one, strong and in excellent training. Voltaire, outraged and humiliated, rushed to his room and told Longchamp to pack their things and prepare to leave at once. He looked as if he had taken leave of his senses. Longchamp, stupefied, went to find out what had happened, and Madame de Châtelet besought him to procrastinate, to delay Voltaire's departure as long as he could, to prevent him from going altogether. She was appalled at the possible consequences of such a stormy rupture with Voltaire, who had been her lover for seventeen years. What would her position be at court, in society, in her family? And what would Monsieur du Châtelet say when he heard that his wife was deceiving Monsieur de Voltaire with a new lover? He would never put up with it. Such a rupture would be as scandalous as a divorce. It must be prevented at all costs.

She went to Voltaire's bedside. He had been so shattered by the scene that he had retired. She sat down on the edge of the bed: if love could not reconcile them, logic still might. Emilie was as expert at one as at the other. Longchamp pretended to be occupied with urgent tasks elsewhere in the room, and Emilie spoke in English. The only words Voltaire's faithful servant recognized were some of the affectionate nicknames they were in the habit of calling each other. As he understood nothing of the rest, and Voltaire still looked glum, Longchamp went out of the room and stood listening at the door. Emilie at once began to speak French.

She began with the immemorial argument: Voltaire hadn't seen properly. He was nearly deaf in one ear, wasn't he? Well, his eyes were no better. Voltaire burst out that he could see perfectly well, and could have touched what he saw. But Voltaire didn't believe his eyes or his ears had deceived him; and seeing how obstinate and angry he was, Emilie changed her tactics. She admitted everything and said they must simply all get used to the situation and then they would be able to go on living and even be happy. All that was needed was for everyone to make an effort.

Having proposed this hypothesis, she then proceeded to prove it in masterly fashion.

What was the thing she valued most in all the world? Voltaire's health. If she had exacted from him all she had a right to expect, what would have become of him? He would have been dead. Voltaire admitted this. And what would have become of her if Voltaire had died in this way? She would have died of grief. Look at how she had suffered when he was in Prussia: a mere absence had brought her to the edge of the grave. The death of her lover would have plunged her over the brink, and she too would have gone to her grave. Voltaire admitted this too. So, if Voltaire had been a satisfactory lover, he would have died and she would not have survived him. But if he was not one, it was she who would die, for the transports that were fatal to him were vital to her. So? Did he want her to waste away and die? He groaned. Or would he allow another to keep her alive in order to go on loving him?

She had taken a lover only to preserve her health and Voltaire's. She argued that Saint-Lambert was not a rival but the physician of their ailing love, their savior.

Voltaire could not hold out against such wisdom and perspicacity. "Ah, madame," he cried, "you are always in the right. But since things are as they are, at least let them not happen before my very eyes."

She might at least lock the door when her "doctor" came. He wept. They embraced. She told him not to upset himself by thinking about such trifles, and left.

So there was one of the lovers soothed. The other now had to be calmed.

Saint-Lambert was still ready to run Voltaire through with a sword. But Emilie did not need to talk so long to him; with him she could use other arguments besides those prompted by reason and logic. She did point out again, however, that it would be neither honorable nor profitable to duel with a sick old man of fifty-four, who was famous into the bargain and had numerous friends who would consider such a duel a crime. Moreover, Monsieur de Voltaire could not be more kindly disposed toward his rival and would be quite ready to make his peace with him if Saint-Lambert would go and apologize for words spoken in anger. Saint-Lambert, thus skillfully handled, in turn handled Voltaire just as skillfully: he went and stammered out some phrases of apology which he was not allowed to finish. Voltaire, moved to tears, fell into the arms of this "physician" and they wept together. Emilie's face must have been a study. "My boy," Voltaire said to his young rival, "all is forgotten, it is I who was at fault. You are at the happy age where one loves and inspires love. Enjoy these moments, for they are all too short. A sick old man like me is no longer fit for pleasure."

So he yielded his place. What was the point of hating? Was it not better to keep Emilie's affection, the memory of seventeen years of love, seventeen years of physical, but above all intellectual, intimacy?

Voltaire had behaved characteristically: he forgave Saint-Lambert, just as he had forgiven Génonville thirty years before.

He was a good loser; too good. Frederick II must have enjoyed a good laugh when Voltaire wrote to him praising his rival. We are a long way from the tempestuous romantic passions that often end up as newspaper items. People have said of Voltaire and his contemporaries that if they escaped so unscathed by their amours it was because they had no hearts. It has also been said that they did not really love at all. They certainly did not love, as people have come to do since, with their viscera, but that is not the best part of man. Madame de Tencin, addressing Fontenelle, who did not sin through any excess of sentiment, laid her finger on his breast and said, "It isn't a heart you have there. It's a brain, just like in your head." The observation could be applied to Voltaire, who introduced reason into everything, even his passions.

The visit to Commercy was interrupted at the end of December 1748 when Madame du Châtelet was summoned to Cirey on urgent financial affairs. At Châlons when they stopped at the bishop's palace, it was raining in torrents. While the horses were being changed, some people present suggested a game of cards. Emilie accepted with alacrity, played, lost, and wouldn't stop. Hour after hour the postilions, waiting in the rain, sent in to ask when they were to start. "Just one more hand," Emilie would answer. Voltaire's patience wore thin. She finally agreed to go at eight o'clock in the evening; she had sat there since eight in the morning.

While they were at Cirey, Emilie, gloomy and anxious, finally told Voltaire that she was pregnant. He took it badly and there was an angry scene, then tears, and in the end laughter. They were laughing over how to convey this piece of news to Monsieur du Châtelet. It was a problem. Monsieur du Châtelet was a model husband, but such perfection has its limits and Voltaire was afraid those limits were about to be crossed. They sent for Saint-Lambert: three heads are better than two. Longchamp was afraid that the two men might quarrel. As was his habit, he listened at the door. They talked for a long time. Finally he heard them burst out laughing: they had found the solution.

Monsieur du Châtelet was sent word to come to Cirey immediately, as there were pressing business matters to attend to. Never was a warrior more warmly welcomed. Normally his stories about his campaigns were so boring that everyone disappeared as soon as he began; he usually took his meals with his children. Now he was enthroned at his own table, pressed to talk about the army, and listened to with feigned enthusiasm by Emilie and Voltaire, who demanded to know every detail of his recent feats in battle.

The marquise, in a low-cut dress and elaborately made up, lavished such admiration on the marquis, she made him blush; she behaved in so enticing a manner that after eighteen years' separation they began sleeping with one another in the same bed. A few weeks later Madame du Châtelet told her husband he was going to become a father again. The delighted marquis spread the news around. Coaches began to arrive with neighbors offering their compliments; the peasants, bribed by Voltaire, organized a fête.

Saint-Lambert modestly added his congratulations to the rest. The marquis was in seventh heaven: never had he felt so well liked, never had his wife's friends seemed so witty. At this point, now that the essential had been accomplished, it was hinted that his place was with the army. So off he went to Silesia. Saint-Lambert returned to Lunéville, and Emilie and Voltaire left for Paris. They were the host and hostess at Cirey: both the marquis and Saint-Lambert seemed like guests.

Voltaire and Frederick still corresponded. Frederick kept on asking Voltaire to Berlin, and Voltaire kept inventing excuses for not coming immediately: his ill-health, or the effects of the waters at Plombières, which he had not taken. Frederick bided his time. He knew the real obstacle was Emilie.

Voltaire liked Lunéville and good King Stanislas liked Voltaire, despite the warnings of his daughter and Father Menou, principally because he was a famous author. Stanislas, like everyone who was anyone in the eighteenth century, was an author too: of a treatise entitled *Un Philosophe chrétien* (*A Christian Philosopher*), a work which according to Voltaire was of little merit. The "philosopher" of the title was there because it was the fashion; and the word "Christian" because the King was afraid of his confessor.

The only King who remained unmoved in the midst of all this enthusiasm for literature and Voltaire was Louis XV. But he was the only one Voltaire would have liked to captivate.

In 1748 there were to be major festivities to celebrate the signing of the Treaty of Aix-la-Chapelle, ending the War of the Austrian Succession. The King was to receive representatives of all the national institutions in the great gallery at Versailles, and each would deliver a speech. The Academy was informed that its turn would be on February 21, 1749. Voltaire prepared a panegyric and had it bound and edged in gilt for the Duc de Richelieu to deliver. Richelieu had to learn it by heart; he begged Voltaire not to make it too long. On the morning of February 21, all the members of the Academy except Voltaire were there waiting for the King. Richelieu was standing in a recess, quietly rehearsing his piece aloud, when someone behind him took it up and recited the rest. Richelieu suddenly saw, or thought he saw, what had happened: Voltaire had played a trick on him and had disclosed the text to make him look ridiculous—a peer playing at being an academician, who couldn't even make a speech without learning it by heart. Richelieu decided to improvise a short speech rather than fall into the trap. He acquitted himself well enough and then sent Voltaire back his panegyric with a cruel and insulting letter. Voltaire was stricken with grief—and with fear. He fell on a portrait of Richelieu, tore it to pieces, and ground them underfoot. But the two of them had known each other from childhood and were bound together by too many links to leave matters thus. They met one day at a dinner party and all was explained. Voltaire had not played a trick on his friend: Madame du Châtelet had given a copy of the speech to Madame de Boufflers, who had lent it to someone else, who had had copies made, and so on. People had been reciting it in salons several days before the ceremony. Richelieu accepted this explanation, and the two were friends again. But Voltaire regretted that his fine, handsomely bound panegyric had served no useful purpose:

Cet éloge a très peu d'effet.
Nul mortel ne m'en remercie
Celui qui le moins s'en soucie
Est celui pour qui je l'ai fait.

This eulogy has little effect./No one gives me any thanks for it/And he
who pays it least heed at all/Is the one for whom I wrote it.

For the King of course had not seen it. And so, no pension!

Money Matters

Voltaire's business affairs did not go badly in 1749. Longchamp had
other things to do besides listening at doors: Voltaire often sent him to
Paris to collect money due him from bankers and notaries. The Abbé
Moussinot was still his business agent.

On his brother's death Voltaire's income had been increased by four
thousand livres. His tragedy *Oedipe* had brought in something but not
much; it was the subscriptions for *La Henriade* that made him start to
grow rich. But that was only a beginning, only a pittance—not the enormous sums that would enable him to live in accordance with his tastes;
that is, like his friends the noblemen with vast fortunes.

When he returned from England he had invested capital in the Cadiz
trade, which equipped ships for the West Indies at a profit of twenty-five
per cent. The Pâris-Duvernet brothers had got him army contracts. And
Voltaire never let his income lie fallow. He lent money out privately. A
list of the payments he received during 1749 shows that all his debtors
were people of quality:

Bills on the city of Paris	14 023 livres
Bill on M. le Duc de Richelieu	4 000 livres
Bill on M. le Duc de Bouillon	3 250 livres
Pension from M. le Duc d'Orléans	1 200 livres
Bill on M. le Marquis de Lezeau	2 300 livres
Bill on M. le Duc de Villars	2 100 livres
Bill on M. le Comte d'Estaing	2 000 livres
Bill on M. le Prince de Guise	2 500 livres
Bill on M. le Président d'Auneuil	2 000 livres
Bill on M. Fontaine	2 600 livres
Bill on M. Marchand	2 400 livres
Bill on the Compagnie des Indes	605 livres
Emoluments as Historiographer of France	2 000 livres
Emoluments as Gentleman of the Bedchamber	1 620 livres
Bill on M. le Comte de Guebriant	540 livres
Bill on M. de Bourdeille	1 000 livres
Bill on the Royal Lottery	2 000 livres
Bill on M. Marchand	1 000 livres
Bill of 2 s.	9 900 livres
Supplies to the army in Flanders	17 000 livres
	74 038 livres

To this was added the income from his father's estate and various other sums. In all, his income that year must have been about 100,000 livres. During his visit to Prussia he was said to have invested 200,000 livres in a shipping company that Frederick had founded at Emden.

The unusual thing about Voltaire's fortune was that it consisted almost entirely of paper profits: in 1750, Voltaire did not even possess a roof over his head. The golden river that ran between his bony fingers had its source in mere notes, swollen by a thousand different sources of credit scattered all over Europe. Monsieur de Voltaire was, in fact, a very modern "capitalist."

Agitation, Work, and Away Again

In the midst of all his recent tribulations, Voltaire had found time to rewrite *Sémiramis*, and the play was ready to take the place of Crébillon's *Catilina*, which had failed in spite of the King's and Madame de Pompadour's support. This failure gave Voltaire great satisfaction; his rival's success "would have killed him." On the other hand he was delighted at the success of Marmontel, and even taught his protégé how to "organize an audience."

The preference which the King and the favorite had shown for Crébillon had wounded Voltaire. He was desperate at the thought of never becoming Versailles's most brilliant courtier. Did it not go without saying that the first king in Europe should choose the first writer of the age to sing his praises? To him it would have seemed quite natural for the King to overlook his nonchalance and even disrespect toward the monarchy and religion. But, for Louis XV, Voltaire's "philosophic princedom" was unacceptable, and Voltaire turned cool toward the court. He asked permission to sell his post of Gentleman of the Royal Bedchamber, and there is a letter from the King granting this permission and allowing him to keep the title. This was a mark of unusual generosity, for Voltaire had not purchased the place and the King could merely have taken back a gift that the recipient no longer wanted. So Voltaire sold the place for sixty thousand livres, pocketed the money, and kept the title without any of its obligations.

What he wanted was the impossible—first place in the friendship, or even the intimacy, of the King. Such a favor was simply not in the order of things at the French court, and Voltaire eventually sought it elsewhere. But he never got over the disappointment of not finding it at Versailles.

Madame du Châtelet was working frenziedly. She appeared at court and in society, but she spent her nights at her books. She was afraid she might die before she finished her monumental translation of Newton's works. She didn't know why she had this fear of death. She had never lived at such a hectic pace: her iron constitution, her natural energy, and her passion made her indefatigable. But in reality she was in torture. Her letters to Saint-Lambert are touching and painful, full of pleas and re-criminations: he neglects her, and never writes except to complain of her reproaches. But after having lamented and threatened, she would weaken and forgive and ask forgiveness. She was worried too about the coming child, who would be an intruder in the Châtelet family. Her eldest son was twenty, and the newcomer would take away part of his inheritance. She was too upright a woman not to be tormented by the idea of this in-justice.

The Duc de Lorraine went to stay at Trianon and Madame du Châtelet was invited. This was in April 1749, and Emilie thought that both she and Stanislas would stay there for the summer. She had her summer gowns sent from Lunéville. Saint-Lambert was angry and wanted her to come back: he didn't wish to be alone all that time. He had never been so insist-ent: no doubt his love for Emilie was less than hers for him, but still he must have been fond of her. For once Saint-Lambert's anger was sweet to Emilie: it told her of his jealousy and desire, and of the concern that made him want to be near her during her confinement. So she would be obliged to return to Lunéville.

She took advantage of her situation to get Stanislas to give her an apartment at Lunéville that she had been hankering after for some time. It was more convenient for her lover's visits and more comfortable, with two staircases and doors opening directly onto the garden. Stanislas gallantly offered her the furniture as well.

But when Stanislas left for Lorraine at the end of April, Emilie stayed on in Paris. She begged Saint-Lambert to understand that she had to finish her work on Newton and that she could do so only in Paris. She was not just amusing herself, she was slaving away frantically. Why should she, a woman in love, and probably for the last time in her life, have bothered about Newtonian physics? She wasn't a scholar: other women made fun of the scantiness of her learning, and most Frenchmen didn't want anything to do with Newton's theories. But her translation would be the means of making them known in France, and she had to finish and publish it. It was to this end that Emilie sacrificed the last weeks of her life and the last pleasures of her passion for Saint-Lambert.

She and Voltaire were living in their Parisian pied-à-terre, a house they rented all the year round in the Rue Traversière-Saint-Honoré. There she worked, with an elderly scholar named Clairaut. They used to bury themselves in their calculations and forget all about time. One day Vol-taire was waiting upstairs for them to join him at dinner. He sent down to tell them it was ready, and they asked for a quarter of an hour more. After half an hour he sent down again. They asked for another quarter of an hour. When it had elapsed, he ordered dinner to be brought in. He waited, the food grew cold, and still there was no sign of them. Unable to contain himself any longer, he hurled himself downstairs at risk of limb and life, knocked, called, and rattled at the door. They had bolted it! Voltaire then proceeded to kick down the door, screaming insults at Emilie for carrying on with an old professor while Saint-Lambert was pining away in Lorraine. "Are you in league together to kill me?" he cried.

During dinner no one spoke, and at the end of it Clairaut vanished as quickly as he could. The other two turned their backs on each other and went to their rooms. Next morning Emilie sent to ask Voltaire if he would take coffee with her. He said he would, and she went down, taking with her a beautiful Dresden cup and saucer. She brought the conversation around to the scene on the previous evening, touching on it delicately, well aware that she was playing with fire. Voltaire remained cold and distant. She grew bolder and eventually ventured a reproach. At this Voltaire leaped up, knocking against Emilie, who dropped her beautiful cup and broke it into a thousand pieces. Longchamp, who ran in on hearing the crash, caught a few withering words in English from Emilie, who then swept out leaving Voltaire alone with the wreckage. He soon recovered and sent Longchamp out to find the best Dresden breakfast sets obtainable from the finest shops in the Palais Royal. He brought back half a dozen, but none was as good as the one that had been smashed. Voltaire kept the most expensive. When he heard that it cost ten louis he said it was a ruinous price and refused to pay it, but finally he did so. He then sent the replacement to Emilie, who melted and came down to thank him. They embraced, wept a little, and everything was all right again. Voltaire, at peace once more, took up his pen and returned to his three works in progress.

He was planning a *Catilina* (as a counterstroke to Crébillon's play of that title), an *Oreste*, and lastly a comedy in verse called *Nanine*, suggested by Richardson's *Pamela*.

Nanine was put on in 1749. It was not very well received. During the performance the audience began to laugh at a passage that was meant to be affecting. Voltaire yelled out from his box, "Be quiet, barbarians!" Astonishingly enough, the laughter ceased. Wagnière, another of Voltaire's secretaries, tells how he disliked having to sit near his employer in the theater: he would start off calmly enough, then gradually fidget about more and more, twitching, shuddering, living the scene on the stage, opening and shutting his mouth, his whole body participating with the actors. "His voice, his feet, his stick would all make themselves heard to a greater or lesser extent: he would half rise out of his chair, sit down again, and suddenly stand up, looking six inches taller than he really was —that was when he made the most noise. Even professional actors dreaded acting in front of him because of all this."

Voltaire was just as dissatisfied with *Nanine* as the audience was, and decided to abandon it and return to Cirey. Emilie was impatient to leave too. She had broken with Clairaut, and Cirey for her meant the briefest possible halt on the way to Lunéville. At this time she was the object of pressing attentions from Frederick, who was trying by every possible means to get her to yield Voltaire up to him. When told for the thousandth time that Voltaire's health would not permit it, he no longer troubled even to reply to such pretexts. He was convinced that the only obstacle was Emilie. So he proposed a bargain. If she would send him the poet he would send by return a geometrician from his new Academy. Voltaire said Emilie could not give Frederick an answer until after her confinement. Frederick did himself no good by replying: "Madame du Châtelet is to be in childbed in September. You are not a midwife. She can be confined perfectly well without your assistance. . . . Remember also that the favors one does people without having to be asked are more gracious and agreeable than those which have to be so much solicited." Voltaire replied, with some firmness: "I am not a procreator of children, nor a doctor, nor a midwife, but I am a friend, and even for Your Majesty I will not leave a woman who may well die in September. It appears that the confinement may be very dangerous, but if she comes through safely I promise you, sire, that I shall come and pay you my respects in September." Frederick would have to wait.

Just as Voltaire was getting ready to leave Paris a young abbé, the protégé of a friend and relation of Madame du Châtelet's, came and asked Voltaire if he would look over a speech which the abbé was to make at the Louvre before the Academy and certain people highly placed at court. It was the chance of a lifetime: if the speech were a success, the abbé would be given a royal appointment. The subject—it was the same every year—was a panegyric on Saint Louis. The problem was to vary the tone and somehow escape platitudes. Voltaire declined the task and went on packing. He was no better acquainted with Saint Louis than with any other saint: the doctors of theology at the Sorbonne would be able to give better advice. But Emilie told him he must do it, and he obeyed. The next morning he gave the abbé his text back entirely rewritten, with almost every line either crossed out or altered. The original speech was so dreadful that the task of revising it had taken Voltaire all night. The young abbé, unable to recognize his own work, was horrified. He went to Madame du Châtelet, and she made Voltaire promise to make a copy of it that was readable. So he spent another night on it. Next morning he handed over an entirely new speech. But it was pointed out to him, rather curtly, that he hadn't clearly separated the exordium from the first point, the first point from the second, the second from the third, and the third from the peroration. The abbé's contribution consisted of writing in the conventional formulae to mark the divisions. It was wise of him to limit himself to that. The panegyric earned him a diocese not long after. His audience was better at judging texts than at choosing bishops.

Last Happy Days in Lorraine

During the summer of 1749, Stanislas kept informal court at Commercy, and it was there that he received Voltaire and Madame du Châtelet. He had had little lodges built in the park to accommodate his entourage and used to go and dine now with one, now with another, with only two or three hours' warning. He was neither a gourmet nor a gourmand, simply downing his meals as if they were a duty rather than a pleasure. In order to get them out of the way as soon as possible he fell into the habit of having dinner earlier and earlier, and one day his administrator, Monsieur de la Galaizière, said: "Sire, if you go on like this you will end by having each day's dinner the day before." His favorite pastime was gambling and his favorite game "Comet," at which Emilie lost with her usual pertinacity.

Madame de Boufflers was still the ornament of this little court. She welcomed the two travelers with delight. She spent her time writing verses, did not bother her head with philosophy, and was amused by everything, including her children's tutor, the Abbé Porquet, who was so thin and cadaverous that he used to say he was "stuffed into his skin."

Saint-Lambert was at the court at Commercy too, writing Les Saisons, a collection of poems which nearly made him famous. The Abbé de Bernis, Madame de Pompadour's favorite, had chosen the same subject, and it was necessary to beat him to the post. The competition between the two made the atmosphere of the mild little court of Lorraine somewhat feverish. Moreover, Voltaire also re-encountered Father Menou, who had warned the King's treasurer, Monsieur Alliot, and his wife against his old enemy. Voltaire did all he could to ingratiate himself with them, but in vain. Madame Alliot in particular was convinced that he was the Devil in person. One day during a storm she asked him to leave her house because she thought he was quite capable of drawing down thunderbolts. Voltaire, who was as terrified of lightning as she was, left protesting to his hostess that he thought more highly of the Almighty than she could possibly say.

His quarrel with the Alliots grew fiercer still over the subject of mealtimes and of the food itself, which did not suit Voltaire's frail health. The squabbling descended to schoolboy level. Voltaire penned Monsieur Alliot a number of letters flaunting his title of Gentleman of the Bedchamber, and the King of Prussia's repeated overtures of friendship. Was he to be worse treated by an Alliot at Commercy than at Versailles or Berlin?

Monsieur Alliot behaved with more wisdom and dignity, and answered the dyspeptic poet's angry letters in measured tones. But this guerrilla warfare of knives and forks was interrupted by much crueler events.

Three Widowers and an Orphan

These days of August 1749 were Madame du Châtelet's last. She enjoyed all the pleasures her condition allowed, but she was filled with sinister forebodings. She had tidied up her papers, bundled up some, sealed others. She had written letters to be delivered "afterward" to her husband and her best friends. Every time Saint-Lambert left her it broke her heart: she was afraid she would not be alive when he came back.

In spite of her fears, on September 4, 1749, she gave birth to a little girl. It was an extremely easy delivery, and at the same time she was delivered of her apprehensions. Voltaire was exultant too: he had been so afraid. He wrote to Monsieur d'Argental: "Last night Madame du Châtelet, scribbling away at Newton, felt a slight call of Nature. She called a chambermaid, who only just had time to hold out her apron and catch a little daughter, whom she then carried off to cradle. Her mother put away her papers, and as I write this they are both sleeping as soundly as dormice."

The child was baptized and handed over to a wet nurse. She thrived, and Emilie was doing very well too, until she characteristically did something foolish. It was hot, she was thirsty, and she drank a great glass of iced orgeat syrup. Almost at once she was seized with terrible pains, and the doctors came running. For a time she seemed to be improving. Mademoiselle du Thil was there and remained at her friend's bedside. The next morning Emilie was still exhausted, and seemed to be dozing. In the evening Monsieur du Châtelet, Voltaire, and other visitors left her, going off to sup with Madame de Boufflers. Only Saint-Lambert, Mademoiselle du Thil, and Longchamp remained with her. Almost at once Emilie lost consciousness and the death rattle began. Monsieur du Châtelet, Voltaire, and Madame de Boufflers were sent for immediately, but by the time they arrived Emilie was dead. They had forgotten to send for a priest. Voltaire wrote: "She experienced nothing of the horrors of death. It was only her friends who felt them."

Voltaire and Saint-Lambert remained alone with her. Voltaire was shattered. He started to roam aimlessly around the palace. He tripped down some stairs, fell near a sentry box, and cut his forehead on the flagstones. When Saint-Lambert, who followed him, tried to help him up, Voltaire said through his tears, "Ah, my friend, it is you who killed my Emilie." Then, waving his bony arms threateningly, he added: "Ah, monsieur, why did you have to get her with child?"

If Voltaire had tried to do so himself, perhaps Saint-Lambert would never have succeeded, with such unhappy results. Now the dreadful news had to be announced to those who had so joyously been told of the birth.

Voltaire suddenly remember a ring that Emilie always wore, with a setting that opened to show a miniature of himself. He asked Longchamp to go and remove it from her finger at once. Longchamp said it had already been given to Monsieur du Châtelet, and Voltaire sent him to try to prevent the marquis from opening it. Fortunately Madame de Boufflers had opened the ring and already taken out the portrait. It was of Saint-Lambert. "I swear to heaven," Voltaire cried, "if that isn't just like women! I took Richelieu's place, and Saint-Lambert took mine. One nail drives out another. That's the way things go in this world."

The huge correspondence between Voltaire and Emilie has been lost, probably destroyed by Saint-Lambert during these sad days. They would have shown us Voltaire wooing and winning Emilie, converting her to philosophy, Newton, and atheism. They would have shown us Voltaire at his freest. But unfortunately they have vanished.

The "divine Urania's" death was met with sarcasms in Paris. Spitefulness manifested itself everywhere, at court, in society, in the theater, the gazettes, and the gutters.

Someone wrote: "I have just learned that Madame du Châtelet died yesterday in childbirth. It is to be hoped that this is the last of the airs she will give herself. To die in childbed at her age is truly to seek singularity and endeavor to do everything differently from other people."

Someone else wrote an epitaph which was read aloud at a supper party amid roars of laughter. It has been attributed to Frederick II, and he was quite capable of it:

> Ci-gît, qui perdit la vie
> Dans le double accouchement
> D'une traité de philosophie
> Et d'un malheureux enfant.
> On ne sait précisément
> Lequel des deux l'a ravie.
> Sur ce funeste événement
> Lequel des deux doit-on suivre:
> Saint-Lambert s'en prend au livre,
> Voltaire dit que c'est l'enfant?

Here lies one who lost her life/In giving twin birth/To a philosophical treatise/And an unfortunate infant./It is not certain/Which of the two was to blame./In this sad case, whom is one to believe:/Saint-Lambert, who says it was the book,/Or Voltaire, who says it was the child?

Emilie was a woman with flaws but she was infinitely superior to many of her detractors. Not one mentioned her monumental translation of Newton or had any respect for the marvelous friendship that had lasted for seventeen years between two difficult characters whose affection owed more to mutual esteem and admiration than to sensuality.

Voltaire had the following lines inscribed beneath Emilie's portrait.

L'Univers a perdu la sublime Emilie.
Elle aima les plaisirs, les arts, la vérité.
Les dieux en lui donnant leur âme et leur génie
N'avaient gardé pour eux que l'immortalité.

The universe has lost the sublime Emilie./She loved pleasure, art, and truth./The gods gave her their soul and their genius/And kept for themselves only immortality.

There is no doubt that the real Emilie is the Emilie of Voltaire. The years of their friendship were the happiest and most fruitful in Voltaire's life. No one could ever take her place. The studious solitude of Cirey snatched him away from the dangerous toils of Paris. The discipline and elegance of life with such a *grande dame* restrained his wildest excesses: he did not escape all the traps set for him, but he avoided the most dangerous ones. Emilie maintained around her an atmosphere of good breeding and of spiritual as well as decorative luxury. She had given him peace, order, and that "superfluity" so necessary to the unfolding of a genius such as Voltaire's.

The Art of Suffering and of Finding Consolation

What was to become of Voltaire now? At fifty-five, for the first time in his life, he was at loose ends and without anywhere to go. The world had never seemed so empty to one who lived only for society and for whom Emilie had come to replace all the rest. Stanislas behaved perfectly as usual, and arranged a magnificent funeral. He visited the bereaved poet in his room three times a day and they mingled their tears. But what was Voltaire to do next? He had always expected he would die young and that Emilie would survive him; he had always thought she would close his eyes for him at Cirey. Where should he go now? He thought first of retiring among the Benedictines at Senones, where the Châtelets had a friend, Dom Calvet, whom Voltaire was fond of. He also considered going back to England, to Lord Bolingbroke. But instead he went back to Cirey with the other widower, Emilie's husband. He dreaded the experience. But it was all right: it was at Lunéville that she had died and he had seen her mortal remains; at Cirey she was immortal, lively and happy as he had always known her. He wrote to D'Argental: "I have not lost a mistress, I have lost half of myself, a spirit for which mine was made, a friend of twenty years whom I saw come into the world. The fondest father does not love his only daughter otherwise than I loved her. I like to find the memory of her everywhere: I like to speak to her husband, to her son. In short, people all have different ways of suffering, and that is mine."

Voltaire's confession is both poignant and revealing. The "paternal" love he felt was not free from sensuality. He seems not to have been capable of distinguishing between paternal and other affections.

Would Emilie's burning passion for Saint-Lambert have allowed her to keep Voltaire, as she had kept Monsieur du Châtelet? Would Saint-Lambert have put up indefinitely with such a situation? Would his kind of love have held out against such a false position, or against the passage of time? And what would have been the attitude of public opinion and of Monsieur du Châtelet? Emilie's husband and the world had been very tolerant, protective even, because it was Emilie and because it was Voltaire. But it is likely that Emilie's future with Saint-Lambert would have been a somber one. He was young, too young; he would soon have flown, and Emilie would have been inconsolable. Whatever happened, she was doomed. By dying she had solved the problem.

With Monsieur de Châtelet's help, Voltaire moved out of Cirey. The things he wanted to take with him—books, certain pieces of furniture, paintings and statues—were packed into straw-lined carts. The huge convoy moved off, and Monsieur du Châtelet and his son were left alone in a house half empty of furniture and quite empty of its soul. Voltaire made no claim for all the money he had spent on Cirey; between him and Monsieur du Châtelet the question of bargaining did not arise.

He wept heartbrokenly on leaving Cirey. It was like losing Emilie a second time. He was ill, too, very ill; it was no pretense. He thought he was going to die, and wanted at all costs to avoid being buried in Paris. He wrote to the Abbé Voisenon: "I have a horrid repugnance for the idea of being buried in Paris." It is not difficult to guess the reason: Like Adrienne Lecouvreur, in Paris he might be refused Christian burial. He was haunted by the fear of the common grave.

He traveled in short stages, correcting *Catilina*. Going through Rheims he discovered an excellent copyist, whom he engaged and took along with him: the man had penned some enthusiastic verses on this dreary tragedy that he had devotedly transcribed for his new employer.

In Paris Voltaire took up residence in the Rue Traversière. Monsieur du Châtelet, not to be outdone in generosity, made over to him the part of the house that Emilie had formerly occupied. Voltaire, lonely and ill, would have liked to let one floor to a friend, but perhaps living with Voltaire did not seem an attractive proposition. At any rate no one accepted his offer.

He was like a soul in torment, overwhelmed with sorrow. He roamed through the rooms talking to Emilie. He told his friends of the state he was in. Frederick did not believe all this grief was sincere: "Voltaire protests too much in his affliction, which makes me think he will soon find consolation," he wrote. No doubt he was right, but he was confusing two things: the rapidity with which Voltaire's emotions succeeded one another, and sincerity. Voltaire emitted great flashes whose nature it was to dazzle rather than to last. But it was pure malice to accuse him of feigning now. He was not the sort to allow grief to lay him low forever, but while his grief lasted it was unbearable. He would have to free himself of it, but that time had not yet come. One night Longchamp found him in a daze, groaning, stumbling, sometimes falling, and murmuring Emilie's name. Voltaire's faithful servant thereupon decided to cure his master of what he considered excessive grief by showing him some letters Emilie was supposed to have written to Saint-Lambert, making fun of Voltaire. According to Longchamp, Voltaire was so upset at the sight of them that his tears immediately dried up. The story is unconvincing. Moreover he had certain consolations which no one else knew about at the time.

He was not so lonely as Longchamp makes out. He had visits from the D'Argentals, Richelieu, Marmontel, the Abbé Mignot, his nephew, and also his niece, Madame Denis. She lived not far away and came often.

And more than anything else, it was the theater that made Voltaire forget his grief. He had renamed *Catilina* and was calling it *Rome sauvée* (*Rome Saved*); he wanted to have it put on to show Crébillon that Voltaire could succeed where he had failed. If Crébillon had been ill with mortification as a result, Voltaire would certainly have given up full mourning for half mourning. But it was a strange plan: Crébillon was the official theatrical censor, and it was he who would have to give permission for the play to be performed. Voltaire went to see him and explained that it was by pure accident that he had come to write on the same subject as the illustrious censor, who had also composed a tragedy on Catiline. Crébillon pretended to be taken in and gave permission. But he said that Voltaire was "a very wicked man."

The first performance got off to a bad start. The spectators in the pit were bored, and talked and blew their noses and didn't listen. Voltaire hid silent in a box. Suddenly one speech made people sit up and take notice and they started to applaud. Voltaire sprang up, leaned out of his box, and cried: "Courage, Athenians, this is Sophocles!" But the Athenians of Paris would go no further, and the play was more or less a failure. Voltaire made a note of the unpopular passages and rewrote them. He went to see the leading actress, Mademoiselle Clairon, to apologize for making other alterations in addition to those she had requested. He always treated stage princesses with as much deference as real ones: they were a good deal more difficult to please.

These innumerable corrections inspired Fontenelle's remark that Voltaire was "a very unusual author: he writes his plays while they are being performed."

It was said that Voltaire himself signaled his claque when to applaud and that, seeing one spectator listening impassively with his hands still idle in his muff, he shouted at him to clap. The other replied that he had no desire to do so.

"What's your name?" cried Voltaire.

"Rousseau," said the man.

"Which Rousseau? The young one or . . ."

This exchange took place in the middle of the performance. Suddenly a big burly woman rose up in front of Voltaire, brandishing an enormous fist in his face, and threatened to use it if he did not keep quiet. Voltaire fled, and the audience laughed. His assailant was Madame Le Bas, who would certainly have carried out her threat. Her husband was famous as engraver to the King and a member of the Academy of Fine Arts; she herself was no less celebrated for the harangues and cuffs she distributed in the pit of the Comédie Française.

Enter Madame Denis

Voltaire was certain that the Rousseau who had flouted him was Jean-Jacques. This was not true, and when the latter heard about it he wrote to explain that he hadn't even been in the theater that day, and that in any case he would never have done anything to offend Monsieur de Voltaire. At this time, in January 1750, the younger Rousseau was still almost unknown. A few months later he was famous.

So, four months after Emilie's death, life, through the theater, was reasserting itself. Frederick's only mistake had been to talk about consolation too soon.

The husband of Voltaire's niece, Madame Denis, had died five years earlier, in 1744, and for five years she had been finding consolation. Her tears were more copious than lasting. On installing herself in the Rue Traversière for Christmas, 1749, she found her uncle almost recovered, and they united their states of bereavement, for better or worse.

Voltaire lavished praises on his niece, but his contemporaries were much less enthusiastic. Her uncle said she had wit; but she was only talkative and an indiscreet gossip. She prided herself on her free and easy ways; but she carried them to the point of licentiousness. If she had had manner, beauty, or charm, and a touch of wit, they might have brought her what they had so many others—a brilliant reputation or a fortune. But she lacked these ethereal virtues. She was greedy and sensual, and soon put on weight and looked older than her years. When she acted in Zaïre her uncle was in raptures. One day, when someone was flattering the niece to please the uncle, she coyly said with mock modesty: "The part really needs someone young and beautiful," and a bystander murmured, "You are ample proof to the contrary."

Marmontel, who was all smiles to both of them, said, "She is an amiable woman in spite of her ugliness." There can be no doubt that the portrait painters flattered her. The fact that she aped her uncle's manners lent her an appearance of taste and wit but it was only a veneer on her fundamental vulgarity.

Unfortunately she also had ambitions as a writer. This alarmed Voltaire, who foresaw the consequences of failure, and he nipped her unpromising genius in the bud.

The court, the town, and the people were all passionate devotees of the theater. Stages were put up everywhere. The King and the nobles acted in the state rooms at Versailles, the others in market places, squares, courtyards, salons, and even attics. At one of these performances Voltaire noticed a young actor of astonishing skill, power, and vivacity. The young man was invited to the Rue Traversière, where he was regaled with coffee and chocolate and dazed with praise. Voltaire had just discovered Le Kain, one of the most gifted actors France has ever had. He was ugly. It was an expressive ugliness, but it was a drawback that he had to overcome by talent and hard work. He told Voltaire that he had not inconsiderable means but that, knowing that he could live only in the glow of the footlights, he was going to devote his money entirely to the furthering of his career in the theater. Voltaire was both delighted and horrified. "Oh," he cried, "you must never do any such thing, believe me. Act for your pleasure, but never make it your only occupation in life." Whereupon he lent the young man ten thousand livres to establish himself: "Pay me back when you can."

It was no small sum. Even Jean-Jacques Rousseau, who wasted no love on Voltaire, recognized the attractiveness of Voltaire's spontaneous acts of generosity: "I know of no man on earth whose first impulses were finer." He implies that the impulses that followed left something to be desired—as indeed they often did.

Le Kain was overwhelmed by such generosity. Before letting him go, Voltaire asked him to recite some poetry, and in his confusion he repeated some lines by Piron. Voltaire recognized them and cried, "Stop! No Piron! No bad poetry. Recite some Racine." Le Kain began to recite one of Abner's speeches, and Voltaire was in tears before the end. He embraced the young man, promising that one day he would hold all Paris under the same spell.

In order to have Racine and Le Kain under his own roof he built a little theater in the attic. He began by putting on his own tragedy, *Mahomet*, for Richelieu, the D'Argentals, his niece, and the servants. A young ingenue who played Palmire lisped her towering lines too simperingly, and Voltaire cried: "Mademoiselle, remember that Mahomet is an impostor—a rogue, a scoundrel, who had your brother stabbed, has just poisoned your father, and, to crown such dastardly acts, means to force you to sleep with him. If all this pleases you in some way, of course you are quite right to be so charming to him. But if you find such things repellent, this is how you should set about it—" and he leaped onto the stage, where he hurled himself about and screamed like a madman, in paroxysms of horror and despair. The poor girl was terrified, but she learned her lesson, perfected her talents, and Le Kain later considered her a good actress.

Voltaire took it into his head to put on his tragedy *Rome sauvée* in his attic theater. Le Kain and his friends threw themselves wholeheartedly into the project and the all-powerful Richelieu ordered delivered around from the Comédie Française all the sets and costumes the King had provided for Crébillon's play on the same subject. The list of guests included Richelieu, the Duc de La Vallière, D'Alembert, Diderot, Marmontel, three abbés of whom two were academicians, and a number of other people distinguished in society or the Church. The play was a success with this audience, and soon all Paris heard about it. Voltaire's attic in the Rue Traversière became overnight the most elegant and the most inaccessible place in Paris. The play had to be given ten times. Voltaire had benches and tiers added at the sides and arranged boxes between the rafters, until the room could hold a hundred spectators. Ministers and ambassadors begged for invitations but did not get them easily.

Voltaire extracted from this success a complex pleasure in which revenge played its part: the actors of the Comédie Française were furious. They had scorned *Rome sauvée*, and now the most fastidious of audiences was praising it to the skies. Even the court smiled on Voltaire: Madame de Pompadour chose *Alzire* to be acted there in private. It was the first time a tragedy had been performed at court in so intimate a theater, and it went off perfectly. Voltaire was graciously invited to the second performance. The King said in an audible voice: "It is astonishing that the author of *Alzire* could also have written *Oreste*." This spoke very well for *Alzire*, but it was a reminder of the failure of *Oreste*. Louis XV too was fond of the exchange of darts at which Voltaire excelled. It was the current style, and it was often cruel.

One day the King said to a courtier, "You are getting old. Where do you want to be buried?"

"At Your Majesty's feet," was the reply.

The Birth of a Serpent

When the Abbé Desfontaines died he had left Fréron as his successor as Voltaire's prime enemy: he was to spy on him, harass him, and drive him to write pamphlets entirely beneath his talent and his dignity. Of all Voltaire's jealous, backbiting rivals, Fréron met with the most success.

Born at Quimper in 1719, Fréron had been a pupil of the Jesuits and even taught at Louis-le-Grand, where no doubt he found traces still of the brilliant young François-Marie Arouet. He was a remarkable teacher; he had taste, moderation, and skill. He knew all the subtleties of dissertation. But he became a critic under the auspices of Desfontaines and his associates, which is a sufficient indication of his literary integrity and of his sentiments toward Voltaire. He was treacherous, malicious, and stubborn. All his talents, natural and acquired, were put at the service of traditional beliefs. But more than he loved these, he hated all new ideas. He attacked them both in the works of the *philosophes* and in their persons, and of all the targets that presented themselves the most obvious was Voltaire.

Enrolling under the doubtful banner of Desfontaines, Fréron collaborated with him in the *Observations sur les écrits modernes* (*Remarks on Modern Writings*) and *Jugements sur quelques ouvrages nouveaux* (*Judgments on Various New Works*). Then on his own account he started a periodical called *Lettres à la Comtesse de X. sur quelques écrits modernes* (*Letters to the Comtesse de X. on Certain Modern Writings*), in which he made such base attacks on a number of authors' reputations that, notwithstanding the "respectability" of his own opinions, the police suppressed his periodical in 1746. He replaced it in 1749 by the *Lettres sur les écrits de ce temps* (*Letters on Present-day Writings*), which in 1754 took the name of the *Année littéraire* (*The Literary Year*). It was in this latter that he aimed at Voltaire his cruelest, best-aimed, and often most successful jibes.

The war between them began through a fit of jealousy on the part of Fréron, who had written a eulogistic poem on Fontenoy which was eclipsed by Voltaire's. Fréron did not show his resentment openly or immediately; he was too clever for that. He even wrote in praise of Voltaire's poem. But how could one be impartial without repeating the criticisms that others had made? So he reproduced the attacks, discussed them, and in short managed to make mincemeat of the poem he was purporting to praise. As Desfontaines had given him access to his archives, Fréron was able to reprint old attacks not only on the work but also against Voltaire himself. Among other piquant items, he revived certain lines written in 1735: "By his familiarities with the great, he consoled himself for the discomfort he felt with his equals; he was sensitive without affection, voluptuous without passion, sociable without a friend, open without frankness, and on occasion liberal without originality." It was a mixture of true and false, and the truth sounded worse than the lies. Voltaire did not forget Fréron, in spite of the latter's disappearance from the literary scene for several years, having been exiled to Bar-sur-Aube in 1746, at the time of the suppression of *Lettres à la Comtesse de X.*, in which he had attacked "France's youngest academician . . . an abbé illustrious for his birth and two little odes" who "on leaving school finds himself elevated to the highest literary honor." Fréron's Comtesse X., referring to this pink and beardless abbé, said, "I regret less than ever that I am a woman." Everyone had recognized the churchman in question as Babet la Bouquetière, the Abbé de Bernis, favorite of Madame de Pompadour.

Fréron returned from Bar in 1749 and began publishing his new periodical. Voltaire immediately scented danger and asked D'Argental whether the prisons were full or if there was still room for Fréron. His fears were well founded: Fréron attacked him in the very first number.

He chose a play to which Voltaire had not signed his name, but no one had been taken in, and Voltaire could neither acknowledge the play nor defend himself. So he remained silent, though choking with rage. Fréron grew bolder and repeated his underhanded tactics. Voltaire applied to the superintendent of police to have Fréron arrested. He applied directly to Monsieur d'Argenson and asked all his friends to besiege the Prime Minister too.

Then Voltaire discovered another crime on the part of Fréron: he was angling to get the King of Prussia to appoint him as his correspondent, informer, and purveyor of books and pamphlets. This would enable Fréron to shape Frederick's opinion on what was going on in Paris, in particular in the realm of literature. The idea of this treachery made Voltaire ill with fury. Fréron knew how to hit where it hurt most. In addition to the blow to Voltaire himself, it was a blow to Thiériot: it was only two years since Voltaire had got his friend appointed to the post of Frederick's informer. Not that it was such a splendid job: Thiériot had still received no payment but words, and Voltaire was always reminding Frederick what he owed for books bought and reports sent. After turning a deaf ear for two years, Frederick finally sent twelve hundred livres; he and Thiériot had been counting on two thousand a year. "I must also tell you that if I am any judge of His Prussian Majesty's character, he doesn't like to be asked for things," Thiériot wrote Voltaire. Voltaire made up the difference: what did he care if he had to pay Thiériot himself, so long as Fréron didn't take his place! After many alarums and excursions, it was learned that Frederick had no wish to take Fréron into his service. Voltaire breathed again but did not swallow his resentment.

The theater in the attic in the Rue Traversière was always full. Voltaire had tickets printed and enjoyed drawing up the lists of guests. Finally, not content with writing the plays, he wanted to act in them as well. In 1750, a the age of fifty-six, ailing and prematurely old, he could be seen onstage rejuvenated by the magic of the theater. He declaimed his parts in stentorian tones which sometimes grated on the audience's ears, but he threw himself into them wholeheartedly and ended the evening's performance half dead with fatigue but overcome with delight. The applause brought the color back to his wrinkled cheeks and made his eyes sparkle with joy. His two nieces, Madame Denis and Madame de Fontaine, also took to acting. The actors of the Comédie Française were anxious lest all authors start acting their new plays themselves, leaving professional actors only the old ones. Voltaire, at their request, sent them two tickets each for four performances. They expressed their enchantment with plays they would probably have rejected three months earlier. Their show of enthusiasm was proof at least that they were good actors.

Voltaire was saving up his *Rome sauvée* with the idea of going to Sceaux and staging it there. But the Duchesse du Maine was slightly older and less energetic now, and she hadn't forgotten how Voltaire had thrown her château open to hordes of undesirables. But she still loved society and the theater. With his usual aplomb, Voltaire simply announced to her that he was about to put on *Rome sauvée* at her country estate. Her answer was not encouraging, but on May 8, 1750, Voltaire set out for Sceaux, settled in, and began to lay siege to his hostess. His wit and gaiety soon won her over, but on one point she was adamant: she did not want to have the actors sleeping in her house. "I dispense my protectress from having to lodge the mummers," Voltaire promised her. He would have them driven back to Paris—but on condition that she supply the coaches.

The tragedy was performed on June 22, 1750, and was a huge success. Voltaire, as Nero, surpassed all the rest—according to Le Kain, who was perhaps somewhat blinded by gratitude. But it is true that Voltaire was as good an actor on the stage as in real life.

In the enemy camp they mocked both Voltaire and his play. "He is like the pastry cooks," one of them said. "The pies they can't sell they eat themselves." They also accused him of sabotaging *Cénie*, a play of Madame de Graffigny's that was being put on just then. This was pure malice; Voltaire was on excellent terms with Madame de Graffigny and wished her nothing but success. But she met with no more of that in the theater than in life.

The triumph at Sceaux had the further advantage of showing the actors of the Comédie Française that they needed Voltaire more than he needed them.

The Siren of Potsdam Tries a New Song

Since Emilie's death Frederick's invitations had become more and more pressing. The King's early enthusiasm seemed to be reviving in all its freshness. Voltaire was touched: "When I read your letter I felt that if I were only slightly restored to health I should set out at once, even if you were in Königsberg." But it was winter, and for one who shivered in the middle of summer the German roads were impossible. He promised to come when the weather turned better. Meanwhile he sent Frederick some poems, to be delivered in Berlin by Baculard d'Arnaud, one of the lovers with whom Madame Denis had consoled herself in her widowhood before doing so with her uncle.

Voltaire had helped him with advice and money at the beginning of his career, but it was not long before Thiériot was telling him how Frederick and Baculard were exchanging verses at his expense. Frederick said that to "a fine sunset" (Voltaire) he preferred "a finer dawn" (Baculard). Baculard replied in verse that in that case he hoped to equal the radiance of Voltaire.

Voltaire was in bed when Thiériot brought him this bit of news. "Let's see those verses!" he cried. When he got to the part about sunset and dawn, he leaped out of bed and began raging at Frederick, crying over and over again: "Why doesn't he stick to being a king?" He swore he would go to Berlin to sort out that monarch's ideas for him. What neither pleas nor bribes had been able to accomplish, a blow at Voltaire's pride achieved in a moment.

Voltaire did not set out for Germany without the usual bargaining between the two parties. The bone of contention was Voltaire's niece. Frederick was quite willing to defray all Voltaire's expenses but, not having wanted Emilie at his court, he certainly didn't want Madame Denis. If she wished to come he would receive her if he must, but let her pay her own expenses. Voltaire drew up a detailed list of all the expenditures the journey would cost him, including the coach, the maintenance of his household while he has away (he could not simply abandon Madame Denis), and expenses arising from the illnesses he was bound to be afflicted with. "I do not want to be a burden on you," he wrote to the King. And he asked for four thousand German crowns by way of an advance. He promised to pay them back, and if Frederick agreed to his proposal he would set out within four days. "Whatever pains my body suffers, I shall force it to go," he added stoically. He could afford to be stoical for four thousand crowns.

Frederick knew that to refuse the advance to a friend, even one who was rich and solvent, would mean a definite rupture. But what agony to have to disburse it! And what if Voltaire balked at repaying it? Frederick would be the laughingstock of Europe if he tried to dun him for it. Voltaire seems to have expected such hesitations. His first rage over the Baculard episode was past, and he was in no hurry to betake himself to Prussia unless it would be profitable for him to do so. Such were the two distinguished friends: their relations were far from olympian despite their aristocratic veneer.

But Frederick gave in, hiding his feelings under a veil of mythological verse in which he played Jupiter to Voltaire's Danaë. Voltaire accepted his role and pocketed the money:

> Votre très vieille Danaé
> Va quitter son petit ménage
> Pour le beau séjour étoilé
> Dont elle est indigne à son âge.

Your aged Danaë/Is about to leave her humble home/For the fine starry abode/Of which at her age she is unworthy.

The elderly "coquette" admitted devotion to:

> Son Jupiter et non sa pluie,
> Mais c'est en vain que l'on médit
> De ces gouttes très salutaires
> Au siècle de fer où l'on vit
> Ces gouttes d'or sont nécessaires.

Her Jupiter and not his rain,/But it is foolish to scorn/This very salutary shower/For in this iron age we live in/These drops of gold are necessary.

It is clear that Voltaire made ready to go to Prussia without enthusiasm. He waited until the last minute for a sign from the French court which would prevent his departure. But none came, either from the King or from the favorite.

When Voltaire, despairing of being kept from leaving, betook himself to Versailles and asked the King's permission to leave France, Louis told him he might go whenever he wished, and turned his back on him.

Madame de Pompadour did not receive Voltaire's farewells quite so unfeelingly, and although she knew that Frederick detested her, she asked Voltaire to convey her respects to him in as cordial a manner as possible. When he did so, Frederick answered curtly: "I do not know her."

The D'Argentals disapproved of his departure. They tried to persuade themselves that this would be only a short visit, like the previous ones, for they were altogether opposed to his settling in Prussia for good. They were not the only ones displeased with his ostentatious departure: his reputation suffered both at court and in society. People were glad enough to be rid of him, but that he should go and shine at Potsdam was another matter. When Frederick applied to Louis XV to abandon Voltaire to him, Louis replied that he could keep him with pleasure: in private he said it meant one madman less at his court and one more at Frederick's. Voltaire's appointment as historiographer was withdrawn and given to Duclos, though the King magnanimously continued to pay Voltaire his pension of two thousand livres. But the air of nonchalance adopted by the King and Madame de Pompadour could not entirely disguise their mortification: Voltaire's attitude seemed to them not so much hostile as unseemly. When this sentiment reached Voltaire's ears he wrote: "It is amusing that men of letters who would have liked to exterminate me a year ago now cry out against my departure and call it desertion. It almost seems as if they were angry at having been deprived of their victim."

His enemies themselves admired his talent and intelligence, and even the bitterest among them considered that he belonged to Paris. Street vendors sold pictures of him wearing a bearskin busby: "Voltaire the Prussian—one sou!" Some people accused him of being motivated by avarice and of going to Prussia to enjoy the pensions of a favorite. It showed how little they knew Frederick. Others, like Lord Chesterfield, puzzled over the problem of Voltaire's desertion without being able to arrive at any explanation: whatever profit he might get out of it, they thought it an absurd move. However, the wily Lord Chesterfield considered that Voltaire would be able to let himself go more freely in future, now that he was out of reach both of the censors and of his enemies. He would be more dangerous than ever to the country and the institutions that had let him escape them, and escape them in a mood of resentment.

Chesterfield was right. Versailles had made a mistake in letting the *enfant terrible* go. The fruitless squabbles of Paris had absorbed a good deal of his aggressiveness, and his ridiculous rages and unworthy pamphlets against opponents such as Desfontaines had caused him to neglect his hatred for tyranny, injustice, and fanaticism in all shapes and forms. Now, in his gilded exile, protected by a philosopher-king, he could give free rein to all this.

If Versailles and its counselors had been less haughty and more clever, Voltaire might have been trapped and even tamed by honors such as an appointment as Master of the Royal Pearls. But now it was no longer a question of court frivolities which might well have absorbed all of his energies but of seeing clearer and farther, of talking too much yet expressing himself better than anyone else, and of scattering throughout Europe the little books that would spread like sparks of fire, setting light to received ideas, superstitions, ignorant self-satisfaction, and injustice.

The break with Versailles and Paris was the great turning point in Voltaire's life. Emilie's death had paved the way for it by severing his strongest links with France. In this spring of 1750, at the age of fifty-six, it was all over, he was leaving. Was it flight, desertion, betrayal, or a need to escape? Whichever it was, it was dramatic. Voltaire, the child of Paris, would never be a Parisian again. He would return there only at the end of his days, entering the capital as an idol, leaving it as a withered corpse. Paris was a finished chapter in his life. One wonders if he sensed it.

After this break Voltaire would no longer be even entirely French. When he came back from Prussia he was a Frenchman without France, a Frenchman without frontiers, a Frenchman of the intellect but not of the flesh. He would return a European, and an exemplar for all humanity.

6. Voltaire's bedroom in his Paris residence, corner of Rue de Beaune and Quai Voltaire. (Photo Roger-Viollet)

7. The house at Rue de Beaune and Quai Voltaire, where Voltaire died. (Photo Roger-Viollet)

8. Frederick the Great with his dinner guests at the Château de Sans Souci, by A. V. Menzel. Foremost among Frederick's guests is Voltaire (left, in profile). (National Museum, Berlin. Photo Roger-Viollet)

9. Engraving of Voltaire being crowned with a laurel wreath by Le Kain, as Madame Denis looks on. (Bibliothéque Nationale. Photo Giraudon)

10. View of the north side of Voltaire's Château de Ferney, by Signy. (Musée Carnavalet. Photo Giraudon)

11. Meeting of philosophers. Engraving attributed to Jean Huber. (Musée Carnavalet. Photo Lauros-Giraudon)

PART TWO

IX

You women have grown accustomed to being the principal moving force of tragedies, as you are of this world. It is necessary for you to be as profoundly in love as madwomen, to have rivals, to create rivals; it is necessary that a man adore you, kill you, regret you, kill himself along with you. But, my dear ladies, Cicero and Cato were not gallant lovers, Caesar and Catiline slept with you, granted, but they were certainly not the sort to kill for you. (Letter to Madame Denis, December 25, 1750)

How many bad books written by witty men! (Letter, March 20, 1751)

One does not know how to approach the public. There is only one secret to please it within one's lifetime and that is to be supremely unhappy. (Letter, December 14, 1751)

We are balloons that the hand of destiny moves about blindly and irresistibly. We bounce two or three times, sometimes on marble and sometimes on a manure pile, and then we burst forever. (Letter, June 10, 1752)

At times I think of everything that I have suffered, and conclude that if I had a son doomed to meet as many setbacks I would wring his neck out of paternal tenderness. (Letter, July 22, 1752)

He who thinks makes others think. (*Fragments on History*)

Pope, who was brought up in the Catholic religion that he sometimes mocks in his epistles, nonetheless did not want to leave the bosom of the Church even though he was a *philosophe*, or rather because he was enough of a *philosophe* to believe that it was not worth the trouble to change. (*The Century of Louis XIV:* "Racine")

Sovereign power can mistreat a good man but not dishonor him. (*The Century of Louis XIV*, Chapter 11)

There have been more than a hundred and twenty battles in Europe since 1600; and of all of them there have not been ten decisive ones. This is blood uselessly shed for interests that change from day to day. (*The Century of Louis XIV*, Chapter 13)

This fury of proselytes is a malady particular to our climates; it has always been unknown in upper Asia. These peoples have never sent missionaries to Europe, and our nations are the only ones who have endeavored to take their opinions, like their trade, to the two farthest ends of the globe. (*The Century of Louis XIV*, Chapter 39)

A good form of government must make punishment serve a purpose. It is wise to make criminals work for the public good; their death is of no use to anyone but executioners. (*The Century of Louis XIV*, Chapter 42)

Europe's Two Kings

At that time Europe had two kings: the King of Prussia and Voltaire. They lived together and, strange to relate, they were friends in their own unusual way. The first, Frederick, directed the policies of other sovereigns as he pleased, imposing war or peace. He overthrew their alliances and caused courts and chancelleries to spend sleepless nights. He poked fun at God and even at the Pope. In addition he wrote poetry in French.

The second, Voltaire, had at first ruled only over the theater, and he continued to be the shining light of French tragedy in Paris and the other capitals of Europe. Then he acquired greater and more insidious power by teaching the art of speaking and writing to all Europe, to its kings, its writers, and its respectable citizens who, almost without realizing it, ended up adopting the master's ideas as well as his language. And so, around the middle of the century, the fine flower of Europe found themselves the willing subjects of a philosopher-poet, the least majestic but the most interesting man in the world.

The first king ruled the force of arms, the second those of the mind. But Frederick was intelligent enough to want to make use of mind also, and he dealt with Voltaire as he dealt with other sovereigns. He tried to annex the latter's finest province; that is, his language and his style.

Voltaire was foolish enough to covet the favor of kings, including, for want of a better, Frederick's. He was not the wiser of the two. He was full of excellent maxims, but he often behaved like a court poet. He was punished for it.

The two "kings" had at least one trait in common: in the eyes of right-thinking Europe they were both equally scandalous and equally uncontested.

They had recognized one another long before they ascended their respective thrones. Each had sensed the sovereignty of the other, and they were irresistibly drawn to one another by both fraternity and complicity. With great intelligence, and on occasion genius, intermingled with much vanity, cupidity, cynicism, and flattery, and the entire mixture well seasoned with duplicity, the two great men earned themselves an extra claim to glory by weaving between them the subtle threads of a strange attachment which history, for want of a better word, calls friendship.

Voltaire left Paris on June 18, 1750. After missed stagecoaches, miserable inns, the dreary landscapes of Westphalia and the smiling countryside of Magdeburg, he arrived in Potsdam on July 10.

He was in the same frame of mind as when he had arrived in London twenty years earlier. He found everything in Prussia perfect: "A hundred and fifty thousand victors, no prosecutors, opera, theater, philosophy, poetry, a hero who is a philosopher and poet, grandeur and grace, grenadiers and muses, trumpets and violins, Platonic repasts, society and liberty! Who would believe it? Yet it is all true."

In reality Potsdam was not the groves of Academe but a vast barracks. Frederick never ceased waging war and preparing for war. In Potsdam no one, from private soldier to crown prince, was allowed to wander abroad without the King's permission. He did not give it very often. Everyone was confined to barracks. Five battalions were shut up like this within the walls of Potsdam. The few women who lived there were hardly allowed out of their houses and were never seen. Few appeared at court. A little later Voltaire wrote, "It is not a court, it is a retreat from which ladies are banished." Some young men were said to have died of boredom there. But Voltaire didn't see this at first, or refused to see it. "My Frederick the Great" occupied all his attention. He even sacrificed for Frederick's sake the corrections of his *Rome sauvée* that he was eager to make. Even for Emilie he would never have sacrificed his work in this fashion. "He takes up my time and soul," he wrote ecstatically of the King.

And then suddenly there were the festivities—apparently lavish, ruinously expensive, and incomprehensible in view of Frederick's avarice. But the army supplied the supernumeraries and the manpower.

These sumptuous displays were designed to dazzle Europe rather than the citizens of Berlin. They were publicity for Prussia aimed at the diplomatic corps and foreign courts. Voltaire sat in the front row and spread the word far and wide that Louis XIV lived again on the banks of the Spree. It was no more than what was expected of him in return for the four thousand crowns that Frederick had advanced him. He also wrote, delighting the princes and the court dignitaries with his descriptions of the entertainments, whose charms were multiplied tenfold in his accounts. Frederick had got himself the best public relations officer alive. "Forty-six thousand Chinese lanterns lit up the square where the carrousel was held. The order was as perfect as the silence, the organization flawless. This country is a fairyland. And all this the handiwork of one man."

Frederick knew Voltaire had made a considerable sacrifice in coming to him, and he knew his friend so well that he lived in constant fear that he would change his mind and leave again. In order to keep him at his court for good he knew he could rely on Voltaire's vanity and greed. Flattering attentions and a few ribbons satisfied him on the first count: Voltaire was appointed chamberlain and chevalier of the Order of Merit. As for the second, Frederick granted Voltaire a pension of twenty thousand livres and promised Madame Denis an annuity of four thousand livres if she would come and keep house for her uncle in Berlin. Though he hated the thought of having her at his court, Frederick knew that the niece's presence would help to keep her will-o'-the-wisp uncle there.

So much for the solid realities cementing the association between Frederick and Voltaire. But the trivialities which were the daily bread of their friendship are not to be forgotten: the letters dispatched from one room to another, the flatteries, all the little attentions that are the small change of friendships at a king's court. The royal family, especially Frederick's brothers, treated Voltaire like a visiting monarch. More than all the money and titles, it was this illusion of living almost on an equal footing with a poet-king that intoxicated Voltaire, who had always felt himself to be, and now was in fact, the king of the poets of his age.

He felt attached to Frederick and Berlin, and thought that he would remain as he was for the rest of his life. He therefore did his best to persuade Madame Denis to come join him. But she made no secret of her unwillingness to do so, and her uncle, outraged by her ignorance, wrote back: "Who can have told you that Berlin is as primitive as Paris in the time of Hugh Capet?" Let her come and see, and she would never want to leave.

But Madame Denis reigned over a salon in Paris frequented by Voltaire's friends. She lived a free life—very free, according to Longchamp. First there had been a giant-sized German musician who had charmed Madame Denis but not her uncle, who had sent him packing. When Voltaire left Paris the musical colossus reappeared. Just as he and Madame Denis were playing nicely in tune, an Italian singer came on the scene and took the German's place. The new harmony did not last long, either because the singer was hard to get along with in private or, as he alleged, because Madame Denis borrowed large sums of money from him which she had no inclination to repay. The two of them had a violent falling out.

Longchamp had to intervene, and Voltaire, to put an end to the scandal, sent the money the Italian claimed was due him. He pocketed it and vanished. Madame Denis liked this kind of excitement and was not certain she would find its equivalent in Berlin.

Longchamp was not above reproach either. He stole manuscripts, copied them, and sold them to booksellers. This was worse than theft, for he not only filched from his master but also placed him in a dangerous position. The authorities were concerned, and wanted to know where the manuscripts came from. Madame Denis took charge of the inquiries and the manuscripts were recovered. Longchamp accused Madame Denis of having wrongfully accused him; she had turned against him since he had intervened between her and the Italian singer and secured the money from Voltaire to pay him off. It may well be that Madame Denis was not as grateful as she might have been for the special services Longchamp had rendered her; it would not have been unlike her. But that does not excuse the misdeeds of Longchamp, who had hitherto been his master's honest and devoted servant. No doubt he had succumbed to the offers of dubious booksellers.

Such was the life that so absorbed Madame Denis that she refused to join her uncle and never set eyes on Berlin.

As soon as Voltaire had unpacked he got down to essentials—that is to say, to the theater first of all, acting in his own plays with the King's brothers. Then he set about removing the man who had cast a shadow on his reputation: Baculard d'Arnaud. Voltaire found it hard to forgive Frederick for having compared the author of *Zaïre* to a setting sun, but he could not forgive Baculard at all for having believed the King and taken himself for a rising one. Voltaire sent him to shine somewhere else. One evening Baculard, together with the princes and Voltaire, was acting *Mérope:* Voltaire had given him only a small part. He mumbled his lines so offhandedly that Voltaire was furious: the coxcomb was committing the double crime of treating both Voltaire and the Theater with contempt. War was declared on the spot, and Voltaire finally demanded that the King send Baculard away. The pretext was a letter his rival was supposed to have written to one of Voltaire's enemies, reporting some anti-French remarks that Voltaire was alleged to have made in Berlin. As Baculard could not compete with Voltaire in Frederick's esteem, he was sent packing, the King taking advantage of the circumstances not to pay his fare. Thus did Baculard's sun set when it had scarcely risen.

Baculard took refuge with the Duke of Saxony, who received him so warmly that Voltaire was jealous. He wrote to the Margravine of Bayreuth, saying Baculard deserved worse than hanging and recommending that, far from welcoming him, she should see to it he was run out of all the courts in Germany. He was wasting his time, for Baculard could live only in Paris, and soon returned there of his own free will. There he sent audiences into floods of tears with gloomy plays that were the melancholy delight of the new "sensibility."

When he had given Paris a good cry, Baculard made his peace with his rival in Potsdam. Remembering Voltaire's kindnesses to him at the beginning of his career, he extended his sincerest apologies and Voltaire, unable to resist any sign of repentance or gesture of friendship, pardoned him his sins.

The King of Prussia's Menagerie

The only exceptional thing about the society with which Frederick II surrounded himself was the number and celebrity of the writers and scholars at Potsdam. Other German courts had created a French society long before him. Everyone wanted to breathe the air of Versailles and assume the manner of Louis XIV, the only king in Europe at the beginning of the century. When Louis died, Frederick William of Prussia simply announced: "Gentlemen, the King is dead," and everyone knew which monarch was meant. The German courts had been so Frenchified that a French traveler, invited to dinner by the Prince of Zoll, found that all the other guests were his fellow countrymen, and exclaimed to the prince: "Monseigneur, this is most amusing: you are the only foreigner present."

When Voltaire arrived, Frederick's entourage already included the Marquis d'Argens, Maupertuis, La Mettrie, Algarotti, and Lord Tyrconnel. The conversation was entirely in French. Frederick had only a superficial command of German, just enough to scold his servants and command his troops. When he wanted to read Racine in German translation he could do so only by following the French text. Intellectually he was French, and temperamentally even Voltairian: there were quite striking resemblances between the two friends.

Voltaire's fellow guests when he dined at Sans Souci were a remarkable gathering. Frederick was very fond of the Marquis d'Argens, who well deserved it. The son of an attorney in the Parlement of Aix-en-Provence, he threw to the wind the lawyer's cap and gown which he inherited, ran away, and embarked on all sorts of wild adventures. Having joined the army, he soon deserted to go to Spain after an actress he wanted to marry. His father succeeded in preventing the marriage, and the young man, in despair, swallowed ground glass. They saved him by stuffing him with oil. Then he fled to Turkey, broke into the Seraglio, was surprised with a dancing girl, beaten, chained, and ordered to choose between Islam and impalement. He chose flight—to Holland. Like everyone else, he began writing, then returned to Aix and became an advocate to please his father. His thirst for pleasure was equaled only by his thirst for knowledge. He was attracted by science, but he was so interested in painting that he went to Rome to get his hand in by copying masterpieces. He won so much money playing roulette that he was able to stay

and admire the Holy City for six months. A young Frenchman introduced him to a prostitute, with whom he fell in love. Unfortunately she
was even more in love with him than he with her, and when he took up
with another girl, she hired a couple of professional cutthroats who almost killed him. He left Rome.

Back in France he entered the army again, was wounded, and pronounced unfit for further service. To make some money he sold pamphlets
to Dutch booksellers, light compositions which skimmed over every subject without going beneath the surface but were never stupid or entirely
without merit. They pleased Frederick, for naturally they were entirely
irreligious. He invited D'Argens to Potsdam. The marquis replied boldly
that he wouldn't feel safe in Prussia, where the kings were well known
for their habit of enlisting by force any strangers of martial size and bearing. "Can I come without danger, I who am five foot seven and passably
well built?" (Voltaire ran no such risk.) As soon as Frederick became
King he reassured D'Argens: "Have no more fear of guards battalions,
my dear marquis. Come and brave them in Potsdam." He promised D'Argens piles of gold for which he made him wait two years. But before trying Berlin, D'Argens had himself made Prussian chargé d'affaires at the
court of the Duke of Württemberg. As the duke was dead, he had to present his credentials to the duchess, who was regent. She received him well
—too well, it was said. D'Argens himself admitted he was alarmed by the
liveliness of her sentiments. He was not the man to flee in the face of this
sort of danger, but whether he thought a few courtesies would suffice, or
whether these courtesies only fanned the duchess' ardor, her temper
soured, and the quarrels between the lovers were the talk of the German
courts. D'Argens took refuge with Frederick: he could be certain there
was no danger of that sort there. But if he suffered from too much emotion at Stuttgart, at Potsdam he suffered from too little, and he put an
end to his amorous deprivation by marrying an actress of respectable
family. But Frederick disapproved, and much tact was needed to apprise
him of the marriage and bring him, reluctantly, to accept it. D'Argens
had risked the favor he enjoyed at Frederick's court. He did not lose it,
but it was slightly tarnished, and eventually it wore thin. The King gave
him a house and had the walls decorated with scenes depicting D'Argens's exploits: D'Argens at war—fleeing before the enemy; threatened
with impalement by the Grand Turk; being treated by a surgeon for
Venus' disfavors. D'Argens, who had got up early to go admire his house,
was wild with rage and summoned workmen to whitewash the walls. His
anger greatly amused Frederick.

D'Argens was very superstitious, like many freethinkers who sneer at
the Eucharist and turn pale when someone spills the salt. He recounts
how one night he shared a room with Maupertuis, a fellow freethinker
from Paris. Before getting into bed Maupertuis knelt down and said his
prayers.

"Maupertuis, what are you doing?" D'Argens asked, astonished.

"My friend, we are alone," was the famous mathematician's only reply.

Atheism was for the public, and for Frederick. We do not know whether D'Argens followed Maupertuis's example; in any event, he did not hold it against him. La Mettrie, the fiercest materialist of the age, trembled like a leaf when it thundered, and resorted to the precautions of a pious old woman.

D'Argens was irreligious and supersitious like La Mettrie, but they had nothing else in common. Julien Offray de La Mettrie was born on December 25, 1709, at Saint-Malo, where Maupertuis had also been born; the latter had helped him and recommended him to Frederick. He was a bit of a fire-eater, even slightly crazy, with ideas that were as often absurd as they were inspired. He was always seething with them, and wine was not unconnected with the ferment. He took holy orders only to leave them and become a doctor. He adored dissection and, having joined the army, found that the war supplied him with plenty of material. He does not seem to have been unduly hampered by sentiments of humanity: one day at table, with footmen present, he said he would like to do certain experiments on servants—he was already trying out some remedies of his own invention on soldiers. He recklessly cultivated the impression that his dispensing caused more ravages than the Borgias, and then was surprised when one day, presenting himself at the bedside of a sick groom, he was greeted by the patient's comrades brandishing pitchforks. Naturally he too was a writer. He won a moment of celebrity in 1746 with his *Politique du médecin Machiavel, ou le chemin de la fortune ouvert aux médecins* (*The Politics of a Machiavellian Physician, or the Way to Fortune Thrown Open to Doctors*). The book was ripped up and burned by order of the Parlement. Frederick needed no better recommendation: he read it and sent for its author. The book is not without color and verve, and its ferocious comedy was deadly to the famous contemporary doctors it was aimed at. But it was La Mettrie's other book, *L'Homme-Machine* (*The Human Machine*) which made him celebrated among the *philosophes* through the controversies it aroused. He maintained that the soul did not exist and that thought is merely the product of an organ called the brain, and thus is simply the result of a mechanism. Even such dogged materialists as Holbach and Diderot were horrified. Frederick was delighted. To make sure his book would cause a scandal, La Mettrie had had the idea of dedicating it to Haller, a mild, worthy, timid scholar who quietly reflected glory on the University of Göttingen. Haller, seeing his name thus blackened, sent protests all over learned Europe, to courts and embassies, swearing that he didn't know La Mettrie and that the dedication was an imposture. La Mettrie had never dreamed his little joke would meet with such success. To add a further turn to the screw, he wrote some *Souvenirs sur Monsieur Haller* (*Reminiscences of Monsieur Haller*), whom he knew no better than the unfortunate Haller knew him. He described the German doctor giving lectures on science in the town brothel before an audience of the "ladies." Poor Haller solemnly set about laboriously disproving the story point by point, and showing that he was innocent and La Mettrie a liar. Europe had no doubt of it but was greatly amused by the learned professor's terror.

The Chevalier de Chasot, born in Caen in 1716, did not detract from the collection. He had moral as well as physical attractions. After killing a man in a duel he had been obliged to flee from France. Frederick took him in and began by investing him with his order "*Sans peur and sans reproche.*" Chasot saved Frederick's life at the Battle of Molditz. Outstandingly brave in war, he was also brilliantly witty and gay, and played the flute enchantingly. Frederick in particular was enchanted. There was a concert at Potsdam every day. The King also practiced every day, and composed every morning at the harpsichord while his hair was being dressed. In the evening there was music in a paneled rotunda, with a fireplace of red marble and a huge crystal chandelier. No one was invited but Frederick's intimates; it was a great honor. The King performed his own sonatas. He liked only the flute, and other instruments merely served as accompaniment. Chasot shone at concerts as on the battlefield. Frederick admired everything about him, except his liking for women.

Voltaire did not become a close friend of Chasot's and quarreled openly with him after becoming involved in a notorious lawsuit in Berlin. But in the early days of his stay the two of them made a journey across Germany together, though Voltaire was none too pleased at being accompanied by the chevalier. Frederick had sent him—to keep an eye on Voltaire, and also to disburse the funds for the journey. That is, to keep a check on them and see that Voltaire didn't spend too much. In one town Voltaire was asked to write something in the distinguished visitors' book. The previous traveler had written: "If God is with us, who can be against us?" Voltaire wrote underneath: "The Prussian battalions." Chasot reported it to Frederick. Even when traveling one shouldn't forget one's duties as a courtier and public relations officer.

When they got back and Chasot presented the list of expenses, Frederick was beside himself. One item he found particularly outrageous: it was for "Soap enemas taken by M. de Voltaire for 2 months at 2 Kreuzen each."

"A kited apothecary's bill!" cried Frederick, preparing to slide out of it.

"I cannot reduce it a jot," Chasot said. "My account is perfectly accurate." He had advanced the money himself.

When he arrived in Potsdam, Voltaire noticed another Frenchman, Monsieur Darget, a silent, discreet individual who was Frederick's valet and secretary. But Voltaire surmised correctly that he was more important than all the princes and marshals. He had formerly been secretary to Monsieur de Valori, the French ambassador, and had saved his master's life in tragic circumstances with such courage that Frederick decided to obtain his services. Monsieur Darget was probably the only man whom Frederick entirely trusted. He had access to all his secrets yet never took advantage and scarcely made use of his limitless authority. He was intelligent and selflessly devoted to Frederick, and admired Voltaire, whom he served as well as he could while never actually becoming his friend. Voltaire repaid him with airy praise:

> Adieu, Monsieur le Secrétaire.
> Soyez toujours mon tendre appui.
> Si Frédéric ne m'aimait guère,
> Songez que vous paieriez pour lui.

Farewell, Monsieur Secretary./Always be my affectionate support./If Frederick did not love me,/Believe me, you would make up for it.

The group also included the Keith brothers, who were Scots, and Lord Tyrconnel, an Irishman who served Louis XV as his ambassador in Berlin. The Keiths had been exiled from England on pain of death for their fidelity to the Stuarts. To annoy George III, whom he hated, Frederick did all he could in favor of the Jacobites. One of the Keiths was known as "Milord Maréchal" and was a great friend of Jean-Jacques Rousseau. When he was sent to Paris as Prussian minister, Voltaire wrote to prepare his niece for her meeting with him. He was traveling with a young Turkish girl, captured in war, who never left his side, "although he does not appear to have great need of her." She was a good Moslem and performed her religious duties regularly. Milord's valet was "a Tartar who has the honor of being a pagan." As for the maréchal himself, "I believe he is an Anglican, more or less," Voltaire wrote. As for Frederick's entourage as a whole, he added: "They form an agreeable group which proves that all men may live together very well even though they think differently. . . . What say you of the fate that sends an Irishman to be French minister in Berlin and a Scot to be Prussian minister in Paris? It looks like a practical joke." It looks even more like a chapter out of *Candide*.

Lord Tyrconnel was one of their number, and Voltaire, like Frederick, was quite fond of him. He was an epicurean, fond of eating and drinking, frank to the point of roughness, and a perfect contrast to the urbane Algarotti. "His role is to sit at table," Voltaire wrote. "His speech is succinct and caustic, with that sort of frankness the English often possess and men of his profession possess rarely."

This was rather a harsh judgment of diplomats, especially since Voltaire fancied himself as one.

At Potsdam there was even that rare thing, a German: Baron Pollnitz. Frederick loved his people but did not have much to do with them. When he did admit a German to the circle of his intimates it was on condition that the man leave his Teutonism outside. Pollnitz had, to be sure, discarded his long since, together with his truthfulness, his integrity, and even, three times, his religion. He had wit, discretion, education, and courage. But morally he was a buccaneer. In 1712 he had been at the court of Louis XIV. The Princesse Palatine adored him, and they enjoyed themselves saying all the rude things they could think of about France. The princess presented him to the aged King, who got the Duc de Duras, First Gentleman of the Bedchamber, to offer him the rank of colonel if he would become a Catholic. Pollnitz haughtily swore he would never do any such thing, then three months later, with great ceremony, was converted. He even went to Rome and returned with a papal benediction. But when he got back to Paris, Louis XIV and official devotion were dead. The court of the Regent laughed at his new Catholicism, and he was given neither his colonelcy nor a pension. His thoughts therefore turned to marriage.

He soon became the delight of a marquise of seventy summers and eighty thousand livres a year. But she had two sons who did their best to prevent the marriage. Anticipating the ceremony, the marquise died in Pollnitz's arms, and he, in despair at the injustice of fate and France's ingratitude, left for Holland—with the marquise's jewels.

But he returned when he heard about Law and his fabulous "system," and passed days and nights in the Rue Quincampoix. One day when things seemed to be going well he pointed to his bulging pockets and exclaimed: "I've got one million four hundred thousand livres in here!" Three days later he had only paper.

But though he didn't have any money he did have one stroke of luck. One day when he was at an inn near Etampes a rather striking young man asked if he might sit at his table. Pollnitz begged him to do so and was soon charmed with his companion's lively and witty conversation. As they were talking about their travels and plans for the future, a little girl started to sing an old song outside the window. The stranger stood up at once, bowed briefly, threw down a louis, hurried outside and leaped on his horse, which had been left saddled at the door. The sound of hoofs was heard galloping away along the road. A few months later it was announced that the famous bandit Cartouche had been caught. He was exposed to public view in a cage, and when Pollnitz, like the rest, went to see him, he recognized his table companion. Cartouche recognized him too: "I dined with you at Etampes, monsieur," he called out. "A song warned me that the constables were after me and obliged me to leave you in haste. But for that, you would be a dead man."

So Pollnitz had lost his elderly marquise, his paper treasure, his Protestantism, and the respect of the world, but he had escaped alive and returned safely to his native country. Frederick made him pay dearly for his venality by making him his butt. It seems odd that Frederick, despising him so openly, should have received him at his table, but the explanation is that the pain Pollnitz suffered at his hands gave him a sadistic pleasure. Pollnitz was not cured of his old faults. He had converted back to Protestantism in order to return to Prussia. One day Frederick said jokingly it was a pity Pollnitz was no longer a Catholic as there was a rich benefice vacant, a canonry in Silesia. At this Pollnitz underwent a third conversion, but when he told Frederick he was quite qualified now to become a canon Frederick only laughed at him; he would never get any Catholic ecclesiastical living. This did not prevent Frederick from treating Pollnitz with the most ruthless severity: he was not allowed to leave Berlin or Potsdam, or to go outside the palace, or to borrow or buy, or to receive guests, or to see anyone outside the royal circle. When Pollnitz was too ill to accompany the King on a journey he was told: "Can't you tell your illness to wait till I get back?"

But the fact that he accorded them favors had never stopped Frederick from despising people. In 1749, when Madame du Châtelet had just died and he was doing all he could to entice Voltaire to Berlin, Frederick penned these words about him to Algarotti: "It is a great pity that so craven a spirit should be joined to so fine a genius. He has both the charm and the mischievousness of a monkey. I will tell you about it [some trick of Voltaire's] when I see you; but I shall pretend to take no notice because I need him for my French elocution. One may learn useful things from a scoundrel. I want to learn his French; I care not a whit about his morals."

And when Pollnitz died, Frederick said to Voltaire: "Old Pollnitz died as he lived; that is, up to knavish tricks to the last. No one will miss him save his creditors."

Perhaps it is a pity that Frederick chose friends who deserved such funeral orations. But perhaps he preferred censure to praise.

Such was the strange fraternity in which Voltaire took his place: as the foremost of them all. However different their characters, origins, education, and talent, they were all men of talent, they all had something to say on either science, history, politics, or art, or about their strange experiences. They were all not only educated but capable of putting their knowledge on brilliant display.

Among these luminaries, Voltaire shone like the sun.

Daily Life with Frederick and Voltaire

The first months of Voltaire's stay at Potsdam marked the zenith of his reign there. He was held in such esteem that the princes of the royal family and the great dignitaries of the court asked audience of him. The King's brothers were flattered at being allowed to play chess with him— and he always let them win. He held court with the greatest naturalness and was always courteous and gay. He mingled wit and exquisite politeness with an almost imperceptible condescension. The King provided for six places every day at his table, but often there were more guests than that. Voltaire always liked to keep open house, and this caused friction with the royal kitchens. He would invite people airily to "come and have a cut off the King's roast." Frederick, who kept a close eye on the budget of his royal household, was offended at this largesse at his expense.

Squabbles over candles, wine, coffee, and sugar soon recalled those Voltaire had caused at Lunéville. He complained of not being given the six candles per evening that he was entitled to by contract. The notary's son had had everything written down! The servants complained that every evening Voltaire collected the candle ends to which *they* were entitled, also by contract; and they accused him of selling them. All this soured his relations with the King's servants. He said the tea and coffee he was supplied with were "marinated"—he meant they had been spoiled by contact with sea water. Frederick was informed by Voltaire himself about this sabotage in his kitchens. He pretended to listen but did nothing. He must have been amused to see the "monkey" howling and shrieking over a piece of sugar or a candle end. Voltaire found a stratagem for dealing with the candle situation. It was his habit every evening before dinner to stroll into the King's apartments. A servant lighted his way there, but he used to light himself back with a good-sized candle picked up in the King's quarters. By paying two or three such visits in an evening he was able to come by three nearly whole candles and would proceed to have orgies of light. This gave him great satisfaction but of course did not go unnoticed by the penny-pitching King. He disapproved strongly but said nothing. Voltaire was still allowed to do anything he pleased.

Voltaire performed services for Frederick in return. In the first place, he took his brothers off the King's hands. He amused them and set them to acting in plays. "My brothers are mumming," said Frederick, with a sigh of relief. While they were mumming they were not cooking up plots against him.

Voltaire also occupied Queen Elizabeth Christina. It is hardly worth mentioning her: she scarcely existed. Frederick had married her against his will and took no notice of her. The poor woman didn't know what to do with herself. Fortunately she enjoyed reading. Voltaire gave her Pierre Bayle's subversively freethinking *Dictionary*, but as she was highly orthodox in her views he directed her to the "good" articles only. Her husband was chiefly interested in the "bad" ones. But Voltaire only made brief appearances in the Queen's apartments, where he, like everyone else, half died of boredom, cold, and hunger.

The Queen Mother was much more amusing, and Voltaire was therefore more willing to pay his respects there. One day when he was in Berlin she unexpectedly invited him to dinner. As she was in mourning he had to wear black; but his wardrobe was at Potsdam. His valet had the idea of borrowing a coat from a rich merchant he knew. As the merchant was fatter than Voltaire, the coat was sent to a tailor to be taken in at the seams. Instead, he remade it entirely. It fitted Voltaire splendidly, but when it was restored to its owner he couldn't get into it. The owner merely laughed. Voltaire never knew what had happened and so could not make amends. Nor did he know that his enemies cited this incident as yet another proof of his avarice and dishonesty.

Frederick's court often moved back and forth between Berlin and Potsdam. But the holy of holies was Sans Souci. Voltaire compared the little society that surrounded the King to a confraternity of irreligion; the abbot was Frederick and the senior monk was Voltaire. Built on a hill overlooking the river Havel, Sans Souci was within walking distance of Potsdam. It was a "folly" on a regal scale, only one story high, with a central pavilion in the form of a domed rotunda. The roofs of the wings formed a terrace, and a wide, majestic stairway led down somewhat theatrically into formal gardens. The general effect was Italianate. The central rotunda contained a great marble salon with a gilded cupola. To the left was the dining room, in which there was a portrait of the Duchesse de Châteauroux, whom Frederick called "Petticoat I" because she was the first of Louis XV's official mistresses. Then came the bedchamber, containing a state bed with a silver balustrade around it. But Frederick slept behind a screen—"on a straw pallet," according to Voltaire. In fact it was a hard, narrow camp bed, on which His Majesty's pet dogs played about during the day. He often carried one about with him in his muff. There was also the clock which he himself wound up every evening, and which stopped at the hour of his death: twenty minutes past two on August 17, 1786. His study was lined with books, none of them in German. In the other wing were the guest rooms. Voltaire's opened onto the terrace and had a splendid view over the tiered gardens. It was there that people came to see him, when he was visible. "My health is much the same as in Paris, and when I have colic I send all the kings in the universe packing. I have given up the divine suppers here, and feel somewhat better." He pretended to turn up his nose, but in fact he missed few of the divine suppers of which he was the life and soul. It flattered him to write: "There are too many generals and princes." He liked Frederick best at intimate suppers. On such occasions, "It is Caesar, Marcus Aurelius, Julian or sometimes the Abbé de Pure that I sup with, and we enjoy the charms of retirement, the freedom of country life, combined with all the pleasures that a nobleman who is also a king can provide for his humble guests."

The charms of retirement consisted of a palace, pensions, honors, a king who was the most intelligent of men for a friend, and a brilliant brotherhood of guests. And behind this façade were ten million subjects, working and fighting for the glory of the king of Prussia and the pleasures of Monsieur de Voltaire. It was the *belle époque*, the real age of gracious living—if you happened to be Voltaire and Frederick, and happened to meet. Fortunately Voltaire had some appreciation of the privileged nature of his position: "My function is to do nothing. I enjoy my leisure. I give an hour or two a day to the King of Prussia to polish his writings in prose or verse a little; I am his grammarian and not his chamberlain. The rest of the day is my own, and ends with a pleasant supper."

These supper parties gave him the opportunity to shine his brightest. Frederick was very skillful at setting ideas and speakers one against the other. He carried teasing and mockery to the point of cruelty, and his "brothers," becoming enemies, became more brilliant than before.

Sometimes the King would abandon his luminaries to sup tête-à-tête with an officer he was very fond of, Monsieur de Balby. These private sessions annoyed Voltaire, who was jealous. When asked "What is the King doing this evening?" he would answer sourly, "*Il balbytie.*"[1]

After a few months Voltaire wrote a letter full of "buts." Everything is splendid at Potsdam, but . . . The acting there is good, but . . . There are fine avenues in the town, but . . . The Brothers are very witty, but . . . And he ends this series of "buts" (which he takes care not to make specific) with a pregnant phrase regarding the change of temperature that has set in since his arrival: "The weather is turning distinctly chilly." The "abbot" is on his guard with one of the "Brothers," and the chill is such that, instead of speaking of "polishing" Frederick's writings, Voltaire now speaks of "pruning" them.

Maupertuis is already less friendly than before. He had had the impertinence to interrupt Voltaire as he was reciting his *Mérope*, in order to make some insignificant remark. He would have to be taught some respect.

The Smell of Money

Voltaire himself gave his enemies their opportunity to renew their attack on him, and in such a way that his friends could not come to his defense. He got together with a Berlin broker, a Jew called Hirsch or Hirschell, to carry out some illegal speculation. It is a sordid affair, difficult to disentangle because of all the lies told by both sides.

After his war with Saxony, Frederick had forced his former enemy to reimburse all Prussians officially holding loan certificates drawn on the state of Saxony. These certificates had fallen far below their face value, but Frederick insisted that Saxony should pay for them at the original rate. Hence a traffic in the certificates began, with Prussians buying them cheaply in Saxony and getting them converted at their face value as official Prussian bearers. Using Hirsch as his agent, Voltaire tried to get in on this. Making allowance for all expenses, he calculated that he ought to get a return of thirty-five per cent on his capital in a few weeks. So he handed over to his associate the equivalent of forty thousand crowns, partly in cash and partly in the form of a bill of exchange in Paris. Hirsch left him some diamonds as security.

Scarcely had Hirsch set out for Dresden than someone warned Voltaire that the man was far from reliable and that his money was in considerable danger. Voltaire, horrified, hastily countermanded the bill of exchange, and when Hirsch presented it in Dresden he was refused payment. He then returned at once to Berlin, determined on revenge. He had not bought any certificates and still had the money Voltaire had given him. There then began a period of reciprocal blackmail. Hirsch demanded compensation for his journey and for loss of profit. Voltaire haughtily refused and boasted of having the protection of the King. Hirsch wanted to test this, for Voltaire had claimed to have launched this affair with Frederick's support. They were both so vociferous, the story soon got around. Hirsch wanted his compensation; Voltaire denied having entrusted him with the matter. But if that was the case, why had he given him all that money? "To buy furs," said Voltaire. Unfortunately you could not buy furs in Dresden. "To buy diamonds," said Voltaire. But you went to Holland to buy diamonds. In any event, he wanted his money back. Hirsch refused to give it back. Voltaire had the diamonds he had left as security assayed and found they were paste. His rage knew no bounds, and he brought a lawsuit against his partner. But although Hirsch was several times convicted of lying in court, Voltaire too was in a very awkward situation. He had to admit that he had commissioned Hirsch to enter into illegal speculations. Not only had Frederick not supported him; he disapproved vehemently.

Voltaire was not the man to compromise as Chasot had hoped: he brought the two adversaries together, but Voltaire only tried to throttle Hirsch. Chasot was obliged to report to Frederick; Voltaire never forgave his countryman. The King ordered Voltaire to leave Prussia within twenty-four hours. Saxony had already complained to Frederick many times about the traffic in bonds. Voltaire's case dragged the whole thing into the limelight and risked compromising the King. Frederick disapproved strongly of Voltaire's having boasted of his protection and of having taken advantage of his hospitality to try to turn a handsome profit. Didn't he pay him enough?

Voltaire, informed of Frederick's anger, holed up in his room. No more notes, no more visits by candlelight. He had people intercede with the judges, lamented, wept and raged. It was not having lost the money that infuriated him so much as the rascality of Hirsch. Finally he plucked up the courage to write to Frederick. It is not a very lively letter; there blows through it the icy wind of disgrace. All he could do was implore, and maintain that nothing was left for him in this world but "the happiness of loving and admiring you."

He went to ask the help of Monsieur Formey, the chancellor. He rushed, all pale and haggard, into a roomful of people he did not even see, threw himself on Monsieur Formey, and dragged him into another room. There, in a nervous state, bordering on madness, he gasped out the reason for his visit. He spoke with great excitement and ended by asking the chancellor to tell the judge to see that he won his case. Monsieur Formey's little daughter, who was present in the room, stared at the strange visitor and tried to touch the diamond cross of his Order of Merit. "A brilliant bagatelle, my child," he snapped, and rushed out.

His opponent made such a poor impression in court that Voltaire's cause seemed slightly less desperate. Certain of his enemies related that when it came time to take the oath on the Bible he said, "What, on a book in such bad Latin? I wouldn't mind swearing on Homer or Virgil." A very unlikely story. Too much depended on the case for him to be in the mood for such pleasantries.

In Paris, people were well aware of what had been going on. Louis XV, who had been informed of Voltaire's shady speculations, said to his friends: "This great poet always has one foot on Parnassus and the other in the Rue Quincampoix."

Voltaire bemoaned his fate to the Margravine of Bayreuth: "Brother Voltaire is in disgrace here. He has a confounded lawsuit with a Jew, and according to the Old Testament it will cost him all the more because he has been robbed."

Many a true word is spoken in jest. He won his case, but he never got his money back, and in fact had to pay out more. In response to Voltaire's supplication, the margravine had written to her brother Frederick to plead in his favor. She received this reply: "You ask me about Voltaire's lawsuit with the Jew? It is a matter of a rascal trying to trick a rogue. It is not permissible that a man with a mind such as Voltaire's should pervert it to such unworthy uses. The affair is in the hands of the law, and in a few days we shall learn from the verdict which of the two is the greater scoundrel. Voltaire lost his temper and threw himself on the Jew. . . . In short, he has behaved like a madman. I am waiting for the case to be ended to give him a good dressing down and to see if at the age of fifty-six he cannot be made, if not a reasonable man, at least less of a knave."

After the verdict, which was merely a technical victory for him, Voltaire wrote to Frederick in a humble and repentant frame of mind. This affair had broken him—for the moment. "I have been guilty of an incredible blunder for a man of my age. I have never been able to cure myself of the cursed desire to push everything too far. . . . I was mad enough to want to prove myself in the right against a man in relation to whom one cannot be in the right. You may be assured that I am in despair and have never suffered so bitterly. Through sheer recklessness I have deprived myself of the one thing I came here for. . . . I have displeased the only man I wanted to please."

In this act of contrition, Voltaire had naturally not said a single word about the illegal speculation. Frederick promptly gave him the promised dressing down, couched in the most glacial words:

"I was very content to receive you as my guest. I esteemed your wit, your talents, and your learning, and could not but believe that a man of your age, weary of fighting with authors and being exposed to the storm, came here in search of peace and quiet. But you began, in a singular enough fashion, by making me promise not to employ Fréron to send me news. I was weak or accommodating enough to yield, although it was not for you to decide whom I should or should not take into my service. You admittedly had genuine grievances against D'Arnaud, but a generous person would have forgiven him. Only a vindictive man pursues grudges. In any event, though D'Arnaud had done me no harm, it was on your account that he left here. You went and talked to the Russian ambassador about matters which did not concern you, giving the impression that it was I who sent you. [This was over a question of protocol.] You meddled in Madame Bentenck's affairs, though it was certainly none of your business. [Madame Bentenck was a worthy but slightly daft lady who had been having difficulties with her husband. Voltaire took her part and rashly interceded with Frederick, who sent him back to his writing desk where he belonged.] You have had this most discreditable business with the Jew. You have caused a dreadful uproar all over town. The affair of the Saxon notes is such public knowledge in Saxony that I have received grievous complaints about it. For my part, I saw to it that my house was a peaceful one until you arrived, and I warn you that if you have a passion for cabals and conspiracies you have come to the wrong address. I like quiet peaceable people who do not display the violent passions of tragedy in their conduct. If you can make up your mind to live like a philosopher, I shall be most happy to see you; but if you allow yourself to be carried away by every flame of passion and are at odds with everyone, you will give me no pleasure by coming here [Potsdam] and might as well remain in Berlin."

After such cutting words the friendship between the two would never again be what it had been before.

In an attempt to mend the damage done, Voltaire wrote back contritely:

Sire, after mature consideration I acknowledge that it was a grievous fault to have brought a lawsuit against a Jew, and I ask forgiveness of Your Majesty, Your Philosophy, Your Goodness. . . . In spite of all this the fact remains that I have devoted my life to you. Do with me what you will. I have told the Margravine of Bayreuth that Brother Voltaire is in disgrace. Have pity on Brother

Voltaire

Frederick yielded so far as to give him permission to reappear at Potsdam, reminding him of the affairs of the bookseller Jore, the violinist at the opera, and the knavish Hirsch—and also reminding him that "these names ought not to figure beside yours." This seems obvious enough. Yet Voltaire only remembered it when things were going badly, and the reminder was not enough to keep him from running into new dangers.

What's Bred in the Bone . . .

Voltaire, who had learned such fluent English in London, made no attempt to learn German. He said there were no books to read in that language. "Do not imagine I make any serious attempts in the Teutonic tongue. I wisely content myself with knowing just enough to speak to my servants and my horses." In this he was only taking the same view as Frederick.

For his lawsuit, which was conducted in German, he had recourse to an interpreter. He happened upon a well-bred, cadaverous young man, Gotthold Lessing, to whom he paid little attention but who was later to become one of Germany's most distinguished poets. Meanwhile, however, he was the innocent cause of yet another row.

Lessing was very proud of working for Voltaire, whom he idolized, and he begged the poet's secretary to let him see the manuscript of *Le Siècle de Louis XIV*—which Voltaire had managed to finish while still in the throes of his lawsuit! Having seen it, Lessing wanted to read it, and after much pleading finally persuaded the secretary to let him have part of the manuscript. He then left for Württemberg, where he had been offered a post, taking the precious text with him. When Voltaire found it missing, there was an outcry: he did not doubt for a moment that it was another case of theft. He can hardly be blamed: at that very moment, in Paris, Madame Denis was having the law pursue Longchamp for the same sort of thing. Naturally Voltaire did not keep his grievance to himself; he too invoked the assistance of the law. When Lessing heard about the scandal he sent the manuscript back. He had merely wanted to read it. But the rumor of his supposed theft had got about, and though Voltaire forgot Lessing, Lessing never forgot the insulting letter his idol had written asking for the "stolen" manuscript back, or the fact that the King had been told, or that all Germany had been made to believe he was a thief. In fact, however, Voltaire had unwittingly done him the service of making his name known and thus creating a potential readership for his poetry.

During 1751, Voltaire left Sans Souci to go and stay at the residence of the Marquis d'Argens, who was then in France. He said the place suited his health; but probably he thought it wise to withdraw from Frederick's court for a while to let the temperature thaw a little.

An Excellent Patient

In his solitude—a very relative one—he looked after his health. His various ailments had intensified during the strain of the lawsuit. He stayed in bed nearly all day, and it was in bed that he received his visitors.

Molière's description of the body as a tattered old garment was never more true of anyone than it was of Voltaire. Yet, knowing this, he looked after himself with the minutest care. His methods of self-treatment throw a horrifying light on the ignorance of doctors in the Age of Enlightenment and tell us a great deal about Voltaire himself.

He did not have a beard. It never grew, so he never used a razor but only pulled out the few odd hairs that appeared now and again. He would pursue this task during a conversation, and always kept a pair of tweezers handy on the mantelpiece or in his pocket.

When he had his horrible stomach cramps he went to bed and dictated to his secretary. Sometimes he composed in his head and set it down on paper later. He never wasted time.

When he had smallpox he was given eight emetics and two hundred pints of lemonade. What a stomach! But he survived, though pockmarked for life, and in even more delicate health than before.

He had no illusions about the medicine of his day. "Medicine consists in introducing drugs about which one knows little into bodies about which one knows less," he said. Nevertheless, with characteristic contrariness, he loved dosing himself and tried every fashionable prescription and every old wives' remedy. At one time in his life he had sworn by Father Aignan's Tranquilizing Balm and had had himself rubbed with Rabel's Water and Varenger's Balm. But they were now a thing of the past. He tried taking the waters, but those of Forges half killed him, as did those of Plombières. A diet of whey with essence of cinnamon he once went on did not actually poison him, and this was enough to cause him to be enthusiastic as to its curative powers. Some charlatan or other made him swallow lead shot as a laxative, saying that that was how dirty bottles were rinsed out. Voltaire suffered agonies but miraculously survived.

He once calculated that in the course of a single month he had had eight purges and twelve enemas. And he endured this sort of treatment for years. Of course, it must be remembered that his enemas were administered with the aid of a marvelous apparatus from England, without which he never traveled. "It is a masterpiece of craftsmanship," he wrote. "You could slip it into your waistcoat pocket. You can use it whenever and wherever you like." And he did so—even in the middle of a day's journey by coach.

In Berlin he discovered Stahl's pills and took to swallowing them all day long. When he got back to France he could not bear to be without them, and wrote and asked Frederick to send him a pound of them. "The pills you ask for," Frederick replied, "are enough to purge all France and kill all three of your Academies. I have commissioned D'Arget to send you this drug, so highly regarded in France, which the late Stahl used to have made up by his coachman." He did not say with what ingredients, but his comments rendered the pills ineffective in Voltaire's case and he stopped taking them.

With age the process of physical disintegration grew more rapid. What he had so clearly observed in Ninon de Lenclos he now observed in himself, but twenty years ahead of the normal time. He soon lost all his teeth and was left with a pinched and sunken mouth. His eyesight grew worse, he had dizzy spells, his hearing became poor, his voice took to breaking. But he was still alive. Between attacks of colic he read, wrote, talked, and laughed. He laughed every day, whenever his ailments allowed him a moment's respite.

He kept to a diet because of his colic, but there were certain temptations he couldn't resist: sweets, and rich pies filled with forcemeat. He paid for his greed afterward, but he didn't mind that. He sometimes would drink twenty cups of coffee in an afternoon, but he ate little. At lunch he took a curious mixture of tea and coffee: the first time Le Kain, the actor, was a guest at his table, all they had was twelve cups of this brew. His best meal was the evening one, which he took at nine o'clock or sometimes later. He often had lentils, which he loved; there was no present that gave him more pleasure than a bag of lentils. He ate little meat and, if he did, preferred mutton. His "diet" consisted of eggs and milk. "There are very good and ancient kinds of food," he wrote, "with which all the sages of antiquity were content. I confess that modern cooking does not agree with my stomach. I cannot endure sweetbreads swimming in salty sauce. I cannot eat turkey, hare, and rabbit all minced up together and passed off as one. I like neither broiled pigeon nor bread that has no crust. I drink wine in moderation and cannot understand those who eat without drinking and do not even know what they are eating. As for cooks, I cannot abide their ham extracts, or all the mushrooms, pepper, and nutmeg with which they smother food that is perfectly good as it is, and which would not even be larded if I had my way. I want only bread cooked in a clean oven. A plain sort of supper such as I propose gives hopes of quiet sleep untroubled by bad dreams."

As soon as he left the table he went to bed. He did not require more than four or five hours' sleep, but he stayed in bed for fifteen or sixteen hours every day. Several candles were kept burning all through the night. His bed was covered with books and papers in ordered disorder. On a table within reach were water, coffee, paper, pens, and ink.

His cleanliness was exceptional for that time, as regards his person, his clothes, his possessions, and his apartments: he was as neat as a squirrel. But he felt the cold so much that even in the middle of summer he was smothered in thick eiderdowns. His body lived in slow motion, parsimoniously: all his enormous nervous energy was concentrated on the task at hand.

While he was living in retirement at the residence of the Marquis d'Argens, a visitor found him in bed.

"I am suffering from four fatal illnesses," Voltaire informed him.

"But your eyes look beautifully bright," said the unsuspecting guest. It was true. For all his wrinkled skin and skeleton-like boniness, Voltaire's eyes shone like those of a twenty-year-old. But it didn't do to say so when Voltaire was feeling ill. He sat up in bed and shouted at his guest:

"Don't you know that people dying of scurvy always have inflamed eyes?"

Bitter Orange Peel

From his bed Voltaire wrote to Paris to lay to rest the rumors that had been circulated about his fall from Frederick's favor. He said Frederick had never been more affectionate or munificent toward him. In his feather bed, swallowing his bread-soups, he pretended the life he was leading was a perpetual banquet: "In January we are eating peaches, strawberries, and pineapples."

But the D'Argentals were not deceived. They were too intimate friends not to be alarmed. They sensed that Voltaire's situation was precarious and that it might become dangerous. Reassure them as he might, they did not believe him. They begged him to come back. Paris was the only city in the world where he could find the society he needed. In Berlin were a king and a few wits. But there was no real court and, behind the façade, no real town. In Paris, if the court did not come up to your expectations, there was always the town; and if that grew cold, Versailles welcomed you with open arms. Their friend maintained that he had left Paris to flee envy. But was he any better off in Prussia? If the Jew Hirsch had been so insolent and strong, how was it possible to avoid the conclusion that he was supported by Voltaire's enemies, perhaps even secretly by Frederick? Voltaire had gone to Prussia in search of freedom, and once there he had found himself bound like a servant. At the King's table he might speak of any forbidden subject he cared to, but apart from that satisfaction, was he free to act? go out? travel? keep company with whomever he pleased? Voltaire could not deny that the D'Argentals were right. But the time hadn't yet come to listen to them. The mirage had not yet faded.

Madame Denis added her counsel and complaints to those of the D'Argentals; but she adapted herself more easily than they to her uncle's absence. She received the Prussian travelers Voltaire sent her way with his personal recommendations. She received the Prussian chargé d'affaires in Paris so warmly that he took fright. She offered him the place left vacant by the Italian singer; but he declined—even though she had lodged him handsomely, fed him on the fat of the land, driven him around the town, and introduced him to all Paris in her box at the Comédie Française. This Prussian's ungratefulness did not encourage her to go and live in Berlin.

She had had hopes of marrying the Marquis de Ximénès, a nobleman who was a bit daft. He did not seem so set on it as she was. Voltaire wrote from Prussia advising against the match. Ximénès had a weakness for young girls, and it was probable that tough Madame Denis, a bluestocking who had long since lost the bloom of youth, would not suit his requirements.

After a few months Frederick seemed to soften. Flattery made its timid reappearance, and the two of them made a pretext of being friends again. This apparently satisfied them both. Voltaire wrote D'Argental that he preferred such treatment to the attacks of Fréron and the contempt of Versailles. He still often had a good laugh with La Mettrie. They were too different to be jealous of one another. La Mettrie's only grudge was against doctors, Voltaire's against writers, and they joined their efforts to tear ecclesiastics to pieces. The favor that La Mettrie enjoyed did not bother Voltaire; he took it as a joke. But Frederick was genuinely fond of La Mettrie and confided in him much more than in Voltaire. He gambled with La Mettrie; he dared not do so with Voltaire for fear of the consequences. But La Mettrie had a heart, and a Breton one, and toward the end of dinner it tended to overflow. He was homesick and wanted to see Saint-Malo again, and when he went into raptures about Brittany he spoke of other things too, and Voltaire was able to question him about what Frederick said to him when they were alone. How much better it would be if we never found out what our "friends" say about us when we are not there. The heedless La Mettrie unconsciously filled Voltaire's heart with vitriol. Frederick had not concealed from him, he said, the fact that everyone was laboring under an illusion as to the favor Voltaire supposedly enjoyed with him. According to La Mettrie, the King had said: "I shall need him for another year at most: once you've squeezed the orange you throw the peel away."

With these unforgivable words reported by La Mettrie, the damage was done. Voltaire no longer felt safe in Potsdam. He and Frederick continued to meet and to exchange smiles and compliments, but Voltaire did not forget either the insult or the threat. He wrote to his niece: "I keep dreaming about the orange peel, rather like the man who dreamed he had fallen from a steeple and, finding himself still floating gently through the air, said: 'If only this could last.'" Others might have preferred to cut short the suspense and leave. If Voltaire stayed on it was perhaps because he still had need of Frederick.

The blow had been such a shock, Voltaire could not believe it and tried to persuade himself that La Mettrie had imagined the whole thing while in his cups. But when he made him repeat it, the words and the circumstances were always the same. One day La Mettrie declined to answer any more questions—he was suffering from indigestion. He had attended Lord Tyrconnel as his physician, and the patient had made him stay to supper. La Mettrie tucked into ten courses and wound up the meal by taking a hearty helping of an eagle, bacon, and ginger pie, whereupon he started to choke. He refused any treatment but bleeding, in order, he said, "to make indigestion accustom itself to being bled." But indigestion refused to so accustom itself. La Mettrie's body then swelled grotesquely, and his soul abandoned it without further ado. Frederick burst out laughing when he heard of this "philosophical" end. "Very pleased to hear it," he said. And Voltaire, on hearing of La Mettrie's death, added: "For once it's the patient who killed the doctor."

Perhaps what prevented Voltaire from leaving Frederick was the fact that *Le Siècle de Louis XIV* was in the process of being printed in Germany. Voltaire heard that pirated editions were being prepared in Breslau and Frankfurt and was furious—with good reason. Such editions not only deprived the author of his rights; they might also endanger him by presenting a text that had been tampered with. Voltaire appealed to the King for justice. But Frederick made it clear that he was weary of Voltaire's pleas and complaints and complications in general. Voltaire was aghast. But it was a question of his work, so he persisted, and finally succeeded in prying his work loose from the hands of the pirating printers.

The first edition of *Le Siècle de Louis XIV* came out in Berlin in 1752, thanks to Monsieur de Francheville, aulic councilor to the King. Friends and admirers congratulated Voltaire on a work which presented an entirely new concept of history. In the first place, everything in it was true. All the facts had been verified, and all the documents and eyewitness accounts were authentic. Voltaire had gone to endless trouble, and he had made his friends and informants and secretaries do the same. The other thing that made the book original was the way it grouped all the leading lights of the age around one central figure. The King was celebrated because the civilization of his age was celebrated. For the first time a monarch was praised not by presenting him as a superhuman being but by praising the people who surrounded him. It was art, literature, and science that made Louis the Sun of Europe. The main character in *Le Siècle* is the King as a symbol—the symbol of civilization, or the human mind.

Lord Chesterfield, an excellent critic, admired everything about the book save for the spelling. Voltaire, who couldn't keep his hands off anything, had taken it into his head to simplify spelling. First he abolished capital letters, but there was such an outcry that he restored them. He used the form *français* instead of *françois*, because that was how everyone pronounced it. Some said that his real reason was to make Corneille and Racine look out of date. But as late as the nineteenth century the pupils of the convent of Marie d'en Haut in Grenoble refused to write *français* with an *a* because that spelling had been made general by the infamous Voltaire.

A Sinister Shadow

The success of the *Siècle* attracted a new enemy just as tenacious as Desfontaines or Fréron, another unknown who became famous simply through his quarrels with Voltaire. When Voltaire treated him as an equal no one was more surprised than he, and he proceeded to make the most of it.

This new enemy went by the name of Monsieur de La Beaumelle, but his real name was Angliviel. He was born in 1726, of a Protestant family in the south of France. As his origins were modest, he had tried to rise a little in the world by becoming a Catholic, but after receiving a free education from the priests he had gone to Geneva to renew his original faith at the sources of Calvinism.

In 1750 he went to Denmark, where he taught in a school, wrote a few little texts for classroom use, and started a paper called *The Danish Lady at the Theater*. He also published a little book called *Mes pensées, ou qu'en dira-t-on?* (*My Thoughts, or What Will People Say?*). No one said very much. But the style was lively and ironic, and hence in the current fashion. From Copenhagen he wrote very politely to Voltaire, who was then in Potsdam, asking permission to publish his works, with the supposed sponsorship of the King of Denmark. Voltaire naturally could not resist a young writer who professed himself in his debt and presented himself in the name of a king.

In 1751 La Beaumelle came to Berlin, and Voltaire received him, never suspecting that he was there only to spy on him and try to catch him out. La Beaumelle was apparently eaten up with envy, and envied Voltaire not so much for his talent as for his fortune and social success.

He sensed straight away that he had an ally in Maupertuis. He went to see him, told him of his hatred of Voltaire, and was delighted to find that Maupertuis shared his feelings. Maupertuis had seen at once that this embittered young social climber might be useful to him, and he did all he could to set Voltaire and La Beaumelle at odds. He had ample opportunity.

La Beaumelle claimed to have based a volume entitled *Memoires de Madame de Maintenon* that he had compiled on unpublished letters he had bought from Jean Racine's son. No one believed that the half-starved-looking La Beaumelle could have made such a purchase, and few people believed that such letters even existed. The court circle at Potsdam was intrigued. Frederick said one evening at supper that, as La Beaumelle had not acquired the letters from either the friends or the family of the favorite, he must have come by them dishonestly. Voltaire was pleased to hear this. He had been very worried about the "letters." Would this source, to which he himself had not had access, invalidate everything he had written about Madame de Maintenon and the King in *La Siècle de Louis XIV?* When La Beaumelle told him how surprised he would be at his mistakes once he saw the *Mémoires de Madame de Maintenon,* he was torn by horrible doubts. This was exactly what La Beaumelle was after: to make Voltaire suffer and to discredit his book.

As soon as *Le Siècle de Louis XIV* appeared, La Beaumelle wrote that it was nothing but a tissue of inadequacies and mistakes. This was mere insult, not criticism. But the worst, for Voltaire, was the fact that La Beaumelle threatened to confront him with authentic sources which Voltaire had neglected, when he had taken such pains to verify every fact in his history of the reign of Louis XIV.

Voltaire was always astonished whenever a new enemy appeared on the scene. La Beaumelle had already given signs that ought to have warned him. On his arrival in Potsdam he had given Voltaire his *Pensées* to read. They contained the observation that "there had been greater poets than Voltaire but none better paid." Voltaire turned down the corner of the page and, when he restored the book to its author, asked why he had attacked him. La Beaumelle airily replied that the remark had been intended as praise.

"I don't know how to read, then," Voltaire said.

"Perhaps not," La Beaumelle answered. He tried afterward to soothe Voltaire with the basest flattery. Voltaire bided his time.

Though he had no money, no name, and no one to support him, La Beaumelle had a certain courage or he would not have dared to attack the most famous writer of his age, and one who was also a power to be reckoned with in Berlin. He also knew that Voltaire, despite his courtesy, could be ferocious when roused. As Madame de Graffigny had put it, he was "capable of digging up a corpse in order to hang it."

A misadventure that befell La Beaumelle gave Voltaire an opportunity for revenge. Coming out of the opera one day, La Beaumelle introduced himself to a pretty woman and persuaded her there and then to give him a rendezvous: he was handsome, bold, and ardent. He didn't notice the lady's husband, who was lurking nearby: Captain Cocchein, a swarthy swashbuckler with few brains. La Beaumelle flew to the rendezvous, and without further ado prepared to show the lady the ardor of his feelings. At that moment a cupboard flew open and out stepped the swashbuckler. La Beaumelle thought his final hour had come; but all Cocchein wanted was his purse, and with the aid of his lady he got it. But they were disappointed by the contents, and to get his revenge the husband brought a charge of adultery. La Beaumelle was arrested and put in prison in no time. He protested both orally and in writing; Berlin was highly amused. Then Maupertuis interceded with Frederick, the Coccheins were imprisoned, and La Beaumelle was released.

A well-meaning lady who wanted him to be reconciled with Voltaire went and told La Beaumelle that Voltaire had defended him, suggested to La Beaumelle that he should get all the French in Berlin to appeal to Louis on his behalf, and finally had him set free by the French ambassador. She then sent La Beaumelle to thank Voltaire. Voltaire, seeing a contrite and grateful La Beaumelle at his feet, magnanimously accepted his thanks for having come to his rescue.

But hardly had La Beaumelle left Voltaire's embrace than he heard an entirely different account of what had happened. He was told that Voltaire had said that prison was the right place for him and that the Frenchmen in Berlin didn't need to concern themselves about someone who was not really French. If by any chance he maintained that he was so by birth, he had ceased to be so by virtue of having been banished from France. And even if he hadn't really been banished from France, he had certainly been banished from Denmark. And anyhow, even if he hadn't been banished from anywhere, his case was desperate because he was a bad Christian, and it would cause a scandal if the ambassador of His Most Christian Majesty were to put himself out for such a notorious unbeliever.

Although La Beaumelle was naturally outraged when he heard all this, nothing is certain about this version except that Voltaire did nothing to get him out of prison, and appeared pleased rather than otherwise to see him thus reduced to silence.

Voltaire had not neglected to show Frederick the offending passage in the *Pensées*. The King had been vexed, and on being informed of this, La Beaumelle went to explain everything to Monsieur Darget, the King's secretary, and to complain that the sentence about Voltaire had been shown to the King. Monsieur Darget's only answer was to tell La Beaumelle not to prolong his stay in Prussia. He was therefore obliged to leave, his only consolation being that Voltaire was still losing sleep over the famous letters of Madame de Maintenon.

La Beaumelle took refuge in Gotha, where he made a conquest of a lady's maid, who ran away with him and her mistress' jewels. Voltaire heard about it and spread the news through all the courts of Germany. The affair ruined La Beaumelle's reputation, but Voltaire did not come out of it very well either. La Beaumelle was under no illusion as to the person responsible for this unwelcome publicity: Voltaire told him himself.

Not long afterward a characteristic impulse made Voltaire offer to make his peace with La Beaumelle if he would give up trying to discredit

Le Siècle de Louis XIV. But La Beaumelle merely interpreted this as a sign of weakness, and in 1753, with effrontery unparalleled even in the eighteenth century, he published in Frankfurt a book entitled *Le Siècle de Louis XIV, augmenté d'un très grand nombre de remarques et de pièces par M. de La B.* (*The Age of Louis XIV, with the addition of many observations and documents by M. de La B.*). When it was pointed out to him that he was guilty of theft and forgery, his only answer was to deplore the fact that the printer had been foolish enough to print the letters "La B." in the title. But in fact this indiscretion scarcely bothered him, as the reward he was most interested in was not the bookseller's fifteen florins but the satisfaction of being sure Voltaire knew where the blow came from. This satisfaction was so considerable that he gave some of Voltaire's other works, including *La Henriade*, the same treatment.

Although Voltaire could often be sufficiently carried away to resort to his enemies' vile methods, he was soon restored to his usual self. This was true in this case as well, and the most deplorable aspect of the affair was not Voltaire's wounded vanity but the fact that a man such as La Beaumelle should have insulted a work of history that offered for the first time a masterful object lesson in respect for the truth.

Meanwhile the Potsdam circle was disintegrating. The quarrels with La Beaumelle scarcely interested any of them, save for Maupertuis. Lord Tyrconnel, who had killed his doctor, soon joined him in his grave for the same reason—overeating. "They killed themselves," Voltaire said, "through believing that God made man only for eating—though they thought He had made him for slandering too." He slandered more than they did, but he ate less. He half died of colic or rage seven or eight times a week, but he lived to bury healthier men. "Who would have thought that that great pig of a Tyrconnel, so fresh and strong and vigorous, would be on his deathbed before me?" he mused.

Darget was also ill but did not die, and in March 1752 he went back to France for treatment. His real trouble was emotional rather than physical. He had lost a beloved wife, and all Frederick's favors could not make up for her loss and for his homesickness for his native country. People said he went because he felt belittled by the presence of Voltaire; in fact the two got on very well, probably because Voltaire did all he could to make Darget his watchful intermediary with Frederick.

Darget was far from being the only Frenchman in Berlin to suffer from homesickness. Even Picard, Voltaire's valet, wept because his master would not go back to France. Picard also suffered from the fact that the Prussians made fun of him for being so short. Voltaire consoled him with the precedents of Frederick II himself, Caesar, and Alexander. The valet, uncomforted, replied that they weren't "picards."[2]

In Paris the D'Argentals and Madame Denis thought they had found a way of making Voltaire return: they would make arrangements for

Rome sauvée to be performed only on condition that he come back. But as he would not give way, they had to, and the play was put on with great success. Le Kain was the most applauded, and was awarded the title of "King's Player." Madame Denis, trading on the fact that she was the great poet's niece, wanted to get her own play, *La Coquette punie* (*The Flirt Punished*), put on, but no one except her cronies supported her, and the actors of the Comédie Française refused it. Voltaire was not at all displeased; Madame Denis had no talents as a writer, and he had done his best to discourage her from following in his footsteps.

So Voltaire stayed on in Potsdam, which had in store an even more bitter disappointment than any it had brought him thus far.

A Traitor

Maupertuis was a Breton from Saint-Malo, born in 1698. His father represented Saint-Malo at the Estates of Britanny and was responsible for sending the reports of its proceedings to the King. Maupertuis was a remarkably intelligent child, and although his father was miserly he gave him a good education. On finishing his studies, Maupertuis wanted to be a sailor, but his mother wept. He became a soldier, and she wept again. To dry her tears he left the army two years later and became a physicist. He went to Paris and moved in learned circles, where he was well received. He had a naïve and exaggerated idea of his own ability, which made his beginnings in the world rather difficult for him. But because of his real intelligence he was made a member of the Academy of Sciences in 1723, at the age of twenty-five. In 1728 he visited England and became a devotee of Newton and gravitation, which he determined to make France accept. No method that attracted attention to himself and Newtonism was disdained. But when an expedition was sent to measure a degree of the meridian in Lapland in 1736, he showed himself full of courage and energy, undertaking the most difficult ascents, never complaining about ice or snow or of having to live on seal oil and blubber. Moreover, his calculations were correct and assured the success of the expedition, from which, along with frostbitten feet, he also brought back a couple of female Eskimos, his favorites, whom he put on display in Paris. He also had a blackamoor called Orion. He married one of the Eskimo girls to a man from Normandy, who lived to regret it, and put the other in a convent. Orion went with him everywhere, even to Prussia, and was on such familiar terms with his master that when Maupertuis, as boastful as a Gascon, was bragging of his exploits, Orion used to say aloud, "I wonder if they believe you."

Maupertuis also drew constant crowds by the peculiarity of his getup: he wore a ginger bobtail wig which he powdered yellow. In short, though he was a most reputable scholar he behaved like a charlatan. But, his grotesque affectations apart, he was handsome and a good rider, had acquired social polish, and was a brilliant conversationalist. He was quick at repartee and, like most people who are ambitious, he had a cutting wit. It was with these excellent recommendations that Frederick invited him to Berlin. Louis XV put no difficulties in his way. Maupertuis gave up his royal pension of four thousand livres. Frederick was offering him fifteen thousand. In 1740 geometry commanded a better price in Potsdam than poetry, though when Voltaire came he caused the rates for poetry to go up. Frederick liked Maupertuis and took his geometer to war with him. After he and his philosopher-king had quarreled, Voltaire used to say that Maupertuis went on a donkey, as Frederick wouldn't go to the expense of providing him with a horse. At the Battle of Molditz, Maupertuis couldn't go as fast as his master (who acquired on that occasion the nickname "the Molditz Flyer"), and was caught by the Austrians, beaten, robbed, and taken prisoner. The court at Vienna, hearing of this mishap, showered him with presents. When he returned to France he was made a member of the Academy. But he made himself unbearable by his conceit, his contempt for Descartes, and his continual boosting of Newton. He set off again for Berlin, where as no one knew anything about either they could not argue with him, and he managed both to establish Newton's reputation and to enhance his own. Known at Frederick's court as "His Importance," he married a girl from a noble Prussian family who would have preferred a little less geometry and a little more genealogy. He installed himself securely in Berlin society, was made president of the Prussian Academy, and ruled like a tyrant over the intellectual life of the country. But he was an enlightened despot, and Frederick paid tribute to the good he accomplished.

Maupertuis had had a great deal to recommend him to Voltaire as well: he had been a visitor at Cirey and had introduced Emilie to Newtonian physics. He and Voltaire had been friends for twenty years. But at Potsdam the two of them didn't get on. They were too close; they were rivals.

Voltaire wrote of Maupertuis: "He was born with great wit and talent, but his excessive pride caused him in the end to become both ridiculous and mischievous." But Frederick wrote of him: "I would rather live with Maupertuis than with Voltaire. His character is more reliable and he is more agreeable to converse with than the poet [Voltaire]: for if you do not take care, the latter is forever preaching sermons." This was said in a moment of ill humor at the time of the poet's lawsuit with Hirsch. But if Voltaire had known about it nothing could have made him hate the mathematician more. The quarrel between them arose out of the constant friction between their two vanities, exacerbated by the interventions of the King. A witness who lived at Potsdam said: "The one is too despotic, the other too irritable. Maupertuis wanted to gain the upper hand. Voltaire crushed him."

War

When Voltaire arrived in Potsdam he and Maupertuis embraced. But Buffon, the great naturalist who knew them both well, had long said that the two luminaries were not made to be in the same room, and Potsdam was not much bigger than a room. During the first few months Voltaire made an effort, but trying to be pleasant to someone who no longer responds is possible only when the two parties seldom meet. At Potsdam the two saw each other every day. It was torture for Voltaire: "Having been unable to soften Maupertuis," he wrote, "I put up with him."

La Beaumelle spread the rumor that Voltaire wanted to drive Maupertuis away so as to take his place as president of the Prussian Academy. But it was Maupertuis's ill humor that enraged Voltaire, not his titles or offices. He had enough of his own. Among the nest of vipers at Potsdam, Frederick himself was not the least venomous. In his entourage people said openly, "If Voltaire loses his case against the Jew he'll be hanged; if he wins he'll be thrown out." Frederick heard and did nothing. This, on top of the memory of the "orange peel" remark, kept Voltaire in bed for three days. He began to lose his sparkle at supper. One evening when he had been gloomy and Maupertuis brilliant, they chanced to share the same coach on their way home. Maupertuis remarked gloatingly: "A charming evening, you must admit." Voltaire, crouched in his fur in the farthest corner, growled, "I have never endured as stupid a one."

It has been said that the rupture between the two of them arose out of this reply. But it arose out of everything about the two of them, and everyone around them. Everybody now began to take sides and heap fuel on the fire.

War actually broke out on the subject of Professor Koenig. Maupertuis had begun by protecting Koenig, despite the fact that the latter was for Leibnitz and against Newton; he had even tried to reconcile Emilie and Koenig. But the only result had been that Emilie had quarreled with Maupertuis too. Koenig had later ventured to make a few remarks about an article published by Maupertuis. They were meant quite innocently, but Maupertuis replied with incredible violence and hauled Koenig before the Berlin Academy. He meant to discredit him completely and cause him to lose all his titles and his post as librarian at The Hague. Frederick did not interfere. Voltaire had no time for either Leibnitz or his disciple Koenig, but when he saw how Maupertuis was abusing his authority as president of the Academy in order to victimize poor Koenig, he took up the cudgels against such flagrant injustice, and incidentally against the overwhelming Maupertuis.

Although Koenig had been Maupertuis's friend for twenty-five years, he did not show him all the respect the latter thought was due him as president of the Berlin Academy. In conversation Koenig one day addressed him as "my poor fellow." Koenig did not take Maupertuis's childish rage at this familiarity seriously, and published his *Observations*. He had in fact asked Maupertuis's permission to do so, and Maupertuis had treacherously given it. Soon after the book came out its author learned that it had been condemned by the Berlin Academy, and when he appealed to its president he was told by Maupertuis that he had had nothing to do with its being condemned and that the Academy had acted perfectly freely. Koenig then drew up his own defense—a dignified, courageous, and accurate one. The Academy pigeonholed it. Voltaire read it.

Maupertuis's illness did not make him any more amenable. He was suffering from inflammation of the lungs, which he treated with copious drafts of brandy. But his illness did not cut him off completely, and he learned that Voltaire was speaking up in Koenig's favor. Voltaire for his part soon learned that in exchange Maupertuis was spreading the sort of dangerous slander "against which there can be no defense." The slander he was referring to was the fact that "Maupertuis had slyly spread the rumor that I found the King's writings very poor." Maupertuis had also told a dozen or so chosen vessels that one day, when Voltaire was brought some of Frederick's verses to correct, he had used "very odd language" in front of several people, having said apropos of the King. "Will he never tire of sending me his dirty linen to wash?"

Voltaire said this was slander, but no one believed him. There is also another version of the same anecdote. This version has it that one day Voltaire was with a German friend called Manstein, helping him with his verses, when the King sent Voltaire a bundle of drafts with the request that he correct them. Voltaire handed Manstein back his own efforts at versifying, saying, "Some other time, my friend. Here is the King sending me his dirty linen to launder. I'll launder yours afterward."

In an hour it was all around the court, in a day it was all around the town. The "dirty linen" was a worthy comeback to the "orange peel" slur. But in conveying this drop of vitriol to the King, Maupertuis was playing as dangerous a game as Voltaire.

On December 18, 1752, Maupertuis was unpleasantly surprised to receive a slim anonymous pamphlet entitled *Réponse d'un académicien de Berlin à un académicien de Paris* (*Reply to a Berlin Academician by an Academician of Paris*). It was a defense of Koenig in the form of a violent attack on Maupertuis. Everyone in Berlin knew it had been written by Voltaire. Frederick did not conceal his anger at this assault on the president of his Academy, whom he had supported. But as he pretended not to know who the author was, and Voltaire pretended not to know that he in fact knew very well, they met with the usual exchanges of flattery.

Frederick now entered the game and wrote an anonymous refutation called *Lettre d'un académicien de Berlin à un académicien de Paris*, taking up his president's defense. At the time only Maupertuis knew that the

King was its author. But where Voltaire's attack was lively and telling, the royal riposte was tedious and unconvincing. Everyone said so—Voltaire among the first.

So Voltaire did not know the source of the attacks on him as author of the *Réponse*, whereas Frederick knew very well on whose back they had landed. The King's pamphlet contained compliments of the following kind to his "Virgil": ". . . this miserable author of an infamous lampoon who spreads his venom; this pamphleteer without genius; this contemptible enemy of a man of merit. The sterility of his imagination does not prevent him from committing a pointless crime which becomes the latest height of infamy." Respectable people could feel only pity and scorn for "this wretch and his like, for their frivolity, knavery, and ignorance." Voltaire shrugged his shoulders: it could only be the work of some hack. Frederick had it reprinted. He still did not sign it, but he had it stamped with his royal coat of arms, which amounted to the same thing. Then he sent a copy to Voltaire, who nearly died of rage.

Between fits of fever and fury, Maupertuis, his meditations fortified with brandy, had written some very farfetched *Lettres* on scientific subjects. He proposed blowing up the Pyramids to see what was inside them, and setting up an international youth town where only Latin was spoken. He also advocated the vivisection of criminals condemned to death, explaining that by dissecting a live brain one could discover the mechanism of the passions. Brandy turned him into a disciple of La Mettrie. But vivisection was something of a family characteristic: Maupertuis's brother used to cut up cats. The Duchesse d'Aiguillon was astonished, because he was a great cat lover. "Madame, we use sub-cats for this sort of thing," he explained.

Maupertuis's high-flown visions drew forth a reply from Voltaire that resounded from Potsdam to Paris, Rome, London, Vienna, The Hague, and St. Petersburg. *La diatribe du docteur Akakia, médicin du pape* (*The Diatribe of Dr. Akakia, the Pope's Physician*) fell like a thunderbolt on the proud president. It was full of sly wit and verve, and made everyone who was anyone roar with laughter. Dr. Akakia, supposed physician to the Pope, reproved a reckless and conceited young ignoramus for writing *Lettres* in which he passed himself off as the learned president of an Academy. As if anyone could believe a real president could sink to those depths! And so on.

Voltaire had read the manuscript to Frederick, who nearly split his sides laughing. But on reflection the King remembered that he really ought to defend Maupertuis and his own authority, mocked in the person of the president of his Academy. Moreover, the *Diatribe* demolished Maupertuis's anonymous defender as well as Maupertuis himself. Voltaire read it to Frederick in fear and trembling, knowing that instead of laughing he might declare himself once and for all for Maupertuis. Fortunately, Frederick the wit assuaged the anger of Frederick the King, and he laughed. But afterward he asked Voltaire, in the name of their friendship, to destroy the manuscript. It was an affecting scene. Frederick said he was well aware of the magnitude of the sacrifice he was demanding: such a great genius, such fame . . . Voltaire couldn't resist the siren's song. They congratulated one another, and embraced, and began to address one another again as "Virgil" and "the Solomon of the North." Carried away with words, Voltaire promised to do anything his philosopher-king wished, and when Frederick, to make sure, said, "Burn your tract!" he replied, "Let's burn it together!" As conscientious connoisseurs they reread it page by page, laughed again, and, finally, with tears streaming down their faces, consigned it to the flames.

Among the many scenes these two consummate actors had played together, this was one of the very best.

Voltaire had already tucked away several copies of the *Diatribe* that had been printed in secret. He had them smuggled out to Saxony just before Frederick seized all those that were lying at the printer's waiting to be distributed. Voltaire swore orally and in writing that there were no more *Diatribes* in the whole of Prussia. When some suspicious wretches said that Voltaire still had a few up his sleeve, he protested vehemently against "this horrible calumny," demanding "justice or death."

Meanwhile the court of Potsdam did not altogether neglect intellectual pleasures. One day at supper Frederick had the idea that they should all write a book in collaboration. Everyone present had to contribute a chapter on a subject, an event, and a character of his choice. Voltaire was enthusiastic and began his section the next morning. He chose *Abraham*, and the prophet's faith came in for some rough handling. By chance, he went on in alphabetical order and a few days later wrote an article on *Atheism*. He was the only one to pursue the game, and out of it sprang the *Dictionnaire philosophique*. It shows how great was his need to create, how tireless his activity, how incomparable his gift for seizing upon an idea. There were many other wits and scholars present, but not one of them got even a couple of dozen lines out of Frederick's suggestion. Voltaire derived from it one of the most intelligent and fruitful works of the century. If it was popularization, it was popularization of the most necessary and laudable kind. Voltaire, presenting his article, described himself as "Beelzebub's theologian," and said that this little piece —in fact far from Christian—would be very orthodox. But what followed promised to be completely heretical and heterodox. This was the irreligion of Voltaire's maturity: grimmer, stronger, and more aggressive than before. Frederick recognized his real, his own Voltaire again.

But the Maupertuis affair was still smoldering underground, and Voltaire did not forget it. He hid in his hole like a hare, trembling. He appeared at supper only at the King's request and shone only on order. He could produce compliments and smiles as required; he had a special gift for such command performances, but life at Potsdam was becoming wearisome to him. And he was gnawed by constant fears in this nest of intrigue.

Frederick was rather pleased with himself for having persuaded Voltaire to burn the *Diatribe*. He himself went to inform Maupertuis of the danger that had threatened him and of how much he owed to his protector. According to La Beaumelle, Maupertuis was on the point of giving up the ghost, and the King's goodness brought him back to life again. To go Voltaire one better, Frederick, thinking he had him at his mercy, tried to humiliate him further by asking him to give a solemn undertaking never to write anything against France, Frederick, or Maupertuis. ("France" was there simply to introduce the name of Maupertuis.) Voltaire signed the paper the King presented. He had been through this sort of thing before, and often. As he signed he no doubt thought with glee of the copies of the *Diatribe* increasing and multiplying in Saxony.

To move—and to lull—his victims before finishing them off, Voltaire wrote a plaintive, humble letter to his adored Frederick, who of course showed it to Maupertuis. Voltaire said he was ready to do whatever the King wanted. Had he not given heart-rending proof of it? He would obey even the cruelest commands so long as he felt loved or even tolerated at court (at that very moment he was trying his best to make his escape from it). All he asked was to be able to contemplate his idol. What was he, after all?: "An old man weighed down with illness and pain, but still as much attached to Your Majesty as the day I arrived at your court."

Frederick and Maupertuis allowed themselves to be lulled. And then, in the time it took to go from Berlin to Potsdam, up rose the *Diatribe* like the phoenix from its ashes, and was in everyone's hands. They laughed at the victim but feared for the author. If one of the King of Prussia's own subjects had allowed himself a quarter of the insolences Voltaire permitted himself, he would never have seen the light of day again. Voltaire knew this and decided a hasty retreat seemed in order. "I cannot make war," he wrote. "All I can manage is a respectable desertion." On December 18, 1752, he wrote to Madame Denis: "I see clearly the orange has been squeezed. Now we must think of saving the peel." But he could not resist a parting jibe, and composed before he left a little dictionary for the use of kings:

My friend signified *My slave.*

My dear friend meant *You are a matter of supreme indifference to me.*

I will make you happy equaled *I will put up with you as long as I have a use for you.*

Sup with me this evening was as much as to say, *I shall make game of you this evening.*

The problem was how to get away. For two months he had been trying to think of a method. He invoked his health, but Frederick was unmoved by this threadbare excuse. Nor was he taken in when Voltaire said he wanted to go and take the waters at Plombières—in the month of November! Frederick dryly suggested those of Bohemia instead. "They are excellent, and I will see that you do not lack for company," he promised. But Voltaire fancied the waters of Bohemia as little as he did Frederick's guardian angels.

Frederick, wild with rage, had the *Diatribe* seized by the police, and summarily ordered that it be publicly burned in the Place des Gendarmes at ten in the morning on December 24, 1752. A fine Christmas present for an infidel! Voltaire's secretary at the time, Cosimo Collini, says he made some very witty jokes. But it is more likely that he made himself as scarce as possible, like a mouse caught in a cat's paw.

To console Maupertuis, Frederick sent him a charming letter and a pinch of the *Diatribe*'s ashes. The Berlin *Gazette* gave an account of the burning and indicated the name of the author, though it had not appeared on the book. Frederick said this form of punishment was more of a disgrace in Prussia than in France; Voltaire, who couldn't stand Prussia any more, would rather have been disgraced in France. Maupertuis was not satisfied, however, and pressed Frederick to punish Voltaire as severely as possible for his crime. But Frederick was not to be persuaded. He wrote to his sister, the Margravine of Bayreuth: "A little too much amour-propre has made him [Maupertuis] too sensitive to the tricks of a monkey, whom he ought merely to despise now that he has been whipped." Much to Frederick's amusement, Maupertuis would have liked to have Voltaire vivisected: the mere burning of a book was nothing to him. But Frederick contented himself with that. It was the only book that Frederick had ever had officially burned. A distinction not to be forgotten.

The End of a Beautiful Friendship

The relationship between Voltaire and Frederick had definitely soured. It was time to end it. As a New Year's present on January 1, 1753, Voltaire sent Frederick back his "cap and bells"—the cross and gold key that were the insignia of the King's chamberlain. But Frederick returned them with a note saying he would rather live with Voltaire than with Maupertuis. Wisely, Voltaire continued to act the courtier, and sent the baubles back to Frederick with a little poem:

> Je les reçus avec tendresse.
> Je vous les rends avec douleur.
> C'est ainsi qu'un amant, dans son extrême ardeur,
> Rend le portrait de sa maîtresse.

I have received them with affection./I return them with pain./Thus does a lover, in the extreme of his passion,/Give back his mistress' portrait.

To all appearances they were back to "Danaës" and "coquettes" again. But Voltaire was looking about him for support; he was no longer safe. And he remembered the other King, at Versailles, the only person who could really protect him if Frederick should come to lend an ear to Maupertuis. The French ambassador, the Chevalier de la Touche, was the obvious person to turn to, and Voltaire besieged him with attentions. Frederick continued to invite him to supper. Voltaire did not want to go, after what had been done to him; besides, didn't the King know he was ill? "Do I have to die to prove I'm speaking the truth?" he said. He very nearly did put himself in his grave, and remained in bed for a fortnight. He never had visitors turned away, however: he received them in bed. And there he also worked; took bread and milk, coffee, pills, and endless enemas; did his accounts; and harried his debtors, booksellers, and friends in Paris.

After a month without Voltaire, Frederick could bear it no longer and made advances. He gave him back his apartments at Sans Souci, which led into his own, and sent a carriage around for him. Voltaire was exultant. Although he accepted nothing, he sent word to Monsieur de la Touche to spread the news in Paris. He himself sent letters out in all directions. And yet, at the same time that he was boasting everywhere that he had never been in such high favor, he was arranging to rent rooms in Leipzig, where he hoped to take refuge. All this was not due merely to a love of complications: he genuinely wanted to leave, but not in anger. There ought to be a marvelous farewell scene, and on a stage closely observed by all Europe the monarch of wit and the monarch of Prussia should separate with verses, tears, embraces, and protestations of the most elegant courtesy and friendship.

Frederick could have played this comedy with the same ease and pleasure as Voltaire, and the same total absence of illusion about the sincerity of the other. But Frederick didn't want a farewell scene: he wanted to keep Voltaire in his "menagerie." He tried to get around him once more. As it was only illness that was presumably keeping Voltaire from returning to court, Frederick sent him some quinine. Voltaire waved it away when he saw it, exclaiming: "That's not what I need! What I need is permission to leave!"

He was living in a suburb of Berlin, in a house with a big garden where he walked about with his secretary from Florence, the worthy and subtle Collini. The walks were kept a secret, for Voltaire was supposed to be on his deathbed. When he wished to be left alone to think he would say to Collini, who accompanied him in silence: "Now let me ponder." What he was pondering, as he walked around the garden, was a plot to escape, disguised as a shepherd and riding on a haycart driven by Collini. Collini pointed out that he didn't know how to drive, but Voltaire was only amusing—and consoling—himself by daydreaming.

Wearying of having all his advances answered with "I want to go to

Plombières," Frederick finally gave him permission to leave. "It was not necessary to use the pretext of needing to go to Plombières in order to ask to depart. You may leave my service whenever you choose, but before you go, send me back the contract of your engagement, the cross, the key, and the volume of poetry I gave you."

The touching parting scene Voltaire had envisioned seemed highly unlikely after this cold dismissal, and Voltaire decided to be off at once. Then he changed his mind and asked Frederick to receive him in audience. The Abbé de Prades arranged it, and Voltaire and Frederick remained closeted together for two hours in the King's study. They could be heard laughing from outside. It turned out they were laughing about Maupertuis. Collini relates that they were reconciled at the expense of the president of the Berlin Academy. For Voltaire, it was just a question of continuing his campaign of revenge. Frederick's role is more difficult to describe.

Voltaire seemed to be taking up the game on the old footing and accepted an invitation to sup with his philosopher-king. But he went in fear and trembling. He was not sure he wouldn't be clapped in irons afterward. He called the last of these parties "the suppers of Damocles."

Despite his contempt for Voltaire's character, Frederick was still fascinated by his intelligence and talent. He did all he could to win him back and thought he had succeeded. But after six days Voltaire came to him one morning when the King was getting ready to go to his parade ground and announced that he was leaving, as he had been given permission to do.

"So, Monsieur de Voltaire," Frederick said icily, "you insist upon going?"

"Sire," Voltaire answered, "I am obliged to do so by pressing business and, above all, my state of health."

"Then I wish you a pleasant journey, monsieur," said the King, and turned on his heel.

And that was all there was to the great farewell scene that Voltaire had dreamed of.

X

Men are indeed mad, but churchmen are the maddest of all. (Letter, March 11, 1753)

There is no more wastefulness than there is economy in nature. (Letter to Koenig, June 1753)

I perceived that in the long run everything that one says and does is not worth the trouble of going out of the house. Illness has certain great advantages; it delivers us from the company of others. (Letter, May 19, 1754)

[Apropos of Jean-Jacques Rousseau's "noble savages" as a model of behavior]: "The examples of our nations have made savages almost as wicked as ourselves." (Letter, August 30, 1755)

The older and more knowledgeable one becomes, the more one must repent of having been a writer. (Letter to Monsieur Cramer, 1757)

I have never written as a theologian; I have merely been a zealous citizen and, even more so, a citizen of the universe. (Letter to Cramer, 1757)

No people has the right to mock another. (*Essay on Morals*, Introduction)

Pure despotism is the punishment visited on men's bad conduct. If a community of men is mastered by a single man or by several, it is obviously because it has neither the courage nor the cleverness to govern itself. (*Essay on Morals*, Chapter 1)

There are only three ways in which to subjugate men; that of disciplining them by proposing laws to them; that of using religion to uphold the laws; and that, finally, of massacring a part of a nation in order to govern the other part; I do not know of a fourth way. (*Essay on Morals*, Chapter 13)

What makes laws fickle, faulty, inconsistent is that they have almost all been established on the basis of passing needs, like remedies applied at random, which have cured one patient and killed others. (*Essay on Morals*, Chapter 17)

One of the achievements of the human mind in this last century has been to have discovered the secret of owing more than one possesses, and to live as though one did not owe a penny. (*Essay on Morals*, Chapter 18)

It is an old tradition among sculptors to put slaves at the feet of statues of kings; it would be better to show free and happy citizens there. (*Essay on Morals*, Chapter 27)

Among the nations of Europe, war makes the conqueror almost as miserable as the conquered after a few years. It is an abuse that swallows up every channel of wealth. (*Essay on Morals*, Chapter 27)

Luther and other monks, by contracting marriages useful to the state, no more violated their vows than those who, having taken an oath to be poor and humble, possessed fabulous wealth. (*Essay on Morals*, Chapter 33)

Unpleasant Consequences

Voltaire scrambled into his great coach and fled for Leipzig, without stopping to pay any visits en route. He took leave of people by letter, pleading his bad health, his age, and so on as an excuse for not bidding them good-by in person. Everything had long been prepared. The coach was pulled by a team of either four or six horses, depending on the state of the roads. It was as big as a room inside, and packed with cases of manuscripts and books, strongboxes, and furs. It also contained Collini, who took notes, listened, talked, and laughed with his master. Voltaire needed to make others laugh in order to be able to laugh himself. As soon as he had a moment's respite, amusing ideas about everything and nothing came crowding in on him.

Voltaire had scarcely departed when Frederick got together with Maupertuis again, and the two of them began to be more worried about Voltaire in flight than they had been about him under their eye in Berlin. Frederick was apprehensive about the epigrams and indiscreet revelations regarding the Solomon of the North with which Voltaire would certainly regale the courts of Europe. But above all he dreaded comments on his poetry.

As soon as Voltaire alighted at Leipzig he wrote an appendix to the *Diatribe*. It was written in the same style as the first part, except that the comedy was broader and more farcical and the public that could laugh at Maupertuis's expense therefore larger. Maupertuis learned about it and wrote an angry, threatening letter, ending: "You may thank the respect and obedience which have stayed my arm hitherto for saving you from the most unpleasant experience you have ever yet had."

Voltaire was greatly amused, and to add to his amusement he published the letter, though he cut out everything after the word "arm," thus leaving out the discomforting allusion to such past misadventures as his cudgeling by Rohan. This made Maupertuis's threat even more ominous, and to make it more ridiculous as well, Voltaire added the word "Tremble!" He then answered Maupertuis in a letter which he duly circulated, and which ended: "As there are some fifty or sixty people who have taken the liberty of laughing heartily at you they would like to know on what day you are planning to murder them." Maupertuis, more furious than ever, thereupon appealed for revenge to Frederick, who was also furious because Voltaire had neglected to return the cross and the golden key and the book of poetry. Frederick's primary concern over the book of poetry could not have been any embarrassing allusions contained in it. Five hundred copies of it had been printed in a room at Sans Souci, and most of them had been distributed. In any case, the poems, although "laundered" by Voltaire, were not at all dazzling: the King's desire to wound was clear enough, but his arrows were blunt. What Frederick was afraid of was that Voltaire was going to reprint the poems with vitriolic comments of his own. The two friends were equally afraid of each other. But Frederick had the advantage of two hundred thousand "mustaches" and almost as many police.

Voltaire knew his own weakness and trembled, but he went on—and did not return either the cross or the key or the book.

At Leipzig he received a very severe letter from Frederick, making it clear that he had never been taken in by the pretext of the waters at Plombières: "Your object was to go to Leipzig to print new insults against the human race." In the language of philosophy and sensibility, "the human race" was becoming popular. But in this case it merely meant Maupertuis. "But as I am an admirer of your adroitness, I gave myself the pleasure of watching your artifices and amused myself by gravely handing over the wherewithal for your imaginary journey to the water at Plombières," Frederick went on.

Then he added: "I doubt not that you are better, since it seems the printers of that town have purged you of an excess of bile. I appeal to your conscience, if you have one." Frederick could not help admiring Voltaire for his very duplicity: he had put Maupertuis's threatening letter in the hands of the Leipzig magistrates. "Admit, with me, that you were born to be Cesare Borgia's prime minister. Did you also give the magistrates the pamphlets you have written against him?" Frederick apparently saw no incongruity in his lecturing Voltaire on morals. "Heretofore you have been continually at odds with the law, but by singular cleverness you find a way of making it useful to you. This is what is called pressing one's enemies into service to further one's own ends." (Frederick ought to have known all about that: it was his methods of recruitment that gave rise to the proverbial expression "to go to war for the King of Prussia"—meaning to be someone else's cat's-paw.) After this letter Voltaire had every reason to fear the worst.

He sent his cases of books on ahead to Hamburg and took the road to Gotha, making a delightful halt at the court of Princess Dorothea of Saxe-Meiningen. Voltaire said she was as witty as the Duchesse du Maine but was gentler, kept a better table, and didn't write poetry. He was so charmed by her that he promised to write the *Annales de l'empire*, a huge tome on the Germans since the time of Charlemagne. She wanted an equivalent of *Le Siècle de Louis XIV* on the subject of the Holy Roman Empire, but of course on an even vaster and more grandiose scale. No poet ever let himself in for a more tedious task. He started immediately and began searching through the huge archives of Gotha. He kept his promise and produced the *Annales*, but they only faintly echo the brilliance of *Louis XIV* and of *Charles XII*. His heart—that is to say, his mind—was not in it.

On March 25, 1753, he set out for Strasbourg, intending to stop at Frankfurt on the way. At one point he thought of making a detour and asking asylum of his beloved Margravine of Bayreuth. But he reflected that it would be putting himself in Frederick's power to go and stay with his sister. The margravine for her part was rather alarmed at the idea, and despite the pleasure she would have found in talking with him, she was relieved when he decided to continue on toward Frankfurt.

By a strange trick of fate he had stayed away from Bayreuth to avoid danger, but it was in Frankfurt that danger awaited him. Between Gotha and Frankfurt he stopped in Cassel. The Landgrave of Hesse and his son were princes after his own heart. Praises and flatteries were exchanged; operas, ballets, and tragedies were performed. But there was a shadow: Voltaire was told that the terrible Pollnitz, Frederick's confidant, spy and thug, was in Cassel. In Berlin rumor had it that one day Frederick, Maupertuis, and others were reviling Voltaire and Pollnitz, who was listening, had said: "Sire, give the order, and I will stab him as he leaves the town." It must be said in Frederick's honor that he was so angry he had had Pollnitz thrown out. But he might change his mind.

Maupertuis too had been seen in Cassel. He had come to have a new pamphlet against Voltaire printed under the name of La Beaumelle, who was in the Bastille at the time. Maupertuis knew the latter wouldn't mind; if the pamphlet succeeded in hurting its intended victim, La Beaumelle would be delighted. Nobody would be taken in by the name. The public was so avid for literary scandal and calumny that authors did not have to trouble about the credibility of the lies they spread.

Voltaire was well aware of La Beaumelle's whereabouts. He had even done his best to help put him there. At his request Madame Denis had run from ministry to ministry to get the authorities to have La Beaumelle thrown in prison. The latter was informed of these attentions by a man called Sabatier who had it from a priest who had been present in the office of the superintendant of police the day that Madame Denis informed Monsieur d'Argental that La Beaumelle's freedom was a threat to France. But in fact he owed his incarceration to the Duc d'Orléans.

This was not Madame Denis's first intervention on behalf of her uncle. The year before she had asked Monsieur d'Argenson to suppress a pamphlet by Fréron that constituted an even more virulent attack against his person than against his work. "The criticism is good, the invective unnecessary," D'Argenson declared, and the pamphlet was suppressed for six months. It was said that it was Voltaire who asked for it to be allowed to circulate again, but though Voltaire can easily be imagined helping Fréron's indigent family out by giving them money, this particular form of magnanimity seems most unlikely.

Voltaire then resumed his journey. On April 30, 1753, he stayed the night in Marburg. At eight the following evening they entered Frankfurt. He was expected.

A Fresh Attack on a Poet and Personal Liberty

In his *Mémoires*, written in 1759, Voltaire gives his own account of the events that befell him in Frankfurt.[1] He tells the story comically rather than tragically, wanting to avenge outrage by ridicule. In any case, what other vengeance was possible against an all-powerful monarch? The one aim of the account of the Frankfurt business in the *Mémoires* was to make Europe laugh at Baron Franz von Freytag, one of Frederick's myrmidons, and at Frederick himself. But the reality was murky enough, and in Voltaire's letters and conversations, and in the account of his secretary Collini, we can follow the sinister yet often farcical story almost hour by hour.

Frederick had ordered his secretary Fredendorff, who hated Voltaire, to write and tell Freytag, Frederick's agent in Frankfurt, that he wanted Voltaire arrested and searched. It must be mentioned that Frankfurt was not part of Frederick's domain, and he had no right to have anyone arrested there. Freytag was supposed to take possession of the insignia and decorations of the fallen chamberlain, of his titles to pensions, and above all of the book of poems and some manuscripts. Freytag was told that it was the poems that were of greatest importance and was warned that the suspect was a very sly customer. The most rigorous precautions should be taken against his tricks, his escape, or worse!

For several days Freytag had been sending spies to all the inns asking after a French gentleman by the name of Maynvillar. There was no such person, but Freytag hoped by this means to get the innkeepers to volunteer the names of any other Frenchmen there. On May 31, 1753, the landlord of the Golden Lion at Frankfurt answered that he had just put up a Monsieur de Voltaire, who had taken a comfortable set of rooms and installed himself with his secretary, Monsieur Collini.

Voltaire slept peacefully under the protection of the Hapsburg eagles, but his pursuer was in a dilemma. He had been told that the suspect was likely to create a great commotion and that this was to be avoided. So Freytag took along with him a hefty assistant who would immediately step in if Voltaire made any sort of outcry or put up a struggle. Freytag was very uneasy because he had been told that when Voltaire shouted he could be heard as far away as London and Saint Petersburg. Such a piece of information might easily have got Voltaire quietly strangled; Freytag, at least, thought that would have been the simplest solution. He wasn't quite sure what crime Voltaire was supposed to have committed. At nine in the morning he and his assistant presented themselves in Voltaire's room. After a few opening courtesies, he informed Voltaire of His Gracious Prussian Majesty's intentions. Voltaire fell back in his chair, shut his eyes, and all but swooned away.

He soon came around and called Collini, who opened the trunks, ferreted about, and produced some papers. But Freytag had been interrupted by Voltaire's swoon and hadn't completed his recital of the King's demands: Frederick wanted more than this. Voltaire passed out for the second time. "He looks just like a skeleton to me," Freytag said at this point in his report. Freytag was so suspicious, he had everything opened and insisted on carrying out the search himself. It took him from nine in the morning till five in the afternoon. Voltaire's nerves were in shreds. Freytag asked if he was sure there was nothing else, and Voltaire swore a hundred times that there was nothing else. What about the book of poems? he was asked. It was in one of the cases Voltaire had sent on to Hamburg. Freytag then said he wouldn't let Voltaire go until he had the book in his hands, whereupon Voltaire swooned for the third time. Finally Freytag signed a guarantee that as soon as he received the book Voltaire would be free to go where he chose. After all this searching Voltaire looked in such poor shape that Freytag felt sorry for him. He had thought he was going to have to face the Devil, and what he was confronted with was the next thing to a corpse. He sent him the best doctor in the town, made him a present of wine from his own cellar, and offered to take him for a walk through the gardens of the town—properly guarded, of course. But Voltaire was appalled at his situation. How long would it take to get hold of the books sent to Hamburg? Would they ever be recovered at all?

Freytag wrote to Berlin for fresh instructions. He wanted a secretary who knew something about "poëhsie" to help him; he was afraid he might have missed something. To show how economical he was being—he knew Frederick would appreciate that—he said that Voltaire had wanted him to send an express letter to Hamburg to recover the trunk, but as three louis had already been wasted on expenses in this business, Freytag had preferred to use the ordinary post. So Voltaire was under arrest for another week.

What is surprising in all this is Voltaire's moderation, when he apparently had every reason to burst into one of his famous rages. But these rages were much less important to him than to spectators. Like all his outbursts of emotion, they were spectacular, but they were also superficial. All the to-do was external; the storm only ruffled the surface. As soon as the sudden crisis was over, he recovered his calm and concentration and resumed his work. He did not consider himself lowered in other people's esteem by his outbursts of temper: he knew they were only sound and fury and did not affect his thinking, his plans, his friendships, or his hatreds.

So on the evening of this maddening day he remained calm. The matter was too serious for anger. He was tonight the other Voltaire, one of the other Voltaires, probably the most profound and the truest: he sat up working all evening and part of the night. He plunged into the *Annales de l'empire*, to please the charming Margravine of Gotha and to remain true to his passion for disciplined work: "Work is a mortal's lot and honor. I perceive afresh every day that it is man's life; it gathers together the forces of the soul and makes men happy." As Collini admiringly observed, the real pleasures of Voltaire, who was thought to be so frivolous, were austere.

Now that the curtain had gone up in Frankfurt, the rhythm changed and the play proceeded with all the verve and all the twists and turns of an Italian comedy. Collini played a part. He was a great help to his master in adversity. It says a good deal about Voltaire that so many of his servants were so attached to him. They very often exploited him, but they loved him, and he forgave them because he knew that and loved them too.

The news of Voltaire's detention had spread all over town, and visitors began to arrive. Some of them came simply out of curiosity, among them the bookseller Van Duren of The Hague. He was the one who had tricked and robbed Voltaire at the time of the *Anti-Machiavel*, and Voltaire no sooner laid eyes on him than he gave him two resounding cuffs on the ear. Van Duren was about to reply in kind, but Collini, by dint of talking and gesticulating, managed to appease him. He explained to Van Duren that he'd been cuffed by such a great man that he should regard it as "a fortunate bit of luck that doesn't happen to everyone." Exit Van Duren quietly, for the moment.

All the other visits were quite peaceful. Voltaire made some charming friends among the people of Frankfurt and soon surrounded himself with an entertaining circle of intimates. He would have created a salon even in a dungeon.

This success made Freytag uneasy. If Voltaire enlisted all Frankfurt under his banner, what would become of him, the representative of a "foreign" and none too well liked sovereign? Voltaire's attack on Van Duren showed he might not always behave like a corpse. Moreover, the people of Frankfurt wanted their town council to intervene in Voltaire's favor, as they should have done from the beginning, for Frederick was violating the city's rights. Voltaire asked if he might go and pay his respects to the Duke of Meiningen. Freytag politely refused. Then Voltaire exploded: "Why does your King wish to arrest me in an imperial city? Why could he not have done it in his own territory? You are a heartless creature, you're killing me, and you scoundrels will certainly find yourself in disgrace with the King."

It didn't worry Freytag unduly that he might be killing Voltaire, but he was very uneasy over the final threat. He wondered if his zeal might not get him into trouble. Stupid though he was, he realized the whole affair was far from clear, and wrote for further instructions. Meanwhile Voltaire wrote to the Holy Roman Emperor, appealing for protection. He did not ask him to raise an army against Prussia, only that Freytag, as a representative of a foreign state, should be reminded that he was exceeding his rights by trying to arrest a French citizen in an imperial city. And he took up the old refrain about having one foot in the grave. "It is in this cruel state that a dying invalid throws himself at the feet of Your Sacred Majesty, begging him to deign to order, with the kindness and secrecy which such a situation forces me to implore, that nothing contrary to the law be done against me in Your Majesty's imperial city of Frankfurt." He recalled that the Emperor's mother, the Duchesse de Lorraine, sister of the former French Regent, Philippe d'Orléans, had been well disposed toward him, and hoped that His Majesty would not be unmoved by this recollection. As soon as he was freed by His Imperial Majesty's intervention, he would go to Vienna to speak with H.I.M. on subjects related to the latter's power and glory. In plain language this meant that, betrayed by the King of Prussia, Voltaire was prepared to betray him by entering the Emperor's service.

The fear that inspired the deplorable versatility was not an imaginary one: an inhabitant of Frankfurt came to warn him that anything might happen. He wrote off at once to H.I.M.'s most intimate counselor, asking that he be authorized to write on his door "M. de Voltaire, Chamberlain to His Imperial Majesty." It was a mad suggestion. Why should the Emperor give him that title? He had acquired it at Versailles and Potsdam only after years as a courtier and thanks to the most influential supporters. But at the same time he wrote quite resignedly to the D'Argentals, perhaps out of a desire not to alarm his friends: "My dear Angel, one must know how to suffer, man is born partly for that." If he did not appeal to Versailles for help, it was perhaps because he was afraid he would be ill received. He was right: the French court had not forgotten his indiscretions, his departure for Frederick's court, his invidious comparisons, and the extravagant praises of Potsdam which were thinly veiled criticisms of Versailles.

Madame Denis lent Voltaire moral support. She knew all about what was going on and had done everything she could to get Lord Keith, the Prussian minister in Paris, to intervene and get her uncle set free. This Lord Keith was the Milord Maréchal who had been Voltaire's friend at Sans Souci and whom Madame Denis had received and introduced to her circle in Paris. They thought they could count on him. But it turned out that Lord Keith was Voltaire's friend when Voltaire was Frederick's, and that his friendship dwindled in direct proportion to the poet's credit. He had enough wit to admire Voltaire's and to keep his end up at the supper parties; but all that was only play. He wasn't the sort to risk an ounce of his own credit to save someone who was discredited. Moreover, Lord Keith had become a "man of sensibility," a Rousseauist; he was therefore full of noble sentiments. But though the "philosophical sensibility" is prodigal with its tears, that is the only form of generosity it practices. Lord Keith made it quite clear to Madame Denis that if she wished to see her illustrious uncle set free the first thing to do was to see that the King of Prussia got back what he was asking for. So far, so good. But the next part of the letter is cynical and has extremely disturbing undertones. Lord Keith says that Voltaire must give everything back, for by so doing "he will avoid being blamed by everyone." He adds, most practically: "He owes this also to his own interest: kings have long arms." Should Voltaire prove obstinate, Lord Keith points out that Voltaire has caused all countries to be closed to him, with the exception of France, where it may be possible for him to live if he behaves himself. He adds, by way of a joke: "He is too old to go to China and become a mandarin." He issues a warning that, if Voltaire should return to France and there begin once again to utter epigrams against "the King my master," a word from himself to Versailles would suffice to get the poet exiled again. What a friend! He was also cultured and sensitive, as he demonstrated by ending his letter with a story which shows that Voltaire was not trembling for nothing. Lord Keith's prophecies were both transparent and sinister.

"When discord began to arise among the Spaniards who had conquered Peru, there was at Cuzco a lady (for my story's sake I would it had been a poet) who was furious with Pizarro. A certain Caravajal, both a partisan of Pizarro and a friend of the lady, paid her a call and advised her to moderate her language. But she was more unbridled than ever. Caravajal, having tried in vain to calm her, said: 'My friend, I see that to silence a woman the only way is to throttle her by the gullet.' And he forthwith had her hanged from the balcony."

Lord Keith added a hypocritical but no less sinister comment: "The King my master has never committed such iniquities: I defy his enemies to cite a single one. But if some big strong *Preisser* [Prussian], upset by something your uncle said, were to hit him on the head, he would certainly flatten him. I am persuaded that when you have reflected upon what I have written you will be convinced. Prevent your uncle from doing anything foolish; he is as good at that as he is as writing poetry."

This letter breathed into the Frankfurt affair the sort of icy draft that blows through the dim corridors of dungeons where prisoners suddenly die. But it is not certain that Frederick himself had the same terrifying intentions as Lord Keith hints at.

Lord Keith advised Madame Denis not to show his letter to Voltaire but to pass on the ideas it contained as if they were her own. After the shock of the letter and a tiresome journey, Madame Denis arrived in Frankfurt almost as ill as her uncle.

When their tears and embraces were over, they turned to more practical matters. Voltaire decided to dictate a formal and absolute renunciation of all rights to any post or pension whatsoever at the Prussian court. Madame Denis took it down. They offered everything: papers, poetry, luggage, renunciations, submissions. She added that her uncle was dying and wanted only to go draw his last breath in France. "So much good faith cannot but disarm Your Majesty," she wrote. She recalled the old friendship, vows, and promises. She might have reminded Frederick of the letter he had sent Voltaire in 1750, when he was trying to lure his "Danaë" to his court: "What slavery, what unhappiness, what change, what inconstancy of fortune can you fear in a country where you are esteemed as highly as in your own, and in the house of a friend who has a grateful heart? What, because you retire to my residence, will it be said that it is your prison? What, because I am your friend, must I become your tyrant! I confess I cannot follow that sort of logic."

Another letter was sent to Monsieur d'Argenson at Versailles, this time with Madame Denis dictating and Collini taking it down. She wasn't strong enough to write: she had been bled twice, she said. Voltaire could apparently neither speak nor write at the moment, but he organized everything. If he was dramatizing a little, it was only his way. On June 18, 1753, there was a ray of hope. The package from Hamburg arrived with the King's book of poetry. Thinking his troubles were over, Voltaire's spirits revived.

But Freytag would not open the box until he had new instructions from Frederick. And Berlin was not in any hurry. Freytag, who was hard put to it to restrain his prisoner's patience, sent a reminder to Fredendorff, who merely replied: "You need pay no attention to anything M. de Voltaire's impatience may lead him to say. All you need do is to go on as you have begun." But Freytag, who had promised to set Voltaire free on receipt of the book, did not know how to go on. The calm that Voltaire had preserved thus far was now cast aside, and he shouted and stamped his feet and had hysterics. Freytag was at his wit's end. He wrote to Voltaire, complimenting him on his admirable resignation and begging him to remain patient until the next post from Berlin. Voltaire maintained it was a trap. He was convinced that what they were waiting for from Berlin was someone to strangle him. Madame Denis wrote to Berlin to De Prades, the abbé for whom Voltaire had secured a post in Frederick's entourage; perhaps he would remember past favors Voltaire had done him. "I dreamt not, three years ago, that it would be the King of Prussia who would cause his death. Forgive my grief."

There appeared to be no way out. But Voltaire thought of one—a comic denouement. He decided to escape. Collini hired a post chaise and waited with it outside a different hotel. Dressed in black velvet, Voltaire slipped into it and they drove off. They managed to get through the city gates and thought they were safe. They had with them only a few valuable papers and a box full of money. Madame Denis and the heavy luggage had been left as hostages. But half an hour later a spy notified Freytag of their escape. Terrified at the possible consequences for him, Freytag sent out couriers in all directions, called upon the services of an aulic councilor known for his severity, Monsieur Schmidt, and asked the burgomaster to order Voltaire's arrest. The burgomaster, who was a subject of the Emperor, refused at first, then yielded. The fugitives were caught just as they were about to enter the territory of Mainz. There had been a quirk of fate worthy of *Zadig* or *Candide:* Voltaire had lost his purse as they crossed the city and went back to look for it. The four minutes thus wasted delivered him into the hands of his persecutor.

Freytag did not begin to enjoy his triumph at once, however. Voltaire, volubly seconded by Collini, publicly accused Freytag of having taken a bribe of a thousand thalers to let them escape.

They were taken back to the hotel, and there, while Freytag tried to get the warrant for Voltaire's arrest, Voltaire set about burning certain papers. To put a stop to this, Freytag proposed to take Voltaire to his house until the warrant came. Voltaire refused to go, insisting on being arrested in a formal manner so that everyone would know about it and so that he would have the right to escape, like anyone who has been imprisoned. Freytag then had Voltaire shut up in the coach and surrounded by guards, and to make quite sure his captive would not escape he sat in the coach beside him. This greatly delighted the crowd that had gathered by then to watch the fun.

At this point the landlord of the Golden Lion now declined to lodge so troublesome a guest any longer, and Voltaire was driven to the house of Councilor Schmidt.

Madame Denis had already crossed swords with Schmidt. She had defended her uncle like a tigress and wasn't in the least afraid of the formidable councilor. But as she was going around all the salons of the town preaching a crusade against the Prussians, Schmidt had her arrested, and Collini as well. Freytag, no Machiavelli, wrote to Berlin that they had arrested her "because she might have spoiled everything."

At the Schmidts' residence Voltaire engineered a scene that was half farce, half ballet. In the drawing room Freytag displayed his prisoners and their belongings to Madame Schmidt, an enormous Prussian lady, surrounded by her servants, her neighbors, her footmen, and even her coachmen. The audience began by dividing up between them the money in Voltaire's box, then turned out his pockets, then took his jewels. He begged to be allowed to keep his snuffbox, or at least the snuff in it, but was shown no mercy. When Collini tried to protest he was threatened with being clapped in a dungeon. Suddenly Voltaire spied a door that had been left ajar and darted through it like a lizard. The door had led only to a closed courtyard and Voltaire was hauled back into the drawing room, where Councilor Schmidt informed him: "Wretch, you will be dealt with severely and without pity." A certain Herr Dorn, a notary, who had been sent after Voltaire, said, "If I'd caught him I'd have blown his brains out." Freytag himself had said that if he had overtaken Voltaire outside the imperial city of Frankfurt he would have shot him rather than go back to Frederick empty-handed. "So seriously did I take the royal letters and instructions," he said. "The King was well served by this henchman who, according to Voltaire, had once been a convict.

Voltaire was given receipts for what had been stolen from him and Dorn the notary was charged with incarcerating the prisoners in a wretched inn called the Goat's Horn, where Voltaire says they each had three sentries with fixed bayonets outside their door. Freytag swore it was only two. Collini protested in vain that he was a subject of the Emperor. "If I lived for centuries I should never forget these atrocities," he wrote.

Madame Denis had not been present at the previous scene since she was still at the Golden Lion. Dorn went there and, on the pretext of taking her to her uncle's room, led her to the door of the inn, whereupon three soldiers seized her and carried her off to the Goat's Horn. She thought her last hour had come on finding herself in a miserable attic where, said Voltaire, "four soldiers with fixed bayonets did duty as curtains and chambermaid." Dorn had his supper served in her room and washed it down with great quantities of wine. Voltaire, unable to resist adding the finishing touch, says that Dorn tried to rape Madame Denis but, frightened by her screams, abandoned "his criminal design."

At last Frederick's answer arrived. He thanked Freytag for his zeal but instructed him to set Voltaire at liberty, on condition that he sign a pledge not to keep a copy of any of His Majesty's writings. If he broke this promise he would become Frederick's prisoner again, in whatever country he might find himself. This was just one more outrageous absurdity in an imbroglio which had been sheer folly from the beginning.

Strangely enough, Frederick did not immediately insist on having the book of poems back but contented himself with the promise that it would eventually be restored.

Why, then, this business of arrests and imprisonments and all the rest? Apparently Frederick's secretary, Fredendorff, had initiated the whole affair through an excess of zeal. This is confirmed by the fact that when things started to go further than he had intended he would have no more to do with the matter and left Freytag without instructions. Freytag, not wishing to fall short, had overshot the mark. Frederick had given only hasty verbal orders in a moment of pique, and when his ill humor was over and he inquired at the end of June what had become of Voltaire, he was astonished to find that his modern Virgil was still in custody in Frankfurt.

But Voltaire had still not escaped his persecutors. They wanted him to purchase his freedom. Freytag brought him the bill for his board and lodging, carefully based on the amount of money Voltaire had in his possession; he was equally careful not to tell Voltaire that the King had set him free. This explains a painfully servile letter that Voltaire wrote to Freytag while still under the impression that he was his prisoner, and the money he slipped Dorn whenever the latter paid him a visit.

The people of Frankfurt were talking about the way Freytag was abusing his authority, and the murmurs reached Voltaire's ears. He sent a report to Berlin via the burgomaster, and Freytag began to be afraid. He had the sentries removed and restored the prisoners' luggage. Voltaire sensed that the wind was changing, and when Freytag and Schmidt asked to see him he refused. They even gave him back his sword and offered him back his money, minus the cost of his board and lodging. He refused the account they rendered and demanded his money back intact. They sent Dorn to persuade him, with a receipt for him to sign in one hand and the remaining money in the other. But Voltaire seized a pistol, cocked it, and aimed it at the notary, and Collini had to disarm him and shut him up in the next room out of harm's way. Voltaire gives another version of the scene, wherein Dorn merely pretended to be giving back the money stolen from the two prisoners' pockets. And according to Voltaire, the pistol had neither powder nor bullets in it. Collini says Dorn nearly broke his neck running down the stairs.

Dorn told everyone of Voltaire's supposed murderous attack on him, and by way of compensation kept the things Voltaire had been robbed of: his precious papers, rings, a bag of gold carolines, a bag of gold louis, a pair of gold scissors, and his diamond shoe buckles. Voltaire's attempt on Dorn's life may well have been a fiction, but Dorn's theft was not.

Dorn even brought charges against Voltaire, and on July 6, 1753, Freytag sent a report to the King saying that, as Monsieur de Voltaire had deposited "a sum of money" with him and Councilor Schmidt, it seemed only just that it should be used to compensate Dorn's wife and daughter for the mental and physical suffering caused them—on learning of the notary's narrow escape from death. Frederick apparently unmoved, did not say a word about the two women in his reply.

On July 2, Frederick had renewed his order to free Voltaire, not even deigning to mention the attempted escape. The foolish Freytag then began to brag about his own zealous efforts to get the prisoners set free. This sort of publicity was not at all to Frederick's liking, and on July 9 he dispatched a brief command in answer to all Freytag's reports: "You must have received the orders to let him and his niece go where they choose."

Freytag sensed Frederick's exasperation and was worried. But Fredendorff reassured him. What did it matter if Voltaire was still under lock and key? Let him shout: if he protested that he was Gentleman of the Royal French Bedchamber, let Freytag suggest sending him to Versailles —where he would doubtless promptly be dispatched to the Bastille. If he threatened to complain to Berlin, Freytag need not worry—Voltaire's slanders would never hurt him. Clearly, Frederick is not the guiltiest party in all this. The King even wrote Freytag to give Voltaire back all his money, his personal effects, his luggage, and his papers. Unfortunately, by the time this letter arrived Voltaire had left Frankfurt, with only the clothes on his back.

Home Again—Almost

Voltaire and Madame Denis left Frankfurt on July 6, 1753, and arrived in Mainz on the seventh. It was a sort of minor triumph: all the Rhineland had hung out its flags to make them forget the insults of Frankfurt. This was the Germany dear to Voltaire's heart. He allowed himself to be consoled and was soon his old gay, courtly, witty self. He stayed there three weeks, to dry out, as he put it, the clothes "that had got wet in the shipwreck." And he also worked, making great progress on the *Annales de l'empire*. On July 28 he was on the way to Mannheim. He spent a night in an inn at Worms and amused himself by posing as an Italian with the proprietor, who spoke Tuscan.

Mannheim was another triumph. The Elector Palatine gave lavish fetes and had operas and comedies performed in honor of Voltaire's visit. His court was one of the most pleasant and cultivated in Germany. Voltaire felt at home and happy there. The Elector put his rich archives at Voltaire's disposal, and Voltaire wrote to the Duchess of Gotha to tell her how the documents contained in them would benefit the *Annales*. In this oasis of peace, politeness, and intelligence, he also had an idea for a new play, the first since he had left France. Prussia had not inspired him. He wrote to D'Argental: "The Elector has paid me the compliment of putting on four of my plays. This has revived my old zest, and I have started, moribund as I am, to draw up the outline for a new play that is all about love. I blush for it; 'tis the daydreaming of an old fool."

It was a tragedy—a charming tragedy that was meant to be terrifying but terrified no one. On the other hand, it was brilliantly witty. It was called *L'Orphelin de la Chine* (*The Chinese Orphan*). This was Voltaire's contribution to the chinoiserie of his age. Just as others painted "Chinese" figures and scenes on china or porcelain or on lacquer screens, so Voltaire wrote a tragedy based on the memoirs of a real-life missionary to China, Father de Prémare.

On August 16, having dragged himself away from the delights of the Palatinate, he arrived in Strasbourg. He took rooms in a humble inn in a rather seedy part of town. Naturally there was malicious comments to the effect that it was a different story when someone else was paying the bill; but once again malice was mistaken. During one halt on his journey Voltaire had been struck by the kindness shown him and Madame Denis by a young servant, and on learning that the youth's father kept the White Bear Inn at Strasbourg and was not doing any too well, he promised to put up there. At the expense of his own comfort and perhaps even his health, he hoped to improve the White Bear's fortunes by staying there.

In Strasbourg he met various people with whom he had corresponded. Wherever he went, Voltaire immediately became the center of a friendly circle, and then soon thereafter of another that was less friendly. Among those well disposed toward him was the learned Joseph Frederick Schoepflin, who undertook to go through Voltaire's notes for the *Annales*.

He went to and fro in Alsace, looking for somewhere permanent to live. Since Cirey he had had no real home. He was weary of the hospitality of princes and dukes; after Prussia and Frankfurt he wanted a roof of his own.

He wanted to buy a fine château with fine grounds. There seemed to be just the place for him at Horbourg, a splendid estate belonging to the Duke of Württemberg on which Voltaire had lent the duke money in return for an annuity. Voltaire had a weakness for this sort of arrangement. The duke did not pay very regularly and was difficult to deal with; but Voltaire was astonishingly patient with people who owed him money. This policy paid off in the end, of course. He went to see the estate that served as guarantee for the enormous sum he had lent the duke and found beautiful vineyards and an ancient, imposing, dilapidated château. But when he learned there was a lawsuit pending as to the ownership of the estate, he prudently withdrew. "I am not about to build myself a retreat with a lawsuit for its foundations," he said.

When he went to Colmar to reconnoiter, Voltaire was required to defend himself against a Jesuit plot aimed at having him expelled from Alsace. His enemies were at work again: wherever he went, the moment he appeared they inevitably joined forces to attack him. The momentary calm of his return was over, and hostilities were about to break out once again.

Without his knowledge a bookseller of The Hague, named Néaulme, had printed and published Voltaire's *Abrégé de l'histoire universelle* (*Résumé of World History*), which had existed in manuscript form since 1740. How had Néaulme got hold of a copy? There were six copies in all, one of them in the possession of Frederick of Prussia. This copy was incomplete and full of uncorrected mistakes and violent attacks which Voltaire had not yet revised. And it was this version that had been printed. It had been stolen from among Frederick's baggage when he was defeated at Sohr in 1745 and obliged to flee in haste. It had fallen into the hands of a valet of Charles of Lorraine, and the valet had sold it to Néaulme. Its publication had come at a very inopportune moment, for Versailles still looked askance at Voltaire and he had not yet been able to go to Paris. The French government, far from supporting him, had forbidden him to return to the capital. As D'Argenson said, the court, while clinging to its policy of displeasing Frederick over great matters, chose to please him over a small one!

This edition of the *Abrégé* was likely to provoke scandal, partly because Voltaire had not revised it and partly because the text had been tampered with. The Church could not tolerate the way it had been insulted in this version of the work, and heads of state had been treated no better.

Madame Denis received letter after letter from her uncle exhorting her to beg ministers and influential friends to have this *Abrégé* banned and to institute legal proceedings against the printer and booksellers, and even readers. But Madame Denis either had other things to think about or was bored; in any event she got nowhere. Voltaire grew angry, for while she could get no reaction from the ministers in her uncle's favor she was very good at getting money out of his bankers for her own purposes. She was a spendthrift and imagined that because she was the great man's niece she ought to live like a duchess. She took offense at Voltaire's strictures and wrote him, in the boldest terms: "You are eaten up by avarice." She apparently had second thoughts, however, for she crossed out this phrase (though it is still legible) and wrote instead: "You are tortured by the love of money." Then, as might be expected, she went on to demonstrate that all the money was being spent on preparing for her uncle's return to Paris, though she knew very well he was forbidden to re-enter the city. The King himself had expressed the hope that Voltaire would stay on the frontier as long as possible. Madame Denis ended her letter: "Do not force me to hate you. You are the meanest of men as regards the heart. I shall conceal its weaknesses as best I am able."

If Voltaire had been as heartless as Madame Denis claimed, this letter would have meant the dismissal of his niece. But he put up with her as he put up with Thiériot, and she continued to monopolize him, to the detriment of her sister, Madame de Fontaine d'Hornoy, who was just as much a niece as she was, and a much more distinguished one.

Madame Denis's outburst made Voltaire very unhappy. He told only the D'Argentals how he felt, and concealed both his grief and Madame Denis's affront from everyone else. He said "she was dying of hurt from all the violences visited upon her in Frankfurt," though in fact she had long since forgotten them. But he himself could not forget the sorrow she had caused him, and wrote: "I would rather have been excommunicated than suffer the injustices that a niece who had been a daughter to me added to my other misfortunes." The curious comparison of their relationship to that of a father and daughter does not make Voltaire's sorrow any less real.

He longed to see Paris again, even if only for a few short days. He was informed that he was being watched, and that if his words and deeds and writings were those of a good subject, with the help of a minister and some powerful friends he would be given permission to return. It was now March 1754, and he and Collini were still in Colmar, under close surveillance. It would soon be Easter. His friends advised him that the authorities were waiting to see if he would do his Easter duty. One day he asked Collini nonchalantly if he were going to do so. Collini said he was. "Very well, then," said Voltaire, as if the idea had just occurred to him, "we'll go together." A Capuchin friar was summoned, and Collini withdrew while his master made his confession. The next day they both presented themselves at the communion table, Collini burning less with holy fervor than with curiosity to see how Voltaire would behave. Though he asked God's forgiveness for so doing, he could not help pretending to cast his eyes heavenward in order to see Voltaire's face at the moment the latter received the host: "He had put his tongue out," Collini wrote, "and was gazing wide-eyed into the priest's face. I know those looks of his." The priest must have felt his hand tremble as he met that no doubt mocking glance.

Voltaire sent the Capuchin a dozen bottles of wine and a loin of veal to express his thanks. In Paris his evil-tongued enemies said there was good news from Colmar: Voltaire had made his first communion.

He was sixty. He wrote to D'Argens: "A devil might go to mass when he is in a papal territory such as Colmar or Nancy." And to D'Argental: "If I had a hundred thousand men I know what I would do, but since I haven't I shall go to communion at Easter and you can tax me with being a hypocrite as much as you please."

Twenty years later he scandalized D'Alembert by repeating the same sacrilegious farce, and wrote to a friend who reproached him: "What should wise men do when surrounded by barbarous enemies? There are times when one must imitate their antics and speak their language. . . . There are some people who are afraid to touch spiders and there are others who swallow them." The idea was Montaigne's, but Voltaire's tone was harsher and would grow more so. The shock of Frankfurt had something to do with it. The recent persecutions in Colmar, though not very serious, were resented more bitterly than previous, graver ones. Before, he had uttered cries of pain; now they were cries of hatred. Fanaticism in others produced a reversed-image fanaticism in him. When his secretary Wagnière asked him what he would have done to survive if he had lived in Spain under the Inquisition, he replied: "I would have worn a big rosary, and gone to mass every day, and kissed all the monks' sleeves, and tried to set fire to all their monasteries."

While Voltaire was living quietly in Colmar, Monseigneur de Porrentruy, Bishop of Basel, under whose jurisdiction Colmar came, had given orders that sermons should be preached against him. Voltaire was obliged to write to Stanislas' confessor, Father Menou, to ask him to have these attacks stopped. As recently as 1735 Monseigneur de Porrentruy had had a goldsmith condemned to death for having had the audacity to request that the statutes of his guild be revised. Custom prescribed that his tongue he pierced first, but the bishop kindly waived that formality and merely had the man's head cut off. In these circumstances, how many who blame Voltaire for going to mass at Easter in 1754 would have beaten him to the confessional?

For some unlikely reason, Gervasi, Voltaire's doctor, had diagnosed his illness as dropsy and advised him against taking the waters, but as the D'Argentals were going to Plombières, Voltaire decided to join them there and take the air at least.

To mark her return to her uncle's favor, Madame Denis was also to be there. On August 8, 1754, Voltaire left Colmar by himself, leaving Collini behind to attend to the printing of the *Annales de l'empire*.

On the way to Plombières, Voltaire stopped at the Benedictine Abbey of Senones to see his friend Dom Calvet. Ever since the days at Cirey he had wanted to make a retreat there, and the stop enabled him to avoid meeting Maupertuis, who was still at Plombières at the time. Voltaire felt at home at Senones. He breathed the air of his schooldays again, the air of his real family, the lycée Louis-le-Grand. He was enchanted by the library: it was as good as that of Saint-Germain-des-Prés! His enthusiasm for the cleanliness, the frugality, the pure and learned language of the monks knew no bounds. Their discipline, diligence, tranquillity, and kindness—all were a realization of his ideal. He said he had had a delightful stay there. No one at Senones had called him to account on the subject of devotion.

Atheists have mocked Voltaire for this pious retreat, but there is no need for them to worry. Voltaire did not betray the cause of anticlericalism, though he did rather betray the good Benedictines. What he was searching for in their library was "not vespers or matins" but material for anti-religious articles for the *Encyclopédie*.[2] As he wrote to the Duchess of Gotha: "It is not a bad military tactic to go behind the enemy lines for artillery to use against them."

Frederick had the Abbé de Prades write to Voltaire, who had continued to correspond, in order to ask for compensation for what had happened at Frankfurt. Frederick thought this an opportune moment to have the abbé write Voltaire that the latter's new devotion ought to have made him forget that old grievance. He inquired what crucifix he was wearing during his retreat. Voltaire gnashed his teeth and wondered how Frederick had learned that he was indeed wearing one. By way of reply he had the crucifix packed and sent to Frederick.

So the rupture between them was not complete after all. Frederick kept a very close eye on everything Voltaire did—if for no other reason than the fact that he was bored. He wrote to Darget: "Gout is a great affliction, but hypochondria is the worst of all. You gave me great pleasure sending me news of Paris and the poet; his character consoles me for missing his wit. I am more lonely than I would like."

Incredible as it may seem, Voltaire was paying court to Frederick through the Abbé de Prades and the Margravine of Bayreuth. He did it out of self-interest and the growing realization that he would not be restored to favor in France unless Frederick so requested. And since he was dying with longing to see Paris again, he humbled himself in order to get Frederick to utter the open-sesame. Frederick was vastly amused. The only thing that made him laugh now was reading the letters in which Voltaire and Maupertuis continued to heap abuse on each other. He said: "They take me for a sewer and dump all their rubbish down it."

Of Voltaire he said: "He is good to read but dangerous company!" Then why had he tried so hard to keep him? Less than a year after the Frankfurt incident Frederick was writing wistfully: "You honor mankind too highly by your genius for me not to be interested in your fate."

Voltaire was unforgettable.

Plombières was a tiny town in the provinces packed with people taking the waters. As soon as Voltaire arrived an amusing little group formed around him. One of its most popular members was Monsieur de Ruffey, a magistrate from the Parlement of Burgundy, full of energy, wit, and invention. Voltaire's presence gave rise to a great many poems and songs, not always brilliant but often amusing. De Ruffey's more youthful vivacities sometimes overshadowed those of Voltaire, who was weak enough to sulk. But all was well again when he was asked to decide a gambling dispute. The Comte de Lorge and the Comtesse Belestat each accused the other of having stolen twelve francs at the gaming table. Voltaire had to pronounce sentence, and he extricated himself by gallantry. He wrote a poem saying that no one had stolen anything from the comtesse: on the contrary, it was she who ravished others' hearts and defended her own all too well. Her sentence:

> Votre coeur attaqué sait trop bien se défendre
> Et la Mère des Jeux, des Grâces, et des Ris
> Vous condamne à le laisser prendre.

Your heart knows too well how to defend itself when attacked/And the Mother of Sport, the Muses, and Mirth/Condemns you to allow it to be taken.

He left Plombières for Colmar at the beginning of September 1754, accompanied by Madame Denis, who traveled enthroned on a mountain of trunks and packages that threatened to crush the puny poet every time the coach turned over, as it did on nearly every journey.

Voltaire still had no roof over his head. At the age of sixty, with a fortune more like that of a successful banker than a man of letters, he did not know where to go. Such a situation seemed much stranger in the eighteenth century than it does today, and Voltaire's nomadic existence may be one reason why at times people did not regard him with due seriousness and respect. He was the greatest writer of his age, but he ruled over empty air.

So Voltaire searched for a house. He looked first in Switzerland, in Bern and then in Lausanne, where he was offered a very fine estate. He was just on the point of setting out to see the property when he was told that the Margravine of Bayreuth was waiting for him to have supper with her in an inn in Colmar. He couldn't believe it, hesitated, then hurried to the inn. It really was the margravine, with her husband. The two of them buried him in compliments and presents and did their best to lull him into forgetting Frankfurt. He was enchanted by the margravine. After the supper party he said: "We may conclude that women are better than men." In other words, Dorothea was better than Frederick. He wrote to everyone he could think of to tell them that the margravine had come to present her brother's apologies and that she had accepted Madame Denis at her table. That was what Voltaire wanted to believe. In fact there had been no apologies; all they wanted was for the matter to be forgotten. But as soon as Voltaire got anywhere near a royal highness the experience went to his head. As for Dorothea, she was not quite sure how her formidable brother would take it, so she wrote him a very different account in which Voltaire was made to look ridiculous. The only real purpose of the encounter, in short, was to flatter the poet's vanity. The margravine had simply amused herself for a moment while she changed horses at Colmar.

Another phantom who also reappeared from the past was Richelieu. He was brilliant, vain, selfish, harsh on occasion, a plunderer of the vanquished, but also the most sprightly grand seigneur, the greatest gallant, the most distinguished nobleman. In spite of the difference in their backgrounds, there was a real fidelity and affinity between him and Voltaire—as with Frederick. These three men "were" their age. Voltaire and Richelieu even resembled one another in tone and manner: the likeness was so striking, they almost seemed to be imitating one another. They had both had the same education at Louis-le-Grand; they had both been initiated in the ways of the *haut monde* by the same duchesses. They slandered each other fiercely, but their quarrels were only temporary. Voltaire lent Richelieu money. The duc had to be pressed for payment, but in the end, and usually in a rage, he paid. The duc solicited favors for his friend at court. It was not always easy, but he never refused. As soon as they started talking or writing to one another their antennae began to vibrate, and all the suns and the stars of the most brilliant civilization shone at their very brightest.

As long as Voltaire had pretended to belong to Frederick, Richelieu had pretended to forget Voltaire. Both decorum and ambition demanded this of a good courtier of Louis XV. But as soon as Voltaire popped up again at Frankfurt, free, Richelieu was glad of the opportunity to renew his close ties with him. He invited him to the Etats of Languedoc,[3] over which he was to preside, but that was too far from Colmar. So they arranged to meet at Lyons. Madame Denis was coming along too, and naturally the two travelers were at the point of death when they set out: "Madame Denis says that you will have to bury us when we arrive," Voltaire wrote Richelieu.

At the moment of departure, the moribund Voltaire behaved very badly toward his faithful secretary Collini. As they had too much luggage, Voltaire wanted Collini to sell all his clothes and take only a bundle of linen undergarments. Collini refused, Voltaire lost his temper, Collini gave notice. Voltaire reckoned up their account: "I owe you nineteen francs. Here is a louis. Keep the change." Collini, outraged, replied: "I owe you a hundred sous, take them, I don't want your present." Madame Denis looked on, let Collini go without a word, and doubtless gave her uncle a dressing down. Voltaire then repented and offered Collini a louis, which he still refused to accept. They argued and argued—and finally made peace. Collini packed his luggage again and the trio gaily set off.

They stopped en route at Dijon where Voltaire was more moribund than usual. As he was too ill to go himself, he sent Collini to present his compliments to Monsieur de Ruffey. Ruffey immediately came around to see how his ailing friend was, and Voltaire was at once restored to gaiety and life. They ordered supper, and Monsieur de Ruffey sent for some vintage wines from his cellar. They ate and drank, Monsieur de Ruffey shone, Voltaire sparkled. They talked and laughed until after midnight and swore to meet again and have a dinner party that would last for a week.

On November 15, 1754, they arrived in Lyons: "It is rather too much of a joke for an invalid to come a hundred leagues to chat in Lyons with Monsieur le Maréchal de Richelieu. He has never made his mistresses go so far, though he has led them enough of a dance." But as soon as they were reunited the mutual charm worked again, and Voltaire resumed with Richelieu the flattery he had once lavished on Frederick. The duc was "My Hero" or "Theseus," as at Fontenoy; Voltaire, who had been neglected, became "Ariadne abandoned at Naxos."

When after five days of verbal intoxication Richelieu had to go on to Languedoc, Voltaire went to pay his respects to the clergy. Cardinal de Tencin, the Archbishop of Lyons, was the D'Argentals' uncle and brother of the Madame de Tencin who had been imprisoned in the Bastille at the same time as Voltaire. The poet, clad in silk, presented himself in the cardinal's antechamber. It was full of people. He had himself announced and was soon received. But Collini, who had accompanied him to the cardinal's, had hardly seen him go in than he saw him come out again. Voltaire seized him by the arm and led him away, saying, "Let us leave immediately—this country is not for me." In the carriage he told Collini that the cardinal had informed him curtly: "You are not in favor at court so I can't ask you to stay to dinner." According to Voltaire, they were the words of a slave, and he broke off relations with the cardinal at once.

As the margravine was in Lyons too, he went to have her dress the wound inflicted by the cardinal, who, Voltaire cynically noted, was known for his practice of simony.

The margravine brought about a reconciliation between the prelate and the freethinking poet. Four days after the rupture they met again and exchanged felicitations and embraces. The cardinal confessed that what he had held against Voltaire was not so much his relations with the court as the fact that in *Le Siècle de Louis XIV* he had called the Council of Embrun a "little" council. Monseigneur de Tencin had been its president. Voltaire immediately agreed that it should henceforth be a grand or even a grandiose one. And he wrote giving instructions to the printer in Paris. The cardinal at once proclaimed that Voltaire was the greatest genius in the world and that in the diocese of Lyons he was a man held in highest esteem. He also recommended Voltaire to his own business agent, Monsieur Jean-Robert Tronchin, a solid banker from an excellent Geneva family.

Voltaire began to find life in Lyons society more pleasant, but the accommodations there were poor. So he and Collini went to Geneva to see whether what they had been told about the Tronchin family was true and whether the Lausanne property was a good bargain. They arrived at Geneva after sunset: the powerful Tronchin family had arranged to have the city gates left open for them. They dined at the Tronchins and were invited by Monsieur Guiguer to stay with him at the Château de Prangins. Voltaire was told that the property at Lausanne was not available after all. So he stayed on at Prangins, which he liked very much. Collini did not like it at all. He wanted to go to Paris, and so did Voltaire. But Voltaire was sixty and Collini not yet thirty, and Collini was ten times less willing to resign himself to living outside France. The people of Geneva had received Voltaire well, the Bern government protected him, the Genevan notables were delighted to welcome a man who told the papists what he thought of them. He was won over and decided to stay there in a country where no one asked you for your certificate of confession. Unfortunately he discovered that Catholics were not allowed to acquire property in the Calvinist republic. But he did not let this put him off: he pulled strings, hoping to secure a special dispensation that would enable him to buy the estate of his dreams. He found it at Morion: the house was cold and there was no garden, but he would buy it just the same. The Tronchins got him a residence permit, which was a step in the right direction. Collini rejoiced over his master's difficulties and hoped the two of them would be expelled. But suddenly the dream came true. Voltaire found a property at the gates of the city, on a terrace overlooking the Rhône and the lake, with a view of Mont Blanc to the south. The place was called Saint-Jean, and the margravine's son had lived there. Voltaire renamed it forthwith—Saint-Jean smelled too much of the sacristy. He called it "Les Délices." For the handsome square house, recently built, and the surrounding land, he paid eighty-seven thousand livres. Thanks to the Tronchins, the formalities were ironed out: the State Council granted him all the necessary permits.

Voltaire then threw himself into the task of doing over the house as feverishly as he had long ago at Cirey. He gathered together battalions of workmen of all kinds. Even the garden was transformed. Trees were dug up and moved; new ones were planted. Voltaire concerned himself with everything. "Les Délices is at present a torment to me. Madame Denis and I are busy building accommodations for our friends and our hens. We have carrots and wheelbarrows brought in, we are planting orange trees and onions . . . we have nothing . . . the foundations of Carthage must be laid."

Voltaire was both exhausted and thrilled: he was in his own home at last.

The first visitor was the actor Le Kain. Voltaire might well have pondered whether it was such a good idea to have his new house given its first benediction by an actor, in a city where theatrical performances were forbidden and the theater considered the gateway to hell. But Voltaire easily persuaded himself that because the citizens of Geneva had received him well they were ready to share all his predilections.

He should have been more careful. Professor Jacob Vernet wrote him a letter warning him to be circumspect, for certain Calvinists had their eye on him. Once again he was being watched. It had been noticed that his ideas were contrary not only to popery but to religion itself. Neutrality was not enough in Geneva. He was expected to aid in diverting youth from the growing tide of irreligion. This was asking a lot of Voltaire, and the new plaster of Les Délices was not yet dry before the seeds of his quarrel with Geneva had been sown.

Voltaire replied to Vernet on February 5, 1755, in the most affable tone: "My dear monsieur, what you say about religion is very reasonable. I hate intolerance and fanaticism and I respect your laws on religion; I love and respect your Republic. I am too old and too ill and a little too severe for young people. I should be grateful if you would convey to your friends my affectionate greetings. . . ."

Voltaire was making a joke of it. But he had fallen among people who didn't understand this sort of joke.

For the moment the citizens of Geneva were most concerned with the large amounts of money Voltaire was spending locally, and they looked forward to his attracting many wealthy visitors. They calculated that he had an annual income of a hundred thousand francs, plus considerable cash that might come from his various business enterprises: a golden shower for the Republic.

At Les Délices the theater had been done over just as soon as the kitchens. Voltaire had written Le Kain that, instead of being reunited with the creator of *Mérope*, he would find only a mason and a gardener. But the moment Le Kain arrived from Lyons they put on *Zaïre*. It was a great success with the Genevans: "Never have the Calvinists been so tenderhearted," said Voltaire. And he wrote to the Tronchins in Lyons: "Calvin never dreamed that Catholics would make Huguenots weep on Genevan territory."

Voltaire thought he was in a position of some strength with the powerful clan of Tronchins as his allies and protectors, but he was forgetting that the Tronchins were not all Geneva. They were only its leading wing and themselves proved unreliable. In fact before very long Théodore Tronchin, the doctor to whom Voltaire had entrusted his delicate health, joined the throng in criticizing his patient's behavior saying, "What can one expect of a man who is always in contradiction with himself and whose heart has always been the dupe of his mind? Since earliest childhood his moral condition has been so unnatural and distorted that he is now a completely artificial being that resembles nothing else on earth."

Tronchin went on to accuse him of having become too rich. It was true: lacking a noble lineage, Voltaire had realized very early on that only a great fortune could make him free. But the reproach is a curious one, coming from an extremely wealthy physician. Would Dr. Tronchin himself have bothered about the health of a poet who was poor?

Next Tronchin accused Voltaire of letting himself be spoiled by praise. This too is true, though if Voltaire was easily intoxicated by flattery he became sober again equally quickly. The learned Dr. Tronchin had not seen that Voltaire's character was a sort of play of mirrors. D'Alembert described Voltaire better when he summed him up as *"Monsieur le Multiforme."*

It might be supposed that Les Délices brought Voltaire all the pleasures he had longed to partake of in a home of his own, and that he could enjoy at last the serenity that age, the peacefulness of Geneva, and a comfortable and elegant life ought to provide. But before he even had an opportunity to enjoy any such serenity a new storm appeared on the horizon. *La Pucelle* was the cause of it. This mock-heroic epic was extremely dear to Voltaire's heart, but no *enfant terrible* ever gave its parent more trouble. When he was still in Colmar he had already been told that there was a plot brewing. Voltaire was always well informed: he had innumerable friends in high places, and also hired spies who often received valuable information from their confreres hired by the police. When he wrote to D'Argenson he could often reproduce the police reports almost word for word. And now there was a scandal about a new and unauthorized edition of *La Pucelle*. As usual "someone" had stolen a manuscript copy. The suspect was Emilie's friend, Mademoiselle du Thil, who was supposed to have found an incomplete manuscript among the papers at Cirey and sold it to the printers, who in turn had presumably completed it themselves, adding their own obscenities, sacrilege, and bad poetry, and signing their edition with Voltaire's name. For the moment it was being sold and read in secret, but it was being read and causing talk everywhere.

Even though he was on foreign soil Voltaire trembled, and sent Madame Denis to Paris to intercede with D'Argenson and enlist the support of all her uncle's friends. But Madame Denis discovered in Paris that the manuscript in question had been stolen from her by her lover Ximénès, who at the very moment that he was dealing Voltaire this blow was trying to get into the Academy and soliciting Voltaire's patronage. Worst of all, D'Argenson thought that Voltaire himself had arranged the new edition, which was proving to be a very lucrative venture. One La Morlière, who acted both as a spy and in a number of other shady capacities for Voltaire, boasted of having sold a good copy of *La Pucelle* for fifty louis. D'Argenson thought that Voltaire felt himself to be beyond the reach of French law in Geneva and was sharing in the profits being made on this clandestine edition. This was not the case, but Voltaire knew that the authorities were only too ready to believe it.

He then had a brilliant idea. Since he couldn't stem the flow of false *Pucelles*, the only thing to do was multiply them into an avalanche and make them so crude that the authorities couldn't possibly believe Voltaire could have connived at such falsifications of his own work. The plan succeeded. Voltaire was thought to be the victim of the false *Pucelles* at the very moment when he had become their fabricator.

He learned that a certain Grasset, a Geneva bookseller who also did business in Paris, was on the point of purchasing a manuscript of *La Pucelle*. Yet another one! Voltaire contacted Grasset, buttered him up a little, then told him that the manuscript was a forgery and that he would get in trouble if he published it. But Grasset was certain he would make a huge profit on the edition he was planning to bring out. Voltaire therefore invited him to Les Délices, wined and dined him, and persuaded him to hand over a page of the manuscript. It was a tissue of outrageous obscenities. Voltaire saw red and flew at the bookseller's throat. Grasset easily shook him off and got hold of him instead. Voltaire shouted for help, all the carpenters, masons, and gardeners came running, and Grasset barely managed to escape in one piece.

Voltaire brought suit before the Geneva magistrates, producing the vile page that Grasset was planning to publish in his name and appealing to virtue, human rights, and the Bible. Grasset was arrested, and soon after was released and expelled from Geneva. Voltaire regretted that Switzerland did not have crueler ways of dealing with criminals.

When Madame Denis related what she swore were the true circumstances surrounding the theft of the first manuscript, he was furious, and she was terrified. She knew he only half believed her, and suspected her of having sold the manuscript herself for six hundred livres. He loved his niece, but he did not have a very high opinion of her, and he wrote and told his Angels the D'Argensons how bitterly disappointed he was with her. He also divulged how much money she had got out of his bankers. "To fritter away six hundred thousand francs and sell a stolen manuscript for six hundred francs is a singular example of the way she brings ruin in her train."

The authorities gave up trying to bring Voltaire before the bar in the matter of the false *Pucelles*, but he did not escape unscathed. There had been another scandal over the edition circulating in Paris, the government and the police had been put to enormous trouble over the whole affair, and friends had been exasperated by all the indiscreet pressures and the contradictory steps that Madame Denis had begged them to take in her uncle's behalf. News of the scandal had spread to Geneva, where the Grasset incident had been made much of and his forged sample page read, copied, and peddled in the streets. The Calvinist city began to find the former purity of its air tainted by the proximity of the great man.

But there were redeeming factors. *L'Orphelin de la Chine*, which was produced at Les Délices, and in which Mademoiselle Clairon was magnificent, was a great success. Although Le Kain was too gentle a Genghis Khan on opening night, he managed to be a proper "tiger" for the second performance. The King wanted to see the play, and since the court was sojourning at Fontainebleau at the time, it was performed there. Queen Marie, whose *sancta simplicitas* merely increased with age, told the King she had heard that the play contained allusions to the orgies at Trianon. He replied that if she would be good enough to tell him which passages she would like suppressed he would see to it that they were. But she didn't know what cuts ought to be made, and so the *Orphelin* was played before the court in its entirety and was a triumph. Voltaire was delighted: such satisfactions always made him forget his troubles.

Collini was now in Paris. Voltaire had let him go to the capital to defend *La Pucelle* and to get some relaxation. Collini thoroughly enjoyed himself and although the affair of the forgeries had died down he did not mention coming back. Voltaire didn't insist but wrote amiably: "When you have had your fill of Paris let me know, my dear Collini . . . stock yourself up with pleasure, and come back when you have nothing better to do. Yours affectionately . . ."

Madame Denis also advised him to take his fill of pleasure, because once he was back in Geneva it would again be a starvation diet for him. She said young Collini was a terrible woman chaser: one day he had suddenly made violent advances to her. Poor Collini hated Geneva. He was young and ardent, and there he was—stuck between an old man and a fat middle-aged woman, in the shadow of snow-capped Mont Blanc. Voltaire understood his feelings only too well.

Comings and Goings in Geneva; the Lisbon Earthquake

The Protestant pastors were none too pleased with the way life was lived at Les Délices, though some of the other citizens of Geneva were charmed by it. They volunteered to perform plays, and acquitted themselves very well. But the Calvinist Consistory met on July 31, 1755, and forbade theatrical performances. When foreign troops had been brought in to restore order during the troubles of 1732 and 1739 they had established a theater which enjoyed an enormous popularity. It was precisely this success that frightened the Calvinist Church, which maintained that the corrupting power of the theater was all the greater when it was exercised on virtuous people. Corneille's *Polyeucte* had been banned on March 18, 1748, though a more pious play can scarcely be imagined. Voltaire, with his private theater, his masquerades, his insolent and sacrilegious sallies, seemed very much out of place in the puritanical atmosphere of this bastion of Calvinism.

He promised to be good. He had been lectured by the Tronchins and by his friend Pastor Vernet. He swore that he would have no more plays performed at Les Délices and that he was deeply grieved to have displeased such respectable people. Of course he was only thinking of a way to get around the difficulty. Play acting was the most delightful of pleasures to him: to make fun of bigots and fools at the same time turned it into the sport of the gods.

Among these lesser stirrings there suddenly occurred the terrible cataclysm at Lisbon. The whole earth had trembled, and the capital of Portugal had been wiped out. History had recorded no such natural calamity since Herculaneum and Pompeii. Voltaire was aghast. He kept saying, "What an awesome argument against optimism." To D'Argental he wrote: "Pope's 'Whatever is, is right,' is rather far removed from reality, and I no longer dare complain about my colics." Out of this state of mind came his *Poème sur le désastre de Lisbonne* (*Poem on the Disaster at Lisbon*), in which he contradicts Pope, attacks optimism, and deals harshly with Providence and the Roman Church. He said the poem was not anti-Christian, but unfortunately the printer, to fill out the poem, had bound the poem up together with Voltaire's unorthodox *Poème sur la loi naturelle* (*Poem on Natural Law*). The volume was sentenced to be burned in 1759, despite Voltaire's preface proclaiming his Catholic zeal.

It was with the Lisbon poem that his quarrel with Jean-Jacques Rousseau began. Since their collaboration in 1745 on *La Fête de Ramire* for the court their relations had been polite, and even respectful on Rousseau's part. He sent Voltaire his book, *Discours sur l'origine de l'inégalité parmi les hommes* (*Treatise on the Origin of Inequality among Men*). On August 30, 1755, Voltaire thanked him in a famous letter: "You will please men because you tell them truths about themselves, but you will not make them any better. . . . Never has so much wit been employed to make us seem stupid; after reading your book one feels like crawling about on all fours. However, since I lost that habit over sixty years ago I regret I am unable to resume it, and I leave that very natural means of locomotion to those more worthy of it than you or I. . . . I content myself with being a peaceful savage in the solitude I have chosen in your native country, where you yourself ought rightfully to be." Voltaire invited Rousseau to Geneva to drink "milk from our cows and to browse on our grass," but apparently Rousseau was not tempted by this rural prospect, though he had answered Voltaire's letter in cordial terms.

But everything changed in 1755 after the *Poème sur le désastre de Lisbonne*. Protestant men of the cloth were no less outraged than the Catholic curés, and one Geneva pastor asked Rousseau to write a refutation. So Rousseau took up the cudgels against Voltaire and in favor of Providence: "Voltaire, though appearing still to believe in God, believes only in the Devil, for his God is a maleficent being who, according to him, takes pleasure only in doing harm." Rousseau frequently mentioned the fact that Voltaire was rich and had no right to complain—hardly a philosophical argument. What became evident in this first skirmish was the fundamental opposition between the two men. Rousseau did not miss the opportunity to moralize, pointing out that his criticism of Voltaire was intended to improve him, to make him write fewer works that were regrettable, and thus to add to his glory. Not daring to send his letter to Voltaire directly, he forwarded it to Tronchin, to whom he wrote: "If he is less of a philosopher than I thought, send it back." Tronchin was under no illusions as to the effect the letter would have: Voltaire wasn't going to become a Providence-worshiper simply because Rousseau had scolded him. "A man cannot be cured at sixty of ills caught at eighteen," Tronchin remarked.

Voltaire did not rise to the bait. "Yours is a very fine letter," he wrote, concluding that he was "too ill to dare to think with you." The question was put off to another time. Voltaire considered the argument boring and beside the point.

He had verses and letters to write, friends, visits, business to attend to, and his property to see to, which he did very efficiently. For all these reasons Rousseau had to wait for his answer to his letter, and when it finally arrived, in another form, he recognized it at once: "It is no other," he says in his *Confessions*, "than the novel *Candide*, of which I can say nothing because I have not read it."

At the time, Jean-Jacques was satisfied with Voltaire's polite letter. He had been so afraid of what his famous correspondent might say that he was inordinately pleased with what he did say: "A man who could take my letter as he did deserves the name of philosopher, and no one could be more willing than I to join to the admiration I have always had for his works my esteem and friendship for his person."

As winter was approaching and it was cold at Les Délices, uncle and niece moved to Montriond at the other end of the lake, just outside Lausanne. There, in the shelter of the vines, out of the north winds, they waited for the spring. All Lausanne visited them and was as cordial as Geneva had been.

On March 10, 1757, they arrived back at Les Délices, and Voltaire immediately set out again on a short visit to Bern. Collini was intrigued and eventually found out that his master was meeting certain emissaries to discuss some mission either to, or perhaps on behalf of, Frederick. Voltaire hinted to Thiériot that they wanted to drag him from his retreat to "put him in a palace." In a letter to the Duke of Württemberg he was more explicit: "I have only to say the word to go to a country where I once paid my respects to Your Highness, but it is not in that country that I would wish to pay them again." This clearly meant Prussia.

Two months later the Empress Maria Theresa invited him to Vienna, but Frankfurt had cured him of hobnobbing with sovereigns. "I would rather scold my gardeners than pay court to kings."

Nonetheless, he and Frederick still exchanged compliments. Voltaire was always sending messages to the margravine and to Frederick's secretary, Darget—full of flatteries to be passed on to the King. Neither Frederick nor Voltaire was taken in by all this, but they were still in touch, and that was the main thing. Each was insatiably curious about what the other said and did.

But along with the compliments Voltaire continued to indulge in the characteristic pinpricks that served as a release for his real resentment. He kept an eagle in a cage and would show people its beak and claws, saying, "Just like the other one"—meaning Frederick, of course. He also had a horrid little monkey called Luc, who had already bitten his master three times, once so severely that he had been obliged to walk on crutches. Among Voltaires' intimates it was known that Voltaire also called Frederick "Luc": "Because he bites everyone," he explained. Someone protested that he couldn't always tell, when Voltaire was writing, whether by "Luc" he meant Frederick or the monkey. "When I mean Frederick," Voltaire said, "you have to read it backward."[4]

All this did Frederick no harm and would do Voltaire no good if it got back to the King. But it amused him no end.

His house was a most enjoyable diversion too. He was very proud of it, and thought it finer than Pope's house at Twickenham, which he had found magnificent. He had four carriages, a coachman, a postilion, two footmen, a valet, a French cook, a groundskeeper, a scullion, a lady's maid for Madame Denis, and Collini, his secretary. The food at his table was always excellent and plentiful.

But Collini was growing bolder and bolder and becoming more and more of a trial. Madame Denis and Voltaire did all they could to humor him, but in vain. "He is mad about women," Madame Denis wrote. "Not that there is anything wrong in that, but they turn his head and make him cantankerous even with his betters."

Collini's head had been turned in particular by a lady from Burgundy who had been ill used by her husband. She had taken refuge with the French ambassador in Geneva, and as she lacked neither beauty nor wit, Collini thought she would make a very suitable guest for Voltaire, to whom he entrusted her. Voltaire made a great fuss over her, but she nonetheless occasionally fell into graceful fits of weeping over her misfortunes. Collini soon persuaded her, however, that he was as unhappy as she and that the two of them should console each other. They made so little attempt to hide their satisfaction with one another that the whole household, from the scullion to Voltaire, could not fail to be aware of it. In spite of Voltaire's tolerance for all religions, he could not allow his house to become the temple of Venus. The lady was asked to leave, and Collini was overcome with grief. Voltaire did not scold him too much, but Madame Denis made certain remarks which caused Collini to dislike her even more than before.

For several months Collini had suspected that Madame Denis's attention to Voltaire was somewhat different from the usual devotion of a niece. He was one of the first to discover that they were lovers. This had been a closely guarded secret, as Voltaire was always discreet about his *affaires d'amour*, even with Emilie. Moreover, Voltaire never flaunted his intimate relations with women; even with Madame du Châtelet he was always extremely circumspect in public. Unlike his secretary, who would describe his transports at great length when a woman caught his eye, Voltaire loved women by looking at them, speaking to them, listening to them.

But letters from Voltaire to Madame Denis definitely confirm Collini's suspicion that the uncle and niece had been lovers for years. Most of these letters were written in Italian, which does not make them any less ardent. In 1746 he was already writing to her: "One of your hairs means more to me than all the locks of Belinda."[5]

On October 15, 1746, he had written: "But I beg you to be sober and to make me so too. I ask your permission to bring along my impotence. It would be best if I could f— but whether I f— or no, I shall love you always, and you will be the only consolation of my life."

In the autumn of 1747 he was still complaining that his bad health interfered with his good intentions. Love is a very fine thing,

> Mais il faudrait se mieux porter
> Pour en parler et pour le faire.

But one would need to be in better form/To speak of it and to make it.

Nevertheless he speaks of it often: "Nature, which has endowed me with the most affectionate of hearts, has forgotten to give me a stomach. I cannot digest, but I can love. I love you, and shall love you until the day I die. I kiss you a thousand times, my dear virtuoso. You write better Italian than I do. You deserve to be made a member of the Accademia della Crusca.[6] My heart and my ——— present you with their most loving compliments."

His transports are intermingled with talk of his ailments: "I hope I shall see you despite my colic. I love you and shall love you more than my life," he writes in one letter. And on February 1, 1748: ". . . I feel every day that I must devote the last days of my life to you, and that after a springtime of folly, a stormy summer, and a languishing autumn, you alone will be able to soften the rigors of my winter."

At that time Emilie was still alive, and there was no reason to suppose that she would be the first to die. Did he already intend, then, to spend the last part of his life with his niece? This would explain why she had focused her ambitions on furthering her uncle's career and his fortune. She had been given assurances, assurances that were repeated at this point. "In truth, I feel I do not have much longer to live. And will it be said that I did not spend the last part of my life with you, that I did not have the happiness of ending in your arms? Write to me, console me, my heart needs your letters more than it needs doctors."

What did Voltaire see in Madame Denis? Could it be that he found in her that sensual "emotion" he no longer found in Emilie or in any other woman? As early as 1740 his niece's cupidity was obvious. They were discussing the will Voltaire intended to make. She wanted to make sure that she would be his heir and wrote to him saying that if he made over all his possessions to her during his lifetime she would still leave him master of all. Only instead of writing "master" she put "mistress." Her uncle was astute enough to see the significance of the mistake. She did not become mistress of the fortune as early as 1740, but mistress of the uncle she did become in 1744, after her husband's death. It was then that Voltaire's love for Emilie gave place to affectionate friendship. When Voltaire was joined by his niece in Frankfurt and they were held under duress by Frederick, she brought him certain secret consolations during his captivity. She was able to turn those consolations to account, and if she did not remarry it was in expectation of inheriting her uncle's fortune. She did eventually become his heir, but much later than she had hoped.

Collini's suspicions did not make him any the better disposed toward Madame Denis. He wrote some harsh truths about her and was foolish enough to leave one letter full of unkind remarks about her lying about. A maid found it and gave it to her mistress, who flew into a rage, passed it on to Voltaire, and insisted that Collini leave his service. Voltaire resigned himself and dismissed Collini, though not in anger. In his memoirs Collini regrets that he did not always understand his master's kindness, and his account of their separation does honor to them both. Voltaire gave him a roll of gold coins. Collini said he had some money. "Take it, take it," Voltaire said, "one never knows what may happen." It was very different from the scene at Colmar. Collini wrote that "nothing is more ill founded than the accusation of avarice made against this great man. . . . Voltaire had the art of both enjoying and augmenting his fortune." He concluded: "I have never known a man his servants could so easily steal from. Is that like a miser? I repeat, the only thing he was miserly with was his time."

Visitors

Visitors from abroad began to turn up at Les Délices. In 1775 two now forgotten poets, Palissot and Patru, came. In a letter to David Garrick, Patru wrote that he had just spent "one of the most agreeable weeks in my life" at Voltaire's. He goes on to describe his host. "Imagine if you can, a man with all the appearance of one who is dying, all the fire of first youth and all the brilliance of his charming stories! If I judge all the other faults or even vices imputed to Monsieur de Voltaire on account of the avarice I have heard him taxed with, his slanderers seem most vile and ridiculous beasts. Never has there been seen more splendid fare at table, conjoined with manners more polite, more affable, more engaging. Geneva is delighted to have him. . . ."

In August 1756 there came a very famous visitor: D'Alembert. The two men had known each other since 1746 and were on excellent terms. D'Alembert was a very great wit and also a very good man. But what really bound him and Voltaire together was the *Encyclopédie*. The project excited Voltaire because of its sheer magnitude, but above all he was thrilled by the spirit that animated it. It was a most formidable weapon aimed at destroying traditional authority and the old order of things. Voltaire admired independence of spirit, as evidenced in Diderot as well as in D'Alembert. He wrote to D'Alembert "Paris abounds in scribblers, but as for eloquent philosophers I know only you and him." He was forgetting Jean-Jacques Rousseau, the most eloquent of all; but Jean-Jacques was soon to remind him of his existence.

As early as 1752 Voltaire offered his collaboration in "this immense and immortal work." He willingly lent his aid, in what we should call the team spirit, though he did not devote himself to this vast endeavor so totally as did Diderot or D'Alembert. He made no effort to trade upon his fame and contributed anonymous stones to the great edifice. With touching modesty he said he wished to serve as "an errand boy in this enormous shop." He was ready to obey orders. D'Alembert was the leader, and it was for him to criticize and correct and cut, for him to direct and co-ordinate the contributors so that each article was free of personal idiosyncrasies and formed part of a whole. Voltaire asked D'Alembert to refuse to admit personal biases and include only those opinions on which sensible educated men were in agreement. "I have obeyed your orders as faithfully as I could," he wrote. "I have neither the time nor the knowledge nor the health to work as I should like. I offer you these essays only as raw material for you to arrange as you see fit in the immortal edifice which you are constructing. Add to or remove from them what you will. I give you my little stones to set into whatever corner of your wall you please. . . ."

D'Alembert was warmly welcomed not only at Les Délices but in Geneva as well, by the Protestant ministers in particular, the most eminent of whom had very frank conversations with him. But when he got back to Paris and wrote his article entitled "Geneva," they raised a great hue and cry. He thought he was praising the Calvinist pastors, but they didn't think so at all. And they were by no means wrong. D'Alembert's hatred of popery caused him to regard himself as being very sympathetic to Calvinism. What pleased him in the talks that he had had with the pastors was their hostility to the rites and dogmas of Rome, from which he concluded that they had freed themselves from the Faith. When they read his article they were up in arms. Did he take them for unbelievers? Voltaire found himself torn between his beloved Encyclopedist on the one hand and the Genevan pastors on the others. "These strange fellows have the temerity to complain of the eulogy you have deigned to bestow on them," he wrote. To Monsieur d'Alembert all religious faith was mere superstition. So he had incurred the enmity of both Rome and Geneva. The only support left him was that of the "devil" of Les Délices.

Voltaire intervened as a peacemaker between the *Encyclopédie* and the pastors. Tronchin courteously requested a rectification, but all he got were "Encyclopedic" politenesses.

There was another point at issue as well. D'Alembert had mentioned Geneva's horror of the theater, and everyone naturally believed that Voltaire was the moving spirit behind D'Alembert's attack on the puritanical bias of Calvinism against theatrical spectacles. Rousseau was so sure of it that he told Pastor Vernet on October 28, 1758, that Voltaire had inspired D'Alembert's remarks on the theater in Geneva. Rousseau preached moderation to Vernet on the religious controversy but not on the subject of public play acting. Jean-Jacques rose up in indignation against "this web of seduction woven in his native land." Out of this arose Rousseau's famous *Lettre à d'Alembert sur les spectacles* (*Letter to D'Alembert on the Theater*), in which all dramatists were dealt with very severely. In a letter to Vernet on July 4, 1758, Rousseau admitted that D'Alembert's article had so "reawakened my zeal that I saw clearly that he made no scruple of flattering Monsieur de Voltaire at our expense. So much for authors and philosophers. . . ."

Attracted both by intrigue and by profit, Voltaire now embarked upon an enterprise about which he was as nonchalant as his contemporaries generally were: the fitting out of ships. Scarcely anyone had scruples about trading in coffee, cotton goods, "black ivory" (i.e., slaves), or anything else. In this instance the ships were going to make war on the Jesuits in Paraguay. Voltaire was delighted at the idea of sponsoring an expedition against the Fathers, while at the same time wringing a handsome profit out of His Most Catholic Majesty—for it was the King of Spain, the land of Loyola and the Inquisition, who was sending the fleet. "The King of Spain is sending four warships against the Reverend Fathers. You may be assured that this is certain fact, for I myself am partly financing the outfitting of one of the ships . . . and to round the joke off nicely, it is called the *Pascal*,[7] which is being sent off to fight against 'a relaxation of morals. . . .'"

Voltaire was also involved in another, even more bizarre, affair. In January 1756 he had learned that Madame de Pompadour, noting a certain decline in the ardor of her royal lover, began to fear that her favor at court might therefore be adversely affected. Voltaire was less surprised by this fear than by what she proposed to do to ward off the consequences of her possible disfavor.

Madame de Pompadour turned to her confessor. He advised her, first of all, to observe Lent. She therefore fasted three days a week, having made sure that it would not harm her health. He then prescribed a course of edifying reading, and to make her religious conversion the more note-worthy, suggested that she should get famous contemporary writers, none of whom had hitherto distinguished themselves in this genre, to en-large the number of elevating works available. On being so advised, she immediately thought of Voltaire.

So on March 1, 1756, the Duc de la Vallière wrote to Voltaire to ask him to "compose a metrical version of the Psalms of David." What was required was not so much scrupulous accuracy as pleasing para-phrase. "You will blot out Rousseau, you will inspire edification, and you will enable me to give the greatest pleasure to Madame. . . . [the name was not given in full]. What we need is not *Mérope* but a touch of David. Imitate him, improve on him."

The reward proposed to Voltaire for the modest feat of improving on David was no less than a cardinal's hat! There is no written proof of the proposal extant, but it was made, and was known to have been made. The prudent Condorcet writes in his *Vie de Voltaire:* "Voltaire was unable to play the hypocrite even to become a cardinal, a hope that was dangled before him sometime thereafter." It would have been a rather unfor-gettable sight to see Cardinal de Tencin, Cardinal de Bernis, and a Cardi-nal de Voltaire sitting side by side in the Sacred College. But Voltaire turned down this proposal to rewrite the Psalms of King David.

In 1756 he also had the pleasure of celebrating his friend Richelieu's victory at Port Mahon. He had rather rashly prophesied this victory in a rhymed couplet when Richelieu set out at the head of the expedition against the English in the Balearic Islands. Unfortunately the predicted victory was an unconscionably long time coming, and people had begun to scoff at Voltaire's prophecy. However, all eventually ended well for Richelieu and his prophet, whereas the English commander, Admiral Byng, came off very badly. Like Voltaire, the English had talked prema-turely about victory: the news of their defeat came like a revelation of betrayal, and Byng was tried and sentenced to death. Voltaire had known him in London, and he and Richelieu were outraged at the treatment he received. Richelieu wrote a fine letter to Byng's judges, and Voltaire added a note of his own that was simple, dignified, and moving. But they obtained only four votes in Byng's favor, and the King refused to pardon the unfortunate admiral.

Voltaire's role in this affair shows him rising above his sometimes ridic-ulous pettiness to reveal himself as a man whose humanity on many occa-sions was as exceptional as his talent.

He would willingly have bartered the cardinal's hat he had been offered for permission to return to France and live in Paris. The delights of Les Délices could only be those of exile, and he himself had said that continual pleasure was no pleasure at all. But by an absurdity of fate it would have been easier for the greatest blasphemer of his time to become a cardinal while residing in the capital of Protestantism than it was for

Monsieur de Voltaire, writer and native of Paris, to live as an ordinary citizen in the Rue Traversière-Saint-Honoré.

Monsieur d'Argenson, Voltaire's great friend who was Minister for Foreign Affairs, had an elder brother who was the Keeper of the Seals[8] at this time. But the elder D'Argenson detested Voltaire, and though application after application was made he refused to give him permission to come to Paris.

Voltaire returned to Montriond, his residence in Lausanne, for a change of air. Here there was no restriction on the performance of plays. The city's inhabitants were far less fanatic than the Calvinists in Geneva and on the whole were most charming, although a few of them proved to be crosspatches. One lady whom Voltaire had forgotten to invite to his theater at Montriond avenged herself by putting on a private performance of a parody on *Zaïre*. Meeting a young relative of the lady's one day, Voltaire said:

"Oh, so you're the one who is making fun of me, eh, mademoiselle?"

To which she answered, terrified:

"Oh no, monsieur! It's my aunt."

What Voltaire really wanted was to return to Paris. He mustered all his friends again and set them on the ministers. But they proved difficult to convince: Voltaire had so often promised to be good, and every time he set foot in Paris a scandal had ensued. He concentrated his efforts on Richelieu and suggested a plan. The first thing to do was to dispel the idea of his attachment to the King of Prussia, which had done him such harm at the French court. "If I might speak of myself for a moment, I should tell you that I have never understood how anyone could hold my coquetries with the King of Prussia against me. If they knew that he one day kissed my hand, skinny as it is, to try to make me stay, they would forgive me for not going out of my way to offer objections." Then, alluding to the proposals that had been discussed in Bern, he added: "And if I told you that I had been offered carte blanche this year, it would have to be admitted that I am cured of my passion."

But unfortunately for Voltaire's case "coquetries" continued to fly to and fro. In between defeats, Frederick wrote an opera based on *Mérope*. "He has never offered me a more gallant present," Voltaire wrote to the Duchess of Gotha, counting on her divulging these flattering words to Frederick. In his *Mémoires*, however, he delivered himself of quite a different opinion of the King's opera: "Without question it is the worst thing he ever wrote," he declared.

There was talk of war between Austria and Prussia, in which event France would be Austria's ally. Voltaire pretended not to understand all this business of alliances but said that if the hostilities reached the point of open violence "at least let us hope Monsieur Freytag will be hanged!"

On February 4, 1757, he wrote to Richelieu: "I have just had a very affectionate letter from the King of Prussia, so things must be going very badly for him." He considered the two possible issues of the war as they would affect both his "friend" and himself. Should Frederick win, "I shall be justified in my former affection for him. Should he be beaten, I shall be revenged." In fact he would gladly have put out flags to celebrate Frederick's defeat. He even went so far as to invent a sort of war chariot intended to pulverize the Prussian army: the designs for it are still extant. He had got the idea from an account of the chariots of Ahasuerus, the ancient King of Persia, and he submitted his plans to Monsieur de Florian.[9] De Florian studied Voltaire's suggestion and passed it on to the minister. Richelieu was interested, or pretended to be, but while the project was being given the bureaucratic treatment, the Austrian infantry crushed the Prussian army at Kolín, and Voltaire's paper tank was returned to him. Nevertheless the reports made on it by Monsieur de Florian and other officers were quite serious ones: they even constructed a model, to the great delight of the inventor. He wrote to De Florian: "They are now making a miniature version. It will be a very fine war machine. They are going to show it to the King, and if it comes off, what a joke it will be that it is I who am the inventor of this destructive engine! What I should like is for you to be in command of the army and kill hordes of Prussians with my little secret."

The war chariot claimed no victims, but the fortunes of war did bring Voltaire some satisfactions. Frederick, with his army routed after Kolín, was in grave danger. Richelieu, who was in Germany doing all he could to contribute to Frederick's defeat, received the following request from Voltaire: "If you should pass through Frankfurt, Madame Denis beseeches you to send her forthwith the four ears of a pair of scoundrels, the one named Freytag, the unpaid representative of the King of Prussia in Frankfurt who never had any wages save what he stole from me, and the other Schmidt, a rascally merchant, councilor to the King of Prussia. The two of them had the impudence to arrest the widow of one of our King's officers carrying one of our King's passports." Although the tone is jesting, Voltaire seriously hoped to get substantial compensation.

It seemed as if nothing could save Frederick from the coalition, and he set about preparing to die in a manner befitting one who had read Marcus Aurelius and learned something from Voltaire about theatrical performances. Voltaire was rubbing his hands at the prospect of revenge. Then suddenly everything changed. When it struck him that Frederick was really in the most desperate straits, Voltaire forgot everything else except the friend, the admirable "Solomon," the enthusiastic admirer who had kissed his hand and bestowed so many royal praises on his modern "Virgil." He wept and called for help. He wrote frantic letters to the margravine, who replied with the tired cliché: "One only knows one's true friends in time of misfortune." She also sent on a note from Frederick, who remarked, "I learn that you are taking an interest in my successes and in my misfortunes. My one choice that remains is to sell my life dearly."

The only thing that could save Frederick was an immediate peace. Austria wanted to crush Prussia totally, but France was less implacable. Frederick offered to make Madame de Pompadour Princess of Neuchâtel if she could contrive to bring about the opening of peace talks: the loss of Neuchâtel to "Petticoat Number Two" would be a trifle to Frederick, and if the peace plan worked he would still be King of Prussia and could prepare for better days. But Madame de Pompadour haughtily refused. Voltaire wrote the margravine to try Richelieu: "I venture to put forward this idea not as a suggestion, still less as a piece of advice, but merely as a simple wish that has no other source than my zeal."

It was a strange sort of zeal on the part of a man who had tried to rouse all Europe against Frederick. Perhaps the explanation of this volte-face was simply the fact that Voltaire was still fond of Frederick, though perhaps self-interest also played a part. For if Richelieu succeeded in negotiating a separate peace with Frederick he would owe it to Voltaire and would certainly reward him. And Richelieu himself would not be negotiating for nothing: he always saw to it that he was well paid for anything he did. His army nickname was *La Père La Maraude* [Father Loot]." Voltaire's old ambition to play a part in politics also entered the picture. Versailles would not allow him to appear onstage, but he could still try to influence the course of events behind the scenes.

Voltaire told Richelieu what he had written to Frederick's sister, and Frederick, who had been informed by the margravine that Richelieu had been informed by Voltaire, admitted that he had received excellent advice. Swallowing his pride, he wrote to Richelieu: "I am certain the nephew of the great Cardinal Richelieu is a man as capable of signing treaties as he is of winning battles. A mere trifle will suffice to make peace, monsieur, if it is truly desired. . . ." And the rest of the letter as well was written with sovereign skill, dignity, and detachment. The plan, however, came to nothing.

Meanwhile Voltaire was overjoyed to receive a poem from his royal friend entitled *Les Adieux à la vie* (*A Farewell to Life*). He expected Voltaire to spread this piece of propaganda all around Europe. Out of habit, Voltaire corrected the verses and then wrote to Frederick to dissuade him from carrying through his resolution to end his life. What Voltaire wanted was Frederick vanquished but alive. He bade him live on as a philosopher: "A philosopher can do without kingdoms." That must have made Frederick laugh. Frederick's idea of self-destruction struck Voltaire as shocking. Such grandiose, despairing deaths were all very well on the stage, but in real life they were exaggerated, unseemly even. The behavior of the heroes of antiquity became ridiculous when carried over into modern times. In Voltaire's eyes, he and Frederick were not heroes but men, and should behave as such in the name of humanity and good taste. "It is the duty of a man of your stamp to await events." Frederick was thinking about his memorial statue and writing what were perhaps his two best lines of poetry:

> Je dois en affrontant l'orage
> Penser, vivre et mourir en roi.

As I face the storm, I must/Think, live and die like a king.

The Abbé de Bernis had just been made a minister, and Voltaire and the D'Argentals judged that the moment had come to obtain permission for Voltaire to return to Paris. But the abbé reminded Voltaire that the court still had not forgotten his sojourn at Frederick's court and looked with a distrustful eye on his assiduous correspondence with Prussia. Appearances were admittedly against him. He was flirting shamelessly with the King of a country that was at war with his own. To this he answered that he was sacrificing himself in the interest of France by maintaining the link with Prussia and that, far from being reproached for so doing, he ought to be rewarded.

Versailles did not consider it necessary to reply.

Voltaire was wasting his time, for French policy was at this moment favorable to Austria. Since the Abbé de Bernis was Madame de Pompadour's protégé, he was obliged to carry out her wishes, and she hated Frederick. She might have overlooked his annexation of Silesia, but she could not forgive him for calling her "Petticoat Number Two." While she supported Austria, Voltaire was applying every possible pressure in the opposite direction. Maria Theresa was apparently unaware of this, for she allowed *L'Orphelin de la Chine* to be performed in Vienna on December 17, 1758. But, as Voltaire knew, letters were constantly intercepted. "I write nothing but what the courts of Vienna and Versailles may read with edification," he noted.

Voltaire continued wandering about in the labyrinth in search of a thread that might save Frederick. France, engaged in the disastrous Seven Years' War, had England to deal with in Canada and elsewhere, as well as the war on the Continent. She would have been glad to extricate herself from the conflict between Austria and Prussia. Voltaire had the idea of suggesting that Prussia, as England's ally, should mediate between Versailles and London, and that France, as Austria's ally, should mediate between Berlin and Vienna.

Voltaire's friend the Abbé de Bernis made no reply to his solicitations, despite D'Argental's reminders. "You may imagine how disagreeable his silence is to me after the request you advised me to make and the manner in which I wrote to him." Not so much as a note to read out to his friends in Geneva. "Just a civil word. . . . Not to reply to a letter is an outrage one should not inflict on a man whom one has lived with and been able to learn from." What the Abbé de Bernis had been able to "learn" was the information Voltaire had characteristically hastened to communicate to him about the Viennese and Berlin courts, the margravine, and so on. And once again Versailles was not grateful. Even the once affable "Babet la Bouquetière" seemed to have become as harsh as Cardinal Fleury.

But at last the note arrived, perfumed and beribboned, and at once Voltaire's bitterness vanished. He shared his exultation with D'Argental: "My dear and esteemed friend, I have had a letter from Babet, who has exchanged his basket of flowers for a minister's portfolio. I am enchanted with it." Madame de Pompadour also wrote, and Babet sent another letter. His missive had been full of flowery phrases that meant as little as ever, as Voltaire well knew. "Bernis is my friend 'as always.' True, 'as always' there are a few bigots who look askance at me, and 'as always' the King is brooding about my chamberlainship," he wrote of this latest bouquet sent by De Bernis from Versailles.

The King of France cared little about the King of Prussia's chamberlain. But he had always disliked Voltaire. He had tolerated him; but now he no longer saw him and had no desire to see him.

Frederick, saved by the Prince de Soubise's disastrous tactics as commander of the allied troops at the Battle of Rossbach on November 5, 1757, regained his interest in life and there was no more talk of dying. Just after winning the Battle of Cüstrin he wrote airily to Voltaire: "I am greatly obliged to the philosopher of Les Délices for the part he takes in the adventures of the Don Quixote of the North. This Don Quixote lives the life of a country player, acting now in one theater, now in another, and sometimes is applauded. I know not what will come of all this, but I believe with our worthy Epicureans that those who stand in the lecture room are happier than those who tread the boards."

Frederick was now dealt a cruel blow, the only one that could draw a murmur from that hard heart: his sister, the gentle Margravine of Bayreuth, died. She had lived only for her brother, and Frederick knew she was probably the only person in the world who really loved him. He asked Voltaire to write a poem to perpetuate her memory. One of the lines of his ode to her read:

Ombre illustre, Ombre chérie, âme héroïque et pure . . .

Illustrious shade, beloved shade, pure and heroic soul . . .

His poetic tribute to the poor margravine was stilted and conventional; Frederick criticized it and asked for another. Voltaire, who knew the weaknesses of his poem better than anyone, ground out another, and this time Frederick was satisfied: "Certainly it will not do you dishonor," he said. "Please have it printed and distributed in the four corners of the earth." He had already said, "Europe must weep with me for a virtue too little known."

The ode made neither Europe nor any other continent weep, but it brought Voltaire and Frederick a little closer to one another again. It was six years since the shadow of Freytag had come between them. But Frederick had the audacity to mention Maupertuis, asking Voltaire not to harass a dying man. Voltaire exploded. Maupertuis dying? Voltaire knew for certain that he was in Basel being prosecuted for giving a girl an illegitimate child. "Would to God that I could be prosecuted for such a thing," Voltaire wrote wryly. His letter to Frederick ended in a different tone: "Soon I shall die without having seen you. You scarcely care, and I shall endeavor not to care at all. I love your verse, your prose, your wit, your bold and firm philosophy. I have been unable to live either with you or without you. I am not speaking to the King or the hero. That is a matter for monarchs. I am speaking to the man who has enchanted me, whom I have loved, and with whom I am always angry."

It was a tortuous and tortured friendship, but it was an inextinguishable one. Voltaire had spoken in this letter not as a courtier but as between equals. But Frederick was not touched by this sincerity. The tone of the letter brought a severe reprimand from Frederick: "Learn, at your age, in what style it behooves you to write to me. Understand that there are some liberties that are permitted and some impertinences that are intolerable to men of letters and intelligence. Become a philosopher at last; that is to say, a sensible man. May Heaven, which gave you so much wit, give you good judgment in equal proportion."

Frederick's recapitulation of their past relations was no less scathing. "I know I idolized you so long as I did not think you cantankerous or malicious. But you played so many tricks of all sorts on me. . . . Let us say no more on the subject, I have forgiven you with an entirely Christian heart. When all is said and done, you have caused me more pleasure than harm. I am more diverted by your books than troubled by your scratches."

They did not quarrel over these exchanges. During the Seven Years' War they exchanged smiles over France's defeats. This may seem shocking, but for Voltaire it was not France but merely the King's army that had been beaten. Half of Paris openly acclaimed Frederick's victories. But Voltaire did not go that far. "The King of Prussia always sends me poems when he gives battle. But you may rest assured that I love my country better than his verses and that I have all the sentiments that I ought to have," he wrote to Thiériot.

Frederick still sent Voltaire his "dirty linen," and in 1759 Voltaire's willingness to continue "laundering" it put him in a dangerous situation vis-à-vis the French court. One day, on receiving a batch of Frederick's verses which grossly insulted Louis XV and Madame de Pompadour, Voltaire sensed that the packet had been opened. He was horrified at the thought that if it were known that he corrected such things he might be suspected of writing or inspiring them. He handed the compromising parcel over to the French ambassador in Geneva, who transmitted it to the Prime Minister in Paris, hoping thus to escape all suspicion of complicity.

Frederick described Louis XV as:

> Jouet de la Pompadour,
> Flétri par plus d'une marque
> Des opprobres de l'Amour . . .

Plaything of Pompadour,/Sullied by more than one mark/Of the infamies of Love . . .

And of the King's favorite, "unworthy offspring of a proscribed financier," he had written:

> Et ces charmes divins que nous n'aurions connus
> Qu'en quelque temple obscur sous les lois de Vénus.

And those divine charms that we should never have known/Save in some obscure temple of the cult of Venus.

Voltaire did not conceal from Frederick that he was afraid to work on this masterpiece with him. To write such things, he said, "a man needs not only genius but also an army of a hundred and fifty thousand men."

Frederick thought Voltaire very timid and laughed at him. "One may write whatever one chooses and with impunity, without having a hundred and fifty thousand men, provided one does not have it printed." He maintained that there had been much more vicious satires than his: "Witness your *Pucelle*." He suspected Voltaire of indiscretion and hinted as much. Voltaire protested at the very idea of such treachery: "My poor niece, who trembled with fear on reading your poem, burned it, and all that remains are a few vestiges in her memory; she remembers only three stanzas too splendid to forget."

In fact Frederick's masterpiece survived in its entirety on the desk of the Prime Minister, the Duc de Choiseul. In response to Frederick's insults, Choiseul sent on to him an ode that dwelt at length on all that monarch's defects and vices. Frederick had laughed, for instance, at Versailles for being the "realm of the Petticoat." This could not be said of the court at Potsdam, but an equally malicious dart was launched at him in the form of a word that hinted at a certain vice and had the added advantage of rhyming with the word *amour* just as well as did the name Pompadour:

> De la nature et des amours
> Peux-tu condamner la tendresse,
> Toi qui ne connus l'ivresse
> Que dans les bras de tes tambours?

Of nature and love/Can you condemn the tenderness,/You who never found ecstasy/Save in the arms of your drummers?

Choiseul was known to have a nimble pen and he let it be thought that this new masterpiece was his creation, but we now know that it was by Palissot, a poet then in fashion. There was one passage that reproached Voltaire for his "culpably fulsome praises," but apart from this remark he liked the poem very much. He mentions it in his anti-Frederick *Mémoires*, replacing the unflattering passage about himself with a few lines of his own. Such were the literary customs of the day.

After another turn of fate's wheel, Frederick's military fortunes took a turn for the worse, and he was eager to cease hostilities. Voltaire wanted peace too, and looked about for a way to serve as an intermediary. He wrote D'Argental, asking him to suggest to Choiseul that he should employ Voltaire to sound Frederick out. Choiseul gave Voltaire permission to write to Frederick. It was not much, but he need no longer tremble over the possibility of his correspondence being intercepted. And he hoped for something better: to be charged with a secret mission to negotiate peace. He had a scheme which D'Argental was to submit to the Prime Minister through vague hints and insinuations. He wrote: "Luc [Voltaire's nickname for Frederick] wants peace. Would there be any harm in letting him have it and leaving a counterweight in Germany?" He added: "Luc is a scoundrel, I know, but is it worth ruining oneself to wipe out a scoundrel whose existence is necessary?" His idea was to make peace and leave Germany divided between Prussia and Austria, with Prussia acting as a counterbalance to the House of Austria. Voltaire was still following Cardinal Richelieu's policy—a century later. For the moment all he did was give Choiseul Frederick's letters to read and vice versa. Austria began to have suspicions about these goings-on. Voltaire was enjoying himself immensely in this atmosphere of lofty conspiracy, into which he naturally soon introduced an element of farce. It was agreed that Frederick should sign his letters "Mademoiselle Pestris," a resident of Gotha (the Margravine of Gotha was acting as a letter drop). When "Mademoiselle Pestris" referred to business and asked what "the banker" thought, the reference was to Choiseul. Voltaire pretended innocence. He said to the margravine: "I confess, madame, I understand nothing of such matters [of state]. All I do is report what is said simply and faithfully for the good of two or three families." Ambition, fame, vainglory, and self-interest all played a part in this game, but above all there was the game itself, the love of masks, the eternal theater, that sublimated form of life.

But "Mademoiselle Pestris" was as touchy and sour-tempered as an old maid. Voltaire complained about her to the Margravine of Gotha. All this was playing at diplomacy as though it were a parlor game. What spies who were even halfway competent would have been taken in by these masquerades?

Voltaire wrote to the margravine in a code reminiscent of the gallantries exchanged in Madame de Rambouillet's salon a century earlier: "Even if my little commerce with you-know-who should prove to be thorny, it will nonetheless bring me a shower of blossoms from a certain Serene Highness. I think she is something of a coquette. I assure you I do not mean you, madame, but the lovely lady [i.e., Frederick] whose beauties and pretentions Your Serene Highness favors. . . . She has told a confidant who hasn't a tender heart of her love [for Silesia], and I believe her lover might well have grown somewhat cold. . . ."

The lover was Choiseul, and the unsympathetic confidant the English statesman William Pitt.

Voltaire delighted in playing these amusing games, but he was also very anxious to see this absurd and ruinous war end. He could see France losing on all fronts. There could be no happy outcome in a campaign that had begun badly and been carried on even more disastrously. Finally he put forward another argument against the Seven Years' War, the sincerity of which could not be doubted: he hated war in all its forms, because it was ruinous, cruel, and above all extremely stupid. War glorified the opposite of everything he loved, destroyed everything he adored, and instituted everything he hated. For Voltaire, man's nature and true climate was polite, ordered society, reason, the arts, luxury, in short the intelligent pursuit of happiness—and that was the climate of peace.

He counted a good deal on the Duc de Choiseul, who had a noble soul according to Voltaire, this being tantamount to saying that his ideas were the same as Voltaire's. He was not fiercely virtuous or fanatical: he was humane. He desired the public good, and his own as well, of course, but did not ruthlessly pursue either of these goals. And he was agreeable; that is to say, perfectly well bred.

All these efforts came to naught thanks to a maneuver on the part of Voltaire's, or Frederick's, enemies who wanted to continue the war. *Les Oeuvres du philosophe de Sans-Souci* (*The Works of the Philosopher of Sans Souci*) were printed in Paris. These texts had been reserved for the few intimate guests at the suppers at Sans Souci; they were very unedifying and not intended for the public. The aim of circulating them in the middle of the war was to discredit Frederick and create a current of opinion favorable to continuing the war to the bitter end.

It was a great blow to the proponents of peace. But Voltaire had allowed himself to be deceived by Choiseul, who did not really want peace. He could have had the entire edition of Frederick's *Oeuvres* seized and destroyed but he let the printers continue turning out copies. And it was Voltaire who was accused of having arranged the publication of these texts. This seems very unlikely, for it destroyed all his efforts and hopes. Frederick himself suspected him, but "Mademoiselle Pestris" did not take the matter very seriously: "I should be very happy if my wrongs were limited to the clandestine publication of my poetry." Either because they had qualms of conscience or were genuinely shocked themselves, those responsible had removed the worst impieties from this edition, but by removing the scandal they had also made the book so dull that few people bothered to read it. Frederick's enemies at Versailles were no more skillful at polemics than they were on the battlefield.

It was at this point that Voltaire decided that the services rendered to "Mademoiselle Pestris" entitled him to compensation for what had happened at Frankfurt, but no compensation was forthcoming, and "Mademoiselle Pestris" disappeared from the scene. Henceforth the correspondence was in plain language, and they flattered and clawed at one another without benefit of code names. Frederick wrote announcing the death of Maupertuis, whom he now perfidiously praised. He also pointedly reminded Voltaire of how cruel he had been to the late president of the Berlin Academy:

> Et gémissez de la noirceur
> De votre coeur incorrigible.

And lament the blackness/Of your incorrigible heart.

Voltaire riposted: "I myself think only of dying, and my final hour is drawing near. Do not trouble it with unjust reproaches. . . . You have done me enough harm; you have caused me to fall forever from the favor of the King of France, you have made me lose my post and my pensions, you ill-used me at Frankfurt, me and an innocent woman of good repute who was dragged through the mire and put in confinement. And thereafter, while honoring me with your letters, you taint the sweetness of that consolation with bitter reproaches. Is it possible that it is you who treat me thus, when for three years I have devoted myself to the task of trying, to no avail, to serve you? . . ."

Frederick enjoyed these complaints and took pleasure in provoking them. He replied that if he had not been "madly in love" with Voltaire's genius the Frankfurt episode might have turned out very badly indeed. But what Frederick liked least was Voltaire's reference to Madame Denis —that "niece who bores me," Frederick had called her, and the verb *ennuyer* had far more pejorative connotations in those days. The niece bored a good many other people too. Voltaire was too fond of talking about her and pushing her into the limelight. "People still talk about Molière's maidservant but no one will talk about Voltaire's niece," Frederick shot back.

In the midst of these squabbles, Frederick and Voltaire still dreamed of peace. They were very nearly the only ones who did. In April 1760 Voltaire received Charles James Fox's son at Les Délices. The Englishman listened politely to his host's paeans to peace and then told him bluntly that his hopes were vain. Voltaire was shocked, but on reflection he realized that his visitor was better informed than he was and that the war would go on. He had been wasting his time and effort.

XI

Parisians spend their time erecting statues and smashing them; they amuse themselves hissing and clapping their hands; and with much less wit than the Athenians, they have all their defects and go to even further lengths. (Letter, 1758)

I am ashamed to be at peace and at ease at home, and on occasion to have twenty persons to dinner, when three-quarters of Europe lives in misery. (Letter to D'Argental, 1759)

I am rather like those weather vanes which stand still only when they are rusty. (Letter, 1759)

Pascal amuses me at the expense of the Jesuits; Swift amuses me at the expense of the human race. How I like English brashness! How I like people who say what they think! To think only by halves is to be only half alive. (Letter to Madame du Deffand, October 1759)

I do not have the rigidity of mind of old men; I am as flexible as an eel, as lively as a lizard, and work continually like a squirrel. As soon as a stupidity of mine is pointed out to me, I quickly put another in its place. (Letter to D'Argental, October 22, 1759)

Except for splitting wood, there is no sort of occupation that is not mine. (Letter to Thiériot 1760)

If the people attended decent theatrical spectacles, there would be many fewer crude and hard souls. (Letter, 1760)

One must always come back to amusement; without it existence would be a burden; this is what causes cards to occupy the leisure of so-called gentlefolk from one end of Europe to the other; this is what sells so many novels. One can scarcely stay by oneself being a sobersides. If nature had not made us a bit frivolous we would be most unhappy; it is because they are frivolous that the majority of people do not hang themselves. (Letter, 1760)

We [French] almost never miss a chance to ruin ourselves and be beaten. But after a few years this is not evident. The industry of the nation makes up for the stupid blunders of the ministry. (Letter, 1760)

I have all the infirmities of old age; but at heart all the predilections of youth; I think this is what keeps me alive. (Letter, 1761)

I am obliged in all conscience to tell you that I was not born more wicked than you and that at heart I am a decent man. It is true that, on having reflected for some years now that scarcely anything was to be gained by being so, I have begun to be somewhat merry because I have been told that that is good for one's health. (Letter to the Abbé Trublet, April 17, 1761)

One must shed one's blood to be of service to one's friends and avenge oneself upon one's enemies, otherwise one is not worthy of being a man. (Letter, 1761)

Every time one draws the portrait of a ridiculous man, someone always turns up who resembles him. (*The Scotswoman*, Preface)

A Little Estate and a Little Book

By the end of 1758 Voltaire had decided to leave Lausanne, and bought a little estate in Lorraine called Ferney. In Paris, where Thiériot (whom he had nicknamed "Thiériot-Trompette") was to spread this piece of news, no one understood why he had made such a purchase. In the same year, in a very complicated deal, he bought the nearby manor of Tournay from Président de Brosses. A year before he didn't even have a roof over his head, and in 1758 he had four châteaux. He liked the neighborhood of Geneva but not Geneva itself: "There are clergymen there like everywhere else," he remarked. He was very pleased because at Tournay he enjoyed full manorial rights and the title of count, which went with the property. There were a few manorial rights at Ferney but no title. All these lands brought in about five per cent annually in rents. His capital brought in three or four times more than that, but it was his lands that made him a lord, and that fact both amused and impressed him. When he wrote to Tronchin in Lyons to tell him that he was leaving Geneva, he said: "Your lawyers are respectable and wise, the society in Geneva is as good as that in Paris, but your people are arrogant and your clergy rather dangerous." So he kept his person in a safe spot in Ferney, in France. He could always go into the most pleasurable exile imaginable at Les Délices if Versailles bothered him.

It is difficult to see what he saw in Tournay, except that it was near Ferney and the two estates could be combined: ". . . the château [at Tournay] is a barn fit only for owls; it is a *comté* but a comic one; a garden that contains nothing but snails. . . . These two estates almost adjoin my Délices. I have made myself a rather nice little kingdom within a republic," he wrote.

He could now call himself "comte" as well as Gentleman of the Bedchamber, a title he had not forgotten. Catherine II, who admired his writing, had also just sent him a sumptuous sable coat. His satisfaction is evident when he writes to Thiériot: "You are mistaken, my friend—I have four legs instead of two: one foot in Lausanne in a fine winter residence; one in Les Délices near Geneva where I am visited by society. So much for the front feet. The two hind ones are in Ferney and the *comté* of Tournay, which I have bought on long lease from Président de Brosses." In his negotiations for this purchase, Voltaire the notary's son and the former clerk of Maître Alain had tried to match wits with the sly président of the Parlement of Burgundy.

This finagling with a gentleman of the robe as clever as himself was to cost him dearly.

The deeds for Ferney were not yet signed when Voltaire began to exercise his seignorial rights against the curé de Moens, who had been persecuting the tenants on the estate. Voltaire took up their defense. A Genevan had encroached on the road; so let him repair it! The new lord of the manor wrote to the Minister of Finance to obtain tax concessions. In short, as soon as Voltaire appeared, a new breath of life swept through the estate, which had long been slumbering in poverty and routine.

In the ministries there was as much talk of Ferney as of Canada. This was only natural, for Voltaire's estate could rightly be considered the center of the civilized world.

Apart from the continual pains in his belly, Voltaire was happier at sixty than he had been at thirty. In his *Mémoires* (written in 1759 but published posthumously), he said: "All the conveniences of life are to be found in my two houses; pleasant society and people of wit fill the moments that my studies and the care of my health leave free."

It was this private and domestic "optimism," endangered by the prodigious misfortunes of the rest of the world, that brought forth *Candide*, published in Geneva in March 1759. Frederick thanked him for it in April. Voltaire had had the main outlines of the tale in mind for a long time. *La Vision de Babouc*, published in 1748, already contained the spirit of it, and the *Poème sur le désastre de Lisbonne* contained its philosophy. But in fact Voltaire himself had been Candide from birth. No book has ever been so completely the image of its author. It contains all his ideas, eccentricities, and tics; it even includes the answer to Rousseau's letter on Providence. While he was basking in pleasures continually and systematically cultivated in luxurious surroundings, he was at the same time haunted and revolted by the spectacle of the world around him: the disastrous earthquake in Lisbon; the Seven Years' War ravaging Europe, Canada, India; France was ruined, Germany was drenched in the blood of all the continental armies, autos-da-fé were being lighted again in Spain and Italy and darkening the Age of Enlightenment with their smoke. Voltaire asked himself whether his happiness was an absurdity in such a world or whether the absurdity resided in the endless and senseless misery to which the world was prey. In any case, this cruel absurdity could not be papered over with the name of Providence. Out of the universal and irremediable scandal he fashioned *Candide*—a lively and entertaining tale that was taken to be licentious. He himself was slightly ashamed of it and called it a *"Coïonnerie"*—mere poppycock—to suggest that it was less scandalous than it seemed. But it is a work of nearly unfathomable despair. He had taken care to provide a few light touches, for total despair would have been excessive, and thus contrary to decorum, good taste, and humanity, which ought to be moderate in everything, even despair. If it had been exaggerated it would have been false, and *Candide* rings as true as crystal. It allows a smile, and in so doing saves humanity from despair. Everything in man is weak and vulnerable, he is the victim of bloodthirsty divinities and blind acts of fate; but man can laugh at them because they are stupid. The game of life is cruel, but man acquits himself honorably, and would win it handily were it not for the absurd senselessness of fate. How sadly this lucid book was misunderstood! In the nineteenth century Madame de Staël, among others, saw it as a burst of diabolical laughter.

Candide is the unsurpassable masterpiece not only of a man but also of a venerable language reaching its apogee and, for a few pages, catching its breath before descending again. It is also the unsurpassable perfection of a supreme frivolity, the frivolity of a man who has entirely understood his misery and above all understood that he can surmount it only by his own lightheartedness. In this tale are crystallized once and for all without illusion, but not without grace or courage, the truths of a civilization about to collapse. In one stroke *Candide* saved those truths for eternity.

The Road to Ferney

Building, planting, and breeding horses did not occupy all Voltaire's days. He was also amassing documents for a *Histoire du Tsar Pierre le Grand (History of Peter the Great)* and writing a new tragedy, *Tancrède*. It was begun on April 22, 1759, and completed on May 18. Voltaire had it performed three times in the theater he had installed in the "barn" at Tournay. It was dedicated to Madame de Pompadour.

Probably the person most delighted by the play was Voltaire himself, who was as excited as in the days of *Zaïre*.

The stage of the theater at Tournay was so tiny that nine actors together could hardly move on it, and they had to have lances and helmets and shields for *Tancrède* as well. But, according to the author, it was a marvelous performance: "I hope the play will be performed in Paris precisely as it has been in my barn." The main difficulty was to find room for the two hundred people who flocked from Geneva to see it.

Around 1760 people began to make pilgrimages to theatrical productions at Ferney. The intendant[1] of Burgundy came with fifty others. They sobbed a great deal listening to Madame Denis on stage, but they ate even more. Monsieur de Chauvelin, the French ambassador in Geneva, also came with his retinue. They applauded and wept, and with equal enthusiasm consumed trout costing twenty livres at the supper that followed. The Duc de Villars, the governor of Provence and the son of the maréchal and of the duchesse who had made gentle fun of young Arouet, dropped by too. The duc was not of the same stamp as his parents: he lacked courage and had many vices. But he had one paramount virtue in Voltaire's eyes; he loved the theater. He played opposite Madame Denis, and when the peer performed, it was before an audience made up of intimates staying at Ferney without the usual guests from Geneva.

As the Geneva Consistory had not said anything regarding the theater for some time, Voltaire began staging performances at Les Délices again. His Genevan friends were delighted to have the theater almost at their door once more. But on October 20, 1760, there appeared a report of the Consistory on the impropriety of Monsieur de Voltaire's having put on a play on the feast of Saint John, despite the promises he had made in 1755. In November 1760 the Consistory made another complaint. Voltaire said he was only trying to entertain his guests and had no intention of defying the laws of Geneva and depraving its citizens. Fortunately, opinions among the members of the Consistory were divided: a number of them wished to punish Voltaire in some way, but others, while agreeing in principle, merely wanted to put a stop to the theatricals without actually quarreling with Voltaire and his powerful friends in the city. Voltaire still had the right to stage plays at Tournay, which was under French rule. Some zealots would have liked to forbid citizens of Geneva from visiting foreign territory to deprave themselves by watching. But as the citizens concerned were the most influential people in Geneva, the affair was simply allowed to die down.

The Encyclopédie

On January 23, 1759, the Paris Parlement stopped the sale and distribution of the *Encyclopédie* and on February 6, 1759, it was ordered burned. Up until that time its articles had been allowed to appear without hindrance, thanks to the protection of the liberal Malesherbes, the director of the royal printing house and the chief censor for printed works, Madame de Pompadour, and Chancellor d'Aguesseau. The Encyclopedists had got a bit too sure of themselves and were not overmodest about their success. Many of their readers, without being bigots, realized that it was not only religion but the whole social order that was being undermined. As well as the *Encyclopédie* the decree also affected lesser works, including Voltaire's poem *La Religion naturelle*. Voltaire was immediately up in arms. He pressed D'Alembert to send him the names of all the people who had taken part in the decision, with notes on their works, talents, and position. Voltaire was told that the "Ass of Mirepoix," Archbishop Boyer, had thrown himself weeping at the King's feet, saying, "Sire, religion is lost if publication of the *Encyclopédie* continues." It was he who had appointed the censors charged with examining, expurgating, or suppressing the articles submitted to the *Encyclopédie*. What had happened, then? Couldn't the theologians appointed as censors see straight? Or had the Encyclopedists, as some people said, submitted harmless texts and printed others far more dangerous that the censors had never set eyes on? The Abbé Tamponet, one of the censors, was a well-known quibbler: according to Voltaire, he said, "I can discern heresies in the text of the Lord's Prayer."

It was at this point that Voltaire's quarrel with the Jesuits came to a head. The *Journal de Trévoux*, a Jesuit paper, announced with a certain amount of satisfaction the names of the works that had been condemned. While Voltaire's dealings with the Jesuits had not always been felicitous, his gratitude to his old teachers had restrained him from inflicting more than pinpricks. In 1749 he had written to Father Vionnet: "I have served for a long time under the standard of your Society. You have few soldiers thinner than I, but none more loyal." In the ten years that had passed since then, Voltaire had become a much more bitter enemy of religion. In 1749 he had not yet begun to speak of *l'Infâme;* in 1759 he did, using the famous phrase *écraser l'Infâme*[2] for the first time. It had become an obsession, and the phrase was henceforth repeated hundreds of times in his writings. Who or what was *l'Infâme?* Some say that it refers to the Roman Catholic Church, but the explanation is probably less simple. Voltaire never explained, probably because the meaning was less precise than is often thought. *L'Infâme* was indeed sometimes the Church of Rome, but the Catholic Church had no monopoly on infamy. *L'Infâme* was also intolerance, fanaticism, and persecution. It was superstition with magic amulets around its neck, armed with poisoned spears and riding astride enormous Stupidity.

Father Berthier, the editor of the *Journal de Trévoux*, was the first Jesuit to be chastised. In November 1759 he, and all Paris, read an anonymous pamphlet of thirty pages entitled *Relation de la maladie, de la confession, de la mort et de l'apparition du Jésuite Berthier (An Account*

of the Illness, Confession, Death and Epiphany of the Jesuit Berthier).
Hardly had he recovered his breath from this surprise than there appeared another pamphlet entitled *Relation du voyage du frère Garassise,
neveu du frère Garassise, successeur de père Berthier* (*An Account of
the Voyage of Brother Garassise, Nephew of Brother Garassise, Successor to Father Berthier*). Everyone cried out at once that this was a product cooked up in the kitchens at Ferney. Voltaire neither admitted it nor
denied it but it meant a complete break with the Jesuits. He did take the
precaution, however, of saying that this war was none of his seeking; he
had merely defended himself. "In any war," he wrote to Palissot on September 24, 1760, "the aggressor alone is in the wrong in the eyes of God
and men." It was rather bold of Voltaire to bring God into his quarrel,
but he was right as far as men were concerned—everyone laughed at
poor Berthier.

This crusade against the *Encyclopédie* found a champion in Jean-
Jacques Le Franc, Marquis de Pompignan, a magistrate of Montauban
who was rich, cultivated, and complacent. He thought he had been born
to be the poet of the century, but unfortunately the position was already
occupied by Voltaire when his commonplace genius first saw the light of
day on the banks of the Tarn. As early as 1739 Le Franc was saying that
Voltaire's tragedies would never be anything but Voltaire's tragedies. It
may have been true, but it wasn't the sort of thing to say if one wanted
to live in peace. However, Voltaire was rarely discourteous, and when he
met Monsieur Le Franc in 1739 at the home of Farmer-General La
Popelinière, he treated him in a polite and even friendly manner. He
wrote him a few affable notes and received in exchange some criticisms
that he pretended not to hear. His letters were full of precisely the sort
of compliments he liked to receive himself. "All men have ambition," he
wrote to Le Franc. "Mine, monsieur, is to please you and enjoy on occasion your support and at all times your friendship."

It was up to Le Franc to preserve these excellent relations. Voltaire
asked nothing more than to be liked, and even when he was offended by
those he had approached in good faith his first reaction was always to be
conciliatory: "Every man of letters who is not a rogue is my brother. I
have a passion for the arts, I am mad about them. The reason why I have
been so distressed when other writers have persecuted me is that I am a
citizen who despises civil war and only takes part in it in self-defense."

It was because Le Franc was impudent enough to provoke Voltaire
that war broke out between them. Le Franc had had a few minor
successes that went to his head. In Paris such intoxications are usually
damped down by the intoxications of others. But Le Franc returned to
his province before he had slept off the heady effects of his first triumph,
and in Montauban he considered himself a full-blown genius. In 1748 he
made his first attempt to enter the Académie Française. He was not
elected but was given reason to believe that he would be soon. In 1760 he

was elected to Maupertuis's chair—one that seemed to be reserved exclusively for Voltaire's enemies. As Le Franc aspired to be tutor to royal princes and princesses, and to please the Dauphin one had to be very devout, he turned his reception speech at the Academy into a head-on attack on impiety, the *Encyclopédie*, literature, and even the Academy for sheltering some of the worst enemies of the faith. He did not mince words; the Academy had never received such a dressing down in place of the expected grateful speech of acceptance.

The devout listened to him devotedly. Dupré de Saint-Maur compared him to Moses. And Le Franc's own brother, who was Bishop of Puy, compared him to Aaron. He said God had chosen both to perform miracles "in Israel"—by which he meant Paris.

A formidable roar of laughter arose on the banks of Lac Leman at Le Franc's speech and the comments it had given rise to. The philosophers also lost no time in marshaling their forces against the new academician. Voltaire felt all the more concerned because Le Franc had of course pronounced a eulogy in praise of Maupertuis.

"It was not right," wrote Voltaire, "to outrage an old man who has retired from the world, especially since he was of the opinion that my withdrawal had been forced upon me; this was merely adding insult to injury, which is most cowardly. I fail to understand how the Academy could have allowed a reception address to be a satire."

As a matter of fact, by drawing attention to Voltaire's connections with the *Encyclopédie*, Le Franc had compromised his enemy's chances of returning to Paris. Meanwhile Le Franc became even more puffed up with pride. He claimed the King had read his speech and liked it, and tried to make Monsieur de Malesherbes agree to its being printed. Malesherbes refused to do so without an order from the King himself. Le Franc then took his speech directly to the royal printing house, intimidated the printers, and had the text set. Malesherbes had the type broken up and to justify his action said: "However reprehensible the Encyclopedists may be, it does not follow that their adversaries are above the law."

A modest-looking pamphlet with an intriguing title now began to appear all over Paris: *LES QUAND, notes utiles sur un discours prononcé à l'Académie le 10 mars 1760 (WHENS, Helpful Notes on a Speech Delivered at the Academy on March 10, 1760)*. There was no author's name given. But it was Voltaire of the best vintage, that is to say, the worst for his victim. It was made up of short verselike paragraphs each beginning with the word "When." The repetition was most effective, and each paragraph had the force of a dagger thrust:

"WHEN one's own works do one's age no honor it is an act of peculiar temerity to decry that age."

"WHEN one is scarcely a writer and not at all a philosopher it is not seemly to say that our nation has only false literature and an empty philosophy."

Voltaire thus skillfully took up the position of defender of the French nation, literature, and philosophy, against a man ironically named Le Franc who so belittled his French heritage.

Finally, a piece of good advice: "WHEN one is admitted as a member of an honorable body, one ought in one's first speech to conceal beneath the veils of modesty the insolent pride that belongs to hotheads and mediocre talents."

No one knew at first where this hail of blows had come from, for rumor had it that Voltaire was dead. This piece of news had been deliberately spread by a friend. This was not the first time. It was Voltaire who had had this information given to a man who was bombarding him with letters trying to convert him. Through an intermediary, the man was told that it was useless to continue to write, since his would-be convert had died. But he was asked to go on praying for him.

He now made haste to reassure his friends in Paris that he was still alive. "My Dear Philosopher," he wrote to D'Alembert, "I admit I am not dead, but I cannot say I am alive. Berthier is well and I am ill. Chaumex [another of his *bêtes noires*] can eat and I cannot. So it is not my hand that writes to you but my heart. . . ."

When impudent slanderers dared to attribute *LES QUAND* to him, Voltaire protested vigorously: "I don't know why they drag me into all these disputes, I who am a plowman, a shepherd, a rat retired from the world in a Swiss cheese. I content myself with laughing in derision and not meddling in anything."

Other work would have been a sufficient alibi for anyone else but him: he was also engaged in farming, stock rearing, and building at Ferney and Tournay. Anybody but Voltaire would have been overwhelmed by all this work, on top of which he had to deal with correspondence, lawsuits, business, and guests. He had a thousand worries, from manuring the fields to the most delicate negotiations with the authorities. There were also the pleasures of the salon, the table, and the theater, not to mention the pangs of colic four days a week. Where could he have found the time to write a pamphlet?

And yet he always found time for polemics and, as he said, for laughter: "I like to laugh. I am old and ill and I'm very fond of gaiety, a surer remedy than all the medicines recommended by my dear Tronchin. I shall make as much fun as I can of people who have made fun of me. It pleases me and does no harm. A Frenchman who is not gay is a man out of his element."

In the present quarrel Voltaire encountered an ally as caustic as himself —Abbé Morellet, theological adviser to the editors of the *Encyclopédie*. Voltaire, who had had great fun writing *LES QUAND*, set everyone to laughing again with a sequel entitled *LES SI (IFS)*. This pamphlet was followed in turn by *LES POURQUOI (WHYS)*, written by the Abbé Morellet. "It was my idea," said the abbé, "that Monsieur de Pompignan ought to be made to run the gauntlet of all the interrogatives." So *LES POURQUOI* was followed by *LES QUI, LES QUOI, LES CAR, LES AH! AH! (WHOS, WHATS, FORS, HA-HAS)*. Pompignan was reminded that he had not always been a servile courtier. In 1756 he had criticized the King and the taxes. "Have pity on a people that has been drained dry; come out from inside your sumptuous palace and you will see an empire that will soon be a desert . . . the fields are sown with tears." He was not trying then to please the King and the Dauphin. "Why is this man in contradiction with himself?" asked Morellet. "It is not because the people's situation has improved but because his own has changed."

In *LES CAR:* "Do not send any more supplications to the King saying that he treats his subjects as slaves FOR it is no longer a supplication but merely a libel."

Le Franc de Pompignan had paid dearly for his speech, for his opponents stripped him of all his pretensions. Voltaire even went so far as to accuse him of deism. An odd criticism coming from him!

But Le Franc launched a counterattack. He hoped to be able to get Voltaire expelled from the Academy. At this idea the saying ran through Paris: "If the name of Monsieur de Voltaire were struck off the list of forty, the figure would have been taken away and all that would remain would be the zero."

Everything went against Le Franc. It became known that if Voltaire were turned out D'Alembert and Duclos would also leave the Academy. "In that case they would have to recruit Capuchins," Favart[3] wrote on May 22, 1760.

What emerges from all this is that in 1760 a few writers could enlist public opinion in their favor, even among those who might hold different ideas. Opinion became "sensitized" by these disputes, which soon drifted from literature to politics. The authorities and Le Franc could only lose by the controversy. Even the court at Vienna, which was far from favorable to new ideas, considered that Le Franc had been very foolish and ought to have confined himself to being modestly content with the honor the Academy had done his modest talent.

But Monsieur Le Franc de Pompignan, though badly wounded, was not reformed. He continued to boast of his talents and, thwarted in Paris, returned to throw his weight about in his native village in the provinces. He published a work entitled *Relation du voyage de M. le marquis Le Franc de Pompignan depuis Pompignan jusqu'à Fontainebleau (Account of the Journey of Monsieur le Marquis Le Franc de Pompignan from Pompignan to Fontainebleau)*. It was of course a triumphal journey, and the King saw him at Fontainebleau, and even stopped for fifteen seconds to tell him he knew his worth. And then: "I was received at Montauban with honors so extraordinary that the memory of them will long linger in my heart and in all this province." This "account" was supposed to be addressed to the chief inspector of taxes of the village of Pompignan. It was pure Molière.

The year 1760 crackled with counterattacks by Voltaire. He wrote a *Poème sur la vanité (Poem on Vanity)* and attributed it to Le Franc.

> Je prétends des plaisants réprimer la licence.
> . . . .
> Pour trouver bons mes vers il faut faire une loi
> Et de ce même pas je vais parler au roi.

I mean to curb the freedom of ridiculous clowns. . . ./There ought to be a law making everyone like my poetry./I shall speak to the King about it forthwith.

At the end of the poem Voltaire recalled Piron, who was right for once when he had inscribed on his tombstone: "Here lies Piron who was nothing"; Voltaire drew the moral:

> Humains, faibles humains, voilà votre devise.

Humans, weak humans, there is your motto.

He recalled vanished empires, monarchs of the past of whom nothing remained, not even their ashes; where, he asked, were the tombs of Alexander and Caesar? And then he added one last barb:

> César n'a point d'asile où son ombre repose
> Et l'ami Pompignan veut être quelque chose.

Caesar has no refuge where his shade may rest/Yet our friend Pompignan wants to be somebody.

Even the Dauphin, Le Franc de Pompignan's protector, laughed at this. Le Franc did not get the post of tutor to the royal princes and princesses, however. But the Dauphin's entourage was extremely devout, and Voltaire was held in abhorrence there. No punishment was too severe for him, and if the Dauphin had come to the throne he would not have lacked counselors to persuade him to put Voltaire to the torture. A lady named Madame du Hausset, who frequented this minor court, was uneasy about the intolerance that prevailed there, and about its consequences for the future. She thought that if Pompignan had obtained the post of tutor he, together with his brother the Bishop of Puy, would instill in his royal charges an implacable hatred of Voltaire and the freethinking *philosophes*. She wrote: "I very much approve of Voltaire and his hounding of Pompignan. Were it not for the ridicule that has been heaped on him, the bourgeois marquis [Pompignan had recently been ennobled] would have become tutor to the princes of the blood, and with his brother Georges would have seen to it that people were burned at the stake again."

Voltaire was delighted to be told that Mirabeau had overheard the Dauphin mockingly quoting the end of the *Poème sur la vanité* to Pompignan himself. "So you see poetry is of some use sometimes. People quote it on great occasions," Voltaire commented. He wrote a new pamphlet in which the marquis was described as going mad and running through the streets of Montauban shouting, "Jehovah! Jupiter! Lord!"— thereby confessing to his crime of deism. Then there were derisive songs about him that were hummed in his presence, and a playbill that by an unfortunate coincidence announced *Didon* by Monsieur Le Franc de Pompignan, and directly underneath *Le Fat puni* (*The Coxcomb Punished*). Pompignan fled to his native province. But Voltaire's revenge was not yet complete.

The philosopher of Ferney turned an act of kindness into an act of vengeance. He took in a poor devil who had been recommended to him by D'Alembert and whose gifts and intelligence had never been properly put to use. Voltaire installed him at Les Délices, made much of him, and got him to tell the sad story of his life. It was a perfect illustration of Voltaire's view of the absurdity of the world and ineptitude of Providence. He wrote a poem entitled *Le Pauvre Diable* (*The Poor Devil*); its hero, Simon Valette, was a native of Montauban, like Pompignan, and also knew Fréron in Paris. So under Valette's name Voltaire was able to get back at two of his enemies. Valette, dying of hunger in Paris, met a strange fellow:

> Cet animal se nommait Jean Fréron.
> ....
> Il m'enseigne comment on dépeçait
> Un livre entier, comme on le recousait . . .
> Je m'enrôlai, je servis le corsaire
> Je critiquai sans esprit et sans choix
> Impunément le théâtre, la chaire
> Et je mentis pour dix écus par mois.

This creature was named Jean Fréron. . . ./He taught me how to take to bits/An entire book and put it back together again. . . ./I enlisted myself in the service of this buccaneer./I criticized without wit or discernment/Both the theater and the pulpit with impunity/And told lies for ten crowns a month.

He also earned a certain celebrity:

> Je fus connu, mais par mon infamie.

I became known, but only for my infamy.

At last he realized his position and left Fréron:

> Triste et honteux je quittai mon pirate
> Qui me vola pour fruit de mon labeur
> Mon honoraire en me parlant d'honneur.

Sad and ashamed I left my pirate,/Who rewarded me for the fruits of my labor/By stealing my honorarium while prating about honor.

Once out of this trap he fell into another:

> Manquant de tout dans mon chagrin poignant
> J'allai trouver Le Franc de Pompignan,
> Ainsi que moi, natif de Montauban.

Entirely without resources, in my sad state/I went to Le Franc de Pompignan,/Like myself a native of Montauban.

But all the high-flown poet did to help his fellow countryman was offer him a copy of his own *Poèmes sacrés* (*Sacred Poems*):

> Votre dur cas me touche.
> Tenez, prenez mes cantiques sacrés,
> Sacrés ils sont, car personne n'y touche!

Your desperate case touches me./Here, take my sacred hymns,/So sacred that no one will touch them!

This joke became proverbial.

Pompignan's "treasure" being worthless, Valette had no alternative but to die of want, but he was saved from this fate by Voltaire, at Pompignan's and Fréron's expense.

Pompignan lived in retirement in his village, where he died quietly in 1784. He had to all intents and purposes been exiled by Voltaire. Voltaire congratulated himself on living far from the noise and agitation of the world, but he had never ceased to take an active part in everything he had supposedly left behind. He was acutely aware of the shifts in public opinion, knew everything that was going on, had a finger in all the intrigues and scandals and speculations. In fact, the world that he prided himself on having repudiated possessed him more than ever.

When Pompignan withdrew to the provinces Voltaire's hostility toward him seemed to come to an end, but he still had a host of other targets at which to launch his darts.

Le Pauvre Diable had also dealt a few scratches to Gresset, the author of *Vert-Vert*, whose prompt success had annoyed Voltaire even more than the parakeet who was the subject of Gresset's mock epic. He said *Vert-Vert* was trivial, compared it to school exercises, and said Gresset enjoyed the twofold privilege of being a wit among schoolboys and a schoolboy among wits.

Voltaire's barbed criticisms, whether justified or not, were always expressed in such a way as to fix themselves both in the public's mind and the victim's heart. He ought not to have attacked Gresset, who was living peacefully in his native town of Amiens, to which he had retired. But Gresset had made the mistake of breaking his silence momentarily to attack the theater, and Voltaire could not leave such a crime unpunished. Gresset lived so far removed from literary squabbles that he did not read the attack until fourteen years later and did not reply. But after his death there was found a description of Voltaire that he had written: "Though he thinks himself the conqueror of literature, Voltaire is only its Don Quixote. . . . He has collected here and there all the results of art, morality, feeling, and nature, and appropriated all these spoils for himself. Those who know no better think everything he puts before the public is his own property. . . . The eternal plagiarist, he has passed off new and as his own creations that could readily be found elsewhere and sometimes everywhere. He will die and be totally forgotten."

The official Voltaire, the academician and tragic poet, even the attacker of *Vert-Vert*, did die. And his contemporaries hardly saw or appreciated anything save the clever and fashionable versifier. But Gresset had forgotten the other Voltaire, the Voltaire of the pamphlets, the tales and the novels, the letters, the *Essai sur les moeurs*, the *Dictionnaire philosophique*—the great man of the age, the incarnation of an entire civilization. When Gresset reproached him for picking up his material everywhere, he saw correctly but he judged wrongly. It was not a weakness: it was Voltaire's genius itself. What he took from elsewhere was nothing until he made it his own.

Voltaire now found a new victim, the Abbé Trublet. The man lacked neither culture nor subtlety, but it was often said that he wanted to appear to have more of both than God had given him. He tried too hard: "He applied to his own little style all the care that coquettes devote to their toilette." He was a priest at Saint-Malo and made no attempt to conceal that he owed much of his success to the confessional. He told D'Alembert that when he preached he turned the heads of all the ladies in Saint-Malo. "The other way perhaps," D'Alembert replied. This was not just a witticism: Trublet was physically repulsive. Grimm said that his person and countenance were coarse, unpleasing, and unclean, hence "his person was even more scorned than his works." He prided himself on the fact that his use of commas bordered on the sublime. Grimm called him "a brute with a great deal of wit," but for all his brutishness his work found admirers, among them Voltaire, until the day Trublet wrote of *La Henriade:* "I don't know why, but it makes me yawn when I read it." He may not have been altogether wrong when he added that it wasn't the poet that made him yawn but the poetry, or rather the versifying.

When he learned that Trublet fell asleep over his epic, Voltaire took it upon himself to rouse him. The Abbé de Voisenon said Trublet wrote his books out of scraps of conversations and things he read; he called him "the ragman of literature." Voltaire seized upon this remark and wrote:

> Au peu d'esprit que le bonhomme avait
> L'esprit d'autrui par supplément servait.
> Il entassait adage sur adage
> Il compilait, compilait, compilait
> On le voyait sans cesse écrire, écrire
> Ce qu'il avait jadis entendu dire
> Et nous lassait sans jamais se lasser.

The little wit that he possessed/Was supplemented by the wit of others./He heaped adage on adage/He compiled and compiled and compiled,/he wrote and wrote/What he had heard others say before/ And wearied us without ever wearying himself.

In fact, everyone pillaged everyone else at that time, for there were no copyright laws to protect writers. But some were much more talented at plagiarizing than others, and what counted was the way they used what they had filched.

The abbé received this trouncing with a smile: it made him a little more famous. He was made a member of the Academy and sent Voltaire a copy of his acceptance speech, accompanied by a flattering letter. As usual this gesture disarmed Voltaire, who replied graciously though with just a touch of irony: "A thousand thanks, monsieur and illustrious colleague, for the reply you have honored me with. It is as ingenious as it is obliging, and better still it is very gay. This is evidence of your good health, the only thing it remained for you to prove. May you long preserve it, and with it all the pleasures and all the fire of your genius. This is the hope even of your enemies, who, though they may not love your person, love your work. There is no exception to this, and woe to those whom it would be necessary to except."

After this the "criminal" was pardoned and his rights to life and literary talent restored.

But there were other criminals, unrepentant hacks who kept endlessly repeating themselves, the worst of whom was still Fréron. In 1759 he had slashed *Candide* to ribbons, and a year later Voltaire pretended to have come across an old number of *L'Année littéraire*, a journal edited by Fréron which had been appearing since 1754. "I was surprised to receive last December a copy of a periodical pamphlet, the *Année littéraire*, of whose existence I was utterly ignorant here in my retreat. And I learned that it was a publication in which the most celebrated of men . . . are insulted," he wrote Fréron. There followed some vague phrases about those feeble minds who set themselves up as censors of other people's work, and the assertion that it would not enter his head to castigate publicly the author of his pamphlet "who is absolutely unknown [to me]. People tell me that he has long been my enemy, but I assure you I know nothing about it." This tone boded no good for the "unknown."

It was an easy task for Fréron to unmask Voltaire's assumed innocence. He offered ample proof that the *Année littéraire* and its author had long been well known to the hermit of Lac Leman. Moreover, he said, it was probable that the letter he had been sent was a forgery and not by Voltaire at all, since it had neither style nor wit.

In August 1760 Voltaire put on a mediocre play called *L'Ecossaise* (*The Scottish Lass*). Everyone said it was by Voltaire, but he maintained that it was only a translation from the English and that the real author was one Jérôme Carré. Fréron rightly criticized the play severely. When it was pointed out to him that a character called Frelon was obviously a caricature of him, he replied adroitly that he did not think Voltaire capable of writing so badly or so basely.

L'Ecossaise really was by Voltaire; it was a success, and he was pleased. The audiences had a fine time looking for insults aimed at Fréron. Voltaire did even better, or worse, in a tragedy called *La Mort de Socrate* (*The Death of Socrates*), which had less to do with antiquity than with his enemies Berthier, Chaumex, and the Abbé Nonnotte. He had *L'Ecossaise* put on again, changing the name "Frelon" to "Guêpe [Wasp]." All Paris, hoping for amusing developments, came to see Fréron attend his own execution in person. Diderot and the playwright Sedaine had mustered all the friends of the *Encyclopédie* and of Voltaire to applaud the speeches in which Fréron was attacked. "Monsieur Guêpe" was described as a spider, a cad, a rogue, a viper, a scoundrel, but while the claque of *philosophes* roared with laughter Fréron calmly sat there in feigned indifference. One hardly dares to imagine how Voltaire would have behaved in similar circumstances. Fréron's calm disappointed him, and so did Fréron's brief and venomus review of the play. According to Voltaire, Madame Fréron met Jérôme Carré, the supposed author, coming out of the theater, and kissed him: "How grateful I am to you," she said, "for punishing my husband. But you will never make him change his ways."

This sounds very unconvincing, but Voltaire had merely revamped a real incident. Madame Fréron did go to the performance, but she was horrified by the attacks on her husband. Someone, to console her, said, "Oh no, madame, it can't be your husband—he isn't an informer, or a forger, or a slanderer." The poor woman answered: "Oh, monsieur, that makes no difference, people will still recognize him."

All Paris squabbled over *L'Ecossaise*, orally and in writing, and the wretched play was a success. It was performed in the provinces and the actors proposed to revive it the following winter. Fréron had been vanquished, and Voltaire was rejoicing over a very minor victory. "My old body, my old trunk, has borne a few fruits this year, some sweet, some rather bitter. My sap is gone. I no longer have either fruits or leaves, and one must obey nature and not try to bully her. The fools and fanatics will enjoy fair weather this autumn and winter, but let them be on their guard against the arrival of spring!"

Tancrède

Written between April 22 and May 18, 1760, *Tancrède* was performed on the third of September. Set in the Middle Ages, by turns fierce, tender, and noble, and full of such high-flown rhetoric that it bordered on the ridiculous, it had a great success, which was far more justified than that of *L'Ecossaise*.

This new masterpiece of classical tragedy delighted not only Madame Denis and the Genevans in the "barn" at Tournay but also the most fastidious Parisians when it was staged at the Comédie Française. Even a claque that had come to avenge Fréron forgot to hiss, and wept with the rest of the audience. It was a triumph—*Zaïre* all over again.

Madame d'Epinay, a writer and benefactress of Rousseau, who would not appear to have been very tenderhearted by nature, reported that she had burst into tears, and wrote, "It makes you die. The princess dies too, but she dies a most heart-rending death. It's a touching novelty that carries you away with sorrow and applause. Mademoiselle Clairon does marvels. There's a certain 'Well, father!'—oh, Jeanne, never say 'Well!' to me like that if you don't want to kill me. Also, if you have a lover, get rid of him tomorrow if he's not a paladin—they're the only men who do women honor."

When Voltaire heard all this he wept, partly for the paladins' fateful glory, partly with pleasure for his own, now vastly enhanced. But he wept with only one eye. He kept the other on Fréron and his cohorts: "It is said that Satan was in the theater in the form of Fréron and that, a lady's tear happening to fall on his nose, he sputtered as if it had been holy water." He was expecting a vengeful review from this "Satan," but what was forthcoming instead were praises mixed with a few justifiable reservations as to the composition and the way the various scenes had been linked together. D'Argental had already pointed out these defects, but Voltaire thought that if he made the audience weep their eyes would be so dimmed by tears that they would not be able to see them. But Fréron did not weep a single tear and saw everything.

Diderot also had certain reservations. When Voltaire heard of this, he begged Diderot to express his criticisms frankly. Knowing how sensitive Voltaire was, Diderot was understandably nervous about doing so, but he took the edge off his slight reservations by burying them beneath extravagant praise of the performance he had seen in Paris. "Ah! My dear *maître*, if you could have seen la Clairon crossing the stage half swooning into the arms of the torturers that surround her, her knees giving way beneath her, her eyes closed, her arms dangling as though she were dead, if you could hear the cry she utters on seeing Tancred, you would remain more convinced than ever that silence and mime have sometimes more pathos than can be attained by all the resources of oratory," he wrote to the "hermit of Ferney."

The key word here is "pathos." Diderot had already sensed the power of sensation, the sensual attraction of the theater. The coldly formal classical style was already being abandoned for the new "drama of sensibility," and Voltaire leaned to the new wind, which he probably approved of for appearance's sake when people admired traces of it in his *Tancrède*, but which he would have disapproved of in other writers.

By way of thanks to Madame de Pompadour, who had supported his claims to the titles of Ferney and Tournay, Voltaire wanted to dedicate *Tancrède* to her. And he began to ponder what he should say. The dedications he had written previously always bore his inimitable stamp, and D'Argental was afraid he might put in some characteristic jests of the sort that seemed overfamiliar and impertinent to certain royal personages and to other aristocrats. Voltaire reassured him and sent him the dedication to read. The D'Argentals went through it with a fine-tooth comb, searching for anything that might conceivably be misconstrued. To make really certain, they passed it on to the Duc de Choiseul, who was to present it to the King's favorite only if he couldn't see any fault in it. In the end everyone had approved of the text, even the King. Voltaire had flattered Madame de Pompadour extravagantly, without overmuch subtlety and without overmuch brilliance; he had groveled, in short. He had it printed and sent a splendid copy of *Tancrède* with the dedication to Madame de Pompadour. Then he waited.

Six months later he was still waiting. By this time he was worried. Only Madame de Pompadour and the King knew why he had had no answer, and they did not want to make the explanation public. The favorite had had an anonymous letter hinting that Voltaire had protected himself by penning a dedication full of flatteries with a hidden sting, for fear of being blamed later on for praising unreservedly someone who was unpopular. Madame de Pompadour, with the approval of the King, preferred to bury the whole matter for as long as possible.

It seemed to Voltaire that the court was unpredictably capricious and constant in only one thing: ingratitude.

But Madame de Pompadour's silence was no reason for making his already strained relations with Versailles worse. Hence when Lord Lyttleton wrote in a preface that Voltaire was living in exile in Switzerland, Voltaire protested: he did not want it to be thought he was playing the martyr. He wrote to Lord Lyttleton: "I live on my estates in France. A retired life is the one most conformable to age, above all when one lives on one's own property. Although I have a little country house near Geneva [Les Délices], my manorial lands and châteaux are in Burgundy, and if my King has been good enough to confirm the privileges belonging to my estates, which are exempt from all taxes, I am all the more devoted to him for having done so."

Lord Lyttleton suppressed the word "exile" and "Switzerland"; but the King still did not invite Voltaire to Versailles.

Dame Bourette, who kept a café in the Rue Croix des Petits Champs, was more amiable. She sold lemonade and pitchers of wine, and made up nice little poems which gave her pleasure and did no one else any harm, and which she used to send to famous authors. They would return the compliment by sending her one of their books or a gift in kind or in cash. Madame Denis had sent her a handsome fan. When she sent Voltaire another batch of her songs, Voltaire asked his niece to send her another gift. Their first thought was to present her with a jug worth sixty livres; then they decided on another present worth thirty-six; and finally they sent a cup with a gold stripe worth eighteen. Dame Bourette proudly invited authors to come and admire it and even drink coffee out of it. But the virtuous Jean-Jacques replied: "I shall willingly come and drink coffee with you, madame, but not, if you please, out of the gilded cup of Monsieur de Voltaire: I do not drink from that man's cup."

He did well to abstain. He might have caught the germ of courtesy or, even worse, of a taste for luxury. So he drank his coffee out of his wooden shoe and kept his soul as pure as his principles.

"Rodogune" was thus in good hands. Voltaire was far from advocating irreligion as one of the cornerstones of education. On the contrary, it was a luxury, and not to be put within the reach of the vulgar or of children. Just as on the one hand he mocked Tartuffes, so on the other he was discreet in the presence of children and of people who were as immature as children. Enlightened people of the upper class were adults intellectually, and for them religious devotion was infantile and ridiculous. But for the common people it was a necessity. Voltaire thought it salutary for the lord of Ferney to accompany his pupil to mass at the local church: and so he went, with "Rodogune" on his arm.

But this did not satisfy the bigots. Heretofore, when she was starving, they had not bothered about the great Corneille's only grandniece. But now they began to be concerned about her soul and to talk of taking her away from Voltaire. At one of the King's levees it was suggested that she be put into a convent. The matter was discussed again at the house of Madame la Présidente Molé, but when someone asked why nobody had suggested doing for Mademoiselle Corneille what Voltaire was doing for her, there was no reply. Voltaire, who had been sent an account of this meeting, wrote to Diderot: "Not one of them offered ten écus. You will observe that Madame Molé had a dowry of eleven million and that her brother Bernard, comptroller to the Queen, defaulted on a debt of twenty thousand, of which the family never repaid me a sou."

In such cases one cannot help being on Voltaire's side. The difficulty is that he used the same methods whether his cause was good or bad. Once again he circulated a pamphlet, *Anecodotes sur Fréron* (*Anecdotes about Fréron*). He swore he had had nothing to do with it and that the real author was La Harpe: he had actually seen the manuscript in La Harpe's handwriting! And, of course, he maintained at the same time that all the facts in the pamphlet were true.

Joining forces with Voltaire, Le Brun published *L'Ane littéraire* (*The Literary Ass*), a pasquinade against Fréron whose title was inspired by the latter's *L'Année littéraire*. Fréron was furious. Voltaire was delighted that Fréron was furious. But Rodogune never saw her fiancé again.

Neither the triumph of *Tancrède*, nor *L'Ecossaise*, nor the Corneille girl, nor the dedication received in silence by Madame de Pompadour, nor the pamphlets were enough to fill the days of the Hermit of Ferney. He decided to rebuild the château. The old one, a "Gothic" ruin which blocked the view of the landscape, was demolished, and Voltaire built the present Château of Ferney, which externally at least remains nearly intact. He built it in accordance with his own taste and that of his contemporaries. There was nothing lavish or majestic about it, only the noble simplicity of an unaffected and pure neoclassic style. There was no suggestion of the *nouveau riche:* Voltaire was a country landowner, wealthy and sensible, who respected his own comfort without neglecting the landscape. "Without taste there is nothing," he said.

Though art was not everything to him, it was the crown of everything. But to raise art to its apogee, the rest was indispensable: and the rest was wealth, whose surest source was work. So Voltaire worked, and made others work, to improve the environs of Ferney, which were beautiful but poor. Having built a fine château, he now wanted a fine village, inhabited by happy, healthy people who worked hard and lived comfortably. "I join to the delight of having a nicely built château and outstanding gardens the solid pleasure of being of use to the country I have chosen to retire in. I have got the council to drain the marshes that used to infect the province and made it barren. I have cleared enormous expanses of heath. In a word, I have put the theory of my *Epistle* into practice."

All the improvements cost Voltaire vast sums of money and endless trouble. He needed all his Arouet tenacity to overcome the obstacles presented by the soil, the climate, the people in the district, and the administration. The last was the worst. Fortunately he had powerful protectors.

Not everyone admired the château unreservedly. Some would have liked it to be grander. Others thought the salon was too small for receiving the finest flower of all of Europe. Apparently Voltaire, acting as his own architect, forgot to allow for the thickness of the walls, hence the size of the rooms was correspondingly reduced.

One of Voltaire's first battles at Ferney was with the curé of the neighboring parish of Moens, who was pressing Voltaire's tenant farmers for a tithe that had gone unpaid for several years. After a long lawsuit in Dijon, the case was decided in the curé's favor, and the peasants, who had never bothered to appear in court and plead their cause, found their possessions being seized. The curé was claiming the arrears of the tithe over several years, plus the expenses of his various journeys to Dijon. The entire village was in despair. Voltaire told the curé he would pay him half of what was owed on condition that he would leave the peasants in peace. The curé refused. Voltaire wrote to the Bishop of Annecy (for though Ferney was regarded as part of Burgundy for administrative purposes, it was under the jurisdiction of Savoy as far as ecclesiastical matters were concerned). Voltaire, who had quoted the prophets and appealed to the Fathers of the Church, had tried his best to make his letter to the bishop a polite and informative one, but to the bishop it sounded as if Voltaire was trying to tell him what to do. Moreover, in his letter Voltaire had stated that no Protestant pastor would do anything so uncharitable as what the curé was doing. The master of Ferney realized too late that he had made an implacable enemy of the Bishop of Annecy.

He wrote to Président de Brosses in Dijon to get him to stay the proceedings against the people of Ferney, who were too poor to pay. But there was nothing to be done: the curé was in the right all along the line, and the peasants must either pay up or have their possessions seized or go to prison. Voltaire was unwilling to let this happen and gave the curé several million francs out of his own pocket to pay the tithes his tenants owed, and they breathed freely again. The curé collected, never suspecting that he himself was going to have to pay a much heavier tithe to the master of Ferney, whose revenge was not long in coming.

One day a few young men, on their way home from hunting, stopped at the house of a widow with whom the curé himself was smitten. The curé was mad with jealousy when he heard of this visit, and surrounded the widow's house with bullies whom he led in person, forced his way in, killed a dog belonging to one of the hunters, and then, when the dog's master protested, beat him with a cudgel. His two friends received the same treatment. As he lost consciousness one of them cried, "Am I to die without confession then?" "Die like a dog," the curé replied. There was a great scandal the next day when he celebrated mass and, as the father of one of the lads who had been beaten put it, "did not hesitate to hold God in his murderer's hands."

This was precisely the sort of thing to kindle Voltaire's anti-clerical zeal. He tried to get the boy's father to pluck up the courage to bring suit against the curé. The boy who had been hurt the worst had been brought to the château and looked after by Voltaire, who was just as furious with his father, who did not dare plead for justice, as with the curé who went on celebrating mass. The patient was between life and death, and still the father hung back.

"They will kill me," he said.

"So much the better," Voltaire replied. "It will make your case all the stronger."

Mademoiselle Rodogune Comes to Ferney

Voltaire discovered that a young woman who bore the great name of Corneille was living in poverty. He could not bear to think that a descendant of the author of *Polyeucte* had been left penniless and without the benefit of a decent education.

The young woman, whose name was Marie-França ise, was the descendant of a brother of the great Corneille's father; his name, like the playwright's, was Pierre. He had a son born in 1662, who was both the playwright's first cousin and his godson and, like him, was named Pierre. Like most of the Corneilles, he was a lawyer in Rouen, and was ruined by standing guarantee to a dishonest client who defaulted on a large loan. He left five children, including the girl's father, Jean-François, born in 1714. Jean-François, though he was unaware of it, was also a cousin of Fontenelle, whose mother had been the famous Corneille's sister Marthe. When he was told of this relationship, Jean-François decided to apply to his famous uncle for help, but unfortunately Fontenelle was nearly a hundred years old and had forgotten that there were two Pierre Corneilles. So when Jean-François was presented as Pierre Corneille's grandson, he was called an impostor, and Fontenelle left his fortune to his nieces. Jean-François brought a lawsuit, which he lost, but the nieces took pity on him, paid their own court costs, and gave him some money, though not enough to raise him out of his poverty. He worked as a wood-molder, earning only forty francs a month to support five people. His case began to be talked of in Paris, and Fréron was the first to lend him a helping hand. The Comédie Française then put on a benefit for the man, and though he had only asked for a slow day, they gave him the box-office receipts for a tragedy and a comedy on one of their busiest days, a Monday. They came to five thousand livres, and he was able to pay his debts and send his eldest daughter, aged eighteen, to a convent as a boarder. But she soon had to be taken away again when the money ran out, and then she was taken in by Fontenelle's nieces. Ponce Denis Ecouchard Le Brun, a poet, had written Voltaire an account in verse of her sad story, together with a long letter explaining the structure and imagery of the preceding thirty-three stanzas. Voltaire was reduced to tears.

"It is only right that one of the great Corneille's faithful soldiers should try to be of use to his general's granddaughter." He had made his decision and now carried it out with his usual energy. Mademoiselle Corneille was to come to the Tronchins' in Lyons, where he would send a conveyance to bring her to Ferney. "If I can be of any help to her I am at her disposal, and I hope to thank you till my dying day for having procured me the honor of doing what ought to have been done by Monsieur de Fontenelle. A part of the young lady's education shall be to see us sometimes perform her grandfather's plays, and we shall set her to writing commentaries on the subjects of *Cinna* and *Le Cid*."

In his enthusiasm to educate the girl, Voltaire had forgotten to find out her precise relationship to the great Corneille. Though suspicious and canny when it came to matters of business, he had simply flung open his doors to a poor young woman bearing a great name. The questions he asked himself are touching. Would she like him? Mightn't she be afraid of him? What had people told her about him and his impiety? He promised to give her "every facility and every help in fulfilling all the duties of religion." He would hire for her all the teachers she wanted: "We shall bring a master here who will be highly honored to be teaching the Great Corneille's granddaughter, though not nearly so highly as I shall be to see her living under my roof." But on reflection he grew a little uneasy. He knew nothing at all about her or her family background, and was Le Brun's recommendation to be trusted? If Voltaire had only known that Fréron was involved! He asked Madame d'Argental to see her, and meanwhile Madame Denis prepared a magnificent wardrobe for her.

Mademoiselle Corneille arrived in December 1760. She was gentle and lively, cheerful and naïve. Her youthful health and grace were attractive. Voltaire immediately christened her Rodogune, after the heroine of Corneille's own favorite play: "We are very pleased with Mademoiselle Rodogune. We find her gay, natural, and unaffected. Her nose is like Madame de Ruffec's, and she has the same little pug face, the most beautiful eyes, lovely skin, and a wide, rather tempting mouth with two rows of pearls," he reported."

He wrote to her father. It was not an easy task, but the way he went about it shows what he was really like: "All who see her are highly pleased with her. She is both gay and modest, gentle and diligent. It is impossible to be more well bred. I congratulate you, monsieur, on having her for a daughter, and thank you for having given her to me."

His generosity provided an opening for his enemies. Without permission, Le Brun published Voltaire's letter thanking him for the information about Mademoiselle Corneille. Fréron seized on this to write that Voltaire's taking in Mademoiselle Corneille was only a pretext to keep his name before the public, and that Le Brun was Voltaire's publicity agent. As for Fréron, as soon as he knew Voltaire was taking an interest in the girl, he decided that it was best to cease befriending her. "The young woman's father is some sort of petty postal clerk who somehow earns fifty livres a month, and his daughter left her convent school to finish off her education at home as a mountebank." Voltaire was all the more furious over this because the charming "Rodogune" had just had a flattering proposal from a young man of a very respectable family in the neighborhood. The suitor was poor, but Voltaire had promised the girl a dowry. On seeing Fréron's article, however, the suitor's family broke off the engagement.

Voltaire called all the thunderbolts in Paris down on Fréron's head. He wrote to D'Argental, Malesherbes, and Monsieur de Sartine, the current commissioner of police.

Unfortunately, neither Monsieur de Malesherbes nor Monsieur de Sartine was inclined to pursue Fréron at Voltaire's request. Voltaire was too obviously connected with the *Encyclopédie*, and Malesherbes was already more involved in that particular enterprise than he cared to be and did not wish to have his name associated with Voltaire. Nor had the recent affair of *L'Ecossaise* been forgotten. Madame Denis wrote one letter after another repeating that she was a noblewoman, the widow of one of the King's officers; that Voltaire was a gentleman and lord of the manors of Ferney and Tournay; that Mademoiselle Corneille's forebears enjoyed titles of nobility as members of the Parlement of Normandy since the sixteenth century and that she was the great-niece of France's most famous tragic poet. It was all to no avail. Monsieur de Sartine went so far as to summon Fréron and give him a dressing down, but that was all.

Voltaire closely supervised Mademoiselle Corneille's education and saw to it that she fulfilled her religious duties. "Our first care must be to teach her to speak her own language nobly and simply. We make her write something every day: she sends me a note and I correct it. She gives me an account of what she reads. . . . We never allow any inappropriate word or mistake in pronunciation to pass unnoticed: practice makes perfect. Nor do we forget handicraft: some hours are set aside for reading, others for petit-point embroidery. I am giving you an exact account of everything. I must not omit to tell you that I myself take her to mass in the village. It is up to us to set an example, and we do so."

Meanwhile Voltaire "worked assiduously to get the curé a job in the galleys." But the curé had supporters. His bullies were arrested but he himself was not, even though he had struck the first blow. This denial of justice infuriated Voltaire so much that he became overexcited and began to do damage to his own cause. Président de Brosses, with whom he was still on friendly terms, advised him to be more prudent. The Bishop of Annecy intended to bring the curé before him and pronounce sentence against him. But Voltaire protested that Ferney was in France and that the matter should be dealt with by the King's tribunals. The authorities wanted only to reconcile the opposing parties and lay the whole business to rest; but Voltaire kept on insisting that the curé be sent to the galleys. To make a long story short, the lad who had been badly beaten and nearly died was awarded fifteen hundred livres damages. Voltaire's comment was that it would cost you nothing to kill a man if you were the curé of Moens. The curé was also obliged to give back the tithes that Voltaire had given him on behalf of the peasants.

While all this was going on, official intermediaries had been advising the curé, intimidating the victim's father, and telling the judges what to do. These intermediaries were the Jesuits of Ornex. Voltaire watched what they were up to and wasted no time launching a counterattack.

"I have all sorts of terrible affairs on my hands," he wrote to D'Argental in January 1761. "I am driving the Jesuits out of an estate they have usurped, I have brought a criminal lawsuit against a curé, I am converting a lady who is a Huguenot, and my most difficult task is to teach grammar to Mademoiselle Corneille, who has no aptitude at all for that sublime discipline."

The Jesuits were his neighbors, and Voltaire had been on excellent terms with them in the beginning. Being naturally inclined to create around himself a friendly circle of well-bred, educated people, he invited them to Ferney and made much of them. They were delighted to be acquainted with the most brilliant product of their schools. They said mass for him whenever he so desired. But then suddenly everything went wrong.

There were four of them in the vicinity, and their leader appeared to be Father Jean Fessi. It was he who went to Dijon to press the magistrates to change their minds should they happen to decide to apply the law fairly. The Jesuits owned large estates near Ferney which they considered not large enough, and they wanted to annex the property of a noble but impoverished family of six brothers, the Messieurs Desprez de Cressy. Their land had been confiscated to pay their debts, but they retained the first option to repurchase their property. They could not afford to buy back their lands, so the Jesuits arranged for the Cressys' creditors in Geneva to expedite matters, with the result that the fathers became owners of the Cressy estates. The six brothers were all officers away at the wars, and between battles they learned the sad news that their estates were irrevocably lost.

But Voltaire sprang to the defense of six helpless victims and made such an outcry that the Jesuits thought it best to give up their claims of ownership of the estates as quietly as possible. The Cressy brothers could still buy back their land from their Genevan creditors; Voltaire had won. "I repeat," he wrote, "that there is no more need to be afraid of these foxes [the Jesuits] than of the Jansenist wolves; what one must do is to boldly pursue these stinking beasts. Let them howl that we are not Christians. I shall soon prove to them that we are better Christians than they."

His new discovery was that he must be more Christian than the Jesuits and Jansenists put together. Morever, when the Jesuits were expelled from France the Cressy brothers were not only able to buy back their own lands; they also bought the estates of the Jesuits. It was then that

Voltaire said there must be such a thing as divine Providence—which he believed in only when priests were its victims.

Since he had become lord and master of Ferney he spoke his mind with the utmost freedom. He felt independent on his own estate, and his boldness redoubled and became more virulent. His attitude became more severe toward timid souls such as Fontenelle, who though he shared Voltaire's ideas always remained "One of those old men as cautious as if they still had their way to make in the world. . . . Anyone looking for old men like that need not come to me." At sixty-five Voltaire had become fully conscious of his power. Heretofore his impiety had been that of an amateur; now he attacked "l'Infâme" with passion. And yet he still claimed to be a "Christian," defending "true" religion against the priests who had monopolized it and distorted it. "Yes, I swear by God's death that I serve God, because I abhor the Jesuits and the Jansenists: because I love my country, because I go to mass every Sunday, because I set up schools, because I build churches, because I am about to set up a hospital, because there will be no more poor people on my estates despite the tax collectors. Yes, I serve God, I believe in God, and I want people to know it," he declared. This strange profession of faith was not mere rhetoric. In a few years Ferney had been visibly transformed in the way he described. As for his intimate faith, that is his business. True, this God whose first commandment was to make war on priests seems rather quarrelsome, in fact more or less the image and likeness of His worshiper.

In 1761 Voltaire played a trick on his enemies who accused him of outright atheism by deciding to make his Easter communion in great style, together with Madame Denis and Mademoiselle Corneille. In March 1761 a Capuchin friar came and confessed everyone: Madame Denis, Mademoiselle Corneille, the maids, the valets, the cooks, the coachmen, the gardeners. Everyone was given absolution, and the priest was just about to leave when he saw Voltaire in the kitchen garden in conversation with the gardener. "Father," said Voltaire, "you have just given a good many absolutions. Will you not give one to me, too, who confess to you here before witnesses that I do no harm to anyone, at least not consciously?" It was an odd Confiteor—administered among Voltaire's lettuces and turnips—but the friar laughed and gave him absolution: if it was as short as the confession it couldn't have been worth very much, but Voltaire nonetheless slipped him six livres as they shook hands. The friar was touched and expressed the hope that the master of Ferney would long continue his kindness toward his monastery, where Voltaire's name was blessed: all for six livres.

During this period of zeal Voltaire also built a church, which is still standing to this day. The old church, which incidentally blocked the road to the château, threatened to fall into ruin, and he wanted the new one to be lighter, more uncluttered, in short more Voltairian. He took advantage of the demolition work to shift the wall of the cemetery, thus gaining a few feet of land. The workmen, it was said, had had to disturb a few old bones. There was also a large cross in the middle of the church-yard directly facing the windows of the château: "Take that gibbet away!" Voltaire ordered.

At this point ominous rumblings began to be heard from the neighboring sacristies. The curé of Moens boasted that he would get Voltaire sent to prison. Voltaire laughed, but the threat was a serious one. Many landowners had done just as he had, and no one had protested, but they were not Voltaire, and they hadn't a curé of Moens at their heels, or a Bishop of Annecy lurking in the background, determined to thwart his plans to build a new church.

Voltaire was first asked to explain what he meant by calling the cross a "gibbet." He swore he had never said any such thing. Of the six workmen who had been present, four backed him up and the other two maintained they knew nothing about it. Finally it was explained to the curé that "gibbet" was not blasphemy but merely a technical word for pieces of wood put together in the form of a cross. The people of Ferney supported Voltaire, but they were devout and easily influenced. The curé of Moens therefore had the tabernacle containing the Sacred Host solemnly removed from the old church in the midst of the demolition and carried in procession to his own church. The people concluded, as they were meant to, that Voltaire was driving God from his estates. The principal official of Gex, the provincial district that included Ferney, was informed, and the ecclesiastical judges came to Ferney to make inquiries on the spot.

Voltaire took it all very lightly. He was more interested in the building of the new church than the demolition of the old. "They are bringing a criminal charge against me for eighteen inches of churchyard and two mutton chops that were mistaken for disinterred bones," he maintained. He said they were attempting to excommunicate him for wanting to move a wooden cross. He had not merely wanted to—he had actually had it removed. "As I am bent upon being master, I have demolished the entire church by way of answer to the complaints that I have already torn down half of it."

He kept the churchbell, the altar, and the fonts and sent the parishioners to attend mass a league away. The ecclesiastics were told that they were asses and sent packing. He informed the prosecutor in Dijon that if there had to be a lawsuit he wanted it to be before the King's judges and not curés and provincial officials. "I fancy I shall be the death of my bishop, if he doesn't die beforehand of melted fat," he concluded.

All his self-assurance was due to the fact that he had written to the Pope, hoping to be able to repeat the process he had gone through for the dedication of *Mahomet* by sending a letter to Rome via Monsieur de Choiseul and Cardinal Pasionei, who was a man of culture with more or less liberal views. Unfortunately the letter was lost in the labyrinths of the Vatican and reached neither the cardinal nor the Pope. Voltaire himself reported that it contained an amusing account of all his acts of sacrilege. Perhaps remembering that he himself had been offered a cardinal's hat, he expected to find fellow spirits in the Sacred College. At any rate he had counted on them rather than on the Pope, whom he described as "an oaf who doesn't know a word of French."

He did not know that things were going very badly in Dijon and that he was on the point of being arrested and tried by the Parlement. If the old law were applied to him, as it still was in certain cases, he risked having his tongue torn out and his hands cut off. His friend Tronchin, who was then in Dijon, said that in the Burgundian capital no one talked of anything else save this curious case. Tronchin managed to placate the judges, who, far from being favorable to Voltaire, as the latter innocently believed, gave way only because of Tronchin, whom they held in high esteem. Thanks to him, the case was shelved.

An Undesirable Citizen

To avenge Geneva's insults to the theater, Voltaire tried to install a troupe of French Catholic actors at Carrouges, just outside Geneva but in territory under the jurisdiction of Savoy. He asked Madame Chauvelin, the wife of the French ambassador in Turin, to obtain permission for the actors to set up a theater in Carrouges; and he succeeded. "Now we shall have a troupe of mountebanks near Les Délices; with our own company, that makes two," he reported gleefully.

It was two too many for the Consistory, which regarded Carrouges as an act of provocation.

Later in the same year, 1761, Voltaire's feud with Jean-Jacques Rousseau erupted again. With the publication of *La Nouvelle Héloïse*, Rousseau's romanticism appeared fully grown. It was a paean to feeling, a work of unabashed sentiment. Rousseau said: "There was only one opinion of the book. Women especially were carried away by it and by its author, to such a degree that there were few, even of the highest rank, whom I might not have conquered had I tried." He added: "It is strange that the book should have enjoyed greater success in France than in the rest of Europe although the French, men and women, are not dealt with very gently in it."

For Rousseau the man, Voltaire felt a kind of contemptuous pity. As far as Rousseau the author was concerned, Voltaire was entirely confused. He simply didn't understand Rousseau's strange ideas. They belonged to two different and incompatible breeds. While Jean-Jacques wrote that "the land of fancy is the only country in the world worth living in," Voltaire was busy twenty-four hours a day plowing, draining, planting, building, doing business by land and sea, speculating, giving dinners for thirty guests, marrying off a girl, defending a man unjustly accused, punishing a bully. In short, he wore himself out creating a world as far removed from the fanciful as possible, in order to attain the most positive and human of happinesses, the happiness that enabled him to say: "The earthly paradise is wherever I am." When he considered what his age called "progress" he concluded: "Do these things make for more happiness? I firmly believe that good houses, good clothes, and good food, together with good laws and liberty, are better than want, anarchy, and slavery." To which Jean-Jacques's reply was: "There is nothing so beautiful as that which does not exist."

Voltaire had long kept his distance from Rousseau, regarding him as a sort of intellectual black sheep and a man difficult to deal with socially. It seemed to him in rather bad taste to take too much notice of him. "For various reasons you have condescended to crush that fool of a Jean-Jacques," he wrote to D'Alembert. "I for my part act like the man whose only answer to all the arguments against motion is to get up and walk. Jean-Jacques proves that theater is impossible in Geneva: I build one."

Rousseau was mortified by Voltaire's attitude, and after penning a letter in 1756 on the *Désastre de Lisbonne,* to which Voltaire's only reply had been *Candide,* on June 17, 1760, Rousseau wrote him a letter overflowing with aggressiveness and hate. "I dislike you very much, monsieur, for you have inflicted wrongs on me of the most painful kind." He was referring to the fact that the Genevans, led astray by Voltaire, had resented Rousseau's virtuous protests against the theater. "Because of you I shall die in a foreign country, bereft of all the consolations of the dying and thrown on a refuse heap." When he wrote this he was living in comfort at Montmorency, the darling of the aristocracy and the triumph of Paris. There followed a litany of "I hate yous," ending with: "Lastly, I hate you because you want me to hate you. But I hate you as a man much more fit to love you had you wanted me to love you."

Voltaire did not reply to this letter. Not because he was angry: when he was angry his fury knew no bounds. He did not answer because he did not consider Rousseau and his emotional outburst worthy of reply. But there was something else as well: Rousseau's letter disconcerted him. He had received many insulting letters and pamphlets—almost as many as he had written. But none of them had been like this: this plaintive self-righteous hatred dragged him into an unseemly world that he did not know and did not care to know. In this sense Voltaire may well have been "limited," as he has been accused of being: for him Rousseau was the strange, the amorphous, the indecorous—a world into which a decent person did not yet venture. Voltaire undoubtedly felt a sort of disgust for Rousseau's sensibility, because he did not understand it. How he would have laughed if anyone had told him that Rousseau was the future.

The most intelligent of men, imprisoned in his intelligence, can sometimes be as shortsighted as any fool imprisoned in his stupidity.

At the root of all Rousseau's accusations was envy. Voltaire's success in Geneva was unbearable to him. It would not have been so bad if Voltaire had been idolized in Berlin or Vienna—but in Geneva, Rousseau's native city, which refused to recognize her own son! He felt he ought to have been in Voltaire's place. Hence he hated his rival. "Do you speak to me of Voltaire? Why do you sully your letter with the name of that buffoon? The wretch has ruined my country. I should hate myself more if I hated him less. . . . Citizens of Geneva, he gives you a fine reward for offering him refuge when he did not know where to turn to do more evil. You will be his last victims. I do not believe there are many other men eager for such a guest."

The prophecy turned out to be truer of Rousseau himself than of Voltaire. It was Rousseau who was left without a refuge, who was everywhere driven away, who quarreled with all his benefactors, and lived and died friendless. Voltaire suffered, if anything, from too many friends rather than too few.

There was something morbid about Rousseau's hatred. When he came back penniless from England after having quarreled with the English, a Monsieur Barth offered him hospitality in Münster. It was a beautiful, romantic place: Rousseau was on the point of accepting but changed his mind abruptly on learning that Voltaire had stayed in Münster in 1753. And this was in 1767!

After receiving Rousseau's letter of June 17, 1760, Voltaire wrote to Thiériot: "I had a long letter from J.-J. R. He has gone quite mad. A pity." When La Nouvelle Héloïse came out, Rousseau did not send Voltaire a copy, but he got hold of one and read it. He was surprised at its success, for it bored him. "I have read it, to my cost," he said, "and it would have been to his as well had I had time to say what I think of this pointless work." But he had more important things to do. "A mason, a farmer, the tutor to Mademoiselle Corneille, and the defender of an unfortunate family persecuted by priests has no time to discuss novels." But he did find some part of the book worthy of praise: "There is an admirable passage on suicide that makes one want to die." This was mere rhetoric: Voltaire was for life. For a complicated life, even: at the same time that he was saying he would not comment on La Nouvelle Héloïse, he was distributing, through Thiériot, four letters signed by four different names, none his, in which he did his best to flay both the book and its author. One of the letters bore the name of the Marquis de Ximénès: Voltaire had been reconciled with him and had even received him at Ferney. In return for Voltaire's hospitality the marquis obligingly signed one of his letters. The Maréchal de Luxembourg, who was then Rousseau's protector, called Ximénès a scoundrel, though he was well aware that Voltaire was the real culprit.

"I Have Done a Little Good, and That Is My Best Work"

At the same time that he was mercilessly hounding Rousseau, Voltaire was acting with admirable generosity toward Mademoiselle Corneille. He badgered the Academy to complete its edition of the French classics, and himself offered to correct the definitive edition of Corneille's *Collected Works*. He even printed them at his own expense, found subscribers, and used the profit to constitute "Rodogune's" dowry. The King subscribed for two hundred copies. Catherine II and the Empress followed suit, Voltaire took a hundred, and Madame de Pompadour and Choiseul fifty each. Noblemen and their friends followed these examples, with English aristocrats heading the list. Voltaire sent free copies to authors who could not afford to subscribe.

He had reread Corneille's works and wrote the introduction. Corneille sometimes seemed rather unpolished to his piercing eye and to his heart long won over by the refinement of Racine's style. But Voltaire felt it his duty to say what he thought, even of this divinity: "I treat Corneille sometimes like a god and sometimes like a clumsy oaf. I told the truth about Louis XIV, I shall not do otherwise with Corneille."

His reservations were bitterly resented by the out-and-out Corneille enthusiasts. Once again Voltaire was accused of impiety and sacrilege. D'Alembert expressed in moderate terms the general feeling of the Academy: "It seems to us that you do not always insist enough on the author's beauties and that you sometimes insist too much on defects which are not apparent to everyone. Where you criticize Corneille, you ought to be so obviously right in your judgment that no one can disagree; otherwise it is better either to say nothing or merely to express doubt."

The truth was that at the age of sixty-seven Voltaire had rediscovered Corneille, and his scrutiny, from which Corneille emerged as a poet of genius despite his faults, was worth far more than the automatic idolatry of those who had not reread him since their schooldays.

After this skirmish with Rousseau, Voltaire turned his attention to his work and wrote *Phèdre* in the record time of six days. "A fury of inspiration seized me one Sunday and did not leave me till the following Saturday. I spent all my time rhyming and scribbling. The subject carried me along full tilt." When he had finished he sent his five acts to the D'Argentals: "Well, I have written the enclosed in six days. Read and judge, but weep," he wrote on October 20, 1761.

They did weep, but only over the play's weaknesses.

While he was trying to patch up the tragedy he wrote a comedy, *Le Droit du seigneur*. As he was not certain of its virtues he had it attributed to Monsieur Le Goux, a young official in the Parlement of Dijon, who saw no objection to Voltaire's camouflage. But his uncle, a friend of Voltaire's and président of the province of Marche, did object, and told Voltaire so. He suggested another pseudo author: Monsieur Picardet, of the Academy of Dijon. The latter thus found himself the "father" of a play he had neither written nor even read the title of—which had been changed to *L'Ecueil du sage* (*The Wise Man's Pitfall*). Crébillon, the theater censor, now ninety, was unwilling to give it a license: he had guessed who its real author was. Old Crébillon did a great deal of tinkering with the text, even going so far as to add a comic scene of his own, and despite Voltaire's fury the strange hybrid was performed with success.

Another pleasant surprise was the news that the King had restored Voltaire's pension, which had been suspended since his visit to Prussia. There was even a rumor in Paris that Voltaire was being recalled to court. But it was false, and even before Louis's refusal to have him back became official, Voltaire, who had guessed the truth, was writing everyone that he did not want to leave Ferney. "I assure you the life I lead there is delightful; it is to the happiness I am enjoying that I owe the preservation of my frail machine."

Crébillon died soon afterward. Voltaire lost no time in publishing, under an assumed name, an unsolicited eulogy which was really a thinly disguised attack. His friends, who recognized his hand in it, did not approve of speaking ill of a dead man. Diderot was shocked. D'Alembert told him what he thought, pretending not to be aware that the piece had come from Voltaire's pen: "Although I am entirely of the author's opinion as to Crébillon's merits, I am very vexed that anyone should have chosen such a moment to cast stones at a corpse. He ought to have been left to rot on his own; it would not have taken long."

But this was demanding the impossible. Voltaire could not leave his enemies to rot. He resuscitated them in order to attack them, and in so doing kept their names alive.

Gracious, and Costly, Living

Voltaire continued his princely way of life at Ferney and Les Délices. He complained that these two residences, together with the war against the English and the loss of the Indies, had cost him a third of his income. But, judging from his expenditures, he did not seem to miss this third. The Duc de Villars was ill, and in the summer of 1762 he came to stay at Les Délices, bringing his household with him. The *Utrecht Gazette* of October 17, 1762, reported: "Geneva, October 6, 1762. Ours is at present one of the most brilliant of cities. Monsieur le Duc de Villars, Monsieur le Comte d'Harcourt, Madame la Comtesse d'Anville, of the house of La Rochefoucauld, Monsieur le Duc, her son; together with many foreigners of distinction. Monsieur le Maréchal-Duc de Richelieu visited the city yesterday. He arrived at Monsieur de Voltaire's at Ferney on the first of this month with a retinue of forty persons, and departed again yesterday for Lyons."

Not all the visitors brought such a train with them, but they came in a constant stream, and the expense of entertaining them can well be imagined, for Voltaire was a magnificent host. The Duc de Villars, after being attended by Dr. Tronchin and lodged, fed and amused by Voltaire, departed cured and radiant.

The next guest to arrive was the Comte de Lauragais, whom Voltaire had known as a child at the house of the comte's grandmother, the Duchesse de Lauragais. The comte wrote tragedies, and Diderot was amazed that such good verses should come out of such an addled head. "Where do you get them from?" he asked slyly, looking out of the corner of his eye at the comte's secretary, whose name was Clinchant and who could also write poetry. The comte was keen on chemistry too: that is to say, he had two hired chemists whom he shut up in a little house at Sevres, saying, "You shan't come out until you've made a discovery for me." No one knows if they ever did come out. The comte was also keenly interested in the actress Mademoiselle Arnould, but in this case without an intermediary. Voltaire made the comte deliriously happy by praising his tragedy *Oreste*, but this was merely a ruse. Voltaire was about to offer the Comédie Française a play of his own on the same subject and wanted to persuade his guest to let his host's play be put on first so that it would eclipse the comte's. The plan worked so well that Lauragais never submitted his play at all. Although the comte may have been scatterbrained, he was not stupid, however, as his enthusiastic reception at Ferney shows. Voltaire did him the honor of personally showing him all around the house and grounds, and Lauragais was surprised to see a donkey grazing in the garden.

"Don't you recognize Fréron?" Voltaire asked.

"Yes indeed," the comte replied. "There is definitely something about the body. . . . But the face is really unmistakable. I wasn't aware that you were on such good terms with Fréron."

"I sometimes need to be angry," Voltaire said, "and when I do, that face does the trick."

He showed his guest the church, with the inscription which caused such scandal and which can still be read today: *"Deo erexit Voltaire* [Built by Voltaire for God]." He had chosen it deliberately to make the clergy furious at the thought of a church built to the glory of God alone. "The church I have built is the only one in the entire world dedicated to God alone. All the others are dedicated to saints. I for my part would rather build a church for the Master than for the servants."

With such pronouncements he threatened to be the death of his bishop. He was sent relics from Rome for his church and sets from Paris for his theater. "I have built a church and a theater, but while I have already celebrated a mystery in the second I have not yet heard mass in the first. On the same day there arrived relics from the Pope and a portrait of Madame de Pompadour." When his niece, Madame de Fontaine d'Hornoy, was about to remarry he wrote her: "I am very sorry not to be having your marriage ceremony celebrated in my own church in the presence of a great Jesus gilded like a chalice with the air of a Roman emperor, [for] I have had his foolish countenance removed." An English visitor remarked that Voltaire had made the statue's face less foolish by having the artist alter it to resemble his own!

Voltaire was delighted with his niece's second marriage to the Marquis de Florian, the officer who had tried to get Voltaire's Assyrian war chariots to crush the Prussian army adopted. The marriage regularized an old and affectionate friendship. "There is nothing as tender or as sensible as marrying one's closest friend," he wrote. The new Marquise de Florian was the younger of the two Mignot girls. She had not been able to devote herself to her uncle as her sister Madame Denis had, for she had two sons and did not become a widow until 1756. It was a pity: she was more artistic, more vivacious, and more disinterested than her sister. She had an ageeable talent for painting, and a gift for gay and spicy conversation that never struck anyone as vulgar, thus proving that even though she had less wit than her uncle she had more than her sister.

Much Ado about Six Faggots of Firewood

In 1761 Voltaire became a member of the Academy of Burgundy, not for the glory of the title but because he was always involved in lawsuits and the majority of the judges in Dijon were academicians.

Also a member of this Academy was Président de Brosses, well known for his amusing *Voyage en Italie* (*Travels in Italy*), published in 1739. He was one of the most representative men of his time. He was learned and a serious scholar, but wore his great erudition with the utmost gaiety and not a trace of pedantry. Nothing disconcerted him: his judgment was rendered swiftly and surely on whatever he saw or read. A true Gaul and a true Burgundian, he dealt with ribaldry with the same ease with which he discoursed formally on Roman law. And he knew how to live as well as to think. Physically he was a small, strong man endowed with extraordinary liveliness, like quicksilver. Diderot wrote: "Président de Brosses, whom I respect in everyday dress, makes me die laughing in his magistrate's garb. How can one prevent the corners of one's mouth turning up when one sees that ironical, merry, satirical little face buried in a forest of wig hanging down on either side and hiding three quarters of the rest of him?"

Voltaire and De Brosses were friends from the very start; the first time they met, in 1756, they talked from nine in the evening till four in the morning, parting on the most affectionate terms. They exchanged letters regularly, each of them convinced of the other's genius.

Voltaire's enthusiasm for the président was reinforced by his enthusiasm for Tournay, which belonged to Monsieur de Brosses. The président wanted to sell, Voltaire wanted to buy. There ensued a few preliminary overtures: Voltaire said he hadn't enough money available to purchase such a magnificent estate and the président replied grandly that he would give his estate and its title away for nothing to the most illustrious writer of the century. Then Voltaire the notary's son and the hard-bargaining magistrate got down to brass tacks. Voltaire pointed out all the defects of the property in order to bring down the price. The defects were real ones: the land was poor, marshy, neglected, and strewn with useless trees; the house a mere "barn." Nonetheless, the président replied, the land carried with it all feudal rights, including the title of count and legal authority. Voltaire was ready to pay the price of a palace but did not wish to show his hand at this stage. The président wanted to get rid of what was for him no more than a liability, which no one but Voltaire was likely to take on. Président de Brosses cleverly upped the price by appealing to Voltaire's desire to play lord of the manor: he harped on his own sentimental attachment to an estate that had been in his family for generations, and mentioned a talisman buried somewhere in the château that caused its inhabitants to live to a hundred. All the old wives' tales and genealogical tables were solemnly trotted out. In short, the two of them bargained like horse traders, but the président did even better than Voltaire, and the deal was concluded at an exorbitant price. Moreover, the deed of sale limited the purchaser's rights, reserving certain privileges, including an option on resale, for the previous owner. The estate was encumbered with various costly obligations, such as that of repairing the house and spending at least twelve thousand livres on upkeep during the three years following the sale. This was more than the estate brought in.

On signature of the deeds it was customary for the purchaser to offer a present. Voltaire sent Madame de Brosses a combined plow and seed drill! She declined to accept it. She had expected pearls, furs, or cash. But among the new equipment he had just bought for Ferney Voltaire must have had a spare·plow. When the président protested he took it back and sent fifty louis instead—a much more useful present for Madame, who was going to spend the winter in Paris.

The day he was formally installed as Comte de Tournay, Voltaire finally had his reward. He was inducted with all the ancient ceremonies: peals of bells, mass, rounds of musketry, and a procession of the inhabitants before the new lord of the manor seated on a canopied throne flanked by his two nieces in diamonds and their most elegant finery. Even the local gentry put themselves out to come. It was a wonderful day for Voltaire.

But all that soon changed. When one of the peasants of Tournay hit a man who he thought was a thief with a saber the attacker was arrested, imprisoned, and was on the point of being hanged. The responsibility of

12. Paris, with view from downstream of the Pont Royal, 1740, by C. L. Grevenbroek. (Musée Carnavalet. Photo Lauros-Giraudon)

13. View of Paris from the Belleville heights, circa 1740, by C. L. Grevenbroek. (Musée Carnavalet. Photo Lauros-Giraudon)

14. The crowning of Voltaire, drawing by Moreau Le Jeune on the subject of Voltaire's "apotheosis." (Reproduced by permission of the Syndics of the Fitzwilliam Museum, Cambridge)

15. Voltaire, at age forty, by Quentin de la Tour. (Photo Arch. Phot. Paris)

16. Voltaire, at age forty-two, by Quentin de la Tour. (Château de Ferney. Photo Arch. Phot. Paris)

paying for the tenant's defense fell on the lord of the manor, Voltaire, and the judges, knowing that he was well off, made the case as complicated and costly as they could. Voltaire made an outcry and appealed to every possible jurisdiction, at Geneva, Gex, and Dijon. He did not want the lord's legal responsibilities any more: such a feudal privilege bid fair to be a ruinous honor. The lawyers let him complain: he would have to pay up. The Gex judges called fifty-two witnesses. Fifty-two witnesses at Voltaire's expense for a handful of nuts and a saber blow dealt by a fool to a scoundrel. And all this at a time when the curé of Moens was also giving him trouble.

While the président was still rejoicing at having unloaded such onerous privileges onto Voltaire, the latter, finding himself short of firewood, had his servants make use of some faggots lying about on the Tournay estate. If he had read the contract properly he would have seen that the wood belonged to the former owner, or at least to his agent, a man named Charlot. Charlot claimed the faggots, Voltaire sent him packing, and Charlot told the président, who already knew what was going on. He had also already pointed out, politely but precisely, that Voltaire was cutting down too many trees, had failed to make the specified repairs, and so on. Charlot was the président's spy: Voltaire's new property was still under the watchful eye of its former owner. The tone between them grew sharper. The président claimed two hundred and eighty-one livres for the faggots; Voltaire would have fought his claim through the courts for the rest of his life rather than pay him. The opponents were both equally tricky, tenacious, and grasping. Voltaire even went so far as to say and write that the président had all the judges in Burgundy under his thumb, and that any verdict that De Brosses had anything to do with was bound to be partial. De Brosses was furious, ordered Voltaire to pay Charlot, and announced that he would sue Charlot for the two hundred and eighty-one livres if Voltaire failed to pay up. Naturally Charlot was now obliged to dun Voltaire, and the président was able to pursue the rich and illustrious lord of Tourney through a third party, a humble farm agent. It would be to the court's honor if the wealthy thief were made to pay for the six faggots he had filched from a poor man.

So these two very rich men made spectacles of themselves for a few armfuls of wood which their servants would have flung on the hearth without even noticing. The Dijon lawyers drove Voltaire to utter exasperation by declining to support him. But even if according to the letter of the law the président or his agent had a right to the faggots, Voltaire considered he had been made to pay enough for the property to be allowed to have them. The président was advised to take this view; but he refused. "What it amounts to, then," he wrote, "is that I must give the wood to him because he is impertinent. People add that he is also dangerous. Is that any reason for allowing him to do wrong with impunity? On the contrary, that is precisely the sort of person who ought to be punished. I am not afraid of him. I am no Pompignan."

In the end, enough people intervened for the matter to be settled out of court. Voltaire gave the two hundred and eighty-one livres to the poor, and the président gave him a receipt as if he had paid for the faggots. Peace was concluded.

This apparent mildness was not quite the end of the story, of course. Président de Brosses was eager to become a member of the Académie Française and made overtures to the academicians to gain admittance. Monsieur de Voltaire thereupon had it conveyed to him that six faggots of wood had irrevocably barred the door to him.

But enough of the petty Arouet side of Voltaire's character, for it is time for Voltaire the great defender of justice to enter on stage.

XII

A bigoted woman had two confessors, one to absolve her from her sins, the other to prevent her from committing any.
"How is it then, madame, that your boat has so often shipped water with two such good pilots aboard?" (*Philosophical Dictionary:* "Director")

How is it that you take so many fools into your order?" a Jesuit was asked. "We need saints," was the reply. (*Remarks*)

Theology is to religion what poisons are to food. (*Dialogues and Conversations*, 26)

Men will always be mad and those who set about curing them are the maddest of all. (Letter, January 1762)

Religions are like games of backgammon and checkers: they come to us from Asia. (Letter, March 1763)

We need good workers and good soldiers, good factory hands and as few theologians as possible; all those little quibblers make a nation ridiculous and contemptible. (Letter, January 1, 1763)

I have done only one reasonable thing in my life, and that is to cultivate land. He who clears a field renders more service to the human species than all the scribblers of Europe. (Letter, March 11, 1763)

I get what I can from my brain, but one's brain is soon dried up. It is only the heart that is inexhaustible. (Letter to D'Argental, 1764)

Superstition is to religion what astrology is to astronomy—the very foolish daughter of a very wise mother. (*Politics and Legislation:* Treatise on Tolerance)

Which is the least bad of all religions?—the one in which one sees the least dogma and the most virtue. Which is the best?—the simplest. (*Philosophical Dictionary:* God and Men)

It is necessary to fight ceaselessly. When one has destroyed one error, there is always someone who will bring it to life again. (*Philosophical Dictionary:* "Mohammad")

If God has made us in His image, we have not returned the favor. (*Remarks*)

Either the stars are great geometers or the eternal Geometer has arranged the stars. (*Dialogues and Conversations*, 24/17)

Why should it be that a grain of opium often provides more felicity than all the treatises of philosophy put together? (*Remarks*)

—What a dreadful condition that of men is!
—That of partridges is worse; foxes and birds of prey devour them, hunters kill them, cooks roast them, and yet there are always some about. Nature conserves the species and cares very little about individuals. (*Dialogues and Conversations*, 24/11)

The Calas Affair

The Calas affair was a milestone in the history of modern Europe. Everyone who has lived after the rehabilitation of Calas is to a certain extent indebted to Voltaire for a better, more lucid, and more humane view of justice before the law.

It is impossible to say how many cases there have been that are comparable to the Calas affair: there were such cases afterward, perhaps there are some such cases today, and perhaps there may be such cases in the future. But the essential point is that before Voltaire men such as Calas were always wrong and the judges were always right. Once the victim stood accused, he was always found guilty. But Voltaire said no to legalized murder.

The affair is well known in its broad outlines, but even after two centuries the roots of the matter remain obscure. It is known, however, that the Calas family were Huguenots and respectable merchants. They lived in the Rue des Filatiers in Toulouse, in a house that is still standing. The ground floor served as a clothier's shop, and the father, mother, and children lived in an apartment on the second floor.

In October 1761 Jean Calas and his wife were upstairs with two of their sons: Marc-Antoine, the eldest, and Pierre, the youngest. That evening the Calases also had with them a young man named La Vaysse. He had come back from Bordeaux to find that his parents had gone away on

a visit and the Calases had invited him to supper in the big living room on
the second floor. After the meal Marc-Antoine got up and went into the
kitchen, where he told the maid that he was too warm and was going out
for a breath of air. The others sat on talking a bit, but as young Pierre was
getting drowsy, La Vaysse got up to go. Jean Calas and Pierre took a
candle and went downstairs to light his way to the front door. The
mother left alone, heard cries and groans coming from downstairs but did
not dare go down. She sent the maid, but the maid did not come back.
Madame Calas then went down herself but met La Vaysse, who barred
the way and begged her to go back upstairs. She did so but could not
resist going down once more. When she did so she found her eldest son
Marc-Antoine stretched out on the floor. When Calas and his son went
down they had been surprised to find the street door open. Approaching,
they found the young man's body dangling from a wooden beam that
was used for storing rolls of calico. They cut him down, but it was too
late. A doctor was summoned and pronounced him dead. In front of the
doctor, Jean Calas, coming out of his shock, said to Pierre: "Don't go
telling everyone your brother has killed himself—save the honor of your
unhappy family." In the eighteenth century the corpse of a suicide was
tried, face downward, and condemned for homicide. So the father's
remark was quite understandable. Nevertheless, though it was uttered
spontaneously, when there was as yet no question of a trial, it was to be
his undoing. When accused of having lied in an attempt to conceal what
they thought was an act of suicide, the Calases admitted having done so,
and their admission was taken as proof that they were guilty of murder.
When the mother came on her son's body, she shrieked so loudly that a
crowd of neighbors and passers-by gathered outside. The police arrived.
The "Capitouls," or municipal magistrates of Toulouse, were alerted: one
of them, David de Beaudrige, was to play the terrible role in what
followed. Outside an excited crowd was asking, "Who killed him? Who
killed him?" And suddenly an anonymous voice said, "Marc-Antoine was
killed by his family because he had become a Catholic convert." David de
Beaudrige heard this accusation and without bothering to make further
inquiry, not waiting even to identify the place, without a warrant, he had
everyone who had been in the house that evening arrested and imprisoned. He did not even have the house searched, though if there had been a
murderer or murderers they might have been hiding there. He did not
even trouble to find out whether there were any signs of a struggle,
though a sturdy young man does not allow himself to be strangled without putting up some defense. If it was true that Marc-Antoine had
wanted to convert to Catholicism, here might have been relevant books
in his room. But even the papers in his pocket were not shown to the
judge. They were thrown away; rumor had it that they had been found
to be obscene verses.

The Calases thought that as soon as their depositions were heard they would be brought back home. Pierre left a candle alight in the hall so that they would be able to see their way. Beaudrige had it put out. "You won't be back as quickly as that," he said. Both he and the crowd had arrived at the same conviction on the basis of a few random words for which there was no corroborating evidence.

Thus began a trial marked by the incredible stupidity of the public and the ambition of a magistrate who thought that the publicity would make his career. He did not dream how far it would spread. Beaudrige said, "I take entire responsibility," and when a fellow magistrate advised him to be more cautious, he replied, "All this is in the cause of religion." He complained that his colleagues did not give him wholehearted support. Thy were not so sure of themselves as he was. One wonders why the minister at Versailles, when he read the reports, did not suspect that the case was in the hands of a fanatic. It is also surprising that no counter-report was made. Beaudrige was well known and mistrusted in Toulouse. He had had La Beaumelle disarmed and arrested illegally, out of sheer hatred for the man.

Marc-Antoine was twenty-eight, and regarded as a thoughtful and studious young man. He had done well as a law student and wanted to carve out a brilliant career for himself as a barrister. For this he needed a "certificate of Catholicity." Such a certificate was not difficult to get. The father of his friend La Vaysse had obtained one, though he was a Protestant in fact and by conviction. But the curé of Saint Stephen's in Toulouse would not give Marc-Antoine a certificate without a written confession of faith. This was a great deal to ask of a Protestant, and young Calas was in despair. He told one of his fellow students that his career was ruined, for he would never agree to declare himself a Catholic. This was exactly the opposite of what the stupid public believed.

So he then devoted himself to business, though he hated it. And here also he met with a setback. He wanted to go into partnership in order to extend his range but missed a good opportunity through not being able to get hold of the required money in time. That made two disappointments one after the other. Moreover he was vain and was eager to cut a fine figure, and his father criticized him for these undesirable tendencies. Monsieur Calas himself refused to take him into partnership; he did not consider him suited to trade. To distract himself from all his sorrows, Marc-Antoine went astray and started to gamble in a café called the Four Billiard Tables. He was fond of the theater and recited well, with a special preference for speeches on the subject of death. Later, people remembered his liking for the monologues of *Polyeucte* and *Hamlet*, and the defense of suicide in Gresset's *Sydney*.

All this could have helped the judges to discover the true explanation of what had happened, if they had really wanted to. But they preferred to pander to the mob, who saw Marc-Antoine as a martyr to his new faith. For three consecutive Sundays the priests read out from the pulpit a hortatory letter demanding exemplary punishment and calling upon all witnesses to come forward. But only evidence unfavorable to Calas was recorded.

Three weeks after this pretense at a preliminary investigation, Marc Antoine's corpse, steeped in lime, was still awaiting burial. Beaudrige, without any evidence, declared that he had been a Catholic and must be interred as such. The priest of Saint Stephen's, who had refused to give Marc-Antoine a certificate of Catholicity while he was alive, ought now of course to have refused to bury a man he knew very well to be a Portestant. But the funeral took place with great ceremony, and the remains were regarded as those of a martyr. The corpse was actually fought over by the curé of Saint Stephen's Cathedral and the priest of another church. Forty priests surrounded the coffin, preceded by penitents of the Carmelite order, which Marc-Antoine was said to have wanted to enter. But no one could produce any trace of such a vocation. This did not prevent the Carmelites from holding a service to which they invited three other confraternities. They erected a catafalque in their chapel with a skeleton representing Marc-Antoine on top: in one hand it held a martyr's crown and in the other a placard reading "Abjuration of Heresy." People said it was Louis, the brother who was already a convert, who had told the Carmelites that Marc-Antoine had wanted to join their order. Later on he retracted his statement. Louis was a strange character. He had brought suit to force his father to grant him a remittance to which he was entitled by law as a convert, though decency might have forbade him to demand it. What reliance could be placed on a son whose only interest in his family was to extort money from them?

Calas's legal counsel, Ducoux, fell into a trap laid for him by the municipal magistrates, led by Beaudrige, and was suspended for three months and obliged to make a public act of repentance in the presence of the judges. This was done in order to discourage other barristers from defending Calas. Another lawyer, Sudre, tried to present evidence proving the Calases' innocence, but no one would deign to listen to him.

There were five persons who stood accused: Jean Calas, the father; his wife; his son Pierre; La Vaysse; and the maid, Jeanne Viguière. In yet another abuse of power the magistrates decided to put Calas, his wife, and Pierre to the torture. By law only royal courts had authority to make such a decision, as the Capitouls knew very well. La Vaysse and the maid were "put to the question," that is to say, subjected to semi-torture. La Vaysse, and even La Vaysse's father were declared to be accomplices. This was sheer fanaticism. La Vaysse's father was so tolerant that he had signed his son's certificate of Catholicity and had even sent him to a Jesuit school.

The unfortunate maid was declared an accomplice because of her blind devotion to her employers. The judges refused to admit the possibility that such a faithful servant could have failed to co-operate with her master and mistress in murdering their son. They might better have taken into consideration the fact that Jeanne was a fervent Catholic who went to mass every morning and took communion twice a week; she had even encouraged Louis's conversion. If Marc-Antoine had really been killed because he had wanted to become a Catholic, she would have been far more likely to denounce the crime than to aid and abet it. When put to the question, she disavowed all guilt and continued to go to confession and take communion, which she would not have done had she committed perjury. It was Voltaire who, on studying the proceedings, discovered this argument against her complicity; it was also a compelling argument against the alleged murder itself.

The case was brought before the Parlement of Toulouse. Its members were all educated men well aware of what the procedure ought to be, and well acquainted with the Christian idea of justice. They nonetheless behaved like a popular tribunal acting under duress and blinded by passion. Its members shared the fanaticism that had possessed the entire city. The streets rang with the cry, "Calas, assassin!" Only one magistrate, Monsieur de la Salle, had the courage to defend innocence. One of his colleagues cried angrily, "Monsieur, you are the image of Calas!" Monsieur de la Salle replied: "Monsieur, you are the image of the mob." If stupidity is a crime, it is sometimes a particularly hideous one. Thirty years later the popular tribunals, also prompted by their sentiments alone, sent the sons and grandsons of these proud magistrates and barristers to the guillotine.

Because of their false sense of self-importance, Jean Calas was condemned to torture, both ordinary and extraordinary. He could see them preparing all the instruments that were to flay, burn, tear, and break his bones. Jean Calas was driven barefoot and bareheaded on a prison cart to the porch of Saint Stephen's. There, kneeling, with a candle in his hand, he asked pardon of God, the King, and the law. Then he was driven back on the same cart to a square where a scaffold had been erected. He was tied to a wheel, and his legs, arms, and back broken with an iron bar. His face turned heavenward, he heard a voice telling him that "he would live there in torment and repentance for as long as it pleased God to give him life." Finally, for there had to be an end sometime for the poor wretch, the executioner strangled him and threw his body on a pyre, and then his ashes were scattered to the winds.

Such was the end of Jean Calas, a good husband and father, an honest merchant, and a loyal subject. He met his death with remarkable courage, serenity, and even grandeur. To Father Bourgès, exhorting him under torture to confess to his crime, he said: "What, Father, do you too believe that a man is capable of killing his own son?" He was pressed to name his accomplices. "There is no crime, hence there can be no accomplices," he replied. His last words were: "I have told the truth. I die innocent."

Beaudrige was still calling on him to confess when the executioner strangled him: such a confession might have done something to ease his conscience and free him of the most dreadful remorse. When he wrote to the Prime Minister, reporting Calas's death, the perpetual banishment of the son, and the freeing of the two women, he said: "This sentence did not fail to surprise everyone, for one and all expected something more severe." After Calas's good name was restored, Beaudrige was removed from office: the pretext was that he had unjustly interfered in the burial of two Englishmen who died in Toulouse in 1764. The minister, Monsieur de Saint-Florentin, had realized rather late in the day the vileness and ambition of this "Capitoul." After his dismissal from office, Beaudrige's conscience apparently awakened to his crime, but not before he had gone mad and been haunted by visions of flames and tortures and executioners. His grandson, David d'Escalonne, who did his best to oppose the excesses of the Terror, died on the scaffold in 1794. He was reported to have failed to show as much courage as Calas.

Voltaire first heard of the trial through one Monsieur Audibert, who had recently arrived from Toulouse and gave him a detailed account. Voltaire could not sleep because of it. It was not clear whether Calas was guilty or innocent. Nothing had been proved or even properly investigated. Voltaire decided to seek evidence of Calas's guilt. If none existed, the judges had been wrong and Calas's good name must be restored. In the beginning Voltaire was not at all sure that Calas was innocent: it was enough for him that his guilt had not been proven. He was always a passionate champion of justice, and in this case he was more fervent than ever. But instead of indulging in violent polemics he brought to this task amazing patience and pertinacity. He asked Cardinal de Bernis what one was to think of "the dreadful business of Calas, who was broken on the wheel at Toulouse for hanging his son. People here say he was quite innocent and called on God as his witness. This affair haunts me; it saddens and poisons all my pleasures. Either the Parlement of Toulouse or the Protestants must be looked upon with horror." Bernis's pleasures were not poisoned, and he did not reply. Voltaire therefore wrote to Richelieu, now the Governor of Guyenne. Meanwhile he met the Calas children, in exile in Geneva. He wrote again to Bernis, who replied like a man of the world, taking sides neither with the judges nor with the condemned man. A miscarriage of justice was none of his concern.

A Monsieur Ribotte, a traveler from Montauban, might prove a better informant. He was a distinguished gentleman who corresponded with Buffon, Necker, and Rousseau. But how difficult it was to find out anything! "Those who could shed more light keep a cowardly silence," Voltaire wrote. This was what Richelieu did. Out of friendship for Voltaire, Richelieu made inquiries in Toulouse, but he was careful not to divulge the results. He advised Voltaire, for his own peace of mind, to concern himself with other matters. For a time Voltaire was on the point of abandoning the whole affair.

It was Tronchin who started everything off again. He had no difficulty proving to Voltaire that Richelieu had got his information from the Parlement of Bordeaux, who in turn had gotten theirs from the Parlement of Toulouse. The gentlemen of the Parlements would stand together: there was nothing to be expected from them. As if to bear this out, Président de Brosses at this point upheld the view of the other Parlements. Tronchin pointed out that Voltaire would have all the magistrates in France against him if he challenged the sentence of Toulouse. But this simply reinforced his conviction that this was precisely what needed to be done. He made contact with all the merchants and lawyers from Languedoc who were in the habit of coming to Geneva. He questioned them, and confronted Pierre Calas with witnesses. Whenever he learned that a traveler from Toulouse had arrived in Geneva, he immediately went there from Ferney. "Tell me the hour that suits you, and I shall come to your place or Monsieur Tronchin's at whatever time you name," he wrote to one of them.

There are those who have attempted to explain Voltaire's role in the Calas affair as mere anti-clericalism. This is to vastly underestimate that role. It is well known that he had as little time for Protestant fanaticism as for any other. And it must never be forgotten that Voltaire's ideas were extremely subtle and fluctuating. We can be sure of nothing with him, save for his sincere passion for justice, truth—and drama.

Voltaire had young Donat Calas brought to see him and questioned him with the utmost suspicion. The other brother, Pierre, had witnessed the hanging, according to the judges; at all events, he had assisted in the cutting down, he was the closest witness, and therefore perhaps the least trustworthy. Voltaire hence viewed him with the greatest mistrust and had him watched for four months. It was an example of professional conscientiousness that the Toulouse judges ought to have followed. He judged Pierre Calas according to everything that could be found out about him. But unlike the mob, crazed by a passion for injustice, his passion for justice caused him to remain cool and levelheaded.

In the end he knew all there was to be known about the members of the Calas family. He proved extraordinarily skillful at laying traps when he questioned them. After several months' investigation he wrote: "There is nothing I have left undone to discover the truth: I have employed several people to frequent the Calases in order to learn about their habits and behavior. I myself have questioned them frequently. I dare be as sure of the innocence of this family as of my own existence." These words were written on February 13, 1763.

His next task was to convince the world. He laid siege to the minister, Monsieur de Saint-Florentin, by invoking the aid of Richelieu, the Duchesse d'Anville, the Duc de Villars, Monsieur Meynard (a clerk), and even the minister's doctor, who was given instructions to administer "a dose of Calas" every morning along with Monsieur de Saint-Florentin's emetic. He harassed the chancellor, Monsieur de Lamoignon, and the chief président, Monsieur de Nicolaï. He re-established cordial relations with Madame de Pompadour, reminding her of the past, flattering her, amusing her, arousing her pity—anything to salvage the truth, even though it was too late to save Calas himself.

The judges were no longer sure of themselves. Calas's last moments had troubled more than one of them: he had met his death in a manner befitting an innocent man. Moreover it was a very improbable murder. How could an elderly man of sixty-two hang a vigorous young man of twenty-eight, alone and unaided? If he had had an accomplice it could only be Pierre, his second son; why, then, had Pierre been acquitted? As for the farce of banishment, Pierre had been exiled through one of the city gates and allowed to re-enter through another. He was sent to stay with the Dominicans and promised his freedom if he would become a convert. He agreed, and four months later joined his mother and younger brother Donat in Geneva. Who was to blame in such a conversion, the one who agreed to it or those who forced him to do so under such conditions?

Surprisingly, one of the first obstacles Voltaire had to overcome was Madame Calas's reluctance even to discuss the question of rehabilitation. Her imprisonment, the "questioning" she had been put to, and her husband's terrible death had crushed her spirit. Voltaire appealed to her maternal instincts. Her two daughters, who had been away from home at the time of Marc-Antoine's death, had been sent to a convent. Their mother's only hope was to be able to see them again, but they would be restored to her only if their father's name was cleared. In this way Voltaire succeeded in securing the poor woman's consent to his plans for seeing posthumous justice rendered her husband. She was taken from her refuge and brought to Paris in the cause of propaganda: the Toulouse mob had cried out for Calas's death; now it was necessary for the Paris mob to cry out for his rehabilitation. Voltaire's appeal to justice was not enough.

Voltaire and his influential friends saw to it that Madame Calas was warmly welcomed in Paris. The D'Argentals surpassed themselves, and Voltaire wrote to them: "What is it we ask? Nothing save that justice should not be dumb as well as blind. Let it speak, and say why it sentenced Calas. What is more horrible than a secret judgment or a motiveless condemnation? Can there be a more hateful tyranny than that which sheds blood as it pleases without giving any reason? 'It is not the custom to give reasons,' say the judges. Well, you monsters, it will have to become the custom. You owe men an explanation for men's blood."

Madame Calas stayed in lodgings on the Quai des Morfondus. She had no money. It was Voltaire who defrayed all her expenses, as well as those of the counterinquiry. But his interest encouraged others, and financial aid poured in. A bank account was opened for Madame Calas, public opinion was obviously on her side, and the real struggle could begin between the friends of Calas, with Voltaire at their head, and the Parlement of Toulouse.

Certain difficulties still seemed insurmountable. Mariette, the barrister who was pleading Madame Calas's case, could not obtain an abstract of the previous proceedings from the Parlement of Toulouse. The abstract was indispensable, but no reply could be obtained to the request for it. This was at the time when the Parlements were opposing the King. The public thought they were defending the rights of the nation, but they were really defending the rights of the Parlements, which had become the refuge of the most shortsighted conservatism. In a word, it was not at all a propitious moment for getting a sentence revised. Even young La Vaysse's father, who was a barrister, trembled at what Voltaire was trying to do: he would have agreed to almost any act on the part of the Parlement rather than revive the horrible affair in which his son had barely escaped hanging. Voltaire could get nothing out of him. It must be remembered that as a lawyer La Vaysse knew better than anyone how ready the magistrates of Toulouse were to put any person with the slightest charge against him to the question. By contrast Voltaire's courage is all the more admirable.

But he came up with a clever solution. As Monsieur La Vaysse could not be tempted by justice, he must be tempted by self-interest. He must come to Paris, and there, out of reach of the cruel "Capitouls" of Toulouse, he would meet German princes and important people from France, England, and the Low Countries, who had subscribed large sums for the Calas affair. "And you will manage all this money, Monsieur La Vaysse," Voltaire told him, adding that these great people had other lawsuits that also needed defending, cases that were less spectacular and dangerous but more lucrative. Hearing all this, La Vaysse began to be a somewhat more eager partisan of justice after all.

It was astonishing how Voltaire managed to combine idealism with common sense, and how skillfully he made use of his friends and connections. He urged on the timid and restrained the overzealous. He knew what to tell people and what not to tell them. "Let us not quarrel with anyone, we need all the friends we can get," he cautioned. Above all, he needed the help of the Calases, who were understandably disheartened. Madame Calas weakened and wanted to give up the struggle. This exasperated Voltaire: "I believe I would have made rather more noise if they had broken *my* father on the wheel," reminding her of her duty to her children.

When he judged public opinion to be ready to listen, he addressed it. In August 1762 he published a pamphlet entitled *Histoire d'Elisabeth Canning et de Calas* (*The Story of Elizabeth Canning and Calas*). It explained the position in twenty pages, without passion, with exemplary clearness, logic, and purity of expression, and was followed by one entitled *Lettre des frères Calas* (*Letter from the Calas Brothers*), which caused a great stir. The lawyers Elie de Beaumont and Mariette also published an article, and so the matter ceased to be merely the Calas case and became the Calas affair. The small difference between the two expressions was tantamount to a result, a reform, or even a revolution. Thanks to all these minor publications, the scandal spread throughout France, and far beyond its borders. The Europe of the Enlightenment became aware of the monstrous defects of a legal system that still belonged to the Middle Ages. But to all this the gentlemen of Parlement remained deaf: there was no appeal from their judgments. One of them said that all this campaign was of no importance because there were more judges than Calases in France. But they forgot that there was also Voltaire.

In support of his campaign, he published in 1763 a work entitled *Traité de la tolérance* (*Treatise on Tolerance*), unsigned. He wanted people to think it was by a respectable priest. On January 24, 1763, he wrote to his friend Damilaville: "Nothing can be done about Jean Calas having been broken on the wheel, but one can make his judges appear abominable, and that is what I hope. . . . Take care not to attribute to the laity this little work on tolerance which is soon to appear. Let us say it is by a respectable priest. There are certain passages to make people tremble, others to make them roar with laughter, for, thank God, intolerance is absurd as well as horrible."

In this *Treatise* the Calas affair became the affair of humanity, and he resolved it for everyone and for every age. It was this little book that won the rehabilitation case. Choiseul was won over to the Calases' cause. Nonetheless, the Parlements, especially those in the south, were still prepared to resort to violence if the Toulouse sentence were changed.

Finally the sentence was quashed by the Royal Council; several ministers of state were present, as were the Duc de Choiseul, the Duc de Praslin, and three bishops. The Council was ratifying the decision of an assembly of eighty judges, who had unanimously quashed the Toulouse verdict on June 4, 1764. A number of the Toulouse judges had been present. One of them, shamefacedly seeking to justify his conduct, said to one of the eighty judges, the Duc d'Ayen: "My lord, even the best horse may stumble."

"Yes," the duc replied. "But . . . a whole stable?"

Madame Calas was received at Versailles and saw the King. But the King didn't see her, for just as he went by someone slipped and fell, distracting his attention and everyone else's.

A Protestant court reporter to the Assembly of the Judges wrote: "What a contrast with the people of Toulouse! Here even the servants of all the judges and of all her [Madame Calas's] protectors look on her with respect and admiration, and there is not one of them who has not read all her memoirs."

During her stay in the convent one of the Calas girls, Nanette, had met with incomparable devotion in the person of a nun who, after questioning and observing her, was convinced of her family's innocence. She wrote Chancellor de Lamoignon a letter which was remarkable for its lucidity, accuracy, and sensitivity. When Voltaire read it he wrote: "The virtuous simplicity and candor of this nun of the Order of the Visitation seems a terrible condemnation of the bloodthirsty fanaticism of the murderous magistrates of Toulouse." But when Nanette wanted to express her gratitude to Voltaire, the nun exclaimed: "Can there be anything great in a man who sets himself up against the author of his being?"

Pierre Calas was at Ferney when news of the annulling of the Toulouse sentence, a step toward rehabilitation, reached Voltaire in the form of a letter from D'Argental. The old man and the young one fell into each other's arms, weeping: "The Calas boy and I both shed tears of emotion, my old eyes supplying just as many as his. We were choked with feeling, dear Angels . . . and yet it is philosophy alone that won the victory."

But the Toulouse Parlement still raised every possible procedural difficulty. Before, the magistrates had threatened to riot; now they refused to communicate the minutes of the trial. The King, in Council, ordered the magistrates to produce them. They replied that they would have a copy made but that Madame Calas would have to meet the expense. Twenty-five quires of paper would be needed, which would cost an enormous sum. "What!" Voltaire exclaimed. "In the eighteenth century, when men are enlightened by philosophy and moral science, an innocent man is broken on the wheel by 8 votes to 5, and they ask five hundred livres to transcribe the scrawl of the abominable trial? And they want the widow to pay?" Voltaire and his friends paid instead. Sometimes Madame Calas wanted to give up. Then Voltaire would remind her of her daughters shut up in the convent, and she would muster her strength again. She had need of it.

The law provided that after the quashing of the sentence the case had to be gone through all over again from the beginning. The accused were therefore arrested and imprisoned again in order to stand trial. Finally, on March 9, 1765, the final judgment was delivered unanimously: it rehabilitated all the Calases and their names were to be erased from the prison records. The clerks of the court were to carry out these decisions under pain of imprisonment. But the judges of Toulouse did not obey: only La Vaysse's father was able to get into the record office one day when everyone was away and strike out the name of his son. Although those who had been rehabilitated were legally entitled to compensation and damages from the judges who had sentenced them unjustly, the judges refused. They did not dare to bring suit to secure their rights; the judges would have tricked them and ruined them, and the King himself could do nothing about it. It would take a revolution to get rid of the magistrates' excessive privileges. The Parlements played a sinister role in the eighteenth century and were one of the primary causes of social injustice, and there-fore of the violence that aimed to sweep that injustice away. It was the King who saw to it that the Calas family were compensated; and he saw to it quickly. The Queen—though she had little inclination to be kindly toward "heretics"—received Madame Calas and her daughters. The throne proved itself more liberal than its law courts.

What Voltaire did for the Calases would be enough by itself to make him immortal. His wit was not only a delight but also the most effective of weapons. Diderot wrote: "Oh, my friend, what a splendid use to put genius to! The man who behaves thus must have soul and sensibility; he must be repelled by injustice and feel the attraction of virtue. . . . If a Christ existed, I swear to you that Voltaire would be saved."

In February 1765 Voltaire had the satisfaction of learning that Beau-drige had been removed from office. "I hope he will pay dearly for Calas's blood," he said. And he wrote to a friend in the capital: "So you were in Paris, dear friend, when the Calas tragedy ended so happily. It is a drama in the classical tradition, with a fifth act that in my opinion is the finest in the world."

Life at Ferney

Meanwhile, life at Ferney had been as fast and furious, as brilliant and hard-working, as ever. "When one is young one should love like a mad-man," Voltaire said. "And when one is old one should work like a demon."

He had his theater repainted, bringing in workmen who had redec-orated the theater at Lyons. They did him a set in perspective for the tiny stage at Ferney that made the actors look as though they were a league away. For *Olympie* there was a lighted funeral pyre on stage. The Genevan pastors refused to accept his invitations, but they sent their daughters. "I have watched Genevans, male and female, weep through five acts," he wrote on January 9, 1762. "I have never seen a play so well acted. And then a supper for two hundred spectators. And then a ball. That is how I have taken my revenge."

Le Kain, the actor, visited Ferney once again. Voltaire had not seen him since 1755, and he had put on weight: "He looks like a big fat canon," Voltaire reported. Le Kain's talent was at its peak, however, and although he was ugly, he seemed handsome when he was playing a role in one of Voltaire's works. But at the end of his stay, when he found it im-possible to act opposite Madame Denis, he suddenly seemed less attrac-tive. Voltaire also gave Mademoiselle Corneille parts to play, but for all his benevolence her performance on stage does not appear to have been a success. "Her voice is faint, harmonious, and tender," he said. Not a very good asset for an actress; but an excellent one for a marriageable young woman.

A Wedding That Attracts a Flock of Guests

Mademoiselle Corneille's first betrothal had not met with success, but Voltaire wanted her to be happy and went to a great deal of trouble to arrange a good marriage for her, hoping to derive a certain amount of glory from his matchmaking. A year after she came to live with him she turned nineteen, could spell a little, and was ready for marriage. D'Argental undertook to find her a husband. The person he proposed was a captain of twenty-six—Henri-Camille de Colmont, also called De Vaugrenant. Voltaire was prepared to make a good many concessions so long as the suitor was a respectable man with philosophical interests. He would even go so far as to have him to live at Ferney if his philosophy proved a suitable one. The fiancé kept them waiting but finally appeared in December 1762. It did not take Voltaire long to discover that the captain was only half a philosopher and that what he was counting on winning was not so much the affection of his bride-to-be as her dowry. Moreover, "this demi-philosopher was not merely semi-poor but completely penniless," as Voltaire put it. And, he added, "his father is not only a semi-hard bargainer, he is a rod of iron." He agreed to give three thousand livres if Voltaire would agree to give forty thousand. This seemed excessive to Voltaire, and as a counteroffer he guaranteed his ward fourteen hundred livres a year and the author's profits from his *Commentaires sur Corneille*. This was equal to the annual income from a principal of forty thousand livres. He also tried to get the captain a diplomatic mission, but the captain was in no hurry, having already installed himself at Ferney, anticipating playing the role of a ne'er-do-well son-in-law. His father thereupon stopped his allowance. All that remained was an arrogant suitor, without fortune, scruple, or even love for "Rodogune," who for her part felt none for him. His only attraction was a handsome nose. He was surly, and his fiancée found him "gloomy, lacking in politeness, and far from eager to please." The Colmont family, it is true, did not share Voltaire's views regarding the glory of the name Corneille. Their view was that their son, a nobleman and an officer, was marrying the daughter of a postal clerk, an object of charity. All they proposed to contribute was their son, and even that with reluctance. "So I am not even semi-embarrassed," Voltaire concluded. "If marriages are made in heaven," he wrote to D'Argental, "the marriage of Monsieur de Colmont and our little marmot has been unmade." The most difficult task still lay ahead. The captain had to be convinced that the marriage that he found so unattractive was equally unattractive to his fiancée. He had dug himself in at Ferney, and it took some doing to pry him loose and force him to leave.

But there was a replacement waiting in the wings. Monsieur Dupuits de la Chaux was twenty-three, an ensign, with an income of eight thousand livres a year and estates near Ferney. Voltaire arranged everything "like a supper party. I shall keep the bride and bridegroom here with me, playing the role of patriarch if you approve," he wrote to D'Argental in January 1763. This time "Rodogune" was really smitten. "They love each other passionately. It puts new heart into me, though it does not prevent me from having a bad eye inflammation. . . . I wish old Corneille could come to life again to see this: old Voltaire escorting the only person who bears his name to the altar." (Though the great dramatist had a number of living descendants bearing his name, Voltaire, as always, insisted on ignoring that fact.)

The picture is very different from the usual caricature of Voltaire. It resembles a genre painting by Greuze, but it is nonetheless a true portrait of him, for this happiness he alone had made possible gladdened his heart.

In order that Mademoiselle Corneille's father might join in the general rejoicing, Voltaire sent him twenty-five louis. "Rodogune's" father was neither very decorative nor very interesting. Voltaire had already received him at Ferney in 1762 when he was preparing his *Commentaires* on the great Corneille, and he wrote at the time to D'Argental: "This fellow will never be commented on unless I am very much mistaken." Mademoiselle Corneille saw no advantage in exhibiting her father, but he, on the contrary, proposed to spend Voltaire's twenty-five louis on a trip to Ferney for the wedding. Voltaire wrote off at once to the D'Argentals to keep him from coming. "It is a strange thing that a father should threaten to be a killjoy at a wedding feast, but that is how it is! . . . May Heaven preserve us. We cast ourselves beneath the protection of our Angels' wings in order that they may prevent him from being present." He then added: "If I consulted no one save myself I should have no objection, but not everyone is as much a philosopher as your humble servant. Patriarchally speaking, I should be very pleased to make the father and mother witnesses of the family's happiness."

All this was both humane and wise. It would have been kind to invite the father but cruel to expose the daughter to the mockery and scorn of the other guests and of the bridegroom's family.

The last touch of sentiment was added to the picture by the pleasure that Voltaire's nieces and nephews displayed at the wedding despite the fact that the dowry given the bride would diminish their own inheritance. Voltaire himself was quite surprised: "My family, far from grumbling, is delighted. It is rather like a novel."

The marriage had other consequences. A flock of Corneilles descended on Ferney from all over France; all poverty-stricken. The first arrival was a deserter who was a direct descendant of the great Corneille. "And we are threatened with a dozen other first cousins of Pertharite [the hero of one of Corneille's tragedies; his first failure], who will come one after the other with open beaks."[1] It was too much. Voltaire explained to them that fate was capricious and that, while a grandniece might wake one morning to find her fortune made, the others still had to make their own way. They went off as the crow flies, to peck what little they could elsewhere.

Voltaire Breaks a Lance Against l'Infâme

Voltaire's anti-Christian sentiments grew more and more bitter during the years he spent at Ferney. The reasons why he grew more violent rather than more peaceful with age were probably partly personal and partly a reflection of the changing mood of contemporary society. Personally, he knew that the prolongation of his exile was due more to priests than to ministers of state. Ministers came and went, their zeal was often capricious and their memories short for anything that did not directly concern their own interests. On the other hand the clergy's memory was much more tenacious. Nor must it be forgotten that after 1750 the persecution of impiety became harsher and intolerance was more easily aroused: religion was losing ground, and for that reason the clergy became more cantankerous and more dangerous. The courts of the eighteenth century dealt more severely with impiety than those of the seventeenth. The tortures inflicted on Calas were a sort of provocation to the spirit of the age. The attacks of the *philosophes* in turn became more uncompromising: "fanaticism" and "superstition" now clearly meant Christianity. *L'Infâme* became a term used frequently in philosophical circles. How could Voltaire resist this current of ideas to which he himself had contributed so much? In 1759 Frederick, mincing no words, wrote him reproaching him for his moderation: "You caress *l'Infâme* with one hand and scratch it with the other. You treat it as you treat me and everyone else." There was a certain amount of truth in this. Voltaire was an insolent and rebellious son of the Church, who had attacked her but not killed her. He behaved toward the Church as he behaved toward medicine: he called doctors ignoramuses but stuffed himself with pills and potions and followed the most farfetched treatments they prescribed. His war cry was *"Ecrasez l'Infâme* [Crush the Beast]," and he signed his letters Monsieur Ecrelinf (*Ecrasez l'Inf*âme), to the bewilderment of those who intercepted his correspondence. But in Voltaire's view "it is not a question of preventing our footmen from going to mass or hearing a sermon, but of rescuing fathers of families from the tyrannical clutches of impostors, and fostering a spirit of tolerance." Religion was necessary for the common people. "In my opinion the greatest service one can render the human race is to separate the stupid mob from decent people forever. It is insufferable impertinence for anyone to say, 'I want you to think the same as your tailor and your washerwoman,'" he wrote to D'Argental in 1765. Voltaire's ideas were very far removed from those of the egalitarian Jean-Jacques. Thanking Monsieur de La Chalotais for his *Essai d'education nationale (Essay on National Education)*, Voltaire said:

"I thank you for forbidding laborers to study. As one with fields to till, I ask you to supply workmen, not tonsured clerks. Above all send me unschooled brethren to drive and harness my plows."

Even allowing for jest, Voltaire's position is clear enough. His friend Damilaville considered it unphilosophical and maintained that true philosophy should support popular education. Voltaire replied, "I doubt whether that class of citizens will ever have the time to be educated: they would die of hunger before they became philosophers."

It was good sense, not inhumanity, that made him take this view. He was convinced that only a dreamer could imagine it possible to educate people bowed down by poverty. The standard of living in the eighteenth century was still very low; famine existed even in France. Even at Ferney, Voltaire's first care was to provide his peasants with bread, work, sanitary housing and drinking water, not schools. We may find his vocabulary shocking when he refers to the "rabble," though he was much more violent when it came to courts and parlements. But in the eighteenth century popular education was something that might be dreamed of but not put into practice. Voltaire was no dreamer; he even thought, rightly or wrongly, that dreaming was a waste of time, and believed that utopianism hampered progress. He knew that humanity was advancing, but it was doing so slowly, cautiously, and not in a straight line.

But a certain Monsieur Linguet, expecting agreement when he maintained that popular education would be fatal to society, drew down a reply which shows once again how subtle and carefully weighed Voltaire's thought was. He quoted the example of Geneva, where the people could read and yet society was in a healthier state than in France. "No, monsieur, all isn't lost when the people are allowed to perceive that they have a mind. On the contrary, all is lost when they are treated like a herd of bulls: sooner or later they will attack you with their horns."

Frederick's criticism of his treatment of *l'Infâme* would appear to have touched Voltaire on a raw spot. At all events he sought a pretext for reopening hostilities. He remembered that Thiériot had obtained for him a manuscript by Jean Meslier, a country priest who had died in 1733 and who had continued to perform his clerical duties after he had lost his faith, out of fear of poverty and the reprisals of his superiors. Before he died he wrote an atheistic, communistic, and revolutionary confession. Voltaire was chiefly interested in his arguments against Christianity and the Scriptures, and made use of them in 1762 in a pamphlet entitled *Extrait des sentiments de Jean Meslier* (*Extract from the Opinions of Jean Meslier*). He was very proud of his discovery of Meslier's confession and the use he had made of it. He wrote to D'Alembert: "All who read it are convinced: here is a man who proves and discusses. He speaks at death's door, when even liars tell the truth—it is the strongest of all arguments. . . . Jean Meslier ought to convert the entire world. . . ." Voltaire's argument as to the truth of deathbed verities was one that the

Church itself often used to its advantage in the case of deathbed recon-
versions. But Voltaire was carried away with enthusiasm: "How lukewarm
you are in Paris!" he went on. "You leave the light under a bushel basket."
He did not think the Encyclopedist set enough store by his Meslier.
D'Alembert replied: "You blame us for being lukewarm, but as I believe
I have already told you, fear of the stake has a very cooling effect." He
reminded the master of Ferney, safe between his two frontiers, that
moderation was more effective than an excess of zeal, and that it was not
desirable to reveal truth, any more than light, too suddenly to eyes
accustomed to the dark. In short, he attacked Voltaire with his own
weapons: "The human race is more enlightened today only because wise
men have taken care to enlighten it little by little. If the sun shone suddenly into a cave, the inhabitants would notice only that it hurt their
eyes."

But Voltaire did not take D'Alembert's sermon on the virtue of prudence to heart. The pamphlet had been written: he was eager for it to appear in print and be read. He was ready to risk the stake in order that
Meslier should unleash controversy. He knew D'Alembert only too well:
"He is bold but not daring; he was born to make hypocrites tremble but
not to give them a hold over him." The *Extrait des sentiments de Jean
Meslier* was published at the beginning of 1762, and his friend Damilaville
received his copy on February 4. Damilaville may not have been a great
thinker, but he was an independent one. He possessed both unshakable
philosophical convictions and a great admiration for Voltaire. Moreover,
since 1760 he had been the director of an important tax office, which
gave him the right to use the ministerial seal for his letters and parcels.
While Voltaire always tried to help his friends, he also expected them to
help him, and it was very useful to him that one of them had the means
of circulating letters, books, and pamphlets out of reach of the censor-
ship. Diderot and other Encyclopedists made use of the same protection.
But despite Damilaville's influence, the Parlement of Paris condemned the
book to be burned. Rome condemned it on February 8, 1765.

A few months later a new pamphlet was circulating: *Le Sermon des
cinquante (The Sermon of the Fifty)*. Damilaville received a copy in
July. As the author was unknown, Voltaire was free to praise the book.
He wrote to Damilaville: "The *Sermon of the Fifty* is attributed to La
Mettrie, Dumarsais, and a famous prince who is very learned; it is altogether edifying. There are twenty copies of these two small works in the
little corner of the world where I live. They have caused a great stir.
Four or five people at Versailles possess copies of these holy books. I myself have contrived to get hold of two, and I find them altogether edifying."

The pamphlet was an out-and-out attack on the Scriptures, on the very
foundation of the Judaeo-Christian religion. Soon afterward religion was
dealt another blow by the appearance of Rousseau's *Le Vicaire savoyard;*

an even more telling blow than Voltaire's keen dart. It has been said that Voltaire was jealous of it, but there is no evidence for this. He wrote to the Marquis d'Argens: "In the third volume of his *Emile* he [Rousseau] introduces a Savoyard vicar who was no doubt vicar to the curé Jean Meslier. This vicar attacks the Christian religion with great eloquence and wisdom." In 1764, when he was at sword's point with Rousseau, he wrote of the latter: "His vicar may do good . . . but the poor fellow himself is impossible. Oh, how we would have cherished this madman had he not been a treacherous brother, and what a fool he was to insult the only people who were capable of forgiving him."

The Other Pompignan Is Dealt with Like His Brother

Le Franc de Pompignan, with whom Voltaire had crossed swords some years earlier, had a brother, Jean-Georges, who was Bishop of Le Puy. In 1763 he published a long and pedantic pastoral letter, far above the heads of his flock of simple mountain folk, in which he attacked Locke and Newton and compared Voltaire unfavorably to Rousseau as a philosopher. All this was at a time when Voltaire and Rousseau were quarreling bitterly, and both philosophers fell into the trap. Rousseau was imprudent enough to thank the bishop: "Of all my antagonists the most moderate and self-respecting is Monsieur the Bishop of Le Puy. There is a man who speaks sincerely. . . . I have been truly edified by his charity and good faith." In fact all the bishop had said with reference to Voltaire was: "One must not expect of his poetic genius the same logical sequence of ideas and the same profundity as Jean-Jacques Rousseau is capable of displaying in his works."

To show how capable *he* was of logical argument, Voltaire wrote his *Lettre d'un Quaker à J.-G. de Pompignan, évêque du Puy* (*Letter from a Quaker to J.-G. de Pompignan, Bishop of Le Puy*), which appeared in 1764. The Quaker of the title was a meek Christian, naïve, pure, and evangelical. But he was very well informed, and he wrote like Voltaire. He remonstrated with the bishop for wishing to show off his erudition to his humble flock and succeeding only in playing the fool. "And when follies are committed," the Quaker went on, "they are perpetuated by slander. Charity and reason are both lost: one loses one's soul by making oneself the butt of people's laughter. Ah, brother! If only I could help you to be converted, to become moderate and modest as you ought rightly to be, to save yourself from mockery in this world and damnation in the next."

The Quaker pointed out the absurdity of talking about Locke and Newton to the shepherds of the Le Puy diocese: "We are all the more astonished because these two Englishmen are no better known to the inhabitants of Le Velay than to Monseigneur himself. To conclude, after moral sin the thing a bishop ought to be most careful to avoid is ridicule.

It is rather too ambitious an enterprise to try to write against the entire age in which one lives."

Perhaps the Church and the authorities thought the bishop deserved something to make up for all this. He was appointed to the see of Vienne on the Rhône, after having become a near celebrity because of Voltaire.

Voltaire came close to paying dearly for all this. The Pompignans had brothers who were army officers, and one of them, enraged at having the family name held up to ridicule, announced that on his next leave he would make a point of coming to Geneva to cut off the ears of the "patriarch" of Lac Leman. Voltaire immediately appealed to Choiseul: "Monseigneur, I know not what I have done to the brothers Pompignan; the one offends my ears and the other wants to cut them off. Protect me, monseigneur, against the assassin; I will take care of the other one, for I need both my ears to hear the echoes of your fame."

One day his Geneva bookseller, Cramer, came to see him at Les Délices. Voltaire was about to read Cramer a piece on valor that he had just written when his guest happened to mention that he had noticed a French officer going about the town clinking his spurs and stroking his mustaches. At this Cramer noticed his host begin to tremble. Madame Denis and the footmen came running and were told to lock all the doors. Cramer's orders were to go back to Geneva and spread the news that Voltaire had died suddenly.

All this was done. Meanwhile, Madame Denis, on making discreet inquiries, learned that the French officer was a Monsieur de l'Espine on his way to Avignon.

As an offering of thanksgiving for his sudden "resurrection," Voltaire wrote *Saül*, a violent attack on the Old Testament. This time it was no longer a question of mixing bitterness with suavity: the pamphlet was written with outright ferocity. Young Goethe, then still a believer, read it and was appalled: "I remember," he wrote, "that in my childish fanaticism I would have strangled Voltaire for his *Saül* if I could have laid hands on him."

Voltaire thought it prudent to disclaim *Saül*, like the other pamphlets. To his nephew D'Hornoy he referred to it as "some burlesque or other entitled *Saül et David*, vilely drawn from Holy Writ and said to be by certain English rogues who have no more respect for the Old Testament than for our navy."

But he did not conceal from Damilaville his satisfaction at the effect *Saül* had produced: "The older I become, the more implacable I become toward *l'Infâme*." This had been amply proved by his three most recent pamphlets, of which the last was by far the most violent.

But before too long Voltaire's violence abated somewhat and became less overt. In 1762 the Jesuits had been driven out of France. Voltaire and the *philosophes* saw this as a victory, and had uttered cries of joy. Voltaire applauded at first but then he changed his mind. Between him and the Society of Jesus there had long been sentimental bonds and affinities of thought and taste. The various quarrels and even the rupture with the *Journal de Trévoux* had never been able to efface what was indestructible. On March 2, 1763, he wrote to the Marquis d'Argental, on the subject of the expulsion of the Jesuits: "I am not certain whether it is such a good thing; those who take their place will think themselves obliged to affect more austerity and pedantry. Nothing could have been fiercer and more acrimonious than the Huguenots, because they wanted to fight against the relaxation of morals."

This mistrust of the recently converted zealots came to the fore again in a little fable called *Les Renards et les loups* (*The Foxes and the Wolves*), in which he expresses regret for the foxes and apprehension concerning the narrow-mindedness and ferocity of the wolves. He was probably thinking of his brother Armand, the Jansenist. In short, his feelings with regard to the expulsion of the Jesuits were very complex, and perhaps could best be summed up by the old saw: Better the devil you know than the devil you don't.

In this, paradoxically, he agreed with Rousseau, who said the Jansenists needed only to become masters to prove themselves harsher and more intolerant than their enemies.

Three fleeing Jesuit fathers, of whom one was Spanish, presented themselves at Ferney. Voltaire laughingly inquired whether they wanted to be taken on as footmen, and the Spanish one said yes. According to a letter from Voltaire to Damilaville, he made them apostatize in his drawing room, asking them: "Do you renounce all the privileges, all the bulls, all the ridiculous or dangerous opinions that the laws of the State condemn? Do you swear never to obey your general or the Pope when obedience to them would be contrary to the interests and orders of the King? Do you swear that you are citizens before you are Jesuits? And do you swear without mental reservations?" Voltaire reported that they all answered each of these questions in the affirmative, and he conceded that they were innocent for the present, but for their past sins he sentenced them to be stoned on the tomb of Antoine Arnauld, the great leader of the Jansenists. The joke over, he helped them and sent them on their way.

The following year, 1764, Voltaire took in Father Adam, a Jesuit professor from Dijon whom he had known slightly at Colmar. Voltaire did not take him seriously, saying of him, even in his presence: "Here is Adam, the first and last of men." On February 12 he wrote: "I nearly forgot to tell you we have a Jesuit who says mass for us, a sort of Hebrew I took in after the transmigrations from Babylon. He is not the slightest trouble, plays chess very well, and says mass in a most proper fashion; in short, he is a Jesuit whom a philosopher can get along with."

It was for chess rather than mass that Voltaire kept Father Adam on at

Ferney for thirteen years. But though Voltaire pretended not to mind that the priest was better at the game than he was, he really hated losing. "But I love chess, I love it passionately, and Father Adam, who is a fool, beats me at it all the time, without mercy! There are limits to everything. Why is Father Adam the first man in the world at chess for me? Why am I the very last of men in the world at chess for him? There are limits to everything." Especially to Voltaire's patience. Father Adam tried to lose. When it appeared that he was bound to be beaten at a game, Voltaire would start to hum a little tune that made the priest tremble with fright. More than once he took flight, pelted with chessmen that stuck in his wig, and someimes took refuge in a closet to escape a hail of blows from Voltaire's cane. Then the storm would quickly blow over, Voltaire would call out: *"Adam ubi es?"* Adam would reappear, and all would be forgiven.

Father Adam also kept visitors company and showed them around the estate. He did Voltaire another more substantial favor as well. Voltaire was having great difficulty obtaining repayment of a huge mortgage loan he had made to the Duke of Württemberg. The duke showered his creditor with politenesses but nothing more, and finally Voltaire grew worried about his money. But how was a reigning duke to be made to pay up? Voltaire remembered that his debtor was very devout and much influenced by his Jesuit confessor. Father Adam was therefore urged to write to his fellow Jesuit and point out that Voltaire was not as irreligious as people claimed, for he had given him shelter at Ferney when everyone else was driving the Jesuits away. The priest promised to write and have the confessor hint to the duke that it was his Catholic duty to pay his debt; in return Voltaire promised to go to mass. The details of these delicate negotiations are not known, though their result is: the duke gave Voltaire his money back.

But when Father Adam reminded his benefactor of his promise, Voltaire the philosopher had forgotten what Voltaire the financier had said, and Father Adam had to go on celebrating mass without him.

A more outspoken ornament of the Ferney household was a Swiss woman named Barbara, very hard-working, very bold, and with the greatest scorn for her master's reputed cleverness. She used to wonder how there could possibly be so many fools in the world as those who came all the way to Ferney to see a man without an ounce of common sense. Voltaire was highly amused by her scoldings.

XIII

A religion whose most essential ceremonies require bread and wine, however sublime, however divine it may be, will not succeed at the outset in a country where wine and wheat are unknown. (*Historical Miscellanea.* "Commentary on *The Spirit of the Laws*")

A hanged man is good for nothing, but a man condemned to public labor continues to serve the fatherland and provides a living lesson. (*Philosophical Dictionary:* "Laws")

Let the public welfare be the supreme law; such is the fundamental maxim of nations; but the welfare of the people is made to consist of slaughtering some of the citizens in all civil wars. (*Philosophical Dictionary:* "Government")

Who is a persecutor? It is he whose wounded pride and furious fanaticism arouse the prince or the magistrates against innocent men who have committed no other crime than the failure to share his opinion. (*Philosophical Dictionary:* "Persecution")

As Caesar put it well: "With money one has soldiers, and with soldiers one steals money." (*Philosophical Dictionary:* "War")

There is no civilized nation in which laws made to protect innocence have not been sometimes used to oppress it. (*Politics and Legislation:* The Trial of General Lally-Tollendal)

I note every day that work constitutes man's life. Society amuses and dissipates us. Work concentrates the powers of the soul and makes one happy. (Letter to the Abbé d'Olivet, 1763)

It was my destiny to be crushed, persecuted, vilified, sneered at —and to laugh at so being. (Letter to D'Argental, April 1764)

The older one gets, the saying goes, the more hardhearted one becomes; that may be true of ministers of state, bishops, and monks; but it is quite false in the case of those who find their happiness in the delights of good company and the duties of life. (Letter to Madame du Deffand, 1765)

Someone has said that glory resides at the top of a mountain; eagles fly up to it and reptiles crawl. (Letter, 1765)

One of the great defects held against the French nation is that the men of merit whom it has produced have almost always been oppressed or demeaned and miserable wretches have been favored instead. (Letter, 1765)

If nature had not given me two excellent antidotes, the love of work and gaiety, I would long since have died of despair. (Letter to D'Argental, April 1767)

I know of nothing so ridiculous as a doctor who does not die of old age. (Letter, November 6, 1767)

All systems having to do with the way we have come into the world have been destroyed by each other. It is only the way we make love that has never changed. (Letter, September 15, 1768)

Philosophes will end up by causing everything that priests have stolen from princes to be given back to them; but princes will nonetheless put *philosophes* in the Bastille, as we kill the oxen that have plowed our lands. (Letter to D'Alembert, 1768)

It is necessary to keep the belly constantly clear in order for the head to be clear. Our immortal soul needs the water closet in order to think well. (Letter, 1769)

Nature is like those great princes who count the loss of four hundred thousand men as nothing, provided that they carry out their august designs. (*Philosophical Tales:* "The Man with Forty Crowns")

By 1763 Ferney was on the way to becoming a sort of luxury caravanserai where the elite of Europe dropped in to stay for a visit, with or without invitation.

What is surprising is that Voltaire was able to bear not only the expense but also the fatigue and loss of time that this constant stream of visitors entailed. But, like many people of that century, he loved society, with all the conversation, hospitality, pomp, and show that entertaining it involved. But the society at Ferney was an elite one. Visitors were allowed in on the basis of their place in the social hierarchy, first of all, and then by a process of selection even more rigorous than that of birth. People with great names or reputations or, failing those, letters of introduction were let in. Otherwise the porters did their duty and kept them out. Nevertheless, worthy visitors were sometimes so numerous that Voltaire was exhausted; yet he always made a point of receiving those who had a right to be received. That was the proper way to behave. One of the secrets of Voltaire's amazing celebrity was that he embodied perfectly what the best of his contemporaries expected of the most civilized and intelligent man of their age.

But all this adulation kept him from working. As a safeguard, he resorted to a system that was not new but which he brought to perfection at Ferney. From 1764 on he decided not to appear at dinner. He was very willing to feed his guests but not to share his own time and energies with them. Madame Denis therefore willingly reigned over the dining table, while Voltaire, safe in his room out of the cold and the noise, worked or nursed his ailments. When he went into the salon to find an unexpected new arrival he would flee to his room, crying, "God deliver me from my friends. I'll take care of my enemies myself." When an importunate visitor was announced he would exclaim, "Quick, some Tronchin!" This meant that the unwelcome guest was to be told he was ill, closeted with his doctor, and unable to see visitors. His ruses were well known and did not always work. One day some English people arrived, very well recommended: he agreed to feed and lodge them but not to see them. But they had made the journey for that very purpose. They were told he was ill but insisted on seeing him nonetheless. "Tell them I'm at death's door!" he cried in exasperation. But they wanted to see him even if he was breathing his last. "Tell them I'm dead!" They wanted to see the body. "Tell them the Devil has carried me off!" Whereupon they were admitted and hastened to his room, for it was the Devil they had come to see.

There were certain intruders who had to be treated politely, even if Voltaire was really in Tronchin's hands: the Duc de Lorge and the Duc de Randon for instance, who installed themselves at Ferney with their own actors, to act in the little theater. In order to protect himself, Voltaire heroically decided to close the theater and convert it into an apartment.

In the midst of all these comings and goings, the Calas affair, and skirmishes with Pompignan and Rousseau, he was ill as always. Yet on many days when he was confined to his bed he wrote up to forty letters to his friends or business associates.

He continued to write plays, though the fortunes of the theater at Ferney declined somewhat. On the advice of the D'Argentals he rewrote *Olympie* and finally after tryouts at Ferney it was performed in Paris on March 17, 1764. There were neither boos nor curtain calls. Public taste had changed since 1730: neoclassic posturing was becoming passé. He nonetheless turned to yet another subject drawn from antiquity, the Roman Triumvirate, which Crébillon had already treated. Voltaire did not put his name to the play and had it attributed to Poisinet, a mediocre and obscure poetaster who strongly protested. The tragedy was put on at the Comédie Française on July 5, 1764, under the title of *Octave et le jeune Pompée* (*Octavius and Young Pompey*). The public did not conceal its boredom, but Voltaire, nothing daunted, rewrote it, promising a masterpiece.

His own failed tragedies had not prevented him from writing his famous *Commentaires* on Corneille and seeing to its publication with his usual care. He was generous toward the great dramatist, whom he admired, but, as he wrote to the Abbé Voisenon in 1763, "I confess that commenting on Corneille makes me worship Racine. I cannot bear bombast and unnatural grandeur." He was aware that a new style of theater was dawning—a style that would one day come to be known as Romanticism.

Meanwhile, Corneille's grandniece gave birth to a daughter whom Voltaire called either Chimen-Marmotte or Rodogune. Like her mother, she was dark-skinned, with brown hair. The Chevalier de Boufflers, the son of Voltaire's old friend Madame de Boufflers, was also among the prominent visitors to Ferney. He was just eighteen, and endowed with every possible gift: he was handsome, amiable, clever, and full of imagination, energy, and gaiety. He was excellent at drawing and wrote poetry—in short, a spellbinder, and Voltaire's ideal of a perfect human being.

Because of his mother he was welcomed with open arms. Voltaire treated him as an equal, and the first thing that struck young Boufflers was his host's simplicity and lack of affectation, though he was not insensible to the luxury and generosity of his welcome. Boufflers was traveling without pomp and circumstance, in order to get to know the country and the people. He sometimes pretended to be a traveling portraitist and paid for the hospitality he received by doing drawings of the ladies who dispensed it. He also paid court to them and noted that the strait-laced ladies of Switzerland put up a merely formal resistance. Voltaire liked to get Boufflers to talk of his experiences and asked him one day what opinion he formed of the Swiss. His guest replied: "They are a people purported to have a good deal of money and a good deal of wit, but they never display either the one or the other."

He also drew a portrait of the baby, who according to Voltaire was more like a *corneille* with a small *c* (i.e., a crow) than with a capital C.

Boufflers wrote of his host to his mother: "You can have no idea of the expense he goes to or the good he does. He is the king and father of the region he lives in, the happiness of those about him, and as good a family man as he is a poet. . . . Whatever prodigies his publishers produce, he will always be the best edition of his works. . . . For the rest, the house is charming, the situation superb, the fare exquisite, and my apartments delightful."

In Madame Cramer, the Parisian wife of the Geneva bookseller, Boufflers found a perfect companion for his leisures. The evenings at Ferney sparkled with gaiety, and in Boufflers Madame Cramer, who found Geneva dull, rediscovered Paris, youth, wit, grace, and love. That winter of 1764 was the last summer of her life.

The chevalier did a drawing of Voltaire—no easy matter, as he was never still and as difficult to pin down physically as spiritually. But the subject had intrigued the artist, who would have liked to stay with Voltaire at Ferney forever. He wrote to his mother: "You cannot imagine how charming he is at home. He would be the dearest old fellow in the world were he not the greatest of men. His one fault is he is very reserved."

Age did not enter into this extraordinary friendship: what mattered was wit, refinement of feeling, and exquisite manners.

The Prince de Ligne came to Ferney during the summer of 1763. Voltaire did not know him, and though there could be no question of turning away so distinguished a visitor, Voltaire did take the precaution of going to bed after downing a purge. He later confessed to the prince that he was so afraid of being bored by unknown visitors that he would gulp down some medicine before receiving them, so that if necessary he had an excuse for ending the interview.

But Voltaire and the prince got on famously. The prince pronounced Madame Dupuits, Corneille's grandniece, "nigra" [dark-skinned] but not "formosa" [beautiful], but found her sister-in-law, Mademoiselle Dupuits, so charming that his attention wandered from Voltaire's conversation to her décolletage. Voltaire hated this kind of inattention, and one hot day, when his guest's interest strayed to the charms of the buxom Swiss maids who were serving cream, Voltaire leaped up, laid hands on the snowy curves of the nearest enchantress, and cried, "Nothing but bosoms, bosoms, all over the place! Clear out of here!" Then he calmly came and sat down again by the prince, whose attention was now back where it belonged. The Prince de Ligne supplies the best portrait we have of Voltaire at this period: "He always wore gray slippers, iron-gray stockings, with the tops rolled down, a large cotton damask jacket down to the knees, a great long wig, and a little black velvet cap. Sometimes on Sundays he would put on a fine bronze-colored suit with coat and breeches to match, but the coat had wide skirts, gold braid, scallops, and embroidery, with lace cuffs down to his finger tips; he said such a costume made one look distinguished."

It was a costume that belonged to 1725 rather than 1764, and his huge bob wigs also dated from the Regency.

The prince observed that almost without exception Voltaire's conversation was good-natured: affectionate toward those around him, complimentary, agreeable, and amusing, and enhancing any subject it lighted on.

One day he mistook the harpsichord tuner who had come to see to Madame Denis's instrument for the shoemaker. When he realized his error he flushed and said, "Ah, monsieur, you are very gifted. I was putting you at my feet, when I am really at yours."

The prince found Voltaire's interviews with his tenants irresistibly comic: he talked to the peasants as though they were ambassadors. Instead of asking his gamekeeper straight out why there had been no hare served at his table lately, he said, "My friend, is there no further animal migration now from my estate at Tournay to my estate at Ferney?" He was ready to talk to anyone, and introduced his inimitable touches of wit into even the most common conversation. According to the prince, he was "inclined to see and believe in the beautiful and the good, convinced of them himself and convincing others."

He found wit in the remarks of others even where it may have been unintentional. One day he inquired of a visitor what his religion was, and the visitor replied: "My parents brought me up as a Catholic."

"A good answer," Voltaire exclaimed. "He doesn't say he is one."

At the time of the prince's visit Voltaire was angry, and with reason, with the Parlements and their unruly chief magistrates, and when he met his donkey browsing about the grounds he used to say, "After you, Monsieur le Président."

The prince also witnessed another amusing scene when a stranger wormed his way into the salon one day and tried to force Voltaire to buy some gray slippers. Voltaire tried to get rid of him, but the man persisted, crying, "Monsieur! Monsieur! I am the son of a woman for whom you once wrote verses."

"I can well believe it," Voltaire answered, making for his study. "I have written verses for so many women."

The stranger ran after him.

"Monsieur! Monsieur! It was Madame de Fontaine-Martel."

Voltaire halted in his tracks.

"Ah yes! She was very beautiful."

The man pursued his advantage.

"Monsieur, how did you acquire the exquisite taste I see exemplified all around me? Your house is charming."

Voltaire came back into the salon.

"It is, isn't it? I drew up all the designs myself. Do you see this staircase . . ." And he proudly pointed out other details.

"Monsieur, do you know what brought me to Switzerland?" the intruder asked. "Monsieur Haller."

Voltaire, of course, could not bear to hear Haller's name. He turned and made for his study again. His visitor, realizing he had lost his potential customer's attention, said quickly:

"Oh, monsieur, what a lot of money this must have cost you. And what a charming garden!"

Voltaire pricked up his ears once more and came back into the salon.

"I did it all myself," he said. "My gardener is an idiot."

"I can believe it. You know, sir, Monsieur Haller is a great man."

Voltaire turned on his heel once more.

"Oh, monsieur, tell me, how long does it take to build a fine house like this?"

The slipper-seller had found the right tack to take, and eventually made the sale.

The prince said that Voltaire was the most amusing friend in the world. But he also paid more serious tribute to the superior being who "made those who were capable of so doing talk and think; gave help to the unfortunate, built houses for poor families and was a kind master in his own. A good man in his village, a good man and a great one as well, a combination without which no one is ever completely the one or the other, for genius gives more scope to goodness and goodness more warmth and naturalness to genius."

Mademoiselle Clairon came to Ferney too, and the theater was reopened in her honor. She had come in order to consult Dr. Tronchin, and he said he would not answer for the consequences if she went on acting. But she acted for Voltaire, who was ill himself, almost dying, on the day of her arrival. He looked like a skeleton, lying there in bed buried in furs. Appalled, she tried to rally his spirits by reciting a speech from *L'Orphelin de la Chine,* and the skeleton stirred, sat up, wept, and began to recite too. It was so strange a scene that the other people present could not help laughing.

At that he lay down again and sulked.

But soon after, although suffering from a severe attack of sciatica, he insisted on making an appearance in the salon. He came in on crutches, supported by a lady on either side, his head drooping down on one shoulder. He was placed in an armchair and the conversation began without him. But soon he came alive and began to take part, made everyone else come alive, and suddenly sprang out of his chair, his crutches in his hand, and began to mime and dance about with the lightness and ease of a born actor. The general laughter reminded him of his sciatica, and he leaned on his crutches again, groaned, and begged to be put carefully back in his chair.

Tronchin tells how one day in 1722 he met a thin young man whose face made an impression on him. When someone asked the young man how he was he answered, "Always ill, but still ticking." The young man's name was Voltaire, Tronchin learned, and those were the first words he heard from this eternal invalid who was to be his patient for nearly sixty years.

The meeting at Ferney with Mademoiselle Clairon became famous because of an engraving that was made of it. People said that the two of them admired one another so much, they used to fall on their knees and embrace one another. But these effusions must have been rare, for if Voltaire could get down on his knees he could no longer get up from them. One day he fell down and had to be helped to his feet. That was just like Voltaire—sublime one moment and a character straight out of a farce the next. One day someone found him stuck in the mud with his crutches in the fields, where it was his habit to go walking alone, inspecting his estate, taking the air, meditating, plotting, calculating, versifying, and singing, dreadfully out of tune. His doctor would sometimes meet him driving himself about the country in a light gig, a dangerous enterprise, for the horse was a troublesome one. One day the doctor called out, "What do you think you're doing, old boy?" That evening he received a note: "A young patient of seventy is not to be seen every day of the week. I was on my way to see you . . . but you are not to draw your usual cruel conclusion that I am well and have an iron constitution. . . . Slander me not, and love me." What one had to do to please him was throw up one's hands at his thinness and weakness, pretend he was older and more worn out than he was, weep for his sufferings and expect his end. It was a superstition with him that to pretend he was dying would prolong his life. No man was ever more delighted when his enemies pronounced his death. No man was ever sorrier to be caught enjoying good health.

In 1764 James Boswell, then twenty-four, presented himself at Ferney. On his way through Basel he put up at an inn where the landlord, Imhof, told him how Voltaire had stayed there on his return from Germany. "He said, 'Voltaire came here. He went to bed. I asked his servant, "Does your master wish any supper?" "I don't know. It all depends. Perhaps yes, perhaps no." Well, I had some good soup made, and a chicken dressed. Monsieur Voltaire wakes up; he asks for supper. I serve him the soup. He takes it. He refuses it. Then he takes it again. "It is excellent soup!" A gentleman had come in, and I gave him half the chicken. I serve the other half to Monsieur Voltaire. He takes it. He refuses it. Then he takes it again. "It is an excellent chicken!" He is annoyed because he has not a whole chicken, and keeps saying, "Half a chicken is no chicken! Half a chicken is no chicken!" In short, he was very well pleased with my house.' . . . I concluded him to be either a very honest fellow, or a very great rogue."

On his way from Basel to Môtiers to see Rousseau before going on to Geneva to see Voltaire, Boswell met a stonecutter who had worked for Voltaire and recounted an anecdote about him. "Sir, there used to be a horse that pulled a cart at Ferney, and Monsieur Voltaire always said, 'Poor horse! you are thin, you are like me.'"

He wrote in his journal: ". . . I took a coach for Ferney, the seat of the illustrious Monsieur de Voltaire. . . . The first object that struck me was his church with this inscription: 'Deo erexit Voltaire MDCCLXI."

His château was handsome. I was received by two or three footmen, who showed me into a very elegant room."

Boswell sent in his letter of introduction but was told: "Monsieur de Voltaire is very much annoyed at being disturbed. He is abed." Boswell was afraid he might not see him, but some other ladies and gentlemen entered the salon, and he stayed on with them, waiting. At last Voltaire "opened the door of his apartment, and stepped forth. . . . He received in such perfection. He had a slate-blue, fine frieze greatcoat night-gown,[1] me with dignity, and that air of the world which a Frenchman acquires and a three-knotted wig. He sat erect upon his chair, and simpered when he spoke. He was not in spirits, nor I neither."

The dressing gown had become Voltaire's uniform at Ferney. He dined, supped, and received visitors in it. As he went to bed and got up again six or seven times a day, it simplified matters.

They spoke of Scotland, and Boswell told of the new Academy of Painting in Glasgow, observing that his native land was no country for that art. "No," Voltaire replied, "to paint well it is necessary to have warm feet."

Boswell mentioned his plan to make a tour through the Hebrides with Dr. Johnson. Boswell reports that Voltaire smiled, and cried, "Very well; but I shall remain here. You will allow me to stay here?" "Certainly." "Well then, go. I have no objections at all."

Asked if he still spoke English, Voltaire replied that he did not. "To speak English one must place the tongue between the teeth, and I have lost my teeth."

One afternoon after a dinner at which Voltaire was not present, everyone returned to the drawing room. "Some sat snug by the fire, some chatted, some sung, some played the guitar, some played at shuttlecock. . . . It was dull to find how much this resembled any other house in the country. . . ." He repaired to Father Adam's room, where he heard sung "the praises of Monsieur de Voltaire's good actions in private life: how he entertains his friends and strangers of distinction, how he has about fifty people in his château, as his servants marry and have children, and how the village upon his manor is well taken care of."

Between seven and eight there came a message that Voltaire was in the drawing room. Boswell stood by Voltaire as he played chess. "He spoke sometimes English and sometimes French. He gave me a sharp reproof for speaking fast. 'How fast you foreigners speak!' 'We think that the French do the same.' 'Well, at any rate, *I* don't. I speak slowly, that's what I do'; and this he said with a most keen tone."

By suppertime Voltaire "had got into great spirits," and Boswell stayed with him when the rest of the guests went to eat; "and so I had this great man for about an hour and a half at a most interesting tête-à-tête."

Despite Voltaire's polite apologies for the accommodations offered, Boswell found that his room was a handsome one. "The bed, purple cloth lined with white quilted satin; the chimney-piece, marble, and ornamented above with the picture of a French toilet."

The next day Boswell heard "part of a mass" in Voltaire's church. His host was ill that day and did not appear before dinner. Boswell repaired to his room and read *Mahomet*. "A good, decent, trusty servant had fire and wax candles and all in order for me. There is at Ferney the true hospitality. All are master of their rooms and do as they please."

In a letter written to his friend William Johnson Temple, Boswell described his conversation with Voltaire. "He was all brilliance. He gave me continued flashes of wit. I got him to speak English, which he does in a degree that made me now and then start up and cry, 'Upon my soul this is astonishing!' When he talked our language he was animated with the soul of a Briton. He had bold flights. He had humour. He had an extravagance; he had a forcible oddity of style that the most comical of our *dramatis personae* could not have exceeded. He swore bloodily, as was the fashion when he was in England. . . .

"Then he talked of our Constitution with a noble enthusiasm. I was proud to hear this from the mouth of an illustrious Frenchman. At last we came upon religion. Then did he rage. The company went to supper. Monsieur de Voltaire and I remained in the drawing-room with a great Bible before us; and if ever two mortal men disputed with vehemence, we did. . . . The daring bursts of his ridicule confounded my understanding. He stood like an orator of ancient Rome. Tully was never more agitated than he was. He went too far. His aged frame trembled beneath him. He cried, 'Oh, I am very sick; my head turns round,' and he let himself gently fall upon an easy chair. He recovered. I resumed our conversation, but changed the tone. . . .

"I demanded of him an honest confession of his real sentiments. He gave it me with candour and with a mild eloquence which touched my heart. . . . He expressed his veneration—his love—of the Supreme Being, and his entire resignation to the will of Him who is All-wise. He expressed his desire to resemble the Author of Goodness by being good himself. His sentiments go no farther. He does not inflame his mind with grand hopes of the immortality of the soul. He says it may be, but he knows nothing of it. And his mind is in perfect tranquillity. I was moved; I was sorry. I doubted his sincerity. I called to him with emotion, 'Are you sincere? are you really sincere?' He answered, 'Before God, I am.' Then with the fire of him whose tragedies have so often shone on the theatre of Paris, he said, 'I suffer much. But I suffer with patience and resignation; not as a Christian—but as a man.' "

After leaving Ferney, Boswell wrote in his journal: "I departed from this château in a most extraordinary humour, thinking hard, and wondering if I could possibly, when again in Scotland, again feel my most childish prejudices."

Voltaire's relations with his neighbors in Geneva had improved. No one tried to pick quarrels with him now over his theater: all the best people were on his side. The pastors were still hostile, but he had appeased them by disowning *La Henriade*, even though he had never acknowledged that he was the author of it. He had also disowned *Candide*, which he had also never owned up to having written. This is what he thought of the pastors: "There are only a handful of scoundrels in Calvin's city who still believe in consubstantiation. People think openly, as in London. 'You know what' is scoffed at." "You know what" was the divinity of Christ. While the Genevans were as eager to "*écraser l'Infâme*" as Voltaire, they had not yet gone that far.

It was not his views on religion but rather his long-smoldering quarrel with Rousseau that was to cause trouble between Voltaire and some of the citizens of Geneva. When *Emile* was sentenced to be burned and Rousseau was exiled from Geneva on June 18, 1762, he was convinced, and loudly maintained, that Voltaire was behind his being banished from the city. This was not so, however; the verdict of Geneva came after a similar one in Paris. Voltaire was very much upset by this slander: he had been persecuted himself—would he act as accomplice to the Calvinists against Jean-Jacques, whom he did not yet hate, and who had just been condemned by a Jansenist Parlement in Paris? The Jansenists, flushed with victory at having driven out the Jesuits, felt it their duty to show there would be no more "relaxation of morals." Rousseau was simply telling the truth when he said he had heard them say that burning books was no good—it was their authors who needed burning.

Far from being the persecuted Rousseau's enemy, Voltaire is known to have offered him a refuge. At the time of the Prince de Ligne's visit to Ferney in 1763, he had said of Rousseau: "If he cannot find shelter anywhere else, let him come here—all I have is his." He may have been slightly carried away, but these words still testify to a genuine feeling of pity and solidarity. If Rousseau had ever come to Ferney the door would have been opened to him. But Rousseau maintained at times that Voltaire had never made any such offer, at times that Voltaire had forgotten about it, that he would rather have starved than accept it. The last is the most likely to be true. There are various other witnesses to Voltaire's offer of hospitality. Deluc, who was Rousseau's friend and Voltaire's enemy, reported that Voltaire had asked him to persuade Rousseau to come and live in Ferney, where he would have a house readied for him. But Deluc and Rousseau both concluded it was a trap, though Deluc was almost convinced that the offer had been made in all sincerity.

The fact was that Voltaire was sorry for Rousseau as a man and felt a genuine admiration for him as the author of the *Vicaire savoyard*. Monsieur Végobre, a lawyer who worked for Voltaire on the Calas case, relates how he was taking coffee with Voltaire and Madame Denis when the post arrived with the news of the condemnation of *Emile*. When Voltaire opened it his face clouded over and he handed the papers to the lawyer. "Monsieur de Voltaire could not restrain himself and began to weep, and in his characteristic voice, half solemn, half sepulchral, he exclaimed several times: 'Let him come here! Let him come here! I shall welcome him with open arms. He shall be more the master than I am, and I shall treat him as though he were my own son.'" If Voltaire had despised Rousseau, as the latter maintained, there would have been no such scene. He had never wept because Fréron, or Jean-Baptiste Rousseau, or La Beaumelle, or Desfontaines, had been exiled.

It was Jean-Jacques himself who kindled Voltaire's hatred. To every advance of Voltaire's, Rousseau replied that it was in Voltaire's interest to remain on good terms with him: after *La Nouvelle Héloïse* and *Emile*, he was a literary celebrity. Of course, in the eyes of the society of their day, it was Voltaire who was the great celebrity, and he had nothing to gain by concerning himself with Rousseau. But Rousseau, in his envy and megalomania, saw it the other way about. "It is certain," he wrote, "that the best service he can render his reputation is to be reconciled with me."

In his *Lettres écrites de la montagne* (*Letters from the Mountain*), written in 1764, Rousseau again accused Voltaire of having him banished from his native country, though it was Rousseau himself who had renounced his Genevan citizenship out of resentment at being exiled. He found friends in Geneva to support him and attack Voltaire. Rousseau, a native of Geneva, a man of virtue and a believer, was persecuted, they said, whereas Voltaire, a foreigner and an atheist, was an honored guest. Why? Simply because one was rich and the other poor, they maintained. Voltaire had no difficulty in pointing out that the city had condemned *La Henriade*, *Candide*, and his theater. Whereupon Rousseau denounced *Saül* to the authorities as a heinous attack on Holy Writ, and Voltaire as its author. Violence broke out between the two factions.

Voltaire was horrified by Rousseau's denunciation and became his bitter enemy. It was the worst sort of treason, in a time of persecution, to betray a fellow author, even if he was a rival or a personal enemy, to the forces of repression. Henceforward Rousseau was the "false brother," the traitor who must be destroyed—by the worst acts of treachery if necessary. Voltaire wasted no time complaining: he wrote to the Genevans, setting aside their pious arguments about good principles and bad books, and summing up the dispute in the most practical terms: "The root of the matter," he said, "is that some of your citizens are outraged at the idea that one of them should be excluded from his native city while a foreigner owns an estate within its territory. That is the real stumbling block."

There were still many people, too, who resented the fact that a nominal Catholic had been allowed to settle in Calvin's city. Voltaire reminded the money-wise Genevans that he was French, that he had paid dearly for his estate, that his rights of ownership had been legally recognized and his money promptly naturalized. And he concluded pointedly: "No doubt this last effort of my enemies appears as contemptible to you as it does to me. I believe their little strategem would be best forgotten about. Any scandal that compromised me would oblige me to create another."

While Voltaire proposed peace he prepared for war. He was already taking up his battle position and counting his allies: the French ambassadors in Geneva and Turin, and the Duc de Choiseul, Louis XV's Prime Minister. Inside the enemy lines he could count on the Tronchins and the most important families in Geneva.

He fired the first salvo without waiting for further provocation. He had collected together a number of articles, begun in Berlin in 1752, under the title of *Dictionnaire philosophique portatif* (*Pocket Dictionary of Philosophy*). He had it printed in Amsterdam and flooded Geneva with copies. He took the precaution of advising the Consistory that a scurrilous pamphlet entitled, he believed, *Le Portatif*, was circulating at Ferney and being maliciously attributed to him. To show his good faith, he warned the Geneva authorities that a package of these pamphlets would be entering the city at such and such an hour through such and such a gate. The pamphlets were duly seized. Who would have dreamed that Voltaire was their author, and that at that very moment he was smuggling in six other packages through six other gates?

The people at Ferney were familiar with this sort of publication. The watchmakers Voltaire had brought there from Geneva even kept secret collections of them. There is a story of one pious mother who deplored her son's reading habits and took her own measures. One day she asked him how he liked the dinner she had just served him, and he said, "Very good, but very hot."

"It ought to be," she replied. "Go and see what has become of your Voltaire collection."

She had burned it.

Voltaire was furious against the informer Rousseau. "If Diogenes' dog and Erostratus' bitch had a puppy, it would be Jean-Jacques," he said. But private insults were an insufficient outlet for his spleen. In December 1764 he published *Le Sentiment des citoyens* (*The Feeling of the People*), an answer to Rousseau's *Lettres de la montagne*, in which Voltaire appears in the unexpected role of the defender of Christ and ministers of the Gospel against Jean-Jacques. "Is it right that a man born in our city should so insult our pastors, most of whom are our friends and relations and who are often our comforters?" Who was Rousseau? A scholar or a great writer? Forgetting all the rest of Jean-Jacques's celebrated works, Voltaire answered his own rhetorical question: "No! He is the author of an opera and two comedies that were hooted off the stage." Was he even a good man? "We confess with pain and shame that he is one who still bears the baleful marks of his debaucheries, and who goes like a mountebank from village to village and mountain to mountain, dragging with him the unfortunate woman whose mother he killed and whose children he abandoned on the steps of an orphanage, rejecting a charitable person's offer to look after them and thus abjuring all the sentiments of nature just as he casts aside those of men and of religion."

But what must have annoyed Rousseau most was the way Voltaire caught the tone of his adversary's own rhetoric, mimicking perfectly Jean-Jacques's humorless eloquence aimed at bringing tears to his reader's eyes.

But Voltaire went further, denouncing Rousseau not merely as the author of unwholesome novels but also as an enemy of religion and of the very foundations of society: ". . . he must be taught that, though the impious novelist may be chastised lightly, the fomenter of sedition meets with capital punishment." Voltaire, in short, turns Rousseau over to the executioner.

This pamphlet upset Rousseau terribly. He did not at first attribute it to Voltaire but to Pastor Vernet of Geneva, whom he proceeded to attack on the mere strength of his "infallible feeling." Voltaire allowed things to take their course. Rousseau continued to tear him to shreds in his correspondence and refused to yield an inch, welcoming the role of persecuted victim. "When the inquisitor Voltaire succeeds in getting me burned at the stake it will not be pleasant for me, I must admit, but you must admit that it could not be better for my cause."

"My dear Philosopher," Voltaire wrote to Pastor Bertrand in August 1764, "I have, thank God, broken off all commerce with kings." Nothing could have been further from the truth. It was quite true that since 1761 Frederick had not answered his letters: but on the other hand Voltaire was seeking the favor of the Tsarina of Russia.

When he was obliged to endure Frederick's sulks, Voltaire professed to be renouncing the vanities of this world. "I know no other life now but retirement. I leave Madame Denis to give dinners for twenty-six guests and act plays for dukes and presidents, administrators and interlopers who are here today and gone tomorrow. I climb into bed in the midst of the din and shut the door." But it was only in order to write coquettish missives to the Empress, who was in the process of replacing the flagging Solomon, whom Voltaire now described as having fallen from his graces.

The idyll with the Russian court began with Voltaire's *Histoire de Pierre le Grand* (*History of Peter the Great*). The conditions under which he was trying to write it were unfavorable: he lacked the necessary documentation. His attitude toward that ruler, on the other hand, could not have been more favorable: he was determined to make Peter even greater than he really was. Although interested, the Russians sent information only rarely, and always with discouraging delays. Voltaire went to a great deal of trouble and attained in return only an indifferent result. The book appeared in 1759 and was reprinted in 1763. When a traveler returning from Russia told him his book was full of errors, Voltaire airily replied: "My dear fellow, they gave me excellent fur cloaks and I am a very chilly mortal." Obviously he did not attach the same importance to this book as to *Le Siècle de Louis XIV*. But he was very pleased to learn that the Tsarina then on the throne, Elizabeth, Peter the Great's daughter, was satisfied. One of Frederick's last letters before the break with Voltaire showed, however, that he was very displeased to see his former philosopher-friend wasting his time on the history of a barbarian. "Luc tells me he is somewhat scandalized that I should have written the history of bears and wolves; yet in Berlin they were only bears that had been properly trained," Voltaire complained to D'Alembert.

He even complained to the Russian ambassador, Count Shuvalov: "Monsieur," he wrote on December 2, 1760, "I must trust your discretion and good will toward me when I confide to you the fact that the King of Prussia is very displeased with me for having worked at the *History of Peter the Great* and for the glory of your empire. He has written to me upbraiding me in the severest terms, and his letter deals no more kindly with your people than with their historian . . . but I trust that your august Empress, the daughter of Peter the Great, will be as pleased with this monument to her father's glory as the King of Prussia has been vexed."

There was another brush with the tyrannnical Frederick over Voltaire's dedication of *Tancrède* to the Marquise de Pompadour. The play was written between April 22 and May 18, 1759, and performed at the Comédie Française on September 3, 1760. For no justifiable reason, Frederick danced with rage when he read the dedication, and wrote Voltaire a harsh and contemptuous letter reproaching him for his platitudes and his flatteries, and reminding him of what he had said about Madame de Pompadour in *La Henriade*. Writing to D'Argens about Voltaire, Frederick said—untruthfully, for he had all the latter's movements watched: "Everything concerning him concerns me hardly at all. Let us leave the wretch to prostitute himself by the venality of his pen, the perfidy of his intrigues, and the perversity of his heart."

The Machiavellian Frederick could not bear to see Voltaire moving toward a rapprochement with Versailles, and still less to see the Tsarina taking his place. Elizabeth sent Voltaire her portrait set in diamonds. It was stolen on the way, but Voltaire valued the friendship more than the miniature. A year after this promising beginning, Elizabeth died. "I have suffered a great loss," Voltaire wrote to his niece the Marquise de Florian. He wasted no time repairing it. The Tsarina was dead; long live the new Tsarina. But one needed to be a Voltaire to reconcile the lurid intrigues of Catherine II with friendship, admiration, and lofty philosophic principles. Self-interest and vanity worked the miracle, however.

In order to ascend the throne Catherine had murdered her husband, Peter III. He was a drunkard and slightly mad, and his wife dethroned him on July 9, 1762, and had him poisoned and strangled a week later.

The philosophers in Paris reproached her as little for this as did the courts and ruling classes of Europe. She was a woman of superior intelligence, culture, and taste, and she knew Voltaire well through his books and by report. She had a special source of information in her secretary, Monsieur Pictet, a native of Geneva who had been a frequent visitor at Les Délices and had even played roles in Voltaire's theater there. She had also consulted the French ambassador at Saint Petersburg, Monsieur de Breteuil, one of Emilie's nephews, whom Voltaire had known as a child. Catherine's fertile brain gradually conceived the idea that Voltaire was the best person to enlighten Europe about her extraordinary virtues.

Pictet wrote to Voltaire hinting as much, but Voltaire, whose antennae in such situations were preternaturally sensitive, had already written to Pictet rejoicing at the fortunate concatenation of circumstances that had providentially brought Catherine to the throne. This letter somehow came to the Empress' eyes; but she was not the woman to be satisfied with mere compliments. She wanted Voltaire to launch what today we would call a press campaign in her favor at all the courts of Europe.

Receiving no reply to his first letter, which was persuasive but not explicit, Pictet wrote again. But Voltaire was in no hurry to sing the praises of a woman who had murdered her husband. And it was as well known at Ferney as everywhere else that there was a rival claimant to the throne, Ivan, who had supporters and the backing of certain classes of the Russian people. Voltaire preferred to wait and see. On August 3, 1762, he wrote to Shuvalov: "There is talk of a violent colic having delivered Peter from the slight annoyance of losing an empire of two thousand leagues. . . . I confess I have a heart sufficiently corrupt not to be as scandalized by this scene as a good Christian should be. A very great good may come out of this little evil. Providence does as the Jesuits used to do: it makes use of everything." Catherine's ambassador did not fail to inform her of Voltaire's attitude, and she knew she could count on him.

To win him over, she asked him for some tragedies to be performed by Russian noblemen at the Russian court. He was to send everything he had, even unpublished manuscripts; secrecy was guaranteed. He was won over, though he still hesitated as to whether he ought to blazon Catherine's glory all over Europe.

Meanwhile she had Ivan murdered; her throne was assured, but her reputation was ruined. Voltaire praised Catherine in his letters and conversation, but not everyone shared his opinion. "I am afraid Monsieur de Praslin does not like my Empress of Russia. I am afraid they will filch her from me, and she is the only crowned head left to me; I must have her," he wrote at the end of July 1763.

He was not the only philosopher who drew a veil over the Tsarina's crimes. D'Alembert, whom Catherine sent for, was not severe with her, though he refused her invitation. Voltaire wrote that D'Alembert would need to be an even better geometrician than he was to solve the problem presented by Catherine's court. "The Ivan Affair," he added, "was carried out in so atrocious a manner, one would have sworn it was done by believers."

To punish Catherine for the atrocity of killing Ivan, Voltaire kept her waiting six months for the *Dictionnaire philosophique portatif* that she had asked for. But that meant he went six months without a letter from the sovereign he had begun referring to as the Sémiramis of the North. "I agree that philosophy cannot boast about such pupils as she, but what is to be done? One must love one's friends with all their faults," he wrote D'Alembert. "I am her champion against all comers. I know people blame her for certain trifles about her husband, but those are family matters in which I do not meddle . . . and her nasty husband would never have done any of the great things my Catherine does every day."

When Madame du Deffand saw this letter she could hardly believe her eyes. She wrote and told Voltaire that even Peter III would have laughed at his references to "trifles" and "family matters" if he could have been brought to life again. Horace Walpole, Madame du Deffand's lover, was harsher. "Voltaire horrifies me with his Catherine. Murdering a husband is a fine thing to joke about," he wrote acidly.

"My Catherine" soon became "my Cateau" in the salon at Ferney, whence spread the legend of an enlightened, liberal, humane sovereign, kind and even sentimental, and with such free and easy ways. Walpole's opinion also spread. Many people abhorred Catherine, and Voltaire along with her.

The Duchesse de Choiseul was shocked by Voltaire's attitude toward "Cateau": "He makes her out to be as white as snow, the darling of her subjects, the glory of her empire, the admiration of the universe, the wonder of wonders." Madame du Deffand told the duchesse she had made him ashamed of his cynical toadying to a ruler he knew to be a murderess. "Let him blush for it!" cried Madame de Choiseul. It seems unlikely that her wish was granted.

When the Tsarina bought Diderot's library and gave him a pension to be the imperial librarian and custodian of his own books, Voltaire was delighted: "Did anyone ever dream that the Scythians would one day reward in Paris the virtue, learning, and philosophy so basely treated among ourselves? Illustrious Diderot, accept my transports of joy." Whatever "Cateau" did, she was right. If she enslaved the Poles, it was merely another "trifle," and the Poles had been wrong for not loving her. When she made war on the Turks, there was no torture Voltaire did not wish on the Sultan and no conquest he did not desire for her. He hinted that if he had been younger he would have gone to fight for her.

Catherine had taken it into her head to civilize her subjects, and she copied and borrowed all she could from the institutions and manners of the West. One of her ideas was to import teachers to educate the children of the Russian aristocracy. She decided on French-speaking Swiss women for this purpose, and asked Voltaire to do what he could to promote the plan with the Genevan authorities. In 1765 the Russian ambassador came to stay at Ferney to supervise the recruitment in person. A number of young women had been found who were ready, and had their parents' consent, to spread the light in Muscovy. But the Council of the Genevan Republic strictly forbade the teachers to leave and recalled those who had already set out. Voltaire was furious and appealed to the Tronchins. Dr. Tronchin sent him an uncompromising reply: "Monsieur de Voltaire, the Council regards itself as the father of all the citizens, and consequently it cannot allow its children to settle in a country whose sovereign is strongly suspected of allowing her husband to be murdered and where the most lax morals prevail unbridled."

Voltaire invoked the right of the individual to dispose of himself as he pleased, and pointed out that girls were allowed to go to France and England without opposition. The Council let his complaint go unanswered, and Catherine had to do without the teachers Voltaire had too airily promised her.

By way of compensation he sent her an unpublished tragedy that had been lying about in a drawer, for young Russian ladies to perform. It was called *Les Lois de Minos* (*The Laws of Minos*), and contained no love interest or, to tell the truth, genius. He pretended it was by an unknown but gifted young man.

While still engaged in "Catherining," as he called it, he seized an opportunity to renew relations with "Luc." Hearing that Frederick was ill, he wrote him a letter and got an answer, though not a very warm one. "I thought you were so busy crushing the Beast that you could not think of anything else," Frederick wrote. From then on letters followed one another quickly and regularly. As their relations improved, Frederick allowed himself to succumb to Voltaire's "charm" once again: ". . . there is no other old fellow in the world so agreeable as you. . . . You have kept all the gaiety and affability of your youth," he wrote. He waxed even more enthusiastic: "You create other beings wherever you live: you are the Prometheus of Geneva. If you had stayed on here, we should have been something now." That "we" is strange and moving. And what was the "something" that the apparently successful Frederick found lacking? "A fatality that presides over the circumstances of life refused to permit us to enjoy so many advantages," he added.

There is no mistaking Frederick's nostalgia and regret. After so many quarrels and unkindnesses, the two of them were still magnetically drawn to one another. None of Voltaire's innumerable admirers was such a prize as this harsh, cruel, yet sovereignly intelligent King. The rapprochement with Frederick gave Voltaire a sort of confidence and serenity: "This prince writes to me once a fortnight. He does anything I wish him to," he wrote to the Marquis de Florian in 1767.

Another Unsavory Business

Just as Voltaire and the *philosophes* were bringing the Calas affair to a triumphant conclusion, Voltaire was told of a similar affair in the same province of Languedoc.

This was the Sirven case, which began in 1760 in the region of Mazamet. The Huguenot family of Sirven consisted of the father, a geometrician and surveyor, the mother, and three daughters, the eldest of whom was married. One day Elizabeth, one of the younger daughters, who was thought to be simple-minded, disappeared. After a day spent searching for her, the father was summoned to the bishop's palace, where he was told that his daughter had sought asylum, having resolved to convert to the Catholic faith. She had thereupon been sent to the convent of the Black Ladies. It seemed strange that a girl who was simple-minded should have shown so much resolution; but on further inquiry it was learned that she had an adviser in the person of the bishop's sister, a collector of lost souls. The father did not conceal that he was unhappy that his daughter had run, or been taken, away, but he admitted that she was in good hands and that he would offer no objection so long as her vocation was sincere.

Not long after, the girl went completely mad. She had hallucinations, tore all her clothes off, and begged to be whipped. The nuns refused, but a servant girl obliged, whereupon the girl screamed that she was being tortured. The only solution was to put her in a strait jacket and keep her out of sight in her cell. After seven months of this the nuns could do nothing with her, and she was restored to her family on October 7, 1760. She was obsessed with the idea of getting married and accosted everyone who came her way. She had fits of violence during which she flew at her father and mother and had to be tied up. The father accused the Black Ladies of having driven his daughter mad. Bent on revenge, the Black Ladies and the bishops resolved to deal with him as he deserved.

The nuns brought charges against Sirven, accusing him of mistreating his daughter because she wanted to be converted to Catholicism. From that point on, Sirven was caught in the same web that had destroyed Calas. He was made to accompany his daughter to services at the convent. But one day when he was out surveying the property of a neighboring landowner he was told that his daughter had disappeared. He arrived home to find his house full of people and his wife prostrate with grief. He was informed that his daughter had got up at midnight, saying it was day and that she was going out to gather wood. She had never come back. The father searched everywhere but she was nowhere to be found. The local curé said: "She is better off where she is than with her parents."

The curé meant that the girl had probably been carried off and put in a convent again by the church authorities, not, as people later thought, that she had been murdered. During the fortnight that followed, everyone, including the girl's parents, believed she had been shut up again somewhere with the nuns. But one day some children found her body in a well on the common. There was no doubt in anyone's mind that she had committed suicide.

But then the rumor gradually spread that Sirven had murdered his daughter rather than see her converted. As he had not been at home on the night of the "crime," it was next his wife who was accused. As Madame Sirven had called for help when she found her daughter gone, the "murder" was then attributed to the elder daughter. The same argument that had proven so successful in the Calas case was invoked: Protestants were murderers on principle, for one of their dogmas was to slay their children who turned Catholic. The rumor of a ritual murder always drove the mob into a frenzy, and a judge was then found who was susceptible enough to hidden pressures to condemn whatever suspect was brought before him. He could deliver his verdict with impunity: the voice of the people was behind him, and he had the support of occult and powerful authorities. A prosecutor named Trinquier was found for the purpose at Mazamet. He was a former merchant who had gone bankrupt, a starveling who had contrived to secure a schoolmaster's salary for himself, though he never actually taught. Since the medical report did not square with the verdict that he had already made up his mind to render, he had the report changed, not once but twice. The case dragged on for four years, for despite such tampering it was difficult to incriminate anyone in the family of the poor mad girl.

People had gradually come around to being on the side of the family when, to the Sirvens' stupefaction, they were told that they were in danger of being arrested and ought to escape as best they could. So they left everything they owned behind and fled, through the rain and the mud and the darkness, to the country. Under frightful conditions they managed to cover six kilometers (about four miles) in five hours. Once they had got away they separated. The father managed to reach Lausanne, on foot like a vagabond, in 1762. The two women hid out in Nîmes. In Mazamet all their possessions were seized, and the judge left no stone unturned to obtain overwhelming evidence against them. But something strange occurred which held up the proceedings: the corpse of the mad girl, which had been fished out of the well and deposited at the town hall, smelled so terrible that the men who were supposed to guard it disappeared. A person or persons unknown then seized upon this opportunity to steal the body. So the authorities were left with a murder without a corpse.

Sentence was passed, and Monsieur and Madame Sirven were condemned to be hanged. The two surviving daughters were to be present at the execution and were thereafter to be banished. But the Sirvens had fled before being arrested, so the execution was carried out in effigy, five months after sentence had been passed, in the Place du Plô at Mazamet.

Sirven was introduced to Voltaire by a Genevan, Paul-Claude Moulton, though the latter was a great friend of Rousseau's. In view of the slanderous things he had said about Voltaire, one is led to wonder why Moulton did not take him to Jean-Jacques, or what reason he had to believe that Voltaire's support would be more ardent, sincere, and effective than that of "the most virtuous and best of men." The fact that it was Voltaire he called upon is proof of the latter's reputation as a fighter for the cause of justice.

When he had heard the sorry tale of what had happened at Mazamet, Voltaire summarized it thus: "Imagine four sheep—the Sirvens—whom the butchers accuse of having eaten a lamb. That is how I see it."

Sirven fell at Voltaire's feet and begged him to help him as he had helped the Calases. Voltaire agreed to do so. On November 7, 1765, he wrote with characteristic irony: "I am greatly concerned by the Sirven affair. It will not be as sensational as the Calas one, since unfortunately no one has been broken on the wheel. So we shall need Beaumont [the lawyers he had hired to defend the Calases] to compensate for this deficiency with his eloquence."

As the case had been heard before a minor judge, the first thing to be done, before asking for a rehabilitation, was to make an appeal—to the Parlement of Toulouse. "Will not the judges there have the wretched Sirvens broken on the wheel, hanged, and burned to avenge themselves for the Calas affair?" Fortunately new judges had been appointed since that debacle.

The D'Argentals were exasperated by this latest act of idealism on Voltaire's part, which in their eyes was a quixotic crusade. At his age, why could he not stay quiet and let his friends do the same, for of course they had all been conscripted too. Voltaire apologized. "Too many murder cases, I know. But, celestial angels, whose fault is it?" He added: "Sirven is here with me, scribbling down his innocence and the barbarism of the Visigoths. We are approaching the end; time presses." This was on April 22, 1765.

The law put every possible obstacle in the way of exoneration, and meanwhile Madame Sirven died. Voltaire canvassed for help among the Toulouse Parlement, knowing he would get it. Finally, after legal maneuvering of all descriptions, Voltaire managed to get Sirven rehabilitated. His activity in 1765 is incredible—the number of people he saw, wrote to, fed, entertained, flattered, and embraced. He also helped liberate a Protestant who had been condemned to the galleys for listening to an unauthorized sermon. Similar cases were brought to his notice, and he set about trying to free these other victims. But Choiseul refused to pardon them: "What was possible yesterday is impossible tomorrow," he told Végobre, Voltaire's lawyer. Végobre commented that Voltaire "would willingly have emptied the prisons of all their Protestants, yet that did not prevent him from making the most cruel jokes about Calvin and his ministers." This was doubtless because in Voltaire's eyes they were as dangerous fanatics as the others.

The Streets of Abbeville Run with Blood: Voltaire Flees to Utopia

The south of France had distinguished itself by committing two atrocious miscarriages of justice. The north was not to be outdone. With one case alone it equaled the horror of Toulouse and Mazamet.

The most refined and civilized of centuries yielded to barbaric impulses that seem stupefying today. The Age of Enlightenment and atheism was also that of the grossest superstition. Charlatanism flourished even in the most intelligent circles. The magicians Cagliostro and Saint-Germian lived as solid citizens and hoodwinked the least naïve of people. Religious quarrels took grotesque forms: the Jansenists went into hysterical convulsions and gained credence for foolish miracles. In fact, in the Age of Enlightenment the sun shone on the heights only: the plain was still plunged in darkness and full of sinister caves.

On August 7, 1765, the inhabitants of Abbeville had noticed that a crucifix on the Pont Neuf had been mutilated: the body had been struck on the sides with a sharp instrument and a toe was damaged. Another crucifix, in a churchyard, had been smeared with filth. Popular feeling against the perpetrators of these blasphemous acts ran high. Seventy witnesses were called but none of them could point to the culprits. Finally suspicion fell on three young townsmen who had attracted attention before by their anti-religious bravado. In August 1765 the police at Abbeville were ordered to seize the three young men, who lived in the town: the Chevalier de la Barre, Gaillard d'Etallonde, and a boy named Moisnel. Gaillard fled, but the other two were taken into custody. Meanwhile the Bishop of Amiens came at the request of the citizens of Abbeville and presented himself barefoot with a rope around his neck before the profaned Christ, to avert heaven's wrath. The bishop also prayed that the divine mercy would let the light of its grace shine on the culprits. He had previously referred to them as "worthy of the utmost tortures," and it was these words rather than those invoking mercy that the crowd remembered and urged upon the judges.

They questioned Moisnel, who was only seventeen. He broke down and admitted everything, and even confessed to offenses he had invented out of whole cloth, seized with such terror that his replies bordered on delirium.

La Barre was only twenty, but he was much more self-possessed. He admitted only to peccadilloes, such as uttering irreverent expressions of the sort he often heard at the table of his aunt, the Abbess of Willancourt, with whom he lived. He saw no harm in repeating what worthy ecclesiastics and worldly guests of the abbess said in such surroundings. Among his belongings were found some bawdy stories and a copy of Voltaire's *Philosophical Dictionary*. Voices were then raised demanding that Voltaire be arrested as the instigator of the profanation and put to the question with the other accused. Voltaire shivered when the echoes of this reached Ferney; and with good reason. La Barre was put to the torture and confessed. If some prosecutor had taken it into his head to arrest Voltaire, he too would have been "questioned," and a goodly number of people would have been only too pleased.

One of the judges had been bribed by a certain Monsieur de Belleval, who had a grudge against La Barre's family. Belleval arranged for Moisnel to exculpate himself by accusing La Barre and the other young men who hung about together. Moisnel threw himself into his part so zealously that he named Belleval's son among the rest, and the boy was arrested. They were all youngsters led astray by books never intended for their eyes, children left too soon to themselves in an adult society that set them a deplorable example. Why did the abbess not keep closer watch on her young nephew? How did it happen that Monsieur de Belleval did not know that his son was a member of this gang of "juvenile delinquents?" It sounds like a very modern problem.

But the Abbeville court did not stop to ask sociological questions. On February 28, 1766, they sentenced La Barre and Gaillard to make the *amende honorable* before the porch of the Church of Saint Wolfran, whither they were to be driven in a tumbril with a rope around their necks. Then they were to have their tongues cut out and be driven to the town square and there decapitated and thrown into the flames.

For Moisnel, Belleval, and two others, the sentence was suspended, and young Gaillard was executed only in effigy.

But La Barre became a victim of fanaticism and treachery. No one, including La Barre himself and his family and friends, believed that the Paris Parlement would confirm the sentence. Président d'Ormesson, who was a relative of La Barre's, was so sure that the sentence was purely formal that, wishing to keep the odious affair as quiet as possible, he took no steps to prevent its confirmation. But a counselor to the Parlement named Pasquier, who had already played an important role in the execution of a lieutenant general wrongfully accused of treason, the Comte de Lally-Tollendal, insisted that an example be made to prevent the spread of impiety, and the Paris Parlement agreed that the Abbeville sentence against La Barre should be carried out.

There still remained the hope of the King's pardon. Voltaire devoted himself to defending the young man, and made him out to be a sort of budding genius. But the pardon never came, and La Barre was doomed. In his last moments he was cruelly shocked by the sight of the enormous crowd in the square and at the windows. Among those in the ringside seats he recognized "those whom I believed to be my friends"—people who had wept over *La Nouvelle Héloïse*. As they began cutting his hair in preparation for execution he cried: "Are you trying to make a choir-boy out of me?" He asked the executioner if he was the man who had botched Lally's execution in Paris. The man said he was but that it was Lally's fault for not placing his head properly on the block. "Don't worry," La Barre assured him. "I shall put my head down properly and not be childish." This time the executioner was so efficient that the crowd applauded.

The Chevalier de la Barre had paid for a relatively minor act of blasphemy with his life. The accused youngsters had merely said and done what they had been taught by the example of those around them. D'Alembert knew that Pasquier, who demanded that an "example" be made of the youths, had a "philosophical" library, was himself an unbeliever, and indulged in anti-religious talk among his friends.

The execution had a profound effect on Voltaire. In 1766, after the execution, he wrote: "I am tempted to go and die in some place where men are less unjust. But I will be silent. I have too much to say. . . . I see nothing on all sides but the most barbaric injustices. Calas and the Chevalier de la Barre sometimes appear to me in my dreams. People think we live in an age that is merely ridiculous, but it is horrible."

Sometimes he allowed himself to think that "Perhaps the rule of reason and true religion will soon be established, and will silence iniquity and madness." But his imagination more often reminded him of how liable he was to be the next one tortured. As at Frankfurt, he was subject to attacks of anxiety so acute that they resulted in delirium. One day he was so frightened of being arrested because of *La Pucelle* that he fell down and rolled on the floor and clutched at the curtains in terror. Dr. Tronchin managed to calm him, and he pulled himself together and said: "Yes, my friend, it is true, I am mad."

He asked Frederick to grant him asylum in his principality of Cleves. Though surprised by the request, Frederick agreed: "This refuge will always be open to you. How could I refuse it to a man who has done so much honor to letters, to his country, to mankind: in a word, to his entire age?" Nevertheless, Frederick was not as indignant as Voltaire at what had happened at Abbeville. In his opinion laws were made to be obeyed.

So Voltaire went to take the waters at Cleves, to hide and to dream. He was so disillusioned with society that he conjured up a vision of a sort of monastic life, a colony of philosophers in Cleves where the laws of reason alone would hold sway. Fear drove him to invent a utopia. Presumably referring to Ferney, he wrote: "One must know how to leave a prison behind and live in freedom and honor." To Diderot, who was to be head of the philosophic settlement, he said: "You would not be alone there—you would have companions and disciples. You could establish a chair there—the chair of Truth. Your library could be brought there by boat;

it would have to travel only four leagues overland. And you yourself would exchange bondage for freedom." He offered Damilaville a printing works and a "truth-manufactory" in this utopia, and added: "You may be sure that people will abandon everything to come and join us."

Everybody in Paris embroidered on this latest fad of the Patriarch of Ferney. He must be failing fast, they thought. If anyone mentioned his project he denied it and claimed he was being slandered. To the chosen few who were to be the colony's founding fathers he referred to it merely as "the manufactory." But these chosen few were not interested. They were all for philosophy, but only in Paris. One wonders, in fact, how long Voltaire himself really believed in his scheme.

His utopia having come to nothing, Voltaire forgot his fears, and before autumn he was back at Ferney.

Il faut cultiver son jardin

One of Voltaire's great pleasures was to slip out of the château, whatever the weather, and go about the fields, supervising the planting and sowing. He even had his own field, which he tried to plow himself, refusing to give up doing so until 1772, when he was seventy-eight.

He loved the land, and agriculture, and even the farm implements. He rhapsodized about a new drill and cried, "Blessed is he who makes the earth bear fruit!" He wrote a long description of a model farm and did all he could to introduce new crops. Sometimes he succeeded, and invariably gave the credit not to miracles but to effort. "I have not been able to overcome the rigor of the climate. The Comptroller General asked me to sow madder: I tried, but it was no good. I planted more than twenty thousand trees that I had brought from Savoy; nearly all of them are dead. I have bordered the main road with walnuts and chestnut trees four times; three quarters of them have died or been pulled up by the peasants. But still I am not disheartened; old and infirm as I am, I shall plant today though certain of dying tomorrow. Others will enjoy the results."

Among the hundred different Voltaires, this one is a respectable, hardworking citizen, useful to his fellow man.

Despite Voltaire's enthusiasm, agriculture at Ferney was doomed to failure. The harsh climate and the poor and marshy soil could produce only indifferent harvests. The draining of one bug-ridden swamp alone took years and cost an immense fortune: but this by itself would have been enough to make Voltaire's name immortal round about Ferney. The solicitations, the work, and the difficulties presented by man and nature in this affair would have been enough to occupy the entire life of an ordinary squireen. Voltaire got rid of this source of malignant fevers and provided his peasants with new lands.

Voltaire had transferred his dreams of a utopia to Ferney. He not only cultivated the land and drained the swamps, but he set up small "manufactories" to improve the life of the peasant.

When, during the trial of La Barre, he felt himself to be in danger, he thought that all was lost in this field, for if he had to abandon his "manufactories" they would be in jeopardy. But as soon as the storms had passed he embarked upon a whole series of ambitious projects. He turned his theater into a rearing house for silkworms. He wanted not only to produce but also to spin and weave silk at Ferney. He succeeded, and the first pair of silk stockings his "manufactory" produced were for the Duchesse de Choiseul. "It was my silkworms that provided me the thread to make these stockings; it was my hands, on my own estate, that worked, together with the Calas boy, to make them; they are the first silk stockings ever to be made in this region. Deign, madame, to wear them, and then show your legs to whomever you choose, and if they do not admit that my silk is beautiful and stronger than that of Provence or Italy, I will renounce silk making. Then give them to one of your women servants: they will last a year."

> Je me mets à vos pieds, j'ai sur eux des desseins.
> Je les prie humblement de m'accorder la joie
> De les savoir logés dans ces mailles de soie
> Qu'au milieu des frimas je formai de mes mains.

I throw myself at your feet, I have designs on them./I humbly beg them to bestow on me the pleasure/Of knowing them to be envelopes in these silken meshes/Which in the chill of winter I formed with my own hands.

Next he started manufacturing blond lace, a silk lace made of two threads, twisted into hexagonal meshes. He acquired a dozen marvelous workwomen and began taking orders at once. He copied models exactly and sold the lace for half the normal price.

With the money he earned he bought plows and seed and materials for houses for the people of Ferney.

As successful as the silk and lace manufactories were, Voltaire's industrial masterpiece was his watch factory. Until his time Geneva had more or less of a monopoly on fine watchmaking, but the watches were made by foreign workmen. When these workmen entered into dispute with their employers Voltaire offered them his heart, his house, and his financial resources. And so they brought their priceless industry to Ferney. It was Madame de Choiseul who was again privileged, receiving this time the first watches manufactured on French soil. The rest of them were to be marketed in Spain, where the French ambassador was to make arrangements for their sale; the charming Duc de Choiseul was asked to instruct him accordingly. Perhaps this watchmaking industry would not have succeeded without the help of such powerful friends; but Voltaire would have undertaken it just the same.

The difficulty was not production but the disposal of the product. He had the best craftsmen in the world, he had capital, but it was still necessary to sell. So he took on the job of salesman for his "manufactory." His clients were the sovereigns of Europe, the nobility, ministers, ambassadors. To them he wrote letter after letter, prodding and pestering them until he finally got their orders. In Rome, Cardinal de Bernis was obliged to take a case of watches and sell them to all the other cardinals; the Sacred College kept track of time thanks to watches manufactured by Voltaire the unbeliever.

The watches were of the highest quality. Voltaire wrote a circular letter about them which Choiseul had distributed among the diplomatic corps in Paris. "Monsieur," it began, "I have the honor to inform Your Excellency that inasmuch as the citizens of Geneva have unfortunately murdered a number of their compatriots, several families of honest watchmakers have taken refuge on a small estate of mine in the region of Gex. . . ." He then went on to praise the watches and their makers, who "deserve Your Excellency's protection all the more because they have the greatest respect for the Catholic religion." Monsieur de Voltaire had to have his little joke.

The harmony that reigned at Ferney between Catholics and Calvinists was quite touching, and Voltaire was very proud of it. "One does not even notice that there are two religions," he said. Perhaps he wondered to himself whether there was even one.

He did not neglect exports. "I should be greatly obliged to Monsieur de Praslin if he would kindly forward the watches to the Dey of Algiers and his army and to the Bey of Tunis and his army." The Duc de Duras bought a caseful for wedding presents at the marriage of the Comte d'Artois. Catherine laid in a stock of them: "I will take them all," she wrote enthusiastically. Voltaire replied: "We all ardently hope that every hour will be an auspicious one for us, and every moment an uncomfortable one for Mustapha [the Sultan, Catherine's enemy]." This did not prevent Voltaire from proposing his watches to Mustapha at the same time.

XIV

Systems are like rats that can get through twenty little holes and then finally find two or three that they cannot. (*Philosophical Dictionary*: "Beard")

Very good remedies are made from poisons, but it is not poisons that keep us alive. (*Philosophical Dictionary*: "Bees")

Divorce is doubtless approximately as old as marriage. I believe, however, that marriage is a few weeks older. (*Philosophical Dictionary*: "Divorce")

To judge an adultery trial fairly would require having twelve men and twelve women as judges, with a hermaphrodite to cast the deciding vote in case of a tie. (*Philosophical Dictionary*: "Adultery")

I always add to my *Pater Noster:* My God, deliver me from the rage to write books! (*Philosophical Dictionary*: "Literature")

A poor Chinese whose mother whipped him every day never cried. But one day he burst into tears. "Ah," he said, "my mother wasn't up to whipping me today; she's declining and will soon be dead." (*Philosophical Dictionary*: "Money")

It is easier to write about money than to have it: and those who earn it make mock of those who know only how to talk about it. (*Philosophical Dictionary*: "Money")

It is true that nothing is more ridiculous than seeing the infinite number of delicate women, and of men no less eternally female than they, call in a doctor for a headache after they have eaten too much, drunk too much, gambled too much, aged too much, address him like a god, ask of him the miracle of making intemperance and health co-exist, and give a crown to this god who laughs at their weakness. (*Philosophical Dictionary*: "Illness")

A passerby says to a beggar [in Madrid]: "Aren't you ashamed to practice this shameful trade when you are able to work?" "Monsieur, it's money I'm asking you for—not advice." (*Philosophical Dictionary:* "Spaniards")

I cultivate my garden, but there is good reason to leave the toads in it; they do not prevent my nightingales from singing. (Letter to D'Alembert, 1767)

In the theater only people who are passionately loved should be put to death. (Letter, 1769)

I think that it is always a very good idea to argue in favor of the existence of a God who rewards and punishes; society has need of such an opinion. I do not know if you know this verse: "If God did not exist, it would be necessary to invent Him." (Letter, 1770)

The Abbé Dangeau, of our French Academy, sent back letters from his mistress when they had spelling mistakes, and broke with her the third time this occurred. (Letter, 1770)

During the year 1770 the relations between Voltaire and Catherine were most cordial. She sent him a gold and ivory box which she had finished with her own hands. When he lifted the lid he was dazzled by a portrait of his "Sémiramis of the snows" set in brilliants. That was a gift for his eyes and heart. For his body she sent him a sable cloak. In his enthusiasm, Voltaire became the champion of the Cross, urging Catherine to take over Greece and deliver the children of Sophocles and Demosthenes.

He was visited at Ferney by a young Italian nobleman named Gorani, full of energy and wit and something of an adventurer. As Voltaire listened to his more or less imaginary anecdotes he had a marvelous idea for a way of contributing, under the aegis of Catherine, to the restoration of the Byzantine Empire. Gorani's sister had just married Count Alexis, the last of the famous Comnenus dynasty, in Vienna. The count was descended in the most direct possible line from the Emperors of Byzantium and Trebizond. Thrilled at the mere mention of this illustrious name, Voltaire besought Gorani to leave at once for Saint Petersburg. This Comnenus was precisely the person Catherine needed to occupy the throne at Constantinople. Gorani, somewhat taken aback, said his new brother-in-law was an ill-bred poltroon; but on reflection he decided that the count could serve as a figurehead, and he and his sister would take care of the Empire. But this light from the East proved no more than a flash in the pan. Gorani went to fetch his sister and never came back. Voltaire returned to his fields and his watches.

Meanwhile Catherine had had thoughts along the same lines. She sounded out the Greeks as to whether they would be in favor of a Greek Empire protected by tsars. But her dream remained as unfulfilled as Voltaire's.

In Geneva, the watches made Voltaire more and more unpopular. When the Elector Palatine sent his engraver to Ferney to make a medal bearing Voltaire's profile, he needed to use a machine in the Geneva Mint. But the citizens were furious and had the medals seized. The devout Genevese scientist Charles Bonnet, who was always carping and caviling at the Patriarch of Ferney, wrote: "Voltaire despises us. He would build houses merely to spite us. He would build for no other reason: everywhere else he tries to destroy. Providence has permitted the existence of earthquakes, floods, heresies, and Arouet."

The Elector had the medal struck somewhere else, and Voltaire was enchanted with it. He bought several dozen and sent them to the citizens of Geneva with his compliments.

At the time of the *Emile* controversy Geneva was divided into two parties: on one side was the Council, which ruled over the city and was highly critical of *Emile*, and on the other side were the citizens, who supported Rousseau. Voltaire, who had friends among the most important families and rather prided himself on his influence, proposed himself as a mediator: "I do not presume to think that I may be useful, but I feel that it is not impossible to reconcile the opposing views," he wrote to the Council. "Hence in the present circumstances I do not think it would be amiss if two of your most conciliatory magistrates were to do me the honor of coming to dine at Ferney and consent to meet here two of the sagest citizens."

Voltaire wrote off at once to Versailles to let the French government know that he would devote himself to the cause of peace in Geneva and the glory of France. The French government had not asked him to do anything at all.

The members of the Council, who had hitherto supported him, disdained the idea of the round-table conference at Ferney. Voltaire then turned to the citizens, who had hitherto insulted him. He prepared a plan designed to avoid violence and sent it to Versailles for approval. Thereafter, he promised, "I will meddle no more. I am merely preparing the way of the Lord."

When Voltaire informed the Council that he had proposed his plan to the citizens, who welcomed it, the councilors were outraged. To soothe them, Voltaire attacked the citizens. When they in turn accused him of treachery, he reassured them by criticizing the Council.

The representative of France in Geneva, Monsieur Hennin, though an admirer of Voltaire and a frequent visitor at Ferney, was greatly embarrassed by the intrepid old gentleman's zeal and respectfully laid down the law to him, ordering him not to interfere in the dispute again. This only made Voltaire laugh, but Hennin wrote to his minister: "Neither one party nor the other [in Geneva] is in any state to appreciate the joke." It was becoming clear that Voltaire would end up by quarreling with everybody.

But at this point a curious change took place. Rousseau, having learned that Voltaire was supporting the citizens, counseled his friends to accept this alliance. "I advise and exhort you," he wrote, on December 30, 1765, "to give him your confidence as soon as you have sufficiently sounded him out. In a word, since he is your only resource, do not deprive yourselves of him. Deliver yourselves forthrightly and frankly into his hands, and win his heart by your trust."

Voltaire was touched when he heard of this letter. He wanted Rousseau brought back from London and he retracted certain diatribes he had written against Rousseau. He characteristically saw the two of them already on the road to reconciliation. He even offered to get Rousseau's Genevese citizenship restored. This was a fatal mistake. Rousseau was indignant. "You cannot have thought that I would wish to owe my re-establishment to Monsieur de Voltaire . . . the faults lie entirely on his side. It is he who should make the advances, which is precisely what he will never do. All he wants to do is pardon and protect. He is sadly wide of the mark." Though Voltaire had indeed made advances there was a certain condescension in his offer of help, and the quarrel went on.

The *natifs* were the sons or descendants of foreign refugees in Geneva. They were not citizens and had no right to exercise certain professions or to work in the administration. But they were subject to extremely heavy taxes and held in contempt. They took advantage of the dissension between the citizens and the Council to try to improve their miserable lot. The *natifs*, including the watchmakers, decided to band together and claim their rights. They drew up a petition for citizenship and took it to Voltaire for him to present. He found the document confusing and made them write it again, but he willingly agreed to be their champion. It is clear that the claims of the *natifs* were justified; it is equally certain that for Voltaire, a foreigner, to act as their champion was bound to increase civil disorder. "My friends," he told them, "you constitute the most numerous section of a free and industrious people, and you live in slavery. All you ask is to be allowed to enjoy your natural advantages, and it is only fair that so moderate a request should be granted. I will serve you with all the influence I possess with the plenipotentiary lords, and if you are forced to leave the country whose prosperity rests upon your work, I shall still be able to serve and protect you elsewhere."

This was promising a great deal. Voltaire next summoned the representatives of the *natifs* and drafted a compliment for them to address to the French ambassador. Four delegates went to see the ambassador. They were dressed in their very best, their hair curled and powdered. But the delegate who was supposed to deliver the complimentary address had left it at home, and after stammering and stuttering for a while, he suddenly launched into violent recriminations. The ambassador, who by that time had lost all patience, replied that he had received no commission to settle their differences with the Council. And so ended the first interview. They went to tell Voltaire of the mishap, and he laughed at them but promised to write them a petition, on condition that they make no mention whatsoever of his name. As if it could be kept secret! "Read it to your friends and say no more than that it comes from someone influential and mysterious," he instructed them. "The people like such words." So fifteen hundred *natifs* assembled to hear the message of their mysterious protector. But they were shocked by the style in which the petition was drawn up, by the way it addressed the members of the Council as "Messeigneurs [My lords]," and by the exaggeratedly courtly and suppliant tone. Even when he engaged in demagoguery on behalf of the proletariat Voltaire continued to use the language of a royal court. The delegates were apprehensive when they came back to report to Voltaire on the assembly's negative reaction; but he accepted the popular verdict and rewrote the petition, which the delegates then took around from door to door. But neither the citizens nor the Council nor the foreign ambassadors would take any notice. The *natifs* were awkward and uncertain and already divided into three factions. After each setback they came and poured out their woes to Voltaire. Their attitude was so depressing that one day he spoke to them in terms applicable to all those in the position of these *natifs*: "My friends, you are not unlike those little flying fishes that are eaten by gulls if they emerge from the sea and are devoured by bigger fishes if they fall back into the water. You are caught between equally powerful parties, and you will fall victims to the interests of either one or the other, if not both at once."

And that is precisely what happened. The citizens and the Council got together to make the *natifs* see reason, and once again they were victimized.

They managed to cause quite a stir nevertheless. The Council was angry to learn that they had been received by the French ambassador, the more so as they boasted of having obtained the promise of energetic support. The ambassador himself, outraged by this falsehood, summoned the four spokesmen and threatened them with prison. They were terrified and confessed that they had lied. He asked them brusquely who had composed their petition. Not wishing to break their word to Voltaire, they answered that poor workmen must be pardoned for writing badly and lacking wit.

"It is not its lack of wit that makes me doubt that you wrote it. On the contrary, it is because there is all too much wit in it that I am persuaded that someone lent you his pen," he replied.

They remained silent, and the ambassador flew into a rage.

"Do you know I can have you imprisoned if you have the audacity to conceal the truth?"

So then they gave Voltaire away. The ambassador smiled and went to see Monsieur de Voltaire for a second time. As on the day of his arrival, Voltaire again received him in his splendid blue and gold dressing gown and served him a fifteen-course dinner—a fitting complement to all the diplomatic services he insisted on rendering in season and out of season. As always, Voltaire succeeded in heading off the attack.

But on reflection Monsieur de Beauteville grew angry, and so did the Council, who disapproved of the ambassador's playing the role of an agitator. In its session of April 30, 1766, it recognized that Beauteville had acted without reproach and with loyalty toward Geneva; it even observed, with obvious satisfaction, that he had acted severely toward Voltaire. "He sent a man to dress him down who did the job thoroughly: he wept, groaned, and was ready to promise anything."

The ambassador had exaggerated the harshness of his reprimand in order to appease the magistrates of Geneva. In his letter to the minister, Monsieur de Praslin, the ambassador minimized the dressing down without attempting to conceal the reprehensibility of Voltaire's attitude. He said that the patriarch seemed very much cast down when he admitted his error. This is how the patriarch put it on April 30, 1766:

"Twenty or so natifs came to see me in much the same way as the fishwives of Paris once did me the same honor: I drew the fishwives up a little compliment for the King which was well received. I did as much now for the natifs, but apparently Messieurs the twenty-five [the Council] are greater aristocrats than the King. I know not if the fishwives have greater privileges than the natifs."

So much for the whole incident: a jest at the expense of the Council, and it was as if the entire affair had never happened. "I am a poor devil of a plowman and gardener, of seventy-two and a half summers, ill, unable to go out, and amusing myself by building a suitable little tomb in my churchyard, without any luxury. I am dead to the world; all I need is a De Profundis," he wrote to Hennin, the French representative in Geneva, playing the role of the simple hermit to the hilt.

All this was to lead up to the fact that the natifs had been to see him; but he was supplying this information one whole month after the scandal. The natifs had come to see him, he said, "to ask me to shorten a boring complimentary address. I took my academician's scissors and trimmed it for them. . . . I know not who is most in the wrong—the citizens, the Council, or the natifs. I play no part in any of their doings."

Nevertheless it was several months before he ventured into the streets of Geneva. He sent Madame Denis to try to patch up things with the ambassador and assure him that he was willing to throw himself humbly at his feet. As to the *natifs* who wished to emigrate, he informed them that he would take in those who excelled as watchmakers. His diplomatic failure thus served to install the watchmaking industry in France.

The Recalcitrant Pastor

Pastor Vernet was a man of worth and learning, and a member of the Geneva Council. He and Voltaire had met in Paris in 1722 and, as usual, in the beginning their relations were all sweetness and light. Vernet had just written a witty pamphlet entitled *Lettre à la lune pour la prier de ne pas se montrer les soirs d'illumination* (*A Letter to the Moon Asking It Not to Shine on Fireworks Nights*), which was praised by Fontenelle. In 1744, when Voltaire published his *Essai sur l'histoire universelle* (*Essay on the History of the World*), Vernet defended it against its detractors, and Voltaire was grateful. The various French residents in Geneva were all on the friendliest terms with the pastor. Montesquieu entrusted him with the task of seeing to the printing of the *Esprit des lois*. So he was a person of some consequence.

When Voltaire, mounting his bitter campaign against *l'Infâme*, added sarcasms against the Old and New Testaments to his *Essai sur l'histoire*, Vernet saw that Calvin had been as harshly dealt with as the Roman prelates, and protested. He was among those who had reservations when Voltaire installed himself at Les Délices. In 1761 Vernet published *Lettres critiques d'un voyageur anglais* (*Critical Letters by an English Traveler*), which were particularly critical of Voltaire and contained a portrait of him which provoked violent reactions. He conceded that Voltaire had gifts as a poet. But not as a philosopher. "If it be true that he is the author of a poem as profane, satirical, and obscene as *La Pucelle*, I should hold him to be a man dishonored. . . . He is a writer born to please, but it is sheer impertinence to set him up, as his supporters do, as a sage or a scholar, born to teach. The more wit he has, the more dangerous he is through his abuse of it."

Monsieur Vernet could not be accused of abusing his own wit, which he had long since prudently put behind him, along with his youth. But Voltaire, who was still as young at heart as ever, reacted violently and accused Vernet of something of which he was entirely innocent. Vernet, who had been denounced as a thief and a forger, had applied to the Council for a testimonial to his probity. Voltaire's account, dated July 18, 1766, read as follows: "The theologian Vernet has complained to the Council that he has been insulted. The Council has given him a testimonial saying he is neither a highwayman nor a pickpocket. This latter affirmation seems rather doubtful." Voltaire followed this up the same year with an anonymous pamphlet, *Eloge de l'hypocrisie* (*In Praise of Hypocrisy*), which was published at Carrouges, near Geneva:

> Mais si j'avise un visage sinistre,
> Un front hideux, l'air empesté d'un cuistre,
> Un cou jauni sur un moignon perché,
> Un oeil de porc à la barre attaché.
> (Miroir d'une âme à son remords en proie
> Toujours terni de peur qu'on ne la voie)
> Sans hésiter, je vous déclare met
> Que ce magot est Tartuffe ou Vernet.

But, if I spy a sinister face,/A hideous brow, a pedant's foul smell,/A yellow neck perched on a stump,/An eye like a trussed pig's/(Reflection of a soul a prey to remorse,/Forever tarnished out of fear of being seen),/Without a moment's hesitation I declare/That this ape is either Tartuffe or Vernet.

Apparently such revenges gave Voltaire a pleasure equal to the hatred they earned him, for he persisted in perpetrating them till his dying day.

More Tricks Against Geneva

Hardly had the unruly patriarch received his "dressing down" from the ambassador than he found a new opportunity to enrage what he called, when he was at odds with it, the "Parvulissima Republic." This time he made use of a grotesque local incident to make the magistrates and institutions of Geneva look ridiculous.

A man named Robert Covelle was brought before the Consistory, accused of having got with child a certain Dame Catherine Ferloz, a *native*. He admitted the fornication but not the child. Dame Catherine admitted both the fornication and the child, and also the child's father in the person of Covelle. The outraged pastors forbade Covelle to approach the communion table and sentenced him to ask God's pardon on his knees. Covelle asked for a week to think the last point over, and his request was granted.

The pastors referred the case to the Council. Covelle, on reflection, and not without assistance from others, maintained that the pastors were not judges and had no right to inflict punishment. He refused to go on his knees. By a strange chance, explainable by Voltaire alone, there began to circulate in Geneva a satirical pamphlet printed in London. It was called *La Guerre civile de Genève ou les Amours de Rob. Covelle* (*The Civil War in Geneva, or the Loves of Rob. Covelle*).

The Council had the lampoon seized, alleging that it contained "expressions insulting to the Consistory and apparently aimed at disturbing the peace." At all events it succeeded in saving Covelle from having to kneel. Questioned as to who had instructed him so well as to his rights and who had written the pamphlet, Covelle readily admitted it had been Voltaire. And in 1769 the punishment of "kneeling" was abolished.

Covelle had been brought to Ferney by certain citizens of Geneva who wanted to put a stop to the pastors' interference in matters before the courts and in the administration of justice. Covelle had merely been Voltaire's puppet, but his success went to his head and he saw himself as the vanquisher of religious tyranny. He called on the French representative in Geneva, Monsieur Hennin, and delivered a long rambling harangue, mixing up Catherine Ferloz, his own heroism, the Consistory, fornication, and tyranny. Hennin's account of the interview concluded: "I am inclined to believe he had sacrificed more liberally to Bacchus than to Mademoiselle Catherine." Voltaire wrote to Hennin: "You are most fortunate to have met Covelle the fornicator, it augurs well. He is a very stout fellow, for he gets the ugliest girls in Geneva with child and drinks the vilest wine as if it were Chambertin. Moreover, he is a great politician, being totally lacking in common sense."

To enrage the pastors even further, Voltaire gave a party in honor of Covelle, solemnly announcing him as "Monsieur the Fornicator," maintaining that this was a newly created title of the Genevan Republic.

But Covelle soon became a nuisance, and to stop him from coming Voltaire had his servants tell Covelle that their master was dead. To make the news more convincing, Covelle was also told that Voltaire had left him three hundred livres a year, and the pension was duly paid.

Voltaire's "epic" on the Genevan civil war bore marked resemblances both to Boileau's mock-heroic *Le Lutrin* (*The Lectern*) and to Rabelais's account of the war against Pichrocole in *Gargantua*. *La Guerre civile de Genève* consisted of five cantos in praise of the

> Noble Cité, riche, fière et sournoise:
> On y calcule et jamais on n'y rit:
> L'art de Barême est le seul qui fleurit

Noble City, rich, proud and sly:/Where people calculate but never smile:/Where the only art that flourishes is that of the ready reckoner.

He chides the Genevans for their irresistible desire for coins, no matter what coins so long as they are gold. He tells how Covelle's Catherine is drowned and an English nobleman comes by and asks, "Is she a Genevan?" "Yes," Covelle replies. "Well, we'll verify that," the Englishman says. He puts a big bag with a hundred pounds sterling into the corpse's hand; Catherine immediately clutches at it and comes to life.

Voltaire also pokes fun at the kneeling episode. But the most insulting passages are those about Rousseau, "that somber energumen, that enemy of the human race," who had taken refuge in Val-Travers. There, according to Voltaire, he kept boredom at bay by making love to Mademoiselle Levasseur, his common-law wife.

> Cette infernale et hideuse sorcière
> Suit en tous lieux ce magot ambulant
> Comme la chouette est jointe au chat-huant.
> . . . .
> Si quelque fois dans leurs amours secrètes
> Leurs os pointus joignent leurs deux squelettes
> Dans leurs plaisirs ils se pâment soudain
> Du seul plaisir de nuire au genre humain.

This infernal and hideous witch/Follows this walking ape everywhere/As the screech owl is united with the tawny owl.
. . . .
If sometimes in their secret lives/Their sharp bones join their two skeletons/In their pleasures, they suddenly swoon/At the sole pleasure of harming mankind.

The poem ends with a general reconciliation, everyone kissing and making up save for the wretch at Val-Travers:

> Le vieux Rousseau de fureur hébété
> Avec sa gaupe errant à l'aventure
> S'enfuit de rage et fit vite un traité
> Contre la paix qu'on venait de conclure

Old Rousseau, dazed with fury,/Roving about with his slut,/Fled in a rage and made a treaty/Against the peace that had just been concluded.

It is not difficult to imagine how Geneva received this poem, in which everyone was given a drubbing except the Tronchins. Never mind, Monsieur de Voltaire had amused himself and got his own back.

Voltaire's relations with Geneva deteriorated to such an extent that he ceased to be on good terms even with the Tronchins. Dr. Tronchin was tired of Voltaire's antics and of getting him out of scrapes. On a visit to Paris to attend the Dauphine, he was asked by the King if he was still Voltaire's friend. "I am not the friend of an infidel," he was reported to have answered. Voltaire would not believe it; but in fact Tronchin was not a friend he could count on.

One evening in February 1768 the wooden theater that had been built in one of the squares of Geneva went up in flames. It was Voltaire who, to his own delight and Rousseau's fury, had succeeded in installing the theater in Calvin's city. It was packed for every performance. When Molière's *Tartuffe* was presented, the audience invariably applauded all the passages denouncing religious hypocrisy. In 1766 Voltaire's *Olympe* was performed there. He was enchanted; for this failure of a play he had all the partiality of a father toward his backward child.

But the public liked flames better than they liked poetry. They came running with buckets of water as soon as they saw the fire; but when they saw it was the theater that was burning, they merely said, "Well, my fine gentlemen, let those who put it up put it out," and left it to its fate. Voltaire could hardly believe such ingratitude and barbarism. "Ah, this Geneva!" he wrote. "You think you have a firm hold on it, and it slips between your fingers." He said the theater had been deliberately set afire. It seemed likely, though no culprit could be found. But Voltaire soon suggested one: Rousseau.

Among the austere, irreproachable, intransigent Huguenots of Geneva was old Deluc, Rousseau's friend and Voltaire's fierce detractor. He was completely intolerant, but so honest that he came in person to show Voltaire the attacks he proposed to publish against him. He urged Voltaire to proclaim himself a son of Abraham, to renounce impiety and recognize the divinity of Christ, in return for which he, the prophet Deluc would refrain from publication. Voltaire used Don Juan's method with Monsieur Dimanche: he smothered him in protestations of friendship and admiration, quoted from his works, appealed to the law and the prophets, and left the old fellow thinking he must have been either mistaken or misinformed about his host. He then confessed that he had devoted seven chapters to tearing him to pieces, and produced the vast manuscript and started to read it. Voltaire, appalled by the prospect of having to listen to every last word of it, said if Deluc would leave it he would read it in a day. "I will leave it with you for three days," said the implacable visitor, "and you can read it three times." Willing to do anything to escape the torture of hearing the entire thing read aloud, Voltaire promised to ponder every word of it, and led his tormentor amiably to the door. Naturally he did not read a single line of this deadly dull denunciation. According to him, Deluc was "a gullible ignoramus resembling the apostles."

He was such a bore that even Rousseau, who praised him to the skies for attacking Voltaire, couldn't stand him. "I feel friendship, respect, and esteem for him," he wrote, "but I shall always dread the sight of him. . . . But I did find him slightly less tedious than in Geneva. He left two books with me. Good heavens! What a chore. I, who sleep poorly, have enough opium now for at least two months."

Deluc envisioned himself as a tribune of the people and wanted to institute a kind of biblical republic. He was the firebrand who had kindled Geneva's civil wars, and Voltaire held him responsible for the poor state of supplies and the near-famine conditions in the city. He cared little whether people had enough to eat so long as he could go from door to door preaching to them. Voltaire, for whom this world was paradise now, had little time for those who strove to turn it into a vale of tears.

He had another enemy in Charles Bonnet, a distinguished scholar but a very devout man who hated Voltaire for his nonchalant impieties. When he first came to Geneva Voltaire had paid visits to people, but Bonnet preferred not to receive him, and so became a disapproving but regular visitor at Les Délices, hoping to ferret out all his host's many sins. One day, seeing a book by Condillac lying about, he asked Voltaire what he thought of it. Voltaire answered that he had never opened it, did not meddle with philosophy, and contented himself with writing a few poor verses. Bonnet thought Voltaire sounded embarrassed. More likely he was bored—by Condillac, or Bonnet, or both.

Bonnet, a friend of Haller's, did his best, together with Deluc and other theologians, to substantiate the rumor that Voltaire didn't really know anything. It is true that in spite of his immensely wide reading he was not so learned a metaphysician as Bonnet or Deluc, but the range of his knowledge is beyond all dispute, and Bonnet, who cast doubt on it, was an ignoramus compared to Voltaire in the fields of science, English, Italian, history, finance, politics, agriculture, law, and even Latin.

What these scholars really held against the master of Ferney was his delightful way of living, his gaiety and frivolity and debonair manner. They would not admit that genius could be amiable, sociable, and elegant. For the Bonnets of this world, one could be distinguished only if one was a bore. "I would not have all Monsieur de Voltaire's talents at the price he pays for enjoying them: in my opinion he is one of the most unfortunate creatures on the face of the earth," the sober-sided scholar opined.

When the *Philosophical Dictionary* was burned Bonnet rejoiced at the fate of "the most detestable book of this pestilential author," which "is to the conscience what arsenic is to the intestines." But, as he truly remarked, "these sorts of executions merely increase the success of the book concerned." When Voltaire simply smiled to see his *Dictionary* burned, the pastor was furious: "This man no longer produces anything but excrement, and countless people are ready to swallow it," he wrote, dipping his own pen in the chamber pot.

When D'Holbach published his materialist *Système de la nature*, Bonnet was both surprised and delighted to see Voltaire refute him with arguments in favor of the existence of God. But in fact the existence of God was a philosophical necessity in Voltaire's conception of the universe: "If God did not exist, it would be necessary to invent Him." Once that was established, however, he was the implacable enemy of all dogmas, rites, and revealed religions, which he banished wholesale under the name of superstition, that infamous force that produced fanaticism and murder. Yet all his life Voltaire had a certain nostalgia for the religion in which his childhood had been steeped. A true atheist would not have built a church at Ferney but simply have allowed the old one to fall into ruins and so avoided a good deal of trouble with his bishop. He was violently anti-clerical, anti-biblical, anti-theological, and anti-metaphysical, but he was a Deist. One day at dinner, when Condorcet and

D'Alembert launched a brilliant attack on the existence of God, Voltaire sent the servants away and said: "Now, messieurs, you may continue talking against God, but as I don't wish to wake up tomorrow with my throat cut it is better that my servants not hear you." When someone argued against the idea of God as the foundation of morality by saying that wives who were religious were as likely to deceive their husbands as those who were not, he answered: "I know one who was held back by the fear of God, and that is enough for me."

He attached great importance to this idea of the fear of God as the key to morality. "Atheism is a pernicious monster in rulers. Whatever you may say, it can encourage Neros and Alexanders, while the opposite opinion can restrain them. Without this restraint I should regard kings and their ministers as wild beasts." He was astonished, at seventy-seven, that men should treat the most important subject in the world so lightly. "The existence of God is the thing which concerns the human race the most."

He was religious, without having a religion. "Why are we here? Why are there living creatures at all? What is thought? O atoms of a day, my companions in infinite littleness, born like me to suffer everything and know nothing, are there any among you foolish enough to think you know the answers to these questions? No, there are none; no, deep down in your hearts you feel your own nothingness as I acknowledge mine, but you are vainglorious enough to want people to accept your black philosophies."

To assert his deism he had the inscription "Dei Soli" engraved on his church at Ferney. As for the soul, he could not bring himself to believe in it. "The I know not what called matter may be just as capable of thought as the I know not what called soul. . . . People have always sought to discover how the soul acts on the body. First of all we would need to know whether we have one. . . . Why do we insist on having one? Perhaps out of vanity. If a peacock could speak it would say it had a soul and that it was located in its tail."

Sometimes, relishing the thought that the great would be punished in the hereafter, he pretended to believe in the soul and damnation. But this was only for the pleasure of the moment. For him there was a universal morality independent of religion or race. "There are actions which everyone finds admirable. A man gives his life for his friend—the Algonquin, the Frenchman, and the Chinese will all say that that is a noble thing." All the wise and decent people in the world combine to make up a society which agrees on the same principles of truth, liberty, and virtue.

He invokes the saints of this morality. "Let us address our prayers to Saint Zeno, Saint Epicurus, Saint Marcus Aurelius, Saint Epictetus, and Saint Bayle." He had a preference for the Stoics, "who rendered human nature almost divine." D'Holbach had written that it would be dangerous to ask men to be virtuous if virtue only made them unhappy, adding, "If vice made them happy, they would be bound to love vice."

"This is an execrable maxim," Voltaire commented. "Even if it were true that a man may not be virtuous without suffering, he still ought to be encouraged to be virtuous. The satisfaction of having conquered one's vices is a hundred times greater than that of yielding to them, which is always a tainted pleasure and one that leads to sorrow. To encourage a soldier we say to him, 'Remember the honor of the regiment.' To every individual we ought to say, 'Remember the dignity of man.'"

It would be a mistake to interpret some of Voltaire's jests as breaches in his ethical theory, or to confuse his anti-clericalism with immorality. But his thought was so volatile and scintillating that it is almost impossible to pin down. When his hero Zadig says that to be wise a man must be without passions, the old hermit in the story replies that the passions "are the winds that fill the sails. Sometimes they cause the boat to sink, but without them the boat would not be able to go forward at all."

For Voltaire, what mattered was the going forward; whether one was an Epicurean, a Stoic, or even a Christian was of secondary importance. Perhaps it was this vitality of his that was at the root of his ethical theory. At any rate, whether one can accept his ethics or not, one must admit that he was profoundly moral, as became a pupil of Louis-le-Grand.

The Patriarch and His Tribe

Voltaire enjoyed young people's company and knew how to make them enjoy themselves.

One of the people who came to see him was young Mallet du Pan, who came from a very good Genevan family and had defended both *Emile* and the *Philosophical Dictionary*. Voltaire secured him a post as tutor in history and literature to the princes at the court of the Margravine of Hesse, where he began by making the naïve assumption that the offspring of sovereigns who professed to befriend the *philosophes* should be taught their new ideas. He was soon shown his mistake, and he returned to Geneva without trailing any clouds of glory but considerably the wiser.

Another visitor was Jean de Muller, a sort of infant prodigy who at seventeen had mastered all the sciences of the day. He looked no more than fifteen, and to remedy this wore an enormous wig that left only his nose and eyes visible. The first time he came to Ferney Voltaire was ill, and the young man had to sup with Madame Denis and several other disappointed visitors. The next time he was preceded by a flattering letter of introduction from Dr. Tronchin and was welcomed by such a charming, sprightly old gentleman he could scarcely believe it. He jestingly asked Muller where his tutor was and gave the answer himself: "This young man of fifteen is his own tutor, and the historian of Switzerland in the bargain." A young American traveler (a rarity on the Continent at that time) was also there that day, whom Voltaire introduced as follows, presumably commenting on the fact that this exotic visitor was not decked out in feathers: "Mesdames, you see before you a man who comes from the land of savages and yet shows no sign of it."

But this pleasant life was upset by the war in Geneva.

Versailles had lost patience with both parties, and in the winter of 1766–67, after Monsieur de Beauteville's mission had failed, Choiseul sent an army to occupy Geneva and bring it to its senses. But Voltaire soon realized that the chief victim of this measure was Ferney. Geneva was receiving food supplies from Savoy; at Ferney they were starving. "There are thirty dragoons around the hen roost known as Tournay. I have no army at Ferney, but I imagine that in this war there will be more wine drunk than blood shed," he wrote to the Duc de Richelieu in January 1767. The soldiers cut down his trees to heat their cooking pot and stole to fill it. They didn't pay for the wine they drank. "Maman Denis can't get any decent beef for her table and is obliged to send to Gex for cow," he reported. Cow meat, for the handsome French officers who were invited to dinner! It was a very hard winter. "We are short of everything save snow. With that commodity we could supply all Europe. It will soon be ten feet deep in the gardens and thirty in the mountains." Father Adam was at death's door, but neither doctor nor medicines could be secured for him. "We are short of everything. . . . And the Genevans are eating fat chickens from Savoy. It is they who are supposedly being punished, and it is we who are suffering."

He wrote and complained to the minister, and was sent a safe-conduct pass to enable him to go through the blockade to get stores from Geneva. He wrote to Monsieur de Beauteville: "The duc [de Choiseul] excepts me from the general rule because I am already infinitely excepted in his heart. I have an unlimited passport for myself and my servants. So come, do come, and Maman will entertain you magnificently, with beef, not cow."

Visitors flooded back to Ferney again—but Voltaire showed himself more and more infrequently. Sometimes he would be glimpsed at a turn of a path in the garden, with his great wig, his cap, and his cloak that flapped around his skinny shanks. If the name of one of the guests impressed him, he would approach and give his infallibly successful performance as the great magician. He liked to make up in this way for a disappointing welcome.

As well as the menagerie of distinguished guests there was also the farmyard, of which Madame Denis was the finest ornament. She had become short-tempered, and in her rages her natural stupidity and vulgarity came to the surface. Her uncle, exasperated, sometimes called her "*la grosse cochonne* [fat pig]." She was probably the only woman Voltaire ever addressed in such an insulting way; other more substantial privileges satisfying her insatiable appetite for money perhaps made up for a member of his mother's family, Charles Daumart, a poor paralytic wretch whom Voltaire sheltered, nursed, and put up with for nine years, until he died.

Nor were parasites lacking. One was a certain Gallien, a dubious gift from Richelieu, who played many a dirty trick on his protector. Another was young Brother Bastian, who had run away from a monastery in Savoy. He was known to the disreputable element in Ferney as Ricard and disappeared one day, taking with him jewels, money, and several of Voltaire's manuscripts. Voltaire did nothing to stop him, though it would have been easy enough to have him arrested, for as he remarked: "He's still wearing the red coat I gave him." But Voltaire never avenged himself on anyone who had been his friend, shared his life, or lived under his roof. He might dismiss them from his mind, but he would never pursue them.

There were also affable parasites such as Durey de Morsan, the son of a farmer-general. He had been immensely rich but had let himself be drawn into shady business and rooked of all his money. But though incapable of looking after himself he was very capable of pleasing, with his agreeable manners, excellent knowledge of Latin, and skill at versifying. Voltaire, who was very fond of him, kept him and tried to reconcile him with his sister, Madame de Sauvigny, wife of the intendant of Paris. Durey copied out manuscripts and helped the overburdened Wagnière. Voltaire dictated faster than three secretaries could write. In Voltaire's eyes Durey had two weaknesses in addition to those that had ruined him: he was religious, and he liked Rousseau. One day Voltaire went into his room and found a portrait of Jean-Jacques beneath a crucifix. His only comment was to write a jest on the wall about idols who did not deserve to be worshiped.

One of the inhabitants of Ferney who frightened Madame Denis was the inscrutable Father Adam. Some people thought he was merely dull and naïve, and out for a comfortable life. Madame Denis thought his placidity was only a hypocritical mask, and that if something weren't done about it Voltaire would one day be in the power of his "chaplain," that is to say, of the Jesuits. The suspicion even crossed D'Alembert's mind. A newcomer to Ferney, Jean-François de La Harpe, hated Father Adam, who might be expected to see through him too easily. The rivalries of this overcrowded hive must have amused Voltaire. Madame Denis later wrote of Father Adam: "Tell me what the Jesuit does; he's a dull beast, if he had had any wit my uncle would have been careful with him [but] as he rightly thinks him a fool what he says to him can have an effect, malicious beasts are very dangerous."

When Voltaire made fun of Father Adam in public, he remained impassive. "Look at Father Adam," Voltaire would say, "he used to be a

Jesuit, and look at him laughing at all my jokes about *l'Infâme*. And yet I suspect the rascal's a Christian. What a hypocrite!"

Father Adam was on very bad terms with his order, and when he went to Dijon to make contact again with his superiors none of them would see him. But he celebrated mass regularly. Voltaire was always talking about "my chaplain," "my chapel," "my mass." When any of the guests at Ferney asked the priest what he was doing there he used to say he was waiting for grace. He was unquestionably waiting for mealtimes. And Voltaire was amused at the idea of having his own private Jesuit.

Father Adam was not always placid. There was a third copyist at Ferney, Monsieur Bigex. On a visit to Paris, Voltaire's cook had met him at Grimm's residence and recruited him for Ferney. He came from Savoy and was a glutton for work; in addition to his secretarial duties he acted as valet. Voltaire not only dressed him in livery but draped him with the mantle of authorship, borrowing his name to put to a pamphlet called *L'Oracle des fidèles* (*The Believers' Oracle*). Father Adam, presumably out of jealousy, took a violent dislike to Bigex and accused him of stealing fruit out of the orchard, and Bigex brought a suit against him for slander.

The copyist wrote Latin verses against the priest: a pamphlet circulated all over Ferney on the subject. Voltaire didn't interfere, saying he wanted the case to be tried. The papers have been lost and the legal outcome is unknown. But Bigex left and Adam stayed.

Also among the guests during the winter of 1768 were La Harpe and Michel de Chabanon, both young, gay, and writers of verses. Chabanon had been introduced by D'Alembert: he was talented not only as a poet but also as a musician and philosopher. La Harpe, who was jealous of him, said he played better on the violin than on the lyre. Chabanon was also well bred—better than La Harpe—and he had brought with him a tragedy. Voltaire was delighted, hoping to see the new generation carry on from his *Zaïre* and *Mérope* as he himself had carried on from *Phèdre*. But he was obliged to tell Chabanon that his play needed to "simmer" a bit longer.

He had them act his own tragedy *Les Scythes* (*The Scythians*). He took a part himself; Chabanon diplomatically said he was unable to judge Voltaire's acting as they were both on stage at the same time. Voltaire was obliged to admit that *Les Scythes* was a failure, even in his own theater. They also acted in his *Adélaïde*, which, though also a flawed play, was a more successful production.

Despite the mediocre quality of the plays, the theater was packed with French army officers and guests from Geneva, for the town was still under siege. Grenadiers from Condé's regiment were used for the crowd scenes, and Voltaire, delighted with them, ordered them to be given supper and whatever payment they considered suitable. The theater always left him in a heady mood, and he was positively intoxicated when a grenadier refused to take any money, saying: "We have seen Monsieur de Voltaire, and that is payment enough for us." Voltaire was so pleased, he threw open his house to them: "Come for a meal whenever you like, my brave grenadiers! The table will be set for you, and if you wish to work you will be paid whatever wages you ask."

Voltaire was on the best of terms with the French officers and their men. The soldiers pilfered a little, but they also mended his roads and planted trees to replace those they had burned. But Voltaire was disappointed when Colonel de Chabrillant and his junior officers, who had been fed and lodged at Ferney, left without a word of thanks to their host. He complained to the minister, and Choiseul replied, "I take it upon myself to thank you for your kindness to the officers and for the blankets you provided for the men." Voltaire had also advanced money for their pay. He wrote to Madame du Deffand that "the officers serve the King so diligently, they could not even find time to write either to Madame Denis or to me."

Despite the fact that Voltaire frequently referred to Madame Denis as "*Grosse Cochonne*," he insisted that others treat her with respect. His severest reproach against Frederick was the brutal way in which his myrmidons had dealt with her at Frankfurt. She was irreplaceable to her uncle—no longer because of her "transporting graces," but because of her love of tragedy. Although four attempts to put *Les Scythes* on in Paris were greeted by booing, Madame Denis remained convinced that the play was a masterpiece and cried each time she saw it. But the critic Collé wrote: "It is not a work of his old age, it is a work of his senility." Voltaire nonetheless sent the play on to Frederick.

Voltaire's interest in La Harpe continued to grow. He wrote to his friend Cideville: "La Harpe has spent a few days in my hermitage, and as I like corrupting youth I exhorted him vehemently to follow the detestable career of poetry. He is a real man. He will surely write some good works, which will earn him the privilege of dying of hunger and being persecuted and despised. But everyone must fulfill his destiny."

He reproached La Harpe for not working hard enough. Voltaire wanted him to win a prize awarded by the Academy and wrote to D'Alembert recommending La Harpe's manuscript. La Harpe won the prize, and Voltaire wrote: "I place my own glory in that of my pupils, and I expect great things of him." But this pupil was to reward Voltaire with something he didn't expect at all.

Voltaire was admittedly given to facile praise, but this was mere politeness. It was not his fault if some fool took his courtly compliments seriously and thought him capable of writing another *Phèdre* on being told that his verses were like Jean Racine's. What is far more worth remembering is the sincere help Voltaire gave his protégés. As early as 1733, when he was by no means the rich lord of Ferney, he wrote: "I would rather have friends than superfluous luxuries, and I prefer a man of letters to a good cook and a pair of carriage horses." At that time he was supporting the indolent Linant and another friend who died of consumption soon afterward.

La Harpe himself was not courtly: on the contrary, he was touchy, brusque, and on occasion behaved like an insolent puppy toward his mentor and benefactor. Voltaire's patience astonished everyone. One wonders how he put up with all those Thiériots and Linants and La Harpes, all those boors who were the very opposite of himself and what he really liked.

Voltaire's affectionate nickname for La Harpe, who was slight in stature, was "*Petit* [Little Fellow]," and one day, on being so addressed, La Harpe responded by calling him "*Papa.*" He altered some lines in one of Voltaire's plays, and Voltaire's only reaction was to thank him. Thus encouraged, La Harpe indulged in a joke that might have cost him dearly. He recited some verses at table without saying who they were by, and Voltaire praised them. When he asked who the author was he was told they were by his old enemy Le Franc de Pompignan. Voltaire turned pale, and everyone held his breath. "Recite the stanza again!" he said at last. He listened amid a tense silence. Then he said, "No doubt about it, it's a very fine stanza."

Voltaire bore La Harpe little malice for this incident and continued in his devotion to the young writer. La Harpe had no pension, so in 1767 Voltaire wrote to the Comptroller General of the Treasury, requesting that La Harpe be paid half the annual pension to which he himself was entitled. He asked the minister to keep the transaction secret. Voltaire wrote of La Harpe that he would "easily be persuaded that the pension is a just reward for his services to literature."

Such an arrangement was not possible, and Voltaire wrote D'Alembert of his anxiety about La Harpe's future: "His talents will keep him from the direst poverty, but that is all he can hope for." He went on to say how useful a pension would be to La Harpe, but made no mention of his own efforts to share his pension with him.

But although Voltaire forgave his protégé his insolence, La Harpe did not forgive his protector's generosity toward him.

When Voltaire wrote *La Guerre civile de Genève* he had no illusions about its literary merits and, despite many past experiences, did not dream it would appear outside his private circle. But it was not long before it was learned that the poem was circulating both in Paris and in Geneva. There followed the usual series of reactions: rage, curses, fever; fear of prosecution; reflection on whether his authorship of the poem could be disavowed and on who could have spirited it away.

Voltaire's suspicions fell first on Brother Bastian, who was hauled before him for a repetition of the horrible scene with Madame de Graffigny at Cirey. Voltaire reviled him and accused him of stealing; Bastian wept and denied all complicity. They fell into each other's arms in tears, forgave each other, and set out to discover the real culprit.

Voltaire conducted the inquiry. But the closer he got to the truth the less he wanted to believe it: the guilty party was La Harpe, and Madame Denis his accomplice. To exculpate himself, La Harpe said that the stolen manuscript had been sent to him by a young sculptor in Paris. Voltaire had the sculptor questioned, but though he admitted having seen the manuscript, he said it was La Harpe who had already had it in his possession and showed it to him. When Voltaire confronted him with this proof, La Harpe, as his benefactors sadly noted, "took on a pallor which is not that of innocence."

The only punishment he imposed on La Harpe was to send him away, and even for that he waited until he was driven to it by impertinent notes the young man sent to his room.

He had a terrible scene with Madame Denis. He told his niece to pack her bags and leave Ferney immediately. To make the housecleaning complete, "Rodogune" and her husband, Dupuits, were also given orders to leave.

According to Wagnière, Voltaire's secretary, seven people in all left Ferney on March 3, 1768. The few guests who were in the house at the time of the row thought it best to go with the others: ". . . despite Monsieur de Voltaire's extreme politeness toward them they saw how much he needed rest and solitude after the agitation and anxieties caused him by this unfortunate occurrence. In a few days he was all alone in the house except for me and the servants," he wrote. Wagnière was forgetting Father Adam, who had survived by clinging to the chessboard.

News of the palace revolution at Ferney soon reached Geneva, Dijon, and Paris. At every stop Madame Denis told everyone who would listen that she was innocent and knew nothing about the theft, that she would unmask the culprit and bring the stolen manuscripts back to her uncle. Not only the Geneva poem but also the *Mémoires secrets sur le roi de Prusse (Secret Memoirs about the King of Prussia)* had disappeared. This latter theft was much more serious, but fortunately these compromising memoirs did not make their way into print.

In Paris rumor was rife. Some said Voltaire had stolen the manuscripts himself as a pretext for turning out all the parasites at Ferney. Monsieur Hennin came by and pleaded in La Harpe's defense. Voltaire listened in silence. He wrote of La Harpe: "He took [the manuscript] out of my library without saying anything. This impudence had most unpleasant consequences for me. But I forgive him with all my heart, he did not sin out of malice. I have done him certain services and I shall do him others as long as I remain alive." Theft, lying, and ingratitude had become, in the space of a few months, "mere imprudence." No one could be more self-effacingly generous and kind than Voltaire.

Madame Denis was the only one who was making a fuss about this latest incident; Voltaire did all he could to draw a veil over it and never accused her of having played a part in the theft. To Richelieu he wrote that the severe climate at Ferney no longer agreed with Madame Denis's health; moreover, there was no longer a doctor available there to treat her.

Voltaire wanted people to believe that Madame Denis was going to Paris to collect some of his debts. But everyone knew that she was stupid as well as avaricious. She grabbed all the money within her reach, but either frittered it away senselessly or hid it like a peasant. Her crazy thriftlessness was the exact opposite of her uncle's spending habits: his expenditures were lavish, but at the same time he kept scrupulous accounts of where every penny went. In fact "Voltaire's" fortune had gone on growing, and this explanation was clearly a convenient fiction.

His worth represented a present-day capital of about ten million francs. Among his recalcitrant debtors was his lifelong friend the Duc de Richelieu, and the departure of Madame Denis for Paris provided Voltaire with a good opportunity to plead his poverty—and to conveniently explain why she had left Ferney.

On April 4, 1768, he wrote to his other niece, the Marquise de Florian, giving her too an explanation of Madame Denis's departure: "It is but right and necessary that I should speak to you in confidence, my dear Picards. You know the unfortunate effects of ill humor. You know how much of it Madame has on occasion shown toward you. Remember the scene that Monsieur de Florian was obliged to endure. She has made me suffer an even crueler one. It is sad that neither her reason nor her kindness can enable her soul to avoid these violent storms that upset and afflict worldly society. I am persuaded that the hidden reason for the outbursts that escape her from time to time was her natural aversion toward country life, which could be overcome only by great numbers of visitors, festivities, and magnificence. But this turbulent life does not suit either my seventy-four years or my weak health."

Everyone knew the uncle was as fond of society as the niece. But his one concern was to stifle any malicious rumors as to the real circumstances surrounding Madame Denis's sudden departure from Ferney.

Voltaire has so often been shown in a bad light that it would be unfair not to point out that in this affair he dealt more generously with Madame Denis than she had a right to expect.

An Old Philosopher's Merry Pranks

In 1768 a monk visited Ferney during Holy Week, and Voltaire airily said to him: "To set a good example I think I shall take Easter communion on Sunday. I imagine you will be good enough to give me the necessary absolution?" "Certainly," the monk replied, "I give it to you here and now." They lunched together, and the monk went on his way.

On Easter Sunday Voltaire took it into his head not only to go to church but to preach to his parishioners on the subject of theft, as there had been some pilfering at Ferney recently. Wagnière pointed out to him that he had no right to deliver a sermon in church. Voltaire took no notice, and during mass the curé was surprised to hear him addressing the congregation in suitably moving and dramatic accents. Recovering from his astonishment, the priest resumed his place on the steps of the altar and went on celebrating the mass. Voltaire sought forgiveness with a few flowery compliments, but the affair had considerable repercussions. All sorts of stories were invented. People said Voltaire had entered the church with an escort of gamekeepers carrying candles; they quoted the things he had supposedly said, making sure that their version was as scandalous as possible. Others added that he had been accompanied by drummers, and that the strangest thing about the whole business was his attitude of solemn reverence. The Bishop of Annecy was soon informed, as was the French court.

The news was welcomed at first at Versailles: they thought Voltaire must have been converted. But when the details became known everyone turned against him. The bigots accused him of sacrilege, the *philosophes* of apostasy. In point of fact, he had simply yielded to the temptation to act a new part before a large and unusual audience.

The Bishop of Annecy wrote him a dignified and temperate letter: "Since you made your Easter communion of your own free will I must believe you behaved as you did in all sincerity. No decent man, even though he were an unbeliever, could take part in such a farce without dishonoring himself, and hence you are a Christian, and I cannot consider you as an enemy of the Catholic religion. Nonetheless your communion was made without repentance, without the amends made necessary by your past writings and conduct, and you should not approach the holy table without giving pledges of your sincerity, and without due reflection no priest will authorize you to do so."

Voltaire sent him a dilatory reply, and the bishop wrote again, in much sharper terms. Pretending to be a humble sheep in the bishop's flock, Voltaire protested his good faith and asked for his prayers, but the bishop replied that faith consists in acts, not words. Voltaire, who wanted to lure the bishop onto his own ground, where he could make him look foolish, was incensed at this bluntness. The bishop, mistrusting his correspondent, had taken certain precautions, which Voltaire recounted to D'Argental: "I still have not recovered from my surprise when I was told that that foolish fanatic of Annecy, the so-called Bishop of Geneva and son of a most inefficient mason, had sent his letters and my replies to the King. The replies are letters from a church father instructing a dolt."

Voltaire used every weapon at his disposal to damage the bishop's reputation. He said the prelate had applied for a *lettre de cachet* to put the master of Ferney behind bars and called the bishop "a foreigner from the mountains more fit to sweep chimneys than to direct consciences." He spread the story that the bishop had begged the King "to do him the favor of driving a sick old man of seventy-five out of the house he had built himself and the fields he had reclaimed, and of tearing him away from a hundred families whose lives depended on him. The King found this proposition improper and unchristian, and conveyed as much to the prelate."

What Voltaire omitted to mention was that he himself had received a letter from the King rebuking him for his excess of piety and zeal. But the bishop saw to it that the letter was made public, and Voltaire vowed to create an even greater furor the following Easter.

And indeed, one day in March 1769, as he lay in bed, he saw two men walking in the garden. He sent Wagnière to investigate: it was the curé of Ferney and a poor Capuchin friar who had come to lend the curé a hand during the crush of Holy Week confessions. Voltaire was suddenly inspired.

"Is it true that the Bishop of Annecy has forbidden anyone to hear my confession or give me communion?" he asked Wagnière. He knew very well that this was the case: it was he who had spread the news. But he wanted to make it clear that what was about to follow was an act not of sacrilege but of defiance.

"Well," he said, "since that is so I am going to confess and take communion despite him. I don't want to go to church; I want to do it all in my own room—in bed would be the best. It could be very amusing, and we shall see who comes off best, the bishop or I. Go and fetch the friar. Have you any money on you? You do? All right then: put a new écu on the table by the bed so that my friend will be able to see it."

Wagnière returned with the friar, and Voltaire put on his best deathbed act—glazed eyes, hollow voice, skinny hands plucking at the lace coverlet. His words were equally touching: "Father, the holy time of Easter draws near, and I should like to perform my duties as a Frenchman, an officer of the Crown, and the lord of the parish. But I am too ill to go to the church. I should like you to hear my confession here."

At this point he put the écu into the monk's hand. The monk was petrified. At last he said he could not comply straight away as several people were waiting for him in the church, but he promised to return in three days if by God's grace the gentleman remained in the same pious frame of mind. Then he hurried off, trembling, and Voltaire resigned himself to losing his newly minted écu.

But he persevered. For three days he had the news circulated that he was at death's door. Still no friar. What was needed was proof. The surgeon, Dugros, was sent for. But he pronounced Voltaire's pulse excellent and congratulated him. At this Voltaire rose up in a fury and ordered him to take it again. The agitated doctor's pulse was now worse than the patient's, but this time he caught on and said: "You have a high fever." "By God, I knew it," Voltaire exclaimed. "I have been on the brink of death these three days. Pray go tell the curé at once. He knows what he must do for a dying man."

But another three days elapsed and there was still no friar. Voltaire sent a threatening note, this time invoking not the curé's Christian charity but the law of the land. "The statutes provide that upon the third attack of fever a sick man is given the sacraments. Monsieur de Voltaire informs Monsieur le Curé of Ferney that he has had eight violent attacks."

No answer. The priests had had orders from the bishop and did not dare budge without counterorders. Afraid both of their superior and of the wrath of the "Devil of Ferney," they scarcely knew what to do, and anxiously awaited an answer to their request for instructions that they had sent by messenger to Annecy. At one in the morning Voltaire got all the servants out of bed and sent them to beg the curé to come: Monsieur was going to die and wanted to set his soul at rest. If the curé still refused, Wagnière, who went with the servants, was to solemnly remind him of the laws of the land, the decrees of the Parlement, and the cannons of the Church. He was to assure the priest that his master was ready to make any declaration the Church might require, in public if they wished. Voltaire had sent along a written promise to that effect, signed before Wagnière and another witness.

But neither the curé nor the Capuchin would stir.

At daylight Voltaire sent a bailiff with a summons, threatening them with a lawsuit before the Parlement for refusing to administer the sacraments.

When the two priests were served the summons Monsieur Bert, the curé, was seized with such a severe colic that some months later he died of it. He had predicted as much, blaming his illness on the shock he had received on being served the summons, to which Voltaire replied that he was a wretched toper who had taken to drinking the communion wine. If the charge was true, one wonders whether Voltaire's gift to him after the row—a fine new communion chalice—was not a deliberately ironic peace offering.

For the moment Voltaire was still in bed trying to force Stepmother Church to give him the last rites to which he was entitled by law. He sent for Maître Roffo, the notary at Ferney, and asked him to record an irrefutably orthodox profession of faith witnessed by Father Adam, S.J. In the midst of this whole carefully staged farce the bishop's reply arrived. The priests were given authorization, doubtless accompanied by a long list of recommendations and reservations, to go to the dying man's bedside.

The friar was shaking with fright. Voltaire began by pretending to have forgotten the *Confiteor* and the Apostles' Creed, which he had just dictated to the notary. On being prompted, he solemnly repeated them.

The friar was in such a state, he kept mixing up the two, whereupon Monsieur de Voltaire would kindly set him right.

Then he made a verbal profession of faith that was a profession of deism, not Catholicism. "I adore God in my own room. I do evil to no one." But the Capuchin was armed for this emergency: he had a profession of faith in his pocket all ready for Voltaire to sign. Voltaire thereupon came out of his make-believe coma to demonstrate to the monk that the Apostles' Creed was all-embracing and that the friar's profession of faith might introduce unorthodox innovations. But the monk insisted that the "dying" man sign his paper. At such obstinacy Voltaire dropped his charade of illness. According to Wagnière, he thundered out an oration full of such sublime rhetoric that everyone was overwhelmed by his eloquence. Seeing out of the corner of his eye that the moment was ripe, Voltaire cried out to the monk in stentorian tones: "Give me absolution at once!" The friar was forced to give in at last. Stammering and stuttering, forgetting all about the profession of faith and the bishop's instructions, before witnesses he pronounced the formula of absolution. Voltaire lay back on his pillow, beaming. The priests tottered out, supported by the doctor, Wagnière, and the notary.

After a time the curé and the notary returned and the curtain rose on another act. The curé gave Voltaire communion, and Maître Roffo recorded the illustrious penitent's words: "With God in my mouth I sincerely forgive those who have written calumnies about me to the King and who have not succeeded in their malicious designs."

The audience then left, and hardly was the last visitor through the door than Wagnière saw his hitherto moribund master leap nimbly out of bed. "I've had a little trouble with that dreary monk, but it's all been most amusing and done me good. Let's take a walk around the garden."

For once the comments of friends and enemies agreed. Even D'Argental was shocked. Their condemnation of this farce was unanimous. Tronchin wrote: "I have been sent Voltaire's confession of faith. He must have lost all sense of shame. Whom does he expect to take in with such nonsense? Fools?" In fact Voltaire had only wanted to get the better of the Bishop of Annecy, but all Europe talked of nothing but his blasphemous prank.

When he heard what people were thinking of this shocking tomfoolery he tried, rather unconvincingly, to justify his behavior. "I have forthrightly received the viaticum despite attacks by those who envy me and expressly declared I was dying in the religion of His Most Christian Majesty and of my native country." He was an excellent actor, but the play he had staged was a poor one. Frederick took him severely to task for this escapade. Voltaire nonetheless went on playing this role he had cast himself in. He had Massillon's Lenten sermons read out to him at meals—"such an excellent style," he would say with mock piety. "What style! What harmony!" Then suddenly he would exclaim: "That's enough of Massillon!"—and would launch into conversation, laughing, as dazzling, as ever young at heart even though he was now well past his seventieth birthday.

The time that followed was an extremely fruitful period for Voltaire. The readings from Massillon served to fill his days, for the house was much quieter now. He had much more time for writing and dictating, and he produced the delightful tale, *L'Homme aux quarante écus* (*The Man with Forty Crowns*), in which his allusions to the cruel rapacity of financiers made him enemies among the royal fiscal authorities. He also wrote *La Princesse de Babylone*, another masterpiece of subtle wit. In 1769 he published the *Lettres d'Amabaal* and numerous *Epistles:* one of them, entitled *Epitre à mon vaisseau* (*Epistle to My Ship*) was dedicated to the Nantes shipbuilder who had named one of his vessels after Voltaire. This had inspired the ever watchful Piron to write:

> Si j'avais un Vaisseau qui se nommât Voltaire,
> Sous cet auspice heureux, j'en ferais un corsaire.

If I had a ship that was named Voltaire,/Under such happy auspices I would turn it into a pirate vessel.

Among many other rapidly completed works written during this period was the more weighty *Histoire du Parlement de Paris,* produced at the instigation of the government in order to cast discredit on the claims of the Parlements. The history was published anonymously but everyone recognized its author. Fearing the wrath of the Parlements, Voltaire denied all responsibility for the work.

On July 7, 1769, he wrote to D'Argental: "As for the history you speak of, my dear angel, there is no truth whatsoever to the claim that I am the author of it. It can only be by someone who has dug about for two whole years in dusty archives." Apprehension drove him two days later to write to D'Alembert: "I find it absurd that people should attribute to me a work in which two or three passages can only have come out of a dusty office in which I have most assuredly never set foot. But calumny takes no notice of such details."

He also wrote yet another tragedy, *Les Guèbres* (*The Parsees*), which took him only six days and was just as tedious as *Les Scythes.* According to him, it was his best work—but with him his latest work was always the best. His real discovery that year, however, was *opéra comique,* light opera in which there was spoken dialogue. Hitherto Voltaire had despised it, but at the age of seventy-five, charmed by the visit to Ferney of André Grétry, one of its foremost practitioners, he fell in love with it. He said to the visitor: "You are a musician and a wit, and that combination is altogether too rare, monsieur, for me not to take the liveliest interest in you."

Grétry was wise enough to smile at this jibe against the general lack of wit among musicians, and they agreed to collaborate in writing an *opéra comique*. They decided to base it on Voltaire's story *L'Ingénu* (*The Innocent*) and to call this version of it *Le Huron* (*The Boor*).

One day when Voltaire fell into a melancholy mood, as he sometimes did after a period of excitement, he sent for a comic-opera troupe from Geneva. There were forty-nine actors and musicians, and he had them put on four *opéras comiques* for him at Ferney.

He also wrote the libretto for another *opéra comique*, *Le Baron d'Otrante* (*The Baron of Otranto*). The dialogue was half in Italian and half in French. Grétry proposed it to the Comédie Italienne in Paris. The company liked it but objected to the Italian dialogue. Grétry had orders to say the text was by a young writer in the provinces who would not agree to any changes, and they therefore refused it. They would have taken it had they known who the author was, but Grétry dared not disobey orders. So the seventy-five-year-old beginner was cheated of his début on the boards of the *opéra comique*.

Brushes with a Learned Jesuit: Monsieur de Buffon Is Wounded

In his innocence Father Niedham, an Irish Jesuit and scientist and the friend and collaborator of the great naturalist Buffon, had the audacity to refute certain ideas in the *Philosophical Dictionary*. He knew "sad Bonnet" of Geneva, but the latter did not warn him of the temerity of his undertaking. The Jesuit thought his scientific experience would be more than enough to defeat a polemicist who was a mere poet. He was forgetting Voltaire's universality and the seventeen years he had spent with Madame du Châtelet, which had given him a scientific background far above that of the other poets and even many of the philosophers of his time.

Voltaire did not like people to be the friends of his enemies, and Buffon, who was the friend of both Niedham and Président de Brosses, was therefore in some danger. He was a levelheaded man and sensibly tried to damp down the quarrel by not interfering and leaving Voltaire's attacks on him unanswered, but he was under no illusions as to the latter's sentiments. "As I do not read any of Voltaire's insults it is only through friends that I have earned of the things he has been pleased to say about me. . . . He is vexed because Niedham lent me his microscopes and because I said he was a good observer. That is the particular reason which, joined to the general effect of his pretensions to universality and his jealousy of anyone else's celebrity, embitters a spleen already exacerbated with age, so that he appears to be bent on burying all his contemporaries before he himself dies." Buffon wrote this to Président de Brosses, who must have read it with great pleasure. In fact, Voltaire had also reproached Buffon for having been taken in by the "eels" which, according to Niedham, could be spontaneously generated in flour moistened with mutton broth. Niedham and Voltaire differed again over the question of how the presence of the fossilized shells on the tops of mountains was to be accounted for. Both sides of the argument seem amazing to us. Voltaire wanted to prove that the whole idea of the creation in seven days as outlined in the Book of Genesis was ridiculous, and his hatred of tradition filled him with a new fanaticism.

Voltaire was confident that he was one of the best thinkers of the age, far superior to men such as Montesquieu and Buffon. Had not Vestris, the famous dancer, said: "There are only three great men in Europe: the King of Prussia, Monsieur de Voltaire, and myself"? On hearing someone praise Buffon's monumental work, *L'Histoire naturelle*, Voltaire exclaimed: "Not so natural as all that!"

At the end of the year 1768 he heard that the King of Denmark had been bold enough to say at Fontainebleau, before the disapproving King and court, "It was Voltaire who taught me to think." This gave the recluse of Ferney as much pleasure as the Capuchin friar's absolution.

But soon afterward he was mourning the death of his friend Damilaville, on December 13, 1768. There is a story that when Damilaville heard that the doctors had given up hope for him he sold his furniture, gathered his friends about him, drank champagne merrily with them for the last time, and died a few hours later. But this is a fable. He died in bed after a terrible illness, leaving a wife no one had ever heard of before, who appeared only to carry off her dead husband's personal effects. He left nothing in the way of liquid assets, not even enough money to pay his faithful servant. Voltaire assumed the responsibility for keeping the poor servant alive—yet another pension—and received the condolences of those who knew of his friendship for Damilaville. "I shall miss Damilaville for the rest of my life," he wrote to D'Alembert. "I hoped that in the end he would come and share my retreat with me." Yet Damilaville was only forty-seven. Grimm, who pretended to be grief-stricken in order to flatter Voltaire, wrote: "So the mourner in the Alps has received the letter from the Prophet of Bohemia [i.e., Grimm himself]. Though a hundred leagues divide them the fearless champion of reason and the virtuous enemy of fanaticism weep together. Damilaville is dead and fat Fréron flourishes."

In reply to a letter from Thiériot, Voltaire wrote: "I am very glad you referred to 'our dear Damilaville,' but for more than two years now I have been under the impression that you and he were no longer friends. . . . He was fearless in friendship." More fearless than Thiériot, whose reconciliation with the dead man was a pretense aimed at pleasing Voltaire so as to remain in a position to exploit his friendship.

Father Adam's Wig and the Pope

Father Adam was bald and during the winter of 1769 he often caught cold celebrating mass. Voltaire undertook to remedy this situation by endeavoring to obtain a papal dispensation permitting Father Adam to wear a wig, a privilege priests did not enjoy. Cardinal de Bernis, who lived in Rome, was charged with this delicate mission. On June 12, 1769, Voltaire wrote to the cardinal concerning the new Pope, Clement XIV, who had recently been elected:

". . . since you have chosen him he is certainly worthy of the small office you have conferred upon him. And, monseigneur, since men in small offices can grant small favors, there is one that I have need of and for which I ask your intercession . . . it is merely a matter of granting permission to wear a wig. It is not for my own poor skull that I request such a favor, but for another old man. . . ." He then described his worthy but chilly chaplain. "He will pray for Your Eminence with all his heart if you will have the goodness to employ the authority of the Vicar of Christ to cover the poor wretch's skull. And I shall be greatly obliged to you, monseigneur, if you will condescend to send me as soon as possible a fine wig-brief."

No answer came, and Voltaire was in despair, not so much on Father Adam's account as because securing a favor from the Pontiff himself would be such an amusing little coup. "I have opened negotiations with the Pope about a wig, but I see I am going to fail."

Not at all—he got his wig-brief. There was one difficulty however: Father Adam had to get confirmation from his bishop, and his bishop was Monseigneur d'Annecy. So they dispensed with that formality, and Voltaire, more delighted with the wig than if it had been the crown of the Holy Roman Empire, wrote quantities of doggerel in its honor. He sent these verses to Bernis:

> Quand on est couvert de lauriers
> On peut donner une perruque.
> Prêtez-moi quelques rimes en uque
> Pour orner mes vers familiers.
> Nous n'avons que celle d'eunuque.
> Ce mot me conviendrait assez;
> Mais ce mot est une sottise
> Et les beaux princes de l'Eglise
> Pourraient s'en tenir offensés.

When one is wreathed in laurels/One can afford to bestow a peruke./Lend me some rhymes in -uque/To ornament my informal verses./The only one there is is 'eunuch,'/Which would be good enough for me/But the world is an insult,/And the fine princes of the Church/ Might be offended by it.

He wrote to Bernis in a bantering tone: "My word, that Pope of yours seems a clever fellow. Has he really done nothing stupid since he came to power?" Bernis showed the letter to the Pope, who merely laughed. "His Holiness," Bernis wrote, "is pleased at your jest, and speaks admiringly of the superiority of your talents. If you turn out to be a good Capuchin, he will dare to love you as much as he esteems you."

These were prelates after Voltaire's own heart, not like his ridiculous bishop, the son of a mason who took the priesthood seriously.

The reference to being a Capuchin was not an idle one. The general of the Order of St. Francis had just sent letters to Voltaire in recognition of the services he had rendered to the Capuchin friars of Gex, his neighbors. Voltaire had treated the Jesuits roughly but helped the poor Franciscans, who were harmless. Their simplicity made him laugh, as did the honor now bestowed on him: "Joan the Maid and gentle Agnés Sorel[1] are both amazed at my new dignity." And he wrote to Bernis: "I must not fail to give you my blessing. Accept it with as much cordiality as I bestow it. For if you are a cardinal, I am a Capuchin." Frederick congratulated him wryly, delighted to see him in such good company but warning him that pending his canonization "The Holy Father is having you burned in Rome." It was true. While Voltaire wore the habit of St. Francis, some pamphlets of which he was the author were condemned and burned in the Holy City.

Do not almost all of us resemble the old general of ninety who, having met a group of young men who were misbehaving with girls, said to them in anger: "Gentlemen, is that the sort of example I set you?" (*Philosophical Dictionary:* "Character")

The princess: "What does the practice of medicine consist of then?" The doctor: "I have already told you; of tidying up, of cleaning, of keeping the house that cannot be rebuilt in good order. Your servants clean your palace, but it was built by the architect." (*Philosophical Dictionary:* "Illness")

The apostles of suicide tell us that it is quite permissible to leave one's house when one is tired of it. This I grant; but most men would rather sleep in an ugly house than sleep outdoors under the stars. (*Philosophical Dictionary:* "Cato. Suicide.")

In all my passions I have detested the vice of ingratitude; and if I were under obligation to the Devil, I would say nice things about his horns. (Letter, 1771)

The fact that the biretta of a Pope governs the fly of a prince by divine right is one of the most ridiculous things about us. (Letter, 1771)

I am passionately fond of speaking truths that others dare not speak and of fulfilling duties that others dare not fulfill. (Letter, 1771)

One's manner of digestion almost always determines our manner of thinking. (Letter, 1772)

It is absurd that we know what a cook serves us for supper and yet know nothing of what a so-called healer serves us when we are ill. (Letter, 1774)

One always goes too far, either when one insists on his rights or when one attacks those of others. (Letter, 1777)

One must combat nature and ill fortune to the very last moment and never despair of anything until one is dead. (Letter, August 1777)

In 1771 Voltaire was overjoyed to learn that his efforts to rehabilitate the Sirvens had met with success, and the family came to Ferney to thank him. "To think that it took only two hours to condemn them, and nine years to have their innocence legally recognized," he wrote.

Soon other affairs, just as horrible as the Sirven case but less well known, were brought to his attention. A peasant, for example, was condemned to death by a provincial judge who sent the dossier to the Paris Parlement, who simply ratified the sentence without even examining the record. Had they done so they would have seen that when the accused was confronted with the only witness the latter said, "That's not him." "Oh," the accused exclaimed, "he doesn't recognize me." This innocent but awkward remark was taken as proof of his guilt, and he was broken on the wheel, protesting his innocence to the last. A year later a tramp was arrested and confessed to a number of crimes, among them the murder for which the peasant had been put to death. The man's family, ruined and dishonored, had fled to Hungary, and although Voltaire forced the Parlement to review the trial, rehabilitation was never granted.

Then there was the Montbailli affair. Monsieur and Madame Montbailli were awakened one morning by a woman who wanted to speak to Monsieur's mother, who slept in an adjoining room. On entering the mother's room they found her on the floor; she had fallen out of bed and received a severe injury when her head hit a piece of furniture as she fell. Montbailli cried, "Oh, God, my mother is dead!" and fainted. The neighbors came running, and a doctor declared that the old woman was indeed dead. Gossip soon had it that the old woman drank and often quarreled with her son and daughter-in-law, and so they had killed her. This was ridiculous: the children had gained nothing by her death. She left nothing but debts, and it was she who owned the lease of the shop in which they worked. Her death deprived them of their very livelihood. Nevertheless they were brought before the bar of justice, if that is the proper word, tortured, and sentenced. The man was to have his hand cut off and be broken on the wheel, his wife was to be burned at the stake. When Montbailli's hand was cut off he said, "That is not the hand of a murderer," and he protested his innocence till his last breath. As the wife was pregnant, her execution was postponed for six months. It was at this point that Voltaire intervened, with the aid of Chancellor Maupeou. The Council of Arras unanimously acquitted the wife and, "nobler and prouder than the Parlement of Toulouse, wept over the irreparable injustice of having caused the death of an innocent man." The wife returned home, where the idiotic villagers who had ruined her life lighted bonfires to welcome her home.

Voltaire also tried to obtain the rehabilitation of Lally-Tollendal, an army officer wrongly accused of high treason; then he busied himself with the case of a man called Morangies; then with the liberation of the serfs of Saint-Claude in the Jura. This tangle of legal proceedings seems a terrible labyrinth to us, but Voltaire could sort out the threads, and tangle them, too, whenever it was in the interests of his protégés. Once he had set himself a goal, he worked tirelessly to reach it, tunneling his way through mountains of evidence, digging through the records till justice was done.

It was not petty considerations or vanity that supplied him with the energy to accomplish this monumental labor. He so often lied and toadied that it is natural that his intentions should sometimes be suspect, but throughout it is impossible to doubt his generosity, his sense of justice, and his humanity.

Could he really have been the man with the "hideous smile" that Musset speaks of?

In the nineteenth-century pedantic village atheists like Monsieur Homais in Flaubert's *Madame Bovary* were considered the true disciples of Voltaire, and Musset, as a fashionable poet, was merely mirroring his public's view of Voltaire as a heartless unbeliever. But did Voltaire wear a "hideous smile" when he wrote to his notary on April 13, 1773, that he would see to it that Sirven, who had had to pay the costs of the unjust trial that had led to condemnation, would receive all the money that was needed to meet these costs?

In 1773, when people were dying of hunger in Gex, he imported wheat from Sicily which he sold below cost. He kept harassing Monsieur Arnelot, the intendant of Dijon: "I am at my wit's end," he wrote. "I have eighty people to feed." More people in want were arriving from Franche-Comté. Voltaire asked permission to buy reserves of requisitioned wheat which were not being used, and gave full details. Passing this request on to the influential statesman and economist Turgot, Condorcet remarked: "I should like it to be discussed in the Privy Council, that the King may see that the nation's greatest writer is also one of the most beneficent of men and the best of citizens."

But as well as this generous Voltaire there was also the Voltaire who was the adversary of men such as Fréron and La Beaumelle. His friends counseled moderation and indifference toward those whom D'Alembert called "caterpillars." But Voltaire still had to break a lance or two.

A new target in 1772 was a pretentious little pedant named Antoine Sabatier who had been expelled from the seminary at Castres. He became a poetaster in Toulouse, then got himself invited to Paris by the philosopher Helvétius. He was supported by the Encyclopedists, whom he renounced when he was no longer hungry, and soon he attacked. His first victim was Voltaire. This would not have mattered had the court not decided to further the fortunes of Sabatier and grant him a pension. Voltaire wrote: "What say you to this wretch who has jumped from his mudhole into a sacristy and got himself a benefice? . . . This is the man who is passing himself off as a father of the Church at court. These are the sort of people who are rewarded. This fine fellow has become a confessor, though he certainly deserves rather to be executed in the Place de la Grève."

Masquerading as a priest at Versailles, Sabatier was sleeping in the apartment of the minister Vergennes and was tutor to his children, while working on a translation of Boccaccio's *Decameron* as well. By the time of the Revolution he was collecting four pensions. He had already won a title to fame with his pamphlet against Voltaire: *Tableau philosophique de l'esprit de M. de Voltaire* (*A Philosophical Portrait of the Mind of Monsieur de Voltaire*). It was so vile a libel that Rousseau himself refused to finish reading it. But Voltaire did, suffering greatly in the process.

Voltaire also had to endure fresh attacks from La Beaumelle, who after several periods in the Bastille had for some time remained prudent and silent. But now Ferney was bombarded with anonymous letters. Voltaire knew who their author was from the very first. They were sent from Lyons and arrived with relentless regularity, each one implanting its poisoned dart. There were ninety-four of them, and on receiving the ninety-fifth Voltaire had a sort of epileptic attack which greatly alarmed those about him. Then, recovering himself, he seized his pen and wrote to Monsieur de Sartine, commissioner of police in Paris, and the Minister for Home Affairs, Monsieur de Saint-Florentin. Monsieur de Saint-Florentin was convinced that the letters were indeed from La Beaumelle. La Vaysse, whom Voltaire had saved from imprisonment and torture, had gone over to the enemy camp and may even have written the letters at La Beaumelle's dictation. The minister wrote to the Governor of Foix instructing him to enjoin La Beaumelle to leave Voltaire in peace, on pain of serious trouble. La Beaumelle swore he had published nothing against Voltaire since he had last come out of prison; but of course the anonymous letters were handwritten, not printed. Meanwhile he was preparing a *Commentaire des oeuvres de Voltaire* (*Commentary on the Works of Voltaire*), still another libelous broadside. But La Beaumelle died in 1773, when he had only got as far as tearing *La Henriade* to pieces. Voltaire succeeded in preventing the publication of the *Commentaire* for the time being, but in 1775 it appeared thanks to the efforts of Fréron, who had added to it with his own libelous biography of Voltaire.

Piron also died in 1773, at the age of eighty-three, unlamented by Voltaire. He had been rid of two of his enemies in the space of a single year. But Fréron still remained, and found a way of spoiling the pleasure Voltaire would otherwise have derived from Piron's death. He spread a rumor that Piron had said that Voltaire, who had not dared attack him while he was alive, would not fail to insult his corpse, as he had Crébillon's. And in order to avenge these posthumous insults, Piron had left behind a sort of delayed-action bomb in case Voltaire should attack him. He had passed on to his heir a box containing a hundred and fifty epigrams against Voltaire, to be left off at the rate of one a week in the direction of Ferney. "They will enliven the solitude of the respectable old gentleman of that canton for three years," he promised. It was a diabolical idea.

We do not know whether Voltaire, duly informed of all this, profited by the warning. At any event, none of the hundred and fifty poisoned darts has come down to us. But before he died Piron had launched some real shafts against Voltaire, whom he accused, among over even older grievances, of having dissuaded Frederick from inviting him to Berlin. This is quite possible. Voltaire defended himself by saying he had never mentioned to Frederick a poet he had only caught a passing glimpse of three times many years before and had never met personally. To refresh his memory Piron had circulated this epigram:

> Sur l'auteur dont l'épiderme
> Est collé tout près des os
> La mort tarde à frapper ferme
> De peur d'ébrécher sa faux.
> Lorsqu'il aura les yeux clos,
> Car si faut-il qu'il y vienne,
> Adieu renom, bruit et los
> Le Temps jouera de la sienne.

Upon the author whose skin/Clings to his bones/Death hesitates to strike/ For fear of damaging its scythe./But when his eyes are shut,/For he will one day reach that point,/Farewell renown and celebrity, and then/Time's scythe will take its toll.

Piron had wished for Voltaire's death, and Voltaire had secretly rejoiced at Piron's. But for once he had sense enough not to gloat over the demise of an enemy.

Madame Denis was living on the Rue Bergère, supported by the extremely generous allowance she received from her uncle. But she feared that if she stayed away from him too long some other influence than hers might jeopardize her privileged place in Voltaire's affections.

She felt that her future inheritance was in danger and did all she could to oppose an arrangement which Voltaire contemplated making with his principal debtor, the Duke of Württemberg. Voltaire wanted to make the duke his chief heir in return for an annuity. By the terms of this arrangement all the debts owed Voltaire would have been passed on to the duke—together with the trouble of collecting them. But Madame Denis cared nothing for her uncle's peace and quiet, which might have been well served by this scheme: what she was worried about was losing her share of Voltaire's immense fortune. The project had been under discussion for several years and had been the cause of violent disagreements between the pair at Ferney. There had even been talk of selling the estate.

The sale of Ferney would have provided income for Madame Denis, but she wanted Ferney as it was, so as to enjoy both the capital it represented and the income it brought in. In Paris she went from notary to notary, trying to get her uncle to give up this project that would mean disaster for her.

She asked to be allowed to resume her old place at Ferney a hundred times and finally succeeded. Voltaire allowed her to come back in October 1769, after an exile that had lasted a year and a half. Voltaire welcomed his niece back with gaiety and open arms; the two of them shed the requisite tears and took up their interrupted conversation as if nothing had happened.

Life at Ferney brightened up again. Visitors became more frequent again and the table was set for guests every day. Voltaire hid himself away more and more, apart from startling appearances in the crowded salon now and again, lively as a lizard and decked in gleaming brocades or "imperial" furs.

He was not forgotten in Paris. Madame Necker, who like her famous husband the financier and economist was from Geneva, gave a banquet in 1770 for the most renowned *philosophes*, and at the end of the splendid dinner someone expressed surprise that as yet no statue of Voltaire had been erected. Everyone agreed that there ought to be one, and the artist chosen to execute it was Pigalle, the greatest sculptor of the century, whom Voltaire called "the French Phidias." At first only writers were to be invited to subscribe, but as at that time they were neither very numerous nor very rich, and as many of them were no friends of Voltaire's, it was decided to admit to the list other important people. One of these was the Duc de Richelieu, who pledged fifty louis but reduced it to twenty on being told he would otherwise outshine all the other subscribers. The minimum was two louis. Two sovereigns subscribed: the King of Denmark and Frederick. Frederick prudently asked how much he ought to contribute and was told: "Your name and an écu, sire." He wrote of Voltaire: "Profane Greece would have made a god of him and erected a temple in his honor. We erect only a statue, a meager recompense for all the persecutions he has undergone."

Pigalle set out for Ferney, where the entire project nearly came to nothing. Pigalle wanted to portray Voltaire "*à l'antique*"; that is to say, naked save for a peplum. Though enchanted at the idea of being sculpted, Voltaire was horrified at the idea of having to pose semi-nude. He wrote to Madame Necker, pointing out that he was seventy-six and physically ravaged after his most recent illness. "Monsieur Pigalle is to come, I am told, to model my face. But, madame, for that I should need to have a face, and it would be difficult even to discern that I possess one. My eyes are sunk three inches, my cheeks are old parchment barely clinging to bones that threaten to cave in. The few teeth I once had are gone. . . . Never has a poor man been sculpted in such a state."

D'Alembert wrote him a beautiful letter of reassurance. "As long as genius breathes it has a face that its brother genius can easily discern, and Pigalle will find in the two carbuncles Nature has given you for eyes the fire with which he will animate your statue. I cannot tell you, my beloved and respected colleague, how flattered Monsieur Pigalle is at having been chosen to erect this monument to your glory and his own, and that of the entire French nation."

But Voltaire, looking in his mirror, was unconvinced, and did his best to get out of it, cajoling Pigalle, entertaining him lavishly and making him waste his time. But at last the day came when he was obliged to pose. Voltaire refused to sit still; as usual he was all over the place, grimacing, dictating to Wagnière, pacing up and down. Pigalle was exhausted and depressed. It was almost time for him to go and he had got nowhere. At last, during the final sitting, the conversation turned to the subject of the Golden Calf. Voltaire maintained that this was a mere fiction like many other stories in the Bible and that it was impossible to cast a statue in four hours. Pigalle explained how a statue was cast and said it took six months. Voltaire listened fascinated, and Pigalle was thus able at last to model him. Pigalle was delighted, and so, for other reasons, was Voltaire, who seized his pen and wrote that the Bible text was a hoax and that Pigalle had just supplied him with further proof that this was so.

When Pigalle unveiled his masterpiece in Paris, some people said it was miraculous and others were horrified. Diderot, who had been an advocate of the "antique" pose, deemed the statue an incomparable success. Voltaire was chary with his praise: he would have preferred to appear decently clad and was apprehensive, not without reason, of sarcastic comment. He tried to joke about it himself, but his detractors did better, publishing verse satirizing the naked statue.

> J'ai vu chez Pigalle aujourd'hui
> Le modèle vanté de certaine statue.
> A cet oeil qui foudroie, à ce rire qui tue,
> A cet air si chagrin de la gloire d'autrui
> Je me suis écrié: Ce n'est pas là Voltaire,
> C'est un monstre! . . . Oh! m'a dit certain folliculaire,
> Si c'est un monstre, c'est bien lui!

Today at Pigalle's I saw/The much-vaunted model of a certain statue./ At the sight of withering gaze, that murderous smile,/That air so vexed at anyone else's glory/I cried: "That isn't Voltaire/It's a monster!" . . . "Oh," said a certain hack,/"if it's a monster, it's him all right!"

Voltaire was deeply hurt by these malicious comments and cursed the statue that had given rise to them. "A statue is no consolation when so many enemies conspire to sling mud at it," he remarked plaintively.

But his friends took up his defense in a very touching manner. Mademoiselle Clairon was "at home" on Tuesdays to the cream of Parisian society, and one Tuesday in September 1773 she asked her friends to excuse her for a moment, then returned to the drawing room to ask them to follow her into the next room. There they found an altar with an illuminated bust of Voltaire on it. A "goddess" then crowned him with laurels, reciting an ode composed by his loyal and charming friend Marmontel.

> Tu le poursuis jusq'à la tombe,
> Noire Envie, et pour l'admirer
> Tu dis: Attendons qu'il succombe
> Et qu'il vienne enfin expirer . . .

You pursue him unto the grave,/Black Envy, and to admire him you say:/"Let us wait until he dies,/Until he gives up the ghost at last. . . ."

The almost religious solemnity with which this ceremony was performed, the fervor of the ode, the beauty of the lady who recited it, and the distinguished audience that had been present all contributed to causing a great stir. Some people protested that it was sacrilege and idolatry; but many more found it a most fitting tribute. Voltaire was overcome with joy, and when La Harpe wrote to him he answered his ungrateful disciple without the slightest trace of bitterness: "So, my dear successor, they have tried to do to my image what they will one day do to you in person. Has Mademoiselle Clairon's house thereby become the temple of fame? It is only right and proper that she should confer laurels, for she herself is wreathed in them."

To thank Mademoiselle Clairon, he sent her these verses from Ferney:

> Les plus beaux moments de ma vie
> Sont donc ceux que je n'ai point vus!
> Vous avez orné mon image
> Des lauriers qui croissent chez vous
> Ma gloire, en dépit des jaloux,
> Fut en tous temps votre ouvrage.

The happiest moments of my life/Are those which I myself did not witness!/You have adorned my image/With laurels that grow beneath your own roof./My fame, whatever the envious may say,/Has always been your handiwork.

Voltaire's heady delight in this breath of friendship from Paris, reminding him of the triumphs of his youth, is very moving in an old man of seventy-nine.

On December 25, 1770, Voltaire received a joyless Christmas gift: the news that his protector, the Duc de Choiseul, had been turned out of his ministry. Madame du Barry had finally triumphed over him. It was a thunderbolt at Versailles, and the repercussions shook even faraway Ferney. Voltaire wrote: "The loss of Monsieur le Duc and Madame la Duchesse de Choiseul is a great blow to me. One can never count on anything that depends on the court. Even the chief minister of the Crown is never sure he will sleep in his own bed." Bravely, and with satisfaction at playing the role of faithful friend, he paid his respects to the fallen minister. He was not the only one. On Christmas Day Madame du Barry's antechamber was empty, and the road to Chanteloup, the country retreat to which Choiseul had retired, was jammed with coaches. But few of Choiseul's friends expressed their loyalty as delicately as Voltaire in a letter to Madame du Deffand, who was a member of the former minister's circle of intimates: "May I entertain the hope that you will be good enough to tell him that, even though I am the least useful and most wretched among the host of his humble servants, I would leave my bed if I could, ask his permission to come and sit by his and read to him."

But when Louis XV and Maupeou dissolved the Parlements that Choiseul had supported, Voltaire approved wholeheartedly. It was to this very end that he had written his famous *Histoire du Parlement* in 1769. It was a fierce attack, for Voltaire never forgot the Parlements' own ferocity and fanaticism. To deliver the country into the hands of these magistrates on the pretext of limiting the prerogatives of the monarch, was to rekindle the flames for books and authors, to revive dying feudal rights and give a new lease on life to the most outmoded of customs. Voltaire had seen through the magistrates who claimed, without proof, that the nation had given them a mandate to set themselves up as legislators. For a long time he had hated them implacably in the person of his brother Armand. He had also realized that in the conditions that prevailed in France at that time the monarchy was the guarantee of civic liberties, and that these could be ensured only by the submission of social classes and privileged bodies to the authority of the Crown. In his eyes the so-called reform of the Parlements was only an absurd step backward, a return to ancient tyrannies embodied in an anarchic administration. If he were forced to choose between tyrannies, Voltaire preferred that of order to that of disorder. "I would rather obey one tyrant than three hundred rats like myself," he wrote. He may not have been an ardent partisan of a representative system of government, but he was an enthusiastic supporter of the progress of enlightenment, well-being, and freedom.

The Choiseuls misunderstood Voltaire's attitude toward the Parlement.

They attributed the basest motives to him for supporting the new anti-Parlement minister and considered him a turncoat. When they read the letters which he wrote to Maupeou encouraging him in his fight against the Parlements and which Maupeou circulated in support of his policy, the fury and scorn of the Choiseuls knew no bounds. They had gone to great lengths to help Voltaire, and this impressed them as the blackest ingratitude. Madame du Deffand told him how they felt, and he wrote to Chanteloup at once to declare his loyalty. But they would not listen. The duchesse wrote: "Poor Voltaire doesn't know which way to turn. He is running with the hare and hunting with the hounds. He praises both the new chancellor and Monsieur de Choiseul, though he has nothing to hope or fear from either of them. But I confess that since his 'Address to the Nobility' his letters disgust me; I cannot understand them. This last one seemed to me a mere farrago."

Actually, Voltaire's attitude was quite sound: he liked and respected the fallen minister, but he had long been convinced that his successor's policy was more in accordance with the best interests of France.

Moreover, Voltaire had the responsibility of his "manufactories" to think of. If the minister lost interest in watches and stockings, what would his hundred workers and their families at Ferney live on? Voltaire's opinion was that ministers came and went and that the minister in power, whoever he might be, must help Ferney.

In her anger against Voltaire, Madame de Choiseul wrote: "He has always been cowardly without danger, insolent without cause, base without object. . . . He is to be lauded and despised, like all objects of idolatry." Voltaire defended himself and wrote to Madame du Deffand: "I am faithful to all my passions. You hate philosophers and I hate bourgeois tyrants. I have always forgiven you your fury against philosophy; I pray you to forgive me mine against the toils of the law." And he explained himself frankly to the Duchesse de Choiseul: "I shall die as true to the faith I swore to you as to my just hatred of men who persecuted me as long as they could and would persecute me still had they the power. I am surely under no obligation to love those who did me such a bad turn in January 1770 [when his *Histoire du Parlement* was prosecuted], who spill innocent blood, who bring barbarism into the midst of civilization, who, occupied solely with their own foolish vanity, give their cruelty free rein, now breaking Calas on the wheel, now torturing and savagely killing a young gentleman [La Barre] who deserved no more than six months' detention at Saint-Lazare and would have grown up to be worth more than all of them put together. They have defied the indignation of all Europe at this inhumanity; they have dragged in a tumbril, gagged, a lieutenant general [Lally-Tollendal] justly hated indeed, but whose innocence was clear to me from the very evidence at his trial: and I could produce twenty acts of equal barbarity that would make them execrable to all posterity. I would rather die in the [Swiss] canton of Zug or among the Samoyeds than be at the mercy of such compatriots."

But despite his implacable hatred of the Parlements, he also proclaimed his undying fidelity to Choiseul. This earned him no credit with the King or the new chancellor. Choiseul installed a weather vane made in the shape of a silhouette of Voltaire on a rooftop, and all Paris laughed at it during the entire month of May 1772.

In the course of that winter Voltaire wrote a tragedy, *Les Lois de Minos* (*The Laws of Minos*). It was another weapon in the war against fanaticism and encouraged abolishing old laws that were no longer necessary. This play was just as tedious as the others. Except to its author—who thought it sublime and was overwhelmed every time he read it. But by 1772 the Welches, or barbarians, as Voltaire called the French, were beginning to tire of tragedies, particularly Voltaire's. And though he expected a dazzling success, mingled with exciting scandal and new attacks, the play was not put on at all, and he sent it to Catherine.

Voltaire concerned himself with very nearly every problem that came to his attention, including that of finding a new wife for his dead niece's husband. Monsieur de Florian, the widower of Elisabeth Mignot, arrived one day at Ferney in tears, apparently inconsolable. Voltaire made much of him and by way of distraction introduced him to a charming little lady named Madame Rillet, who was separated from her husband. Monsieur de Florian wanted to marry her on the spot. But in order to do so he had to have a dispensation from Rome, because she was a Calvinist with a husband still living. Florian could scarcely wait to lead her to the altar.

Madame Denis professed to think it unseemly that her dead sister was being replaced in such haste, but Voltaire was touched by the revival of Florian's youthful ardor. To tell the truth, he himself had not been left entirely unmoved by young Madame Rillet: but his flame was merely metaphorical, and since jealousy in affairs of the heart was entirely foreign to Voltaire's nature, what he could not have himself he was delighted to see Florian obtain. He wrote to Cardinal de Bernis again, asking him to hurry things along in Rome, as delay might make the lovers fall into sin at any moment. Bernis replied that this was a more serious matter than Father Adam's wig and that the fact that Madame Rillet was a Calvinist was an insuperable obstacle. So Florian took his lady to a Protestant country where no questions were asked. They went to Constance and were married on the shores of the lake, "like barbarians."

Voltaire wrote to Bernis: "I told Your Eminence and His Holiness quite plainly that you would both have poor Florian's sin on your conscience. He got married as best he could. People may say the marriage is null and void, but the bride and groom have made it very real. What is the good of being Pope if you can't give permission to marry to whomever you like?"

The "little canary," as Voltaire called the new Marquise de Florian, fell ill and went to Montpellier with her husband for treatment while Voltaire built them an exquisite little house at Ferney, a miniature Marly which can still be seen today. But scarcely had the little canary settled into her new cage than she died, and Florian was once more left forlorn. But once again he married quickly. He lived with his new wife, Mademoiselle Joly, in the new house, and on their return from Paris the fourth Marquise de Florian presented Voltaire with a cordial letter from Buffon and a copy of his *Histoire naturelle* which he had given her to pass on to Voltaire when she was passing through Montbard. This meant that Voltaire and Buffon were reconciled, and in his delight Voltaire gave his charming messenger a gold repeating watch made in the Ferney workshops. Then he thanked Buffon, addressing him as Archimedes I. Buffon replied, calling him Voltaire I. Voltaire, recalling their quarrel on the subject of fossils, said: "I knew all the time that I couldn't continue to be at odds with Monsieur Buffon over a few shells."

During the previous year Voltaire had brought Le Kain to Ferney and there had been great theatrical activity. His own theater now housed silkworms, but he had built another on the road to Geneva. Traveling companies often acted there. It provided them their longest run after Dijon, because of the well-equipped theater and the wealthy Geneva audiences. The Genevans used to go there on foot in warm weather and sometimes linger in the country taverns so long on the way back that they would find the city gates shut. Then they would organize all-night parties and not go home till morning. Taverns, a café, and a billiard parlor had been set up near the theater.

When Le Kain arrived it was like the descent of the Holy Ghost for Voltaire, but they soon began squabbling over Le Kain's fee. "I have incurred ruinous expenses building and keeping up my colony," Voltaire claimed, "and building Monsieur de Florian's house has been the last straw." But Le Kain refused to give an inch, and Voltaire paid up. He did not regret it. He was mad with joy and admiration, and the citizens of Geneva flocked out to these purlieus of perdition.

This was all very much frowned on by the Council, and also by two Englishmen, Lord Stanhope and his son Lord Mahon, who were led by their hatred of France to stir up the Genevans against the theater, Voltaire, Ferney, and France itself. They hired hooligans to stand at the gates of the city and hurl insults at people coming back from the theater. It led to a great scandal, for among the people treated in this way were members of very respected families, and even an English ambassador. For once the Council and people of Geneva were in agreement: they declared that, even though they might be eager to set fire to the theater (and some of them made no secret of it), they preferred to burn it down themselves without any assistance from foreigners. Their quarrel with Voltaire had become a family quarrel, though none the less bitter for all that. The French ambassador protested to the Council, and the two Englishmen received a reprimand that tempered their zeal.

But nothing could dim the splendor of Le Kain's success, which was so prodigious that it probably marked the end of Geneva's prejudice against the theater. A number of pastors came to see the performances, and even those most set in their views often admitted the grandeur, nobility, and dignity of tragedy. What a triumph for Voltaire! He sat in a stage box, never missing a single performance. He would weep and exclaim and groan, or fall back overcome with emotion, projecting himself into each of the actor's parts. And though he was seventy-eight he would sometimes leap onto the stage and run about among the actors. If anyone in the pit dared to fidget he would fly into a rage and lean out perilously over the edge of his box, brandishing his stick. "Magnificent and honored lords!" he would shout. "This is my house, and if you don't keep still I'll have you given the soundest thrashing your Republic has ever seen." And indeed he had a guard of army veterans with cudgels stationed at the door. He wrote to D'Argental: "My dear Angel, I am in ecstasies over Le Kain. He has made me know *Sémiramis* as I never knew it before. All our Genevans have cried out with pain and pleasure, women have felt faint with emotion and been delighted. . . . I did not know the honor he did my works and how he brought them to life. . . ."

If Voltaire's hyperboles seem extravagant, we also have the evidence of a Genevan pastor, Antoine Mouchon. He describes the people's eagerness to flock to Ferney: the week that *Mahomet* was staged they forgot all about the lottery! People would pay a *louis* to hire a coach. "And I myself," he admits contritely, "shared this general folly. . . . I was witness to things so sublime, they even surpassed what I had expected, knowing the great actor's reputation." He then praised Le Kain in terms just as superlative as Voltaire's. "The thrill he produced was so universal it was the triumph of nature."

The worthy Mouchon went on to speak of the man behind it all: "But not the least part of the entertainment was Voltaire himself, sitting immediately adjoining the wings and expressing his approval like one possessed, either by thumping with his stick or uttering exclamations." Voltaire suddenly rose to his feet and took one of the actors by the hands. The audience laughed, but he saw and heard nothing. His stockings were falling down over his ankles, his coat dated from the Regency, and his knees trembled. The sight of him may have been grotesque but when he shouted "This is my house!" he was speaking not only of the building but also of his whole realm, the realm of the theater, that magic world in which he was the magician enchanted by his own spell.

In the midst of all these pleasurable excitements there came the news of Thiériot's death. He saw again the friend of his youth, Maître Alain's chambers, forgetting the long history of Thiériot's tricks and betrayals, and his own repeated forgiveness of the man. He had already passed judgment on Thiériot in a letter he had written to Damilaville in 1764: "I am getting as lazy as Brother Thiériot, but I don't change masters as he does." Thiériot fluttered about serving whoever amused him and whoever paid him well. His protectors changed, but they were always very rich. He had eaten fine bread from La Popelinière's gilt plate, he had made great inroads in the savings of the Comtesse de Fontaine-Martel, he had lived off the Comte de Montmorency and other great noblemen. He had even been a parasitical retainer of the Archbishop of Cambrai, the Abbé Charles de Saint-Albins, the illegitimate son of the Regent and an actress. Thiériot had found him a very gay patron, and Thiériot had liked everything about the espiscopal palace, particularly the champagne. Voltaire had never really broken with Thiériot, but the news of his death did not leave him grief-stricken. Thiériot had made too many mistakes to merit his enduring affection.

But suddenly there occurred to Voltaire a more practical consideration: Thiériot had had in his possession a great number of letters, manuscripts, and unpublished poems, all of which could be dangerous if they fell into the hands of Voltaire's enemies. So D'Argental was dispatched to recover this explosive material, and with all possible haste in view of the fact that a certain Mademoiselle Taschin who had been living with Thiériot might be tempted to turn the papers into ready cash. "How grateful I am to you for having prevented Mademoiselle Taschin from becoming my heir! For the young lady who killed Thiériot is named Taschin. . . ." Voltaire maintained he had outlived Thiériot because he had had no Taschin to deal with, whereupon D'Argental jokingly offered to send him one.

A story began to circulate in Paris and Geneva that Voltaire, finding himself in his room one day with a beautiful and cold young woman, had fainted. The truth of this particular matter was that a girl, Mademoiselle de Saussure, niece of the famous Genevese physicist, had indeed visited him in his bedroom, that Wagnière had been present, and that Madame Denis had come in and out several times, manifesting some irritation at the young lady's visit. Wagnière maintained that it was the foolish jealousy of Voltaire's niece, and the ridiculous terms in which she expressed it, that was at the root of the gossip. Voltaire's niece hoped that by making trouble between Voltaire and Monsieur de Saussure she would put a stop to the visits of the girl. Richelieu was intrigued by the story and asked Voltaire whether there was any truth in it. Voltaire told him all: Mademoiselle de Saussure was tall, beautiful, and Junoesque, very majestic and very frigid. If she made Voltaire faint, it was with cold. "I swear to you I could sooner have composed a scene about Scylla than offered a couplet to that lovely creature," he confessed.

Voltaire was homesick for France and for Paris. He besought the King's favorite to get his banishment revoked. But alas, she could not send him a passport.

Richelieu and D'Argental did all they could, and were on the point of succeeding when in 1773 *Les Lois de Minos* appeared. In the best of good faith they had tinkered with the text, cutting, adding, and rewriting. Despite all the trouble some of Voltaire's friends had taken to edit the play, the censor objected and wrote Voltaire an intolerable letter. The censor was Jean Marin, a very indifferent writer as vain as a peacock, who terrorized the whole literary profession and got Voltaire to support his candidacy for membership in the Académie Française. To be just, it must be remembered that Voltaire supported him not only in hopes of a passport but also to counterbalance the candidacy of Président de Brosses.

When Beaumarchais went on freely flaunting himself in Paris even though a warrant had been issued for his arrest, Voltaire was much more surprised at his young colleague's impunity than at his triumphant literary success. Repression was now much less effective than it had been at the beginning of the century: the power of the State was much more seriously impaired than Voltaire suspected.

"It is strange," he wrote, "that a young lockmaker with a warrant out for his arrest should be in Paris, while I am not. . . . Beaumarchais's *Mémoires* are the strongest, boldest, most comic and interesting thing I have ever seen, and the most humiliating for the author's enemies. He ends up fighting ten or twelve people at once, and fells them all like Harlequin vanquishing an entire patrol of constables."

Finally he learned that he had not got his passport because Marin had betrayed him. Though Voltaire did not really need him for his passport, he was still in Marin's power because he had been foolish enough to entrust him with some dangerous papers. So, as Voltaire wrote to Condorcet, "To crown all, I am obliged to hold my tongue. That is exceedingly painful for someone who has something to say and loves to talk." And in addition he still had to wait for his passport.

New enemies arose to take the place of those who had died. One was in the same class as Fréron and La Beaumelle. His name was Jean Marie Bernard Clément, and Voltaire called him "Inclément Clément" to distinguish him from the others, the "Cléments Marauds,"[1] who were mere rascals. At the age of seventeen Clément had written letters to Voltaire praising him and asking for help and advice. He got both, and Voltaire even helped him secure a post as master of a boarding school in Dijon. But "the little toad of Parnassus," as Voltaire later called him, lost his job after some unsavory quarrel with his colleagues, leaving behind a letter of resignation so scandalous that a warrant was issued for his arrest.

The Toad then went to Paris to make a name for himself. Voltaire had recommended him to La Harpe, but once Clément had got what he could out of him, he broke with him. Fréron finally set him on the right track, and Clément attacked first the Abbé Delille, then Saint-Lambert, for whom Voltaire had preserved a warm friendship, and then Voltaire himself. Clément wrote that "Voltairian tragedy was a magic lantern," that he had plagiarized Racine, and that the public was so corrupt that it preferred Voltaire's tinsel to Racine's gold.

Saint-Lambert was not an easygoing man, and when he learned of Clément's attacks he started looking for him. He also advised the authorities, and both the libelous pamphlet and its author were seized. Clément was imprisoned in Fort l'Evêque, which at least spared him a cudgeling from Saint-Lambert.

Rousseau's protests at Clément's imprisonment brought about his release, though Rousseau defended Clément's right to freedom only because it was Saint-Lambert who had had him arrested: Madame D'Houdetot had rejected Rousseau's love and accepted Saint-Lambert's. Jean-Jacques saw in the lives of men such as Voltaire and Saint-Lambert nothing but the depravity and hyprocrisy of civilization. Voltaire, warned by Saint-Lambert, wrote of Rousseau: "He is very proud of this little Clément. He issues decrees like the Parlement, without giving reasons. I shall shortly have the honor of rendering him the most scrupulous justice." So the unknown Clément became famous thanks to the fuss made by Saint-Lambert and a pamphlet by Voltaire, entitled *Les Cabales* (*Plots*). This lampoon appeared in 1773, and everyone wondered who it was who could have provoked it.

> Je ne m'attendais pas qu'un crapaud du Parnasse
> Eût pu dans son bourbier s'enfler de tant d'audace.
> Monsieur, écoutez-moi, j'arrive de Dijon
> Et je n'ai ni logis, ni crédit, ni renom.
> J'ai fait de méchants vers et vous pouvez bien croire
> Que je n'ai pas le front de prétendre à la gloire
> Je ne veux que l'ôter à quiconque en jouit.
> Dans ce noble métier l'ami Fréron m'instruit.
> Monsieur l'abbé Propred m'introduit chez les dames
> Avec de beaux esprits nous ourdissons nos trames.
> Nous serons dans un mois l'un et l'autre ennemis
> Mais le besoin pressant nous tient encore unis.
> Je me forme sur eux dans le bel art de nuire
> Voilà mon seul talent; c'est la Gloire où j'aspire.

I did not expect that a toad of Parnassus/Could swell with such audacity in his mudhole./Monsieur, lend me your ear, I have just come from Dijon/And I have neither a roof over my head, nor credit, nor reputaiton./I have written some vile verses and you may rest assured/That I have not the impertinence to pretend to fame./All I want to do is take it away from whoever enjoys it./In this noble profession I am instructed by friend Fréron./Monsieur l'Abbe Propred [the historian and philosopher Gabriel Mably] introduces me to the ladies/And we weave our plots with wits./In a month we shall all be enemies/But for the moment pressing need keeps us together./I learn from their example the fine art of doing harm/That is my only talent; my one claim to fame.

Clément thereupon attacked Voltaire personally: "With what sagacity you sifted all the little bills of avarice. I shall not trouble to mention all the laments of printers, and of Jews beaten at their own game." He then accused Voltaire of cleverly cheating his booksellers and squeezing every last possible penny out of them. The legend of Voltaire's avarice was often deliberately perpetuated by the very people he had helped. What some of them could never forgive him for was his fame and fortune. "He is the most well heeled of all the wits," Clément wrote—that was what was so intolerable.

Clément next spread the story that Voltaire's sister's husband, Monsieur Mignot, was the poisoner referred to in one of Boileau's satires. That made the Abbé Mignot, Madame Denis, and Madame de Florian all the children of a poisoner. For good measure Clément added that Voltaire himself was the grandson of a poisoner. The Abbé Mignot, who was a conseiller of the Parlement, complained to the minister. Clément was sent for, rebuked, and made to apologize to the abbé, but he did so saucily, and returned forthwith to the attack.

It was a pity Voltaire did not share Buffon's lofty disdain for those who attacked him. "Everyone has his own sort of fastidiousness," said Buffon. "Mine goes so far as to cause me to believe that certain people are incapable of insulting me."

A month after his eightieth birthday Voltaire nearly died. During his slow convalescence a piece of news arrived that made him hop out of his sickbed and skip about for joy: Fréron was said to be dead. But the news turned out to be false, and Voltaire took to his bed again.

The people about him were very alarmed, especially people such as the watchmakers at Ferney, who depended entirely on him. Monsieur Hennin, the French representative in Geneva, was certain he would recover and live to be a hundred. Voltaire was furious: "There are people barbarous enough to have claimed I am well!" he cried.

The measures to be taken in case of his death had already been decided upon. The State intended to recover all documents relating to political matters in which Voltaire had been involved since Cardinal Dubois's ministry. Everything was to be sealed, and all his papers seized. Detailed instructions to this effect were sent from Marly, where the court was staying in July 1774, to the Governor of Burgundy, the Deputy Governor of Gex, and Monsieur Hennin. They were signed by Louis XVI. It was one of the first documents signed by the young King on ascending the throne.

The death of Louis XV in May 1774 had scarcely affected Voltaire at Ferney. He had the decency not to rejoice in it but, like most Frenchmen, he did not conceal the hopes the sick nation placed in its new ruler. But Louis XVI did nothing to improve matters for Voltaire when he chose Maurepas as Prime Minister. Maurepas was one of Voltaire's old enemies, an expert in all the intrigues of Paris and the court. Finally the *philosophe* Turgot was appointed Minister of Finance, and everyone thought that the Enlightenment was about to illuminate the labyrinths of politics. Voltaire shared this hope, but it was soon to perish.

Voltaire's watchmaking industry was once more in danger. Geneva was at peace now, recovering from the civil wars, and began to think it was time to recall her best workmen from banishment and give them the rights they had so long demanded. The "manufactory" at Ferney was not very secure: everything depended on Voltaire's wishes and capital, and on the aid he could get from ministers.

Madame Denis helped him. She occupied herself with the workers' families and their welfare. The people on the estate were careful to show their gratitude, knowing they were flattering their future mistress. Voltaire was eighty and in worse health than ever, and the reign of Madame Denis seemed imminent. But, ironically, it was she who nearly died first. Her illness caused great anxiety, and the people greeted her recovery with a great celebration on May 18, 1775. There was a military parade of both infantry and cavalry, complete with flags, banners, and posters, led by officers in cockaded hats and accompanied by drums, kettledrums, and trumpet fanfares. After the procession three hundred people sat down to an open-air banquet, with speeches written by Monsieur de Florian. "Joy has changed us into warriors," the speaker said. Madame Denis was in ecstasies, and listened with tears in her eyes to the peroration: "Be so good, madame, as to honor always with your bounty this rising colony founded by the immortal Voltaire; we shall do all we can to be worthy of it through our work and diligence."

As soon as Madame Denis was up and about, visitors started to come to Ferney again. One amusing couple were the Marquis and Marquise du Luchet. She was always laughing, and in order to be able to keep it up even invented some occasions for laughter which were not in very good taste. The word "mystification" dates from this time, and was apparently first used in the marquise's salon, where she received some people who moved in high society and some who did not. One of her "mystifications" or hoaxes caused a lady of quality to complain to the police, and Madame du Luchet was summoned and given a severe dressing down. Grimm wrote: "A woman who is taken up by the police is dropped by everyone else." It was at this point that the marquis felt that he and his wife ought to go and visit some mines or other he owned in Savoy. It was obviously gold mines that they needed. Voltaire, after being diverted by their confessions to the police, had remarked, "In every confession there is some sin that is now avowed." In the case of the Luchets that sin was the fact that they were ruined. "Madame du Luchet cannot write about either her affairs or yours for the very good reason that she understands nothing about them. She has never dreamed about doing anything but laughing. But to hope to do nothing but laugh, like the wife, or to hope to make a fortune from mines, like the husband, is tantamount to seeking the philosopher's stone, which can never be found," Voltaire wrote one of his friends.

During their visit, Ferney was like a hospital, with Voltaire, Madame Denis, and the servants all in bed. Madame du Luchet took care of all of them, made them laugh, and cured them. So she had accomplished what she had set out to do. Her husband, on the other hand, found nothing in his mines. But they left Ferney as they had arrived, smiling.

Their place was taken by Madame Suard and her brother Charles-Joseph Panckouke, a famous publisher in Lille, who had come to propose a complete edition of Voltaire's works. Madame Suard lived in Paris and kept a distinguished salon frequented by the most brilliant *philosophes*, in which Voltaire was worshiped. She was pretty and agreeable, cultivated, unaffected, and possessed of the most discriminating taste. Though she admired and loved Voltaire to a degree just short of idolatry, she would chide him gently but firmly if he joked about Christ, and be rewarded for her reproof with a compliment. If Voltaire attacked one of the people who frequented her salon she would stop him: "He is a friend of mine. You speak only from hearsay, but I know him personally," she would write.

On the day of her arrival she was so frightened at the thought of meeting her idol that she nearly went away without seeing him. But she was told that he was out in the grounds, and as she waited in the salon with other visitors she had time to overcome her nervousness. Suddenly he came in, carrying a letter announcing her arrival: "Where is this lady? Where is she? I am told you are all soul, and it is a soul I come in search of."

"Monsieur, this soul is steeped in you, and has longed for many years for the happiness of approaching yours."

Also among the visitors was Monsieur Audibert from Marseilles, the friend of the Calases who had kept him informed of developments in the course of their struggle with the law; handsome young D'Etallonde, anxious over his prospects for rehabilitation; and the Cramers, the booksellers from Geneva who acted as skillfully on the boards as they sold Voltaire's works in their shop. There was also a Russian visitor named Soltikoff, and a Monsieur Poissonnier, a learned and talkative man who was Catherine II's physician. Madame Suard describes a scene in which Voltaire congratulated Poissonnier on his learning and his services to humanity in discovering a process for taking the salt out of sea water. "Oh," said the scholar, "that's nothing compared to what I've just invented: I can preserve meat for several years without salting it."

Madame Suard was struck by Voltaire's exquisite politeness toward this vain and pedantic pseudo scholar. But she was even more struck by the fact that her host was not nearly as gaunt and cadaverous as he was usually depicted. "It is impossible to describe the subtlety of his eye or the charms of his countenance. What an enchanting smile! And there is not one wrinkle that is not a grace in itself. How surprised I was when, instead of the decrepit face I expected, there appeared this physiognomy full of fire and expression; when instead of a stooping old man, I saw one upright, elevated, noble without being affected, with a firm and even nimble step, and a tone, a politeness which, like his genius, belongs to him alone."

She saw Voltaire with the eyes of faith. If the fire of genius played a certain part in the transfiguration of wrinkles, so also did Madame Suard's amiability. Grimm has also left us a portrait of Voltaire, composed a short time before Madame Suard's, which gives us a very different view of him: "Monsieur de Voltaire . . . is thin and of a dry humor, splenetic, with a pinched face, a witty, caustic manner, and sparkling mischievous eyes. All the fire one finds in his works is also there in his actions: lively to the point of giddiness, he is ardor personified, dazzling and sparkling. A man of such a constitution cannot but be a valetudinarian: the blade wears out the sheath. Gay by temperament, serious by self-discipline, open without frankness, politic without subtlety, sociable without friends, he sees the world and forgets it. He loves grandeur and despises the great; at ease with them, but constrained with his equals. He is polite to people in the beginning, then turns cool and ends up disgusted with them. He loves the court but is bored when he frequents it. He cares for nothing by choice, for everything out of caprice. Possessed of delicate sensibilities but without a fondness for others, voluptuous without passion. Rational without principle, his reason is as fitful as his attacks of madness. Vain to excess, but even more self-seeking, he works less for fame than for money, after which he hungers and thirsts. To conclude, he forces himself to work in order to live. He was made to enjoy, but he wants to amass. Behold the man." Though the man we see here is partly Grimm himself, rather than Voltaire, it is still a searching portrait, malicious in intent yet for all that full of thought-provoking insights.

The day after Madame Suard had drawn her charming portrait she no longer recognized her model. He looked as though he were at death's door. She threw herself at his feet and kissed his hands three times every quarter of an hour. He felt obliged to return the compliment. What had happened to make him look like this? He confessed: he had eaten too many strawberries the previous evening and was suffering from indigestion. He put himself on a strict diet consisting only of cream and coffee —but a fowl was always kept ready in case he should suddenly feel ravenously hungry. Peasants and villagers were forever going in and out of the kitchen, eating at all hours. What with the visitors in the kitchen and the visitors in the salon, the château at Ferney was a veritable caravanserai.

After having confessed about the strawberries Voltaire bade life farewell, talking on and on. Madame Suard listened entranced. "Monsieur de Turgot has three terrible things against him: the financiers, the rogues, and the gout." Madame Suard preferred Necker to Turgot. Voltaire bridled. She let go of his hands and took up the cudgel for Necker. "Come, madame, calm yourself. God bless us, you know how to love your friends." And they kissed each other's hands again. "You bring me back to life!" he cried. "Ah, how charming she is! I am glad I am such a miserable old wretch—she would not be so good to me if I were twenty." Madame Suard told all this to her husband, adding, "And indeed, his eighty years set my passion perfectly at ease."

During the early days of her visit Voltaire was not sure that her feelings were sincere, and he had not been willing to put her up in the château itself. But as soon as he was sure of her friendship he had her given a room. She was so happy she was unable to sleep the first night. At six in the morning she posted herself in the salon to wait for the moment when the patriarch was brought his coffee and cream, and sent word asking to be admitted to his bedroom. She found Voltaire sitting very upright in a simple, very clean and tidy bed. He was wearing a silk waistcoat and a nightcap tied with dazzling white silk ribbon. Everything in his room was perfectly clean and neat, the books and papers all in order. When he asked Wagnière for a file he specified the third on the left, on top of such and such a dossier. Wagnière found it without any difficulty. The poet wrote in bed, with a chessboard across his knees for a desk. The table was laden with pens, and when Madame Suard asked for one as a souvenir he delighted her by choosing the one he had used most often. They kissed hands once more. Then they spoke of Condorcet, the most estimable man in the world, according to Voltaire, who admired and revered him for his intelligence, knowledge, and virtue. He had just written such a fine, inspired encomium on Pascal that Voltaire was both overwhelmed and terrified: "If Condorcet believes Pascal's faith to be sincere, the rest of us are great fools not to be able to think as he does. There is nothing untoward in the fact that Racine was a good Christian: he was a poet, a man of imagination. Pascal, on the other hand, was a man of reason, and such people should not be set up against us. But he was also a morbidly religious man and as insincere as his antagonists." Voltaire was forgetting that Pascal too was a man of extraordinary imagination.

Faced with such problems, Madame Suard's head began to spin. She let Voltaire talk, and was silent.

Voltaire stayed in bed almost all day, but about eight o'clock in the evening she sometimes had the good fortune of seeing him appear and partake of scrambled eggs, his fare at supper for the last three months. One evening he received an official from Gex who had come to ask protection for a friend dismissed by Turgot. The visitor said Turgot was destroying France by dismissing all men of merit. "You are like the woman who cursed Colbert every time she made an omelette because he had levied a tax on eggs," Voltaire replied.

Some afternoons Voltaire would get out of bed and come and give his puppet show in the salon. She would hurry to kiss his hands, keep him prisoner, and make him talk. It was not difficult, for that was what he had come downstairs for. One day as she was still kissing his hands he cried, "Give me your foot, give me your foot!" She offered her cheek, and he accused her of coming to Ferney merely to corrupt him. She replied that all she was afraid of was tiring him. "Madame," he said—with what she described as "an inclination of the head of inexpressible gallantry"—"I have listened to you and such a thing is altogether impossible."

In the evening Madame de Florian and her high-spirited young sister used to go and wish him good night in his room. He would reproach the cruel creatures for abandoning such a handsome young man to his solitary couch.

Madame Suard was touched to discover in the antechamber an engraving of the Calas family taking leave of their father before his execution. She was surprised that Voltaire should keep so painful a scene constantly within his sight. "Ah, madame," he said, "for eleven years I was preoccupied with that unfortunate family, and with the Sirvens, and during all that time, madame, I reproached myself for the least smile that crossed my lips, as though it were a crime." He said this in a voice full of such emotion that she could not do less than kiss his hands once more. Not far from the engraving of the Calases, there was another of Madame du Châtelet, the incomparable and unforgettable Emilie.

He explained to Madame Suard that the victory of the Enlightenment was far from certain, that fanaticism was still rampant everywhere, unvanquished if not invincible. He explained that it was fanatical education that made fanaticism persist from generation to generation, and then proceeded to attack Christ, whereupon gentle Madame Suard bristled. He seemed both amused and touched: "Oh yes," she describes him as saying with a glance and smile full of the most charming mischievousness, "he treated you women so well, you must always spring to his defense."

Sometimes they talked of friends they had in common: Saint-Lambert, La Harpe, Condorcet, D'Alembert, Marmontel, and Richelieu. All were praised to the skies, save Richelieu, who had opposed the admission into the Academy of Madame Suard's friends, who were also Voltaire's friends. This was an unpardonable crime in their eyes, and that was why they criticized him for still leading a dissolute life at his advanced age. Madame Suard quoted two of Voltaire's own lines:

Qui n'a pas l'esprit de son âge
De son âge a tous les malheurs.

Whoever has not the spirit appropriate to his years/Has the sorrows that belong to them.

"Alas, madame, that is very true," said Voltaire with a sigh. Richelieu, however, did not seem to be suffering unduly.

One evening he appeared in a sumptuous dressing gown and a very fine cap, which made all the ladies cry out in admiration. Madame Suard remarked that this evening Voltaire looked as handsome as Pigalle's statue of him, which she had been to see in Paris. She kissed his hands and told how she had also kissed the statue.

"Pray tell me, did it kiss you back?" Voltaire asked. "It didn't? But I am right, am I not, that it wanted to?"

Monsieur Soltikoff was amazed to see Voltaire surrounded with all this affection. When he congratulated him, Voltaire whispered to him: "I owe it all to the fact that I'm eighty."

Madame Suard noticed that Madame Denis was not as tender and considerate with Voltaire as she herself would have been if she were in her place. When he complained of being tired and wanted to go to his room, Madame Denis scolded him. "They will hardly ever admit that he might not feel well, and they seem not to allow him the right to complain," she noted. But Madame Denis was more used to Voltaire and his ways than the gentle Madame Suard. And no one had ever yet succeeded in stopping him from complaining, about either his real ailments or his imaginary ones. As soon as he had lamented his decrepitude, invoked death, and breathed his supposed next to last gasp, he was up and about again, as sprightly as ever. "In his life there is not a single empty moment," Madame Suard wrote.

He told her about the time that Séguier, the président of the Parlement, had come to see him. "He sat there in that very chair where you are now, madame, and threatened to denounce me to the Parlement, which would burn me if it got hold of me."

"Monsieur!" she cried in horror. "They wouldn't dare!"

"What would prevent them?"

"Your genius, your age, the good you have done mankind, the outcry there would be all over Europe, all that is decent, all that you have made humane and tolerant would rise up in your favor."

"Ah, madame," he replied, shrugging his shoulders, "they would come and see me burn, and that evening perhaps they would say: 'What a pity!'"

La Barre's executioner had been applauded by the crowd. Perhaps Voltaire was right. Eighteen years after this conversation took place, the people of Paris flocked to watch the guillotine lop off heads as they applauded. But Madame Suard was horrified.

"No," she cried, "I could not bear it—I shall go and stab the executioner."

"You are a sweet child," said Voltaire, kissing her hand. "I shall count on you."

Needless to say, he and Madame Suard both wept when it came time for her to leave. They clasped each other to their bosoms, she said. The scene was a perfect expression of the new "sensibility" that was bringing audiences to the theater in droves.

Quite Another Matter

Madame de Genlis was an altogether different sort. She was regarded as a bluestocking, but above all she was a pedagogue, or at least she possessed the ideas and principles of one. She made no secret of them, and she detested Voltaire. But at the same time she was to the manner born. Had she not been redeemed by the education she owed to her milieu and the age in which she lived, she would have been insufferable despite her genuine merits. The Duc d'Orléans had entrusted her with the education of his sons, and she was thus the governess of Louis-Philippe, who was to become King of France in 1830.

She wangled three or four visits to Ferney during a stay in Geneva. In order to get herself invited she wrote a polite letter to Voltaire, at the same time making it clear that she did not propose to make any concessions. To mark her independence—not that Voltaire threatened it—she took care to date her letter "Août," not "Auguste," which was the form Voltaire preferred. She expected him to comment on this spelling and had prepared her reply. But Voltaire did not mention it. On the contrary, he invited her to dinner and received her graciously. He appeared in a frock coat, rather than a dressing gown and nightcap. She had drawn up a plan of their conversation, knew what she wanted to say, and would discuss nothing else. She did her best to show no sign of emotion or interest in the patriarch's presence, and was visibly irritated by the enthusiasm of Monsieur Ott, the German painter she had brought with her. She was so preoccupied by the lecture she proposed to deliver to her host that she forgot to look at the clock, and arrived at Ferney an hour early. Madame Denis delegated another guest, Madame de Saint-Julien, to keep her amused until dinnertime. Little Madame de Saint-Julien, in a plain morning petticoat and lowheeled slippers, trotted Madame de Genlis out under the arbors, which was unfortunately too low to accommodate a long-legged lady in court dress with several feet of flowers and feathers piled atop her head. Madame de Saint-Julien pattered ahead, chattering gaily, with Madame de Genlis crouching in her wake, her headdress rapidly falling to pieces.

At last the agreed hour arrived. Madame de Genlis's coiffure was set to rights, torn flounces were pinned in place, and everyone met in the salon with all the ceremony that Voltaire loved to indulge in at his receptions. He kissed Madame de Genlis's hand with his usual grace, smothered her in compliments, and, like everyone else, she was completely won over. But the spell was soon broken. As everyone was admiring a painting of the Virgin and Child, Voltaire made some highly uncalled-for remarks concerning the virginity of the parent and the divinity of the infant.

Madame de Genlis immediately turned her back on him. It was no more than he deserved, and naturally her description of him was influenced by the unfavorable impression this incident made on her. She reported that he was now only the ruin of a man; that he dressed barbarously; that his voice was atrocious to listen to, sepulchral one moment and shrill the next; that he refused to tolerate any difference of opinion. She ends by saying that the habit of solitude had made him forget the ways of the world—a ludicrous remark, since the most distinguished people in Europe constantly flocked to Ferney, and even Voltaire's enemies admitted that he was extraordinarily courteous and thoroughly at home in high society.

But even Madame de Genlis was captivated by Voltaire's eyes: "They were indeed the most intelligent I ever saw, but at the same time there was something velvety about them, an inexpressible gentleness: the soul of Zaïre inhabited those eyes completely." She also surrendered before all the improvements Voltaire had brought about in the surrounding countryside: "He is greater because of this than because of his books, for everywhere one sees proof of ingenious goodness, and it is difficult to believe that the same hand that had written so many impieties can have performed works so noble and wise. He showed the village to all the visitors, but with perfect modesty, speaking of it simply and good-naturedly, explaining everything he had done without seeming the least bit boastful, though I know of no one else who could have done as much."

She was quite right on this particular point, but in general she had completely failed to understand her host. She speaks of him as Balzac was to speak of the country doctor in his novel *Le Médicin de campagne*, hailing him as a "good citizen." But she was forgetting that he was also Voltaire, the author of the *Lettres anglaises*, the *Dictionnaire philosophique*, the *Essai sur les moeurs*, and *Candide*. Already imbued with the attitude of the virtuous, upright bourgeois of the following century, her portrait of the greatest writer of the Age of Enlightenment reminds one of a favorable report by a visiting social worker.

In August 1776 Voltaire received a sort of ultimatum: "Monsieur, I have an infinite desire to pay my respect to you. You may, I fear, be ill. I also know that you often are obliged to pretend to be, and that is what I do not wish to happen at this time. I am a gentleman in ordinary to the King, and as you know better than anyone, people never close their doors to us. I therefore claim the privilege of having your door flung wide open to me." The letter was signed Vivant Denon, followed by the writer's titles, merits, and travels. Despite the peremptory tone of his letter, he was invited to come to Ferney: Voltaire hoped he might have a little fun with such an impertinent guest. He wrote: "Monsieur, my honorable friend, not only is it possible that I may be ill; I am so, and have in fact been these eighty years. But, dead or alive, your letter makes me ardently desire to take advantage of your thoughtfulness. I do not dine, but I sup a little, and shall therefore expect you to have supper with me in my cave."

Vivant Denon's brashness was proverbial. He planted himself in the way of the King so frequently that Louis XV one day asked him what his purpose was in so doing. "To see you, sire!" Denon answered. He had wits and looks, and became an intermediary between Madame de Pompadour and the artists she employed. He installed himself at Versailles, and at the age of twenty-two was named one of the King's gentlemen in ordinary. He was even sent on a mission to Saint Petersburg, and he had been on his way back from there when he wrote his letter to Voltaire. The Revolution did not inconvenience him: he emerged a baron of the Empire.

He amused Voltaire and the rest of the company with the story of his journey and the gossip going the rounds at Versailles and Saint Petersburg. He asked Voltaire for a portrait, but Voltaire did not have one, and replied as he always did, even to Pigalle: "Copy the bust of me at Sèvres." He did not like any of his portraits. He hated being painted: he was not good at posing, he knew he was an "impossible subject," and, realizing full well what he really looked like, he had no great fancy for the role of Narcissus. It should also be remembered that he was not very sensitive to the arts. He sang very badly and had no ear. In painting he was only interested in "subjects," in sculpture only in "nobility" and "a good likeness," which was what he meant by "the natural." In architecture he shared the neo-classic taste of his age for harmony and symmetry: he was even in advance of his time with his predilection for the cold, stiff Louis XVI style which prefigured that of the Empire twenty years later.

Denon took offense at Voltaire's refusal and was seen at Ferney no more. But a few months later Voltaire received an engraving of himself. Denon had done the portrait from memory. It was a monstrosity. Everyone at Ferney was furious at this outrageous caricature of their idol, but Voltaire waited for his own rage to subside before he answered. He thanked Denon and sent him a little casket of boxwood which a skillful mountain craftsman had made and decorated with a portrait of Voltaire. "Permit me, monsieur, to send you a little casket of boxwood lined with tortoise shell made in one of our villages. You will see it is a decent, respectable pose and a perfect likeness. It is a great fault in any genre to seek after the unusual and shun the natural." Denon was not about to admit that a mountaineer could teach a royal gentleman anything about the art of portaiture, and answered rudely, whereupon Voltaire sent him advice from a sculptor in Rome and asked him to retouch the portrait. But Denon took no notice: he had his horrible caricature printed and circulated it all over Paris, where people laughed at this likeness of a Voltaire looking "ugly as sin."

In this same year, 1776, a print appeared which Voltaire found very shocking. It was called "Monsieur de Voltaire's luncheon," and depicted him in bed, thin and grimacing, with a plump, even bloated, Madame Denis in attendance. Fortunately his mountain craftsman made him little likenesses of himself in ivory, boxwood, and plaster which were entirely to his taste, and to that of other quite important people. These little Voltaires were sold by the dozen to Catherine II and Prince Poniatowski, King of Poland.

That same year he was visited by an Englishman, Mr. Martin Sherlock, chaplain to Lord Bristol. Sherlock saw him for the first time leaning on the arm of his nephew, Monsieur d'Hornoy, son of the first marriage of his young niece. He was exhausted, his voice almost inaudible. Nevertheless he offered to conduct his visitors around the garden. "It is in the English style," he pointed out. "You will like it. It was I who introduced this style into France." They discussed Shakespeare, and Voltaire said he was badly translated, that he was overfond of buffoonery, a taste which he had got from Spain, a country in fashion in his day: "A country of which we know no more than we do of the wildest parts of Africa." It must be remembered that the Spanish Inquisition banned and burned Voltaire's works, and that he considered Spain even more backward and dangerous than Italy. His Europe consisted of Paris, London, Amsterdam, Brussels, Berlin, and Vienna. He added, of Spain: "It does not deserve to be known. If a man wishes to travel there he must take his own bed with him. When he enters a town he must go into one street to buy a bottle of wine, into another to buy a slice of mule, and in a third he finds a table where he can eat his supper. A French nobleman passing through Pamplona sent for a spit, only to learn that there was but one in the town, and that one had been lent out for a wedding."

As they went through the village of Ferney, Voltaire confided to his guest: "Yes, we are free here. Cut off a little corner of land and we are no longer in France. I have asked for several favors for my children here, and the King has granted everything I asked, and declared the region of Gex free of all the farmers-general's taxes, so that salt, which used to be sold at ten *sols* a pound, is now only four. I have nothing left to ask for save to live."

It was true that after countless efforts he had managed to get his unfortunate peasants out of the clutches of the *"pandours,"*[2] as he called he farmers-general, in return for a sort of subscription of thirty thousand livres a year. Voltaire had gone in person to the Estates of Burgundy to arrange the details of the dispensation, and the entire populace turned out to greet their benefactor's return. The citizens surrounded his carriage on horseback, the peasants came on foot waving branches and showering him with flowers and laurels. He and Madame Denis were nearly smothered to death with kisses. Voltaire sobbed with happiness and called the villagers his children.

This success had some regrettable consequences.

The deputy governor of Gex, Monsieur Fabry, took alarm at Voltaire's growing popularity. He thought that Voltaire was going to take over the administration of the entire region. Other officials were of the same opinion: Voltaire did too much, and did it too well. Allied with them were those who considered that Voltaire was too rich and did not do enough. They all searched for a leader and found one in Président de Brosses. He was easily persuaded that Voltaire was setting up a veritable tyranny in Gex, that the people were terrified of him because of his influence with the government, and that he was flouting the power of the King and usurping that of his representatives.

Still smarting from his failure to get into the Academy, Prèsident de Brosses made the journey to Versailles to beg Monsieur de Malesherbes, now Minister of the Royal Household, to reduce Voltaire to inactivity "by every means at the state's disposal." Monsieur de Malesherbes instituted the necessary inquiries, but Monsieur Hennin, the French envoy in Geneva, wrote such an enthusiastic report on the squire of Ferney that Monsieur de Malesherbes took no measures against him.

Mr. Sherlock went through Voltaire's library with him and noted his comments on the numerous English authors who were represented. "Lord Chesterfield? He has much wit. Lord Hervey? Equally brilliant, but more solid. Bolingbroke? He said you had no good tragedy. Addison's *Cato* is well written, with much taste. But there is a gulf between taste and genius. Shakespeare had genius but no taste. He has spoiled the taste of the nation for two hundred years, and the taste of the nation for two hundred years will remain the taste of the nation for two thousand. It becomes a religion. There are many fanatics of Shakespeare in your country."

After dinner Sherlock and Voltaire went into a small drawing room containing portraits and busts. They admired the likeness of the Duchess of Coventry, then Voltaire took hold of his guest's arm and stopped in front of another bust.

"Do you know who this is?" he asked. "It is the greatest genius who ever lived. If all the geniuses in the world were gathered together, he would be their chief." It was Newton.

Sherlock noticed the arms of Arouet-Voltaire on the doors of the salon: "azure with three flames or." They were also on the silver plate. There were two sittings at each meal, and five servants waiting at table, three in livery. No foreign domestic was ever allowed to serve at table.

"On the two days I saw him," Sherlock observed of Voltaire, "he wore white cloth slippers, white woolen stockings, red breeches, two waistcoats and a dressing-gown. His jacket was of blue linen sprinkled with yellow flowers and lined with yellow. He wore a grey wig with three bobs, surmounted by a silk night-cap embroidered in gold and silver."

This was not the getup of a sick and brooding old man. Sherlock summed up his visit with this perspicacious comment: "The soul of this man is extraordinary: he wanted to be a universal man of letters, he wanted to be rich, he wanted to be noble, and he has attained all these goals."

Madame de Saint-Julien occupied a special place in Voltaire's heart. She played an active role in his local good works, but even if she had not he would still have been fond of her: she was made of the stuff the people he loved best all his life had been made of. He called her the "Butterfly Philosopher": she was lively, gay, fond of sport, and indefatigable. Her maiden name was La Tour du Pin, and she was the niece of the Marquis de La Tour du Pin-Gouvernet, who had married Suzanne de Livry, the young lady Voltaire had been in love with in his youth. Her first name was Diana, a most fitting one, for she was a remarkable shot and would stay on horseback from morning till night. Voltaire adored her. She was not only bursting with vitality but intelligent and well read, and could discourse on serious subjects. She pressed all her friends at court into Voltaire's service and was of genuine help to him, especially in the matter of getting him exempted from taxes. In fact when the great fete to celebrate the dispensation took place at Ferney, Voltaire had a gold medal of Turgot struck, to be awarded as a prize to the best shot in the district of Gex. The workers Voltaire had brought from Geneva were fond of shooting and there were a number of experts among them. But it was the "Butterfly" who won the medal, and the workers presented it to her in triumph. She was enchanted with her prize and wore it everywhere.

Madame de Saint-Julien performed other services for Ferney, too. She recommended a young priest, Rouph de Varicourt, from a poor family, who ended up Bishop of Orléans in 1822. In the same family there was also a daughter, Renée-Philiberte, who was destined for the cloister. She accompanied her relatives on their visits to Voltaire and heard the old gentleman's ribald jests without apparently being shocked in the least. She was eighteen, with a pretty face, a noble bearing, and an amiable character. Voltaire looked at her with amazement and resolved to put up a fight against her becoming a nun. He asked her relatives to entrust her to him, they agreed, and Voltaire introduced her to the Marquis de Villette. Villette was amused at the patriarch's ecstasies over his ward: "In the evening, with the caresses she lavishes on him, and the solemn air with which he kisses the pretty governess' hands, you cannot imagine what a touching picture it makes."

Villette was the son of an immensely wealthy financier who had been made a marquis. The young man was a great rake, and his reputation was deplorable. Yet he composed quite elegant light verse and had a taste for the philosophy of the Enlightenment. He often corresponded with Voltaire. Villette liked to let it be thought that Voltaire, who had been on intimate terms with his mother, Madame de Villette, was his father; and he found people to believe him.

Three months after meeting Mademoiselle de Varicourt at Ferney, Villette announced that he was taking her as his wife: "I am going to marry at the Château of Ferney a young person who has been adopted by Voltaire. She brings me for dowry a charming face, a pretty figure, an untouched heart, and a pleasing mind. I have preferred this to a good million that I was offered in Geneva. The fathers of the Church would never have converted me; the feat was reserved for the temporal father of the Capuchins [Voltaire], who is today the spiritual father of Europe."

Voltaire played his role to perfection: it was not tragedy now, but middle-class drama, and he was the first to be moved and flattered by it: "Our cottage at Ferney is not the place for keeping daughters," he wrote. "We have married off three of them: Mademoiselle Corneille, Mademoiselle Dupuits, and Mademoiselle de Varicourt. She hasn't a penny but her husband is nonetheless making an excellent bargain. . . . As for me, I remain alone in my bed and drivel away in verse and in prose . . . the newlyweds are working away night and day to provide me with a new little philosopher. This raises my spirits in the midst of my horrible sufferings."

Voltaire Haunted by Fréron's Ghost, and Shakespeare's

In March 1776 Fréron died at the age of fifty-seven. One evening while he was partaking of a copious supper he learned that his paper, *L'Année littéraire*, had just been banned. His wife ran to petition the minister, but when she got back she found her husband dead—either of indigestion, as rumor had it, or of the shock of having his paper banned, since he was in dire financial straits.

Voltaire would have said nothing on the occasion if a strange message hadn't come to reawaken his hatred. An anonymous letter asked him to take pity on Fréron's poverty-stricken daughter, just as he had on Mademoiselle Corneille. He grew angry, suspecting the letter of being the handiwork of Fréron's wife, and spread it about everywhere that Fréron's widow was asking him for help: "I replied that if Fréron had written *Le Cid* and *Cinna* I would have easily been able to marry off his daughter."

Fréron's son wrote a harsh and insulting article against the old fool who imagined that the family would accept charity from him. In fact, the original letter eventually proved to be a hoax. By the time one is eighty-three and has received anonymous letters all one's life one ought to have learned merely to throw them on the fire. But in this case the eighty-three-old was Voltaire, and his wrath was as easily kindled as ever.

More fuel was added to the fire when he learned that an "unknown" had had the audacity to praise Shakespeare at the expense of Racine. There had recently appeared the first two volumes of a French edition of Shakespeare's works by Pierre Letourneur, who claimed it was a much more faithful translation than Voltaire's versions of a number of Shakespeare's plays. Letourneur's renderings were not quite so inaccurate as Voltaire's, but there was not much to choose from between them. To modern eyes, Letourneur's translation of *Othello*, for instance, seems to free the original from the elegant artificialities of Versailles, but at the time it was as if all the forces of barbarism had been let loose to destroy the nobility of the French classical theater.

Voltaire was seized with an absurd and magnificent fury because Letourneur had taken it into his head to write in the preface of his translation that Shakespeare was the greatest genius the theater ever had. From his study at Ferney he wrote to D'Argental on July 9, 1776: "Have you read this wretch's two volumes in which he tries to make us regard Shakespeare as the sole model for tragedy? He calls him the God of the theater."

Voltaire's aversion to Shakespeare at this point is astonishing, since he himself had helped introduce Shakespeare to France in his younger days when all things English seemed to him superior to things French. But Voltaire had come to believe that the great English dramatist's tragedies, with their sweep of passion and their totally unclassical form that observed none of the "unities," were not only tasteless but dangerous "barbarisms." Failing to change with the times, Voltaire was unable to foresee that in just a few short years Shakespeare's theater would become the foremost model for the Romantic revolution led by Victor Hugo.

The Atmosphere at Ferney Changes for the Worse

A new enemy now made his appearance. He was no substitute for the irreplaceable Fréron, but he revived Voltaire's fighting instincts. He was a disconcerting enemy, polite, calm, serious, extremely cultivated, and his attacks on Voltaire were carefully planned. Voltaire had all he could do to keep up with him. His adversary stuck to his guns and responded to Voltaire's counterattacks only when they contained erroneous facts, misquotations, or wrong dates—the sort of mistakes that were not exceptional in Voltaire's writings.

When the patriarch received a work entitled *Lettres de quelques Juifs portugais* (*Letters from Certain Portuguese Jews*), which pointed out errors in his interpretations of certain passages in the Bible, he wondered who the author could be. When D'Alembert wrote, identifying him as a certain Abbé Guénée who had penned them for Cardinal de la Roche-Aymon, a distinguished prelate whose one shortcoming was that he could neither read nor write, Voltaire replied: "The secretary of these Jews is not without either wit or knowledge; but he is as sly as a monkey, and he bites to the bone while pretending to kiss your hand." Although Voltaire did not underestimate his enemy, he could not overcome him. Though still as sharp as ever, his darts no longer wounded his enemies, for they were beginning to be wide of the mark. Fashion and the world had changed, but Voltaire had stayed the same. People do not always grow old through losing their talents, but through retaining the same talents in a world where they are no longer appreciated. In spite of his unimpaired vivacity, the Voltaire of 1776 was an old man because he too closely resembled the Voltaire of 1730.

The Hope of an Imperial Visit and a Crushing Disappointment

At Ferney Voltaire had many a boring visitor, and was not above staging "fainting spells" to get rid of them. But in June 1777 he awaited one possible visitor with the liveliest anticipation: the Emperor Joseph II, Marie-Antoinette's brother, who would be passing by Ferney on his way home to Vienna from Paris. Frederick had written Voltaire a letter telling him of the Emperor's itinerary and expressing the hope that "new acquaintances" would not make Voltaire forget old ones. D'Alembert too was certain that the Emperor would stop to pay homage to Voltaire, and wrote that such an imperial visit would "add several years to the life of the Patriarch of Ferney." Just in case, Voltaire had all the loose stones removed from the road to his property, and on the day that the Emperor was due to pass by, the peasants on Voltaire's lands turned out to stand for hours along the roadside in their Sunday best. But alas, when the postilion announced to the sovereign that he had reached Ferney, the latter's only words were: "Coachman, whip the horses on!" and the coach roared past the village and on into Switzerland. Joseph had driven through without stopping not only because his mother, the Empress Maria Theresa, had forbidden a visit to Voltaire as too great an encouragement to atheism, but also because he had been told too often in Paris that he *ought* to call at Ferney.

There was no getting away from the fact that Joseph's behavior had been humiliating, for in Paris he had made a number of visits a good deal more uncalled for: to Mademoiselle Guimard, the dancer, for instance, and to Madame du Barry, now banished to Louveciennes. Joseph's intention must have been to humiliate Voltaire deliberately, as a further detail shows. When he stopped later in Bern, Joseph paid a lengthy call on the poet Albrecht von Haller, a notorious and implacable enemy of Voltaire's. But the learned Haller was quite devoid of vanity and not at all overwhelmed by the honor the Emperor did him.

Voltaire tried to soothe his wounded feelings by spreading a story that two watchmakers had stopped the Emperor's coach and asked Joseph rude questions about his travels and opinions, calling him "Monsieur l'Empereur" and informing him that at Ferney everyone was a republican. It was this incident, invented by Voltaire out of whole cloth, that had supposedly caused Joseph to order his coachman to whip the horses and drive on.

But Voltaire's enemies rejoiced loudly over his discomfiture.

When intolerance and barbarism are the most powerful forces, one must accept them.

What ought wise men to do when they are surrounded by mad savages? There are times when one must imitate their contortions and talk their language. There are people who are afraid to handle spiders and others who eat them. (Letter to D'Alembert, on the clergy, 1761)

I would like every public figure, when he is about to commit a great stupidity, to repeat endlessly to himself: Europe is watching you. (Letter to D'Alembert, 1765)

Ridicule gets the better of anything; it is the most powerful of weapons. It is a great pleasure to laugh while taking one's vengeance. (Letter to D'Alembert, 1766)

No, sire, everything is not lost when the people are put in a position to see that there is such a thing as a mind. On the contrary, everything is lost when they are treated like a herd of bulls, for sooner or later they attack you with their horns. (Letter to Monsieur Linguet, March, 15, 1767)

The Exile Re-enters Paris

To distract himself Voltaire wrote some more tragedies: his "French verse factory" was still ticking regularly. At the age of eighty-three he produced *Irène* and *Agathocle*. The second was never finished; but the first was a different matter. He wrote to the Marquis de Thibouville, who was in charge of the Comédie Française, telling him to be ready to receive *Irène*, to read it, and to put it on. Only three acts were ready as yet, but the remaining two would soon be completed. He had been working at it for three months. This was one of the horrors of old age—twenty years before, he could turn out a tragedy in a week. He announced that the subject of *Irène* was incredibly novel and daring: it dealt with the remorse of a woman who loved her husband's murderer. Voltaire realized that five acts entirely devoted to the remorse of a woman in love was a difficult task to bring off without boring the audience to death. So he tore the entire draft up and started over again. But the new version was very much like the old one. "I find it both moving and humiliating," he wrote. "A father is never very happy about strangling his own child. There go three whole months quite wasted, and at my age time is precious." He found a comforter in Madame Denis, who wept when she read the play. But when Cordorcet read it he did not weep. As well as fine passages he saw many faults, and was of the opinion that it should be rewritten. So Voltaire rewrote it yet again. But then came a thunderbolt: the Comédie Française had already accepted and cast it. There was only one actor who refused a part: Le Kain. Voltaire had written the role especially for his idol, but his idol was inflexible. Voltaire's friends begged, raged, and threatened, but Le Kain was immovable: at the age of fifty, he was in love and was about to be married again, to a Madame Benoît, who for him eclipsed all the Irènes and Zaïres and Iphigenias in the repertoire. The only person who understood Le Kain's irresistible passion for some other object than the theater, the only one who did not accuse him of treachery and ingratitude, was Voltaire. Le Kain was a friend, and therefore above suspicion. Voltaire insisted that people were being too hard on Le Kain—every actor, he maintained, had the right to refuse a role. This was a very different Voltaire from the one who used to fight every inch of the way with his actors, his printers, and his detractors.

At Ferney, he received tributes of admiration and respect which gave him great pleasure. La Harpe, whose tragedy, *Les Barmécides,* was due to be put on before Voltaire's, offered to allow *Irène* to be staged first. Voltaire declined but La Harpe insisted. It was no small sacrifice from an author at the beginning of his career. Another even more surprising gesture moved the old poet to tears. Barthe, a young man from Marseilles whose comedy *L'Homme Personnel (The Egoist)*, had come close to boring Voltaire to death when it was performed at Ferney, was going to have it put on at the Théâtre Français and withdrew it to make way for *Irène.* Barthe had doubtless gone to endless trouble to get it performed, but he was generous enough to efface himself before Voltaire in spite of the memory of his unfortunate visit to Ferney.

Barthe wrote to Monsieur de Thibouville: "You were ready to put on *L'Homme personnel.* You have a decision to make. That decision must be to forget it. I know that new plays are performed in the order in which they are received and that there are regulations to that effect, but what writer would invoke them in such a case as this? Monsieur de Voltaire is, like monarchs, above laws. If I have not yet had the honor of contributing to the pleasure of the public, I nonetheless do not wish to delay that pleasure, and I request you to give the public the earliest possible opportunity to enjoy a work by the author of *Zaïre* and *Mérope*. May he, like Sophocles, go on writing tragedies until he is a hundred, and live as you do, messieurs, to the sound of applause."

The moment came when *Irène* had to be put on, with or without Le Kain. It was to be the pretext for Voltaire's return to Paris. No official order of banishment had ever been pronounced against him, but he had been given to understand, in the plainest of terms, that if he went back to Paris severe measures would be taken against him: prison or exile, or first one and then the other. Though these were only verbal warnings, they were dangerous enough. Louis XV could not endure his presence and showed a rare pertinacity in his severity toward Voltaire. The most authoritative and the most beloved voices were raised in the self-banished exile's favor. But it was always in vain, and after encountering the King's adamant refusal to allow him to return, Madame de Pompadour, Madame du Barry, Richelieu, D'Argental, and others all solemnly advised him not to force matters by turning up in Paris.

But the new King, Louis XVI, was favorable to reform, and it was natural that people should expect him to show more clemency toward Voltaire. But, like his father, he had a horror of the author of *La Henriade*. Voltaire was more hopeful of gaining the favor of Queen Marie-Antoinette, though at this time she did not yet have the authority she later acquired. There was Turgot, and public opinion, which was more turbulent, more influential, in short more Voltairian, than it had been in 1750. Turgot and public opinion were Voltaire's best hopes. But the court still had to become aware of their power.

Voltaire called Louis XVI "Sesostris," implying that he was as heroic an empire builder as the legendary King of Egypt celebrated by Herodotus, but Louis apparently did not understand such erudite flattery and made no overtures to him. Voltaire still had his titles, Gentleman of the King's Chamber and Historiographer of France, however, and could ask to be allowed to fulfill those functions. At Ferney, the more time went by the more painful his longing for Paris became, and Madame Denis shared his impatience. Her eighteen months' sojourn in the capital had made her desire to go back even keener. She kept nagging her uncle: "Let us go! Let us not just languish here and die!" But if Voltaire was going to Paris merely to die in prison, he preferred to stay where he was and die at Ferney in his own bed.

Villette, D'Argental, and Thibouville did all they could to sound out Voltaire's friends and especially his enemies and the authorities. They asked what would happen if one fine evening Voltaire were to appear in his box at the Comédie Française. If he went to a meeting of the Academy. If he gave a dinner party. When Voltaire's "guardian angels" were sure that the immense majority of Parisians would applaud, and that the authorities would pretend to see and hear nothing, they wrote him to come. He needed no second bidding.

On February 5, 1778, he set out by coach for Paris with his secretary, Wagnière. Madame Denis had already left two days earlier. The joy of departure was dimmed by the sorrow of parting. All the people of Voltaire's little kingdom were in tears: they were sure their "Father" was leaving them forever. He promised he would be back in six weeks, and he believed it. He was so sure of it that he left all his papers as they were in his room—he who was always so well organized and meticulous. He probably thought of the journey as simply a "lark." He knew his "children" couldn't live without him and that he himself would be glad to get back to Ferney once he had made his reappearance on the Parisian scene —and perhaps even at Versailles.

He had said: "I am preparing to make a little journey to Paris and eternity." He had spoken so often of that departure for eternity, and despite the many delays during his eighty-odd years it could not be put off forever.

Father Adam was not among the luggage. He had been turned out of the house. That too was bound to happen in the end: Madame Denis had done her best to bring it about. Father Adam had become more and more exacting and tiresome. But Voltaire did not abandon him: he made provisions for him to be given a pension of seven hundred livres.

On the first evening of the journey the patriarch's coach stopped for the night at Nantua. The ostler had an unsatisfactory horse that had been hitched to the coach changed and said to the coachman: "I don't give a ——— if you kill my horses, but go as fast as you can, you're driving Monsieur de Voltaire." On February 7 they arrived in Dijon. The news of his arrival got about. Voltaire saw only his lawyer and another legal adviser: he was still wrangling over details concerning his estates at Tournay and Ferney. But that evening, at supper, the young people of Dijon made their way into the inn. They bribed the maidservants to leave the doors open so that they could see the patriarch at table, and some of them even substituted themselves for waiters. At Joigny the journey was interrupted by a broken axle. Monsieur de Villette came specially from Paris to pick up the old gentleman, who had been shaken up by the accident, and asked the coachman to drive as slowly as possible to ensure that Voltaire would arrive in as good condition as possible. At six o'clock on the evening of February 10, 1778, they arrived at the gates of Paris. At the tollhouse the travelers and their belongings were inspected, and to the official who asked him if he had anything to declare Voltaire replied, "By my faith, I believe that there is no contraband here save myself."

The customs officials recognized him. This seems to be proof that the popular prints in circulation bore some resemblance to him, though they always made him furious. "They make me like a monkey," he used to complain, "as ugly as the Devil and with as evil grimaces as the Seven

Deadly Sins." Voltaire himself had talked a thousand times of his gauntness, his wrinkles, and his toothlessness, but he did not like to have anyone else describe or, worse still, depict him in this state of decrepitude.

"Good heavens! It's Monsieur de Voltaire!" said the men in the tollhouse. He, courteous as ever, prepared to alight to allow them to search the carriage, but they politely waved him on.

Madame Denis and the Marquis de Villette had arranged everything. Voltaire drove to the Rue de Beaune, to Villette's town house, where his apartment had been splendidly prepared for him. It was here that Paris was to flock to worship its idol.

The Intoxication of Fame and the Infirmities of Age

Voltaire wanted first of all to visit D'Argental, but he was not at home. But hardly had Voltaire returned to the Rue de Beaune than D'Argental walked in. The two men were the same age and had been fast friends since childhood. Though they had seen each other only at intervals they had never ceased to be close to one another. The scene of their reunion would have made a worthy subject of a sentimental painting by Greuze. When they had choked back their sobs, dried their tears, and put away their enormous handkerchiefs, they talked, and D'Argental told Voltaire the latest news: Le Kain had died the previous day. Voltaire uttered a loud cry and dramatically expressed the grief befitting the occasion of a great actor's death. It was a great scene of "sensibility": everyone tried to weep even more copiously than Voltaire, who was passed from one pair of arms to another. He was informed that Le Kain had given up the ghost after appearing in *Adélaïde du Guesclin*. He had made his debut in *Brutus,* and thus his career had both begun and ended with tragedies by Voltaire. The poet let out another cry at the thought that Le Kain had actually died onstage while playing in his tragedy. But Tronchin reassured him: Le Kain had died not of *Adélaïde* but of Madame Benoît.

The Paris celebration of his return began at once. It was perfectly organized. These people so gifted for social life and dramatics knew how to stage with ease and seemliness the expression of their feelings, the succession of their visits, their flattering attentions, and even their own antics. What might seem a frivolous game was fundamentally a matter of style; this worldly homage to intelligence was itself a matter of intelligence.

Madame Denis and Madame de Villette received the constant stream of visitors in an outer salon. Madame de Villette, the "*Belle et Bonne* [Beautiful and Good]," contributed her graciousness and charm. Plump Madame Denis represented the family: she was the antechamber in which people tried out on the niece the compliments intended for the uncle.

These preliminaries gave a footman time to warn Monsieur de Voltaire what sort of people were on the way in, so that he could prepare himself.

Then Monsieur de Villette and Monsieur D'Argental went to take over the visitors from the ladies and usher them in. Between the visits Voltaire would join Wagnière in the next room and dictate a letter or corrections for the text of *Irène*.

The days began early and ended late. They were busy and frantic ones, obliging the old gentleman to deal with a hundred different subjects, to give advice, turn a fresh compliment for everyone, remember names, recognize faces, disinter buried memories. He made the utmost demands on himself in order to please, to shine without showing the slightest sign of fatigue or inattention. He succeeded perfectly because he had had nearly a century's training at the game. But at the age of eighty-three . . .

Linguet, the lawyer, wrote at the time: "Monsieur de V. has suddenly left the woods of Ferney which he planted, the houses of Ferney which he built, and the peace of Ferney which so pleased him, for the mud and the bustle and the praise of Paris. Only he will be able to say, in a little while, whether he has gained or lost by the exchange."

All day long he received visitors in this fashion, in his dressing gown. La Harpe found him unchanged since the time of their quarrel, now forgotten. The old man read an act of *Irène* to his visitors: as soon as he found an audience he had to act.

The Academy sent a deputation, consisting of Monsieur le Prince de Beauvau and Messieurs de Saint-Lambert and Marmontel, to tell him that they were going to hold an unprecedented extraordinary session in his honor. He was moved to tears and asked Monsieur de Beauvau to express his gratitude to the Academy: he would go and thank them himself as soon as his health permitted.

Dr. Tronchin appeared also, but not spontaneously: he waited for Voltaire to send for him. The latter was so unsure of Tronchin's friendship that for a moment he was afraid that the celebrated physician would not come. His fears were by no means unjustified, but as always he preferred to give friends the benefit of the doubt and welcomed Tronchin with open arms. On his first visit the doctor thought that Voltaire appeared to be in excellent health. But he was soon to change his opinion.

Then the composer Gluck came to pay his respects, which was no small honor coming from a man who thought that there was only one genius in the world, and that his name was Gluck. Voltaire found a way to convey how much Gluck's homage had touched him. There was a controversy at the time between Gluck's supporters and Puccini's. As Gluck was leaving the room, Puccini was announced, and Voltaire, always quick to seize upon an occasion for flattery, said, "That's the proper order—first Gluck, then Puccini."

In every salon and even in every little shop, no one spoke of anything but the return of Voltaire. His presence disturbed certain bigots and certain authorities, who saw a sort of provocation in the attitude of Voltaire and of his worshipers. They hoped to get him exiled by invoking the ex-

17. Voltaire, 1775, at age eighty-one, in an engraving after V. D. Denon. (Musée Carnavalet. Photo Lauros-Giraudon)

18. Voltaire in his last years, a bust by Houdon. (Reproduced by permission of the Victoria and Albert Museum)

19. Counselor of the Parlement, after an engraving by Sebastien Leclerc (1637-1714). (Bibliothèque Nationale. Photo Roger-Viollet)

20. Illustration for La Fontaine's *Contes*. Engraving by J. Dambrun, after Fragonard. (Bibliothèque Nationale. Photo Roger-Viollet)

21. Rue Quincampoix. Engraving showing crowds besieging Law's bank. (Bibliothèque Nationale. Photo Bulloz)

pulsion order against him: everyone believed that an order for his arrest existed, though none turned up. Voltaire's friends nonetheless were terrified for him and sought Marie-Antoinette's aid. She sent the Princesse de Polignac to the Rue de Beaune to reassure him on her behalf.

The following Monday he was to have gone to the theater, where the actors had promised to put on a performance for him. But he fell ill with a severe inflammation of the bladder, and Dr. Tronchin forbade him both to attend the theater and to receive visitors. His orders were followed for the theater, but not for the visitors.

The announcement of Voltaire's illness merely produced an even greater number of callers. The salon was full all day long. The crowd filed past as though before a shrine, bowed, gazed, and moved on to leave room for the next. Madame Denis was ecstatic. The Marquis de Villette shared this triumph: many people who had looked askance at him because of his escapades came back when Voltaire was staying in the Rue de Beaune, to ask Villette for permission to come see him. Villette used to tell them cynically: "To see Voltaire you have to go through me. You want some Voltaire: you can have some. But first you must bow and scrape to Villette. . . ."

Madame Necker came, though for her the call was merely a most unpleasant duty. As a Genevan, she knew the Varicourt family and was not at all pleased to see one of their daughters married to this cad of a Villette. Voltaire took no notice of her disdain. Her husband was the Minister of Finance, and the greatness of the husband was enough to make Voltaire find the wife an acceptable caller despite her coldness.

He also received Benjamin Franklin. They embraced each other philosophically and, of course, wept. Were they not both the same age and did they not share the same belief in deism? Voltaire spoke in English, and when someone reproached him for it he replied at once:

"I beg your pardon—I could not resist the honor of speaking the same language as Franklin."

Franklin had brought his grandson of fifteen with him and asked the patriarch to give him his blessing. Voltaire climbed up on his three-legged stool, stretched his bony hands out over the child's head, and said, first in French and then in English: "God and Liberty." Twenty people looked on, greatly moved. The "philosophical" climate tended to be very damp.

The English ambassador, Viscount Stormont, also came to call, and smiled at Voltaire's attacks on Shakespeare, which were both sharp and salacious.

But Voltaire's bladder was still giving him a great deal of trouble. A famous harpsichordist gave him a few moments' respite by entertaining him on Madame de Villette's instrument, but by the end of that day Voltaire's legs were swollen and he was exhausted. Dr. Tronchin was not pleased, and publicly said so. Madame Denis and Monsieur de Villette were clearly exploiting the situation at the expense of the old gentleman's life. Tronchin had no illusions about Voltaire's entourage, and to cover himself he had a note inserted in the *Journal de Paris:* "I should have preferred to tell Monsieur le Marquis de Villette to his face that since Monsieur de Voltaire has been in Paris he has been living on the capital of his strength, while all his true friends surely wish him to live only on the income. At the rate things are going his strength will soon be exhausted and we shall be the witnesses of, if not the accomplices in, Monsieur de Voltaire's death."

But Tronchin's warnings went unheeded. No sooner had the swelling in Voltaire's legs gone down than the old pace started up again, as frantic as ever. The matter of *Irène* had to be settled and the cast decided on without more delay. The Duc de Richelieu's candidate for the leading role was Mademoiselle Molé, but Voltaire now wanted Mademoiselle Jainval to play it. It must have been a strange sight to see these two aged specters debating the merits of their favorites: one in a damask dressing gown and ribboned nightcap, the other weighed down with his maréchal's gold braid and decorations; both determined and both as cunning as the Devil himself, veiling their assaults in phrases of exquisite courtesy. The maréchal won: Voltaire could not baldly say no to his childhood friend, his protector—and his debtor. But at rehearsal he managed to save everyone's face. He promised Mademoiselle Molé that he would write a play with a much finer part in it for her if she would withdraw from the cast of *Irène;* and she gave in. A third candidate then dropped from the skies to arrange everything satisfactorily. This was Mademoiselle Arnould, who was a star of the first magnitude and soon swept play, author, and maréchal all into her orbit. The effort that such a change of cast entailed in the way of talk, scheming, and hysterics made Voltaire's days exhausting. He saw several hundred people a day while passing blood in his urine and bearing the burden of more than eighty years on his shoulders.

Wagnière complained that he did not even have time to dress himself. As for his master, he stayed in his dressing gown. But every so often he would have to put on a coat and wig to receive Madame du Barry. Their conversation is not recorded, but Voltaire later compared the true spontaneity of Madame de Villette with the artificial naturalness of the great favorite. He did admit, however, that the favorite was excellent at her profession, and he spoke as an expert.

Monsieur Le Brun left a few notes on the visit he paid to Voltaire. When Voltaire said to him, "I am eighty-four years old and have done a hundred foolish things," he was at a loss for a reply. But Mademoiselle Arnould thereupon remarked that she was only forty, had committed a thousand follies, and felt none the worse for them.

On February 20 Voltaire received a letter from a priest, the Abbé Gautier, who asked if he might come to see him. The letter was dignified and modest, and made no secret of the fact that the writer wanted to help Voltaire save his soul. He wrote that he was praying for him and, without being too insistent, expressed the hope that Voltaire might be so kind as to answer his request.

Voltaire was touched by the letter and wrote to tell the abbé he might come, recalling in his reply how he had imparted an unorthodox blessing on Franklin's grandson.

The abbé was a former Jesuit: there was always one somewhere in the neighborhood of Voltaire. Such things do not happen by chance. When people exercise such an attraction on one another it is for life, and even beyond. When Voltaire heard the word "Jesuit" it stirred some fiber in him: the child who had not known his mother or loved his father or brother had loved his teachers and been loved by them. He had rebelled against them, but he had remained their most sensitive and adroit as well as their proudest pupil. It was impossible for them to keep his loyalty to them intact: to do so they would have had to applaud his pranks and acts of sacrilege.

Instead, they had put him in his place, and he was annoyed with them —the more so as he was certain that the majority of them had no more illusions than he about the "sacred mysteries," and found pompous popery as ridiculous as he did.

The first interview with the Abbé Gautier was cordial. Voltaire asked him straightaway who had sent him. The abbé declared he had come of his own free will, but he did not conceal the fact that he intended to give an account of his visit to his superior, the Abbé de Fersac, curé of Saint-Sulpice. This frankness pleased Voltaire. Three people interrupted the interview, one of whom was Monsieur de Villette. "Come, monsieur," Voltaire said, "pray leave me with my friend the abbé—he does not flatter me." Madame Denis and Wagnière also came in on various pretexts. Finally they said the visit was tiring Voltaire; the truth was that it was making them uneasy. But the Abbé Gautier said he would return later— and did. Meanwhile another priest, the Abbé Marthe, a fanatical cleric, appeared on the scene. He went straight up to Voltaire and said: "You must confess to me without further ado. There is no question about it, no drawing back, that is what I am here for." He was politely persuaded to leave, but he returned several times to try his luck.

Voltaire now realized that in Paris he was to be a bone of contention between various parties contending for his soul. If he weakened, he could not tell who would carry it off: he decided to keep it for himself. But to do that he needed not to be ill. Yet he was ill, more ill than he thought. But he was also intoxicated with adulation, and no longer either spared his strength or gave in to his weakness.

Madame du Deffand made two appearances. To the note she had sent when he arrived Voltaire had replied: "I arrive dead, but I mean to come to life again merely to throw myself at the feet of Madame la Marquise du Deffand." But it was she who came to see him, despite her fears that she would find herself surrounded by all the intellectual mountebanks of Paris. How right she was! A Monsieur Wiart who called on Voltaire the day before she did said he met three hundred people: "All Parnassus was there, from the mire at its base to the summit. He will not survive this fatigue—he might easily have died before I saw him." So Madame du Deffand made haste to see Voltaire, or rather to hear him, for she had been blind for some years now. She met Madame Denis—"a slut"; and Villette—"a comedy character, low comedy even."

Voltaire kept her waiting a good quarter of an hour before emerging from his room. Was it his bladder that kept him, or was it *Irène?* He spoke only of *Irène.* "That is all he thinks of," said the marquise. He told her about the Abbé Gautier's visit. Villette wanted to give an account of it, but Voltaire shut him up by saying he did not know how to tell a story. He seems to have found it more difficult to endure Villette in Paris than at Ferney. He concluded his own account of the abbé's visit by saying: "This will preserve me from either ridicule or scandal."

The good news arrived that the King had commissioned Pigalle to make a bust of Voltaire. Voltaire thought he was back in favor, but unfortunately it turned out that Pigalle had received from Versailles an order for a large number of busts, among which Voltaire's had somehow been included. The King had had nothing at all to do with it.

On February 25 Voltaire was in bed dictating letters to Wagnière when he was seized with a violent fit of coughing and his nose and mouth filled with blood. "Oh! Oh!" he cried. "I'm spitting blood!"

Madame Denis sent for Dr. Tronchin, and Voltaire gave Wagnière a note for the Abbé Gautier. Wagnière threw it away. On February 26 Voltaire sent for the abbé again. He gave orders that a letter should be sent to him, saying to the people who thronged his room: "At least, messieurs, you will bear witness that I have asked to be able to fulfill what people here call one's duty." He added that he did not want his body thrown on the refuse heap.

He was provided with a young nurse who was able to turn away visitors, and a surgeon was summoned to sleep every night in his room. Apparently those about him had realized the danger at last.

The Abbé Gautier did not come until the following day. On his way in he passed the old Maréchal de Richelieu, who was on his way out, and Richelieu begged him not to frighten his "little friend from Louis-le-Grand." Voltaire received the abbé very kindly. He reminded him that he had promised to confess before he died, and since his last moment seemed close at hand, he said: "If you agree we shall attend to that little matter right away." The abbé said that the curé of Saint-Sulpice had authorized him to hear Voltaire's confession but that he insisted on a recantation first. Voltaire agreed and asked everyone else present to withdraw. Wagnière, as was his habit, put his ear to the door, which consisted only of a wooden frame pasted over with cloth and paper. He maintained that he would have considered it disobedient in this instance to obey his master's order and leave him alone. Wagnière was so upset at what he overheard that in his agitation he prevented anyone else from overhearing. For he was not the only eavesdropper. There were also the Abbé Mignot and Monsieur de Vieilleville, though these two were ashamed of what they were doing. Voltaire called for Wagnière and asked him for writing materials. His secretary, who felt more like dashing the inkstand to the floor, trembled as he brought it. Voltaire's hand did not tremble at all as he wrote his recantation. Mignot and Vieilleville came in and witnessed it.

Wagnière was politely asked to sign too, but he was up in arms at the idea. When asked why, he replied that he was a Genevan and a Protestant. They apologized and did not trouble him further. When Wagnière was alone with his master he asked what he really intended. What would people say about his recantation? What could his faithful secretary say to defend his memory? Voltaire took a sheet of paper and wrote: "I die worshiping God, loving my friends, not hating my enemies, and detesting superstition."

Voltaire did not take communion. According to Wagnière, he got out of it by saying to Gautier: "Monsieur l'Abbé, you will note that I am spitting blood, and we must be careful not to mix my blood with God's." D'Alembert wrote Frederick II a rather different version, according to which Voltaire is supposed to have said that he refused to take communion "because I am spitting blood and might easily spit out something else." Frederick wanted to know everything, down to the last detail. D'Alembert painted a sympathetic portrait of the Abbé Gautier, picturing him as a poor devil of a priest who had come to save Voltaire's soul out of the mere goodness of his own. It was this goodness that was supposed to have opened Voltaire's heart. Yet when the abbé presented himself again a few days later he was told that the patient was not well enough to receive visitors. The abbé thought he knew what had happened: he believed it was all the doing of certain *philosophes*, including D'Alembert, whom he had seen in the salon. But poor Gautier was much mistaken: it was all the doing of the curé of Saint-Sulpice. Monsieur de Fersac thought his subordinate had gone too far too fast and complained to Monsieur de Villette and Monsieur de Voltaire. The salvation of this impious but illustrious soul belonged to him. Voltaire realized at once that things were going to become complicated, and for the sake of peace and quiet he turned the Abbé Gautier out. The abbé declared he had only acted on the authority of his superiors; his superiors denied this. Whom was one to believe? On April 13 the curé of Saint-Sulpice came on his own and made no secret of his annoyance at having been preceded by an insignificant abbé. The porter of Villette's town house was instructed to let in no other priest save the curé of Saint-Sulpice.

Voltaire's health improved. He heard that the Abbé Gautier had another penitent, a freethinker by the name of L'Attaignant, who had recanted and confessed when he was at death's door, and thereupon recovered. As the abbé was also chaplain of the Hospital for Incurables, a verse was composed on his ministrations to the two *libertins*, L'Attaignant and Voltaire:

> L'honneur des deux curés semblables
> A bon droit était réservé
> Au chapelain des Incurables.

The honor of two such curates/Was rightly reserved/For the chaplain of the Incurables.

Since he had been feeling better Voltaire had regretted his recantation. But he could not free himself of the awful fear that had never ceased to haunt him—the fear of being buried like a dog. "I don't want my body to be thrown on the refuse heap. All these shavelings get on my nerves, but here I am in their power, and what I have to do is get out of it. As soon as I can be moved I shall go from here. I hope their zeal will not pursue me to Ferney. If I'd still been there this would never have happened," he insisted.

All this is not exactly dignified. But a dignified silence was not to be expected of Voltaire. He had lived in an uproar and he would die in one too.

To the quarrel between priests was added the quarrel between doctors. Monsieur de Villette, who disliked Dr. Tronchin, sent for a fashionable physician named Lorry. The two doctors met and reconciled their differences in the interests of the patient. But Villette could no longer stand the sight of Tronchin, and Tronchin refused to allow Villette into Voltaire's room.

Some days the quarrels among the doctors, Madame Denis, Villette, and various visitors were so violent that Voltaire's room was like an inn. He was improving but still spitting blood. The constant stream of callers had begun again. La Harpe read out an act of a tragedy he had just written: it was about a violent combat, and La Harpe gave a realistic performance, complete with shouts and thrusts and parries and stamping of his feet. People outside in the street stopped to listen to the din. The patient endured it to the end, then said: "Messieurs, you ought to ask them to give me the Cross of St. Louis." Everyone thought he was delirious. "Not at all," he retorted, "but I deserve it for having endured that awful battle so bravely."

The time has now come when to all the many different sentiments Voltaire's life has inspired the entirely new one of pity must be added. There is no one so cruelly used as an idol in mortal pain sacrificed to his public.

Dying as he was, he still dreamed of yet another success: he wanted to go to Versailles. It was the dream of his life; it would be his crowning glory. Europe had its kings, its emperors and empresses, but above all there was the real King, his King. That Louis XVI should be unfriendly was almost as intolerable as to die without Christian burial. If only he could have a smile, a word from the King before dying . . . All his friends tried to dissuade him. Those who came and went freely at Versailles told him it was the most formal place on earth and that the King would not be able to think of a word to say to him, nor would the Queen, or Monsieur and Madame, the King's brother and sister-in-law—they were all the dullest people. But in Voltaire's eyes his was only a bastard glory until the King had recognized it. This attitude on the part of one who was regarded, with good reason, as having mocked all authority, throws considerable light on what faith in the monarchy still meant a few years before the Revolution.

The most that could be got out of Versailles was the assurance that the King would continue to "ignore" Voltaire's presence.

Another Reprieve, Public Favor, and Private Bickerings

Hardly was Voltaire up and about again than Madame Denis started him off on the same turbulent round of popular idolization. Tronchin repeated his warnings and said the old gentleman ought to be bundled up and sent to Ferney. Instead the doors were flung open, and the procession of visitors recommenced.

A Monsieur de Farian de Saint-Ange, a very boring orator, began to read a speech he had prepared: "Today I have come only to see Homer, but I shall come back another day to see Euripides, then Sophocles, then Tacitus . . ."

"Monsieur," Voltaire interrupted, "I am very old—couldn't you make all your visits at once?"

Someone else congratulated him on his longevity and predicted that he would live longer than Fontenelle. "Ah, monsieur," said Voltaire, "Fontenelle was a Norman, and managed to trick even nature." On a recommendation from the Ministry for Foreign Affairs, he even received the Chevalier or Chevalière d'Eon, a French secret agent who spent most of his life in female dress. The servants and even the visitors were all agog, but the visit was spoiled by their curiosity as to whether this caller was a man or a woman: the "chevalière" hid her face in her muff and left as soon as possible after a few rapid courtesies.

With the social merry-go-round, the rehearsals for Irène began. They were a terrible drain on his health. Although he did not attend all of them, those he did left him gasping for breath. The actors were dull; they had none of the passion of Mademoiselle Duclos's day. The insatiable Madame Denis suggested they come and rehearse in her uncle's room, but he found the strength to protest. Mademoiselle Clairon came to see him. He complained of the acting and read one act in an incredibly strong voice. Mademoiselle Clairon said no actress had the power to act like that, and that to ask as much of Mademoiselle Vestris would simply kill her.

"That is precisely what I intend, mademoiselle," Voltaire replied. "I should like to do the public that service."

When a duke idly referred to the acting as very good Voltaire replied, "It may be good enough for a duke, but it is no good to me." He had so many worries and raised so many protests that he fell ill again. For four days he seemed at the point of death and his friends never left his bedside. He would murmur to visitors: "Voltaire is dying, Voltaire is spitting blood," and fall back on his pillow again, only half conscious. He revived once again, and rose from his bed like a ghost from the tomb.

Meanwhile all Paris echoed with resounding praise of him: compliments, poems, articles, and countless rhapsodic speeches. A few anonymous insults arrived by post, and he philosophically observed that at Ferney such things had to be paid for on delivery whereas in Paris they were paid in advance. "I gain on the exchange," he said.

March 14 was the opening night of *Irène*, and no performance at the Comédie Française was ever so splendid. The Queen, the princes, all the court, and all the ambassadors attended, and the audience in the pit was as brilliant as that in the boxes. It is hard to know which to admire most—Voltaire's fame or the public's good will in according their homage to a play that was poor and did not succeed in disguising that fact. Madame Denis was present in one of the boxes to represent her uncle, who was in bed. It was said that the Queen scribbled down notes on the performance. At each intermission a courier ran as fast as he could to bring the latest news of his triumph to the moribund author in the Rue de Beaune. After the first and second acts the response was marvelous; after the third and fourth merely polite. The last act was so dull that the audience's patience was the real masterpiece of the evening.

On the days that followed Villette and Madame Denis again exhibited the dying Voltaire, strutting about as if they were the objects of all the adulation. The Duc de Praslin paid Voltaire a very charming visit. The Académie Française sent another deputation, and he asked them to allow him to dedicate *Irène* to the Académie. He sent them the text, asking them to make any necessary corrections. They made a few slight changes and declared themselves delighted with the whole business. All was going well in that quarter.

But receiving visits was not enough for him, he wanted to pay some too. On March 21 he hired a coach and visited the Place Louis XV, now the Place de la Concorde. He was delighted with what the architect Gabriel had done. It was the architecture of the age—noble, pure, and classical. The crowd recognized him and escorted him back to the Rue de Beaune.

When he got home he was enchanted to find a delegation from the "Loge des Neuf-Soeurs" (Masonic Lodge of the Nine Sisters) waiting for him. Monsieur de Lalande, worshipful master of the lodge, had come with an invitation. Voltaire was told that at a meeting the Freemasons had recited verses in honor of Voltaire, and then they had drunk his health. Voltaire was not a Mason, but his love of liberty and his struggles against injustice and fanaticism had made him a Mason in spirit. His outing had done him good, Monsieur de Lalande found natural and cordial terms in which to express his homage, and Voltaire recovered the ten years he had just lost. He was sparkling, light, caustic, and tender, and for every member of the delegation he found words that made it seem as if he had known them for years. He promised to visit the lodge, and they all parted friends and already "brothers."

After all these pleasures came the storm. Before going to see *Irène*, Voltaire wanted to reread the script as performed. He was suspicious, and to make sure he had the same text as the actors themselves he sent for the prompt copy. When he read it he saw that senseless alterations had been made without consulting him, lines had been cut and others changed. He was seized with a fury much more dangerous to himself than to those responsible for the changes, but he could no longer control himself. He sent for his niece, who, frightened by his shouts and threats, admitted that it was at her instigation that the emendations had been made. Wagnière says that in twenty-four years he had never seen Voltaire in such a fury. He set upon his niece and gave her such a shove that she fell into a chair, in which one Monsieur Duvivier happened to be sitting. She had chosen a good place to fall: Monsieur Duvivier was to become her husband not long after. Actually, it was not the first time she had fallen into his arms; but it was the first time in public. This incident allowed Madame Denis to say later that she had married Duvivier because her uncle pushed her into it.

The tinkering with *Irène* may not have mutilated a masterpiece, but it came close to killing Voltaire. The worst of it was that D'Argental and Thibouville had also been involved. They were prudently kept out of the way while he was still in a rage, then D'Argental, hearing that Voltaire had calmed down, timidly appeared and provoked another storm. Voltaire accused him of alterations going back forty years and demanded stolen manuscripts back without an instant's delay. Madame Denis was told to go on foot and get them at once.

"I have been treated as no one would dare to treat even young Barthe," Voltaire cried. Alas, Monsieur Barthe was present, among some thirty other visitors who happened to be there. Voltaire collapsed and was carried off. But young Barthe considered himself insulted, and started to stamp about and shout, "Vengeance! Hold me back!" He wanted to fight the old man. Voltaire then reappeared and soothed him, saying there had been nothing offensive in what he had said—on the contrary. Everyone laughed, including Barthe. At this point, a civil engineer entered, and Voltaire greeted him: "Ah, monsieur, how lucky you are! You can build your fine bridges without any D'Argental coming along and adding his own arches to them."

But the next day he apologized. "Forgive me, dear Angel—my head is eighty-three and behaves as though it were fifteen."

How could a man like D'Argental not accept such an apology? Voltaire got around Thibouville too, and the storm blew over.

He went to see "My Sully," as he called Turgot, convinced that his greatness equaled that of Henry IV's great minister. Condorcet records how his admiration for Turgot was constantly evident in his conversation: he saw him as proof that the age was not as decadent as it was said to be. He kissed his hand, saying in a voice breaking with emotion: "Permit me to kiss the hand that signed the nation's salvation." When he first saw him he had said: "When I see Monsieur Turgot it's as if I saw a statue of Nebuchadnezzar." "Yes," said the minister, who had just fallen from power, "with feet of clay."

"But with a head of gold," cried Voltaire. "With a head of gold!"

Apotheosis

On March 30 he really became King Voltaire, consecrated and crowned in Paris.

On his way to see *Irène* he paid his visit to the Académie. He went in his fine carriage, upholstered in sky blue with gold stars. It made its way with difficulty through the crowd, which pressed as close as it could around the horses and the wheels, acclaiming Voltaire. In the courtyard of the Louvre, the headquarters of the Academy, several thousand people waited, applauding. The Académie Française then filed before him in procession, an unprecedented honor. Of course, there were certain absentees: the members who were prelates had stayed away. Voltaire was obliged to accept his nomination as chairman of that day's session, which was carried unanimously by all those present. D'Alembert read a speech in praise of Boileau, into which he introduced various compliments to the illustrious member who had not been present among his colleagues for twenty-eight years. He concluded with a panegyric which brought the audience to its feet, and in which encomiums to the genius of Boileau, Racine, and Voltaire were intermingled.

Voltaire gave thanks with his usual wit, and as time pressed, he left for the Comédie Française. It was not easy to get there: the crowd had grown, and so had its enthusiasm. The journey to the theater was a triumphal march, and the triumph was a popular one, kindly, informal, genuine. People climbed on the wheels and springs of the carriage and put their heads in through the windows. One man asked permission to kiss

Voltaire's hand, and without waiting for an answer seized hold of a hand and saluted it.

"By my faith," he cried, "a good plump hand for a man of eighty-four!"

He had got hold of that of "Belle et Bonne" (Madame de Villette)—perhaps not by mistake.

It was the women who were the most violent in their admiration: they tore the fur of his pelisse out in handfuls—the Tsarina's sables!

He had dressed for the occasion—but as people had dressed under the Regency. He looked as though he had stepped out of another century, out of the *Memoirs* of Saint-Simon. The monumental wig that he had been wearing since 1720 and that he combed every morning with his own hands might have made people laugh; but nothing is ridiculous in someone become a national monument. When he entered the theater he was greeted by an ovation that seemed as though it would never end. He was in the box belonging to the Gentlemen of the Privy Chamber, facing that of Monseigneur le Comte d'Artois. Madame Denis and Madame de Villette sat in the front of the box and Voltaire made a move to sit down behind them, but the pit shouted for him to come forward, and he seated himself between the two ladies. The atmosphere in the theater was electric, and the excited audience began to chant: "The Crown! The Crown!" All Paris was in on the secret. At that moment Brizard, the actor, appeared at Voltaire's side and placed a crown of laurels on his head. The audience became delirious, there were thunderous bravos and cheers. Voltaire was overwhelmed; laughing and crying at the same time, he murmured: "Good heavens, you want to kill me with glory." He transferred the crown to Madame de Villette's head, but the audience roared, insisting that he should take it back. The Prince de Beauvau entered the box, took the crown from Madame de Villette, and crowned the reluctant Voltaire once again. The noise was deafening, the auditorium full of dust from the stamping of the crowd. The aisles and even the wings were packed. When the curtain finally went up, the stage itself was seen to be full of people.

Scarcely anyone paid any attention to the performance of *Irène*: the only thing that could be heard was the applause for Voltaire. People had come to see not the play but the author. Everyone sensed that this was a grand finale, a solemn lowering of the curtain that must be made a success at all costs. No one really knew quite how, until someone remembered Mademoiselle Clairon's little ceremony a few years before. Voltaire's bust was hurriedly sent for and set up on its pedestal in the middle of the stage. Again the audience became delirious, realizing that what they had been waiting for was going to happen. Mademoiselle La Chassagne, in a moment of inspiration, had invented the appropriate rite: she wound wreaths of flowers around the bust, and the actors formed a semicircle, like priests—with Brizard dressed like a monk! Flowers were strewn lavishly on the divinity on the stage. Voltaire had hidden in the recesses of his box. But the crowd roared for him to appear. It was too much; he was overwhelmed. He came forward, unable to resist the cries, the magnetic appeal emanating from the auditorium. He bent down his head and leaned it on the sill of the box, overcome. When he raised it again, his face was bathed in tears.

Madame Vestris then came to the front of the stage with a sheet of paper in her hand. There was silence, and she recited a verse in his honor:

> Aux yeux de Paris enchanté
> Reçois en ce jour un hommage
> Que confirmera d'âge en âge
> La sévère postérité.
> Non, tu n'as pas besoin d'atteindre au noir rivage
> Pour jouir de l'honneur de l'Immortalité.
> Voltaire, reçois la couronne
> Que l'on vient de te présenter.
> Il est beau de la mériter
> Quand c'est la France qui la donne.

Before the eyes of an enchanted Paris/Accept this day an homage/Which will be from age to age confirmed/By harsh posterity./ No, thou needst not wait to reach the dark shore/To enjoy the honor of Immortality./ Voltaire, accept the crown/That has just been offered thee./It is a splendid thing to deserve it/When it is France that bestows it.

Madame Vestris was obliged to give an encore. As she read the lines again, the audience memorized them. One actress, carried away with enthusiasm, kissed the bust. Everyone else followed suit. The auditorium was in a frenzy.

Then a rather indifferent comedy of Voltaire, *Nanine*, was performed. The script did not matter, for the applause drowned out the actors' lines. When Voltaire left the theater he walked through corridors lined with smiling, curtseying women: it was the exit of a king. There was no jostling: he felt he was surrounded by admiration, deference, and affection.

Respect had kept the crowd at a distance in the theater, but as soon as he entered the street the crowd threw itself on him. He was nearly smothered to death. As many in the crowd were unable to reach the master, they embraced his horses. They wanted to unharness them and pull his coach themselves. But he was terrified of crowds and begged them to let his carriage take him home in the usual way. The coachman parleyed with the ringleaders and promised to go at a walking pace so that everyone along the route would be able to see Voltaire. Finally he arrived safe and sound in the Rue de Beaune. He wept for a long while. He hadn't the strength to speak, and simply collapsed into a deep, deathlike slumber.

After Olympus, Back to Normal

The next day he was down to earth again. He knew what all such excitement amounted to. "Ah, my friend," he wrote, "you don't know the French. They did the same for Jean-Jacques . . . and afterwards a warrant was issued for his arrest and he was obliged to flee the country." In the oscillation that is natural to nervous temperaments, he had swung back from exaltation to depression.

He learned that the Queen, who had been at the opera the previous day, had intended to go to the Comédie Française to see Voltaire but had been forbidden to do so by an order of the King. On April 2 *Irène* was performed at court, but Voltaire was not invited. All Paris commented on the court's latest blunder in insulting the capital's idol. It was just a clumsy pinprick, not a show of strength. But it proved to Voltaire that the best of his visit was over and that it would be wise to cut his stay short.

But there was Madame Denis to be reckoned with: she was enjoying herself and wanted the party to go on. She bristled at the suggestion that they return to Ferney and was supported in her resistance by D'Argental, Thibouville, and some of the *philosophes*, who wanted to exploit Voltaire's triumph to the fullest. "God protect me from my friends," he wrote.

But others saw the danger: Dr. Tronchin and Monsieur Dupuits, the husband of Corneille's grandniece, counseled a return to Ferney. They even got him a special soft-sprung coach in which to make the journey as comfortably as possible. Madame Denis never forgave Tronchin for this, though she still would not admit defeat. She had an invincible ally in Voltaire's vanity. When he felt weak he was willing to leave but was in no state to travel. When he felt better and could have traveled he didn't want to go. So in both cases he stayed, and Madame Denis won. She even succeeded in getting him to buy a splendid town house, the Hôtel de Villarceaux, near Madame de Saint-Julien's and opposite the Hôtel de Choiseul, in the Rue de Richelieu.

On April 6 he went to an ordinary session of the Academy. He betook himself there on foot, exchanging greetings with passers-by and with a crowd escorting him. At the entrance to the Tuileries a woman selling books at a stall ran up to him and said: "Kind Monsieur de Voltaire, sign some books for me. If you give them to me to sell, my fortune will be made. You have made other people's fortune, and I'm a very poor woman." It is curious to see this contrast between Voltaire's popular reputation for kindness and generosity, and the literary and official one that has represented him as malicious and mean.

He pretended to believe he would eventually return to Ferney. He said he would spend several months there, and the Duc de Condé, the Governor of Burgundy, was waiting to welcome him in Dijon. Madame de Saint-Julien, Voltaire's "butterfly philosopher," had promised to go with him. Dr. Tronchin said that if he went back to his hermit's existence at Ferney he might live another ten years.

Parisian Pleasures, Great and Small

On April 7 he went to the "Loge des Neuf-Soeurs" to return the visit the Freemasons had paid him. But this time it turned out to be a ceremony rather than a mere visit. The lodge was in the Rue du Pot-de-Fer near Saint-Sulpice, in what had formerly been the novice house of the Jesuits. Yet another link with Loyola. Brother Cordier de Saint-Firmin announced that he had the honor to present Monsieur de Voltaire to be apprenticed as a Mason. The Worshipful Master de Lalande had already received the recommendations of the most worthy Brother Bacon de la Chevalerie, Grand Orator of the Grand Orient of France, and those of all the brothers of this lodge. He had chosen the most worthy brothers Comte Strogonoff, Cailhava, Président Meslay, the Marquis de Lort, Brinon, the Abbé Roney, and others, to receive and prepare the candidate.

"After being given the words, signs, and tokens, Brother Voltaire was placed by the side of the Worshipful Master, to the east. A brother of the Column of Melpomene placed on his head a crown of laurels, which he made haste to remove. The Worshipful Master tied around his waist the apron of Brother Helvétius, which the philosopher's widow had presented to the Loge des Neuf Soeurs."

The Marquis de Villette was present, and when Voltaire was handed a pair of ladies' gloves he passed them on to him. "Because they imply a tender, honorable, and deserved affection, please give them to Belle et Bonne," he told him. A very gallant gesture, though perhaps not very Masonic.

Monsieur de Lalande delivered a very lofty speech in praise of Voltaire: ". . . Thus, most dear brother, you were a Freemason even before you were given the name, and performed the duties belonging to the order even before you assumed its obligations."

More eulogies and honors followed. Several brothers asked permission to recite poetry—and recited their own verses. Each read what he considered his best work; they were all remarkably long. Voltaire expressed his gratitude: the lavish praise lent him patience. After these interminable speeches there was a concert, and then finally the banquet. Voltaire's only helping of this love feast was a few spoonfuls of mashed beans, a secret panacea that had been passed on to him by a bluestocking.

The feast was not as copious as the speeches, and Voltaire at last was able to make his escape back to the Rue de Beaune. There he appeared on the balcony between D'Argental and Thibouville to reward the crowd that had been waiting all day in the street and around the corner by the river. Their applause for him was long and loud.

Everyone agrees that whenever he appeared the people were radiant with joy. Madame du Deffand, who knew everything, wrote—regretfully—that all France acclaimed Voltaire. Everyone except the court, that is to say. And for the court to hold aloof from all the people was something new in France. Can those who govern a people afford to turn up their noses at that people's idol? They should rather make that idol idolize them. And it would have been so easy—Voltaire was merely waiting for the signal to do so. What an ovation Louis XVI would have been given if he had allowed Voltaire to conduct him to his box at the Comédie Française. And if the King had asked him to, Voltaire would have gone on his knees and offered His Majesty holy water at high mass in Notre Dame. All the patriarch's glory would have been reflected on his sovereign, whereas instead the court's contempt for his popularity made that popularity turn into resentment against the throne.

That evening he went to see a great lady, the Comtesse de Montesson, who was supposed to be secretly married to the Duc d'Orléans and had one of the most brilliant salons in Paris. Plays were performed there; Madame de Montesson was an accomplished actress and the rest of her company was not lacking in talent. It reminded Voltaire of the theatricals at Ferney. But here it was all even better. The charm, wit, and courtesy of the most brilliant and attractive society that had ever existed offered Voltaire the best possible climate for the display of his talents. How could he have thought, that evening, of returning to Ferney? The day had been filled with all sorts of satisfactions, and he felt in excellent form. His vivacity was captivating, and the comtesse received him like an adored sovereign. So long live Paris, and make the most of it!

He had owed Madame du Deffand a visit for a month: she thought he was taking his time, and resented it. She received him in the convent to which she had retired. The only people present besides herself and Voltaire were her secretary and another lady living in the convent. What happened during the visit was not recorded. Perhaps Voltaire made some imprudent references to religion which were reported by Madame du Deffand's friend. Perhaps his mere presence in a convent seemed like sacrilege to the other pious ladies in retirement there. At any rate Madame du Deffand had to endure their angry reproaches, and on Voltaire's death, when they heard he had been refused a religious funeral, they came and created a disturbance under the blind marquise's windows. This was nothing new to Madame du Deffand, who was not unduly disturbed thereby, and must have laughed to herself at being criticized, at her age, for the company she kept.

The lively Voltaire continued to trot to and fro through the streets of Paris. At the end of April, on his way back from nagging Monsieur de Villarceaux to make up his mind as to whether or not he was going to sell him the house in the Rue de Richelieu, Voltaire decided to take a stroll in the gardens of the Palais Royal. He noticed a couple of pretty children playing with their governess and saw that one of them bore a striking resemblance to the Regent, whom he had met in those same gardens about sixty years before. He learned that the child was Monsieur de Valois, son of the Duc d'Orléans and the Regent's great-grandson. The little boy was then five years old and was one day to become King Louis-Philippe. The governess invited Voltaire into the palace to see the other children, who were asleep. The Duchesse d'Orléans, who was in the midst of having her hair done, left it just as it was and came flying to see him in her wrapper and petticoat, overjoyed at having the opportunity to meet him. The duc was not there, and the duchesse told the patriarch how disappointed she was that her husband had missed him.

In the same neighborhood he clambered up the stairs to see Sophie Arnould, a princess of the theater and therefore, in Voltaire's eyes, quite the equal of those of royal blood. The important thing was to be a princess of some kind. He also paid other visits, or pilgrimages, to people dating like himself from the previous century. Among them was the Comtesse de Ségur, who started to talk to him about God and His Church. As it was one of his good days and he was feeling well, he responded with typical vivacity and eloquence, all the boldness that so charmed some people and so horrified others. More than sixty people gathered around to listen to him.

He was fulminating against the priests to whom he had not a fortnight before made an *amende honorable*. When he had finished his diatribe he resumed his natural affability and did his hostess, who was in very weak health, a good turn. He passed on a remedy for fatigue which had helped him at Ferney: all the patient had to do was swallow yolks of eggs beaten up with potato flour, and he was cured. In those days the ingredient that represented a sensational innovation was the potato. Everyone present went into ecstasies at the universality of Voltaire's genius.

He still had a visit to pay to Madame la Marquise de La Tour du Pin-Gouvernet, the former Suzanne de Livry, the actress he had culled like a wild rose from under the branches of Sully in his youth. After her sad adventures in London she had married the marquis and, wishing to forget her theatrical past, had ordered her door closed to Voltaire. He had forgiven the insult, and she was now willing to receive him. But the meeting was a catastrophe. They scarcely recognized each other, and each was horrified by the other's decrepitude. The patriarch of Ferney still had his sparkling gaze, his power of mimicry, and his characteristic expressions at least; but of the wild rose there was nothing left. They could scarcely find a word to say to each other. In the room he might have seen the portrait of a young man radiant with intelligence and wearing a quizzical smile: it was himself, painted by Largillière. It was this young man that Suzanne had hoped to find again. They took leave of each other in consternation. But she had the charming idea of sending to Monsieur de Villette's the Largillière portrait, the best we have of Voltaire, which she had kept so long, and perhaps cherished.

Voltaire went home from that visit feeling that he had been contemplating two deaths: his own and Suzanne's. "I return from one bank of the Styx to the other," he remarked.

As soon as he had concluded the purchase of the Hôtel de Villarceaux on April 29, he sent Wagnière to Ferney, to prepare for his own return. But here his lifelong quarrel with religion began once again. The Abbé de Beauregard, preaching at Versailles, attacked the *philosophes* violently, saying that as a reward for their impiety they were crowned with laurels. It was an unmistakable reference to Voltaire. The King's aunts led the ultrareligious party, with the support of Louis XVI himself, and this party wanted to know why no attacks against impiety had been published since Voltaire's return. In fact the Keeper of the Seals, Monsieur de Miromesnil, had decided, as a measure of appeasement, not to let anything be published against Voltaire during his stay in Paris. But now, alarmed by this protest from such lofty quarters, he canceled his instructions to the censor. Voltaire wondered what to do. To go to Ferney would be to retreat before the bell, book, and candle of the Abbé de Beauregard. He decided to stay. It was a good opportunity, moreover, to disobey the doctors. And he was feeling quite well: Paris was smiling even if Versailles frowned.

He even went secretly to the theater. One day at a performance of his own *Alzire* he listened enchanted, hidden at the back of a box. But during Act IV he could contain himself no longer and sprang forward exclaiming, "Splendid! Oh, how splendid!" The audience recognized him and gave him an ovation. Act V was a fresh triumph: the actors, stimulated by the presence of Voltaire and the enthusiasm of the audience, surpassed themselves. Laurel wreath excepted, Voltaire received another apotheosis as resounding as that for *Irène*. He left the theater intoxicated and exhausted.

Last Labors

After *Irène* had finally been performed, what Voltaire subsequently turned his attention to was first and foremost the Academy. It is true to say that he devoted his last efforts and all that remained of his strength to the Academy's essential task, the compiling of its Dictionary. He attended meetings regularly, and urged the members with a passion that astonished everyone to get down to the recasting of the Dictionary. He argued that the French language was becoming impoverished for want of renewal. Voltaire, the pure, classical, "conservative" Voltaire, declared: "Our language is a beggar and must be given alms whether she likes it or not." It was therefore the Academy's responsibility to choose rejuvenating new words. He quoted the example of the word *tragédien*, which was not then admitted as a noun, for an actor who played roles in tragedies. He suggested a work scheme so vast that his fellow academicians were aghast. Among them were a number of worldly aristocrats who did not care at all for the idea of pledging themselves to a task that would occupy them for years. But no one could help admiring the enterprise, intrepidity, tenacity, and farsightedness of this old man of eighty-three who made plans as though he were only thirty. Nor did he remain content with plans. He practiced what he preached, and began assigning the work. The academicians' admiration changed to surprise and uneasiness. There were murmurs when he started assigning each of them specific tasks. But he gave himself the most taxing task of all—the letter A, involving more words than any other section of the Dictionary. Each word was to be gone over and gone into from the point of view of both etymology and meaning, with examples of various usages drawn from reputed authors. The conjugation of irregular verbs was to be re-examined. And in the end Voltaire's enthusiasm overcame the indifference of his colleagues and they accepted his project. When everyone had adopted a letter to work on, he said, "Messieurs, I thank you . . . in the name of the alphabet." And the Chevalier de Chastellux replied with equally elegant formality: "And we thank you in the name of literature."

Voltaire then returned, exhausted, to the Rue de Beaune and drank five cups of coffee.

His flagging strength did not prevent him, two days later, from going to a meeting of the Academy of Sciences. The news spread that he was there, and great and lovely ladies came running to catch a glimpse of him. It was another magnificent but exhausting session. It revived ironic memories of the old days at Cirey, when he had tried to get a seat in this very Academy with an article on the nature of fire. As chance would have it, that day's session was also distinguished by the attendance of Benjamin Franklin. The two most famous and "philosophical" old gentlemen of the age once again fell into each other's arms.

Monsieur d'Alembert rose to his feet to pronounce a funeral oration on Trudaine, a friend of both Turgot and Voltaire. D'Alembert took the opportunity to praise Voltaire at the same time as the deceased, and the audience was delighted. The last item on the agenda was less amusing—a lecture on how to make sweet wine out of sour grapes. Everyone dozed off, including Voltaire. Thanks to the sour grapes, he returned to the Rue de Beaune relatively refreshed.

The following day he resumed his social rounds with a visit to the wife of the Maréchal de Luxembourg. Rousseau was a protégé of hers, but Voltaire did not hold that fact against her. They talked about the war with England. They were both concerned about all these endless, exhausting, pointless wars. But how were they to be brought to an end? The maréchale was for peace at any price, but Voltaire's thin frame shook with anger and, pointing fiercely to the sword of the Maréchal de Broglie hanging on the wall nearby, he said, "Madame, there is the pen with which peace should be signed."

He too was against war, but at the same time he was not in favor of peace without honor. During the early days of May he could not go to the Académie Française because he had been obliged to take to his bed once again. He was apprehensive, about his dictionary, fearing that colleagues had accepted his project only out of a temporary excess of enthusiasm and politeness.

Voltaire at Grips with Doctors, Apothecaries, and Friends

On May 11 he went out again, though feeling poorly. He met Madame Saint-Julien and Madame Denis and told them he was going home to bed. He had violent kidney pains and complained of difficulty passing water. Wagnière records that he tried to cure himself by drinking twenty-five cups of coffee that day.

When Madame de Saint-Julien saw him again two days later, she thought he looked far from well, and advised them to send for Dr. Tronchin. But Madame Denis was angry with Tronchin and refused to ask him to come see her uncle. Two days later the patient's condition was worse, but Villette did nothing more than call the local apothecary. The latter offered a potion of his own invention, which Voltaire fortunately refused to take. Madame de Saint-Julien tried just a little sip and it burned her tongue so badly that she could not eat any supper. The Duc de Richelieu came in the evening and suggested an opium potion which he himself used as a painkiller. Voltaire was in great pain from both his bladder and his kidneys, and asked Richelieu for some of his medicine. A number of the people watching over Voltaire ventured to suggest that it was dangerous and would do him no good. But Madame Denis and Villette were for it—Villette said the only danger was that Voltaire might possibly be out of his head for a few days, but after that he would be cured. So, through the good offices of his niece and of Villette, Voltaire was given a strong dose of Richelieu's potion. Some said that Villette smashed the vial afterward; others maintained that Voltaire sat up and swallowed the entire contents under Villette's eyes. When she heard this, Madame de Saint-Julien is reputed to have asked indignantly: "And didn't you do anything to stop him?" Nothing is precise in all this. But it is beyond doubt that neither the attitude of Madame Denis nor that of Villette was one of affection. Without going so far as to believe Wagnière's allegation that it was this medicine that killed his master, one may draw the conclusion that Voltaire was very badly looked after. No doubt his strength was almost exhausted. But nothing was done to make things easier for him. On the contrary. Of course the fault was not entirely other people's. The stream of visits, the constant alteration of emotions, the public triumphs—all these constituted the worst type of treatment, but one that was eminently Voltairian. In short, Voltaire died of what he had lived by: ceaseless activity. It had given him eighty-three years of marvelous life. There is no need to lament the fact that it killed him, after allowing him to enjoy himself so much until the very end.

He was now seriously ill but not yet dead. He still had a few words to say.

Taking Richelieu's opiate resulted in terrible suffering: his body seemed to be set aflame from his throat to his bowels, and for two days he was wildly delirious. He thought Richelieu, his childhood friend, had poisoned him, and would refer to him only as "Brother Cain." Finally they were obliged to send for Dr. Tronchin, but by then it was too late. He managed to calm the patient a little, but the excessive dose of opium had brought on a paralysis of the stomach. Voltaire was unable to digest either solids or liquids, and his weakness became alarming. He kept asking for Wagnière; the others wanted to send for him and, though Madame Denis objected, Monsieur d'Hornoy, Voltaire's grandnephew, insisted, and sent for him just the same. Madame Denis thereupon wrote to Wagnière instructing him to be sure to see to all the domestic details at Ferney —and to "everything that belongs to me," she added with her usual sense of what she considered her rightful due. She informed him that Voltaire was better. This was an outright lie, but it prevented Wagnière from returning to Paris forthwith and gave him time to bring all the things she had requested, especially the silver plate.

In the midst of his torment Voltaire was told that Lally-Tollendal, whom he had defended, had just been rehabilitated thanks to his son's efforts. He raised himself up in bed, his eyes brightening, and dictated a few lines. Using an oft-repeated phrase, he said: "A dying man comes to life again on hearing this great news." He then added: "He embraces Monsieur de Lally fondly, and will die happy in the knowledge that the King is the champion of justice." He had them pin on the wall, where he could see it, a piece of paper on which was written: "On May 26, 1778, the judicial murder committed on the person of Lally by Pasquier, counselor to the Parlement, was avenged by the King." He remembered the names of the enemies of justice till the end, and remained faithful to the King, in spite of the differences between them, to the very end.

How can it be alleged that he engaged in his terrible struggles against injustice and fanaticism only to satisfy his vanity, his love of publicity and play acting? A man might pretend for eighty-three years, but when he is in his death throes he ceases to pretend. The over-all picture is clear: the real Voltaire is the Voltaire of liberty and justice. The piece of paper on the wall by his bed was a cry of truth, his last cry, the cry whose echoes we still hear.

The End

Since Voltaire had become so ill Madame Denis and Villette stopped "exhibiting" him. Nonetheless the visits did not cease: Madame Denis simply seized upon the callers for herself. She drank up flattery and engaged in witty conversation while her uncle was dying in horrible circumstances. He had been put away out of sight in a cottage at the bottom of the garden. The niece's only concern was to get hold of any scrap of paper he might scribble on in his easier moments: she was terrified lest he might revoke the will that made her his heir. As for Villette, he was preoccupied with the thought of the trouble his guest's death would cause him. He was illustrious while he was alive, but once he was dead he would become the object of scandal and reprobation. Monsieur de Villette was wondering how he was going to get rid of the corpse.

The first thing to do was gain time by keeping the seriousness of Voltaire's illness a secret. The story was given out that Monsieur de Voltaire was suffering from one of those frequent illnesses from which he had always recovered. They even invented jests he was supposed to have made. But the audience was growing restive. The intermission was lasting too long, and it was time for the star to reappear and get on with his performance.

In the dark cottage where he was dying, watched over by two women chosen by Madame Denis—Bardy, a cook, and Roger, a nurse, who sat by him chattering, laughing, and drinking—he was visited from time to time by Tronchin. Tronchin examined him perfunctorily but did nothing; there was nothing to be done. He might at least have insisted that his friend Voltaire be allowed to die decently and be rid of these harpies. But all Tronchin did was make observations which were far from friendly. He remembered Voltaire saying, "If I can, I shall die laughing," and this provided Tronchin the theme for his inappropriate remarks about his patient: "I should be very much surprised if he really did die cheerfully, as he has vowed to do. He won't bother to keep up appearances with his intimates who are there at his bedside, he will simply yield to the promptings of his character, to cowardice, and to the fear of leaving the certain for the uncertain. . . . For Voltaire the end will be an awful moment. If he remains clear in his mind to the last he will make a poor exit from this world."

It is necessary to hear all the evidence about a man as closely observed, spied on, adored, and hated as Voltaire, and to take the truth where one finds it, whether amid flowers or in the mire. The face that Voltaire, the great grimacer, would make at death seemed a good joke to Dr. Tronchin. This was all he had to say at the deathbed of the most brilliant intelligence of the age, the defender of Calas, Tronchin's own coreligionist. Was all that already forgotten?

The truth about Voltaire's condition finally leaked out. The Abbé Gautier, hearing of it, wrote to Voltaire and declared himself ready to resume hearing his confession and preparing the dying man to make a good end. The Abbé Mignot, Voltaire's nephew, was there, and offered to summon the Abbé Gautier. This time the latter had taken precautions and brought with him the text of a more complete recantation than the last time, including an *amende honorable* and a detailed profession of faith. Gautier also insisted that the Abbé de Fersac should be allowed to accompany him: his superior's previous reprimand had not been forgotten. The Abbé Mignot agreed to everything. When the two clerics arrived at the Rue de Beaune, Monsieur de Villette asked to see the recantation, which he read and approved. The two priests were taken to the patient's bedside. He did not recognize the Abbé de Fersac, but he recognized the Abbé Gautier, taking his hands and showing signs of friendship. But when the subject of recantation was mentioned, Voltaire began to repeat: "Monsieur l'Abbé Gautier presents his compliments to the Abbé Gautier . . ." and other disjointed phrases. The abbé thought he was delirious and withdrew, saying he would come back when Voltaire was lucid. This was on the afternoon of May 29, 1778. Two days later the abbé was told that Voltaire had died the previous evening at eleven o'clock. "If I had known he was going to die so soon," he said, "I would not have abandoned him. I would have done all I could to help him to die well." A charitable word at last. They were rare enough in this entire affair.

La Harpe and Grimm give another version of the priest's visit. They were not present themselves but were given a detailed account of what happened. It seems the worthy Abbé Gautier did not really understand what was going on. Voltaire's delirium was not so severe as the abbé had thought. When he asked him if he recognized the divinity of Christ, Voltaire replied: "Christ? Christ? Let me die in peace!" and made a sign for the abbé to go away. The curé of Saint-Sulpice observed: "You can see he is not in his right mind!" And they left. As they did so, Voltaire stretched out his hands toward them and said, "I am dead."

This account sounds convincing. Afterward, Voltaire's "witticisms" were improved on. It was reported that at the mention of the divinity of Christ Voltaire answered, "Don't mention that man to me!" or "In God's name, don't talk to me about him!" Would even Voltaire have been so prodigal of sarcastic remarks a few hours before his death? His "Let me die in peace" seems more probable.

But not much peace surrounded Voltaire as he lay on his deathbed.

Tronchin, his doctor, who had witnessed everything, wrote and told Charles Bonnet, his friend in Geneva, about it the following month. Neither of them was kindly disposed toward Voltaire but, malicious as it is, Tronchin's evidence is of capital importance. He wrote, in his involved style, that there was a great difference between the end of a wise man, which as everyone knows is as serene as the end of a fine day, and "the awful torment of the man for whom death is the king of terrors!" This was a reference to Voltaire, but before speaking of him Tronchin spoke of himself and the magnificent eulogy Voltaire had bestowed on him as he died. We shall see the thanks he got. Then he goes on to relate how his patient said, "Have pity on me, I am mad—send for the doctor for the insane." It is true that the opium had made Voltaire deranged. He presented an awful picture "of madness and despair"—"I cannot remember it without horror," said Tronchin. He maintained his patient had gone mad because he knew he was dying. But was that true? To all the other witnesses Voltaire seemed comatose, in torture from the internal burning sensation, but unconscious nearly all the time. He implored Tronchin: "Monsieur, help me out of this!" To which Tronchin made the Spartan reply, "There's nothing I can do, monsieur. You'll have to die."

The object of Tronchin's account was to demonstrate that the death of an unbeliever must necessarily be a horrible one, an exemplary and therefore edifying agony. The moral this usually kind friend drew was this: "I wish all those who have been led astray by his books had been witnesses of his death. It is impossible to hold out against such a sight." The *Gazette de Cologne* improved on Tronchin's account, adding further details: "Just before his death Monsieur de Voltaire was seized with dreadful agitation, crying furiously, 'I am forsaken by God and my fellow men!' . . . He gnawed his fingers, put his hands in a chamber pot, drew out what was in it, and ate it."

Numerous people were ready to contribute lurid details of this sort. A certain Abbé Depery said he had been told by Madame de Villette—fifty years after Voltaire's death—that Voltaire saw the Devil at the side of his bed and cried out like the damned soul that he was, "There he is! He's trying to get hold of me! I can see hell!"

Hell, in the same room as that last sentence on the wall about the King avenging the innocent? The Abbé Depery also lent credence to the rumor that priests had supposedly been forbidden to enter the room and had been driven away by the *philosophes*. But the Abbé Gautier and the curé de Saint-Sulpice both shortly maintained that they had been courteously received at the Hôtel de Villette.

If hell were to be seen during those last hours, it was rather in all this false witness and in the dreadful greed and cruelty of Madame Denis. There is no need to read the *Gazette de Cologne* or the Abbé Depery's foolish visions or the moralizings of Tronchin to be filled with pity and terror. The reality itself is awful enough: despite the horde of onlookers, Voltaire died forsaken.

In his wretched room the servants strolled in and out as they pleased: the two nurses had whatever visitors they fancied. Wagnière went in once and received the impression that the room was "full of drunken peasants spoiling for a fight." None of the medicines prescribed by the doctor were anywhere to be seen. In a passing moment of consciousness Voltaire cried out that he was being murdered. It was not exactly true; but he was being made to die faster and more painfully than simple humanity would have allowed. Monsieur Racle, a doctor from Geneva, managed to make his way into the place; he found Voltaire—the neat and fastidious Voltaire—in a state of unspeakable filth. What a humiliating end for the spruce little squirrel! Dr. Racle does not go into detail, for, as he says, "I should make your heart bleed with pain and horror." While he could still speak, Voltaire had said to Tronchin: "If I had taken your advice I should not be in the terrible state in which I am now. I should be back at Ferney. I should not have got drunk on the fumes that turned my head . . . yes, all that I swallowed was fumes."

He hated the people around him. Madame Denis did not go to see him; if he had recognized her he would have insulted her.

The nurse, Roger, was charged with the task of taking note of any blasphemies that the dying man might let fall from his lips, in order to testify against him should the family ask for a religious burial. She spied on him closely but did not nurse him. When he emerged momentarily from his coma, he would shout threats and insults at her; once he even threw a vase at her head. When he was delirious she listened, in order to repeat and testify afterward to "the eloquence and fertile inventiveness of his insanity." He still felt as if his insides were on fire, and to soothe the burning sensation he asked for a "pool of ice." He sometimes writhed naked on the bed. He begged for something to drink, but no one took any notice. It was during one of these attacks of thirst that he seized his bedpan and attempted to drink from it. But whose fault was that? People said it was the act of a madman. But what madness possessed nurse Roger to refuse him a glass of water? And what possessed Madame Denis when she was told of this scene and merely said: "What! Monsieur de Voltaire, the cleanest of men, who changed his linen three times a day rather than tolerate the slightest mark on it—what vile level is he reduced to? What revolutionary change does this represent?"

At ten o'clock in the evening on May 30 the end was obviously near. When Dr. Lorry and Dr. Thierry came in, the patient's pulse was almost indiscernible. They massaged his temples vigorously. He opened his eyes and said, "Let me die." The two doctors went out. He was left alone for a moment, then the two women started rubbing his temples again. Suddenly Voltaire uttered a long, long, terrible cry. It was eleven o'clock. Nurse Roger was frightened, and the cook, Bardy, is supposed to have remained in a state of terror for several months. Dr. Tronchin was called and was present during Voltaire's last moments. "What a death! I shudder at the mere thought of it," he said, remembering the terrible suffering Voltaire had had to endure in order to die.

Thus, after using up all his powers with indefatigable energy, Voltaire died. The Light of the Age of Enlightenment was forever extinguished.

There are two monsters that desolate the earth in peacetime: one is calumny, and the other intolerance; I shall fight them till my dying day. (*Literary Miscellanea*, Refutation)

The science of history is merely that of inconstancy, and all that we know for certain is that everything is uncertain. (*History of the Parlement, Introduction*)

We dare to question whether the intelligent soul is spirit or matter, if it was created before us, if, after having animated us on earth for a day, it lives after us in eternity. These questions appear to be sublime, but what are they? Questions of blind men who say to other blind men: "What is light?" (*Philosophical Dictionary:* "Soul")

Everything I see is sowing the seeds of a revolution that is certain to come about, which I shall not have the pleasure of witnessing. The French are late in getting around to everything, but in the end they get there. The light has spread so gradually that there will be an explosion at the first opportunity, and there will be quite a rumpus. Young people are very happy; they will see some splendid things. (Letter to Monsieur de Chauvelin, April 2, 1764)

What our eyes and mathematics prove to us must be considered true; as for all the rest, the only thing to say is "I don't know." (Letter, December 23, 1768)

Is Voltaire Dead?

What remained, on the night of May 30, 1778, of the most brilliant and turbulent of men? There remained a corpse, an immense fortune, a huge pile of famous books, a tumultuous tribute to Voltaire's glory that still filled the Rue de Beaune and the nearby quais along the river, and something else, almost nothing: a breath of the spirit that was felt throughout the world.

What was to become of all this?

The corpse still lay on its pallet. It turned out to be the liveliest and most Voltairian of corpses.

Though Voltaire was already dead, the crowd still acclaimed him and kept calling for him to come out on the balcony. The others had concealed the fact of his death, which presented them with serious problems. In fact, while the crowd was still applauding him in the Rue de Beaune, Monsieur de Voltaire was posting along the road to Troyes. The fear that had haunted him all his life, the fear of having his body thrown on the rubbish heap, came very near to being fulfilled. His nephews, the Abbé Mignot and Monsieur d'Hornoy, did all they could to prevent such a scandal. Even before his death they had begged the ecclesiastical authorities to accord their uncle a Christian burial. They based their appeal on his first recantation and confession, but it was not difficult to prove that Voltaire's later utterances following this repentance had deprived it of any value. They went to Monsieur Lenoir, superintendent of the Paris police, and Monsieur Amelot, the minister, who tried to intervene in Voltaire's favor with the archbishop and Monsieur de Fersac: but they met with an absolute refusal. Both the Abbé Mignot and Monsieur d'Hornoy were members of the Paris Parlement: they were informed that if they made an official request it would be refused and they would be required to resign. The King himself was sounded out on the subject, but his reply on this occasion was the forerunner of many others: he washed his hands of it: "There was nothing to be done save to allow the priests to deal with it." Louis XIV had managed to save Molière from a pauper's grave. But in Voltaire's case the priests were not the worst of the fanatics. The merciful impulses of the coterie of bigots, led by Madame de Nivernais and Madame de Gisors, had the same effect as though they had been inspired by the bitterest hatred.

The Abbé de Fersac refused to conduct the funeral, but he did not object to the transferral of the corpse to Ferney, where Voltaire had prepared his tomb. It was half inside the church and half outside: malicious tongues, Voltaire had said, would not fail to point out that "he was neither in nor out."

The Abbé Mignot, together with his cousin Monsieur d'Hornoy, made a heroic decision: he decided to take his uncle's corpse in secret to the Abbey of Seillières, near Troyes, of which he was the commendatory abbot. He was certain that his prior would agree to give Voltaire religious burial, and scandal would thus be avoided and his uncle be allowed to rest in peace, as he had wished.

But before Voltaire's final appearance, there had naturally to be a certain amount of scene-setting. During the early morning of May 31, Monsieur Try, a surgeon from the Rue du Bac, Monsieur Mithouart, an
apothecary from the Rue de Beaune, and Monsieur Brizard, their assistant,
came to perform an autopsy and embalm the corpse. Voltaire had died
on the evening of the 30th, but Paris did not know this. The doctor and
his assistants had only a candle and a few instruments to help them in
their task. They found the kidneys and bladder terribly infected and per-
forated. The apothecary opened the skull, and a third doctor who seems
to have been present, a Monsieur Rose de l'Epinoy of the Academy of
Medicine, observed that it was on the small side, with very thin walls, but
that the size of the brain was much larger than average. In return for his
trouble Monsieur Mithouart asked to be allowed to keep the brain, which
he boiled in alcohol and took home in a jam jar. Monsieur de Villette, as
friend and host of the deceased, claimed the heart and had it put in a
gold-plated silver box.

Then came the business of sewing up, which they managed after a
fashion, clapping the skull together and covering it with a tight cap. The
corpse was then dressed and finally put into a handsome dressing gown,
which Madame Denis saw go with some reluctance. They had already
cut up three good sheets to bandage the body so as to make it sit upright.
Monsieur de Voltaire's last role was to be that of a mummy. They sat
him in the fine coach lined with blue silk sprinkled with gold stars. Six
horses were hitched to the coach: speed was essential, for he had now
been dead for forty-eight hours, the weather was hot, and the embalmers
were none too confident of their handiwork. Voltaire was propped up
against the cushions, held in place by hidden straps. A footman sat beside
him to keep him company to Seillières.

The nephews followed in another carriage.

At the gates of Paris Monsieur de Voltaire and his fine turnout were
saluted discreetly by the customs officials—and they were off. The journey went well, except for the footman, who was nearly in the same state
as his companion on arrival—almost dead from fright and from the
dreadful smell from the corpse. The mummy was got out and dumped, in
a sitting posture, on a table in a low-ceilinged room. The abbey at this
time was nearly in ruins. The prior made no difficulties about doing what
he had been asked to do, and it was decided to bury Voltaire in the
church itself, near the choir. They took up a flagstone, dug a little hole,
knocked a coffin together out of four planks , and stuffed the body into
it. This took up the afternoon. Madame Denis had been asked to authorize a lead coffin, but she had said: "What for? It's very expensive and
there's no point in it." The gravedigger from Romilly, the neighboring
village, and the priests and monks were all summoned for five o'clock the
next morning. The clergy were in proper liturgical vestments and the
Office for the Dead was sung. All the curés wanted to say a mass, so Vol-

taire, who had been refused one low mass in Paris, had six sung ones in Champagne. The coffin was lowered and the slab replaced. In order that the grave could be recognized later, a stone was placed upon the coffin, with the inscription: "A 1778 V."

When, a little while later, the nephews learned that various parts of Voltaire's body had been divided up, they protested. They were supported by public opinion, which drove them to start a lawsuit for the restoration of the pieces. But what was done could not be undone, and they did not insist.

Madame Denis did not bother her head about such trifles. All her attention was taken up by her troubles as residuary legatee, by Monsieur Duvivier, and by the task of trying to get hold of as many of her uncle's possessions as possible. Things got lost so easily. A heart or a brain were not important, but furs, jewels, and unpublished manuscripts were another matter.

The Archbishop of Paris learned of Voltaire's death in Paris at the same time as he learned that he had been buried at Seillières. He immediately informed his superior the Bishop of Troyes of what had been going on in his diocese. The bishop asked the prior of the abbey to account for himself and ordered Voltaire's body to be exhumed. The prior affected innocence and protested that he had acted in good faith: he had been shown a regular recantation and certificate of confession. He recalled aptly, but to no avail, that as Voltaire had never been excommunicated he had a right to a Christian burial. For the sake of appearance, the bishop pretended to be furious and the prior was dismissed, but his superior, the Abbé Mignot, was left unpunished. The prior received very respectable compensation from the two nephews, and Voltaire was allowed to rest in peace, for the moment.

The newspapers were requested not to mention Voltaire, and the theaters were asked not to perform his plays. This went on for a month—a long silence for Voltaire, even when he was dead. In July the Comédie Française performed *Mahomet*. There were neither cheers nor boos. It seemed as if peace were his at last.

But it was only a truce. The Académie Française would have liked to follow their usual custom of having a mass said for their deceased member in the Cordeliers, the church of the Franciscan friars. But the Archbishop of Paris forbade it. D'Alembert and all the Encyclopedists thereupon began campaigning for a mass for Voltaire. This irony amused some people, but not the Archbishop. Many priests differed from the official view, and many said they would have buried Voltaire had they been asked. D'Alembert wrote to Frederick II that the curé of Saint-Etienne-du-Mont would willingly have buried Voltaire in his church between Pascal and Racine, and would have had his profession of faith carved as an epitaph.

The Lodge of the Nine Sisters had a solemn ceremony performed to take the place of the one that the Church refused to accord Voltaire. It took place on November 28, 1778, in the presence of Madame Denis and Madame de Villette. The high spot was the appearance of Benjamin Franklin. It was very splendid, very long, and very boring. Representatives of all the arts had been invited, and music alternated with speeches in verse and prose. Most of the audience ended in the arms of Morpheus; Voltaire's spirit certainly left the ceremony before the end.

At D'Alembert's insistence, Frederick II had a mass said for Voltaire in Berlin Cathedral. Frederick's comment was: "I am embarking in Berlin on the famous negotiations for the service for Voltaire, and though I have no notion of what the immortal soul may be, a mass shall be said for his. Our actors in this farce are better acquainted with monetary rewards than with good books."

The object of all these various pieces of play acting was to tell the world that the Archbishop of Paris, the French Church, and France itself were the only ones to refuse a Christian burial to the illustrious Christian named Voltaire.

Monsieur de Villette worshiped the golden heart in his possession with all the requisite publicity. He sent the relic to Ferney to be installed in Voltaire's room, which had been left precisely as it had been in his lifetime. Villette also prided himself on having had a marble monument put up there too: a truncated fluted column in a black-draped niche. Wagnière, who had no desire to spare Villette's feelings, maintained that it was only a cheap piece of clay painted to look like marble. Nonetheless, Villette's inscription over the door of the shrine was authentic enough: "His heart is here, his spirit is everywhere."

Villette later bought the estate at Ferney from Madame Denis. He lived there for a time, until financial setbacks forced him to rent it to an Englishman. Sensitive souls reproached him for having rented out Voltaire's heart along with the rest of the furniture, and he finally sold Ferney and took the heart to his own estate at Villette. Even in pieces Voltaire was still a wanderer.

At the outbreak of the Revolution Monsier de Villette became an enthusiastic supporter and renounced his title of marquis. He replaced the plaque outside his house, which read "Quai des Théatins," with another reading "Quai Voltaire." It was a good idea: Voltaire had lived there in his youth, and he had come there to die. But the authorities, urged on by Voltaire's enemies, protested. So the accommodating Villette left the two plaques side by side, saying that people could call it by whichever name they preferred.

Villette's mind was seething with an even more sublime idea—the transferral of Voltaire's remains to Paris—which he put forward in a little journal of the day entitled *La Chronique*. The idea spread through Paris, and there were soon a dozen people who claimed to have originated it. The

Abbey of Seillières happened to be on the point of being sold, having become state property. It was in ruins and due for demolition, and Voltaire's bones were in danger of being thrown into a common grave together with those of the monks. But where in Paris was Voltaire to be buried? Some, seeing him as the father of the new France and the Revolution, proposed that his body should be placed beneath the altar of the Federation, like St. Peter's beneath the throne of the Pope. Never had so irreligious a man been called upon to do so much service as a relic. Others, revering him as the author of *La Henriade,* wanted to bury him under the hoof of the horse of the equestrian statue of Henri IV near the Pont Neuf. Others thought of a tomb at the end of the Champs Elysées, a site now occupied by the Tomb of the Unknown Soldier.

During a performance of Voltaire's *Brutus,* in which the audience of the day looked for political allusions in every line, Villette, always eager to serve himself by serving Voltaire's reputation, went up on the stage and delivered an impromptu speech. He called the Parisians "Romans" and Voltaire "Brutus," descriptions which were both about equally apt, and arrived at the natural conclusion that Voltaire's remains ought to rest in the Panthéon—the church of Sainte-Geneviève before the Revolution.

To remove any lingering hesitations he promised to undertake all the expense himself, and was acclaimed for the offer.

The Abbey of Seillières was due to be sold on May 3, 1791; what was to become of Voltaire's remains if nothing was decided before then? He was no surer of a resting place dead than he had been alive. The commune of Romilly was prepared to give Voltaire refuge; and so, worked on by Villette, was the municipality of Paris. The Troyes Society of Friends of the Constitution also claimed to have rights over the skeleton. As the lesser are obliged to give way to the greater even in times of revolution, Romilly yielded to Troyes and Troyes to Paris . . . but they both wanted at least a few relics. Romilly said it would be satisfied with the right arm and Troyes asked for the skull. (They did not know that the brain had been removed.) Certain people were indignant at these requests for dismembered parts of Voltaire's remains, since it recalled all too vividly the customs of the Roman Church.

On May 10, 1791, after being buried thirteen years, the body was exhumed. People from both Romilly and Troyes were there, competing to be the first to carry off the bones. The inhabitants of Troyes were showing the most determination, when suddenly a decree arrived from the Constituent Assembly declaring Voltaire's remains the property of the State. This meant hands off to Romilly and Troyes, but still they all competed feverishly, digging up the flagstones to find the inscription "A 1778 V." Suddenly there was a shout: "Here it is!" A pick had gone through the boards of the coffin.

It was lifted out of the hole, and two surgeons advanced and pronounced the body intact. According to them, all that was missing was a small portion of the left foot. They declared that there was no sign of it; the truth was that it had just been stolen, but no one wanted any trouble with the Paris authorities. The report noted that the shroud was black and rotten and stuck to the body. The corpse was completely withered and could not be detached from the bottom of the coffin. So the coffin would have to be taken as well. The Romilly national guard fired a salute, and the mummified corpse was crowned with oak leaves and carried in full view to the neighboring village. The way was crowded with local women throwing leaves and flowers. Some even made their children kiss the gruesome object as it passed.

At Romilly the mummy was given a new coffin and a guard of honor, less actually to honor it than to defend it. They were afraid of a raid by neighboring localities bent on carrying off the relic, or an attack by "myrmidons of superstition" determined to steal the body and throw it into the river. They were as apprehensive about their friends as about their enemies, and with good reason. First the calcaneus had disappeared, and now the metatarsus had disappeared as well. (Apparently at one time Voltaire's foot was on view in the museum at Troyes, from which it later vanished.) Somebody also stole two teeth.[1]

One of these teeth was given as a souvenir to Monsieur Charon, an official of the city of Paris who had been sent on a mission as "organizer of the celebration of the translation of Voltaire's ashes." The other tooth was given to an "enlightened" journalist named Lemaître, to persuade him to keep quiet about the missing foot. He had the tooth made into an amulet which he wore around his neck on a chain. He eventually went insane and died in the mad ward at Bicêtre in Paris, whereupon the relic passed on to a cousin of his of the same name who was a dentist in Paris. After that it can no longer be traced.

A legend came into being in Romilly concerning a tall stranger who appeared there during the night and spirited the corpse away. The mayor and the guards were so terrified at what Paris might do to them for their negligence that, according to the story, they removed the body of a gardener taken from the churchyard to fill the empty coffin. The tall stranger was supposed to have been a Russian sent by Catherine II to procure Voltaire's body for her. The story has no foundation in fact, but it does show the state of mind people had fallen into over these magical remains.

By a strange coincidence the date for the transferral of Voltaire's remains to the Panthéon was fixed for July 11, 1791, the day of the King's flight to Varennes, his arrest, and his sad return to Paris. The two processions almost passed one another, Louis XVI a prisoner in his closed carriage surrounded by soldiers, and Voltaire, dead but triumphant, returning on a catafalque surrounded by regal pomp to a Paris from which the monarchy had once banished him.

The progress of the catafalque was unhindered: every township threw flowers, fired salutes, and pronounced speeches in honor of Voltaire. At the entrance to Paris the mayor, Monsieur Bailly, came in great state to meet the cortege. The procession across Paris was splendid. Hundreds of thousands of Parisians acclaimed the coffin, just as they had acclaimed the author of *Irène*. Cavalry rode at the head, and infantry escorted the long procession. The catafalque did not arrive at the Panthéon until seven in the evening. All along the way there had been only one discordant note: a priest who could not bear to see such idolatry and had cried: "Lord, thou wilt be avenged." He was merely hissed at by the crowd. The thirst for blood had not yet been awakened.

The catafalque was preceded by a statue of Voltaire and a cardboard model of the Bastille. Albs and surplices had been "borrowed" from monasteries and churches to provide "antique" costumes for the hundreds of choristers singing civic hymns. There were innumerable people carrying "philosophical" banners. One of them read: "If man is born free, he must rule himself." On another was written: "If man has tyrants, he must overthrow them" (this was a quotation from Voltaire's *Poème sur l'envie;* the next line ran: "We know only too well that our tyrants are our vices").

The procession passed the Tuileries to cross the Seine via the Pont Royal. All the windows in the palace were open, filled with the people of the King's household. The whole building resounded with cheers, save for one window behind which sat the King and Queen, silent and impassive. What could they have been thinking?

The mayor and his retinue followed the impressive antique catafalque in a calash. People threw down flowers from their windows, some of which missed and fell into the mayor's carriage. A witness dryly remarked that "Monsieur Bailly gave thanks with a show of emotion as though the triumph had been for him."

The procession, modeled on the procession for Corpus Christi, halted after it had crossed the Pont Royal: Monsieur de Villette had transformed his house into a sort of ingenious "station." He had had a placard made, on which was written in big letters: "His heart is here, his spirit is everywhere." The front of the house was hidden up to the first story by tiers of pretty girls, dressed in white and singing cantatas composed by Chénier. When the statue drew level with this stand there appeared a sort of goddess, as at the Opéra, borne on the shoulders of attendants. She emerged from the first-floor windows just opposite the statue, which drew to a halt. The goddess was Citizeness Villette, who took the statue in her arms and covered it, according to a reporter, with "the delicious tears of sensibility." She then crowned it with a laurel wreath. Five hundred thousand Parisians massed by the river, on the bridges, and in the Louvre shed similar tears and wept for joy. Then Madame de Villette set her four-year-old daughter between the arms of the statue: "She thus consecrated her, so to speak, to reason, philosophy, and liberty," said the reporter. It was all highly religious, except for the absence of religion.

The procession of the relics halted at another station by the old Comédie Française, in the Rue des Fosses-Saint-Germain, opposite the Café Procope. On the front of the building was a bust of Voltaire—crowned, of course—with the inscription: "At the age of seventeen he wrote *Oedipe*." At seven in the evening the procession reached the Odéon, and there the inscription read: "At the age of eighty-four he wrote *Irène*." The Opéra had sent its choruses along. It was at this moment that a storm broke over Paris and the rain began to pour down. The crowd fled, women dressed as goddesses with their thin shifts drenched and clinging, fashionable befeathered ladies running like wet hens for the shelter of the colonnades. One journalist wrote that "the aristocratic heavens wished to be revenged." The catafalque was left alone in the rain. When the storm was over it continued its journey and arrived that evening, with a sparse escort, at the Panthéon. Without further ceremony the coffin was placed in the crypt. The rain outside did duty for holy water.

For the next twenty-five years France and Europe were to be at each other's throats. The living were to be bathed in blood, but the dead author was left in peace at last.

As for Voltaire's heart, Madame Villette kept it in the little apartment where she took refuge during the troubles, in the Cul-de-sac Férou, off The Rue de Vaugirard. Afterward she returned to the Château de Villette, which had become a sort of Voltaire museum and therefore sacred to the Jacobins. Madame de Villette took advantage of this immunity to turn the house into a refuge for priests who were threatened by the Reign of Terror.

In 1819 Madame de Villette became patroness of a Masonic lodge which took her name: this was a bold thing to do under the Restoration, especially in view of the fact that her brother was Bishop of Orléans. She had in her possession papers and clothes that had belonged to Voltaire, including the handsome dressing gown in which he had been wont to make his appearances in the salon. It was also she who preserved the Largillière portrait. At her death all these things passed to her son, the Marquis de Villette, who died childless in 1860 and left all his property to Monseigneur de Dreux-Brézé, Bishop of Moulins. The bishop wanted nothing to do with these impious relics and had them put up for sale. They were all dispersed: the portrait went for six thousand francs,[2] and the heart was given to the nation. Napoléon III had it deposited in the Bibliothèque Nationale, and there it still remains.

As for the brain, Monsieur Mithouart kept it in his jar for the rest of his life, but his son and heir thought it ought to be in some national museum and offered it to the Directory, who declined the offer. So "the seat of Monsieur de Voltaire's genius," as it was then called, remained in the Mithouart family. Time passed, and the Empire with it. Mithouart knew the Restoration would not be interested in such a gift, so the brain was put away in a cupboard. In 1830 he thought the liberal monarchy might accept it, but when he proposed this he received no answer. It was about this time that he showed the brain to a group of scientists he had invited to his house one evening. They decided to remove a few pieces and see what happened when they were held in a candle flame. One of them solemnly noted their astonishment and admiration when "the brain still emitted rays of light." He added: "This brain will leave its mark on the future."

In 1858 a relation of the Mithouarts who had inherited the jar offered it to the Académie Française, which refused. "The Academy has no suitable reliquary in which to put this unexpected object," the prospective donor was told.

In 1870 the brain is heard of again in the possession of a Mademoiselle Mithouart, a spinster living in the Rue des Bons Enfants in Paris. At her death she left it to an employee called La Brosse at the Mithouart apothecary's shop in the Rue Coquillière. When he died in 1875 his goods were auctioned: the names of all the buyers are recorded, save for that of the person who bought the jar with the brain in it. So disappeared, almost a hundred years after his death, "the seat of Monsieur de Voltaire's genius."

His skeleton had been left lying in the crypt of the Panthéon. But in 1814 certain extremists came to the conclusion that to leave the remains of an infidel in what had once been a church was an outrage against France. They therefore decided to remove the remains in secret and deposit them where they belonged—on the rubbish heap.

One night in May 1814 Voltaire's coffin, together with that of Rousseau, nearby, was opened, emptied of its contents, and carefully closed again. Nobody breathed a word about it. The remains were taken to a piece of waste land at Bercy used as a dump for refuse and scrap, buried in quicklime, and covered with rubbish. The conspirators stamped down the ground to hide their traces.

It was not until the Second Empire that a journalist revealed what had happened. He declared that it was a scandal to let visitors come and pay solemn respects to an empty coffin. At the Emperor's order an inquiry was instituted and Voltaire's coffin opened. It was indeed empty. What had happened would never have been discovered if, after a long police search, the son of one of the conspirators had not decided to reveal what his father had told him. But it was now fifty years later, and it was impossible to find the remains of Voltaire in the lime. Moreover the ground had been disturbed by building. The Halle aux Vins has since been put up on the site.

Voltaire's life had been a restless odyssey, and that of his remains, down to the last handful of dust, a no less turbulent one.

And what is left of his great fortune? That fortune so skillfully built up, in itself an economic and financial history of the eighteenth century, went at Voltaire's death to his niece Madame Denis, who was soon to become the wife of Duvivier.

An inventory of Voltaire's property in 1775 showed an income of 197,000 livres, not counting the 8,000 livres that Ferney brought in. The present-day equivalent would be an annual income of about 120 million old francs, or a capital approaching a billion old francs.[3]

Madame Denis did not inherit the whole of Voltaire's capital, since he had invested large sums in life annuities to assure himself a large income. But she inherited about half of it, which left her in no danger of penury. Voltaire's will of September 30, 1776, left 100,000 livres each to his nephews Mignot and D'Hornoy. They did not do as well as the overbearing niece. He left Wagnière 8,000 livres—not a great deal for such a devoted secretary, but Wagnière's cause had been damaged by Madame Denis. Each of Voltaire's servants received a year's wages, and 300 livres were to be divided among the poor of Ferney, "if there are any such left." Thanks to Voltaire, there were very few. He seems to have assumed that Madame Denis would keep on Wagnière and the servants, but she did not.

To begin with, she encountered certain disappointments. She had to give back the Tournay estate to the De Brosses family, which immediately carried on the old président's tradition by bringing a lawsuit for wrongful possession and neglect, claiming a compensation of 71,000 livres. Wagnière, by patience and skill, got the case settled out of court for 41,000 livres. Madame Denis dismissed him nonetheless. She was interested only in her young husband, though he cost her more than the whole De Brosses family put together.

In June 1778, a few days after her uncle's death, she visited Madame du Deffand, who said she was "a good common sort of woman without wit but with a good deal of common sense and a way of talking well which she no doubt acquired from her uncle." She noted the heiress' words on the subject of her uncle's papers: "They are a very valuable possession," Madame Denis said. "I would sell them all, save for the fact that I have resolved not to part with them." Yet they were the first things she sold. It is true that the purchaser was Catherine II, Empress of All the Russias. The library at Ferney was not unusually large: it consisted of between six and seven thousand volumes. But they were all annotated, full of corrections and lively observations. The books were not the treasures of a bibliophile but the tools of a workman. Voltaire was in the habit of turning a book into a kind of digest. He had scissors and paste at hand as he read, and would reduce one fat volume to fifteen, twenty, or fifty essential pages, which he would then have rebound. Rabelais, for instance, was reduced by nine tenths. Voltaire's library was a sort of "Temple of Taste." He scribbled in the margins and between the lines, and sometimes stuck in extra leaves between the original pages.

Madame Denis replied to Catherine's first offers with purely formal refusals, waiting for the Tsarina to name a suitable figure. When she did so it was a truly imperial one: 135,000 livres. This was more than half the sum Madame Denis got out of the whole Ferney property, house, land, village, factories and all. But she pretended to be reluctant to part with her uncle's library and was finally persuaded by the additional gift of a diamond-studded box containing the Tsarina's portrait and some magnificent furs. Wagnière was summoned to Saint Petersburg to arrange the books and papers as they had been at Ferney.

Catherine received him in front of a bust of Voltaire. She curtsied to it and said, "Monsieur, there is the man to whom I owe all I know and all I am."

When she was certain that Madame Denis was going to part with her uncle's papers in return for the money, the diamonds, and the furs, Catherine wrote to her: "No one before him ever wrote as he did, and to the future he will serve as an example and a stumbling block. I greatly appreciate the esteem and confidence you repose in me: it is a great pleasure to me to find that these qualities are hereditary in your family. The nobility of your dealings is a guarantee of your sentiments toward me. I have charged Monsieur de Grimm to convey to you a few poor tokens which I beg you to make use of, Catherine." This letter was addressed "To Madame Denis, niece of a great man who was very fond of me."

Frenchmen must regret that the letter was not from Louis XVI.

As for the Ferney estate, Madame Denis disposed of it the very year Voltaire died. She sold it to Villette for 230,000 livres. There is every reason to suppose that if Voltaire had left it to his nephews they would have preserved Ferney and his papers as well. As early as September 29, less than four months after her uncle's death, she wrote to Wagnière: "I only wish Ferney had been burned to the ground." Certainly she had been bored to death there in the "mountains"; she had been attached to the patriarch by self-interest alone. But though such sentiments may be explained they are difficult to forgive.

She sold everything she could: her one concern was money, in order to enjoy to the fullest her amazing marriage during the few years that were left to her.

They made a strange couple—she a fat woman of over sixty and he an ex-dragoon thirty years her junior. But her income was a thousand times larger than his. He had been Commissioner for War in Santo Domingo and had returned with little glory and less profit. All Paris laughed at the news of the marriage, except a few who were angry on Voltaire's behalf. Duvivier was known in the army as "Nicolas Toupée," being more expert at frizzing his friends' hair than at making cavalry charges. He was a versatile fellow: as well as being hairdresser to the whole barracks room he also acted as secretary and miscalculated the accounts a bit—in his favor. Madame Denis loved him to distraction, as she had loved all his predecessors. But this was her last fling, and she married him.

One day when he had annoyed her she wrote to him: "I declare to you I am ready to share with you my thoughts, my life, and everything I possess. If you are not willing, put a bullet through my head and you will be doing me a kindness."

The captain naturally preferred to share everything she possessed. As to her thoughts and her life, he left them entirely at her own disposal.

It was the Academy that found the marriage most offensive. Its members made no attempt to disguise their disapproval, and relations were broken off between the Academy and Voltaire's niece. D'Alembert was the first to stop seeing her. La Harpe met her in the street shortly after the marriage and asked her in a sorrowful voice if at least it made her happy. "Happy?" she exclaimed. "So happy I could burst!" The remark is a portrait of her in a nutshell.

She already spoke like Duvivier rather than like Voltaire. But she was not happy long. She was obliged to live in the style that suited her husband, who wanted to eat and drink and sleep at whatever hour suited him, and brought home noisy crowds of hungry, thirsty guests. She gorged herself along with them and put on even more weight. People said Duvivier led her this life deliberately to make her die of apoplexy as soon as possible.

D'Alembert had great success with a story he used to tell about Madame Denis's mustache. Early one morning one of her tenant farmers came to pay his rent. He was told that Madame was still asleep, but insisted on forcing his way in. Advancing toward the double bed, he was puzzled as to which of the two more or less hairy chins he ought to address. "Beg pardon, gentlemen," he said. "But which of you gentlemen is the lady?"

To revenge herself on the Academy, Madame Denis gave the Houdon statue of Voltaire, which she had promised to them, to the Comédie Française instead, where it may still be seen. Alfred de Musset saw it there and was revolted by what he called Voltaire's "hideous smile." The Largillière portrait Madame Denis gave back to Madame de Villette.

All that remains of Ferney is the house, the grounds, and the little church with Voltaire's name on the front in letters larger than those of God. The house would be an empty tomb like the grave in the Panthéon, were it not for a portrait of Emilie, by Nattier. The visitor feels nothing; he can only imagine what Ferney was like in Voltaire's time. Thanks to the miracle performed by Mr. Theodore Besterman, Voltaire's house in Geneva, Les Délices, has been snatched back from the void, and Voltaire seems to live there still.

Usually a man takes his name from a place, but in the case of the village of Ferney-Voltaire, it is the other way round. But Voltaire's soul has vanished from the place. As for Voltaire's money, that vanished too, in the hands of Madame Denis and her Duvivier. Of both the heiress and the fortune, nothing remains.

What is left, finally, of the mountain of written works that Voltaire left—epic and other poems, tragedies by the dozen, pamphlets by the hundreds, stories scattered like so many unstrung pearls, letters by the thousands and the ten thousands flung prodigally into the world like handfuls of diamond dust? Voltaire's true monument is his works, not a porphyry catafalque or a golden casket. When he died, the first step necessary to build this monument out of this mountain of papers he left was to preserve everything in order to give the best a chance to survive.

Charles-Joseph Panckouke, the member of a famous family of publishers who had once proposed that Voltaire authorize an edition of his complete works to be printed by Panckouke's firm in Lille, was the first to address himself to the task of collecting Voltaire's works. Thanks to his sister, the charming Madame Suard, Voltaire had given him permission and access to his manuscripts, for the current editions were often unreliable. Madame Denis was moved to send Panckouke several boxes of her uncle's papers, and Panckouke had the intelligence to realize that the best of Voltaire's writings were in his letters. Voltaire himself would never have believed it; he had doubts even about the *Contes,* which he thought would give him a reputation for frivolity. Collecting the correspondence, the most difficult of undertakings, was also the most necessary. It was the letters that revealed most profoundly the man and his time. They had presented his contemporaries with a mirror of their age, of their civilization, ideas, and aspirations. Kings, princes, ladies of fashion, lawyers' clerks, and judges—all were reflected in these gay, courteous, spontaneous, lucid missives. As they flew from capital to capital, Europe and the eighteenth century discerned in them their own character, their own unity. Voltaire, addressing the elite of that civilization, found the tone that most truly belonged to the Europe of the Enlightenment between 1715 and 1778. As they read his letters his contemporaries must have thought, "He is I and I am he. We understand each other better than men have ever done before."

He thought for them, like them, with them, but always just that instant ahead that was necessary in order to surprise without shocking, and to seem continually new and novel, though often he was merely anticipating the thoughts of others. He thought for his world—only faster, more subtly, more clearly. Above all he expressed himself exactly as all enlightened people would have liked to express themselves—as, in fact, they all thought they could. His letters gave both the greatest and the most obscure of his correspondents the marvelous feeling that they were hearing their own thoughts perfectly expressed, so that each of them adopted the language and tone in which Voltaire clad his own thoughts—as naturally as they accepted the air they breathed and the water they drank. No man ever gave his fellows such delight in understanding, accompanied by the illusion of being as intelligent as the most intelligent man alive. The miraculous thing was that the more Voltaire was himself, and the more brilliant he became, the more limpid his writing grew and the closer his correspondents felt to him. His detractors have tried to present this prodigious gift for spreading light as an elegant but superficial gift for popularization. But to the patronizing fool who said to Napoleon: "In short, Voltaire was everybody," Napoleon replied: "But everybody is not Voltaire."

If so many people have believed themselves the equal of Voltaire, it is because he breathed his spirit into them. They might have the illusion that they could have written *Candide;* but they were only *Candide*'s reflection. It is a divine gift of geniuses to be not only witty and intelligent themselves but to inspire wit and intelligence in others who do not know they possess such gifts. Voltaire used to say that he had sometimes blasphemed against Christ but that that would be forgiven him; whereas those who had blasphemed against the Holy Spirit[4] would be damned.

Panckouke suffered some of the torments of the damned here below in his search for Voltaire's letters. Many were of too recent date to be published. Too many people still alive were criticized in them, too many families would be made uncomfortable, too many influential people preferred a discreet silence. Frederick II, who had clamored for a complete edition of the correspondence, turned a deaf ear when asked for the letters in his possession. He had his reasons. He had just learned that among Voltaire's as yet unpublished works, which were not likely to remain unpublished long, were the famous *Mémoires secrets destinés pour servir à la vie de Voltaire (Secret Memoirs for Use in Writing the Life of Voltaire)*—which had also been intended for use in damaging Frederick's reputation. Voltaire had written them in 1759 to avenge himself for the affront dealt to him in Frankfurt and had been keeping them up his sleeve ever since. Madame Denis, only too delighted to do her enemy Frederick an ill turn, had given the manuscript to Panckouke. The *Memoirs* are extremely amusing, their ferocity couched in language of exquisite elegance and carefree spontaneity. It was their very exquisiteness that rendered them so intolerable to Frederick, to whom an informer had sent a copy. Frederick's rage expressed itself silently. He had bought in Paris a bust of Voltaire by Houdon, and it arrived in Berlin shortly after he had read the *Memoirs*. He gave orders that the packing case was not to be opened. The bust was never taken out of its straw until after Frederick's death. It was still smiling quizzically.

The first edition of the correspondence was the one worth-while monument that his contemporaries raised to the true glory of Voltaire. He still lived on in those enormous heaps of paper: the work he had put into them proved too much for those who were trying to work on them in his behalf after his death. Panckouke and his colleagues were obliged to seek the help of another, and Panckouke made a good choice in Beaumarchais, who was powerful, skillful, rich, and an excellent businessman—in short, a man after Voltaire's own heart. The complete edition of the letters was a matter of great financial consequence. Beaumarchais acquired three paper mills in the Vosges and bought the Baskerville type for an enormous sum. After sinking all this money in the project he was unpleasantly surprised to discover that the Parlement and clergy intended to ban the publication. So Beaumarchais got permission from the Margravine of Baden to set up his printing house in the fortified town of Kehl, on the banks of the Rhine opposite Strasbourg. The Kehl edition was brought into France clandestinely and distributed secretly to subscribers. It consisted of seventy-two octavo volumes, printed between 1784 and 1789. Condorcet was responsible for the notes.

Beaumarchais needed someone professional but exceptional to collate, correct, and if possible set up the edition. So he enlisted the aid of the controversial "erotic" writer Restif de la Bretonne, who had been trained as a printer. Unfortunately he was an autodidact whose notions of spelling and grammar were almost as eccentric and bizarre as his totally unorthodox ideas and morals, and Beaumarchais was obliged to get rid of him.

This admirable edition of the correspondence was the ruin of Beaumarchais. His only really honorable undertaking among countless suspect business deals was the one that lost him a million livres. There were not enough subscribers and those who did sign up failed to pay promptly. People had stopped being interested in Voltaire's tragedies, epics, and pamphlets and had not yet begun to be interested in the *Contes* and the letters. It was one thing to applaud a laurel-crowned author for three hours without stopping, and quite another to subscribe to an edition of his works.

Still, in those days it was Beaumarchais who deserved every credit for his monumental endeavor. In our time it is Mr. Besterman, who, at Les Délices, has brought to life again Voltaire's incomparable *Correspondance* and its enchanting author.

Who dares say Voltaire is dead? He is of the nature of fire and light. Just as in the prophetic arms of the Arouets the golden flames of the Holy Spirit are constantly rekindled and reborn, so Voltaire himself is an unfailing, radiant source of intelligence; a breath of the spirit that blows through every heart that loves freedom and justice; life itself.

NOTES

Part One, Chapter I

1. We also have a certificate of baptism—not the original, which was burned during the Revolution, but a copy made at Voltaire's death by a worthy parish priest who could not have been very fond of him, for he copied it out on wrapping paper and in such a scrawl that his irritation and disgust are almost visible. The copy confirms the date and the names of the witnesses. The godfather was "Master François de Castagnier de Châteauneuf, Abbé de Varennes," and the godmother "Dame Marie Parent, wife to Daumart, esquire, comptroller of the royal constabulary." Not exactly brilliant godparents, such as those chosen for his older brother Armand; but François-Marie would choose others for himself later. At any rate the Abbé de Châteauneuf would start him off in the right direction: along the road of libertinage, where François-Marie would rename himself Voltaire.

2. *Le Bourgeois gentilhomme* was a cloth merchant. But Voltaire's much wilier grandfather resembled Molière's Monsieur Jourdain only in his wealth and its origin. He did not want to be the Great Panjandrum: he was content to start by becoming a citizen of Paris, and ten years after he founded his business in the capital, that is what he became.

3. *Conseiller du roi* was an honorific title given to almost any crown official; most often a *conseiller* was a magistrate in theory, but in practice was something like a royal notary. (*Editor's note.*)

4. Broadly speaking, the livre in the eighteenth century was about equal to the U.S. dollar in the late 1960s. In the currency of the time 12 deniers=1 sou (or sol); 20 sous (sols)=1 livre tournois or 1 franc; 3 livres=1 écu; 10 livres=1 pistole; 24 livres=1 louis. (*Editor's note.*)

5. In the eighteenth century a *Parlement* was primarily a multichambered law court, one of the principal duties of which was also the registering of the King's edicts in order to give them the force of law. When the Parlement is mentioned with no qualifying adjective in the text, the Paris Parlement is meant—the most important in the country, since its jurisdiction extended over half of France. (*Editor's note.*)

6. One of them, captain of the Château of Rueil, took out a coat of arms on his appointment as comptroller of the Royal Constabulary. His bearings were azure with turret argent, and he married one Mademoiselle Parent from Poitou. The Parents were already related to the Arouets, and he had been en-

nobled in the sixteenth century. These cloth merchants knew how to weave family connections.

7. Armand was baptized on March 23, 1685. His godfather was "the most high and mighty lord, Monseigneur Armand-Jean du Plessis, Duc de Richelieu et de Fronsac, peer of France," who was the great-nephew of Cardinal Richelieu, so the link with that family dates from before Voltaire's birth. Armand's godmother was "the most mighty lady, Dame Charlotte d'Aubespine de Châteauneuf, Marquise de Ruffec, wife to the most high and mighty lord, Monseigneur Claude de Rouvroy, Duc de Saint-Simon, peer of France and knight of the King's orders." This Saint-Simon was father of the author of the famous *Memoirs*. François Arouet thus chose excellent godparents for his elder son.

8. They had three children. First Marie-Louise, born in 1712—plump Marie-Louise, who in 1738 married Nicolas-Charles Denis, Esquire. As Madame Denis she was to be well known to all Voltaire's friends and enemies. The younger daughter, Marie-Elisabeth, born in 1715, was married in 1738 to Monsieur Joseph de Dompierre de Fontaine. The two sons of that marriage provide a direct descent from the original Arouets to the present day, under the name of Dompierre d'Hornoy, in Picardy. The third child, born in 1728, was to become the Abbé Vincent Mignot, clerical counselor and Commendatory Abbot of Seillières in the *département* of Aube.

9. When, in an ode to Boileau, Voltaire wrote "I was born your neighbor, in the palace courtyard," he was quite accurate: Boileau's father was a magistrate and the family lived in the Palais de Justice. It has been said that the squalling of the Arouet children got on the misanthropic Boileau's nerves and that he scolded François-Marie for chattering and being too familiar. But this cannot have happened: Voltaire never actually met Boileau.

10. In the eighteenth century an abbé was not necessarily a member of the clergy but rather anyone entitled to wear ecclesiastical dress after undertaking some sort of theological studies. (*Editor's note.*)

11. The French Academy, founded by Cardinal Richelieu in 1635, was the equivalent of a Royal Academy of Letters. (Membership was limited to forty, as it still is today; hence this body is often known as "The Forty Immortals.") (*Editor's note.*)

12. This young man married Mademoiselle de Noailles when he was only thirteen, and two years later was shut up in the Bastille for too boldly accosting the Duchesse de Bourgogne, heiress to the throne! The friendship between him and François-Marie was so well known that later, when Cardinal Fleury was in a rage with Richelieu, he exclaimed that he and Voltaire made a good pair.

13.   Adieu, ma pauvre tabatière!
Adieu, je ne te verrai plus.
Ni soins, ni larmes, ni prières
Ne te rendront à moi, mes efforts sont perdus. . . .
Adieu, ma pauvre tabatière!
Qu'on oppose entre nous une forte barrière!
Me demander des vers! Hélas! Je n'en puis plus!
Adieu, ma pauvre tabatière!
Adieu, je ne te verrai plus.

Poor snuffbox, good-bye/Adieu for aye./No tears nor prayers nor assidu-ity/Will bring you back to me./Adieu, poor snuffbox!/What greater obstacle 'twixt us could come/Than to ask verse of one who must be dumb?/Farewell, then, snuffbox!/Adieu for aye.

14. Mademoiselle de Lenclos had already been delighting Cardinal Riche-lieu's contemporaries sixty years before, and though legend has it that she was as fresh in her seventies as at the time of *Le Cid*, by the time we are speaking of she certainly bore all the marks of her advanced age. But the abbé shut his eyes to what had grown wrinkled or withered and was all eagerness to be charmed through his ears: Ninon's conversation "had the effect on him of beauty itself." This appealing relationship had already been going on for two or three years: Ninon was just seventy-seven when she yielded to the abbé, then in his fifties. Afterward he mildly reproached her for letting him lan-guish two or three days after he had declared himself. Was it necessary to tarry so long? His charmer replied that she had waited for that particular mo-ment because she thought it would be elegant to install a new lover on her seventy-seventh birthday. Voltaire called this "a fine gala." After a few more birthday parties, however, Ninon requested the abbé to confine himself to words. But they went on loving each other tenderly nonetheless.

15. A group so called because they met at the Temple, once the head-quarters in France of the Knights Templar, and in Voltaire's time the home of the Knights of St. John of Jerusalem. The *libertins* who met there, in the words of Theodore Besterman, "though not necessarily libertines, were as free in their behaviour as in their ideas: they were a living demonstration of the fact that free thought is not necessarily as dull as many of its twentieth-cen-tury devotees, and that the life of reason does not exclude a passion for beauty and poetry, and the love of women, good food and good wine." (*Editor's note.*)

16. A *président* in the eighteenth century was a judge of *parlement;* a *président à mortier* was a senior judge who had the right to wear a mortor-board and judicial toga; and a *premier président* was a chief justice of a *parlement*. (*Editor's note.*)

17. Strictly speaking, a *lettre de cachet* was any order signed and sealed by the King. The term, however, was generally applied to an order of imprison-ment or exile, without trial. (*Editor's note.*)

Part One, Chapter II

1. A member of the King's inner council. (*Editor's note.*)

2. A royal fiscal administrator. (*Editor's note.*)

3. She was soon to change her name to Adrienne Lecouvreur and become the reigning star of the Comédie Française. (*Editor's note.*)

Part One, Chapter III

1. Assiduity, however, was not his strong point. He apologized most cour-teously to his colleagues for his irregular attendance and, to convince them that he suffered more than they did when he was absent, donated a portrait of himself so that he would always be present among them in spirit at least. Some

members of the Academy resented this: the only previous portraits were those of Cardinal Richelieu, the King, and Queen Christina of Sweden. The maréchal took up too much space for someone who didn't even bother to appear at meetings. So portraits of Racine, Corneille, Bossuet, and Fénelon soon arrived to restore the balance, and others have been arriving ever since.

2. Voltaire's epic is a poem modeled on Virgil's *Aeneid*. In its final form it is in ten cantos and contains approximately 4,300 lines. The subject is purportedly the siege of Paris by Henri IV at the end of the sixteenth century, but in reality it is a brilliant panorama of religious fanaticism and political despotism. The poem is revolutionary from the very first verses, which equate the excesses of Catholicism and those of Protestantism. Many episodes in the poem are meant to underline how easily bloody crimes can be committed in the sincere belief that they are dictated by God. (*Editor's note.*)

3. Today the splendid château no longer exists: those who knocked it down sold its stones to make roads. But just before Voltaire's visit the duc himself narrowly escaped destruction: he had been found to be involved in a plot to hand over Bayonne to the Spaniards. The Regent said that Richelieu's crime was enough to cost him four heads if he had had them. The Duc's uncle, the great cardinal, would certainly have cut off one of them. What saved the duc was the love of Mademoiselle de Valois, the Regent's daughter: in return for her father's promise to spare Richelieu's life she agreed never to see him again and to marry the Duke of Modena, whom she had hitherto refused. The Duc de Richelieu, lucky as usual, was merely banished to his own château, where he was allowed to entertain Voltaire by way of distraction.

4. Today the Place des Vosges.

5. Jansenism was a religious movement founded by Cornelius Jansen, a Dutchman, closely based on the teachings of Saint Augustine and bearing a marked analogy to those of Calvin. Jansen's views were expounded at length by his disciple, Antoine Arnauld, in a book called *Frequent Communion,* published in 1643. This book was the first manifestation of Jansenism to the general public in France and it raised a violent storm. The Jansenists soon entered into violent conflict with the more easygoing Jesuits, and Louis XIV, a fanatic for uniformity, whether civil or religious, wrote to the Pope at the instigation of the Jesuits, asking for a papal bull excommunicating the Jansenists. In 1730 this bull, the *Unigenitus,* was proclaimed part and parcel of the law of France, but the quarrel dragged on indefinitely throughout the eighteenth century. (*Editor's note.*)

6. Louis XV had ascended the throne on September 1, 1715. (*Editor's note.*)

7. Louis XV's great predecessor on the throne, Louis IX, had dispensed justice beneath a great oak tree at Vincennes. (*Editor's note.*)

8. The literal meaning is: "I am not a king. I do not deign to be a prince. I am a Rohan," but there is perhaps also a play on *suis,* which means both "am" and "follow." (*Translator's note.*)

Part One, Chapter IV

1. These had been drafted during Voltaire's stay in England and were first published there under the title *Letters Concerning the English Nation.* (*Editor's note.*)

Part One, Chapter VIII

1. Lorraine had been an independent duchy since the time of the Holy Roman Empire. France occupied parts of it from 1552 to 1766, when the whole of it was ceded to the French crown. (*Editor's note.*)

2. An Italian theater company that merged with the Opéra Comique in 1762. (*Editor's note.*)

Part Two, Chapter IX

1. A pun on *balbutier*, to stammer, mumble. (*Translator's note.*)

2. Literally, natives of Picardy. (*Translator's note.*)

Part Two, Chapter X

1. The *Mémoires* appeared in 1784, but they were not published by Voltaire himself. A copy had been stolen from him in 1768 by Madame Denis and La Harpe, the young writer he had welcomed to Ferney.

2. One of the most remarkable literary enterprises of the eighteenth century, the famous *Encylopédie, ou Dictionnaire raisonné des sciences, des arts, et des métiers (Encyclopedia or Rationally Ordered Dicitonary of the Sciences, the Arts, and Trades)* was begun under the editorship of Denis Diderot and Jean d'Alembert, and included such noted contributors as Marmontel, Montesquieu, Condillac, and Holbach. The first volume was published in 1751, and after many difficulties with the royal censors, the last thirty-three volumes appeared in 1772. Embodying the most enlightened thought of the period, many of its articles were considered heretical. No other encyclopedia has perhaps occupied so large a place in the political, civil, intellectual, and literary history of its century. The compilers were known as the Encylopedists, and the doctrines set forth in their articles are regarded as major factors in bringing about the French Revolution. (*Editor's note.*)

3. Under the *ancien régime*, the Etats were provincial administrative bodies, convoked at irregular intervals by the King. (*Editor's note.*)

4. *Luc* backward spells *cul*, a vulgar word for "backside" or "asshole." (*Editor's note.*)

5. The heroine of Alexander Pope's mock-heroic satire, *The Rape of the Lock*. (*Editor's note.*)

6. An academy founded in 1582 for purifying the Italian language and literature. (*Editor's note.*)

7. Blaise Pascal had written a famous attack on the Jesuits, the *Provincial Letters*. (*Editor's note.*)

8. The equivalent of a minister of justice. (*Editor's note.*)

9. A talented officer who in 1762 married as his second wife Voltaire's younger niece, Marie-Elisabeth, formerly Madame de Fontaine d'Hornoy.

Part Two, Chapter XI

1. A royal provincial administrator under the system introduced by Cardinal Richelieu. (*Editor's note.*)

2. Literally, "Crush the infamous." The expression is often translated in English as "Crush the Beast." (*Translator's note.*)

3. Charles—Simon Favart was a dramatist and director of the Opéra Comique. (*Editor's note.*)

Part Two, Chapter XII

1. "Corneille"=crow, rook, and Voltaire frequently plays on the word and its derivatives. (*Translator's note.*)

Part Two, Chapter XIII

1. I.e., a dressing gown cut like a greatcoat. (*Editor's note.*)

Part Two, Chapter XIV

1. A contemporary of Joan of Arc; the mistress of Charles VII of France. (*Editor's note.*)

Part Two, Chapter XV

1. A pun on the name of the famous sixteenth-century writer Clément Marat. (*Translator's note.*)

2. A local military force organized in 1741 by a Croatian baron to repress brigands on the Turkish frontier; hence brutal marauders. (*Editor's note.*)

Part Two, Chapter XVII

1. This macabre taste for relics was nothing unusual: Descartes's skull was sold for 100 francs in 1820: when the remains of Heloise and Abelard were transferred to the Petits Augustins, an Englishman offered 100,000 francs for one of Heloise's teeth; another Englishman bought one of Newton's teeth for 16,595 francs, which he had mounted in a ring.

2. This portrait now belongs to Theodore Besterman. A copy of it was donated to the Musée National de Versailles by Massimo Uleri, and a third copy is in the Musée Carnavalet.

3. One hundred old francs=one new franc. (*Editor's note.*)

4. In French, *le Sain Esprit*—a pun, since *esprit* means both "wit" and "spirit."

CHRONOLOGY

WORLD EVENTS	ARTS AND SCIENCES

1694

Foundation of the Bank of England/D'Iberville occupies Newfoundland/Birth of Lord Chesterfield.

First edition of the *Dictionnaire* of the French Academy/Regnard: *Attendez-moi sous l'orme*/Bossuet: *Réflexions sur la comédie*/Leibniz: *Système nouveau de la nature*/Huygens: *Traité de la lumière*/Gobelins workshops closed/Saint-Simon begins *Mémoires*/Death of Madame Deshoulières; Téniers the younger; Pujet; Puffendorf; A. Arnauld/Birth of Quesnay, Charles-Antoine Coypel.

1695

William of Orange conquers Navarre/Death of Achmet II.

Cabinet des fées published/Fénelon named Archbishop of Cambrai/Bossuet condemns Quietism/Death of La Fontaine; Purcell; Domat; Huygens/Birth of Pannini; J.-B. Pater.

1696

Treaty of Turin/Death of Jean Sobieski.

Rigaud: *Portrait de Rancé*/Regnard: *Le Joueur*/Charles Perrault: *Vie des hommes illustres*/Death of Madame de Sévigné; La Bruyère; Molinos; P. Mignard; P. Elzevier/Birth of Tiepolo; Toqué.

LIFE OF VOLTAIRE	EVENTS IN FRANCE
	1694
Sunday, November 21: Birth in Paris of François-Marie Arouet.	Famine/Victory of Jean Bart over the Dutch/Bombardment of Dieppe, Le Havre, and Dunkirk by the English.
	1695
1 year old.	Palace of Versailles completed/Introduction of poll tax.
	1696
2 years old.	Birth of Louis-François-Armand de Vignerot du Plessis (later Maréchal de Richelieu)/Peace of Paris/Madame Guyon imprisoned in the Bastille.

WORLD EVENTS

ARTS AND SCIENCES

1697

October 30: Treaty of Rijswijk: end of War of the League of Augsburg/Death of Charles XI of Sweden/Accession of Charles XII.

Bayle: *Dictionnaire historique et critique*/Fénelon: *Explication des maximes des saints*/Perrault: *Contes de ma mère l'Oye*/Regnard: *Le Distrait*/Death of E. de Witte/Birth of Prévost; Hogarth; Canaletto.

1698

Convention of The Hague.

Louis XIV writes *Manière de montrer les jardins de Versailles*/Madame d'Aulnoy: *Les Illustres Fées*/Birth of Bouchardon; Metastasio; Gabriel; Bodmer.

1699

Creation of the principality of Liechtenstein/Death of Christian V of Denmark.

First Salon in the Grande Galerie of the Louvre/Du Fresny: *Amusements sérieux et comiques*/Fénelon: *Télémaque*/Madame Dacier translates the *Iliad*/Death of Jean Racine; M. Preti; J.-B. Monnoyer/Birth of Chardin; Subleyras.

1700

Death of Charles II of Spain/Accession of Philip V (grandson of Louis XIV) to throne of Spain/Death of Innocent XII/Election of Clement XI/Treaty of London: division of the Spanish succession.

Fénelon: *Dialogue des morts*/Leibniz: *Nouveaux essais sur l'entendement humain*/Congreve: *The Way of the World*/Death of Rancé; Le Nôtre; Dryden; Siberechts/Birth of Natoire.

1701

Accession of Frederick I of Prussia/The Stuarts barred from the throne/Death of James II of England/James III recognized as King of England by Louis XIV/Coalition of The Hague against France and Spain.

Beginning of the publication of the *Journal de Trévoux*/Rigaud: *Louis XIV en pied*/Death of Madeleine de Scudéry; Segrais; Boursault/Birth of La Condamine.

LIFE OF VOLTAIRE	EVENTS IN FRANCE
	1697
3 years old. His godfather, the Abbé de Châteauneuf, makes him recite the *Fables* of La Fontaine.	Torcy named Foreign Minister/Expulsion of company of Italian actors/Fénelon exiled to Cambrai.
	1698
4 years old.	The King in camp at Compiègne with Madame de Maintenon.
	1699
5 years old.	Torcy appointed Minister of State/Pontchartrain made Chancellor/Chamillard named Minister of Finance/Death of Pomponne.
	1700
6 years old.	Memoranda of Royal Intendants.
	1701
7 years old.	Louis XIV preserves Philip V's rights to the throne of France/Death of Louis XIV's brother; Barbezieux; Tourville.

WORLD EVENTS	ARTS AND SCIENCES

1702

Death of William III/Queen Anne ascends the throne of England/War of Spanish Succession begins.

The Daily Courant: first English daily/Farquhar: *The Inconstant*/Birth of Aved; Liotard; P. Longhi.

1703

Battle of Höchstädt/Savoy enters the Coalition/Peter the Great founds Saint Petersburg/Death of Mustapha II/Birth of Marie Leczinska.

Lalande: *Musique pour les soupers du roi*/Bach: first *Organ Works*/Death of Saint-Evremont; Charles Perrault/Birth of Boucher; Wesley.

1704

Stanislas Leczinski accedes to throne of Poland/The English occupy Gibraltar.

Salon at the Louvre/Regnard: *Les Folies amoureuses*/First French translations of Saadi/Swift: *Tale of a Tub*/Jurieu: *Histoire critique des dogmes et des cultes*/Newton: *Treatise on Optics*/Bach: *Cantata No. 1*/Handel: *Almira*/Death of Bossuet; Bourdaloue; Locke; J. Parrocel/Birth of Duclos; Jaucourt; La Tour.

1705

Death of Leopold I, King of Hungary and Holy Roman Emperor/Accession of Joseph I/Bull *Vineam Domini.*

Crébillon: *Idoménée*/Regnard: *Les Ménechmes*/Rigaud: *Portrait de Bossuet*/Buxtehude: *Musique sacrée*/Halley calculates the trajectory of comets/Death of Ninon de Lenclos; Giordano; Madame de Grignan; E. Pavillon/Birth of C. Vanloo.

1706

Act of Union between England and Scotland/Madrid lost and recaptured by Philip V/Death of Dom Pedro of Portugal/Birth of Benjamin Franklin.

Coysevox: *Le Rhône*/Rameau: *Premier livre de clavecin*/Farquhar: *The Recruiting Officer*/Death of Bayle.

LIFE OF VOLTAIRE	EVENTS IN FRANCE
	1702
8 years old.	Saint-Simon made a duke and peer of the realm/Revolt of the Camisards/Villars named Maréchal de France/Death of Jean Bart.
	1703
9 years old.	Death of "The Man in the Iron Mask" in the Bastille.
	1704
10 years old/His mother dies/Enters Jesuit school of Louis-le-Grand/December 19: Ninon de Lenclos bequeaths him two thousand livres to buy books.	End of the Camisards' revolt.
	1705
11 years old.	Louis XIV makes peace offers to Heinsius.
	1706
12 years old/Birth of Emilie Le Tonnelier de Breteuil (later Marquise du Châtelet)/François-Marie writes his first tragedy, *Amulius et Numitor*, lost without trace/He is introduced to the Grand Prior, Vendôme, at the Temple.	Defeat of Villeroi at Ramillies/Louis XIV makes new peace offers/Defeat of La Feuillade at Turin.

WORLD EVENTS   ARTS AND SCIENCES

1707

Siege of Lérida/Peter the Great
invades Poland/Death of Aurangzeg,
Emperor of Hindustan.

Vauban: *La Dîme royale;* falls from
favor and dies/Crébillon: *Atrée et
Thyeste*/Lesage: *Le Diable boiteux,
Crispin rival de son maître*/Death of
Coypel; Edelinck; Buxtehude/Birth
of Linnaeus; Goldoni; Buffon; Euler;
Fielding; L. M. Vanloo.

1708

Pope condemns Jansenist arguments
of Father Quesnel/Birth of Pitt.

Regnard: *Le Légataire
universel*/Berkeley: *Theory of
Vision*/Boerhaave: *Institutiones
medicae*/Handel:
Resurrection/Death of Maucroix; De
Hooghe; Hardouin; Mansart/Birth of
Voisenon; Nonotte.

1709

Charles XII defeated by the Russians
at Poltava.

Lesage: *Turcaret*/Cristofori makes
the first *pianoforte*, in Florence/First
opera buffa, in Naples/Boettger
invents porcelain/Death of Thomas
Corneille; Regnard; Hobbema/Birth
of Gresset; Tronchin; Charles de
Brosses; Collé; Mably; Samuel
Johnson; Le Franc de Pompignan; La
Mettrie; Vaucanson.

1710

Victory of Vendôme at Villaviciosa:
Philip V master of Spain.

Handel in England/Leibniz: *Essais
de théodicée*/Swift: *Journal to
Stella*/Death of Fléchier/Birth of
Pergolesi; (Gentil-)Bernard.

1711

Death of Joseph I, Holy Roman
Emperor/Accession of Charles VI.

Crébillon: *Rhadamiste et
Zénobie*/Chardin: *Voyage en
Perse et aux Indes orientales*/Vivaldi:
Concerti/Death of Boileau; G. de
Lairesse; Feuquière/Birth of Hume.

LIFE OF VOLTAIRE	EVENTS IN FRANCE

1707

13 years old.

Official values of paper money
set/Death of Madame de Montespan.

1708

14 years old.

Defeat of Audenarde/Siege of Lille.

1709

15 years old.

Famine/Bankruptcy of Samuel
Bernard/Plate melted down at the
Mint/Fall of Chamillard/Voysin
appointed Secretary of
State/September 11: Battle of
Malplaquet/October 23: removal of
nuns from Port Royal/Death of
Father de la Chaise/Father Tellier
named confessor of Louis XIV.

1710

16 years old.

Destruction of Port Royal/February
15: birth of the Duc d'Anjou (later
Louis XV)/Death of Mademoiselle
de la Vallière.

1711

17 years old/August: ends studies at
Louis-le-Grand and becomes law
student.

Death of the Grand Dauphin of
France.

WORLD EVENTS	ARTS AND SCIENCES

1712

Birth of Prince Frederick of Prussia (later Frederick the Great)/End of religious war in Switzerland/Congress of Utrecht/Birth of Infante of Spain/Philip V renounces crown of France.

Spectator ceases publication/ Marivaux: *Pharsamon*/Berkeley: *Dialogues between Hylas and Philonous*/Arbuthnot: *History of John Bull*/Death of La Fare; R. Simon; Van der Heyden/Birth of Jean-Jacques Rousseau; Cassini; Guardi; Gournay.

1713

Clement XI: Bull *Unigenitus*/Charles VI issues Pragmatic Sanction in favor of his daughter Maria Theresa/Treaty of Utrecht: end of France's political hegemony/England acquires monopoly of slave trade/Decline of Dutch power/Russian capital transferred from Moscow to Saint Petersburg.

Hamilton: *Mémoires du comte de Grammont*/Discovery of ruins of Herculaneum/Couperin: *Premier livre de clavecin*/Death of Jurieu; Corelli/Birth of Diderot; Sterne; Raynal; Soufflot; Ramsay.

1714

Death of Queen Anne/George I succeeds to throne of England/Treaty of Radstadt/Russia acquires Finland

Fénelon: *Lettre à l'Académie*/Marivaux: *Télémaque travesti*/Leibniz: *Monadologie*/Fahrenheit invents alcohol and mercury thermometers/Death of D. Papin/Birth of Gluck; Pigalle; J. Vernet; Cassini de Thury.

1715

Scottish Rebellion: defeat of James Stuart.

Lesage: *Gil Blas*/Massillon: *Oraison funèbre de Louis XIV*/Rigaud: *Louis XV enfant*/Death of Fénelon; Malebranche; Girardon; Quellyn/Birth of Vauvenargues; Helvétius; Condillac; Bernis; Cochin; Mirabeau the elder; Perroneau.

LIFE OF VOLTAIRE	EVENTS IN FRANCE

1712

18 years old/Birth of his niece Marie-Louise Mignot (later Madame Denis).

Smallpox epidemic/Death of the Duc de Bourgogne/July 24: Battle of Denain: end of War of Spanish Succession/Rohan named Cardinal/Death of Catinat.

1713

19 years old/September: goes as ambassador's secretary to The Hague/Writes *Ode sur les malheurs du temps*/December 24: returns to Paris.

Villars captures Fribourg/Place Bellecour built in Lyons.

1714

20 years old/Resumes law studies/Fails to win French Academy prize with his poem *Le Voeu de Louis XIII*/Publishes two scandalous poems, *Le Bourbier* and *L'Anti-Giton*.

Louis XIV forces Parlement to register bull *Unigenitus*/Edict concerning succession of royal bastards.

1715

21 years old/Frequents Temple and associates with the *libertins*/Reads his *Oedipe* to the Duchesse du Maine at Sceaux.

Persian embassy to Versailles/September 1: death of Louis XIV: accession of Louis XV (Regency until 1723)/Maurepas named Secretary of State.

WORLD EVENTS	ARTS AND SCIENCES

1716

Alberoni named Prime Minister to Philip V of Spain/Prince Eugene takes Temesvar: Turks driven out of Hungary.

Death of Leibniz; Charles de la Fosse; Caffieri/Birth of Saint-Lambert; Vien; Melendrez; Falconet; Daubenton.

1717

Christianity forbidden in China/Siege of Belgrade/Triple Alliance of The Hague against Philip V/Prince Eugene takes Belgrade.

Retz: *Mémoires*/Galland: *Les 1001 Nuits*/Watteau: *L'Embarquement pour Cythère*/Death of Madame Guyon; Jouvenet/Birth of Winckelmann; D'Alembert; Horace Walpole;Vergennes.

1718

Death of Charles XII of Sweden/Founding of New Orleans/Quadruple Alliance/Peter the Great executes his son, the Tsarevitch Alexis.

Piganiol de la Force: *Description de la France*/Massillon: *Petit Carême*/Watteau: *Gilles*/Cassini measures Paris meridian/Abbé de Saint-Pierre: *Discours sur la polysynodie*/Death of Fagon/Birth of Fréron; Roslin.

1719

Franco-Spanish War/Alberoni dismissed.

Defoe: *Robinson Crusoe*/Houdart de la Motte: *Fables*/Handel: *Acis and Galatea*/Vertot: *Histoire des révolutions de la république romaine*/Death of Addison; Quesnel/Birth of Sedaine; Vadé; Cazotte.

1720

Walpole named Prime Minister of England/Spaniards occupy Texas/Founding of English colony in Honduras/Philip V of Spain joins Quadruple Alliance.

Dangeau completes his *Journal*/Marivaux: *Arlequin poli par l'amour*/Foundation of the Royal Print Collection/Hochbrucker invents pedal harp/Death of Hamilton; Chaulieu; Heinsius; Dangeau; Coysevox; Madame Dacier/Birth of Piranesi; Gozzi; the Abbé de Prades.

LIFE OF VOLTAIRE	EVENTS IN FRANCE
1716	
22 years old/May 5: exiled to Tulle, then to Sully-sur-Loire/Liaison with Mademoiselle de Livry.	John Law founds General Bank/Creation of Civil Engineer Corps/Voysin resigns/Reopening of Comédie Italienne in Paris/Death of D'Artagnan.
1717	
23 years old/Return to Paris, Rue de la Calande/Sees the Tsar/Begins drafting *La Ligue,* a first version of *La Henriade*/May 16: imprisoned in the Bastille.	Peter the Great in Paris/Founding of French Indies Company/Dubois appointed to Council of Foreign Affairs/Daguesseau named Chancellor/Regent buys the "Regent" diamond.
1718	
24 years old/April 11: leaves Bastille for exile at Châtenay/November 18: first performance of *Oedipe*/Görtz offers him post as secretary.	Law's bank becomes Royal Bank/Dubois appointed Foreign Secretary/Cellamare conspiracy/Abolition of Councils/Building of Elysée Palace.
1719	
25 years old/February: adopts the name Voltaire/Publication of *Oedipe*/Frequents aristocratic circles.	Law takes over direction of Mint/Death of Madame de Maintenon; Schomberg.
1720	
26 years old/February: first performance of *Artémire*/Visits Lord Bolingbroke at La Source/Reads extracts from *La Henriade*.	Plague in Marseilles/Law appointed Comptroller General of Finance/Closing of the Rue Quincampoix/Riots in Paris/Resignation and flight of Law to England/Parlement registers bull *Unigenitus*/Construction of Château de Champs.

WORLD EVENTS   ARTS AND SCIENCES

1721

Death of Pope Clement XI/Innocent XIII succeeds to papacy/Walpole named Chancellor of the Exchequer/Saint-Simon appointed ambassador to Spain.

Montesquieu: *Lettres persanes*/Berkeley: *Treatise on Motion*/Scarlatti: *Griselda*/DeFoe: *Moll Flanders*/Death of Watteau, shortly after completing *L'Enseigne de Gersaint*; Trudaine; Maupertuis/Birth of Eisen.

1722

Founding of French settlement at Mahé/Death of Marlborough.

Bach: *Das wohltempierte Klavier*/Rameau: *Traité d'harmonie*/Lebat: *Nouveau voyage aux îles de l'Amérique*/Marivaux begins publication of his paper *Le Spectateur français*, and his *La Surprise de l'amour* is published/Holberg: *Der politiske Kandestöber (The Pewterer Turned Politician)*/Death of A. Coypel; Gillot.

1723

Rehabilitation of Bolingbroke.

Marivaux: *La Double Inconstance*/Bach: *Magnificat*/Holberg: *La Chambre de l'accouchée*/Beginning of Yung-Cheng porcelain/Death of Leeuwenhoek/Birth of Adam Smith; Holbach; F.-M. Grimm; Reynolds; Marmontel.

1724

Death of Pope Innocent XIII/Benedict XIII succeeds to papacy/Abdication of Philip V of Spain; death of Don Luis; Philip V returns to the throne/Founding of Bahia Academy/Correr Palace in Venice constructed.

Bach: *Saint John Passion*/Marivaux: *Le Prince travesti*/Chaulieu: *Poésies*/Defoe: *Roxana*/Handel: *Tamburlaine*/Metastasio: *Didone abbandonata*/Death of Dufresny; Chikamatsu/Birth of Kant; Klopstock; Maulpertsch; Bellotto.

LIFE OF VOLTAIRE	EVENTS IN FRANCE

1721

27 years old/November: Voltaire offers the manuscript of *La Henriade* to the Regent, and profits from the debacle of Law's speculative financial ventures.

Foundation of first Masonic lodge in France/Cartouche arrested/The Pâris brothers take over from Law/The "visa" of Duverney/Franco-Spanish entente/Dubois named cardinal/Death of Chamillard; D'Argenson/Birth of Antoinette Poisson (later Madame de Pompadour).

1722

28 years old/January: death of François Arouet, his father/Voltaire solicits secret mission in Germany/July: goes with Madame de Rupelmonde to Brussels and Holland/Meets the poet J.-B. Rousseau/Writes *Le Pour et le contre*.

Dubois named Prime Minister/Death of the Princess Palatine/Establishment of the Bureau of Commerce/Arrest of Villeroi/End of plague in Marseilles.

1723

29 years old/Finishes *L'Essai sur les guerres civiles*/Liaison with Madame de Bernières/Publication of *La Henriade* (originally entitled *Poème de la Ligue*)/November–December: Adrienne Lecouvreur nurses him through smallpox/Writes *Mariamne*/Death of Génonville.

Louis XV comes of age/Death of Dubois; the Regent; Lauzun/the Duc de Bourbon named Prime Minister.

1724

30 years old/March 6: first performance of *Mariamne*/July–August: at Forges with Richelieu/Voltaire's health deteriorates.

Founding of the Paris Stock Market/Founding of the Club de l'Entresol/Declaration against the Protestants/Decree against mendicancy.

WORLD EVENTS	ARTS AND SCIENCES

1725

Death of Peter the Great/Catherine I ascends the throne of Russia/Discovery of the Bering Straits/Treaty of Herrenhausen/Philip V breaks the Quadruple Alliance/Diamonds found in Brazil/Founding of Academy of Sciences in Saint Petersburg.

Foundation of porcelain factory at Chantilly/Destruction of rood screen of Notre Dame/Salon at the Louvre/Couperin: *L'Apothéose de Lulli*/Vico: *Scienza Nuova*/Montesquieu: *Le Temple de Cnide*/Marivaux: *L'Ile des esclaves*/Pope: English translation of the *Odyssey*/Death of Scarlatti; Wren/Birth of Casanova; Greuze; P. Paoli; Cugnot.

1726

Spaniards found Montevideo.

Swift: *Gulliver's Travels*/Bernoulli: *Traité du mouvement*/Rollin: *Traité des études*/Crébillon: *Pyrrhus*/Thomson: *The Seasons*/Madame de Sévigné: *Lettres à sa fille*/Salon of Madame de Tencin/Mademoiselle Camargo's debut at the Opéra/Vivaldi: *Le Quatro Stagioni*/Death of Delalande/Birth of Philidor; Chodowiecki.

1727

Death of Catherine I of Russia/Peter II becomes Tsar/Death of George I of England/Union of Mannheim/First printing works founded at Constantinople/First Masonic lodge in Madrid founded.

Destouches: *Le Philosophe marié*/Montesquieu: *Réflexions sur la monarchie*/Marivaux: *Eloge de la raison*/Moncrif: *Histoire des chats*/Gay: *Fables*/James Bradley discovers aberration of light/Birth of Turgot; Morellet; Gainsborough; G. D. Tiepolo; Drouais.

1728

Founding of Jaipur.

Jean-Jacques Rousseau leaves Geneva/Marivaux: *La Seconde Surprise de l'amour*/Chambers: *Encyclopaedia*/Pope: *Dunciad*/Abbé Prévost: *Mémoires et aventures d'un*

LIFE OF VOLTAIRE	EVENTS IN FRANCE
1725	
31 years old/August 18: first performance of *L'Indiscret*/October 6: sends *La Henriade* to George I of England/November: receives a pension from the Queen's privy purse/First encounter with Desfontaines.	Louis XV marries Marie Leczinska/Imposition of the *Cinquantième* tax/First Masonic lodge established in Paris.
1726	
32 years old/February 4: cudgeled by the Chevalier de Rohan's men/April 17: imprisoned in the Bastille/May 5: at Calais, on way to exile in England/July: secret visit to Paris.	Fleury, the Prime Minister, re-establishes the corps of Farmers-General.
1727	
33 years old/January: presented to George I of England/April 8: attends Isaac Newton's funeral in Westminster Abbey/December: publishes two works in English: *Essay on Civil Wars, Essay on Epick Poetry*/Begins history of Charles XII, meets Swift, Pope, Congreve, Gay.	The episode of the Convulsionaries of Saint-Médard/Chauvelin named Foreign Minister/Death of Pontchartrain.
1728	
34 years old/*La Henriade*, dedicated to the Queen of England, published by subscription in London/November: returns to France, though not to Paris.	Controversy over bull *Unigenitus*.

WORLD EVENTS	ARTS AND SCIENCES
	homme de qualité/Montesquieu made a member of the French Academy/Museum of Antiquities established at Dresden/Death of La Monnoye/Birth of Goldsmith; Burke; Mengs.

1729

Birth of Catherine of Anhalt-Zerbst (later Catherine II)/Natchez Indian rebellion in Louisiana/Treaty of Seville.	Bach: *Saint Matthew Passion*/Montesquieu in England/Goldoni: *The Venetian Gondolier*/Gray discovers transmission of electricity/Bouguer: photometry/Haller: *Les Alpes*/Death of Congreve/Birth of Lessing; Ecouchard-Lebrun; Monsigny.

1730

Abdication of Victor Amadeus II of Savoy/Walpole's ministry/Death of Pope Benedict XIII/Clement XII succeeds to the papacy/Deposition of Achmet III/Death of Frederick IV of Denmark/Christian VI succeeds him/Death of Peter II of Russia/Anna Ivanovna becomes Tsarina.	Salon of Madame du Deffand/Hamilton: *Contes*/Rollin: *Histoire ancienne*/Marivaux: *Le Jeu de l'amour et du hasard*/Buffon in England/Goldoni: *Don Juan*/Metastasio: *Alessandro nell' Indie*/Use of sextant introduced/Birth of Gessner.

1731

Dupleix at Chandernagore/English replaces Latin entirely in English courts.	Holberg: *Danish Plays*/Marivaux: *La vie de Marianne*/Abbé Prévost: *Manon Lescaut*/Fielding: *Tragedy of Tragedies*/Tull: theory of enclosures/Death of Defoe; Houdart de la Motte/Birth of Cowper.

1732

Foundation of Georgia/Treaty of Warsaw/Birth of Washington; Necker.	Berkeley: *Alcyphron*/Metastasio: *Demetrios*/Destouches: *Le Glorieux*/Montesquieu initiated as a Freemason in England/Founding of

LIFE OF VOLTAIRE   EVENTS IN FRANCE

1729

35 years old/April: authorized to live in Paris/Writes: *Histoire de Charles XII, Brutus, Lettres philosophiques*/May: visit to court at Lorraine/Invests funds with Pâris brothers.

First cabaret opened in Paris/Vogue for English-style gardens/Death of John Law.

1730

36 years old/March 15: death of Adrienne Lecouvreur: poem on *La mort de Mademoiselle Lecouvreur*/Summer: takes the waters at Plombières with Richelieu/December: first performance of *Brutus*.

Orry named Comptroller General.

1731

37 years old/January: police seize first edition of his *L'Histoire de Charles XII*/June: in Rouen/December: lodges with Madame de Fontaine-Martel/Reads *Brutus* to ten Jesuit fathers.

Dissolution of the Club de l'Entresol/Affair of la Cadière/Foundation of Academy of Surgery.

1732

38 years old/March 7: first performance of *Eriphyle(Sémiramis)*/May: Begins *Le Siècle de Louis XIV*/June: first

Closing of cemetery of Saint-Médard.

WORLD EVENTS	ARTS AND SCIENCES
	London Magazine/Lesage: *Don Guzman d'Alfarache*/Marivaux: *Les Serments indiscrets*/Boerhaave: *Elementa Chemiae*/Maupertuis: *Discours sur la figure des astres*/Bach: *Coffee Cantata*/Death of Boulle/Birth of Fragonard; Lalande; Haydn; Beaumarchais.

1733

War of Polish Succession/Conscription in Prussia/Villars in Italy/Treaty of Turin/Founding of Spanish colony in the Philippines.	Benedictines of Saint-Maur begin publication of *Histoire littéraire de la France*/Rameau: *Hippolyte et Aricie*/Bach: *Mass in B Minor*/Pope: *Essay on Man*/Marivaux: *L'Heureux Stratagème*/Franklin: *Poor Richard's Almanac*/Pergolesi: *La Serva Padrona*/Kay invents flying shuttle/Death of Couperin/Birth of Priestley; Wieland; Mesmer; Ducis; Malfilâtre; Zoffany; Borda; H. Robert.

1734

The Emperor declares war on France/Battle of Parma/Russians take Danzig/Union of Moravian Brothers/Founding of University of Göttingen.	Montesquieu: *Considérations . . . de la grandeur et de la décadence des Romains*/Hogarth: *A Harlot's Progress*/Bach: *Christmas Oratorio*/Réaumur: *Histoire des insectes*/Gresset: *Vert-Vert*/Goldoni: *Belisario*/Tartini: *Violin Sonatas*/Death of S. Ricci/Birth of Restif de la Bretonne; Dorat; Ruhlière; Romney.

1735

Franco-Austrian armistice/La Bourdonnais appointed governor of Ile-de-France.	Dom Calmet: *Histoire universelle*/Marivaux: *Le Paysan parvenu*/Nivelle de la Chaussée: *Le*

LIFE OF VOLTAIRE	EVENTS IN FRANCE

edition of his *Oeuvres*/August 13:
success of *Zaïre*/December: writes
Le Temple du goût.

1733

39 years old/January: publication of
Le Temple du goût/May: at St.
Gervais/June: liaison with Madame
du Châtelet/July: adds *Remarques
sur Pascal* to his *Lettres
philosophiques*/During this year,
works on *Le Siècle de Louis XIV*,
writes *Alzire* and two operas,
Tanis et Zélide and *Samson*.

Tax of *dixième* introduced/Madame
de Mailly becomes the King's
mistress/Franco-Bavarian and
Franco-Dutch treaties/Death of
Forbin.

1734

40 years old/January 18: first
performance of *Adélaïde du
Guesclin*/March: witness at marriage
of Richelieu to Mademoiselle de
Guise/June 10: *Lettres
philosophiques* condemned to be
burned/*Lettre de cachet* against
Voltaire; he goes into hiding at
Madame du Châtelet's residence at
Cirey/Begins *La Pucelle*/July: visits
camp at Philippsburg/Duke of
Holstein offers to take him into his
service.

Death of Berwick; Villars.

1735

41 years old/Works on *La Pucelle*
and *Le Siècle de Louis XIV*/Quarrel
with Desfontaines/March: receives

Decree concerning wills.

WORLD EVENTS	ARTS AND SCIENCES
	Préjugé à la mode/Hogarth: *The Rake's Progress*/Salvi: the Trevi Fountain in Rome/La Condamine and Maupertuis measure the earth's meridian/Madame de Tencin: *Mémoires du comte de Comminges*/Du Halde: *Description de l'empire de la Chine*/Lemoyne decorates Hôtel Soubise/Rameau: *Les Indes galantes*/Bach: *Italian Concerto*/ Death of Stradivarius/Birth of the Prince de Ligne; Lépicié.

1736

Indian rebellion in Louisiana/Bank of Copenhagen founded/Construction of Summer Palace in Peking/Beginning of Italian Opera in Saint Petersburg.	Marivaux: *Le Legs*/Lesage: *Le Bachelier de Salamanque*/Chardin: *Le Château de cartes*/Pergolesi: *Stabat Mater*/Glass factory at Murano founded/Hull patents steamship/Death of Pergolesi; Pater/Birth of Lagrange; Watt.

1737

First theaters in Prague and Stockholm.	Salon at the Louvre/Linnaeus: classification of plants/Marivaux: *Les Fausses Confidences*/Goldoni: *The Man of Accomplishments*/Rameau: *Castor et Pollux*/Gluck in Italy/Walpole in France/Death of Lemoyne/Birth of Bernardin de Saint-Pierre; Parmentier.

LIFE OF VOLTAIRE	EVENTS IN FRANCE

permission to return to Paris/May:
Lorraine/August 11: first
performance of *La Mort de Jules
César*/September: meets Curé
Meslier.

1736

42 years old/January 27: first
performance of *Alzire ou les
américains*/Beginning of quarrel
with Le Franc de Pompignan/Cirey:
Madame du Châtelet learns
English/July: Paris/August 8:
beginning of correspondence with
Prince Frederick of Prussia/October
10: first performance of *L'Enfant
prodigue*/publication of *Epître à
Mme du Châtelet sur la
calomnie*/November: in Holland for
several weeks because of threat of
prosecution for writing *Le Mondain*.

Franco-Austrian agreement.

1737

43 years old/March: returns to
Cirey/Death of Nicolaï, his old
teacher/Active correspondence with
Frederick, who sends much
documentary information about
Russia/December: finishes *Mérope*.

Fall of Chauvelin.

WORLD EVENTS	ARTS AND SCIENCES

1738

Treaty of Vienna: end of War of Polish Succession/Stanislas Leczinski becomes Duc de Lorraine/England signs the Treaty of Vienna/Franco-Swedish treaty/Riots among English workers/Preaching of Whitefield.

Piron: *La Métromanie*/Salon at the Louvre/Paul invents spinning frame/Handel: *Israel in Egypt*/Rollin: *Histoire romaine*/Crébillon: *Les Egarements du coeur et de l'esprit*/Bernoulli: *Hydrodynamica*/Cassini, Thury, Maraldy, and La Caille measure the speed of sound/Porcelain factory at Vincennes founded (later transferred to Sèvres)/Lancret: *Les Quatres Saisons*/Death of Boerhaave/Birth of Beccaria; Herschel; Boufflers; Delille.

1739

French settlement founded at Karikal, India/Philip V signs Treaty of Vienna/Turks besiege Belgrade/Walpole declares war on Spain/Foundation of Academy of Sciences in Stockholm.

Madame de Tencin: *Le Siège de Calais*/Salon at the Louvre/Hume: *Treatise of Human Nature*/Bouchardon: Fountain in the Rue de Grenelle, Paris/Tocqué: *Portrait du Dauphin*/Deluze makes first industrially printed fabric/De Brosses: *Lettres familières d'Italie*/Clairaut does research in integral calculus/Handel: *Susanna*/Birth of La Harpe.

1740

Death of the of the "Sergeant-King" (Frederick I) of Prussia/Frederick II ascends the throne: he invades Silesia/Death of Pope Clement XII/Benedict XIV succeeds to the papacy/Death of Anna Ivanovna/Ivan VI becomes Tsar of Russia/Death of Charles VI/Maria Theresa succeeds to the Austrian throne/Beginning of War of Austrian Succession/First Greek newspaper.

Pellerin printing works founded at Epinal/Salon at the Louvre/Coustou: *Les Chevaux de Marly*/Chardin: *Le Bénédicité*/Richardson: *Pamela*/Crébillon: *Le Sopha*/Marivaux: *L'Epreuve*/Abbé Goujet: *Bibliothèque française*/Birth of Sade; Oberlin.

LIFE OF VOLTAIRE	EVENTS IN FRANCE

1738

44 years old/January: writes first of the *Discours sur l'homme*/Scientific experiments with Madame du Châtelet/February 25: his niece Marie-Louise Mignot marries Nicolas-Charles Denis/Lawsuit against bookseller Jore/Publication of *Eléments de la philosophie de Newton*/writes *L'Envieux*/December: Madame de Graffigny at Cirey: readings from *Le Siècle de Louis XIV* and the Bible.	Decree concerning *la corvée*/Mademoiselle de Nesles becomes Louis XV's mistress/Completion of Crozat canal, in Picardy.

1739

45 years old/May 15: he and Madame du Châtelet leave for Holland/August: publication of *Vie de Molière*/In Paris: writes *Réponse à toutes les objections principales faites en France contre la philosophie de Newton*/November: Cirey/*Pièces fugitives en vers et en prose* seized on publication.	Louis XV fails to take Easter communion/Buffon made superintendent of the King's gardens.

1740

46 years old/January: revises Frederick's *Anti-Machiavel*/June 8: First performance of *Zulime*/July: Holland/September 11: first visit to Frederick II at Cleves/November: Berlin/December: returns to Belgium.	Louis XV sends England an ultimatum.

WORLD EVENTS	ARTS AND SCIENCES

1741

Franco-Prussian alliance/Walpole defeated in elections/Franco-Bavarian alliance/Sweden declares war on Russia/Franco-Hanoverian entente/Secret Austro-Prussian armistice/Elizabeth of Russia overthrows Ivan VI/Charles Albert has himself proclaimed King of Bohemia.

Handel: *Messiah*/Windows of Notre Dame destroyed/Gabriel made First Architect to the King/Salon at the Louvre/La Tour: *Portrait du président de Rieux*/Hume: *Essays Moral and Political*/Favart: *La Chercheuse d'esprit*/Abbé Prévost: *Histoire d'une grecque moderne*/Death of J.-B. Rousseau; Vivaldi; Rollin/Birth of Lavater; Laclos; Houdon; Chamfort; Fuseli.

1742

Benedict XIV condemns Jesuit policy in China/Austrians retake Linz/Charles Albert of Bavaria, King of Bohemia, elected Holy Roman Emperor (Charles VII)/Resignation of Walpole/Franco-Danish alliance/Treaty of Berlin/Fall of Prague.

Salon at the Louvre/L. Racine: *La Religion*/Fielding: *Joseph Andrews*/Young: *Night Thoughts*/ Piranesi: *Carceri*/Tresaguet perfects macadam process/Death of Massillon.

1743

French war against Sardinia/Second family pact/Frederick II reforms Berlin Academy, which is to publish the King's works in French/Founding of Danish Academy/The La Vérendrycs discover the Rocky Mountains.

Mademoiselle Clairon begins her career at the Comédie Française/Handel: *Joseph and His Brethren*/Salon at the Louvre/Fielding: *Jonathan Wilde*/D'Alembert: *Traité de dynamique*/Death of Grécourt; Ghislandi; Rigaud; Desportes; Lancret; Claude Lorraine/Birth of Cagliostro; Lavoisier; Condorcet; Jacobi.

1744

First General Methodist Conference/Frederick II takes Prague/Construction of castle of Schönbrunn.

Albinoni: *Symphonies*/Pigalle: *Mercure*/Hogarth: *Marriage à la Mode*/Gluck: *Sophonisba*/Frederick II: *Le Miroir des princes*/Hénault:

LIFE OF VOLTAIRE	EVENTS IN FRANCE
	1741
47 years old/April: first performance of *Mahomet*, at Lille/visit of Lord Chesterfield/June: begins *Essai sur les moeurs*/October: Paris/December: Cirey.	New controversy over bull *Unigenitus*.
	1742
48 years old/January: visit to Franche-Comté/August: Brussels/*Mahomet* forbidden in Paris/Visit to Aix-la-Chapelle/November: Paris/Forgeries of his works grow more and more numerous.	Beginning of the "reign" of the King's mistresses.
	1743
49 years old/February 20: first performance of *Mérope*/March: portrait by Maurice Quentin de la Tour/April: fails to get into the French Academy/June: diplomatic mission to Berlin; Frederick tries to make him stay/November: returns to France/November 3: elected a member of Royal Society (London)/*Mahomet* published.	Death of Fleury/D'Argenson, Voltaire's friend, named Secretary of State for War/The Marquise de Tournelle becomes the King's mistress/Birth of Jeanne Bécu (later Madame du Barry).
	1744
50 years old/*Mérope* published/March: liaison with Mademoiselle Gaussin/April: writes *La Princesse de Navarre* at	November 28: D'Argenson appointed Minister for Foreign Affairs/Louis XV declares war on England and Austria, invades Piedmont and the

WORLD EVENTS	ARTS AND SCIENCES
	Abrégé chronologique de l'histoire de France/Metastasio: *Antigone*/Death of Vico; Pope; Campra/Birth of Herder; Lamarck.

1745

Convention of Aranjuez/Charles Stuart lands in Scotland/Death of the Holy Roman Emperor/Election of François III of Lorraine (François I), husband of Maria Theresa of Austria.	Morelly: *Essai sur le coeur humain*/Swedenborg: *Of Religion and the Love of God*/Servandoni: portal of Saint-Sulpice/Tiepolo: frescoes in the Palazzo Cornano/Salon at the Louvre/Gluck: *Hippolyte*/Destouches: *Oeuvres*/Rameau: *Pygmalion*/Death of Swift; Guarnerius; J. B. Vanloo/Birth of Volta; Goya; Huet.

1746

French take Brussels/Battle of Plaisance/Death of Philip V of Spain/Accession of Ferdinand VI to the throne of Spain/Surrender of Genoa/Battle of Raucoux/Founding of Princeton University.	Salon at the Louvre/Diderot: *Pensées philosophiques*/Vauvenargues: *Réflexions et maximes*/Abbé Prévost: *Histoire générale des voyages*/Marivaux: *Le Préjugé vaincu*/Handel: *Judas Maccabaeus*/Death of Walpole; Largillière; Coustou/Birth of Monge; Pestalozzi.

1747

Orangist revolution in Zeeland/War between France and Holland/French take Berg-op-Zoom.	Le Breton asks Diderot and D'Alembert to edit the *Encyclopédie*/Bach: *The Musical Offering*/Salon at the

LIFE OF VOLTAIRE	EVENTS IN FRANCE
Cirey/September: at Champs, visiting the Duc de la Vallière/October: Paris.	Low Countries, takes Fribourg/Law claims underground deposits state property.

1745

51 years old/At Versailles at the beginning of the year/February 18: death of Voltaire's brother Armand/February 23: first performance of *La Princesse de Navarre*/April 1: appointed royal historiographer/Elected to Royal Society of Edinburgh/May: publishes poem *La Bataille de Fontenoy*/Writes *Le Temple de la gloire*/Visit to Champs/August–September: correspondence with the Pope/Writes *Précis du siècle de Louis XV*/November 27: first performance of *Le Temple de la gloire*/December 15: meets Jean-Jacques Rousseau/Begins love relationship with Madame Denis.	May 11: Battle of Fontenoy/Madame de Pompadour comes into favor/Machault named Comptroller General of Finance.

1746

52 years old/April 25: elected to French Academy, succeeding Jean Bouhier/May 9: reception at the Academy/the Travenol affair/June 28: elected a member of Academy of Saint Petersburg/August: writes *Sémiramis*/November: named Gentleman of the King's Chamber/December: meets D'Alembert.	Christophe de Beaumont named Archbishop of Paris/Death of Torcy/Jean-Jacques Rousseau abandons his first child on the doorstep of the Foundling Hospital.

1747

53 years old/July: writes first version of *Zadig*: difficulties at court/October: incident at the Queen's gaming table.	Fall of D'Argenson from favor/Birth of Louis-Philippe d'Orléans (later King Louis-Philippe, known as the "Citizen King").

WORLD EVENTS	ARTS AND SCIENCES
	Louvre/Franklin invents the lightning rod/Trudaine founds the School of Mines in Paris/Gresset: *Le Méchant*/La Tour: *Portrait de Monsieur de Saxe*/Samuel Johnson: *Dictionary*/Gluck: *Les Noces d'Hébé et d'Hercule*/Nivelle de la Chaussée: *L'Amour castillan*/Death of Vauvenargues; Lesage; Solimena/Birth of Galvani.

1748

| Treaty of Aix-la-Chapelle: end of War of Austrian Succession. | Crébillon: *Catilina*/Handel: *Samson*/Vestris at the Opéra/Construction of Opera at Bayreuth/Salon at the Louvre/Grimm arrives in Paris/Diderot: *Les Bijoux indiscrets*/Montesquieu: *L'Esprit des lois*/Hume: *Philosophical Essays*/Richardson: *Clarissa Harlowe*/Klopstock: *The Messiad*/Goldoni: *La Vedova Scaltra (The Clever Widow)*/Euler works on mathematical analysis/Needham's theory of spontaneous generation/Discovery of the ruins of Pompeii/Pigalle: *Vénus*/La Tour: *Portrait of Louis XV*/La Mettrie: *L'Homme-machine*/Birth of Berthollet; David; Jussieu; Bentham; Coraïs. |

1749

| Italian League against North African pirates. | Huntsmann casts steel/Salon of Madame Geoffrin/Bach: *The Art of the Fugue*/Salon at the Louvre/Buffon: *Histoire naturelle*/Fielding: *Tom Jones*/Swedenborg: *Arcana coelestia*/Tournefort: *Etudes d'anatomie comparée*/Diderot: *Lettre sur les aveugles*/Death of Magnasco; |

LIFE OF VOLTAIRE   EVENTS IN FRANCE

1748

54 years old/February–April: visits
to Nancy, Lunéville, and Commercy,
at the court of Stanislas Leczinski,
father-in-law of Louis XV/August
29: first performance of
Sémiramis/September: ill/Publishes
Panégyrique de Louis XV and
Pandore/October: discovers Madame
du Châtelet in the arms of
Saint-Lambert.

"Reign" of Madame Henriette as
Louis XV's mistress.

1749

55 years old/January: works on
Histoire de la guerre de 1741/April:
Emilie wants to finish her work on
Newton/June: performance of
Nanine/September 10: Madame du
Châtelet dies in childbirth.

Battle over *vingtième* tax/Fall of
Maurepas from favor/Diderot
imprisoned in Vincennes.

WORLD EVENTS   ARTS AND SCIENCES

J. van Huysum; Clérambault/Birth of
Goethe; Alfieri; Mirabeau the
younger; Subleyras.

1750

Death of João V of Portugal/José I
accedes to the throne/Pombal named
Prime Minister of Portugal.

Goldoni: *La bottega del
caffé*/Jean-Jacques Rousseau:
*Discours sur les sciences et les
arts*/Distribution of the prospectus
of the *Encyclopédie*/Pigalle:
L'Enfant à la cage/Marmontel:
Cléopâtre/Death of Bach;
Muratori; Oudry/Birth of Berquin;
Valenciennes.

1751

Portuguese government forbids
autos-da-fé.

Salon at the Louvre/Diderot: *Lettre
sur les sourds et muets*/Burlamaqui:
Principes du droit politique/Handel:
Jephtha/Gozzi: *Rimes
burlesques*/Fielding: *Amelia*/Hume:
*Enquiry concerning the Principles of
Morals*/Duclos: *Considérations sur
les moeurs de ce siècle*/First volume
of *Encyclopédie*, with preliminary
discourse by D'Alembert/Death of
La Mettrie/Birth of Sheridan;
Gilbert; Jouffroy d'Abbans.

1752

Construction of Place Stanislas begun
in Nancy/Construction of palace at
Caserta.

Réaumur's experiments on
digestion/Hume: *Political
Discourses*/Jean-Jacques Rousseau:
Le Devin du village/First
condemnation of
Encyclopédie/Maupertuis: *Oeuvres
complètes*/Wieland: *Die Natur der
Dinge*/Goldoni: *La
Locandiera*/Gainsborough: *Portrait
of Mr. and Mrs. Sandby*/Death of
J.-F. de Troy; Charles-Antoine
Coypel/Birth of Filangieri.

LIFE OF VOLTAIRE	EVENTS IN FRANCE

1750

56 years old/Voltaire in Paris; Madame Denis comes to live with him on the Rue Traversière Saint-Honoré/Fréron appears/June: Voltaire leaves for Berlin on being appointed chamberlain to Frederick II; he will not return to Paris until the year of his death.

Dissolution of the States of Languedoc/Riot in Paris/Machault appointed Keeper of the Seals.

1751

57 years old/Recovers manuscripts stolen by his secretary Longchamp/Works all year on *Le Siècle de Louis XIV*, printed in December/A month before, La Beaumelle arrives in Berlin.

"Reign" of Madame Adélaïde as Louis XV's mistress.

1752

58 years old/Hirschel scandal/May: La Beaumelle leaves Berlin after quarrel with Frederick and Voltaire/ October: finishes *Histoire de la guerre de 1741*/Quarrel with Maupertuis, director of Berlin Academy.

Affair of *billets de confession*/Last persecution of Protestants.

WORLD EVENTS   ARTS AND SCIENCES

1753

War in America and
Canada/London conference on
Indian questions.

Favart: *Bastien et
Bastienne*/Holberg: *The Haunted
House*/Salon at the Louvre/La
Tour: *Portrait of Rousseau, Portrait
of D'Alembert*/Beginning of
Grimm's *Correspondance
littéraire*/Buffon elected to French
Academy: *Discours sur le
style*/Gabriel starts to build opera
house at Versailles/Richardson: *Sir
Charles Grandison*/Liguori:
Theologia moralis/Third volume of
Encyclopédie with preface by
D'Alembert/Death of Berkeley/Birth
of J. de Maistre; Utamaro; Parny;
Rivarol.

1754

Dupleix leaves India/Foundation of
King's College in New York/Jesuits
expelled from Brazil.

Rousseau: *Discours sur
l'inégalité*/Beginning of Fréron's
review, *L'Année littéraire*/Condillac:
Traité sur les sensations/Diderot:
*Pensées sur l'interprétation de la
nature*/Gabriel starts construction of
the Place Louis XV (today the Place
de la Concorde)/Hume: *History of
England*/Winckelmann in Italy/
Boucher: *Mlle O'Murphy*/Falconet:
Milone de Crotone/Death of
Holberg; Fielding; Piazzetta/Birth of
Bonald.

1755

Foundation of Moscow
University/First Russian
grammar/France and England break
off diplomatic relations/November 1:
Lisbon earthquake/Jesuits expelled
from Uruguay.

Salon at the Louvre/Volume V of
Encyclopédie/Black works on
carbon dioxide/Morelly: *Code de la
nature*/Lessing: *Miss Sarah
Sampson*/Greuze: *Le Père de
famille*/La Tour: *Portrait of
Madame de Pompadour*/Death of
Montesquieu; Saint-Simon;
Gentil-Bernard; Maffei/Birth of

LIFE OF VOLTAIRE	EVENTS IN FRANCE

1753

59 years old/March 27: quarrel with Frederick; leaves Berlin/May: visit to Duchess of Saxe-Gotha, at whose request he writes *Annales de l'empire*/June: arrested and detained in Frankfurt/October: visits Colmar, since Louis XV has forbidden him to come to Paris/The quarrel with La Beaumelle grows more heated.

Louis dissolves the Parlement after numerous quarrels over jurisdiction.

1754

60 years old/Works on *Essai sur les moeurs* in library of the Benedictine scholar Dom Calmet, at the Abbey of Sénones/August: takes the waters at Plombières/December: Geneva/La Beaumelle publishes numerous pamphlets against him.

August 23: Birth of the Dauphin (later Louis XVI)/Machault named head of Navy Office.

1755

61 years old/Pirated editions of *Histoire de la guerre de 1741*/Reunion with Richelieu/February 10: Les Délices/August: performance of *L'Orphelin de la Chine*/The Consistory of Geneva forbids theatrical performances at Les Délices.

Louis XV's Deer Park/Construction of Château of Compiègne/Execution of Mandrin.

WORLD EVENTS	ARTS AND SCIENCES

Fourcroy; Corvisart; Florian; Quatremère de Quincy; Collin d'Harville; Fabre d'Eglantine; Debucourt; E. Vigée-Lebrun; Prony.

1756

Beginning of Seven Years' War/Montcalm in Canada/Pitt Prime Minister of England.

Jean-Jacques Rousseau: *Lettre sur la providence*/Birth of Lacépède; Mozart; Raeburn.

1757

November 5: Frederick crushes the French army at Rossbach.

Salon at the Louvre/Diderot: *Le Fils naturel*/Helvétius: *De l'esprit*/Madame Leprince de Beaumont: *Le Magasin des enfants*/Rameau: *Les Surprises de l'amour*/Burke: *European Settlements in America*/Death of Fontenelle; Réaumur; Vadé; R. Carriera/Birth of Blake.

1758

Death of Pope Benedict XIV/Succession of Clement XIII to the papacy/English capture Frontenac, Gorée and Saint-Louis in Senegal/Lally-Tollendal in India.

Jean-Jacques Rousseau: *Lettre à d'Alembert*/D'Alembert leaves *Encyclopédie*/Diderot: *Le Père de famille*/Quesnay: *Tableau économique*/Swedenborg: *De Coelo et ejus mirabilis, et de inferno*/Birth of Prudhon; C. Vernet.

1759

Jesuits expelled from Portugal/Battle of Minden/Surrender of Quebec/English in Guadeloupe.

Salon at the Louvre (Diderot)/Parlement orders *Encyclopédie* to be burned/Wieland: *Cyrus*/Sterne: *Tristram Shandy*/Gossec: *Symphonies*/Founding of British Museum/Death of Handel; Montcalm/Birth of Schiller; Burns; Wilberforce.

LIFE OF VOLTAIRE   EVENTS IN FRANCE

1756

62 years old/November: suggests   Troubles in the Dauphiné.
idea for "tanks" to Minister for
War/December: tries to intercede
for Admiral Byng/Writes article on
Histoire for *Encyclopédie*/*Essai sur
les moeurs* published/D'Alembert
visits Les Délices.

1757

63 years old/February: at request of   January 4: Damiens attempts to
Russian ambassador, undertakes   murder Louis XV.
Histoire de la Russie/August–
September: acts as intermediary
between France and Frederick in
attempt to make peace/December:
scandal over *Encyclopédie* article on
Geneva, inspired by Voltaire.

1758

64 years old/Works on *Histoire de la*   Choiseul named Secretary of State
Russie/October: buys Ferney and   for Foreign Affairs.
Tournay (from Président de
Brosses)/Lawsuit against the
publisher Grasset.

1759

65 years old/January: *Candide*   M. de Silhouette reforms
published/May: *Tancrède* published   administration of tax farming.
(performed in October at
Tournay)/October: his first attack
on *"l'Infâme"*: publishes *Relation de
la maladie . . . du Jésuite
Berthier*/Finishes first part of
Histoire de la Russie.

WORLD EVENTS	ARTS AND SCIENCES
	1760
Death of George II of England/Succession of George III to throne/Russians sack Berlin/Surrender of Montreal/Siege of Pondicherry.	D'Alembert: differential equations/Macpherson: *Ossian*/Spallanzani: *New Physiological Researches*/Gainsborough: *Portrait of Admiral Hawkins*/Palissot: *Les Philosophes*/Birth of Cherubini; the Comte de Saint-Simon; Hokusai.
	1761
Surrender of Pondicherry.	Salon at the Louvre (Diderot)/Rousseau: *La Nouvelle Héloïse*/Gozzi: *The Crow*/Greuze: *L'Accordée de village*/Death of Richardson/Birth of Boilly.
	1762
January 5: Death of Elizabeth of Russia/Peter III becomes Tsar/July 9: Catherine II seizes power/English at Manila and Havana/Peace preliminaries between France, England, and Spain.	Rousseau: *Emile, Du Contrat social*/Meslier: *Mon testament*/Lord Chesterfield: *Letters*/Gluck: *Orpheus*/Pigalle: *Louis XV*/Gabriel: Le Petit Trianon/Birth of Fichte; A. Chénier.
	1763
Treaties of Paris and Hubertsburg.	Salon at the Louvre (Diderot)/Beccaria: *Dei delitti e delle penne*/Reynolds: *Portrait of Miss O'Brien*/Death of Marivaux; Abbé Prévost; L. Racine.
	1764
Wilkes affair	Rousseau: *Lettres écrites de la montagne*/Soufflot: Panthéon/Winckelmann: *Geschichte der Kunst des Altertums*/Houdon: *St. Bruno*/Walpole: *The Castle of Otranto*/First *Almanach de*

LIFE OF VOLTAIRE	EVENTS IN FRANCE
	1760
66 years old/Difficulties with the Consistory of Geneva/Rupture with J.-J. Rousseau/September: *Tancrède* performed in Paris/Visit of Mademoiselle Corneille/Quarrels with Pompignan/*L'Ecossaise* performed in Paris.	Postal system established for Paris/Taxes rise.
	1761
67 years old/Begins *Commentaire sur Corneille* and intercedes on behalf of Pastor Rochette/Quarrels with Jesuits of Ornex, Curé de Moens, and Bishop of Annecy.	February 18: Execution of Rochette/October 13: suicide of Marc-Antoine Calas/Choiseul named Secretary of State for War and the Navy/Negotiations at Versailles: the family pact.
	1762
68 years old/Festivities at Ferney/Quarrel with Président de Brosses/April 4: Beginning of Calas affair/December: New edition of *Essai sur les moeurs*.	March 10: execution of Jean Calas at Toulouse/Parlement orders suppression of Jesuits/Parlement condemns Rousseau's *Emile*.
	1763
69 years old/Mademoiselle Corneille marries, with dowry from Voltaire/July: publication of Volume II of *Histoire de la Russie*/August: Gibbon visits Ferney/Publication of *Traité sur la tolérance*.	February 10: Peace of Paris, ending the Seven Years' War.
	1764
70 years old/February: intercedes for Huguenots condemned to galleys/*Olympie* performed/March: suggests French Protestant colony in Guiana/June: publication of *Dictionnaire philosophique*/Lettre	May 18: death of the Maréchal of Luxembourg/Trial and condemnation of Sirven/Death of Madame de Pompadour.

WORLD EVENTS   ARTS AND SCIENCES

Gotha/Death of Hogarth;
Rameau/Birth of M.-J. Chénier; A.
Radcliffe.

1765

Frederick founds Bank of Berlin.   Salon at the Louvre
(Diderot)/*Encyclopédie*
finished/Greuze: *La Malédiction
paternelle*/Sedaine: *Le Philosophe
sans le savoir*/Turgot: *Formation et
distribution des richesses*/Cavendish
does research on hydrogen/Death of
the Comte de Caylus; Pannini; C.
Vanloo.

1766

Death of Stanislas Leczinski/Stanislas   Rousseau in London with
Poniatowski becomes King of   Hume/Founding of veterinary
Poland/Jesuits condemned in Spain.   school at
(Maisons-)Alfort/Saint-Lambert:
Les Saisons/Goldsmith: *The Vicar of
Wakefield*/La Tour: *Portrait de
Belle de Zuylen*/Bougainville sets out
on his scientific expedition around
the world/Death of Nattier;
Aved/Birth of Germaine Necker
(the future Madame de Staël)
Malthus; Maine de Biran.

1767

Denmark acquires Schleswig and   Salon at the Louvre (Diderot)/Watt
Holstein.   invents the steam
engine/Jean-Jacques Rousseau:
Dictionnaire de musique/Priestley:
History of Electricity/Lessing:
Minna von Barnhelm/Holbach: *Le
Christianisme dévoilé*/Death of
Malfilâtre/Birth of B. Constant;
Schlegel; W. von Humboldt; Girodet;
Isabey.

LIFE OF VOLTAIRE	EVENTS IN FRANCE

d'un Quaker/July: *Le Triumvirat*
performed/Publication of *Le
Sentiment des citoyens*, against
Rousseau.

1765

71 years old/March 9: rehabilitation
of Calas/May: publication of *La
Philosophie de l'histoire*/Russian
ambassador visits Ferney/Sirven
affair.

Trade open to all the King's subjects.

1766

72 years old/July 1: execution of
Chevalier de La Barre/Voltaire
suggests that the *philosophes*
emigrate to Prussia/Undertakes
rehabilitation of Comte de
Lally-Tollendal/Seeks aid of
Genevan watchmakers.

Lorraine becomes part of France
again.

1767

73 years old/Troubles in
Geneva/*L'Ingénu*
published/Voltaire intervenes in
Genevan troubles/Publishes *La
Guerre civile de Genève*.

Reconsideration of Sirven case.

WORLD EVENTS	ARTS AND SCIENCES

1768

Boston convention/Russo-Turkish War.

Cook's first voyage/Quesnay: *La Physiocratie*/Carmontelle: *Proverbes dramatiques*/Sedaine: *La Gageure imprévue*/Diderot and Madame d'Epinay take over Grimm's *Correspondance littéraire*/Euler: *Institutiones calculi integralis*/Monge: *Géométrie descriptive*/Gainsborough: *Portrait of Elia Linley*/Death of Winckelmann; Canaletto; Sterne/Birth of Chateaubriand; J. Crome.

1769

Death of Pope Clement XIII/Succession of Clement XIV to papacy.

Salon at the Louvre (Diderot)/Birth of Cuvier; A. von Humboldt; Napoléon Bonaparte; Thomas Lawrence.

1770

Dumouriez sent to Poland.

Jean-Jacques Rousseau finishes his *Confessions*/Saint-Lambert elected to the French Academy/Holbach: *Le Système de la nature*/Raynal: *Histoire des établissements européens dans les Indes*/Goldsmith: *The Deserted Village*/Gainsborough: *The Blue Boy*/Death of G. B. Tiepolo; Boucher; Moncrif; Hénault/Birth of Beethoven; Hölderlin; Wordsworth; Gérard; Hegel.

1771

Abolition of serfdom in Savoy/Russian troops conquer the Crimea/Gustav III crowned King of Sweden.

Salon at the Louvre (Diderot)/Poinsinet: *Le Cercle*/Bougainville: *Voyage autour du monde*/Lavoisier analyzes the composition of air/Houdon: *Diderot*/Goya decorates Saragossa Cathedral/Death of Helvétius; L.-M. Vanloo/Birth of Bichat; Walter Scott; Gros.

LIFE OF VOLTAIRE   EVENTS IN FRANCE

1768

74 years old/Quarrel with Madame   Maupeou made Chancellor of
Denis, whom Voltaire sends away   France/Madame du Barry becomes
from Ferney/February: *L'Homme*   King's favorite/Acquisition of
aux quarante écus published/June: Corsica
Work started at Versoix/*Précis du*
siècle de Louis XV and *La Princesse*
de Babylone published/Visit from La
Harpe/Voltaire makes his Easter
communion.

1769

75 years old/*Histoire du parlement*   Abolition of privilege of French East
de Paris published/Visit from   India Company.
Grétry/Incident with Capuchin
monk.

1770

76 years old/Works on *Questions sur*   Marriage of the Dauphin and
l'Encyclopédie and campaigns for   Marie-Antoinette/Conflict between
freeing of serfs of   Louis XV and the
Mont-Jura/Intercedes for   Parlement/December 24: fall of
Montbaillis/National subscription for   Choiseul from favor.
his statue/Return of Madame Denis.

1771

77 years old/November 25: Sirven   The Duc d'Aiguillon named
acquitted/Renewal of quarrel with   Secretary for Foreign Affairs.
Parlements: quarrel with the
Choiseuls.

WORLD EVENTS	ARTS AND SCIENCES

1772

Catherine II crushes Cossack revolt/Trial and execution of Struensee/First Partition of Poland/Warren Hastings appointed Governor of Bengal.

Lagrange: *Addition à l'algèbre d'Euler*/Priestley: *Observations on Air*/Goldsmith: *She Stoops to Conquer*/Cazotte: *Le Diable amoureux*/Wieland: *Der goldener Spiegel*/Diderot finishes *Jacques le fataliste*/Cook's second voyage/Death of Swedenborg; Duclos; Tocqué/Birth of Novalis; Coleridge; Broussais; Ricardo; Geoffroy-Saint-Hilaire; Fourier.

1773

Pope Clement XIV dissolves the Society of Jesus/Diderot in Russia/First iron bridge built, at Coalbrookdale.

Salon at the Louvre/B. de Saint-Pierre: *Voyage à l'Ile-de-France* (Mauritius)/Goethe: *Götz von Berlichingen*/Diderot replaced by Meister as editor of *Correspondance littéraire*/Death of Piron/Birth of John Stuart Mill.

1774

Death of Pope Clement XIV/Potemkin comes into favor with Catherine II.

Wieland: *Die Abderiten*/Goethe: *Werther*/Priestley's studies on oxygen/Scheele discovers chlorine/Herschel builds his great telescope/Death of Goldsmith; Quesnay; La Condamine/Birth of Southey; C. D. Friedrich.

1775

Beginning of American War of Independence: Washington commander-in-chief/Pius VI succeeds to the papacy.

Salon at the Louvre (Diderot)/Gentil-Bernard: *L'Art d'aimer*/Beaumarchais: *Le Barbier de Séville*/Diderot: *Le Rêve de d'Alembert*/Sheridan: *The Rivals*/Death of Voisenon; F.-H. Drouais/Birth of Ampère; Turner; C. Mayer; Boieldieu; Schelling.

LIFE OF VOLTAIRE	EVENTS IN FRANCE

1772

78 years old/Composes ode for two hundredth anniversary of Saint Bartholomew's Day massacre/*Les Lois de Minos*, tragedy-pamphlet against fanaticism, published/Le Kain performs at Ferney/Death of Thiériot.

The country is faced with partial bankruptcy.

1773

79 years old/September: publication of *Fragments historiques sur l'Inde*/Gives watches from Ferney to Madame du Barry/A new enemy: Clément.

Foundation of the central Masonic lodge in the country, Le Grand Orient de France/The Beaumarchais-Goezman affair.

1774

80 years old/Publication of *Le Crocheteur borgne*.

May 10: Death of Louis XV/Louis XVI ascends the throne/Maurepas appointed the new King's *conseiller intime*/Vergennes named Secretary of State for Foreign Affairs/Turgot appointed as head of the Navy Office and Secretary of Finance: free circulation of grain, reduction of the powers of the Farmers-General, re-establishment of the Parlement.

1775

81 years old/Publication of a first bound edition of his supposed *Oeuvres complètes*/Supports Turgot/People of Ferney stage a fete in honor of their benefactor.

Food shortage in Paris: riots over the price of bread and flour.

WORLD EVENTS	ARTS AND SCIENCES

1776

July 4: American Declaration of Independence/First trade union founded in England.

Jouffroy sails a steamboat on the Doubs/Cook's third voyage/Beginning of publication of four supplementary volumes of the *Encyclopédie*/Restif de la Bretonne: *Le Paysan et la paysanne pervertis*/Gibbon: *The Decline and Fall of the Roman Empire*/Holbach: *La Morale universelle*/Mably: *Principes des lois*/A. Smith: *The Wealth of Nations*/Death of Hume; Fréron/Birth of Constable; Avogadro.

1777

La Fayette in America/Constitution of the Swiss Federation.

Salon at the Louvre/Beginning of publication of *Le Journal de Paris*, the first French daily/Lavoisier: theory of combustion/Sheridan: *The School for Scandal*/Houdon: *Diane*/Pigalle: *Monument to the Maréchal de Saxe*/Death of Gresset; Natoire/Birth of Gauss; Kleist; Dupuytren.

1778

Cook in Hawaii/Frederick II invades Bohemia.

Rousseau finishes his *Rêveries d'un promeneur solitaire*/Parny: *Poésies érotiques*/Buffon: *Les Epoques de la nature*/Mozart: *Divertissements*/Lamarck: *La Flore française*/Houdon: *Molière*/Death of Piranesi; Linnaeus; Pitt/Birth of Foscolo; Gay-Lussac; Bretonneau.

LIFE OF VOLTAIRE   EVENTS IN FRANCE

1776

82 years old/Publication of *La Bible enfin expliquée*/Many visitors/A serious enemy: the Abbé Guénée/Louis XVI dislikes Voltaire.

Temporary abolition of the *corvée* and guild restrictions/Resignation of Malesherbes/Fall of Turgot/Necker appointed assistant to the Comptroller General of Finance/Benjamin Franklin arrives in Paris.

1777

83 years old/July: Emperor Joseph II passes by Ferney without stopping to see Voltaire/He writes *Irène*.

Necker appointed Director General of Finance/Creation of the French War College/Franco-Swiss treaty.

1778

Nearly 84 years old/February 10: arrives in Paris/Reads the *Mémoires* of Saint-Simon/March 30: Apotheosis: session at the Academy, performance of *Irène*/Meets Franklin, Diderot/April 7: received at the Masonic Lodge of the Nine Sisters/May 11: so ill he remains in bed/Dies on May 30/July 2: death of Jean-Jacques Rousseau/Clandestine burial of Voltaire's remains at the Abbey of Seillières at 5 A.M. a few days after his death, after having been refused burial in consecrated ground in Paris.

Founding of discount bank in Paris.

INDEX

Abbeville, 392–94
Abelard, Peter, 512
Abrégé de l'histoire universelle, 282
Académie des Sciences (Academy of
    Sciences), 123, 127, 128, 158, 257, 484
Academies. *See* Académie des Sciences;
    Académie Française; specific locations
Académie Française (French Academy),
    10, 15, 34, 116–17, 157–58ff., 171, 174,
    175, 210, 342, 449–50; De Brosses and,
    348, 442; La Harpe and prize, 415; Le
    Franc and, 318–19, 321; Marin and,
    442; and marriage of Mme. Denis, 503;
    Maupertuis and, 258; Mithouart offers
    Voltaire's brain to, 500; and *Oedipe*,
    30; poetry competition, 18; and Treaty
    of Aix-la-Chapelle, 205; Voisenon and,
    326; and Voltaire's death, 494;
    Voltaire's election, 181–83; and
    Voltaire's last days in Paris, 466, 474,
    476, 479, 483–84, 485; Ximénès and, 291
Accademia della Crusca, 297
*Account of the Illness, Confession,
    Death and Epiphany of the Jesuit
    Berthier, An*, 317–18
*Account of the Journey of Monsieur le
    Marquis Le Franc de Pompignan . . . ,
    An*, 321–22
*Account of the Voyage of Bro.
    Garassise . . .* , 318
Adam, Father, 369–70, 379, 412, 413–14,
    417, 421, 426, 464
Addison, Joseph, 86, 455
Adélaïde du Guesclin, 414, 465
Adieux à la vie, Les, 304–5
Aeneid, 510
Agathocle, 461

*Age of Louis XIV, The. See Siècle de
    Louis XIV, Le*
Aguesseau, d' (chancellor), 99, 317
Ahasuerus, 303
Aiguillon, Duchesse d', 261
Aix-la-Chapelle, 156; Treaty of, 205
Alain, Master, 25, 27
Alembert, Jean d', 320, 321, 323, 342,
    365–66, 372, 385ff., 399, 413ff., 423, 425,
    430, 459, 461, 471, 511; attacks existence
    of God, 410; calls Voltaire "Monsieur
    Multiforme," ix, 291; Catherine II and,
    386; and Chabanon, 414; and
    Encyclopédie burning, 317; and
    Father Adam, 413; funeral oration to
    Academy of Trudaine, 484; and
    Geneva, Calvinists, religion, 299–300;
    Madame Suard and, 449; and marriage
    of Mme. Denis, 503; and mass for
    Voltaire, 494, 495; and Pasquier,
    Abbeville troubles, 394; and Pigalle
    sculpture of Voltaire, 434; at *Rome
    sauvée* performance, 219; and
    Rousseau, 340; scandalized by
    Voltaire's sacrilegious performances,
    283; and Trublet, 325; and Voltaire's
    attack on Crébillon, 343
Alexis, Count, 399
Algarotti, Francesco, 148, 149, 151, 234,
    240
Algiers, Dey of, 397
Aligre, Maréchal de, 60
Alliot (treasurer), 211
Alliot, Madame, 211
Alsace, 281
Alzire, 101, 110, 115, 219, 483
Amelot (minister), 167, 168, 492
Amsterdam, 117, 127

Amulius et Numitor, 12
Anecdotes sur Fréron (Anecdotes about Fréron), 331
Ane littéraire, L', 331
Anet, Château d', 186, 188–89
Anjou, 64
Annales de l'empire, 270, 273, 280, 281, 284
Anne, Queen, 88
Annecy, Bishop of, 332, 335, 338, 419–20, 426
Année littéraire, 220, 326–27, 331, 457
Anti-Giton, L' (The Anti-Pansy), 28, 29
Anti-Machiavel, 144, 147, 149, 150
Anville, Comtesse d', 343, 356
Anville, Duc d', 343
Anville, Duchesse d', 356
Argens, Marquis d', 234, 235–36, 247, 250, 283, 367, 385
Argenson, Marc Pierre de Voyer de Paulny, Comte d' (the D'Argensons), 161, 162, 168, 169, 173, 175ff., 180, 198, 276, 282; and Desfontaines, 134; and Fontenoy battle, 172; and Fréron, 221, 271; and *La Pucelle,* 291, 292; and Voltaire's meeting with the Pope, 175, 176
Argenson, René Louis de Voyer de Paulny, Marquis d' (elder brother; the D'Argensons), 292, 302
Argental, d' (friend), 106, 108, 111, 130, 143, 151, 156, 164, 167, 191, 212, 280, 283, 294, 306, 309, 312, 335, 336, 349, 364, 369, 371ff., 419, 423, 440ff., 458, 463, 465, 466, 479, 480 (*see also* Argentals, the d'); and *Alzire,* 110; and Desfontaines, 133; at Emilie's death, 214; and Fréron, 221; introduces Voltaire to Bolingbroke, 64; and *Irène* contretemps, 475, 476; loves Adrienne Lecouvreur, 93; and Mademoiselle Corneille, 362, 363; and Pierre Calas, 360; and *Puero regnante,* 35; shocked at Voltaire's farcical confession, 422; and *Tancrède,* 328, 329; and Thiériot letters, 441
Argental, Madame d', 82, 181, 334. *See also* Argentals, the d'
Argentals, the d', 123, 164, 181, 196ff., 216, 256–57, 283, 288, 305, 328; disapprove Voltaire's departure from France, 224; and Madame Calas, 357; and Mademoiselle Corneille's wedding, 363; at *Mahomet* performance, 218;

and *Olympie,* 373; and *Phèdre,* 342; to Plombières, 284; and *Sémiramis,* 197; and Sirven affair, 391; Stanislas invites to Commercy, 198; and *Tancrède* dedication, 329; and Voltaire's relationship with Frederick, 250
Arget, d'. *See* Darget
Arnaud, Baculard d'. *See* Baculard d' Arnaud
Arnauld, Antoine, 369, 510
Arnelot (intendant), 430
Arnould, Sophie, 344, 468, 482
Arouet, Armand (brother), 5, 8–9, 55, 81, 85, 125–26, 369, 436, 507; death, 169–70
Arouet, François (father), 3ff., 14, 16, 17, 19, 24, 25, 28, 29, 31, 39, 46, 85; death, 54–55; at *Oedipe* performance, 41
Arouet, François (grandfather), 6
Arouet, Madame François (mother), 4, 6–7, 9
Arouet, François-Marie. *See* Voltaire, François-Marie Arouet de
Arouet, Hélènus, 5
Arouet, Marie (grandmother), 6
Arouet, Pierre, 6
Arouet family, 4–9
Arras, 429
Artémire, 51–52, 66
Artois, Comte d', 397, 477
Audibert, and Calas family, 355, 446
Augustine, St., 510
Augustins. *See* Grands Augustins; Petits Augustins
Austria, 57–58, 154, 302ff., 309. *See also* Holy Roman Empire; Seven Years' War; Vienna; War of the Austrian Succession
Autrey, Comtesse d', 152–53
Ayen, Duc d', 359

Babouc, 190
Backbiter, The, 160
Bacon de La Chevalerie (Freemason), 480
Baculard d'Arnaud, 222, 233–34, 246
Baden, Margravine of, 506
Bailly (mayor), 498
Balby, de, Frederick and, 243
Balearic Islands, 301
Balzac, Honoré de, 452
Barbara (servant), 370
Barbier (lawyer), 70
Bardy (cook), 487, 490

Barmécides, Les, 462
Baron d'Otrante, The (The Baron of
  Otranto), 424
Barry, Madame du. See Du Barry,
  Jeanne Bécu, Comtesse
Bar-sur-Aube, 220
Barthe (author), 462–63, 475–76
Basel, 307, 378
Basel, Bishop of, 284
Bastian, Brother, 413, 416–17
Bastille, Le, 43
Bastille, the, 34ff., 37–39, 43, 58, 79–80,
  81–82
Bath, Lord, 87
Bayeux, Bishop of, 160
Bayle, Pierre, 71–72, 241
Bayreuth, 163–64, 170
Bayreuth, Margrave of (husband), 286
Bayreuth, Margravine of, 151, 163–64,
  245, 264, 270, 285, 286, 288, 303–4;
  death, 306
Bazin (police officer), 35
Beaudridge, David de, 351ff., 355, 361
Beaumarchais, Pierre de, 163, 442, 506
Beaumont, Elie de, 359, 391
Beauregard, Abbé de, 483
Beauregard, Captain, 35, 58–59, 134
Beauregard, Prince de, 150
Beauteville, de (ambassador), 402–3, 412
Beauvau, Prince de (1778), 466, 477
Beauvau, princes of, 193
Belestat, Comtesse, 285–86
Belgium. See Brussels
Believers' Oracle, The, 414
Belleval, de, and Abbeville affair, 393
Benedict XIV (Pope), 175–76, 181, 183
Benedictines, 284–85
Benoit, Madame, 462, 465
Bentenek, Madame, 246
Berger (friend), 101, 146
Berlin, 152, 155, 160ff., 179, 204, 222, 223,
  231ff., 237, 240, 242, 246, 249ff., 263,
  265–66, 272, 276ff., 385, 432 (see also
  Frederick II; Prussia); Academy in
  (see Prussian Academy); and first
  edition of Siècle de Louis XIV, 252;
  La Beaumelle in, 253ff.; mass for
  Voltaire in Cathedral, 495; Tyrconnel
  ambassador in, 238
Berlin Gazette, 264
Bern, 286, 289, 295, 302, 460
Bernières, Marquis de (Président),
  65–66, 72, 130. See also Bernières, the
Bernières, Marquise de, 46, 55, 65–66,

74–75, 78, 81, 85, 91, 131–32. See also
  Bernières, the
Bernières, the, 65–66, 68, 73, 77, 91, 131
Bernis, Cardinal de (formerly Abbé de
  Bernis; "Babet le Bouquetière"), 159,
  177, 220, 301, 305–6, 355, 397, 426–27,
  438–39
Berry, Duchesse de (Regent's daughter),
  31, 35–36
Bert (curé of Ferney), 420, 421
Berthier, Father, 317–18, 320, 327
Bertrand, Pastor, 384
Bessières, Mademoiselle de, 85
Besterman, Theodore, 503, 506, 509, 512
Bible (scriptures), 365, 366. See also
  New Testament; Old Testament
Bibliothèque Nationale, 499
Bièvres, Marquis de, 6
Bigex (copyist), 414
Black Ladies, 389
Boccaccio, Giovanni, 431
Boileau, Nicolas, 9, 108, 180, 406, 444, 476
Bolingbroke, Lord, xi, 52, 64, 84, 455;
  and wife (Lady Bolingbroke; the
  Bolingbrokes), 64, 85
Bond (actor), 122
Bonnet, Charles, 400, 408–9, 488
Boor, The, 424
Bordeaux, Parlement of, 356
Bosleduc (doctor), 75
Bossuet, Jacques, 134, 510
Boswell, James, 378–80
Boufflers, Chevalier de, 374–75
Boufflers, Marquise de, 159, 193, 194, 197,
  205, 211ff., 374
Bouhier, Jean, 181
Bourbier, Le, 28, 42
Bourbon, Duc de, 54, 76, 81
Bourbon, Louis de. See Conti, Louis de
  Bourbon, Prince de
Bourbon-Vendôme, Philippe de, 15, 30
Bourette, Dame, 330
Bourgeois gentilhomme, Le, 507
Bourgès, Father, 354
Bourgogne, Duchesse de, 508
Boursoufle, Le, 192
Boyer (Bishop of Mirepoix), 159ff., 317
Braneas, Maréchal de, 102
Breslau, 252
Breteuil, de (Emilie's nephew), 386
Breteuil, Abbé de, 139–40
Breteuil, Baron de, 39, 102, 158
Breteuil family, 39, 102
Brinon (Freemason), 480

Bristol, George Digby, Lord, 454
Brizard (actor), 477
Brizard (surgeon's assistant), 493
Broglie, Maréchal de, 485
Brosses, Charles de, 313, 314, 332, 335,
    345–48, 356, 424–25, 442, 455
Brosses, Madame Charles de, 346
Brosses family, 501
Brumoy, Father, 11–12
Brunschwig, Duc de, 166
Brussels, 41, 59, 60, 61, 62–63, 65, 96, 117,
    122, 133, 149, 151, 152, 156, 166
Brutus, Lucius Junius, 92
Brutus, 92, 465, 496
Buffon, Georges Leclerc, Comte de, 259,
    355, 424–25, 444
Burgundy, 329, 332 (see also specific
    towns); Academy of, 345; Estates of,
    455; governor of (see Condé, Duc de)
Bussy, Abbé de, 51, 121
Byng, John, 301

Cabales, Les, 443–44
Cadiz, 206
Caen, 19
Caesar, Julius, 94. See also Jules César
Café Cradot, 109
Café Procope, 199
Cagliostro, Alessandro, Conte, 392
Cailhava (Freemason), 480
Calais, 82
Calas, Donat, 356, 357
Calas, Elisabeth (mother; wife), 350ff.,
    357–58, 359–60
Calas, Jean (father), x–xi, 350ff., 364,
    394, 437
Calas, Louis, 353, 354
Calas, Marc-Antoine. See Calas affair
Calas, Nanette, 360
Calas, Pierre (son), 350ff., 360
Calas affair, 350–61, 446, 449. See also
    Calas, Jean
Callet, Jacques, 135
Calvet, Dom, 284
Calvin, John, and Calvinism, 20, 289–90,
    392, 404, 510. See also Geneva
Cambrai, 60–61
Cambrai, Archbishop of. See Dubois,
    Cardinal; Saint-Albins, Charles de
Camisards, 20
Canada, 305, 315
Candide, x, 11, 295, 314–15, 326, 340, 381,
    382, 505
Canilhac, Abbé de, 175

Canteleu, 94
Capuchins, 427
CAR, LES, 321
Carmelites, 353
Carré, Jérôme, 327
Carrouges, 339, 405
Cartouche (bandit), 239
Cassel, 270
Catherine II, 183, 314, 342, 385–88, 397,
    399–400, 446, 454, 497; and Laws of
    Minos, 438; purchases Voltaire's
    papers, 501, 502
Catholicism. See specific Catholics;
    places
Catilina (Crébillon), 199, 207, 209, 219
Catilina (Voltaire). See Rome sauvée
Cato (Addison), 455
Caumartin, Abbé de, 34, 80
Caumartin, Marquis de, 28–29, 34, 50
Cavalier, Jean, 20
Caylus, de, and Temple du Goût, 98
Cénie, 222
Century of Louis XIV, The. See Siècle
    de Louis XIV, Le
Chabanon, Michel de, 83, 414
Chabot, Vicomte de, 190
Chabrillant, Colonel de, 415
Châlons, 171, 198, 200, 204
Champbonin (son), 125, 126, 138, 139
Champbonin, Madame, 112, 125, 138, 140,
    142, 158, 192
Champs, 177
Champs Elysées, 496
Chanteloup, 436, 437
Chantilly, 73
Chapelain, Jean, 110–11
Chapelle, Claude, 32
Charles VI, Emperor, 57
Charles VII, King, 512
Charles XII, 42. See also Histoire de
    Charles XII
Charles of Lorraine, 282
Charlot, and incident of faggots, 347
Charon (Paris official), 497
Charonne, 75–76, 102
Chartres, Duc de, 191
Chasot, Chevalier de, 237, 244
Chastellux, Chevalier de, 484
Châteauneuf, Marquis de, 19, 21, 24
Châteauneuf, François de Castagnier de
    (Abbé de Châteauneuf), 4, 9, 12, 15,
    507
Châteauroux, Duchesse de, 160, 167, 242
Château-Thierry, 200

Châtelet, du. *See* Du Châtelet
Châtenay, 3, 39
Châtillon (wigmaker), 90
Châtillon, estate at, 42
Chaulieu, Abbé de, 15, 18, 31, 99
Chaumex (enemy), 320, 327
Chauvelin, de (ambassador), 316, 491
Chauvelin, Madame de, 339
Chénier (composer), 498
Chesterfield, Philip Stanhope, Lord, 156, 172, 224, 252–53, 455
Child on the Throne, A. See Puero regnante
Chinese Orphan, The. See Orphelin de la Chine, L'
Choiseul, Duchesse de (the Choiseuls), 387, 396, 436–37
Choiseul, Etienne François, Duc de (the Choiseuls), 308–9, 310, 329, 338, 342, 359, 368, 383, 436–37, 438; and Geneva war, 412, 415; and Sirven affair, 391; and watch sales, 396, 397
Christian VII, King of Denmark, 425, 433
Christian Philosopher, A, 205
Christina, Queen of Sweden, 510
Chronique, La, 495
Chronology, 513–59
Cicero, 84
Cideville, Pierre, 31–32, 65, 92, 105, 152, 415
Cirey, 109ff., 117, 119–21ff., 144, 152, 154, 158, 167–68, 191ff., 209–10, 258, 291; life at, 135–42
Civil War in Geneva . . . , The. See Guerre civile de Gèneve . . . , La
Clairaut, Alexis, 208, 210
Clairon, Mademoiselle, 199, 216, 328–29, 377–78, 435–36, 474, 477
Clarke, Samuel, 86
Clement XII (Pope), 510
Clement XIII (Pope), 338–39
Clement XIV (Pope), 426–27
Clément, Jean Marie Bernard, 442–44
Clermond, Bishop of. *See* Massillon, Jean Baptiste
Clermont, Comte de, 182
Cleves, 142, 148–49, 394–95
Clinchant (secretary), 344
Cocchein, Captain (and wife), 254–55
Colbert, Jean Baptiste, 29, 86
Collé (critic), 415
College d'Harcourt, 112
Collini, Cosimo, 264, 265, 268, 272, 273,

276ff., 283, 284, 287ff., 293, 295ff.
Colmar, 281–84, 286, 291
Colmont, Henri-Camille de, 362
Colmont family, 362
Cologne Gazette (Gazette de Cologne), 489
Comédie Française, 29, 49–50, 78–79, 88, 199, 217, 251, 333, 476–78, 479, 481 (*see also* specific productions); Thibouville in charge of, 461
Comédie Italienne, 201, 424
Commentaire des oeuvres de Voltaire (Commentary on the Works of Voltaire), 431
Commentaires sur Corneille, 362, 363, 374
Commercy, 198, 201–4
Comnenus dynasty, 399
Condé, Duc de (Governor of Burgundy), 444, 479–80
Condé's regiment, 414
Condillac, Etienne de, 409, 511
Condorcet, Marie Caritat, Marquis de, 301, 409–10, 430, 442, 448, 449, 462, 476, 506
Confessions (Rousseau), 295
Congreve, William, 86–87
Constance, 438
Constantinople, 399
"Conseiller du roi," 507
Contant d'Orval, 3, 27, 45, 83, 84, 174
Contantin (husband of Dunoyer daughter), 20
Contest, 88
Conti, Louis de Bourbon, Prince de, 14, 41, 54, 80
Conversations on the Plurality of Worlds, 54
Convulsionaries, 125
Copenhagen, 253
Coquette punie, La, 257
Cordeliers, the, 494
Cordier de Saint-Firmin (Freemason), 480
Corneille, Jean-François (father of Marie-Françoise Dupuits), 333, 334, 363
Corneille, Marie-Françoise. *See* Dupuits de la Chaux, Marie-Françoise
Corneille, Marthe, 333
Corneille, Pierre, 9, 18, 56, 96, 253, 293, 330, 333, 334, 342, 363, 374, 510
Corneille, Pierre (cousin of playwright), 333

Corneille, Pierre (uncle of playwright), 333

Corneille family, 363–64

Correspondance. See Letters

Couet, Abbé, 76

Courtanvaux, Marquis de, 190–91

Covelle, Robert, 405–6

Coventry, Duchess of, 455

Cramer (bookseller), 267, 368; wife (the Cramers), 374, 446

Crébillon, Prosper Jolyot de, 92, 160, 183, 198ff., 207, 209, 219, 373; death, 343

Cressy brothers, 336

Critical Letters by an English Traveler, 404

Cumberland, William Augustus, Duke of, 178

Cüstrin, 306

Damilaville (friend), 359, 365, 366, 368, 369, 395, 425, 441

Dangeau, Abbé, 399

Danish Lady at the Theater, The, 253

Darget (D'Arget; Frederick's secretary), 237–38, 249, 255, 256, 285, 295

Daumart, Charles, 413

Daumart, Marie, 507

Daumart family, 6–7, 8

Death of Socrates, The, 327

Decameron, 431

Deffand, Marquise du. *See* Du Deffand, Marie de Vichy-Chamrond, Marquise

Délices, Les, 289–302, 311, 314, 316, 323, 329, 339, 343, 368, 386, 404, 409; Besterman and, 503, 506

Delille, Abbé, 443

Deluc (enemy), 381

Demoulin (lawyer), 59, 101, 128–29

Denis, Marie-Louise (Madame Denis; niece), 125, 126, 152, 201, 216ff., 229, 232–33, 247, 256–57, 263, 271, 280ff., 293, 316, 335, 368, 373, 381, 384, 404, 411, 412, 415, 432–33, 444ff., 451, 455, 462ff., 508, 511; and Duvivier, 475, 494, 501ff.; and Easter communion, 337; and Frankfurt incident, 275ff., 298, 303, 415; and Frederick II, 223, 232, 250–51, 275ff., 343, 415; helps with manufactory workers, 445; and *Irène,* 462; Le Kain finds it impossible to act opposite, 361; love of tragedy, 415; as lover of Voltaire, 297–98; and Mademoiselle Corneille, 334; Madame Du Deffand characterizes, 470; at Plombières, 284; and remarriage of brother-in-law, Florian, 438; sends fan to Dame Bourette, 330; takes to acting, 221; and *Tancrède,* 328; and theft of *Pucelle* manuscript, 292; thrown out of Ferney, 417, 418; and Voltaire's death, funeral, estate, 493ff., 501ff.; and Voltaire's last return to Paris; his illness, 463ff., 472ff., 477, 479, 485, 487, 489, 490; and Ximénès, 251, 291

Denis, Nicolas-Charles (husband), 126, 217, 508

Denmark, 253, 255, 425, 433

Denon, Vivant, 453–54

Depery, Abbé, 489

Descartes, René, 54, 98, 108, 258, 512

Deschauffours, executed for sodomy, 77

Desfontaines, Pierre Guyot, 59, 77–78, 89–90, 112–14, 116, 117, 129–30, 132ff., 138, 142, 182, 219, 220; and *Henriade (La Ligue),* 72

Desmaret, Léopold, 142

Devaux, "Pampan," 136, 137, 141

Dialogues and Conversations, 3, 27, 45, 100, 146, 349, 350

Diatribe du docteur Akakia . . . , La (The Diatribe of Dr. Akakia . . .), 261–62ff., 269

Dictionary, Academy's, 483–84, 485

Dictionnaire historique et critique (Bayle's Dictionary), 241

Dictionnaire philosophique. See Philosophical Dictionary

Diderot, Denis, 219, 236, 299, 327ff., 344, 345, 361, 366, 387, 394, 434, 511

Didot (printer), 157

Dijon, 287, 331, 336, 338, 339, 345, 347, 414, 417, 430, 464, 480

Directory, the, 499

Discours pronouncé à la porte . . . , 181, 183

Discours sur l'origine de l'inégalité . . . , 294

Dominicans, 357

Dompierre d'Hornoy (grandnephew; M. Hornoy), 368, 486, 492ff., 502, 503

Dompierre d'Hornoy, Comte de (present-day), 5

Dompierre d'Hornoy, Marie-Elisabeth (Fontaine d'Hornoy; later Marquise de Florian), 125, 126–27, 221, 283, 345, 385, 388, 418, 438, 444, 508, 511

Dompierre d'Hornoy, Nicolas-Joseph

(Fontaine d'Hornoy; husband),
126–27, 170, 508
Dompierre d'Hornoys, the, 508
Dorn (notary), 278, 279
Dorothea, Princess (Frederick's sister),
124
Dorothea of Saxe-Meiningen
(Margravine of Gotha), 270, 273, 280,
285, 302, 309–10
Dresden, 244
Dreux-Brézé, Monseigneur de, 499
Droit du seigneur, Le, 342–43
Du Barry, Jeanne Bécu, Comtesse, 460,
463, 468
Dubois, Cardinal, 57, 58, 60, 61
Du Châtelet, Marquis (husband), 102,
109, 112, 114, 117, 121, 131, 137, 138,
141–42; wife attempts to get pension
for, 193, 197; and wife's death, 214, 215
Du Châtelet, Gabrielle-Emilie, Marquise,
39, 102–4, 105, 108ff., 119ff., 123ff., 128,
130ff., 142ff., 147, 149, 151ff., 160–61,
162, 166ff., 177–78, 179, 186, 188ff.,
204ff., 259, 297, 298, 449; attempt to get
pension for husband from Stanislas,
193, 197; birth of child; death, 174,
212–16; and gambling, 189, 204, 211;
and life at Cirey, 135ff.; on Madame
Bernières, 132; Nattier portrait, 503;
pregnancy; hard work; fear of death,
204, 207–9; and Saint-Lambert;
deterioration of Voltaire relationship,
195–97, 201–4ff.
Du Châtelet family, 102, 114
Du Châtelets (sons), 112, 171, 208, 215
Duclos (academician), 224, 321
Duclos, Mademoiselle. See Lecouvreur,
Adrienne
Ducoux (lawyer), 353
Du Deffand, Marie de Vichy-Chamrond,
Marquise, 82, 103, 104, 142, 154–55, 312,
372, 387, 415, 436, 437, 469–70, 481, 501
Dufay, Madame, 91
Dugros (doctor), 420–21
Du Hausset, Madame, 322–23
Dujarry, Abbé, 18
Du Luchet, Marquis, 445, 446
Du Luchet, Marquise, 445–46
Du Maine, Duchesse, 31, 51, 186, 188,
190, 191, 221–22, 270
Dumarsais, and Sermon of the Fifty, 366
Dumesnil, Mademoiselle, 159, 199
Dunoyer, Captain (husband of Dame
Dunoyer), 20, 21

Dunoyer, Dame, 19–22
Dunoyer, Mademoiselle (actress), 44
Dunoyer, Olympe (Pimpette), 20–26
Du Pin-Gouvernet. See La Tour du
Pin-Gouvernet
Dupré de Saint-Maur, on Le Franc, 319
Dupuits, Mademoiselle, 375
Dupuits de la Chaux (husband of
Corneille's grandniece), 362–63, 417,
479
Dupuits de la Chaux, Marie-Française
("Rodogune"; grandniece of
Corneille), 330, 331, 333–35ff., 342,
361–64, 374, 375, 417
Duras, Duc de, 239, 397
Durey de Morsan (visitor), 413
Du Thil, Mademoiselle, 175, 189, 211, 291
Duvernet, Théophile, 10
Duvivier (husband of Madame Denis),
475, 494, 501ff.
Duvivier, Madame. See Denis,
Marie-Louise

Easter, 197, 283–84, 337, 418–19. See also
Lent
Eccentrics, The, 191
Ecossaise, L' (The Scotswoman), 313,
327, 335
Ecueil du sage, L', 343
Egoist, The, 462
Eléments de la physique de Newton, Les
(Elements of Newtonian Physics),
123, 127, 129
Elizabeth, Tsarina, 172, 382–83
Elizabeth Christina, Queen, 241
Eloge de l'hypocrisie, 405
Embrun, Council of, 288
Emden, 207
Emile, 367, 381, 400, 411
Encyclopédie; Encyclopedists, 285, 299,
300, 316–17ff., 327, 366, 431, 494. See
also specific contributors
Enfant prodigue, L', 117, 191
England; the English, 20, 60, 84–90, 93,
178, 301, 305, 343, 484–85. See also
Lettres philosophiques; London
Entretiens sur la pluralité des mondes, 54
Envieux, L', 130
Eon de Beaumont, Charles, Chevalier d',
473
Epinay, Louise d', 328
Epitre à mon vaisseau (Epistle to My
Ship), 422

Epitre à Uranie (*Epistle to Urania*), 62, 63, 99, 117

Epitre aux Mânes de Génonville (*Epistle to the Spirit of Genonville*), 69

Epitre des tus et des vous (*The Epistle of Thees and Yous*), 88

Eriphyle, 95–96

Escalonne, David d', 355

Esprit des lois, 404

Essai d'education nationale (*Essay on National Education*), 364–65

Essai sur l'histoire universelle (*Essay on the History of the World*), 404

Essay on Morals, 267–68

Essonnes, 190

Estrées, Gabrielle d', 15

Etallonde (visitor), 446

Etampes, 239

Etienne-du-Mont, curé of, 494

Etioles, 177

Eugene, Prince, 58

Evénements de l'année 1744 (*The Events of the Year 1744*), 169

Extrait des sentiments de Jean Meslier (*Extract from the Opinions of Jean Meslier*), 365, 366

Fabry (Deputy Governor of Gex), 444, 455

Falkener, Sir Everard, 85–86, 178

Farewell to Life, A, 304–5

Farian de Saint-Ange, de (orator), 473

Farnese Venus and Hercules, 136

Favart, Charles Simon, 321

Feeling of the People, The, 383

Fénelon, François de la Mothe, 60, 510

Ferdinand VI, King of Spain, 300

Ferloz, Catherine, 405–6

Ferney (estate and village), 313ff., 320, 329, 330, 331–38, 343–45, 361–64, 369–70, 372–80, 383, 388, 393, 395–97, 399ff., 412–27, 429ff., 439, 445–57, 458–60, 462ff., 472ff., 479–80, 483, 486, 501; church at, 337–38, 344–45, 378, 380, 409, 410, 414, 492, 509; disposal of, 502; library at; disposal of, 501–2; Madame Denis ordered to leave, 417–18; manufactories; watchmaking, 396–97, 400ff., 444, 445; present-day, 503, 504; rebuilding of Château, 331; tomb for Voltaire at, 492

Ferney, curé of, 420, 421

Ferney-Voltaire (village), 504. *See also* Ferney

Ferriole, Madame de, 84

Fessi, Jean, 336

Fête de Ramire, La, 180, 294

Flammarens, Mademoiselle de, 102

Flanders, 60–61, 142

Flaubert, Gustave, 430

Fleury, André Hercule, Cardinal de, 78, 97, 107, 150, 151, 154–55ff., 306, 508; death, 158

Flirt Punished, The, 257

Florian, Marquis de, 303, 345, 438–39, 445

Florian, Marquise de (née Joly), 439

Florian, Marquise de (née Rillet), 438–39

Florian, Marie-Elisabeth, Marquise de. *See* Dompierre d'Hornoy, Marie-Elisabeth

Foix, 431

Fontaine d'Hornoy. *See* Dompierre d'Hornoy

Fontainebleau, 177–78, 186, 187, 292–93, 321–22, 425

Fontaine-Martel, Comtesse de, 95ff., 153–54, 376, 441

Fontenelle, Bernard le Bovier de, 54, 57, 123, 158, 182, 183, 203, 216, 333, 334, 337, 404, 473

Fontenelle, Marthe (sister of Corneille), 333

Fontenoy, 172, 176, 178, 180, 220

Forcalquier, Comte de, 112

Forges, 72–73, 76, 248

Formey (chancellor), 244–45

Formont, letter to, 118

Fouquet, Nicolas, 48

Fox, Charles James, son of, 311

Foxes and the Wolves, The, 369

Fragments on History, 229

France. *See* specific citizens, places, wars, works

Franche-Comté, 430

Francheville, de (King's councillor), 252

Francis I, Emperor, 274

Franciscans, 427, 494

Frankfurt, 271–80, 285, 298, 310, 415

Franklin, Benjamin, 467, 484, 495

Fredendorff (secretary), 271, 276, 279–80

Frederick II (Frederick the Great; King of Prussia), 118, 121–22, 124–15, 132, 144–45, 146–47ff., 160ff., 179, 183, 195, 203, 204–5, 210, 221ff., 230–32, 234–66, 268ff., 295, 296, 302–5, 306–11, 384, 385, 388, 394, 422, 427, 432, 471; and *Abrégé de l'histoire universelle*, 282; and *Candide*, 314; and Cleves estates of

Châtelets, 141; concludes peace with Austria, 154; and death of Emilie, 174, 215; and death of Voltaire, 494, 495, 505; and Emden shipping company, 207; escritoire sent to Voltaire, 137; and Frankfurt incident, 271–80, 285, 298, 310, 415; and Joseph II's trip near Ferney, 459; on *l'Infâme*, 364; meets Voltaire, 148–49; and opera based on *Mérope*, 302; and statue of Voltaire, 433

Frederick William, King, 122, 234

Freemasons; Masonic lodges, 475, 499

Frequent Communion, 55

Fréron, Elie, 13, 178–79, 219–21, 248, 271, 323–24, 334–35, 344, 443, 444; and *Ane littéraire*, 331; and *Zaïre*, 328

Fréron, Madame Elie, 327, 457–58

Freytag, Franz von, Baron, 271–80, 303

Fronde, the, 4

Gabriel, Jacques Ange, 474

Gaillard d'Etallonde, 392

Gallien (visitor), 413

Gargantua, 46, 406

Garrick, David, 298

Gâtine, 5–6

Gautier, Abbé, 468–69, 470–72, 488, 489

Gay, John, 84

Gazette de Cologne, 489

Gedoyn, Abbé, 9, 12–13

Genesis, Book of, 425

Geneva, 288–302, 307, 313–14, 316, 328, 329, 336, 339ff., 361, 365, 368, 380–81ff., 400–9, 412, 414, 417, 439ff., 451 (*see also* Délices, Les); Calases in, 355, 356; *natifs*, 396, 397, 400, 402–4, 445; and teachers for Catherine II, 388; and watchmaking, 396, 397, 400, 402–4, 445

Genlis, Madame de, 451–52

Génonville (friend), 33, 42, 69–70, 71

George I, King, 85, 89

George III, King, 238

Germany, 149ff., 315. *See also Annales de l'empire;* Prussia; specified places, rulers

Gervasi (doctor), 71, 284

Gex, 338, 347, 427, 430, 454–55, 456; Deputy Governor of (*see* Fabry)

Gisors, Madame de, 492

Glasgow, 379

Gluck, Christoph von, 466

God, existence of, 410

Goertz, Baron, 42, 51

Goethe, Johann Wolfgang von, 368

Golden Calf, 434

Gontaut, Duc de, 191

Gorani (Italian nobleman), 399

Gotha, Margravine of. *See* Dorothea of Saxe-Meiningen

Gotha, 255, 270

Gouvernet. *See* La Tour du Pin-Gouvernet

Graffigny, brutality of, 135

Graffigny, Madame de, 124–25, 133, 135–37ff., 158, 222, 254

Grands Augustins, monastery of the, 46

Granval (actor), 199

Grasset (bookseller), 292

Greece, 399–400

Grécourt, Abbé, 64–65

Grenoble, 253

Gresset, Jean, 117, 160, 324–25

Grétry, André, 423–24

Greuze, Jean, 362

Grimm, Friedrich, 325, 424, 425, 445, 447, 488, 502

Guèbres, Les, 423

Guénée, Abbé, 459

Guerre civile de Genève . . . , La, 405–7, 416–18

Guiguer (host), 289

Guînard, Mademoiselle, 191, 459

Guise, Duc de, 94, 104

Guise, Duchesse de, 104

Guise family, 104ff.

Guitant, Comtesse de, 49

Gustave, 98

Hague, The, 19–23, 65, 147–48, 149, 161, 162, 282

Halle aux Vins, 500

Haller, Albrecht von, 236–37, 376, 377, 409, 460

Hamburg, 270, 273, 276

Harcourt, Comte d', 343

Haroué, M., 92

Hausset, Madame du. *See* Du Hausset, Madame

Heloise and Abelard, 512

Helvétius, Claude, 431, 480

Hénault (Président), 48, 52–53, 65, 92, 154, 155, 167–68, 169, 191

Hennin (French representative), 400–1ff., 406, 417, 444, 455

Henri IV, 52, 496. *See also Henriade, La*

Henriade, La (La Ligue), 38, 52–53, 58, 63ff., 68ff., 71–72, 84, 85, 88–89ff.,

131, 159, 175, 206, 381, 382, 385, 496;
Desfontaines and pirated edition, 113;
Frederick and, 144; Jean-Baptiste
Rousseau and, 14, 63; La Beaumelle
and, 256, 431; Stanislas of Poland and,
76; Trublet on, 325
Hérault (police superintendent), 99, 111,
115, 116, 134, 157, 201
Herodotus, 463
Hertford, 150
Hervey, Lord, 455; and wife, 87
Hesse, Landgrave of, 270
Hesse, Margravine of, 411
Hippocrate amoureux (Hippocrates in
Love), 34
Hirsch (Hirschell; broker), 243–44, 247,
258
Histoire de Charles XII (History of
Charles XII), 42, 83, 88, 91ff., 104
Histoire d'Elisabeth Canning et de
Calas, 358–59
Histoire du Parlement de Paris (History
of the Parliament), 423, 436, 437, 491
Histoire du Tsar Pierre le Grand
(History of Peter the Great), 315,
384–85
Histoire naturelle, L', 425, 439
Historical Miscellanea, 83, 174, 371
Hogguers, Baron, 42, 50, 51
Holbach, Paul Thiry, Baron d', 236, 409,
410–11, 511
Holland, 122–23, 162. See also
Amsterdam; Hague, The
Holy Roman Empire. See Annales de
l'empire; Austria; specific places,
rulers
Homer, 37
Homme aux quarante écus, L', 423
Homme Machine, L', 236
Homme Personnel, L', 462
Horbourg, 281
Hornoy. See Dompierre d'Hornoy
Hôtel de Lambert, 154
Hôtel de Villarceaux, 479, 483
Hôtel de Villeroy, 169
Houdetot, Madame d', 195, 443
Houdon, Jean, 503, 505
Hugo, Victor, 458
Huguenots, 19ff. See also Calas affair;
Geneva; Sirven case
Human Machine, The, 236
Huron, Le, 424

IFS, 320–21
Imhof (landlord), 378

India, 315
Indies, the, 206, 343
Indies Company, 55
Indiscret, L', 73, 76
Inès de Castro, 68, 77
Infâme, l', 317, 337, 364, 365, 368, 404
Ingénu, L', 424
Innocent, The, 424
In Praise of Hypocrisy, 405
Irène, 461–63, 466, 468, 470, 473–74ff., 499
Isabeau (police officer), 35, 36–37
Italy, 315. See also Rome
Ivan, Catherine II and, 386–87
I've seen . . . See J'ai vu . . .

Jacobins, 499
Jacobites, 238
Jacquier, Father, 168
Jainval, Mademoiselle, 468
J'ai vu . . . , 34, 35
Jansen, Cornelius, 510
Jansenism, 55, 72, 125, 156, 170, 369, 381,
392
Jealous Man, The, 130
Jesuits, 9–12, 72, 77, 181, 219, 281, 317–18,
336–37, 368–69, 413–14, 427, 480, 510
(see also specific persons); and Mort
de César, 94; and Newton book, 127;
in Paraguay, war on, 300
Jesus Christ, 156, 381
Joan of Arc, 110–11, 512. See also
Pucelle, La
John, feast of St., 316
Johnson, Samuel, 379
Joigny, 464
Jordan, Charles-Etienne, 151
Jore, Claude-François, 94, 106ff., 115–16,
128, 247
Joseph II, Emperor, 459–60
Journal de Trévoux, 127, 317, 369
Jugement de Pluton (Judgment of
Pluto), 63
Jugements sur quelques ouvrages
nouveaux (Judgments on Various
New Works), 220
Jules César, 160, 161

Kehl, 506
Keith, George (Lord Keith), 275–76
Keith brothers, 238. See also Keith,
George
Keyserling, Baron von, 124–25, 148
Knights of Saint John of Jerusalem, 15,
509
Koenig, Samuel, 143, 168, 259–60, 267

Kolin, 303
Königsberg, 222

La Barre, Chevalier, 392–94, 396, 437, 450
La Beaumelle, de (enemy), 158, 182, 253–56, 259, 263, 270–71, 352, 430, 431
La Brosse, and Voltaire's brain, 500
La Chalotais, de, essay on education, 364–65
La Chassagne, Mademoiselle, 477
La Condamine, de, letter to, 100
La Fare (poet), 15, 18
La Fare, Madame de, 46
La Fare, Marquis de, 46–47
La Faye, M. de, 52, 117
La Fonds, de (amateur historian), 7
La Fontaine, Jean de, x, 12
La Fosse, Madame, 75–76
La Galaizière, de (administrator), 193, 195, 211
La Grange-Chancel (author), 51
La Harpe, Jean-François de, 331, 413, 414, 415–17, 435, 442, 449, 462, 466, 472, 486, 503, 511
Lalande (Freemason), 475, 480
Lally, Thomas Arthur, Baron de Tollendal, Comte de, 393, 394, 430, 437, 486
La Marche, Fyot de, 10
La Mattrie, Julien Offray de, 234, 236–37, 251–52, 261, 366
Lamoignon, de (chancellor), 357, 360
La Morlière (aide to Voltaire), 199, 291
La Motte, Inès de Castro by, 68, 77
Lampoon Concerning Divorce, 113
La Neuville, Madame de, 112
Languedoc, 287, 288, 356, 389–92
La Noue, de (actor), 152
Lapland, 257
La Popelinière (general), 179, 318, 441
La Popelinière, Madame de, 180
Largillière, Nicolas de, 38, 482, 483, 499, 503
La Roche-Aymon, Cardinal de, 459
La Salle, de (magistrate), 354
La Touche, Chevalier de, 265
La Tour du Pin-Gouvernet, Marquis de, 88, 456
La Tour du Pin-Gouvernet, Marquise de. See Livry, Suzanne de
La Tour du Pin-Gouvernets, 88
L'Attaignant (freethinker), 472
Lauragais, Comte de, 198, 344
Lauragais, Duchesse de, 344
Lausanne, 286, 288, 289, 295, 302, 390

La Vallière, Duc de, 219, 301
Lavasseur, Mademoiselle, 407
La Vaysse, and Calas affair, 350ff., 431
Law, John; Law system, 53–54, 55, 67, 239
Lawfeld, 188
Laws of Minos. See Lois de Minos, Les
League, The. See Henriade, La
Le Bas (engraver), 217
La Bas, Madame, 217
Le Blanc (statesman), 58, 59, 86
Lebrun (author of lampoon), 34
Le Brun, Charles, 154
Le Brun, Ponce Denis Ecouchard, 331, 333, 334, 468
Le Coq (friend), 10–11
Lecouvreur, Adrienne (Mademoiselle Duclos), 28, 29, 51, 70ff., 78, 79; death, 93
Lectern, The, 406
Le Franc, Jean-Georges (Bishop of Puy), 319, 322–23, 367–68
Le Franc, Jean-Jacques, Marquis de Pompignan, 115, 318–24, 367, 416
Le Goux (nephew), 342
Le Goux (uncle), 342–43
Leibnitz, Gottfried Wilhelm, Baron von; Leibnitzians, 158, 259
Leipzig, 268–69
Lejay, Father, 10
Le Kain (actor), 218, 219, 222, 249, 257, 289, 290, 292, 361, 462; death, 465; in Ferney, 439, 440
Lemaître (journalist), 497
Lenclos, Ninon de, 4, 9, 12–13
Lenoir (superintendent of police), 492
Lenormand d'Etioles (married to Madame Pompadour), 176
Lenormand de Tournehem (general), 176
Lent, 61, 300. See also Easter
Léopold, Duc, 135
Lepelletier (comptroller of finances), 91–92
L'Espine, de, 368
Lessing, Gotthold, 247
Le Sueur, Eustache, 154
Letourneur, Pierre, 458
Letters, x, 504–6. See also specific correspondents
Letters Concerning the English Nation. See Lettres philosophiques
Letter to . . . See Lettre à . . .
Lettre à d'Alembert sur les spectacles

(*Letter to D'Alembert on the Theater*), 300

Lettre à la lune . . . (Letter to the Moon . . .), 404

Lettre des frères Calas (Letter from the Calas Brothers), 359

Lettre d'un académicien de Berlin, 260–61

Lettre d'un Quaker (Letter from a Quaker), 367–68

Lettres à la Comtesse de X. sur quelques écrits modernes (Letters to the Comtesse X. on Certain Modern Writings), 220

Lettres aux anglais. See Lettres philosophiques

Lettres critiques d'un voyageur anglais, 404

Lettres d'Amabaal, 423

Lettres de quelques Juifs portugais (Letters from Certain Portuguese Jews), 459

Lettres écrites de la montagne (Letters from the Mountain), 382, 383

Lettres historique et galantes (Letters Historical and Gallant), 25

Lettres philosophiques (Lettres aux anglais), 94, 97, 98–99, 106–8, 115–16, 131

Lettres sur les écrits de ce temps (Letters on Present-day Writings), 220

Le Vau, Louis, 154

Levi, Salomon, 57–58, 60

Le Vier (printer), 65

Libelle du divorce, 113

Liège, 144, 148, 149

Ligne, Prince de, 375–77

Ligue, La. See Henriade, La

Lille, 152, 504

Linant (visitor), 112, 416

Linguet, and Voltaire correspondence, 365, 461, 466

Lisbon, 294, 315

Literary Ass, The, 331

Literary Miscellanea, 83, 491

Literary Miscellanea in Honor of Monsieur Lefebre, 84

Literary Year. See Année littéraire

Livry, Suzanne de (Marquise de La Tour du Pin-Gouvernet), 32–33, 36, 50, 69, 88, 456, 482–83

Lixin, Prince de, 106

Locke, John, 367

Loge des Neuf-Soeurs, 175

Lois de Minos, Les, 388, 438, 442

London, 82, 84ff., 106–7, 122, 124, 301

Longchamp (butler; later secretary), 119, 186–87, 190, 198, 200, 202, 204, 206, 209, 216, 232, 247; and Emilie's death, 212, 213

Lorge, Comte de, 285–86

Lorge, Duc de, 373

Lorraine, Duc de. *See* Stanislas, King of Lorraine

Lorraine, Duchesse de, 274

Lorraine, 92, 108–9. *See also* Stanislas, King of Lorriane; specific places

Lorry (doctor), 472, 490

Lort, Marquis de, 480

Louis (Dauphin), 170, 319, 322, 323

Louis IX (St. Louis), 210, 510

Louis XIII, 6, 18

Louis XIV, 16, 18, 21, 29, 30, 40, 70, 234, 239, 254, 342, 510. *See also Siècle de Louis XIV, Le*

Louis XV (King), 74, 76–77, 91, 122, 150, 155, 157, 158, 160, 161, 165, 167, 176ff., 183, 187–88, 191, 201, 205–6, 207, 218, 219, 224, 242, 245, 282, 287, 307, 330, 343, 407, 420, 425, 430, 436, 453, 463; and Calas affair, 358ff.; and Corneille's *Collected Works*, 342; and Crébillon's *Catilina*, 199, 207, 219; death, 445; and dissolving of Parlements, 436; and Easter devotions, 197; and *Enfant prodigue*, 191; and Fontenoy poem, 176; and *Henriade*, 65; and Le Franc, 319, 321–22; letter to Tsarina drafted by Voltaire, 172; marriage to Maria Leczinska, 76; and Maupertuis' move to Berlin, 258; and *Orphelin de la Chine*, 292–93; Paris celebrates recovery from illness, 168–69; and *Princess de Navarre*, 170–71; and *Siècle de Louis XIV*, 114; and *Tancrède* dedication, 329; and *Temple de la Gloire*, 176ff.; Tyrconnel as Berlin ambassador for, 238

Louis XVI (King), 444–45, 454, 463, 470, 473, 479, 481, 483, 492; as prisoner, 497, 498

Louis XVI style, 453

Louis-le-Grand, 9–13, 219, 287

Louis Philippe, Duc d'Orléans. *See* Orléans, Louis Philippe, Duc d'

Louis Philippe, King, 451, 482

Louvois, François le Tellier, Marquis de, 29

Low Countries, 110. *See also* Holland; specific cities

Luçan, Bishop of. *See* Bussy, Abbé de

Luchet, du. *See* Du Luchet

Lucretius, 61

Lunéville, 112, 192–93ff. *See also* Stanislas, King of Lorraine

Lutrin, Le, 406

Luxembourg, Duchesse de, 141, 159

Luxembourg, Maréchal de, 341

Luxembourg, Maréchale de, 484–85

Luynes, Duchesse de, 178

Lyons, 287, 288, 290, 431

Lyons, Archbishop of. *See* Tencin, Cardinal de

Lyttleton, Lord, 329–30

Machault, de (minister of police), 50

Madame Bovary, 430

Mahomet, 144, 152–53, 155–56, 175, 176, 218, 230, 440, 494

Mahon, Lord, 439–40

Maid, The. See Pucelle, La

Mailly, Madame de, 155

Maine, Duchesse du. *See* Du Maine, Duchesse

Maintenon, Françoise d'Aubergné, Marquise de, 15, 21, 253ff.

Mainz, 280

Maisons, de (Président), 69, 70–71, 94–95

Maisons, Madame de, 71

Maisons, Château de, 70

Malesherbes, Chrétien de Lamoignon de, 317, 319, 335, 455

Mallepart family, 6, 8

Mallet du Pan (visitor), 411

Man about Town, The. See Mondain, Le

Mannheim, 280–81

Mannory, Louis, 184

Man of the World, 3

Mansart, Jules, 70

Manstein (friend), 260

Man Who Was All Puffed Up, The, 192

Man with Forty Crowns, The, 423

Marais (barrister), 80

Marat, Clément, 512

Marburg, 271

Marceton family, 6

Marchand (cousin), 161

Marchant, Marie, 6

Marchant, Mathieu, 6

Marianne, 66, 70, 72ff., 83, 98

Maria Theresa, Empress, 41, 295, 305, 342, 459

Marie-Antoinette, Queen, 463, 467, 474, 479, 498

Marie d'en Haut, convent of, 253

Marie Lesczynska (Maria), Queen, 91, 178, 191, 194, 198, 201, 293, 361

Marie Louise (Dauphine), 169, 198, 407

Mariette (lawyer), 358, 359

Marin, Jean, 441

Marivaux, Pierre Carlet de Chamblain de, 88, 185

Marlborough, Duchess of, 87–88, 89

Marlborough, John Churchill, Duke of, xi

Marly, 444

Marmantel, Jean-François, 186, 207, 216, 217, 219, 435, 449, 466, 511

Marot, Clément, x

Marquet (army contractor), 162

Martel, Madame de. *See* Fontaine-Martel, Comtesse de

Masonic lodges, 475, 499

Massillon, Jean Baptiste, 57, 422–23

Maupeou, René de, 429, 436, 437

Maupertuis, Pierre, 98–99, 106, 109, 111–12, 148, 158, 183, 234, 235–36, 243, 257–63ff., 368–69, 270, 285, 307; at Cirey, 140; death, 311; and Koenig, 143; La Beaumelle and, 253, 255, 256; Le Franc gets Academy chair, 319; at Plombières, 284; president of Academy in Berlin, 179

Maurepas, Jean Phélippeaux, Comte de, 91, 116, 142, 144, 159, 160, 445

Mazamet, 389ff.

Mazarin, Jules, 29

Méchant, Le, 160

Meddler, The. See Indiscret, L'

Medicin de campagne, Le, 452

Medina (Portuguese Jew), 85

Meiningen, Duke of, 274

Melun, Duc de, 73

Memnon, 190

Mémoires (Voltaire), 271, 302, 314

Mémoires de Madame de Maintenon, 253–54

Mémoires secrets destinés pour servir à la vie de Voltaire, 505

Mémoires secrets sur le roi de Prusse, 417

Menou, Father, 193, 194, 284

Mercure, Le, 113, 114

Mérope, 4, 11–12, 144, 158–59, 194, 233, 243, 302, 414

Merville, Guyot de, 25

Meslay (Président), 480
Meslier, Jean, 365–66, 367
Mes pensées, au qu'en dira-t-on?, 253ff.
Metz, 168
Meynard (clerk), 356
Michel, Charles, 153
Michelet, Jules, 53
Micromégas, x, 190
Mignot (husband of Voltaire's sister), 9, 444
Mignot, Marie-Elisabeth (niece). *See* Dompierre d'Hornoy, Marie-Elisabeth
Mignot, Marie-Louise (niece). *See* Denis, Marie-Louise
Mignot, Marie-Marguerite (sister), 9, 81, 85, 125
Mignot, Vincent (Abbé Mignot; nephew), 216, 444, 471, 488, 492ff., 502, 503, 508
Milton, John, 87
Mimeure, Marquis de, 67
Mimeure, Marquise de, 49, 67ff., 75
Mirabeau, Honoré Riquetti, Comte de, 17, 323
Mire, The. See Bourbier, Le
Mirepoix, de, Frederick sends Voltaire's letters to, 165
Mirepoix, Bishop of. *See* Boyer
Miromesnil, de (Keeper of the Seals), 483
Mithouart (apothecary), 493, 499
Mithouart (son), 499–500
Mithouart, Mademoiselle, 500
Mithouart family, 500
Modena, Duke of, 510
Moens, curé de, 314, 332, 335–36, 338, 347
Moisnel (in Abbeville case), 392
Molditz, 152–53, 237, 258
Molé, Madame, 330, 468
Molé, Bernard, 330
Molière, Jean Baptiste Poquelin, x, 248, 407, 492, 507
Mondain, Le, 121, 136
Monjeu, 106
Montaigne, Michel Eyquem, Seigneur de, x, 284
Montauban, 318, 322, 323
Montbailli affair, 429–30
Montesquieu, Charles de Secondat, Baron de, 181, 183, 404, 425, 511
Montesson, Comtesse de, 481
Montmorency, 340
Montmorency, Comte de, 441
Montpellier, 439

Montriond, 295, 302
Morangies case, 430
Morellet, André (Abbé), 320–21
Morion, 289. *See also* Délices, Les
Mort de César, La, 94
Mort de Socrate, La, 327
Mouchon, Antoine, 440
Mouhy, Chevalier de, 129
Moulins, Bishop of, 499
Moulton, Paul-Claude, 391
Moussinot, Abbé, 7, 123, 125, 128, 129, 206
Moylard, Château of, 148
Mullet, Jean de, 411–12
Münster, 341
Musée Carnavalet, 512
Muses rivales, Les, 179–80
Musset, Alfred de, 430, 503
Mustapha (Sultan), 397
My Thoughts, or What Will People Say? See Mes pensées, au qu'en dira-t-on?

Nadal, Abbé, 73–74
Nancy, 92, 200
Nangis, 192
Nanine, 209, 478
Nantua, 464
Napoleon, 505
Napoleon III (Emperor), 499, 500
Nattier, Jean Marc, 503
Natural History. See Histoire naturelle, L'
Néaulme (bookseller), 282
Necker, Jacques, 355, 448, 467
Necker, Madame Jacques, 433, 434, 467
Netherlands. *See* Holland
Neuchâtel, 304
New Testament, 404
Newton, Isaac (and Newtonianism), 86, 98, 105, 106, 108, 111–12, 123, 127ff., 158, 168, 207, 208, 213, 257ff., 455; Bishop of Puy attacks, 367; teeth, 512
Nicolaï, de (Président), 357
Niedham, Father, 424–25
Nîmes, 390
Nivernais, Duc de, 191
Nivernais, Madame de, 492
Noailles, Cardinal de, 75–76
Noailles, Marechal de, daughter of, 56
Nointel, Madame de, 71
Nonnotte, Abbé (Father), 40–41, 327
Normandy, 92–93
Notre-Dame, 18, 481
Nouvelle Héloïse, La, 339, 394

Observations (Koenig), 260
Observations sur les écrits modernes, 220
Octave et le jeune Pompée (*Octavius and Young Pompey*), 374
Ode à la Chambre de Justice, 47
Ode à l'ingratitude, 117
Odéon, 499
Ode to Posterity, 63
Ode to Sainte Geneviève, 13
Oedipe, 18, 29, 30, 31, 40–41, 43, 44, 50, 55, 61, 64, 93, 206, 499
Oedipus. *See Oedipe*
Oeuvres du philosophe de Sans-Souci, Les, 310–11
Old Testament, 368, 404; Genesis, 425
Olivet, Abbé d', 10, 116, 183, 184, 371
Olympie, 361, 373, 407
On the Ill Use Men Make of Life, 77
Opéra, the (Paris), 15, 183, 185, 499
Opéra Comique (Paris), 201
Oracle des fidèles, L', 414
Oreste, 209, 219, 344
Originaux, Les, 191
Orion (blackamoor), 257
Orléans, Bishop of, 499. *See also* Varicourt, Rouph de
Orléans, Duchesse d' (dowager), 44
Orléans, Duchesse d' (wife of Philippe Egalité), 482
Orléans, Philippe II, Duc d' (Regent; 80
Orléans, Louis Philippe, Duc d' (father of Philippe Egalité), 271
Orléans, Louis Philippe, Duc d' (Philippe Egalité), 451, 481, 482
Orleans, Philippe II, Duc d' (Regent; Regency), 16, 31ff., 39, 42, 43, 46, 47, 51, 67, 70, 239, 482; and alchemy, 56; and Bourbon-Vendôme, 30
Ormesson, d' (Président), 393
Ornex, 336
Orphelin de la Chine, L', 281, 292–93, 305, 377
Orry (Comptroller General), 169
Osseville, Madame d', 19
Othello, 458
Ott (painter), 451

Palais Royal, 15, 17, 34, 95, 96, 482
Palissot (poet), 298, 309
Pallou, Father, 10
Pamela, 209
Panckouke, Charles-Joseph, 446, 504ff.
Panegyric of Louis XV, 174

Panthéon, 497, 498, 500
Paparel (contractor), 46–47
Paradise Lost, 87
Paraguay, 300
Parent family, 6, 507
Paris, 24–25, 32–33ff., 39–41, 42, 52ff., 64, 70, 73ff., 82, 85, 88, 91, 94–99, 101ff., 109ff., 114, 115, 121, 133, 137, 139, 143–44, 149–50, 153–56, 157–61, 166–67ff., 182, 187, 190, 191, 201, 204ff., 215ff., 225, 230, 231, 233–34, 239, 245, 250, 251, 256–57, 282, 283, 285, 289, 291, 293, 299, 301–2, 305, 313, 317, 320, 327, 343, 386, 407, 417, 418, 431ff., 441, 442 (*see also* specific citizens, institutions, works); and acclaim for Frederick's victories, 307; Arouet family in, 6–9ff.; birth of Voltaire in, 3; and Calas affair, 357; celebration of Louis XV's recovery, 168–69; Law affair, 53–54; Parlement, 63, 70, 122, 316, 366, 381, 393, 423, 429, 450, 492; *La Pucelle* read aloud in, 142; and Voltaire's death, 491–92ff.; Voltaire's return to; last days, 461ff., 465–90
Paris, Archbishop of, 99, 492, 494, 495
Pâris-Duvernet brothers, 54, 55, 68–69, 161, 206
Parlements, 358ff., 423, 436ff., 507. *See also* specific locations
Parsees, The, 423
Pascal (ship), 300
Pascal, Blaise, 448, 494, 511
Pasionei, Cardinal, 338–39
Pasquier (counselor), 393, 394, 486
Patru (poet), 298–99
Pauvre Diable, Le, 323–24
Peter I (the Great), Tsar, 315, 384–85
Peter III, Tsar, 385–86, 387
Peterborough, Charles Mordaunt, Lord, 87
Petition of the Curé of Fontenoy, The, 172–73
Petits Augustins, 506
Phèdre, 342, 414, 415
Philippe II, Regent. *See* Orléans, Philippe II, Duc d'
Philippe Egalité. *See* Orléans, Louis Philippe, Duc d'
Philippiques, 51
Philosophe chrétien, Un, 205
Philosophical Dictionary (*Dictionnaire philosophique*), 118, 262, 349, 350, 371, 383, 387, 393, 398–99, 409, 424, 428, 491

Philosophical Letters. See Lettres philosophiques
Philosophical Portrait, A, 431
Philosophical Tales, 372
Philosophy of Newton, 146
Pigalle, Jean Baptiste, 433–35, 450, 453, 470
Piron, Alexis, 66–67, 67–68, 98, 147–48, 165, 199, 218, 322, 423, 431–32
Pitot, letter to, 118
Pitt, William, 310
Place de la Concorde, 474
Plaideurs, Les, 61
Plombières, 92, 204–5, 248, 264, 266, 284, 285–86
Plots, 443–44
Pocket Dictionary of Philosophy. See Philosophical Dictionary
Podewik, Count, 162
Poème de Fontenoy, 172–73, 176, 182
Poèmes sacrés, 324
Poème sur la loi naturelle (Poem on Natural Law), 294
Poème sur la vanité (Poem on Vanity), 322, 323
Poème sur le désastre de Lisbonne (Poem on the Disaster at Lisbon), 294, 314, 340
Poème sur l'envie, 498
Poisinet, play attributed to, 374
Poisonnier (Catherine II's physician), 446–47
Poisson, Madame, 176, 177
Poitou, 5, 187–88
Poles, 387
Polignac, Princesse de, 467
Politics and Legislation, 349, 371
Politique du médecin Machiavel . . . (Politics of a Machiavellian Physician . . . , The), 236
Pollnitz, Baron, 238–40, 270
Polyeucte, 56, 293
Pompadour, Jean Antoinette Normand d'Étioles, Marquise de (King's favorite), 176–77, 180, 187, 193, 201, 220, 300–1, 304ff., 357, 442, 453, 463; and *Alzire*, 219; and Corneille's Collected Works, 342; and Encyclopédie, 317; and *Enfant prodigue*, 191; *Histoire du Tsar Pierre le Grand* dedicated to, 315; and *Tancrède* dedication, 329, 385; and Voltaire's visit to Frederick, 224
Pompignan, Marquis de. See Le Franc,

Jacques, Marquis de Pompignan
Pompignan (village), 322, 324
Pompignans, the, 368. See also Le Franc
Poniatowski, Jozef Anton, Prince, 454
Pons, Prince de, 106
Pontcarré, de (parlementarian), 92
Poor Devil, The, 323–24
Pope, Alexander, 84, 89, 294, 296, 345
Porée, Father, 11, 12
Porrentruy, Monseigneur de, 284
Port Mahon, 301
Potsdam (Sans Souci), 224, 231, 234, 237–39, 242, 246–47, 252ff., 308, 310
POURQUOI, LES, 321
Poussin (actor), 50
Prades, Abbé de, 266, 277, 285
Prangins, Château de, 289
Praslin, Duc de, 359, 386, 397, 474
Prémare, Father de, 281
Préservatif, Le (The Preservative), 129
Prie, Madame de, 76, 80
Princesse de Babylone, La, 423
Princesse de Navarre, La, 179, 182
Prodigal Son, The. See Enfant prodigue, L'
Provence, governor of. See Villars, Duc de (mid-1700s)
Providence, 294–95, 315
Provincial Letters, 511
Prude, La (The Prude), 191
Prudhomme (husband of Madame de Bernières), 131–32
Prussia, 156, 162, 302ff. See also Frederick II; Seven Years' War; War of the Austrian Succession; specific cities
Prussian Academy (Berlin), 179, 210, 258, 259
Psalms of David, 301
Puccini (composer—1778), 466
Pucelle (Chapelain), 110–11
Pucelle, La (Voltaire), 110–11, 125, 140–41ff., 291–92, 293, 308, 394, 404
Puero regnante, 35–36, 192
Puy, Bishop of. See Le Franc, Jean-Georges

QUAND, LES, 319–20

Rabelais, François, 46, 406, 502
Racine, Jean, 29, 50, 61, 96, 114, 218, 342, 374, 415, 443, 458, 476; buried in Saint-Etienne-du-Mont, 494; portrait in Academy, 510

Racine, Louis (son), 115, 253
Racle (doctor), 490
Rambouet (magistrate), 148
Rambouillet, Catherine de Vivonne,
    Marquise de, 310
Rameau, Jean Philippe, 104, 105, 168, 176,
    179–80
Ramire's Feast. See Fête de Ramire, La
Randon, Duc de, 373
Réaumur, René de, 128, 158
Regent. See Orléans, Philippe II, Duc d'
Reginard (playwright), 139
Relation de la maladie de la confession
    de la mort et de l'apparition du Jésuite
    Berthier, 317–18
Relation du voyage de M. le marquis Le
    Franc de Pompignan . . . , 321–22
Relation du voyage du frère
    Garassise . . . , 318
Religion naturelle, La, 317
Remarks, 3, 27, 83, 101, 174, 349, 350
Remarks on Modern Writings, 220
Reminiscences of Monsieur Haller, 236
Remusberg, 149, 151
Renards de les loups, Les, 369
Rennes, Bishop of. See Vauréal, Abbé
Réponse d'un académicien de Berlin . . .
    (Reply to a Berlin Academician . . .),
    260–61
Requête du curé de Fontenoy, La,
    172–73
Restif de La Bretonne, Nicolas, 506
Restoration, the, 499, 500
Resumé of World History, 282
Revolution, French, 431, 453, 495, 496,
    511
Rheims, 156, 215
Ribotte (traveler), 355
Richardson, Samuel, 209
Richelieu, Duchesse de (née Guise),
    104–5, 106, 109, 111
Richelieu, Duchesse de (née Noailles),
    508
Richelieu, Armand, Duc de (de Fronsac;
    Voltaire's friend), 10, 15, 46, 51, 52, 91,
    94, 98, 116, 123, 126, 160, 161, 176, 179,
    183, 189, 201, 205, 216, 286–87, 288,
    301ff., 343–44, 412, 413, 418, 441, 442,
    449, 450, 463, 470; appointed
    ambassador to Vienna, 74; in Bastille,
    79–80; and Calas affair, 355–56; duel
    with Lixin, 106; escorts Emilie in
    Versailles, 178; and final illness of
    Voltaire, 485, 486; at Forges, 72–73, 76;

and Indiscret, 76; and Irène, 468; at
    Mahomet performance, marriage to
    daughter of Duc de Guise, 104–5, 106;
    and Muses rivales, 179–80; and Pigalle
    sculpture of Voltaire, 433; at
    Plombières, 92; Port Mahon victory,
    301; and La Pucelle, 111; and Rome
    sauvée performance, 219
Richelieu, Armand-Jean du Plessis, Duc
    de (1685), 508
Richelieu, Armand-Jean du Plessis, Duc
    de (Cardinal de Richelieu), 57, 182,
    309, 508ff.
Rival Muses, The, 179–80
Rivière-Bourdet, La, 65, 66, 68, 73, 131
Rochebrune, de (visitor), 4
Roffo, Maître, 421, 422
Roger (nurse), 487, 490
Rohan-Chabot, Chevalier de, 78–81, 82,
    89, 92, 269
Roi (poet), 181–85
Romanticism, 458
Rome, 92, 175, 300, 366, 397, 426, 427, 438
Rome sauvée (Rome Saved; formerly
    Catilina), 209, 215, 216, 219, 221–22
Romilly, 496, 497
Roney, Abbé, 480
Rose de l'Epinoy (doctor), 493
Rossbach, 306
Rottembourg, de (ambassador), 166
Rouen, 65, 66, 92–93, 94, 106
Rousseau, at Rome sauvée performance,
    216–17
Rousseau, Jean-Baptiste, 12, 13–14, 18, 41,
    42, 58, 60, 62–63, 65, 117, 122, 135, 143,
    147–48; and Temple du Goût, 98; and
    Voltairomanie, 133
Rousseau, Jean-Jacques, 136, 179–80, 195,
    217, 218, 238, 299ff., 339–41, 355,
    366–67, 381–82, 383–84, 391, 400, 401,
    406–7, 408, 431, 479; and Clément's
    imprisonment, 443; and Dame
    Bourette's coffeecup, 330; Durey de
    Morsan and, 413; and Jansenists, 369;
    Maréchale de Luxembourg and, 484;
    and Providence, 294–95, 315
Ruffec, Madame de, 334
Ruffec, Charlotte d'Aubespine de
    Châteauneuf, Marquise de, 508
Ruffey, de, in Plombières, 285, 287
Rupelmonde, Marquise de, 6off., 72, 99
Russia, 384–88. See also Catherine II;
    Saint Petersburg

Sabatier, Antoine, 271, 430–31
Sacred Poems, 324
Saint-Albins, Charles de, 441
Saint-André-des-Arcs, chapel of, 85
Saint-Ange, Château de, 28–29, 34
Saint-Claude, 430
Saint-Cloud, 94, 104
Sainte-Marguerite, 75
Saint-Florentin, de (minister), 355, 356–57, 431
St. Francis, Order of. *See* Franciscans
Saint-Germain-en-Laye, 89–91
Saint-German (magician), 392
Saint Gervais, Church of, 101
Saint-Hyacinthe (author), 134
St. John, Henry, Lord Bolingbroke. *See* Bolingbroke, Lord
Saint-Julien, Madame de, 451–52, 456, 479, 480, 485
Saint-Lambert, Marquis de, 195–97, 200, 201–3, 204, 208, 212, 213, 215, 216, 442, 449, 466
Saint-Loup, 5–6, 187–88
Saint-Malo, 236, 257, 325
Saint Petersburg, 386, 399, 453, 502. *See also* Catherine II
Saint-Pierre, Duchesse de, 102, 109
Saint-Pierre, Bernardin de, 41
Saint-Simon, Claude de Rouvroy, Duc de, 508
Saint-Simon, Louis de Rouvroy, Duc de (author of *Memoirs*), 29, 60, 67, 608
Saint Stephen's Cathedral (Toulouse), 352ff.
Saisons, Les, 195, 211
Samson (opera), 104
Sans Souci. *See* Potsdam
Sartine (police commissioner), 335, 431
Saül, 368, 382
Saussure, Mademoiselle de, 441
Sauvigny, Madame de, 413
Savoy, 332, 339, 412, 446
Saxony, 243. *See also* War of the Austrian Succession
Saxony, Duke of, 233
Scaramouche, 190
Sceaux, Château de, 31, 51, 190–91, 221–22
Schmidt (Frankfurt councilor), 277–78, 279, 303
Schmidt, Madame, 278
Schoepflin, Joseph Frederick, 281
Scotland, 379
Scottish Lass, The. See Ecossaise, L'

Scriptures, 365, 366. *See also* New Testament; Old Testament
Scythes, Les (The Scythians), 414
Seasons, The. See Saisons, Les
Second Empire. *See* Napoleon III
Secret Memoirs about the King of Prussia, 417
Secret Memoirs for Use in Writing the Life of Voltaire, 505
Sedaine (playwright), 327
Séguier (Président; Voltaire's contemporary), 450
Séguier, Pierre, Duc de Villemor (d. 1672), 183
Ségur, Comtesse, 482
Seillières, Abbey of, 492ff., 496
Sémiramis, 186, 187, 197, 198–99, 207, 440
Senones, Abbey of, 284–85
Sens, Archbishop of, 160
Sentiment des citoyens, Le, 383
Sermon des cinquant, Le (The Sermon of the Fifty), 366
Servien, Abbé, 15–16, 32
Sesostris, 463
Seven Years' War, 305ff., 315. *See also* specific participants
Sèvres, 59
Shakespeare, William, 108, 454, 455, 458, 467
Sherlock, Martin, 454–56
Shuvalov, Count, 385, 386
SI, LES, 320–21
Siècle de Louis XIV, augmenté . . . , Le, 256
Siècle de Louis XIV, Le (The Century of Louis XIV), 29, 125, 143, 229, 230, 247, 252–53, 254, 256, 270, 288
Silesia, 150, 151, 204, 305, 310
Sirven case (Sirven family), 389–91, 429, 430, 449
Sohr, 282
Soltkoff (visitor), 446, 450
Sophia Dorothea, Queen (wife of George I), 89
Sophia Dorothea (Queen Mother; mother of Frederick II), 165, 241
Sophocles, 40
Sorbonne, 127, 128
Soubise, Charles de Rohan, Prince de, 306
Source, La, 52, 64
Souvenirs sur Monsieur Haller, 236
Spain, 60, 61, 284, 300, 315, 396, 454

Speech Delivered on the Threshold . . . *See Discours prononcé à la porte* . . .
Staal, Baronne de, 188
Staël, Germaine de, 315
Stahl's pills, 249
Stanhope, Lord, 439–40
Stanislas, King of Lorraine (Duc de Lorraine), 92, 112, 192–94, 197ff., 205, 208, 211, 214
Stanislas, King of Poland, 76
Stoics, 410
Stormont, Viscount, 467
Story of Elizabeth Canning and Calas, The, 358–59
Strasbourg, 270, 281
Strogonoff, Comte, 480
Stuarts, the, 238
Stuttgart, 235
Suard, Madame, 446–51, 504
Sudre (lawyer), 353
Sully, 32–33, 51–52, 54
Sully, Maximilien de Béthune, Duc de (the great), 89
Sully, Maximilien-Henri, Duc de, 15, 32, 73, 79, 89
Sur le mauvais usage qu'on fait de la vie, 77
Sweden, 42; Ulricka, Queen of, 164–65
Swift, Jonathan, 84, 86, 89
Switzerland; the Swiss, 286, 288–302, 387–88. *See also* specific estates, towns
Système de la nature, 409

Tableau philosophique . . . , 431
Tamponet, Abbé, 317
Tancrède, 315–16, 328–29, 385
Tartuffe, 49, 407
Taschin, Mademoiselle, 441
Temple, William Johnson, 380
Temple, the, 14–16, 30–31ff., 131
Temple de la gloire, Le (The Temple of Glory), 176ff., 182
Temple du goût, Le (The Temple of Taste), 97–98, 101
Tencin, Cardinal de, 169, 288, 301
Tencin, Madame de, 82, 203, 288
Thibouville, Marquis de, 461ff., 475, 476, 479, 480
Thiériot (friend), 11, 27–28, 52, 53, 59, 65, 68–69, 71, 74, 78, 82, 85, 87, 90, 91, 93, 106, 107, 113, 115, 118, 130–31ff., 146, 222, 295, 307, 312, 313, 341, 365, 440–41; brother, 184; and Damilaville,

425; death, 440–41; and wedding of Voltaire's niece, 127
Thierry (doctor), 490
Thil, Mademoiselle du. *See* Du Thil, Mademoiselle
Thoriguy, 77
Tolignon, Abbé de, 175
Tomb of the Unknown Soldier, 496
Toulouse, 350–56ff., 391
Tournay, 313ff., 320, 328, 329, 346–47, 376, 412, 464, 501
Tournemine, Father, 11, 23, 24
Traité de la tolérance, 359
Travels in Italy, 345
Travenol (violinist), 183–85
Treatise on the Origin of Inequality . . . , 294
Treatise on Tolerance, 359
Trianon, 198, 208, 293
Trichâteau, Marquis de, 142
Trinquier (prosecutor), 390
Triomphe de la poésie, Le (The Triumph of Poetry), 181
Tronchin, Jean-Robert, 288, 295, 313, 339, 356
Tronchin, Théodore (doctor), 290–91, 373, 377, 388, 394, 407, 411, 422, 465ff., 470, 472, 473, 480, 485ff.
Tronchin family, 288ff., 293, 333, 388, 407, 492, 496, 497
Troyes, Bishop of, 494
Trublet, Abbé, 313, 325–26
Trudaine, death of, 484
Try (surgeon), 493
Tulle, 32
Tunis, Bey of, 397
Turgot, Anne Robert Jacques, 430, 445, 448, 449, 456, 463, 476, 484
Turin, 383
Turks, 387
Twickenham, 296
Tyrconnel, Lord, 234, 238, 252, 256

Uleri, Massimo, 512
Ulricka, Queen of Sweden, 164–65
Unigenitus, 55
Ussé, Marquis d', 64, 65
Ussé, Château d', 64–65, 66
Utrecht Gazette, 343–44
Uzès, Comte d', 30

Valenciennes, 143
Vallette, Simon, 323–24
Valois, de. *See* Louis Philippe, King

Valois, Mademoiselle de (Regent's daughter), 510
Valori, Abbé, 152
Valori, de (ambassador), 152, 165, 237–38
Van Duren (printer; bookseller), 147, 149, 273
Varennes, Abbé de. *See* Châteauneuf, François de Castagnier de
Varicourt, Rouph de, 456
Varicourt family, 467
Vauban, Sébastien le Prestre, Marquis de, daughter of, 64
Vauréal, Abbé, 48–49
Vauvenargues, Luc de Clapiers, Marquis de, 171, 185–86
Vaux, Château de, 48–49. *See also* Villars, Claude Louis Hector, Maréchal-Duc de
Végobre (lawyer), 381, 391–92
Vergennes, Charles Gravier, Comte de, 431
Verner, Jacob, 289–90
Vernet, Pastor, 293, 300, 384, 404–5
Veronese, Paolo, 137
Versailles, 58, 94, 149, 154ff., 161ff., 170ff., 234, 265, 304, 306, 308, 311, 330, 359, 366, 400, 419, 431, 453, 455, 464, 470, 473 (*see also* specific courtiers, kings); Musée National de, 512
Vert-Vert, 324
Vestris (dancer), 425
Vestris, Lucia, 474, 478
Viau, Théophile de, 77
Vicaire savoyard, Le, 366–67, 381
Vie de Marianne, 88
Vie de Voltaire (Condorcet), 301
Vieilleville, de, and Voltaire's confession, 471
Vienna, 41, 74, 258, 295, 305, 321
Vignerot, Madame, 104
Viguière, Jeanne, 353–54
Villarceaux, de, Voltaire attempts to buy house from, 481–82
Villars, Duc de (mid-1700s), 316, 343, 344, 357
Villars, Duc de (son), 316
Villars, Duchesse de (younger), 159
Villars, Maréchale-Duchesse de, 41, 48–49, 55–56, 316
Villars, Claude Louis Hector, Maréchal-Duc de, 48, 51, 52, 55ff., 69, 81, 116, 316
Villars, Château of. *See* Villars, Claude Louis Hector, Maréchal-Duc de

Villefort, Chevalier de, 119–21
Villeroi, François de Neufville, Duc de (Maréchal), 57
Villette, Chevalier de, 64
Villette, Madame de (mother of marquis), 457
Villette, Marquis de, 64, 457, 463, 465ff., 469, 471, 472, 474, 480, 483, 485, 487, 488; and *Brutus*, 496; buys Ferney estate, 502; and Voltaire's funeral procession, 498
Villette, Marquis de (son), 499
Villette, Renée Philiberte, Marquise de (Madame de Villette), 456–57, 465, 468, 477, 489, 495, 498–99, 503; and Voltaire's funeral procession, 498–99
Villette, Château de (estate), 495, 499
Vinache (doctor), 56
Vincennes, 30
Vionnet, Father, 317
Virgil, 37, 510
Vision de Babouc, La, 314
Voisenon, Abbé de, 115, 158–59, 196, 215, 326, 374
Voltaire, François-Marie Arouet de (*see also* specific places of residence, relationships, works): and art of conversation, 139, 375–76; in Bastille, 35–39, 81–82; and beard, 248; begins law study, 16; birth; family background; childhood; schooling, 3–14; and cardinalcy, 301; ceremony at *Irène* performance, 477–78; ceremony with laurel crown at Mademoiselle Clairon's, 435; and chess, 370; cleanliness, 250; as comte, 314; corpse, disposal of; estate, 490–506; and court appointment, 169, 187; death of brother, 169–70; and death of Emilie, 212–14ff.; death of father, 54–55; death of sister, 85; decides not to be courtier, 154; and deer-hunting, 139; discretion about women, 296–97; enters Academy poetry competition; loses, 18; eyes, 250, 452; first love affair, 19–26; first verses, 12; and fitting out of ships, 300; and friendship, 69, 185 (*see also* specific friends); and German language, 247; insensitivity to many arts, 453; invests in making paper out of straw, 101; involvement in murder case (*see* Abbeville; Calas affair; Sirven case); last illness; death, 487–90; lends money,

206; loses money, 85–86; and loss of sexual vigor; Emilie and lover, 195–96, 201–3; lover of Madame Denis, 296–98; manufactories; watchmaking, 296–97, 400ff., 437, 439, 445, 446; and *opéra comique*, 423–24; pension, 43, 45, 343; plans for death, 444–45; political ambitions; as secret agent, 57–58, 161ff. (*see also* specific relationships); poor health; illnesses, 10, 30, 72, 73, 86, 97, 108, 144, 151, 153, 154, 188, 199–200, 248–50, 256, 284, 373, 375, 377, 378, 445, 446, 467–68ff.; and popular education, 364–65; portrait by Largillière, 38 (*see also* Largillière, Nicolas de); and religion (anti-clericalism; attempts at piety; Catholicism), 40–41, 62, 93, 156, 174–76, 197, 283–85, 289ff., 364ff., 397, 404ff., 410, 418–23, 426–27 (*see also* Ferney: church at; *l'Infâme;* specific relationships); and science, 111–12, 123–24, 127–28, 129 (*see also* Newton, Isaac); secretaries (*see* Longchamps; Wagnière); sensitivity to stimulants, 58–59; speaks English, 87, 140, 380, 467; statue by Pigalle, 433–35, 450; and theater, 29–30, 49–50, 139–40, 143–44, 216–17, 221–22, 233, 300, 325, 339, 340, 361, 373–74, 381, 407–8, 414–15, 439, 440 (*see also* specific plays); and utopia, 394–96; works for Paris notary, 24, 27–28

Voltairomanie, La (*Voltairomania*), 130, 132, 133–34

Voyage en Italie, 345

Wagnière (secretary), 284, 417, 419ff., 434, 441, 448, 464, 466, 468ff., 475, 483, 485, 486, 489, 495, 502

Walpole, Horace, 87, 387

War of the Austrian Succession, 172, 205. *See also* Austria

Watteau, Antoine, 137

West Indies. *See* Indies

WHENS, 319–20

WHYS, 321

Wiart (visitor), 470

Willancourt, Abbess of, 392–93

Windischgrätz, Prince, 61

Winterfeldt, Comtesse de. *See* Dunoyer, Olympe

Wise Man's Pitfall, The, 343

Works of the Philosopher of Sans Souci, The, 310–11

Worms, 280

Württemberg, Duchess of, 235

Württemberg, Duke of, 235, 247, 281, 295, 370, 433

Ximénès, Marquis de, 251, 291, 341

Yart, Abbé, 118

Young, Edward, 87

Zadig, 47, 190, 191, 200, 201, 411

Zaïre, 96–97, 98, 122, 154, 175, 217, 290, 302, 414, 452

Zoll, Prince of, 234

Zoraïde, 115